The Literature of Nature

The British and American Traditions

Robert J. Begiebing
Owen Grumbling

Plexus Publishing, Inc.
Medford, NJ

Cover painting: "Kindred Spirits" by Asher B. Durand, courtesy of New York Public Library.

Plexus Publishing, Inc.
143 Old Marlton Pike
Medford, NJ 08055-8750
U.S.A.

Manufactured in the United States of America

ISBN 0-937548-16-2 (Hardbound)
ISBN 0-937548-17-0 (Softbound)

For our children
Megan
Brie
Amy
Emily
Kate

and for the earth they will inherit.

Preface

In constructing this anthology of British and American nature writing since the eighteenth century, we had to make many hard choices. From among such a vast field of materials we were bound, like all editors, by the physical limitations of a manageable text. For that reason alone we have passed over many authors we would have liked to include. Many fine twentieth-century works (e.g., Hemingway's *Big Two-Hearted River,* and Ted Hughes' *Pike*) were left out simply because the permissions costs proved prohibitive. We summarily excluded the huge literature of travel and field sport, as well as essentially polemical or technical works. Excerpts from novels were rejected in the belief that such truncating violates the artistic integrity of the work.

Despite these limitations we believe that our selections represent, or at least suggest, the enormous field of nature writing in England and America during, roughly, the past two hundred years. Our historical background introduction surveys nature writers, and the major social factors that influenced them, from the Greeks up through the Industrial Revolution; our period introductions, in addition, survey the breadth of the modern nature writing tradition, including many—but certainly not all—minor authors and tangential literary trends, such as regionalism. Together, the introductions and selections should provide many points of departure for readers interested in the literature of nature.

. . .

We want to thank colleagues who generously offered their judgments and advice on various portions of the manuscript. Our thanks go to Jacque Carter, Robert Craven, Carl Dawson, Michael DePorte, Loftus Jestin, Joseph Mahoney, John Richardson, Paul Roberge, Eleanor Sabaski, and Don Sieker.
The Editors
1990

Foreword

As the twentieth century draws to a close, the crucial issue before humanity becomes apparent: the profound role that human beings have assumed in altering the environment. The abiding desires of humanity—basic needs, just government, peace, artistic expression, human love—all endure, but they depend more and more obviously upon a precarious balance between human activity and natural process.

In our time, for example, war means more than the death of soldiers or even the murder of civilians; in a real sense, war holds the potential to annihilate nearly all forms of life on our planet. Similarly, the political-economic problem of producing from the earth the necessities of food and shelter, once a mundane task, has—because of increased population and consumption rates—become profoundly complex. With each furnaceful of burning coal, with each holding tank of toxic waste, we seriously alter our material relation to nature. We alter the relationship by means of our technical knowledge; and increased technical knowledge has so long preoccupied society at large that it has become an end in itself.

Attempts to deal with pollution have proceeded from the assumption that pollution is merely technological error, remediable if the problem is rationally analyzed and adequately funded. And this idea itself depends upon a prior, implicit assumption: that our power to act, as well as the world in which we act, is limitless. Now, however, grotesque new problems—loss of the ozone layer, mass extinction of species, global warming—are forcing us to consider the limits of human action in the biosphere; indeed, evidence of carbon dioxide loading leads us to ask whether we have already exceeded our limits.

These problems, it has been argued, proceed from the persistent attitude that humans are independent of nature, that we can analyze and exploit the natural world as an object separate from ourselves. Given the seriousness of current environmental problems, humanity—particularly industrialized humanity—now faces an eminently practical task: to reconsider its relationship with the remainder of the natural world.

We contend, however, that such reconsideration has been happening right along. Throughout the history of industrial society, and long before, there has existed a counter traditon of nature writing, a tradition characterized by reverence and humility. Sometimes harkening back to western culture's own tribal origins, sometimes influenced by foreign and "primitive" cultures, the tradition of nature writing has remained critical of the conventional attitude that nature is a lifeless resource to be exploited.

In its depiction of natural objects, nature literature explores how the natural world meets human needs beyond the merely physiological, economic, or technological. What do we feel atop a snowy mountain or amidst a roaring river? What relations can we have to the sounding whale or the soaring hawk? What primordial needs does intimacy with the natural world satisfy? The nature writers attempt to refine our human values—to find in our relationships with nature lasting insights about eternal human questions: integrity, strength, loyalty, love. Moreover, nature writers attempt to explore nature as a realm alien to our conscious, rational, human-centered perspective. They write of a marvelous world in tune with strange, non-human songs. And the message even from science, here at the close of the twentieth century, is that nature's songs are not necessarily always in tune with human melodies.

In making this anthology we have limited ourselves to modern nature literature in Britain and America. The British selections begin with works written during the onset of the Industrial Revolution, a period when a sense of separation from nature began to enter modern consciousness. The American selections begin somewhat earlier, with the accounts of that marvelous wilderness encountered by the Europeans. To provide prior background, a General Introduction surveys the evolution of western attitudes toward nature from the ancients down to the close of the eighteenth century.

Yet our anthology deals with only one strain of the world's vast abundance of nature literature. Our task here has been to validate the existence of the British and American canons, which, though various, are part of a common tradition. Literary criticism has been reluctant to define and validate the tradition of nature literature, even though its consistent critique of the assumptions underlying modern culture grows increasingly relevant to the future of the culture.

We look forward to future work that enlarges the tradition: editions of texts authored by women and by indigenous peoples, as well as studies by critics whose perspectives can enlighten the tradition. The tradition of nature literature will grow with the work of deep ecologists, feminists, eco-feminists, Native Americans, historians of science and the environment, and those, like Joseph Campbell, who posit the need for globally shared myths that will sanction attempts to sustain the biosphere. What good is a fine house, asked Thoreau, if one does not have a decent planet on which to place it?

Even in the face of potential ecotastrophe, the age-old personal value of nature literature remains vital. People seem awakened to the sense that something is missing in their lives, in the tortured landscapes they see, in the sterile environments where they live and work. One of the deepest human needs of our age is to encounter at first hand the sight, sound, smell, taste, and feel of the natural world in all its rich variety of dress and mood. Nature writers throughout literary history, in responding to the same need, can lead us to experiences of nature that provide a deeper understanding of our own human nature, as well as renew our sensitivity to the niche we occupy in the natural world.

We hope that this anthology will gather readers to the tradition of nature literature—to writers distant in time and place who observed acutely, thought deeply, and wrote artfully in forms that continue to delight, about the natural world that surrounds and nourishes us all.

Owen Grumbling
Bob Begiebing
1 November 1989

CONTENTS

The love of nature is a passion for those in whom it once lodges: it cannot be removed.

Mary Webb, *The House in Dormer Forest*

The Background of Nature Literature

Origins: The Greek and Roman Worlds

Modern nature writing has roots deep in the past. By uncovering these roots we can define some of the essential qualities of the best nature writing in all times as well as examine the basis of more modern developments. The earliest nature writings, for example, were recorded myths, or explorations of natural phenomena in terms of divine activity. In archaic times people lived closer to nature—the earth, the sea, the animal kingdom—in order to satisfy their basic needs. But as time passed and human activities became more specialized, more dependent upon sophisticated tools, daily human life became more divorced from natural processes. This very alienation from the natural world has always produced a reawakening to it.

The literature of Greek culture, which has strongly influenced the development of our own literature in English, began about a thousand years before the birth of Christ with the poems of Homer, whose epics celebrate the legendary activities of ancestral heroes. *The Iliad* is the story of the Greek/Trojan war and *The Odyssey* is the story of Odysseus' voyage home from the war. These two heroic poems became something like a bible in subsequent Greek culture. Their chief concern is *arate*, or excellence in human society. Nature itself does not figure as a topic, but serves rather as a means of explaining the human action central to the works. Indeed, the Greeks felt an intimacy for the natural world that is difficult for moderns to comprehend. Their literature, for example, was firmly rooted in the bodily senses, senses so respected that their intimate power over man's life and imagination was deified.

Homer, eighth-century B.C. Greek poet who composed the Iliad *and the* Odyssey

To the Greeks, natural processes were literally divine, that is, conceived in terms of divine personalities. The ocean was Poseidon; the changing wave, his son Proteus; the sun, Apollo, god of light and learning. The scholar F.F. Zielinski captures the Greek attitude very clearly:

> Out of the earth, from a crevice in the rocks, gushes a cool spring, creating green life around it and quenching the thirst of the flocks and of their Shepherds: this is a goddess, a nymph, a naiad. Let us thank her for her good will, let us shelter her current with a roof, let us hollow out a basin beneath her, in order that in its gleaming surface she may contemplate her divine form.

The German philosopher Friedrich Von Schiller (1759–1805), as many after him, argued that during the classical period the attachment to nature was "naive," marked by an unconscious harmony between man and nature. Homer's poetry is the prime example of the expression of this harmony. In contrast, the conscious view of nature as a fit subject for her own sake was the result of modern man's separation from nature in his social life. Artistic "awareness" of nature then became self-conscious, studied, at times artificial. Schiller termed the conscious attitude toward nature "sentimental," for in self-consciousness man is most aware of the separation from nature and yearns most deeply for some renewed, perhaps idealized unity. Schiller's vision of the ancient as naive may apply to the earliest periods of Greek and Roman culture, but as those cultures aged and became more urban, more decadent, and more politically oppressive, mankind turned consciously to nature, hoping to find sources of inspiration, expression, and vitality.

While the literature of early Greece focused on human excellence and conflict, the economy was based on agriculture. The corn crop was thought of as the goddess Demeter, and the earth as the goddess Hera. Farming thus proceeded less as exploitation than as prayer. The ninth-century B.C. georgic, Hesiod's *Works and Days*, recommended agricultural labor because it was pleasing to the gods. Natural description in *Works and Days* occurs in the context of practical advice. Even here, the farmer does not exploit a "dead" resource: he secures a living relationship with entities that were, to the Greeks, truly divine.

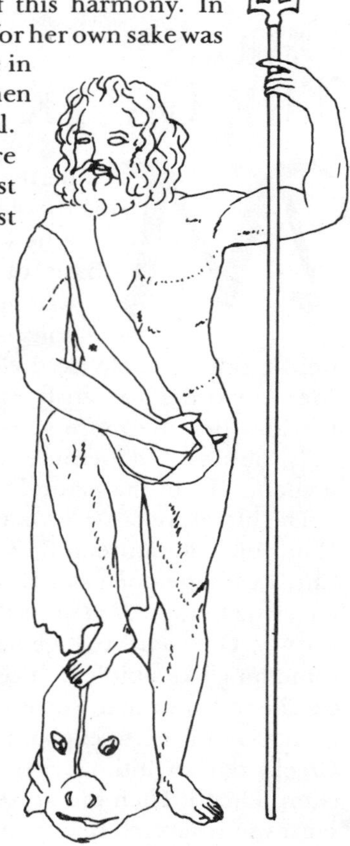

Poseidon, the god of the ocean

The young Apollo in the Temple of Zeus, Olympia, Greece

Striking natural description occurs in the work of two early Greek lyric poets, Sappho and Pindar. In the seventh century the poet Sappho intertwined description of her native Lesbos, a beautiful Aegean island, with personal accounts of exotic love. Typical Sapphic lines depict "breezes rustling amid apple branches by cool water, where quivering leaves are drowsy with cool slumber." Sappho's predilection for love in the countryside may imply a reaction against the restrictions of the increasingly urban Greek culture. Two centuries after Sappho, the lyric poet Pindar clearly celebrates what we call today "the wilderness." He sings of the awe that mountains inspire, and in this, he is unique among premodern nature writers. Pindar ascribes personal importance to landscapes, scenes which he often bathes in brilliant light. His attitude sometimes approaches the modern conviction that humanity finds completeness in the natural world: "Man is a mere dream of a shadow; but when a gleam of sunshine cometh as a gift of heaven, a radiant light resteth on man, aye, and a life of sweetness."

The evolution of Greek culture might be viewed, then, as a pattern typical of subsequent cultural evolutions. As society became more sophisticated, natural phenomena attracted more attention of an artistic as well as a "scientific" bent, culminating in the descriptive natural science of Aristotle, who began the systematic classification of plants and animals during the fourth century before Christ.

The conquests of Alexander the Great ushered in the Hellenistic age, a period of much greater social sophistication. After Alexander's death in 323 B.C., Greek culture gradually grew decadent and self-conscious. Nature became an increasingly popular subject for literature as individual sentiment filled the void left by vanishing traditions. An effort emerged to observe nature closely in both art and science and to find in the natural world a source of pleasant feeling.

In the third century B.C., for example, the Sicilian poet Theocritus wrote his *Idylls*, the first pastoral poems, in which he celebrates the simple pleasures of labor close to the natural world. His heroes are shepherds and goatherds, and his settings are richly depicted landscapes. In these works the poet consciously prefers the natural world to human civilization. There is a yearning for the simpler life, a nostalgia for the beauties of nature that foreshadows the modern theme of alienation from nature. In the following lines from "Idyll VII," or "Harvest Home," Theocritus recalls the pleasure of an autumn day spent with fellow poets:

> . . . there we lay
> Half-buried in a couch of fragrant reed
> And fresh-cut vineleaves, who so glad as we?
> A wealth of elm and poplar shook o'erhead;
> Hard by, a sacred spring flowed gurgling on
> From the Nymphs' grot, and in the sombre bough

Demeter, from the red-figure vase by Makron

> The sweet cicada chirped laboriously.
> Hid in the thick thorn-bushes far away
> The treefrog's note was heard; the crested lark
> Sang with the goldfinch; turtles made their moan,
> And o'er the fountain hung the gilded bee.
> All of rich summer smacked, of autumn all:
> Pears at our feet, and apples at our side
> Rolled in luxuriance . . . .

The landscapes of the *Idylls* are lovely and ideal, yet described concretely. Life in the countryside is idealized as leisurely and easy. Work, when it appears, harmonizes with the natural world. In these ways, Theocritus provides an important theme for subsequent pastoral writing.

The Romans, who conquered Greece during the first century B.C., employed Greek literature as a model for their own culture and amplified the pastoral tradition. The Romans were an agricultural people with a deep affection for the land they cultivated. Rome's most renowned writer, Vergil (70–19 B.C.), imitated the *Idylls* of Theocritus in his *Eclogues* and employed similar themes: love among the shepherds, rivalry in country pursuits, and a longing for "the Golden Age" when life was rural, simple, and pleasurable. Like Theocritus, Vergil offers concrete descriptions of shady nooks and sunny meadows. As a young man Vergil had hoped to be a natural philosopher, and his writing reflects the scientist's eye for the subtle details of plant and animal life.

Inspired by Hesiod's *Works and Days*, Vergil also wrote his *Georgics*, a series of poems offering practical advice on agricultural concerns such as gardening and raising grapes. The *Georgics* gave their name to what would become a lasting genre of poetry. Compared to the eclogues, the georgic poem treats work and nature in a realistic way. Vergil's *Georgics*, however, are more than mere technical studies. His tone implies that the objects of his study are alive and sentient, bearing a living relation with humankind. The opening line of the first *Georgic*, for example, is "What makes the crops happy?" Throughout, Vergil voices the human satisfaction generated by the countryside. In the springtime: "Pathless copses ring with birds melodious, and in their settled time the herds renew their loves. The bountiful land brings forth, and beneath the West's warm breezes the fields loosen their bosoms; in all things soft moisture abounds, and the grasses safely dare to trust themselves to face the new suns." Like some of the most intelligent and imaginative scientists of the post-Industrial world, Vergil combines his acute scientific knowledge of the plants and animals with an emotional and aesthetic appreciation of his subjects.

A contemporary, Catullus (84?–54? B.C.) wrote a famous poem celebrating the restorative powers of nature, which he experienced at his rural retreat, an island on a lake in northern Italy. He specifically contrasts the pleasure of rural landscape with the disillusionments of society and politics. Landscape becomes therapeutic:

> O my little almost island, little island Sirmio,
> this brave eye, this green-bright jewel set in Neptune's fair estate
> of lucid waters and broad seas.
> And it's good to look upon you; even now I can't believe
> that the plains lie far behind me, weary Thrace and Bithynia.
> You are still secure my own.
> After many months of travel, nothing's better than to rest
> relaxed and careless; sleep is heaven in our own beloved bed.
> Here's enough reward for exile, and long roads through foreign lands;
> now, my Sirmio, greet your master, make these waves bring laughter up
> til the Lydian lakes re-echo all the laughter in my home.

The Middle Ages: Retreat from Nature

Medieval culture in Europe grew out of the fallen classical world. Disturbed by internal strife and decay, finally dismantled by external assault from the Teutonic peoples of the North, first Greece (after the fifth century B.C.) and then Rome (after the fourth century A.D.) fell. The Germanic culture that replaced the classical culture combined with the new Christian religion to shape the medieval world from roughly 500–1450 A.D., a world far different from its classical predecessors.

The Germanic people—especially the Saxon and Frisian tribes—brought with them a tradition of pagan feeling for nature expressed in Teutonic mythology, fairy tales, folklore, and "woods-worship." Medieval charms, riddles, and lyrics demonstrate the extent of this pagan feeling for nature during the Christian medieval period. The Anglo-Saxon people, for example, preserved much of their pagan heritage in folklore and charms. The dates of the charms are unknown, but as handed down to us in manuscripts dating from the tenth century A.D., they show a curious mixing of the older pagan and the newer Christian religions. They arose from a still more ancient oral tradition. In the charm "Land Remedy," for example, we see the expression of humanity's relationship to the earth and the earth's relationship, in turn, to the gods and God:

> Here is the remedy with which thou canst mend thy field, if they will not produce well, or if anything harmful is done to them by sorcery or witchcraft.
>
> Take then at night before dawn four sods from four sides of the land and observe their former position. Then take oil and honey and yeast and milk of all cattle which are on the land, and part of every kind of tree which grows on the land, except hard trees, and part of every known herb, except burdock only; and then put holy water thereon, and then let it drop thrice on the bottom of the sods, and say then these words: "Crescite grow, et multiplicamini and multiply, et replete and replenish, terram the earth. In nomine patris et filii et spiritus sancti sitis benedicti." Face east and bow humbly nine times, and then say these words:
>
> "Eastward I stand, I pray for mercies;
> I pray the great Lord, pray the mighty God,
> I pray the holy Guardian of heaven,
> I pray earth and sky
> And the righteous holy Mary
> And the might of heaven and the lofty temple,
> That this charm by the grace of God
> I may utter; by strong resolve
> Raise crops for wordly use,
> Fill these fields by firm faith,
> Make beautiful these meadows; as the prophet said
> That he found favour here on earth who gave
> Alms wisely, according to the will of God."

The sense of the earth's sanctity is clear, as is the sense of humanity's need to focus its ceremony and energy on the earth's cycles of death and rebirth.

Like their classical predecessors, the Germanic people also developed a poetry that sang of the exploits of heroes. But in the predominant medieval culture, the Germanic experience was effectively countered, or absorbed, by the rising force of Christianity. It was the Christian religion that played the greatest role in shaping medieval life.

A horned hare reputed to live in Saxony

Konrad Gesner's Beasts & Animals in Decorative Woodcuts of the Renaissance, Edited by Carol Belanger Grafton, Dover Publications, Inc.

Some characteristics of Christianity that flourished during the Middle Ages tended to make the relationship between man and his natural environment, in an intellectual sense, artificial. As St. Augustine argued, too much attention to earthly beauty might steer man away from the proper business of saving his soul, might cause man to focus his attention on this world instead of the next. Medieval literature reflects the principal focus of intellectual energy during the age. The duty of man was to solve the question of his relation to his Redeemer. Though the denial of humanity's world is one definition of asceticism, an impulse that left its mark on the age, some theologians and writers also cautioned against too much sensual indulgence of any kind, including sensual indulgence in the natural world.

The medieval period, however, was not without religious and secular voices speaking about the impressions nature made upon humanity, as Alfred Biese pointed out in *The Development of the Feeling for Nature in the Middle Ages*. The Greek fathers of the Catholic church, for example, maintained at least an awareness of the classical feeling for nature and its salutary effect on the inner life. The building of medieval monasteries on scenic, mountainous, or fertile areas—like the garden culture within the monastic walls—suggests at least one conscious connection to the seasons and awesome beauties of the natural world. And the earliest poem in Old English, sung by the Christian poet Caedmon in the latter half of the seventh century, does praise God's creation of the earth as a place of natural wonders where man will dwell:

> Now must we render praise to the Ruler of heaven,
> To the might of God and the thought of His mind,
> The glorious Father of men, since He, the Lord everlasting,
> Wrought the beginning of all wonders.
> He, the holy Creator, first fashioned
> The heavens as a roof for the children of earth.
> Then this middle-earth the Master of mankind,
> The Lord eternal, afterwards adorned,
> The earth for men, the Prince all-powerful.

In Europe, St. Francis of Assisi taught that plants, animals, and even the sun and moon were our brothers and sisters. And in Ireland, the monastic movement from the eighth to the twelfth centuries produced lyrics praising the healthful effects of nature's creatures and beauties on the scholarly mind. The following poem, for example, describes the stimulating influence of a bird song on a "Scribe in the Woods":

> A hedge of trees overhangs me;
> A blackbird's lay (a herald I won't hide) sings to me.
> Above my lined book,
> The chanting of birds sings to me.
>
> A clear-voiced cuckoo sings to me—happy sound!
> In his gray cloak from a bushy mound.
> *Debarth!* The Lord befriends me:
> Well do I write beneath a wooded stand.

Some medieval literature that described natural beasts and objects, however, resulted not from the observation or emotional experience of nature but from traditional descriptions of natural phenomena as expressions of Christian morals. Though medieval people were quite aware that the popular bestiary *Physiologus*—a kind of zoological handbook that taught morals as well—was allegorical rather than scientific in the modern sense of the word, natural curiosities were nonetheless described according to the "doctrine of signatures" that viewed the particulars of external reality as images of God's moral teachings. On the one hand, this doctrine of signatures demonstrates the medieval mind's appreciation and love of the natural world as the creation and symbol of God. On the other, it shows how the religious tendencies of the age could at times obscure genuine scientific curiosity about the external world. Such scientific curiosity had begun with Aristotle and, in the Roman period, with the writer Lucretius, whose *On Natural Things* was an attempt to explain the processes of nature as independent of divine intervention. Lucretius argued that natural processes must be examined closely, objectively, for their own sakes. But in the medieval *Physiologus* each creature is assumed to have been created for the moral instruction and use of mankind. A whale appears to be useless in itself and must supply ready morals for proper doctrines:

> He, the proud voyager, has another habit, yet more wondrous. When on the ocean hunger harries him, and the creature feels a craving for food, then the warden of the ocean opens his mouth, his wide lips. A pleasant smell comes from within, so that other kinds of fish are betrayed thereby; they swim swiftly to where the sweet smell issues forth. They enter there in a thoughtless throng, till the wide jaw is filled. Then suddenly the fierce jaws snap together, enclosing the plunder. Thus is it for every man who in this fleeting time most often looks heedlessly upon his life; he lets himself be snared by a sweet smell, a false desire, so that is he guilty of sins against the King of glory. After death the cursed one opens hell for them who, unmindful, have evilly followed the false joys of the flesh. . . .

This side of medieval vision represents, as you will discover, a vision almost exactly the opposite of the post-industrial nature writer. When nature was not treated as a moral backdrop or ornament in literature, it typically appeared in lyric moments that express genuine delight in barnyard scenes, in seasonal flux, in nature, as one sees in the following lyric, "The Cuckoo Song":

> Summer is a-comin' in,
> Loudly sings the cuckoo!
> Groweth the seeds, and bloweth the meadow
> And springth the wood now.
> Sing cuckoo!

Ewe bleats after lamb.
Loweth after calve cow,
Bulloch leaps, breaks wind
Merrily sing cuckoo!
Cuckoo, Cuckoo,
Well you sing Cuckoo:
Cease, you, never now!

Barring such notable exceptions, most medieval lyric poetry is religious, often using the Virgin Mary as a central figure. At times, however, even Mary becomes something like a nature goddess, as in the following song that celebrates the Annunciation and becomes a kind of hymn to spring: "Now the fowls sing and make her blissful/And the grass springs up and puts forth leaves. . . ." It would also be difficult to ignore the symbolic and allegorical treatment of nature that, despite a primary concern with Christian moralizing, does express a profound respect for God's order as evidenced by the natural order. Europeans such as Dante, Alan of Lille, and England's Chaucer in *Parlement of Foules* and the "Physician's Tale" all personify Nature as the goddess-figure Natura. Natura represents creative force or principle in the cosmos, a force secondary to God that mediates between God and humanity.

It is through the allegorical Natura figure that the poet, in poems of philosophical dialogue, tries to understand the order of creation, the proper order of society, the continuity of our world, and the creative principle that performs, but is subordinate to, God's will. The extent to which man deviates from that order typically becomes the extent to which chaos, decay, and moral degeneracy eat at the God-ordained foundations of social order. The medieval treatment of nature as Natura is largely allegorical and moralizing, but it represents the beginning of a philosophical position that pastoral writers and modern nature essayists will adopt and expand. What medieval literature and philosophy may have in common with modern nature literature is (to recall Schiller's phrase) the "sentimental" longing for a distant goal—unity with natural harmony. This longing was a basis for the criticism of the social order, and emphasized the distance that the social order, and hence humanity, had come from that order in nature.

Four figures from a colored copy of Brock's *Kreüter Buch:* I. Peach, II. Spruce, III. Feathered Pink, IV. Butterbur.

The Renaissance: Art and Artifice

The transition from the Medieval to the Renaissance world was neither sudden nor isolated. What we call the Renaissance (roughly from the fifteenth century to the seventeenth century) was a flourishing of certain qualities rooted in Medieval Europe. In thirteenth-century Gothic architecture and in one school of fourteenth-century landscape painting, for instance, the natural world was already becoming a proper theme and source of inspiration. Still, in the transition from Medieval to Renaissance times, five broader changes are significant for our understanding of the evolving relationship between humanity and the natural world: 1) the revival of classical learning and literature (including the pastoral tradition); 2) the Reformation of Christianity and the rise of secularism; 3) the discovery of new worlds through heroic voyages; 4) the emphasizing of the individual; and 5) the laying of the foundations of pragmatic, rational modern thought and science.

It would be hard to overestimate the role of this last quality in transforming the way humanity viewed nature. Joseph Wood Krutch, in his introduction to *Great American Nature Writing*, traces this transformation for us. By the fifteenth century, Krutch notes, botanists began to draw and describe plants realistically, not as signs of a Christian moral. Sixteenth-century zoologists, exemplified by Konrad Von Gesner in *Historia Animalia*, widened the horizons of the Medieval mind so that people could begin to see and study plants and animals in a more realistic fashion. By 1646 Sir Thomas Browne, in *Vulgar Errors*, undertook to disillusion those who still held misconceptions fostered by medieval bestiaries like the *Physiologus*. Most significantly, Browne appealed to common experience and observation to debunk fantastic notions about nature's creatures. An extreme example of scientific rationalism was mathematician-philosopher René Descartes's deduction that animals were without souls and therefore did not feel pain. The most cruel extensions of such a view were effectively countered by empirical seventeenth-century scientists more interested in observation and by the eighteenth-century scientist Carlos Linnaeus.

We can also easily imagine how Spain's and Portugal's great voyages of discovery in the fifteenth and sixteenth centuries stimulated the observation of startling new natural worlds. Columbus's *Diary* is one record of such observations. And the discovery—earlier in the Crusades as well as in the world voyages—of a great variety of landscapes, peoples, and religions paved the way for an increasingly relativistic world view, for a clearer sense of the incredible variety of life in humanity and nature, and for the new requirement of accuracy in describing what was discovered and observed.

If the great achievement of Spain and Portugal was to bring to Europe a vision of an infinitely varied external world, the earlier achievement of Italy, the cradle of the Renaissance, was to prepare Europe for the discovery of the infinitely varied internal world of the individual personality. And that subjective focus, perhaps best represented in Shakespeare, is the real spirit of the modern world, the spirit of individualism.

IN THE JUNGLE.

An Indian drawing, reduced to about two-thirds the scale. Executed about 1570.

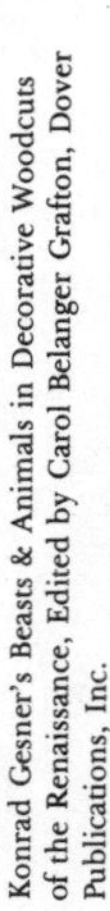

A greyhound drawn by Konrad Von Gesner in his 16th century book, Historia Animalia

Sensual delight and meditative joy in nature, even the therapeutic effects of vista, wood, and field, is the response expressed by the Italian poets Dante (1265–1321) and Petrarch (1304–74) in the thirteenth and fourteenth centuries. Dante was perhaps the first person since late classical times to write that he climbed mountains for the view. Petrarch, also a lover of vistas, closely observed the natural world and, like Dante, found nature to be an intellectual stimulant. His ascent of Mt. Ventoux near Avignon in 1335 is now as famous as it was unusual at the time, as are his odes on the delights of mountainous heights and solitudes. "At first, owing to the unaccustomed quality of the air and the effect of the great sweep of the view spread out before me, I stood like one dazed. I beheld the clouds under our feet, and what I had read of Athos and Olympus seemed less incredible as I myself witnessed the same things from a mountain of less fame." Such pleasures were not without their taint of guilt for men who arose from the thousand-year culture of ascetic Christianity. Even before his descent, Petrarch read a troubling passage of Saint Augustine's about the vanity of mountainous pleasures that lead men to forget the salvation of their souls, so that Petrarch would later admit to his confessor, "nothing save the soul [is] marvellous."

Yet when writing *On the Life of Solitude*, written by the Sorgue River, Petrarch early voiced the Renaissance delight in rural retreat and solitary meditation. The continuing Renaissance themes of self-discovery and transcendence in retreat, which would climax in the works of Andrew Marvell, were established here. The list of those who soon followed Dante and Petrarch in Italy and France is long. Pope Pius II wrote descriptions of the beauties of nature in his *Commentaries;* Jacopo Sannazoro paved the way for the rebirth of pastoral poetry with his *Arcadia* (1504); Luigi Alamanni's *Husbandry* in the same century was inspired by Vergil's *Georgics*. In sixteenth-century Italy, some thirty pastoral plays were composed. In France, the poet Ronsard (1525–85), whose influence on British writers was great, gave personality and divinity to his landscapes.

In England, such writers as Spenser, Drayton, Shakespeare, Jonson, Herrick, Milton, and Marvell expressed Renaissance approaches to nature and invigorated the classical pastoral tradition. After Henry VIII's accession to the throne in 1509, the revival of classical learning that previously had liberated Italy from the ascetic ideal now began to shape the English world view. Its humanistic spirit had been best expressed by Cicero when he wrote that in the active, engaged life men realize their full potential. Perhaps the greatest difference between the Medieval and Renaissance periods is exemplified by the advent of printing. Books became available not only to the wealthy but to the middle class. Mankind would come to be seen optimistically as master of earth, where the aspiring mind and body of the individual, through art, science, philosophy, politics, and trade, might lead to a position closer to angels, who ranked above human beings, and farther from "unthinking beasts," who ranked below them in the cosmic hierarchy or "Chain of Being."

Dante climbed mountains for the view

Nature was order and truth, one manifestation of God. Everything within this order had its place and, as Aristotle had taught, its use. By discovering and conforming to that order, man united himself with cosmic harmony. Yet today there may seem to be a strange paradox in the Renaissance approach to nature. For if Renaissance man loved nature for what it is, he also loved what he could make of it, or shape it into. The idea that nature was the art of God, and art the apelike imitation of nature, led to more than a century of debate about humanity's role in the order of nature. Despite the complexity of that debate, it remains obvious that the prevailing Renaissance attitude viewed man as a part of nature endowed with an ingenious mind to exercise craft and art. And what the gardener, the architect, the jeweler, and the field sportsman could do beyond "nature's art," the poet could match. Sir Philip Sidney (1554–86) said, "Nature never set forth the earth in so rich tapestry as diverse poets have done, neither with pleasant rivers, fruitful trees, sweet-smelling flowers. . . ." Hence the ornate artifice of madrigal music and Elizabethan poetry, poetry that was written in such ordered and complex forms as the sestina, the sonnet, and the Spenserian stanza. For the Renaissance mind, artifice expressed the unique, creative powers of humanity.

Yet for our time, for a people intensely interested in humanity's actual and biological, not idealized, relationship to the natural environment and in the survival of our species and the earth, the predominantly "artificial" view and use of nature in Renaissance literature is what makes the age's pastoral tradition often seem least useful to our contemporary understanding. The huge body of pastoral literature developed during the English Renaissance, for example, is admittedly an idyllic, or idealized, vision of landscape, farming, rural people, and rural life. Sidney was as much aware that his *Arcadia* (1593) was a nostalgic dream and a myth

Old English Country Illustrations for Decoupage and Other Crafts, Selected by Eleanor Hasbrouck Rawlings, Dover Publications, Inc.

as Spenser was that his Book VI of *The Faerie Queene* (1590, 1596) was an idyll. Spenser's great pastoral fantasy poem draws on past ages, other lands and myths, and fantastic landscapes to create an ideal natural world (as in Book VI) or, conversely, on a dark view of the primitive (as in Book IV) to create a wholly "savage" vision of nature and natural man. In place of a close observation of the English countryside, we find witches, tigers, lions, mythic creatures and beasts, a flora and fauna that never existed in England. And Spenser's twelve pastoral eclogues "The Shepheardes Calendar" (1579), although presented as a dialogue between shepherds remotely modeled on Vergil and Theocritus, is really a debate about the function and purpose of poetry in Spenser's time. It is perhaps the bold unreality, the fantastic ingenuity, and the allegorical content and satire that is the

Same as on page 14

Manticora, a fierce monster allegedly caught in Saxony in 1530

distinguishing quality of the Elizabethan regeneration of their ancient models.

The one element in Renaissance pastoral writing that relates to our contemporary social and environmental interests is the use of the idyllic vision as a critique of, if not really an escape from, the worst attributes of humanity's social organizations. For the pastoral, from Theocritus onward, is an urban and usually nostalgic interpretation of rural life. Even while approaching a dream state, the pastoral still looks for a serious response from the reader. The myth of the Golden Age, that fruitful Edenic Garden before the Fall, is a strong component of the pastoral. And that myth's purpose is to present an ideal of permanence and stability of values in opposition to the fluidity of civilization, its fashions, its corruptions, and its strifes. The poet might contrast the world of power, commerce, wealth, and politics to rural simplicity, leisure, and bucolic concerns. Or, the frustrations and intrigues of life at royal court might be contrasted to the life of rural retirement. Christopher Marlowe's "Passionate Shepherd to His Love" (1599) lyrically expresses the values of the pastoral ideal in opposition to those of urban and courtly life. The philosophical examination of the difference between rural and urban values is perhaps the most viable theme coming to us today from the Renaissance pastoral.

When the critique of urban values is harshest, as it is in Michael Drayton's *The Shepheardes Garland* (1593) and *Poly-Olbion* (1612–1622), his long topographical poem celebrating the English countryside, or when the landscapes or forces of nature are most accurately described, as in Drayton, or used in image and metaphor, as in Shakespeare, the reader today finds perhaps his surest ground for sympathy with the Renaissance literature of nature.

It was Drayton who, quoting Vergil, pointed out that though the subject and language of pastoral may often be coarse or silly, "Nevertheless, the most High, and most Noble Matters of the World may be shadowed in them, and for certain sometimes are." His *Garland* is frankly impatient with the quest for mythical Arcadia. The Golden Age is gone and there is no hope for any return to it. In the sixteenth century, London was changing from a medieval town to a modern capital of manufacturing, trade, and politics. Drayton is one of the first to censure the rape

Same as on top of page 16

Old English Country Illustrations for Decoupage and Other Crafts, Selected by Eleanor Hasbrouck Rawlings, Dover Publications, Inc.

of the land for the exploitation of natural resources. In *Poly-Olbion*, a long georgic with an encyclopediac use of English provincial lore, he describes the death of a landscape, Charnwood Forest, as it is cleared for commercial use and profit.

> The Driades that were wont about thy lawnes to rove,
> To trip from wood to wood, and scud from grove to grove . . .
> Exil'd their sweet aboad, to poore bare commons fled,
> They with the okes that liv'd, now with the okes are dead.

A land stripped of its natural flora and fauna is a land, as the American writer Aldo Leopold would suggest four hundred years later, stripped of its spirit. In *Poly-Olbion*, moreover, the accurate description of the landscape and its life dominates the poem, as in Drayton's description of the sun's rays in trees:

> Suppose twixt noone and night, the sunne his halfeway wrought
> . . . Who with a fervent eye lookes through the towrying glades,
> And his dispersed rayes commixeth with the shades,
> Exhaling the milch dews, which there had tarried long,
> And on the ranker grasse till past the noone-sted hong.

William Shakespeare (1564–1616) also had a realist's eye for the landscape and seasons of his homeland, and he used the pastoral tradition in complex and ambiguous ways in his drama. Shakespeare was a country lad before he settled in London as a professional actor and playwright, and his realism speaks of a practical experience of country life and lore that is closest perhaps to the practical realism of Hesiod before him. In his sonnets, the seasons and the exact character of the natural world are often the basis of his imagery, metaphor, and personification.

> That time of the year thou may'st in me behold
> When yellow leaves, or none, or few, do hang
> Upon those boughs which shake against the cold,
> Bare ruined choirs, where late the sweet birds sang.

The striking attributes of the natural imagery in Shakespeare's plays are its quickness and originality, its precise detail based on observation. Here, too, natural phenomena often describe people's moods and states, and nature sympathetically reinforces the personalities and actions of the plays, as in the November night of

Hamlet, or the heath storm in *King Lear*: "Blow, blow thou winter wind,/Thou art not so unkind/As man's ingratitude." When Romeo and Juliet love, all nature loves—stars, moon, and garden. And from MacBeth's guilt, nature itself would recoil: "Stars hide your fires!/Let not light see my black and deep desires." Man and nature are in accord.

Shakespeare uses the pastoral conventions, often as dramatic masques or interludes, in his own original way. *As You Like It*, a mock-pastoral, depicts shepherds as non-idyllic low-life characters. A play based on classical myth and English fairy lore, *A Mid-Summer Night's Dream* celebrates love and marriage in a presentation combining comic pastoral fantasy and striking, accurate description:

> I know a bank where the wild thyme blows,
> Where oxlips and the nodding violet grows,
> Quite over-canopied with luscious woodbine,
> With sweet musk-roses and with eglantine:
> There sleeps Titania sometime of the night,
> Lull'd in these flowers with dances and delight;
> And there the snake throws her enamell'd skin,
> Weed wide enough to wrap a fairy in. . . .

In Shakespeare's *A Winter's Tale*, pastoral life emerges as a serious alternative to the jealousy and tyranny of court politics. Through a long pastoral episode in that play the corrupt court is improved by its contact with the rural people and ritual

Same as on opposite page

described in a naturalistic setting. Here shepherds are presented more as real people than as idealized, conventional swains. And in *The Tempest*, Shakespeare takes us to the enchanted, primitive Bermudas and contrasts the isles with the civilized world. The natural and the supernatural converge as we see the magical, fluid, spiritual power in nature through the shaman Prospero and the contrasting "brute matter" without spirit in dull, monstrous Caliban.

After Elizabeth's death in 1603, and during Shakespeare's retirement to Stratford from 1610–16, the way of living and the view of life began to change dramatically in seventeenth-century England. The changes culminated, first, in the Civil War of 1642 between the King, Charles I, and his Parliament with its Puritan leadership and, second, in the Restoration in 1660 of Charles II and the death of the Puritan ruler Cromwell. It was a century of revolt, turmoil, radical change, the decline of absolute monarchy, and the explosion of learning in all fields from religion and philosophy, to law and history, and perhaps most important for us, to science. Men like John Selden, William Camden, Thomas Hobbes, Francis Bacon, Robert Boyle, and William Harvey led the country through an intellectual revolution that would change how English-speaking people viewed the world. The Medieval and Elizabethan concepts of uniformity, hierarchy, and divine signature and analogy gave way to concepts of multiplicity, objective or scientific "truth," and individualism. The Puritans changed the relationship between God and man to an individual one; cosmic hierarchy in heaven and earth gave way to the opposition of good and evil, of saved and sinner. The scientific discoveries of the time, from Galileo's decentering of the planet in the cosmos to Boyle's and Harvey's discoveries in physical and medical science, led to an increasing faith in scientific method and enabled humans to manipulate their environment more accurately. Thus began the long process—which has borne nourishing as well as poisonous fruit in our own century—of placing physical science in the service of money, commerce, and material improvements.

When the clergyman and naturalist John Ray published *The Wisdom of God Manifest in the Works of the Creation* (1691) at the end of the century, he spoke of another approach to nature that, during the next two centuries, would have tremendous credibility. Not only did Ray insist on the exact, scientific observation common to his time, he fused his scientific observations with the opposing romantic vision of nature and its creatures as teachers of mankind, as not fitting for us alone but fitting in themselves. Such a view lays the groundwork for humility in one's approach to animal life as much as it establishes the emotional and "religious" basis of nineteenth-century Transcendentalism in America.

The seventeenth-century was a time of the steady rise of the power of land, as well as the rise of the tradesman and the bourgeois class. Puritan industriousness,

Same as on page 18

common sense, and scientific materialism led to the tearing down of the theaters and maypoles and to the lessening of legend and folklore. The Pastoral Age that some associated with Medieval or Elizabethan life had disappeared. The most influential poets of the metaphysical school (Donne, Herbert, Crashaw, Vaughan) were not much interested in the pastoral, but focused in their poetry on salvation, political struggle, and the mercantile age.

Though some political poems did emerge—often as experimental eclogues on various vocations—the conventional ideas underwent changes from the earlier Renaissance. The theme of retreat from city to country life became, as it did for Abraham Cowley (1618–67)—a poet, accomplished botanist, and a medical man from Oxford—a meditative turning inwards as much as a joy in the pleasures of the country life. Beyond such pleasures, one could learn, through occasional glimpses, of the harmonious universe of God. That harmony is best glimpsed through science, as Cowley argues in "To the Royal Society," but the country life provides the naturalist with the most opportunities for discovery. The interest in country life also reflects the growing interest in individualism, for it is in the rural retreat that the person is free to find himself. The group ritual of the conventional pastoral gives way to the emphasis on the individual's relationship to his land.

The country becomes at times a specific geographical alternative to the urban, not an ideal or a nostalgic past. The real or imagined escape from the city is an escape from the economic pressures of urban life and provides economic freedom for the artist. If courtly patronage is losing its old predominance, a self-sufficient small farm may become a source of retirement and an escape from artistic penury. In his poem "The Wish," Cowley says that those who live in the beehive of the city deserve his "pity," and that "This busy world and I shall ne'er agree." What does Cowley seek? "May I a small house and large garden have!/And a few friends, and many books, both true . . ./And a mistress moderately fair." With these pleasant accoutrements Cowley would then be the "happy tenant" of fields and woods, enjoying "Nature's treasury" in the same manner as the lucky "Grasshopper" described in his poem of that title as having all of nature at his service.

Ben Jonson, Robert Herrick, John Milton, and Andrew Marvell are among the writers of this century who represent the connection to, and the changes in, the pastoral tradition. Jonson's (1572–1637) "To Penshurst," for example, is in the classical tradition of celebrating the rural mansion. The Roman poets Martial, whose celebration of Faustinus' estate contrasted sterile order with virile productivity, and Ausonius, who emphasized the influence of the environment on man, are echoed in Jonson's "To Penshurst," in Marvell's "Upon Appleton House," and in Milton's "Il Penseroso." In Jonson's poem the old nostalgia for a past time remains, but he describes a way of life which includes the vegetation, the creatures, the fruitfulness, and the owner in one harmonious, proportionate environment. It is the landscape that symbolically describes the larger richness of the Sidney family life.

> Thou are not, *Penshurst*, built to envious show. . . .
> Thou joy'st in better markes, of soyle, of ayre,
> Of wood, of water: therein thou art faire. . . .
> The lower land, that to the river bends,
> Thy sheepe, thy bullocks, kine, and calves doe feed:
> The middle grounds thy mares, and horses breed.
> Each banke doth yeeld thee conveyes; and the topps
> Fertile of wood, *Ashore*, and *Sydney's* copp's
> To crowne thy open table, doth provide
> The purpled pheasent, with the speckled side:

The rural richness and values described here endure into the present and future.

> Now, Penshurst, they that will proportion thee
> With other edifices, when they see
> Those proud, ambitions heaps, and nothing else,
> May say, their lords have built, but thy Lord dwells.

In another poem, "To Sir Robert Wroth," Jonson would write, "How blest art thou, canst love the countrey, Wroth,/Whether by choice, fate, or both;/And, though so neere, the city, and the court,/Art tane with neithers vice, nor sport."

Robert Herrick (1591–1674), a Londoner who accepted a church living in rural Devonshire, wrestled with the contrast between city and rural life, but he eventually came to love the Devonshire countryside and people. Herrick's poetry was polished and steeped in classical learning, and its uniqueness lies in the expression of the simple delights experienced by a sophisticated and urbane man in the rural and natural world. His pastoral dialogue on the birth of Prince Charles ends:

> Come let's away, and quickly let's be drest,
> And quickly give, *The swiftest Grace is best.*
> And when we before him have laid our treasures,
> We'll bless the Babe, Then back to country pleasures.

Herrick's poem "The Hock-Cart" develops the theme of the bond between the landowner and his rustic laborers—a bond that stands as a moment of unity during the harvest feast ritual, even though the laborers return to their toil the next day. The feast is akin to a fertility rite, suggesting the eternal myth and natural world that lie behind local Devon customs. We are invited, as we are in "Corinna's Going a

Same as on page 18

Maying," to become involved in natural cycles and simple rural customs, to celebrate fertility of earth and rural labor in procession, feast, and orgy:

> Come sons of summer, by whose toile,
> We are the Lords of Wine and Oile:
> . . . .The Harvest Swaines, and Wenches bound
> For joy, to see the Hock-cart crown'd . . . .
> Some crosse the Fill-horse; some with great
> Devotion, stroak the home-borne wheat:
> While other Rusticks, lease attent
> To Prayers, then the Merryment,
> Run after with their breeches rent.

And in "His Content in the Country," Herrick celebrates his and his maidservant "Prew's" independence from landlord and usurer. He blesses their good fortune that they are independent of others' favoritism and whim, and that they have "beloved privacie."

With Andrew Marvell (1621–78) the uses of the pastoral tradition approach a climax. Marvell wrote debates and dialogues and found transcendence in retirement. He used the ambiguities and paradoxes of the tradition with a peculiarly modern, skeptical viewpoint. If nature is not sacred to him in an identifiable Christian sense, nature nevertheless has divinity; nature is the source of religious feeling in retirement. Marvell's garden is at times a place of past innocence and grace that has been violated by human experience, but at other times the garden is a source of pure Edenic ecstasy. His "Mower" poems—"The Mower Against Gardens," "*Damon* the Mower," "The Mower to the Glo-Worms," and "The Mower's Song"—suggest not only the Golden Age myth but also the modern impossibility of harmony between humans and the natural environment. Here a cultivated garden speaks not of order in nature but rather of the artificiality of urbanized life and the products of humanity after the Fall. Marvell sees a destructive relationship between humanity and nature, and in him the anti-pastoral reaches maturity. In the "Mower" poems Marvell, as would many a writer after him, decries the luxurious or commercial manipulation of plants—an action symbolic of man's unnaturalness—and the scientific manipulation of nature:

Luxurious Man, to bring his Vice in use,
Did after him the World seduce:
And from the fields the Flow'rs and Plants allure,
Where Nature was most plain and pure.

The colors and perfumes of plants grow strange and "double," "forbidden mixtures" are created, and no "Plant now knows the Stock from which it came;/He grafts upon the Wild the Tame." All this is the work of arrogant man, "that sov'raign thing and proud." And herein lies the danger of the "Mower mown" by "his own Sythe." Man is no longer the rational half-angel he seemed at the height of the Elizabethan Renaissance. He is a kind of death upon the land—"For Death thou art a Mower too."

Although Marvell's other pastoral vision can be seen in the unaltered paradise described in "Bermudas," his pastoral vision is best exemplified by "The Garden." Cannot the individual, Marvell asks, reconstruct natural paradise for himself by turning inward? Cannot he transcend through removal and meditation the industrious hum of fallen, arrogant, striving humanity: "To weave the Garlands of repose," to retire "To a green Thought in a green Shade" where "My Soul into the boughs does glide:/There like a Bird it sits and sings, Then Whets, and combs its silver Wings."

And both themes—the difficulty of retirement, perhaps even the need to stay engaged, and the healing potential of retirement—are joined in his long estate-poem "Upon Appleton House, to my Lord Fairfax," written in the pastoral tradition of Martial and Jonson. As tutor to Lord Fairfax's daughter from 1650–53, Marvell lived on the great estate after Fairfax, who had been a leader in the victories of the Parliamentary armies, retired to his rural family seat. In part the poem condemns Fairfax for retreating from a tumultuous world that needs him, and in part the poem praises Fairfax for finding such a beautiful garden of retirement and escape.

But Nature here hath been so free
As if she had said leave this to me.
Art would more neatly have defac'd
What she had laid so sweetly wast;
In fragrant Gardens, shaddy Woods,
Deep Meadows, and transparent Floods.

By turning inward, Fairfax transforms Appleton House, once a cloister of Cistercian nuns, into a truly religious place in accordance with the new theology of private meditation, of personal transcendence and salvation:

And what both *Nature* and *Founders* will'd
'Tis likely better thus fulfill'd.
. . . 'Twas no *Religious House* till now.

The Enlightenment: Scientific World View

During the eighteenth century Europeans came to view the natural world as comprehensible. What had been thought orderly in an obscure way became, during the Enlightenment, reassuringly lucid. The scientific, philosophical, and political forces of change at work during the Renaissance yielded cumulative and therefore dramatic effects in a period when the rate of change itself escalated. Six general developments were important: 1) a radically new conception of the physical forces moving in the universe; 2) immense gathering of details about natural objects; 3) a new understanding of human psychology; 4) a religious outlook called "deism" or "natural religion" that found basis for faith in the glory of the created world; 5) a new cult of personal feeling, linked to a preoccupation with picturesque and sublime landscape; and 6) rapid industrialization, including a great reorganization of economic relations between town and country.

Dramatic changes in attitudes became possible because a few seminal ideas, growing since the Renaissance, were extended in ways that rendered them exciting rather than troubling. As early as 1609, for example, Galileo had shown in *The Starry Messenger* that the earth was not the center of the universe. An immediate implication was that humanity literally did not stand at the center of things. Gradually another implication emerged: that the earth was not a shadowy mystery designed to test human morality for the next world, but an open book by which humanity might gain wealth in this one.

This idea assumed both clarity and optimism when the Englishman Sir Isaac Newton (1642–1727) asserted that all the universe worked according to uniform laws, comprehensible by means of mathematical principles. Newton's laws of motion and gravitation and his assumption of uniform, infinite space dispelled the conviction that the world of things showed divinity only by mysterious or obscure emblem. Physical things could be explained by clear and simple laws. The very word "nature" came in the eighteenth century to mean ordered and predictable, in fact, reasonable. Newton rendered the physical world not only reliable but fascinating: a delightful puzzle to be solved piece by piece, demonstrating the reason and ingenuity of an increasingly distant Workman. More than forty years after the publication of Newton's *Principia* (1687), Alexander Pope expressed this view:

> Nature, and Nature's Laws lay hid in Night.
> God said, *Let* Newton be! and All was *Light*.

On one hand humanity lost its privileged position as focal point of the created universe; on the other hand, humanity increased its ability to unlock the "delightful puzzle" of the world, and by amassing technological power found it possible to dominate nature in order to satisfy its needs and desires. In *The Death of Nature,* environmental historian Carolyn Merchant argues persuasively that the birth of empirical science during the Renaissance and its rapid growth during the

Enlightenment validated the violent exploitation of the earth as a passive object, a thing important only for its usefulness as an economic resource to humanity.

The immense gathering of details about natural objects initiated by the explorations of the Renaissance was given order by the widely published *Systema Naturae* of Linnaeus, which provided a relatively simple, uniform method for recognizing likenesses among plants. Even the amateur could place genera and species. In *Great American Nature Writing*, Joseph Wood Krutch writes: "The eighteenth century was the first during which some knowledge of natural history became almost an inevitable part of the cultivated man's equipment." As early as 1720 an illustrated *Natural History of English Insects* appeared and was reprinted in many editions. In the popular journals such as *The Gentleman's Magazine*, natural history became a stock topic.

A direct effect on poetry, as John Arthos noted in *The Language of Description in Eighteenth-Century Poetry*, was the evolution of a "poetic diction," that is, a proper vocabulary created largely out of the urge to classify. Fish became a "finny tribe" and birds a "feathery horde." The aim of such metaphor, which may sound artificial today, was to capture the physical essence of a thing.

The changing world view suggested by natural science was magnified by a new psychology of the human mind. John Locke (1632–1704) believed with Newton that physical matter was composed of tiny bodies, the motions of which caused all physical processes. In his *An Essay Concerning Human Understanding* (1689), Locke argued that the human mind holds no innate ideas; its entire stock of knowledge stems from sensations received by the mind. Sensations occur when "atoms" emitted by external physical things penetrate the senses and cause our ideas of size, color, shape, and so on.

For Locke the mind resembled a blank page on which was written the data of sense experience. Abstractions, including moral and aesthetic abstractions, came from a generalizing power in the mind, the "understanding," which acted upon sensations presented to the "imagination." The mind was *not* endowed with prepared ideas of goodness or beauty; rather, it refined them entirely from sensations received out of nature. Even the idea of God, Locke explained, came from the mind's reflecting upon sensations gathered from the physical world.

The ideas of Newton and Locke struck the eighteenth-century mind as utterly reasonable, and revolutionized the thinking of the modern world. For nature writing, the most far reaching corollary was the idea, not fully articulated until the end of the century, that divinity was *immanent* in natural things, not in terms of "superstitious" pantheism or "obscure" emblems, but in the workings of nature itself, as perceived by the senses of the individual. In 1798 William Wordsworth inaugurated modern nature writing with what has become a classic statement:

> [I am] well pleased to recognize
> In nature and the language of the sense
> The anchor of my purest thoughts, the nurse,
> The guide, the guardian of my heart, and soul
> Of all my moral being.

But during the eighteenth century, the more obvious implication for the growth of nature writing was simply that every detail of the natural world became the substance of education: every detail became important. Since nature itself was uniform, there should be at least a rough concordance among the ideas arrived at by different people, though some understandings might be brighter, some dimmer. To a degree, the function of poetry was then to correct the understanding by presenting it with clear, accurate images.

Because of these scientific and philosophic influences the pastoral tradition diverged into several streams during the eighteenth century. The georgic, a distinct form of pastoral since ancient times, enjoyed great popularity, partly as a consequence of the rising interest in natural history. The lighthearted *Cyder* by John Philips (1676–1709) and *The Fleece*, a comprehensive analysis of the wool industry by John Dyer (1699–1758), are the most notable examples. Another genre tending toward realistic natural description was the mock-pastoral. Though a parody, it often treated country sports and manners realistically, and with appreciation. John Gay (1685–1732) prefaced *The Shepherd's Week* with a warning to the reader:

> Thou wilt not find my Shepherdesses idly piping on oaten Reeds, but milking the Kine, tying up sheaves, or if the Hogs are astray, driving them to their styes. My Shepherd gathereth none other Nosegays but what are the growth of our own fields, he sleepth not under Myrtle shades, but under a Hedge, nor doth he vigilantly defend his Flocks from Wolves, because there are none. . . .

The new psychology of Locke, as applied to natural observation, clearly influenced *The Seasons* (1726;1746) of James Thomson (1700–1748) in contrast to the more traditional *Pastorals* of Alexander Pope (1688–1744). Pope's poems on the four seasons proceed deductively, consciously in imitation of the eclogues of Vergil and Theocritus. Pope's description of natural scenes is accurate and exquisite, almost like a well-composed landscape painting. The poem's landscapes are idealized because they depict the timeless Golden Age of Arcady, a "perfect" rural spot where human concerns about love and art are acted out by shepherds removed from the exigencies of actual work.

The Seasons, on the other hand, differs in design. Rather than deduce the content of description from models out of the pastoral tradition, Thomson investigates actual images of the seasons in a comprehensive way, traveling from village to town, from country to country, viewing various occupations and various manners.

Same as on page 13

Generally, the focus remains on particular images, both common and unique: a snowstorm, a pack of arctic wolves, the fabulous ice palace of Catherine the Great.

Joseph Warton, an eighteenth-century critic of nature writing, noted that since the classical poet Theocritus had written his *Idylls*, every nature poet "except Thomson in *Seasons*, hath copied his images from [Theocritus], without ever looking abroad into the face of nature themselves." Thomson's famous description of an impending snowstorm shows his ability to look "into the face of nature":

> Lo! from the livid East, or piercing North,
> Thick Clouds ascend, in whose capacious Womb,
> A vapoury Deluge lies, to Snow congeal'd:
> Heavy, they roll their fleecy World along;
> And the Sky saddens with th'impending Storm.
> Thro' the hush'd Air, the whitening Shower descends,
> At first, thin-wavering; till, at last, the Flakes
> Fall broad, and wide, and fast, dimming the Day,
> With a continual Flow.

The action of *The Seasons* is essentially the process of change in the natural cycle. With the poem focused on natural process, human characters assume a secondary role, acting almost as foils to the natural drama. Thomson's inversion of the pastoral pattern made it acceptable for the naturalist as well as the poet to treat natural occurrences as interesting and attractive in themselves. This, and the accuracy of his description, would strongly influence future nature writers.

By changing the relative importance of humanity and nature, *The Seasons* made possible the future theme of *inter*action, and eventually even intimate interaction, between people and the natural world, the theme that distinguishes the first great harvest of modern nature literature written during the Romantic period of the early nineteenth century. Subsequent nineteenth-century writers would strive to remove common human bias and sentiment, what John Ruskin called the "pathetic fallacy," from their interpretation of nature. Much later, our contemporaries like Annie Dillard, aware of the inevitability of human bias in the very act of interpretation, would consciously fathom the strangeness of non-human life, at the same time remaining aware of its potential to arouse the most profound human feelings.

In contrast to Thomson's *Seasons*, humans remained central in a genre of landscape poetry that grew popular early in the century. The "topographical poem," as Robert Arnold Aubin points out in *The Topographical Poem in the Eighteenth Century*, "described specifically named actual localities" and followed a classical Roman tradition. It relied upon actual images specific to the place but, more so than in *The Seasons*, often used images as small emblems of larger human concerns in keeping with the historical themes that dominate the entire work. The earliest example, Sir John Denham's *Cooper's Hill* (1655), depicts a place offering views of London and Windsor Palace, and meditates upon the various degrees of regal authority exercised in English history. Alexander Pope continued the topographical tradition with *Windsor Forest* (1713), a description of the hunting preserve of the British royalty. Both poems, and their numerous imitations, present the pastoral assumption employed in Marvell's poem of praise to Lord Fairfax, "Upon Appleton House": namely, that retreat to a rural place renews the spirit. In *Windsor Forest* Pope delivers a classic statement of that assumption:

Same as on page 18

Happy the Man whom this bright Court approves,
His Sov'reign favours, and his Country loves;
Happy next to him who to these Shades retires,
Whom Nature charms, and whom the Muse inspires,
Whom humbler joys of home-felt Quiet please,
Successive Study, Exercise and Ease.

As the century progressed, the tendency in the topographical poem and in nature writing in general was to prefer the country to society. That natural landscape could be a stimulus to meditation, Pope eloquently maintained:

Or wandring thoughtful in the silent Wood,
Attends the Duties of the Wise and Good,
T'observe a Man, be to himself a Friend,
To follow Nature, and regard his End.
Or looks on Heav'n with more than mortal Eyes,
Bids his free Soul expatiate in the Skies,
Amid her Kindred Stars familiar roam,
Survey the Region, and confess her Home!

Subsequent writers would emphasize more and more the personal value to be found when one turns attention from the world of society to the world of natural influences.

Such were the major eighteenth-century pastoral forms and impulses, based on the scientific and philosophical influences discussed. We need now to look more closely at the broader cultural consequences of these influences. The new knowledge in physics, natural history, and psychology harmonized with an evolving "natural religion," a cult of personal feeling, and an industrialism marked by the ongoing reorganization of economic relations between the country and the town.

The topographical poems, and especially *The Seasons*, were enormously popular, reflecting the age's enthusiasm for the details of natural history, an enthusiasm greatly advanced by new religious attitudes. Well aware that the old Puritan "enthusiasm" of personal righteousness had helped bring about the bloodshed and anarchy of the Civil War, the eighteenth century turned by degrees to a "natural religion" in which God was perceived less as a mentor of personal salvation and more as the master architect of a complex, beautiful creation. God became worshipped more in works, which science was rendering more comprehensible. Newton's precise formulation of physical law presented a glimpse of the vast clock-like mechanism—to use the metaphor that Pope popularized in his *Essay on Man*—by which God imparted motion to the universe.

"Deism," as this informal religion came to be called, somewhat modified the medieval doctrine of signatures. The deist still saw divine significance in natural things, but the significance was less mysterious than reasonable. Small things remained emblems of the macrocosm, but in a more systematic, comprehensible way. There was more attention paid to the "Divine Works" themselves, the functional testimony of an increasingly distant, impersonal Designer. Slowly there grew the conception that in the comprehensible natural order, man governed as prime intelligence, but fit into the Design as one of many necessary parts. Perception of order and intricacy in natural processes ensured that this conception remained optimistic. The Anglican clergyman John Ray (1627–1705), whose *The Wisdom of God Made Manifest in the Works of Creation* was published in 1691 and republished regularly, made the point that the beauty of nature lay in its own intricate design, not just its usefulness to humanity. This idea was endorsed by Alexander Pope in his immensely popular *Essay on Man*, where he warned against the arrogant presumption that all life was created for the pleasure of humanity:

> Has God, thou fool! work'd solely for thy good,
> Thy joy, thy pastime, thy attire, thy food?
> Who for thy table feeds the wanton fawn;
> For him as kindly spread the flow'ry lawn:
> Is it for thee the lark ascends and sings?
> Joy tunes his voice, joy elevates his wings.
>
> . . .
>
> While Man exclaims, "See all things for my use!"
> "See man for mine!" replies a pampr'd goose:
> And just as short of reason he must fall,
> Who thinks all made for one, not one for all.

Yet the intellectual conviction that "one is made for all" is actually a question of usefulness and thus differs from the modern nature writer's exploration of emotional interplay between man and mountain, or beast, or plant. To arrive at the understanding, as did Wordsworth at the end of the century, that "the meanest flower that grows/Lends thoughts that lie too deep for human tears," would require further development of emotional sensitivity.

Such a development began in the "Cult of Sensibility," an artistic movement that exploited heightened personal emotion in art. Around mid-century, it arose widely as part of the continued desire for social moderation and individual calm. No doubt it filled a vacuum created by the alteration in religious sentiment. In literature its proponents looked to the style and certain themes of John Milton (1608–1674), an anti-royalist leader during the Civil War and author of the great epic *Paradise Lost*. The power of his poetry provided a model for eighteenth-century writers unsatisfied with the prevailing taste for decorous, "correct" verse; the theme of two earlier works, *L'Allegro* and *Il Penseroso*, inspired those concerned with exploiting personal moods. *L'Allegro*, set in the morning, celebrated anticipation and joy, while *Il Penseroso*, set in the evening, celebrated gloom and melancholy. The latter especially provided a theme for mid-century devotees of sensibility, many of whom found in the natural world a fit stimulus for emotion.

William Collins (1721–1759) coupled emotional intensity with apt description in his "Ode to Evening." His highly educated friend Joseph Warton (1722-1800) preferred primitive life to corrupt civilization in *The Enthusiast: or, the Lover of Nature* (1744). Warton's descriptions are sometimes exquisite:

> But let me never fail in cloudless nights,
> When silent Cynthia in her silver car
> Through the blue concave slides, when shine the hills,
> Twinkle the streams, and woods look tipped with gold,
> To seek some level mead.

But nature remains an escape, for the poet seeks the meadow to "invoke Old Midnight's sister, Contemplation sage." Landscape is merely the background of Warton's contemplation; its object, the corruption of English society, allows for little imaginative interaction with the landscape. Warton concludes his thought with a wish to fly away to "western climes" where he will "hunt the wild boar and tiger through savannahs wild." Obviously, there is little accurate knowledge of the "western climes": natural objects are much less the object of genuine emotional attachment than the emblems of a social rhetoric. Warton's younger brother Thomas (1728–1790) extended the influence of Milton's *Il Penseroso* in celebrating wild nature complemented by gloomy ruins. But these were sentiments derived more from books than from first-hand intimacy with natural things.

Nonetheless, these writers were exploring personal emotion to a depth that had not been sanctioned since the end of the Elizabethan period, and their ostensible stimulus was not religious enthusiasm but natural landscape. They were influenced not only by Milton but also by the vogue of French and Italian landscape painting that had become very popular in England by mid-century. Two painters, Claude Lorraine and Salvator Rosa, made a strong impression with their depictions of extensive vistas and romantic ruins, respectively. They graphically showed the awesomeness and power of nature that Locke had argued was the means by which the human understanding conceived of God. In 1757 Edmund Burke explored the ways in which the mind reacted to magnificent natural scenes in *A Philosophical Enquiry into the Origin of Our Ideas of the Sublime and Beautiful*. It became more and more popular to hunt for "picturesque" views, so that by the end of the century William

Same as on page 13

Gilpin and others actually developed a critical method of evaluating landscapes, and published a multitude of "Guides" to the Lake Country in England and other picturesque regions.

The last and most far reaching influence upon nature writing from the eighteenth century to the present is the force of industrialism—the transformation it has effected not only upon physical landscapes and human demographics, but also upon the conceptual framework from which individuals perceive the natural world.

It is a peculiar though obvious paradox that as man comes to understand the subtler workings of nature, he acquires greater power to alter it. The more his alteration detracts from natural beauty, the more he consciously yearns for it. Finally, and most paradoxically, the more he pursues his yearning, the more the object eludes him. The seekers of picturesque views at the end of the century, for example, could attain them—in massive numbers—because of significantly improved roads, paid for with revenues generated by a very rapidly expanding economy, which in turn had long since drawn a great portion of the population away from rural areas to cities, where those people became conscious that natural beauty was lacking in their lives.

From 1700 to 1800 the population of England and Wales rose from five and one-half million to nine million and moved away from its overwhelmingly rural base to an increasingly urban one. From the early years of the century a growing number of factories utilized water power, and the invention of an effective steam engine by James Watt in 1776 caused huge new factory towns to sprawl above coal deposits and near deep harbors. Workers left their farms and villages to man the factories. The land left behind, or from which rural cottagers had been evicted, was bought up with the new industrial and commercial wealth, and combined into huge holdings to facilitate the industrial-scale agriculture necessary to feed the new urban proletariat. The yeoman who farmed a small holding and shared pasturage on a village common saw the common and his own leasehold bought and enclosed, that is, fenced off by newly planted hedgerows, or perhaps he sold the family cottage to a newly enriched entrepeneur who pulled it down to permit a "picturesque" view from a newly erected mansion.

The changing landscape resulted in two literary developments: the poem lamenting loss of the "idyllic" life (a version of the pastoral) and a new emphasis on rural life itself. In 1770 *The Deserted Village* was published with great success by Oliver Goldsmith (1728–1774). The poem begins as pastoral, with an idyllic view of "Sweet Auburn, loveliest village of the plain":

> How often have I blest the coming day,
> When toil remitting lent its turn to play,
> And all the village train, from labor free
> Led up their sports beneath the spreading tree
> While many a pastime circled in the shade,
> The young contending as the old surveyed;
> And many a gambol frolick'd o'er the ground
> And slights of art and feats of strength went round.

But after castigating the luxurious wealth that had transformed the scene, Goldsmith presents an unidealized, though pleasant, narrative of mundane life:

> Sweet was the sound, when oft at evening's close,
> Up yonder hill the village murmur rose;
> There as I past with careless steps and slow,
> The mingling notes came softened from below;
> The swain responsive as the milkmaid sung,
> The sober herd that lowed to meet their young;
> The noisy geese that gabbled o'er the pool,
> The playful children just let loose from school,
> The watch-dog's voice that bayed the whispering wind,
> And the loud laugh that spoke the vacant mind;
> These all in sweet confusion sought the shade,
> And filled each pause the nightingale had made.

There follows a kind of georgic—an appreciative survey of the work of the village preacher, schoolmaster, and innkeeper—and further attacks on large-scale trade (in which Goldsmith includes industrialization) for turning the nation's values from land to money.

Whether or not his nostalgic picture is entirely accurate, Goldsmith is asserting the value of rural culture in the integration of natural objects with basic human activity, and therein lies a great deal of its pleasantness. *The Deserted Village* lies squarely within what the scholar W. J. Keith calls the "rural tradition," as opposed to the pastoral tradition. Recall that pastoral literature traditionally arose from impulse born of urban life. As a sophisticated artifice it idealizes the country as the setting for discussion of values away from the social and political realities of the city. The perspective is that of the city dweller.

In the rural tradition, on the other hand, writers focus on realistic, though appreciative, descriptions of rural society. Often such writers have lived or spent their youth in the countryside and formed concrete impressions of its pleasures. Keith traces the beginnings of rural writing in England to a particular work, Sir Isaac Walton's *The Compleat Angler* (1653). Written amidst the turmoil created by the Civil War, it is both handbook and celebration of fishing and the rural life in general, not only an escape from a divisive society, but also the deliberate seeking out of a particular English locale where familiar and concrete rural activities are narrated with affection.

Same as on page 18

John Dyer's *Grongar Hill* (1726) also seems to fit into the rural tradition. An early topographical poem, it concentrates on the natural attractions of the locale, to the exclusion of historical and political themes. The classic example of rural writing, however, and one that has remained popular into the twentieth century with both naturalists and scientists, is *The Natural History of Selborne* (1791). This journal of vivid observations on local flora and fauna is rendered into literature not by form but by the sensitive appreciation of life that colors the observations of Gilbert White (1720–1793), an otherwise obscure country curate.

A final example of a rural writer, and a transitional figure who just precedes the era of modern nature writing, is William Cowper (1731–1800). Cowper also lived a rural life on intimate terms with the natural world. As a shy young man, he had become so anxious at the approach of an examination in law that he attempted suicide three times and subsequently fell insane, convinced that he was eternally damned. After leaving an insane asylum, he converted to evangelical Christianity and retired to a country life in the company of religious advisors. In his case, condemnation of urban pleasures arose from deep personal feelings; he spent his country retirement practicing acts of charity, gardening, and working at carpentry. In *The Task*, a long poem that eventually made him the most famous English poet of his day, Cowper sought "to discountenance the modern enthusiasm after a London life, and to recommend rural ease and leisure, as friendly to the cause of piety and virtue." In Book III, "The Garden," Cowper delivers a vivid georgic on the art of culturing vines. He foreshadows the insight of the modern nature writer by describing the harmonious impressions afforded the gardener by the objects of his work:

> Scenes form'd for contemplation, and to nurse
> The growing seeds of wisdom; that suggest
> By ev'ry pleasing image they present
> Reflections such as meliorate the heart,
> Compose the passions, and exalt the mind. . . .

Nineteenth-Century Britain: Seed-Time For Modern Nature Literature

At the beginning of the nineteeth century in England, what had been a gradual evolution in literature assumed revolutionary new characteristics, and modern nature writing emerged. The essential new quality, present in both form and theme, was an emotional interchange between human and natural object, a sense, noticed even in its absence, of potential kinship between the individual and the non-human. In the "meditations" of most eighteenth-century landscape poems, nature had served as a setting in which to express feelings that the writer had carried preformed to the scene. In modern (i.e., post-eighteenth century) nature writing, on the other hand, natural objects generate emotional, philosophical, and even religious responses from the writer, who in turn depicts the objects as symbols and invests them with meaning. As William Wordsworth (1770-1850) wrote, "to me the meanest flower that blows can give/Thoughts that do often lie too deep for tears."

The readiness to find human meaning in the natural world evolved in part from the eighteenth century's fascination with the concrete details of nature, which produced an ever-increasing body of scientific knowledge, as well as such popular renderings of that knowledge as Erasmus Darwin's *Loves of the Plants* (1789). The eighteenth-century cult of the picturesque was advanced by faster carriages and, later, the steam-driven railway. "View taking," with the aesthetic instruction of writers like William Gilpin in *Observations on the Mountains and Lakes of Cumberland and Westmoreland (1786),* became a popular pastime of the middle class, which increased and prospered after the conclusion of the war with France in 1814. Reports of newly explored lands, such as

William Bartram's *Travels . . . in America* (1741), which had slaked the thirst for more exotic details of natural history, provided imagery to English writers like Samuel Taylor Coleridge (1772-1834).

Imagery employed by nature writers in the nineteenth century, then, grew more concrete. Furthermore, the previous century's preoccupation with personal feeling became more and more integrated with the details of natural scenes; the natural setting became less the stage for declaiming emotion than the stimulus to emotion. This innovation, along with the further tendency to find profound meaning in nature, were hallmarks of modern nature literature, which was in some ways identical with the tradition known as Romantic Literature. A good example of the richness in the Romantic description of nature is found in the poem "To Autumn" by John Keats (1795-1821):

> Season of mists and mellow fruitfulness
> Close bosom-friend of the maturing sun;
> Conspiring with him how to load and bless
> With fruit the vines that round the thatch-eves run;
> To bend with apples the moss'd cottage-trees,
> And fill all fruit with ripeness to the core;
> To swell the gourd, and plump the hazel shells
> With a sweet kernel; to set budding more,
> And still more, later flowers for the bees,
> Until they think warm days will never cease,
> For Summer has o'er-brimm'd their clammy cells.

Keats's images not only depict the season vividly, but also evoke in the reader the feeling (shared with the bees) that "warm days will never cease."

In the Romantic nature writers of the nineteenth century, concrete natural detail embodies not simply emotion, but also religious thought, another radical extension of an eighteenth-century assumption. From the time of the naturalist John Ray (1627-1705), it had become an increasingly common assumption that scientific understanding of the workings of the natural world revealed divine wisdom, to the greater glory of God. Knowing God more intimately was a strong motive for studying His works. Furthermore, the psychology of John Locke (1634-1704), which assumed that all knowledge came from sense perception of the images generated by external things, lent further justification to the idea that all had the opportunity to study God in the world of nature.

Among the Romantic poets nature tended to become a source of religious feelings for its own sake. The work of some Romantics approaches pantheism, or the worship of nature itself. The contrast with the eighteenth-century view is clear. Lines written in the middle of the eighteenth century by Edward Young (1683-1765), for example, equate nature with Christian morality:

> Read Nature: Nature is a friend to truth;
> Nature is Christian; reaches to mankind;
> And bids dead matter aid us in our need.

By contrast, in 1798 William Wordsworth (1770-1850), the most influential of all modern nature writers, described in "Tintern Abbey" the moral imperative immanent in nature herself:

> (I am) well pleased to recognize
> In nature and the language of the sense
> The anchor of my purest thoughts, the nurse,
> The guide, the guardian of my heart, and soul
> Of all my moral being.

In the passage nature refers to the concrete particulars of an environment as these interact with "the language of the sense," that is, with sense perceptions. The morality that nature teaches is, throughout Wordsworth's poetry, a joyful morality. "All that we behold," he writes, "is filled with blessings!" On an early spring day he feels

> There is a blessing in the air,
> Which seems a sense of joy to yield
> To the bare trees, and mountains bare,
> And the grass in the green field.

Wordsworth's celebration of nature's redemptive power became widely popular as the century advanced. The most renowned rationalist of his age, John Stuart Mill (1806-1873), recorded in his *Autobiography* that as a young man he had come to find life "a vapid, uninteresting thing" until he found relief in the poetry of Wordsworth, who taught him that "there was real, permanent happiness in tranquil contemplation."

The Romantic writers came to view the universe as a living organism in which all things shared complex relationships. If science had painted for the previous age a world whose workings were mechanical and simple, during the nineteenth century science more and more revealed the complexity of natural laws. The discovery of oxygen, for example, by Joseph Priestly in 1785 demonstrated a dynamic relationship between living organisms and the physical world. Among the Romantic nature writers the mechanical world of Newton, which Edward Young called "dead matter" in the lines quoted above, assumed great vitality. In "The Eolian Harp" (1796), Samuel Taylor Coleridge brilliantly portrays the Romantic conception of unity between the human and non-human realms:

> O! the one life within us and abroad,
> Which meets all motion and becomes its soul,
> A light in sound, a sound-like power in light,
> Rhythm in all thought, and joyance everywhere—
> Methinks, it should have been impossible
> Not to love all things in a world so fill'd. . . .

The "universal love" spoken of in this passage was central to the "religion of nature" that developed during the nineteenth century. Early in the century disillusionment with the outcome of the French Revolution stimulated the first great wave of modern nature writing, and the religious fervor that had accompanied political idealism found an outlet in the natural world. Later in the century traditional Christian belief was increasingly shaken by scientific discovery. Sir Charles Lyell's *Principles of Geology* (1830) showed the incredible ancientness of the world, and Charles Darwin's *On the Origin of Species by Means of Natural Selection* (1859) argued forcibly that evolution in nature, not divine creation, established the forms of life. The response of many thoughtful persons was to develop their religious feelings by meditating among fields and forests. Basil Willey in *The Religion of Nature* relates how walks in the countryside became a preferred worship on Sunday morning for many.

Religious appreciation of nature among the century's nature writers could rise beyond moral persuasion to mystical union with the organic life of the universe, as recorded in the last section of Wordsworth's *Tintern Abbey:*

> . . . I have felt
> A presence that disturbs me with the joy
> Of elevated thoughts; a sense sublime
> Of something far more deeply interfused,
> Whose dwelling is the light of setting suns,
> And the round ocean and the living air,
> And the blue sky, and in the mind of man:
> A motion and a spirit, that impels
> All thinking things, all objects of all thought,
> And rolls through all things. Therefore am I still
> A lover of the meadows and the woods,
> And mountains; and of all that we behold
> From this green earth . . .

The term "universal love" presumes another revolutionary idea developed by the romantic writers, an idea that has become an assumption for modern nature writing: all persons possess at least the potential to feel an emotional reponse to nature. The eighteenth-century psychology had set up reason (or logic) as the most important faculty of the mind, but the philosophy of sensation made the additional assumption that logic and emotion, dependent upon sensation, were common to all humans. Belief in shared emotions and a common reason tended to raise the value of the ordinary person in relation to received authority, such as religious dogma, and temporal authority, such as the upper classes of society. If all of us, from prince to pauper, depend upon the same means of logic and experience the same range of emotional states, why should we revere the prince, or, by the same token, why should we not care for the pauper, who feels anxiety and joy as we do?

These democratic ideas culminated in the tremendous upheaval of the French Revolution, and until France became hostile, a simultaneous demand for political democracy in England. In France aristocratic privilege was questioned, denounced, and then violently attacked in the name of the common good as interpreted by the "common reason."

The French Revolution affected nature writing in two ways. First, it forcefully elevated the status of common emotions—the feelings shared by everyone. Second, its violence caused many former sympathizers in England to turn away from bloodthirsty emotion approved by abstract reason. They did not abandon the idea of common feelings among men, but they sought the calm, benevolent emotional relations proven by time: the love among members of a family, the friendship of a neighborhood, and, especially, the affections connected with rural places.

In 1798 these ideas gave shape to a book of poems called *Lyrical Ballads,* which can be considered the beginning of the modern genre of nature writing. Its young authors, William Wordsworth and Samuel Taylor Coleridge, had welcomed the French Revolution as a liberation of the human spirit. In its early stages they saw a new age of equality that, together with the scientific fruits of reason, would put an end to poverty and ignorance. But when the Revolution became preoccupied with beheading aristocrats and conquering foreign nations, Wordsworth and Coleridge grew skeptical of the benevolence of abstract logic. Instead they investigated the means by which emotions are formed in an individual, and the means of generating joyful, benevolent emotional states. "All good poetry," Wordsworth wrote in a "Preface" to the *Lyrical Ballads,* is the spontaneous overflow of human feelings." He locates the stimuli for these emotions in

> humble and rustic life . . . because in that condition, the essential passions of the heart find a better soil in which they can attain their maturity, are less under restraint, and speak a plainer and more emphatic language; because in that condition of life our elementary feelings co-exist in a state of great simplicity, and, consequently, may be more accurately contemplated, and more forcibly communicated; because the manners of rural life germinate from those elementary feelings, and, from the necessary character of rural occupations, are more easily comprehended, and are more durable; and, lastly, because in that condition the passions of men are incorporated with the beautiful and permanent forms of nature.

Wordsworth went on to speak of the poems' various "purposes," one of which became the hallmark of his subsequent career: to show "the strength . . . of moral attachment when early associated with the great and beautiful objects of nature." The poet's general purpose was "that the understanding of the reader must necessarily be in some degree enlightened, and his affections strengthened and purified." He is arguing that the faculty of reason itself is enlightened by true, balanced emotions, and that the emotions are best made true if a person lives in close contact with natural scenes and objects, especially during the formative years. *Lyrical Ballads* overflowed with the optimism of a revolutionary age. Salvation, however, lay not in a political system or in economic theory, but in properly tuning one's imagination to the objects of nature.

The crowning achievement of nineteenth-century nature writing was its discovery that the imagination is "well-fitted" to understand the natural world. It is an insight continually rediscovered down through contemporary nature literature as the interpretation of nature is continually renewed and expanded.

The democratic influence of the French Revolution had initially stimulated investigation of the imaginative faculty that endowed all people with creative power. Slowly, there arose a new conception of the imagination that radically transformed the very eighteenth-century psychology from which it had evolved. The older view had pictured the mind as an initially blank page upon which sensations of the world impressed themselves, rejecting the idea that God placed "innate" ideas in each person's mind at birth. The imagination, according to the eighteenth-century conception, combined the sensations, or images, in a rigidly mechanical way. But a new conception of the mind, originated by Immanuel Kant in Germany, stressed its active role of modifying and fusing the images presented by sense perception. Nineteenth-century nature writers saw an analogy between the mind and the universe itself, which increasingly seemed composed of complex, organic relationships.

William Wordsworth devoted years to analysis of the grand power afforded by the healthy imagination in its contemplation of nature. He expressed his conclusions in an autobiographical poem, *The Prelude; or the Growth of a Poet's Mind* (1850), which he conceived of as a true epic, carrying on in modern days the tradition of Homer's *Odyssey*. In the final book of *The Prelude,* Wordsworth delivers a classic description of the imagination. He has experienced a moonlit scene while climbing Mount Snowdon in Wales and is struck by nature's "transcendent power" to mold and transform the objects of sense so as to impress even the "least sensitive" persons; suddenly he realizes that the human imagination similarly molds and transforms what it perceives. The power of even the most sublime natural scene, he asserts,

> . . . is the express
> Resemblance of that glorious faculty
> That higher minds bear with them as their own.
> This is the very spirit in which they deal
> With the whole compass of the universe.

Elsewhere in *The Prelude* Wordsworth asserts that not only "higher minds," but every human mind, possesses the power to create, to give shape and emphasis in the very act of perception. This power, he argues, is akin to the divine act of creation. Wordsworth's conception of the "transcendent power," coupled with his description of the redemptive joy offered by nature, worked a profound influence upon nineteenth-century nature writing, inspiring several divergent trends in England and, in America, unleashing the energy of Emerson, Thoreau, Bryant, and the entire transcendental movement.

The idea of the creative imagination, and the conviction that it was well fitted to a living universe, together led to the use of natural detail as literary symbol, a practice of great significance to modern nature writing. The artist's imagination calls up from memory its images of natural things and considers emotional responses; the imagination also synthesizes the images and emotions with intellectual insights into the meanings a particular image holds. These meanings derive from its own "real" existence as well as from the artist's feelings about the natural thing.

Theory of symbolism is certainly abstract and complicated, but if we examine a particular symbol concretely we can see how nature writing is enriched by this creation of the imagination. A clear example of a symbol drawn from natural images is found in William Blake's "The Sick Rose" (1794):

> O Rose, thou art sick.
> The invisible worm,
> That flies in the night
> In the howling storm:
>
> Has found out thy bed
> Of crimson joy:
> And his dark secret love
> Does thy life destroy.

Although the rose is a physical entity suggesting beauty and vitality, it dies from what could be a natural process, parasitic attack. But the human feelings attracted to the description invest it with potential for human meaning: the death of innocence, or the end of romance, or the ability of evil and corruption to conquer goodness and beauty.

Further examples of natural symbolism appear when the American author Henry

David Thoreau names Walden's pickerel "animalized water," when Samuel Taylor Coleridge in *The Rime of the Ancient Mariner* sees a "blessing" in the shining water snakes, and when Matthew Arnold (1822-1888) hears "the eternal note of sadness" in the grinding of pebbles beneath the ocean tide. These nature writers are creating thought-filled symbols, fruit grown from the seed of an imaginative interpretation of nature that reached full bloom in nineteenth-century England.

Now that we have traced the major stream of nineteenth-century nature literature in England, three important trends or characteristics can be examined in more detail through to the end of the century.

One major trend is the tendency toward accurate, concrete description. A tradition can be traced from James Thomson in the eighteenth century through Wordsworth, John Clare (1793-1864), and John Keats early in the nineteenth century. Clare was an uneducated farm worker in his youth; his depictions of wildlife are unsentimentally realistic, sometimes startlingly so, as when he describes violence in poems such as "The Badger." Keats became a major figure in the history of British literature for many reasons, not least among them the vivid sensuality of his natural description. Though he died young, his work deeply influenced subsequent generations of poets in both England and America.

Alfred Lord Tennyson (1809-1892) in the early years of his career wed Keats's lush, sensual style to themes of romantic love in poems such as "Marianna" and "Locksley Hall." Although Tennyson's poetry became increasingly preoccupied with social themes, he still frequently demonstrated his descriptive power in the ballads and meditations he set in rural backgrounds, inspired, as he was throughout his life, by the Roman poet Vergil. Tennyson was the last major English poet who had known England as a rural nation; his death symbolizes a turning point in the tradition of nature literature.

The scientific variety of concrete natural description is represented in this anthology by selections from the writings of Charles Darwin (1809-1882), who was both naturalist and theoretician. For more than five years Darwin sailed on the *Beagle* as Naturalist in a scientific expedition around the tip of South America. The journals he kept in this role of wilderness explorer bear similarities to the writings of the eighteenth century Americans William Bartram and William Byrd, who are discussed elsewhere in this volume. Darwin's *Voyage of the Beagle* is especially characterized by the breadth of the intellectual framework with which he attempts to ascertain pattern in the minute details of natural history he records.

Though it is not commonly known, the famous theory of natural selection was deduced almost simultaneously by Darwin and another naturalist, Alfred Russel Wallace (1823-1913), who actually read many of the same authors as Darwin in arriving at his deduction. Wallace wandered even more widely than Darwin in the pursuit of his naturalist studies, carrying with him a deep religious faith. Where a search for pattern had characterized Darwin's naturalist writing, Wallace's work is distinguished by his sense of the marvelous.

Concrete natural description in painting and sculpture as well as literature was the goal of the Pre-Raphaelite Brotherhood, a group of young artists whose collaboration began in 1848. Among other goals, the Pre-Raphaelites paid special attention to the depiction of naturalistic detail in their painting. In execution, they often used the effects of light to render almost fantastical detail. The writers associated with the Pre-Raphaelite Brotherhood employed vivid natural description to reveal intense, sometimes morbid, feelings of romantic love. Dante Gabriel Rossetti (1828-1888), for example attempted in *The House of Life* to let natural scenes symbolize a wide variety of emotions. The emptiness of foresaken love is forcibly depicted in "Barren Spring":

> Once more the changed year's turning wheel returns:
> And as a girl sails balanced in the wind,
> And now before and now again behind
> Stoops as it swoops, with cheek that laughs and burns,—
> So Spring comes merry towards me here, but earns
> No answering smile from me, whose life is twined
> With the dead boughs that winter still must bind,
> And whom today the Spring no more concerns.
>
> Behold, this crocus is a withering flame;
> This snowdrop, snow; this apple-blossom's part
> To breed the fruit that breeds the serpent's art.
> Nay, for these Spring-flowers, turn thy face from them,
> Now stay till on the year's last lily-stem
> The white cup shrivels round the golden heart.

The second important trend of nature writing in nineteenth-century England was an interest in philosophical speculation. This tendency had roots in the eighteenth century's fascination with the "sublime" effect of mountain scenery. In the nineteenth century, both Wordsworth and Coleridge (in passages previously quoted) sought profound philosophic enlightenment in their contemplation of nature, their thoughts at times moving some distance from direct observation of natural scenes. In the following generation Percy Bysshe Shelley (1792-1824) sought to create a new philosophy of man and nature by retelling classical myths and inventing new ones. George Gordon, Lord Byron (1788-1824), is often remembered for his "purple passages" of philosophical speculation inspired by the Alpine scenery of *Childe Harold's Pilgrimage,* though the greater portion of his work does not concern itself with natural description.

Throughout the nineteenth century many writers, shaken by scientific and technological innovation, sought to develop new explanations of man's role in nature. Joseph Warren Beach's *The Concept of Nature in Nineteenth-Century English Poetry* provides an excellent scholarly history of the philosophy of nature. Beach shows that even writers like Thomas Carlyle, who composed very little natural description, nonetheless applied the philosophical implications of other nature writers to his own criticism of society.

Not only philosophy but society were informed by nature in the work of John Ruskin (1819-1900). His career was extraordinarily multi-faceted; he was painter, art critic, historian, teacher, moral philosopher, and social reformer. His *Modern Painters* (1843-1860) championed the paintings of J.M.W. Turner, whose imaginative depictions of land and seascapes dramatized the energy and grandeur of natural forces. Ruskin was preoccupied with the moral effects upon human feeling of mountains, and, for that matter, all art. *Modern Painters,* composed of five substantial volumes written over a period of seventeen years, developed the aesthetic sensibility of the English middle classes, teaching them the importance of natural landscapes to society as a whole.

With the growing awareness of landscape's value there developed a sense of outrage over the exploitation of nature by modern industrial, commercial society, the third important characteristic of nineteenth-century nature writing. Once again, the trend can be detected in the previous century, most notably in Oliver Goldsmith's *The Deserted Village* (1770). Wordsworth, clearly a seminal influence, offers one of the earliest prophetic warnings against commercial exploitation, foreshadowing the theme of protest that grew strong among nineteenth-century American nature writers and that has become a major theme in our own age, even outside the tradition of nature literature. In "The World Is Too Much With Us" (1807), Wordsworth focuses, typically, on the individual's interaction with natural objects, directing his anger against what even today is the ultimate source of environmental destruction: permitting one's desire for personal acquisition to gain precedence—in consciousness—over the awareness of natural splendor. He wrote:

> The world is too much with us; late and soon,
> Getting and spending, we lay waste our powers;
> Little we see in Nature that is ours;
> We have given our hearts away, a sordid boon!
> This Sea that bares her bosom to the moon,
> The winds that will be howling at all hours,
> And are up-gathered now like sleeping flowers,
> To this, to everything, we are out of tune;
> It moves us not.

The *Songs of Experience* of William Blake record an uncannily contemporary-sounding dismay with the oppressive materialism of industrial society. Blake, who in some ways anticipated the socialist criticism at the end of the century, saw an intertwining of the dynamics that governed modern society. In "The Garden of Love" he symbolizes these oppressive forces in the image of the priest "binding with briars my joys and desires."

Other writers throughout the century—Byron, Keats, Tennyson, Carlyle—asserted that the quality of life had been corrupted, simple enjoyment of the environment suppressed by the artificiality of commercial taste, the environment itself destroyed by industrial exploitation of natural resources. John Ruskin argued in *Traffic,* a lecture delivered to the London Society of Guilds, for repudiation of the kind of "progress" that eradicated natural features and created dirt, crowds, poverty, and ugliness. His *Modern Painters* advancing an awareness of the moral value of forest and field, Ruskin was a major factor in the eventual formation (1895) of The National Trust for the Preservation of Places of Historic Interest or Natural Beauty, a private foundation that was empowered by act of Parliament (1907) to acquire and preserve undeveloped land. Today the National Trust is the largest private landowner in Great Britain.

Ruskin's social criticism was carried on by his disciple William Morris (1834-1896), poet, illustrator, inventor, successful entrepreneur, and in later life, persuasive socialist. Morris designed immensely popular home furnishings that replicated patterns and colors of natural motifs. In *News from Nowhere* (1890) he describes a socialist Utopia seen through the eyes of a man who falls asleep for a century and awakens to find Trafalgar Square transformed into a beautiful orchard. Morris envisions landscapes freed from obtrusive technology, and in those landscapes he envisions human labor restored to intimacy with the seasons of the natural cycle.

A key passage taken from *News from Nowhere* offers a vision of humanity restored to non-exploitative harmony with nature:

> Romantic as this Kensington Wood was, however, it was not lonely. We came on many groups both coming and going, or wandering in the edges of the wood. Amongst them were many children from six or eight years old up to sixteen or seventeen. They seemed to me to be especially fine specimens of their race, and were clearly enjoying themselves to the utmost; some of them were hanging about little tents pitched on the greensward, and by some of these fires were burning, with pots hanging over them in gypsy fashion.
>
> "O," said Dick, "these children do not all come from the near houses, the woodland houses, but from the countryside generally. They often make up parties, and come to play in the woods for weeks together in summer-time, living in tents, as you see. We encourage them to it; they learn to do things for themselves, and get to notice the wild creatures; and, you see, the less they stew inside houses the better for them. Indeed, I must tell you that many grown people will go to live in the forests through the summer; though they for the most part go to the bigger ones, like Windsor, or the Forest of Dean or the northern wastes. Apart from the other pleasures of it, it gives them a little rough work, which I am sorry to say is getting somewhat scarce these last fifty years.

Nineteenth-century England, indeed, provided seed-time for modern nature writing. Here meaningful emotional interplay between individuals and the surrounding physical world became thoroughly legitimized. Inheriting ideas about perception and religious truth, drawn by revolutionary ardor for human equality, the Romantics wrote about nature with such conviction and vitality that they created a revolution, not in politics, but in taste, one that was consolidated during the remainder of the century. The possibility that "there is a blessing in the air," an inspiration to nineteenth-century literature, has become its permanent legacy. Subsequent writers have questioned that legacy, but it remains at the heart of an enduring tradition, a tradition resilient enough to be enriched by change, and rich enough, in its own right, to inspire the contemporary imagination.

William Blake
1757-1827

The nature writing of William Blake is at once the simplest and the most complex in the tradition. He was, literally, a visionary profoundly affected by the revolutionary changes of his age, and his work reveals the complex prophetic cast of his mind. His writing also reflects the influence of his trade: a painter and engraver of books. In volumes like *Songs of Innocence* (1789) and *Songs of Experience* (1794), Blake illustrates his poems with his own colored sketches.

Many of Blake's briefer poems depict scenes or persons in a few deft descriptive details. But even his most simple art relates to larger and more complex issues, reflecting a uniquely creative mind. From his youth onward, Blake not only saw a brighter and more colorful world than the rest of us, he also saw some things that most of us never see. When reading "The Marriage of Heaven and Hell" (1790), one is startled not so much by the fact that Blake narrates a conversation with the prophet Ezekiel, as by what Ezekiel says:

> I then asked Ezekiel why he ate dung and lay so long on
> his right and left side? He answered, "the desire of raising
> other men into a perception of the infinite."

That same desire motivated Blake as an artist. In his longer poems, such as *The Four Zoas* and *Jerusalem,* he explains his radical thought about intellect, religion, society, knowledge, and their relations to the individual. In simple terms, Blake felt that the natural world offers non-factual, intuitive understanding. We remain unaware of this level of knowledge because we are limited by our senses, especially in the ways society has conditioned us to use them. But every physical thing possesses an infinite variety of meanings. "If the doors of perception were cleansed," says Blake, "everything would appear to man as it is, infinite." It is possible "to see a world in a grain of sand," if we could learn to free ourselves of the meaning we habitually ascribe to it.

In many of his superficially simple lyrics, such as "The Lamb" (1789), Blake depicts natural objects with clear physical detail, seeming to rely upon some very conventional ways of viewing nature. "The Ecchoing Green" (1789), likewise, is a lovely straightforward depiction of rural life in a village community unaltered by industralism.

But other poems on natural topics show the complexity of Blake's thought. "The Tiger" (1794), for example, uses the animal as a symbol for the power of nature that mankind was unleashing with his technical knowledge. It is more: a symbol of the very power of human consciousness apprehending the universe.

A theme common to Blake's work is the inhibition of natural desires by social restrictions. Often he contrasts the "natural" world of desire with the artificial world of society. In "The Garden of Love" (1974), he symbolizes the oppressive forces governing modern society in the image of the priest:

I went to the Garden of Love,
And saw what I never had seen:
A Chapel was built in the midst,
Where I used to play on the green.

And the Gates of this Chapel were shut,
And "Thou shalt not" writ over the door;
So I turn'd to the Garden of Love,
That so many sweet flowers bore,

And I saw it was filed with graves,
And tombstones where flowers should be:
And Priests in black gowns were walking their rounds,
And binding with briars my joys and desires.

Blake's contribution to the tradition of nature writing is, essentially, to remind us of the interdependence of the natural world with human consciousness, and the need to expand that consciousness to a higher circle of understanding.

from SONGS OF INNOCENCE*

INTRODUCTION

Piping down the valleys wild,
Piping songs of pleasant glee,
On a cloud I saw a child,
And he laughing said to me:

*This and the following poems of William Blake are from *The Poetical Works of William Blake,* ed. John Sampson (Oxford: Clarendon Press, 1905).

'Pipe a song about a Lamb!'
So I piped with merry cheer.
'Piper, pipe that song again;'
So I piped: he wept to hear.

'Drop thy pipe, thy happy pipe;
Sing thy songs of happy cheer:'
So I sang the same again,
While he wept with joy to hear.

'Piper, sit thee down and write
In a book, that all may read.'
So he vanished from my sight,
And I pluck'd a hollow reed,

And I made a rural pen,
And I stain'd the water clear,
And I wrote my happy songs
Every child may joy to hear.

THE ECCHOING GREEN

The Sun does arise,
And make happy the skies;
The merry bells ring
To welcome the Spring;
The sky lark and thrush,
The birds of the bush,
Sing louder around
To the bells' cheerful sound,
While our sports shall be seen
On the Ecchoing Green.

Old John, with white hair,
Does laugh away care,
Sitting under the oak,
Among the old folk.
They laugh at our play,
And soon they all say:
'Such, such were the joys
When we all, girls and boys,
In our youth time were seen
On the Ecchoing Green.'

Till the little ones, weary,
No more can be merry;
The sun does descend,
And our sports have an end.

Round the laps of their mothers
Many sisters and brothers,
Like birds in their nest,
Are ready for rest,
And sport no more seen
On the darkening Green.

THE LAMB

Little Lamb who made thee?
Dost thou know who made thee?
Gave thee life, and bid thee feed,
By the stream and o'er the mead;
Gave thee clothing of delight,
Softest clothing, wooly, bright;
Gave thee such a tender voice,
Making all the vales rejoice?
Little Lamb who made thee?
Dost thou know who made thee?

Little Lamb, I'll tell thee,
Little Lamb, I'll tell thee:
He is callèd by thy name,
For he calls himself a Lamb.
He is meek, and he is mild;
He became a little child.
I a child, and thou a lamb,
We are callèd by his name.
Little Lamb, God bless thee!
Little Lamb, God bless thee!

from SONGS OF EXPERIENCE

THE TIGER

Tiger! Tiger! burning bright
In the forests of the night,
What immortal hand or eye
Could frame thy fearful symmetry?

In what distant deeps or skies
Burnt the fire of thine eyes?
On what wings dare he aspire?
What the hand dare seize the fire?

And what shoulder, and what art,
Could twist the sinews of thy heart?
And when thy heart began to beat,
What dread hand? and what dread feet?

What the hammer? what the chain?
In what furnace was thy brain?
What the anvil? what dread grasp
Dare its deadly terrors clasp?

When the stars threw down their spears,
And water'd heaven with their tears,
Did he smile his work to see?
Did he who made the Lamb make thee?

Tiger! Tiger! burning bright
In the forest of the night,
What immortal hand or eye,
Dare frame thy fearful symmetry?

AUGURIES OF INNOCENCE

To see a World in a grain of sand
And a Heaven in a wild flower,
Hold Infinity in the palm of your hand,
And Eternity in an hour.
A robin redbreast in a cage
Puts all Heaven in a rage.
A dove-house filled with doves and pigeons
Shudders Hell through all its regions.
A dog starved at his master's gate
Predicts the ruin of the State.
A horse misused upon the road
Calls to Heaven for human blood.
Each outcry of the hunted hare
A fibre from the brain does tear.
A skylark wounded in the wing,
A cherubim does cease to sing;
The game-cock clipped and armed for fight
Does the rising sun affright.

Every wolf's and lion's howl
Raises from Hell a Human soul.
The wild deer, wandering here and there,
Keeps the Human soul from care.
The lamb misused breeds public strife
And yet forgives the butcher's knife
The bat that flits at close of eve
Has left the brain that won't believe.
The owl that calls upon the night
Speaks the unbeliever's fright.
He who shall hurt the little wren
Shall never be beloved by men.
He who the ox to wrath has moved
Shall never be by woman loved.
The wanton boy that kills the fly
Shall feel the spider's enmity.
He who torments the chafer's sprite
Weaves a bower in endless night.
The caterpillar on the leaf
Repeats to thee thy mother's grief.
Kill not the moth nor butterfly,
For the Last Judgment draweth nigh.
He who shall train the horse to war
Shall never pass the polar bar.
The beggar's dog and widow's cat
Feed them and thou wilt grow fat.
The gnat that signs his summer's song
Poison gets from Slander's tongue.
The poison of the snake and newt
Is the sweat of Envy's foot.
The poison of the honey-bee
Is the artist's jealousy.
The prince's robes and beggar's rags
Are toadstools on the miser's bags.
A truth that's told with bad intent
Beats all the lies you can invent.
It is right it should be so;
Man was made for joy and woe;
And when this we rightly know,
Through the world we safely go.
Joy and woe are woven fine,
A clothing for the soul divine.
Under every grief and pine
Runs a joy with silken twine.
The babe is more than swaddling-bands;
Throughout all these human lands
Tools were made, and born were hands,
Every farmer understands.

Every tear from every eye
Becomes a babe in Eternity;
This is caught by Females bright,
And returned to its own delight.
The bleat, the bark, bellow, and roar
Are waves that beat on Heaven's shore.
The babe that weeps the rod beneath
Writes revenge in realms of death.
The beggar's rags, fluttering in air,
Does to rags the heavens tear.
The soldier, armed with sword and gun,
Palsied strikes the summer's sun.
The poor man's farthing is worth more
Than all the gold on Afric's shore.
One mite wrung from the labourer's hands
Shall buy & sell the miser's lands;
Or, if protected from on high,
Does that whole nation sell & buy.
He who mocks the infant's faith
Shall be mocked in Age & Death.
He who shall teach the child to doubt
The rotting grave shall ne'er get out.
He who respects the infant's faith
Triumphs over Hell & Death.
The child's toys and the old man's reasons
Are the fruits of the two seasons.
The questioner, who sits so sly,
Shall never know how to reply.
He who replies to words of Doubt
Doth put the light of knowledge out.
The strongest poison ever known
Came from Caesar's laurel crown.
Naught can deform the human race
Like to the armour's iron brace.
When gold and gems adorn the plow
To peaceful arts shall Envy bow.
A riddle, or the cricket's cry,
Is to Doubt a fit reply.
The emmet's inch & eagle's mile
Make lame Philosophy to smile.
He who doubts from what he sees
Will ne'er believe, do what you please.
If the Sun & Moon should doubt,
They'd immediately go out.
To be in a passion you good may do,
But no good if a passion is in you.
The whore & gambler by the state
Licensed, build that nation's fate.

The harlot's cry from street to street
Shall weave Old England's winding-sheet.
The winner's shout, the loser's curse,
Dance before dead England's hearse.
Every night and every morn
Some to misery are born.
Every morn and every night
Some are born to sweet delight.
Some are born to sweet delight,
Some are born to endless night.
We are led to believe a lie
When we see not through the eye,
Which was born in a night, to perish in a night,
When the Soul slept in beams of light.
God appears, & God is light,
To those poor souls who dwell in Night,
But does a Human Form display
To those who dwell in realms of Day.

William Wordsworth
1770-1850

Wordsworth remains the most significant and influential nature writer in the tradition. Many of the writers whose works are printed in this anthology read Wordsworth's work and took inspiration from its characteristic qualities. As a poet he was attracted to a wide variety of plants and animals; his poems about daisies and primroses and skylarks evoked human affection and uncovered moral significance. He wrote, "To me the meanest flower that blows can give/Thoughts that do often lie too deep for tears." Wordsworth's greatest influence lay in the theme running through much of his poetry, that the human mind was well fitted to comprehend the world of nature, and that such comprehension could lead to a mystical communion that strengthened one's soul.

Wordsworth was born and raised in the beautiful and isolated Lake District of England. When he was seven years old, his mother died, and young William began to love the mountains and lakes as a foster mother. With his three brothers he boarded at the home of a woman who allowed the boys to find adventure out-of-doors from morning to night: fishing, boating, skating, hiking, and even climbing the wildest mountain peaks in search of birds' eggs! During his boyhood in the Lake District, Wordsworth acquired a store of memories he could later depend upon to recall joy. The experience and the memory of the presence of nature, he came to feel, could build a sound mind and a sympathetic soul.

After graduation from Cambridge University, Wordsworth spent some time in London before beginning a series of walking tours in Wales and France. The times were charged with the political upheaval of the French Revolution. An idealistic young man, Wordsworth strongly sympathized with the Revolution that promised to right injustices and do away with poverty. After the Revolution took a violent turn, however, Wordsworth became disillusioned with politics. While in France he had fathered an illegitimate child, but remained separated from her and the mother because of the war between England and France. Political disillusionment and personal guilt overwhelmed him to the point of a mental breakdown.

But healing power came from his memories of natural scenes when he returned to a quiet meditative life in the country. He was reunited with his beloved sister Dorothy, and the two set up housekeeping, at first in a cottage at Racedown, near the ocean, and later at Alfoxden in the Quantock Hills, near his friend Samuel Taylor Coleridge. In these settings Wordsworth began to write poems about his feelings toward natural things, often trying to recreate the freshness and strength of his boyish perceptions, what he called the hour "Of splendor in the grass, of glory in the flower."

When depicting the moods that nature could inspire, Wordsworth incorporated his still-strong democratic sympathy for ordinary human beings. One of his great accomplishments was to depict people in natural scenes as if, like trees and clouds, they belonged there. In his poems humans are a part of the natural world, drawing strength and significance from its cycles while imparting human meaning to its phenomena.

Wordsworth himself no doubt felt that his greatest accomplishment lay in demonstrating "How exquisitely the individual Mind. . . to the external world is fitted." He wrote that the human imagination could attain ecstatic joy in its contemplation of nature's whole presence: the force of wind and water, the vitality of animal and season. At this level, nature revealed "that glorious faculty that higher minds bear with them as their own," that is, the sympathetic imagination that makes possible the intellectual love of others.

In 1798 Wordsworth and Coleridge published *Lyrical Ballads,* a classic in the tradition of nature writing. Two years later he justified his poetry in a "Preface." In 1807 he published his *Poems in Two Volumes* and in 1814 *The Excursion,* a long narrative poem interesting for its criticism of the beginnings of modern industrial society. Wordsworth remained in his native Lake District for the rest of his life. After his death came the publication of his great autobiographical poem, *The Prelude: or The Growth of a Poet's Mind* (1850).

TO A BUTTERFLY*

I've watched you now a full half-hour,
Self-poised upon that yellow flower;
And, little Butterfly! indeed
I know not if you sleep or feed.
How motionless!—not frozen seas
More motionless! and then
What joy awaits you, when the breeze
Hath found you out among the trees,
And calls you forth again!

*This and the following poems by William Wordsworth are from *The Poetical Works of William Wordsworth,* ed. Thomas Hutchinson (London: Oxford University Press, 1907). Courtesy of Oxford University Press.

This plot of orchard-ground is ours;
My trees they are, my Sister's flowers;
Here rest your wings when they are weary;
Here lodge as in a sanctuary!
Come often to us, fear no wrong;
Sit near us on the bough!
We'll talk of sunshine and of song,
And summer days, when we were young;
Sweet childish days, that were as long
As twenty days are now.

TO THE SMALL CELANDINE

Pansies, lilies, kingcups, daisies,
Let them live upon their praises;
Long as there's a sun that sets,
Primroses will have their glory;
Long as there are violets,
They will have a place in story:
There's a flower that shall be mine,
'Tis the little Celandine.

Eyes of some men travel far
For the finding of a star;
Up and down the heavens they go,
Men that keep a mighty rout!
I'm as great as they, I trow,
Since the day I found thee out,
Little Flower—I'll make a stir,
Like a sage astronomer.

Modest, yet withal an Elf
Bold, and lavish of thyself;
Since we needs must first have met
I have seen thee, high and low,
Thirty years or more, and yet
'Twas a face I did not know;
Thou hast now, go where I may,
Fifty greetings in a day.

Ere a leaf is on a bush,
In the time before the thrush
Has a thought about her nest,
Thou wilt come with half a call,
Spreading out thy glossy breast
Like a careless Prodigal;
Telling tales about the sun,
When we've little warmth, or none.

Poets, vain men in their mood!
Travel with the multitude:
Never heed them; I aver
That they all are wanton wooers;
But the thrifty cottager,
Who stirs little out of doors,
Joys to spy thee near her home;
Spring is coming, Thou art come!

Comfort have thou of thy merit,
Kindly, unassuming Spirit!
Careless of thy neighbourhood,
Thou dost show thy pleasant face
On the moor, and in the wood,
In the lane;—there's not a place,
Howsoever mean it be,
But 'tis good enough for thee.

Ill befall the yellow flowers,
Children of the flaring hours!
Buttercups, that will be seen,
Whether we will see or no;
Others, too, of lofty mien;
They have done as worldlings do,
Taken praise that should be thine,
Little, humble Celandine.

Prophet of delight and mirth,
Ill-requited upon earth;
Herald of a mighty band,
Of a joyous train ensuing,
Serving at my heart's command,
Tasks that are no tasks renewing,
I will sing, as doth behove,
Hymns in praise of what I love!

TO THE CUCKOO

O Blithe New-comer! I have heard,
I hear thee and rejoice.
O Cuckoo! shall I call thee Bird,
Or but a wandering Voice?

While I am lying on the grass
Thy twofold shout I hear;
From hill to hill it seems to pass
At once far off, and near.

Though babbling only to the Vale,
Of sunshine and of flowers,
Thou bringest unto me a tale
Of visionary hours.

Thrice welcome, darling of the Spring!
Even yet thou art to me
No bird, but an invisible thing,
A voice, a mystery;

The same whom in my schoolboy days
I listened to; that Cry
Which made me look a thousand ways
In bush, and tree, and sky.

To seek thee did I often rove
Through woods and on the green;
And thou wert still a hope, a love;
Still longed for, never seen.

And I can listen to thee yet;
Can lie upon the plain
And listen, till I do beget
That golden time again.

O blessèd Bird! the earth we pace
Again appears to be
An unsubstantial, faery place;
That is fit home for Thee!

A NIGHT-PIECE

The sky is overcast
With a continuous cloud of texture close,
Heavy and wan, all whitened by the Moon,
Which through that veil is indistinctly seen,
A dull, contracted circle, yielding light
So feebly spread that not a shadow falls,
Chequering the ground—from rock, plant, tree, or tower.
At length a pleasant instantaneous gleam
Startles the pensive traveller while he treads
His lonesome path, with unobserving eye
Bent earthwards; he looks up—the clouds are split
Asunder,—and above his head he sees
The clear Moon, and the glory of the heavens.
There in a black-blue vault she sails along,
Followed by multitudes of stars, that, small

And sharp, and bright, along the dark abyss
Drive as she drives: how fast they wheel away,
Yet vanish not!—the wind is in the tree,
But they are silent;—still they roll along
Immeasurably distant; and the vault,
Built round by those white clouds, enormous clouds,
Still deepens its unfathomable depth.
At length the Vision closes; and the mind,
Not undisturbed by the delight it feels,
Which slowly settles into peaceful calm,
Is left to muse upon the solemn scene.

NUTTING

It seems a day
(I speak of one from many singled out)
One of those heavenly days that cannot die;
When, in the eagerness of boyish hope,
I left our cottage-threshold, sallying forth
With a huge wallet o'er my shoulders slung,
A nutting-crook in hand; and turned my steps
Tow'rd some far-distant wood, a Figure quaint,
Tricked out in proud disguise of cast-off weeds
Which for that service had been husbanded,
By exhortation of my frugal Dame—
Motley accoutrement, of power to smile
At thorns, and brakes, and brambles,—and in truth
More ragged than need was! O'er pathless rocks,
Through beds of matted fern, and tangled thickets,
Forcing my way, I came to one dear nook
Unvisited, where not a broken bough
Drooped with its withered leaves, ungracious sign
Of devastation; but the hazels rose
Tall and erect, with tempting clusters hung,
A virgin scene!—A little while I stood,
Breathing with such suppression of the heart
As joy delights in; and with wise restraint
Voluptuous, fearless of a rival, eyed
The banquet;—or beneath the trees I sate
Among the flowers, and with the flowers I played;
A temper known to those who, after long
And weary expectation, have been blest
With sudden happiness beyond all hope.
Perhaps it was a bower beneath whose leaves
The violets of five seasons re-appear
And fade, unseen by any human eye;
Where fairy water-breaks do murmur on

For ever; and I saw the sparkling foam,
And—with my cheek on one of those green stones
That, fleeced with moss, under the shady trees,
Lay round me, scattered like a flock of sheep—
I heard the murmur and the murmuring sound,
In that sweet mood when pleasure loves to pay
Tribute to ease; and, of its joy secure,
The heart luxuriates with indifferent things,
Wasting its kindliness on stocks and stones,
And on the vacant air. Then up I rose,
And dragged to earth both branch and bough, with crash
And merciless ravage: and the shady nook
Of hazels, and the green and mossy bower,
Deformed and sullied, patiently gave up
Their quiet being: and unless I now
Confound my present feelings with the past,
Ere from the mutilated bower I turned
Exulting, rich beyond the wealth of kings,
I felt a sense of pain when I beheld
The silent trees, and saw the intruding sky.—
Then, dearest Maiden, move along these shades
In gentleness of heart; with gentle hand
Touch—for there is a spirit in the woods.

O NIGHTINGALE!

O Nightingale! thou surely art
A creature of a "fiery heart":—
These notes of thine—they pierce and pierce;
Tumultuous harmony and fierce!
Thou sing'st as if the God of wine
Had helped thee to a Valentine;
A song in mockery and despite
Of shades, and dews, and silent night;
And steady bliss, and all the loves
Now sleeping in these peaceful groves.

I heard a Stock-dove sing or say
His homely tale, this very day;
His voice was buried among trees,
Yet to be come-at by the breeze:
He did not cease; but cooed—and cooed;
And somewhat pensively he wooed:
He sang of love, with quiet blending,
Slow to begin, and never ending;
Of serious faith, and inward glee;
That was the song—the song for me!

THREE YEARS SHE GREW IN SUN AND SHOWER

Three years she grew in sun and shower,
Then Nature said, "A lovelier flower
On earth was never sown;
This Child I to myself will take;
She shall be mine, and I will make
A Lady of my own.

"Myself will to my darling be
Both law and impulse: and with me
The Girl, in rock and plain,
In earth and heaven, in glade and bower,
Shall feel an overseeing power
To kindle or restrain.

"She shall be sportive as the fawn
That wild with glee across the lawn
Or up the mountain springs;
And hers shall be the breathing balm,
And hers the silence and the calm
Of mute insensate things.

"The floating clouds their state shall lend
To her; for her the willow bend;
Nor shall she fail to see
Even in the motions of the Storm
Grace that shall mould the Maiden's form
By silent sympathy.

"The stars of midnight shall be dear
To her; and she shall lean her ear
In many a secret place
Where rivulets dance their wayward round,
And beauty born of murmuring sound
Shall pass into her face.

"And vital feelings of delight
Shall rear her form to stately height,
Her virgin bosom swell;
Such thoughts to Lucy I will give
While she and I together live
Here in this happy dell."

Thus Nature spake—The work was done—
How soon my Lucy's race was run!
She died, and left to me
This heath, this calm, and quiet scene;
The memory of what has been,
And never more will be.

A SLUMBER DID MY SPIRIT STEAL

A slumber did my spirit seal;
  I had no human fears;
She seemed a thing that could not feel
  The touch of earthly years.

No motion has she now, no force;
  She neither hears nor sees;
Rolled round in earth's diurnal course,
  With rocks, and stones, and trees.

I WANDERED LONELY AS A CLOUD

I wandered lonely as a cloud
That floats on high o'er vales and hills,
When all at once I saw a crowd,
A host, of golden daffodils;
Beside the lake, beneath the trees,
Fluttering and dancing in the breeze.

Continuous as the stars that shine
And twinkle on the milky way,
They stretched in never-ending line
Along the margin of a bay:
Ten thousand saw I at a glance,
Tossing their heads in sprightly dance.

The waves beside them danced; but they
Out-did the sparkling waves in glee:
A poet could not but be gay,
In such a jocund company:
I gazed—and gazed—but little thought
What wealth the show to me had brought:

For oft, when on my couch I lie
In vacant or in pensive mood,
They flash upon that inward eye
Which is the bliss of solitude;
And then my heart with pleasure fills,
And dances with the daffodils.

TINTERN ABBEY

Five years have past; five summers, with the length
Of five long winters! and again I hear
These waters, rolling from their mountain-springs
With a soft inland murmur.—Once again
Do I behold these steep and lofty cliffs,
That on a wild secluded scene impress
Thoughts of more deep seclusion; and connect
The landscape with the quiet of the sky.
The day is come when I again repose
Here, under this dark sycamore, and view
These plots of cottage-ground, these orchard-tufts,
Which at this season, with their unripe fruits,
Are clad in one green hue, and lose themselves
'Mid groves and copses. Once again I see
These hedge-rows, hardly hedge-rows, little lines
Of sportive wood run wild: these pastoral farms,
Green to the very door; and wreaths of smoke
Sent up, in silence, from among the trees!
With some uncertain notice, as might seem
Of vagrant dwellers in the houseless woods,
Or of some Hermit's cave, where by his fire
The Hermit sits alone.

These beauteous forms,
Through a long absence, have not been to me
As is a landscape to a blind man's eye:
But oft, in lonely rooms, and 'mid the din
Of towns and cities, I have owed to them,
In hours of weariness, sensations sweet,
Felt in the blood, and felt along the heart;
And passing even into my purer mind,
With tranquil restoration:—feelings too
Of unremembered pleasure: such, perhaps,
As have no slight or trivial influence
On that best portion of a good man's life,
His little, nameless, unremembered, acts
Of kindness and of love. Nor less, I trust,
To them I may have owed another gift,
Of aspect more sublime; that blessed mood,
In which the burthen of the mystery,
In which the heavy and the weary weight
Of all this unintelligible world,
Is lightened:—that serene and blessed mood,
In which the affections gently lead us on,—
Until, the breath of this corporeal frame
And even the motion of our human blood

Almost suspended, we are laid asleep
In body, and become a living soul:
While with an eye made quiet by the power
Of harmony, and the deep power of joy,
We see into the life of things.
                                                    If this
Be but a vain belief, yet, oh! how oft—
In darkness and amid the many shapes
Of joyless daylight; when the fretful stir
Unprofitable, and the fever of the world,
Have hung upon the beatings of my heart—
How oft, in spirit, have I turned to thee,
O sylvan Wye! thou wanderer thro' the woods,
How often has my spirit turned to thee!

    And now, with gleams of half-extinguished thought,
With many recognitions dim and faint,
And somewhat of a sad perplexity,
The picture of the mind revives again:
While here I stand, not only with the sense
Of present pleasure, but with pleasing thoughts
That in this moment there is life and food
For future years. And so I dare to hope,
Though changed, no doubt, from what I was when first
I came among these hills; when like a roe
I bounded o'er the mountains, by the sides
Of the deep rivers, and the lonely streams,
Wherever nature led: more like a man
Flying from something that he dreads than one
Who sought the thing he loved. For nature then
(The coarser pleasures of my boyish days,
And their glad animal movements all gone by)
To me was all in all.—I cannot paint
What then I was. The sounding cataract
Haunted me like a passion: the tall rock,
The mountain, and the deep and gloomy wood,
Their colours and their forms, were then to me
An appetite; a feeling and a love,
That had no need of a remoter charm,
By thought supplied, nor any interest
Unborrowed from the eye.—That time is past,
And all its aching joys are now no more,
And all its dizzy raptures. Not for this
Faint I, nor mourn nor murmur; other gifts
Have followed; for such loss, I would believe,
Abundant recompense. For I have learned
To look on nature, not as in the hour
Of thoughtless youth; but hearing often-times

The still, sad music of humanity,
Nor harsh, nor grating, though of ample power
To chasten and subdue. And I have felt
A presence that disturbs me with the joy
Of elevated thoughts; a sense sublime
Of something far more deeply interfused,
Whose dwelling is the light of setting suns,
And the round ocean and the living air,
And the blue sky, and in the mind of man:
A motion and a spirit, that impels
All thinking things, all objects of all thought,
And rolls through all things. Therefore am I still
A lover of the meadows and the woods,
And mountains; and of all that we behold
From this green earth; of all the mighty world
Of eye, and ear,—both what they half create,
And what perceive; well pleased to recognise
In nature and the language of the sense
The anchor of my purest thoughts, the nurse,
The guide, the guardian of my heart, and soul
Of all my moral being.

Nor perchance,
If I were not thus taught, should I the more
Suffer my genial spirits to decay:
For thou art with me here upon the banks
Of this fair river; thou my dearest Friend,
My dear, dear Friend; and in thy voice I catch
The language of my former heart, and read
My former pleasures in the shooting lights
Of thy wild eyes. Oh! yet a little while
May I behold in thee what I was once,
My dear, dear Sister! and this prayer I make,
Knowing that Nature never did betray
The heart that loved her; 'tis her privilege,
Through all the years of this our life, to lead
From joy to joy: for she can so inform
The mind that is within us, so impress
With quietness and beauty, and so feed
With lofty thoughts, that neither evil tongues,
Rash judgments, nor the sneers of selfish men,
Nor greetings where no kindness is, nor all
The dreary intercourse of daily life,
Shall e'er prevail against us, or disturb
Our cheerful faith, that all which we behold
Is full of blessings. Therefore let the moon
Shine on thee in thy solitary walk;
And let the misty mountain-winds be free

To blow against thee: and, in after years,
When these wild ecstasies shall be matured
Into a sober pleasure; when thy mind
Shall be a mansion for all lovely forms,
Thy memory be as a dwelling-place
For all sweet sounds and harmonies; oh! then,
If solitude, or fear, or pain, or grief,
Should be thy portion, with what healing thoughts
Of tender joy wilt thou remember me,
And these my exhortations! Nor, perchance—
If I should be where I no more can hear
Thy voice, nor catch from thy wild eyes these gleams
Of past existence—wilt thou then forget
That on the banks of this delightful stream
We stood together; and that I, so long
A worshipper of Nature, hither came
Unwearied in that service: rather say
With warmer love—oh! with far deeper zeal
Of holier love. Nor wilt thou then forget
That after many wanderings, many years
Of absence, these steep woods and lofty cliffs,
And this green pastoral landscape, were to me
More dear, both for themselves and for thy sake!

THE WORLD IS TOO MUCH WITH US

The world is too much with us; late and soon,
Getting and spending, we lay waste our powers:
Little we see in Nature that is ours;
We have given our hearts away, a sordid boon!
This Sea that bares her bosom to the moon;
The winds that will be howling at all hours,
And are up-gathered now like sleeping flowers;
For this, for everything, we are out of tune;
It moves us not.—Great God! I'd rather be
A Pagan suckled in a creed outworn;
So might I, standing on this pleasant lea,
Have glimpses that would make me less forlorn;
Have sight of Proteus rising from the sea;
Or hear old Triton blow his wreathèd horn.

COMPOSED BY THE SIDE OF GRASMERE LAKE

Clouds, lingering yet, extend in solid bars
Through the grey west; and lo! these waters, steeled
By breezeless air to smoothest polish, yield
A vivid repetition of the stars;
Jove, Venus, and the ruddy crest of Mars
Amid his fellows beauteously revealed
At happy distance from earth's groaning field,
Where ruthless mortals wage incessant wars.
Is it a mirror?—or the nether Sphere
Opening to view the abyss in which she feeds
Her own calm fires?—But list! a voice is near;
Great Pan himself low-whispering through the reeds,
"Be thankful, thou; for, if unholy deeds
Ravage the world, tranquility is here!"

LINES WRITTEN IN EARLY SPRING

I heard a thousand blended notes,
While in a grove I sate reclined,
In that sweet mood when pleasant thoughts
Bring sad thoughts to the mind.

To her fair works did Nature link
The human soul that through me ran;
And much it grieved my heart to think
What man has made of man.

Through primrose tufts, in that green bower,
The periwinkle trailed its wreaths;
And 'tis my faith that every flower
Enjoys the air it breathes.

The birds around me hopped and played,
Their thoughts I cannot measure:—
But the least motion which they made,
It seemed a thrill of pleasure.

The budding twigs spread out their fan,
To catch the breezy air;
And I must think, do all I can
That there was pleasure there.

If this belief from heaven be sent,
If such be Nature's holy plan,
Have I not reason to lament
What man has made of man?

TO MY SISTER

It is the first mild day of March:
Each minute sweeter than before,
The redbreast sings from the tall larch
That stands beside our door.

There is a blessing in the air,
Which seems a sense of joy to yield
To the bare trees, and mountains bare,
And grass in the green field.

My sister! ('tis a wish of mine)
Now that our morning meal is done,
Make haste, your morning task resign;
Come forth and feel the sun.

Edward will come with you;—and, pray,
Put on with speed your woodland dress;
And bring no book: for this one day
We'll give to idleness.

No joyless forms shall regulate
Our living calendar:
We from to-day, my Friend, will date
The opening of the year.

Love, now a universal birth,
From heart to heart is stealing,
From earth to man, from man to earth:
—It is the hour of feeling.

One moment now may give us more
Than years of toiling reason:
Our minds shall drink at every pore
The spirit of the season.

Some silent laws our hearts will make,
Which they shall long obey:
We for the year to come may take
Our temper from to-day.

And from the blessed power that rolls
About, below, above,
We'll frame the measure of our souls:
They shall be tuned to love.

Then come, my Sister! come, I pray,
With speed put on your woodland dress;
And bring no book: for this one day
We'll give to idleness.

from THE PRELUDE: Retrospect—Love of Nature Leading to Love of Man

What sounds are those, Helvellyn, that are heard
Up to thy summit, through the depth of air
Ascending, as if distance had the power
To make the sounds more audible? What crowd
Covers, or sprinkles o'er, yon village green?
Crowd seems it, solitary hill! to thee,
Though but a little family of men,
Shepherds and tillers of the ground—betimes
Assembled with their children and their wives,
And here and there a stranger interspersed.
They hold a rustic fair—a festival,
Such as, on this side now, and now on that,
Repeated through his tributary vales,
Helvellyn, in the silence of his rest,
Sees annually, if clouds towards either ocean
Blown from their favourite resting-place, or mists
Dissolved, have left him an unshrouded head.
Delightful day it is for all who dwell
In this secluded glen, and eagerly
They give it welcome. Long ere heat of noon,
From byre or field the kine were brought; the sheep
Are penned in cotes; the chaffering is begun.
The heifer lows, uneasy at the voice
Of a new master; bleat the flocks aloud.
Booths are there none; a stall or two is here;
A lame man or a blind, the one to beg,
The other to make music; hither, too,
From far, with basket, slung upon her arm,
Of hawker's wares—books, pictures, combs, and pins—
Some aged woman finds her way again,
Year after year, a punctual visitant!
There also stands a speech-maker by rote,
Pulling the strings of his boxed raree-show;
And in the lapse of many years may come
Prouder itinerant, mountebank, or he
Whose wonders in a covered wain lie hid.
But one there is, the loveliest of them all,
Some sweet lass of the valley, looking out

For gains, and who that sees her would not buy?
Fruits of her father's orchard are her wares,
And with the ruddy produce she walks round
Among the crowd, half pleased with, half ashamed
Of her new office, blushing restlessly.
The children now are rich, for the old today
Are generous as the young; and, if content
With looking on, some ancient wedded pair
Sit in the shade together, while they gaze,
"A cheerful smile unbends the wrinkled brow,
The days departed start again to life,
And all the scenes of childhood reappear,
Faint, but more tranquil, like the changing sun
To him who slept at noon and wakes at eve."
Thus gaiety and cheerfulness prevail,
Spreading from young to old, from old to young,
And no one seems to want his share.—Immense
Is the recess, the circumambient world
Magnificent, by which they are embraced:
They move about upon the soft green turf:
How little they, they and their doings, seem,
And all that they can further or obstruct!
Through utter weakness pitiably dear,
As tender infants are: and yet how great!
For all things serve them; them the morning light
Loves, as it glistens on the silent rocks;
And them the silent rocks, which now from high
Look down upon them; the reposing clouds;
The wild brooks prattling from invisible haunts;
And old Helvellyn, conscious of the stir
Which animates this day their calm abode.

With deep devotion, Nature, did I feel,
In that enormous City's turbulent world
Of men and things, what benefit I owed
To thee, and those domains of rural peace,
Where to the sense of beauty first my heart
Was opened: tract more exquisitely fair
Than that famed paradise of ten thousand trees,
Or Gehol's matchless gardens, for delight
Of the Tartarian dynasty composed
(Beyond that mighty wall, not fabulous,
China's stupendous mound) by patient toil
Of myriads and boon nature's lavish help;
There, in a clime from widest empire chosen,
Fulfilling (could enchantment have done more?)
A sumptuous dream of flowery lawns, with domes
Of pleasure sprinkled over, shady dells

For eastern monasteries, sunny mounts
With temples crested, bridges, gondolas,
Rocks, dens, and groves of foliage taught to melt
Into each other their obsequious hues,
Vanished and vanishing in subtle chase,
Too fine to be pursued; or standing forth
In no discordant opposition, strong
And gorgeous as the colours side by side
Bedded among rich plumes of tropic birds;
And mountains over all, embracing all;
And all the landscape, endlessly enriched
With waters running, falling, or asleep.

But lovelier far than this, the paradise
Where I was reared; in Nature's primitive gifts
Favoured no less, and more to every sense
Delicious, seeing that the sun and sky,
The elements, and seasons as they change,
Do find a worthy fellow-labourer there—
Man free, man working for himself, with choice
Of time, and place, and object; by his wants,
His comforts, native occupations, cares,
Cheerfully led to individual ends
Or social, and still followed by a train
Unwooed, unthought-of even—simplicity,
And beauty, and inevitable grace.

Yea, when a glimpse of those imperial bowers
Would to a child be transport over-great,
When but a half-hour's roam through such a place
Would leave behind a dance of images.
That shall break in upon his sleep for weeks;
Even then the common haunts of the green earth,
And ordinary interests of man,
Which they embosom, all without regard
As both may seem, are fastening on the heart
Insensibly, each with the other's help,
For me, when my affections first were led
From kindred, friends, and playmates, to partake
Love for the human creature's absolute self,
That noticeable kindliness of heart
Sprang out of fountains, there abounding most,
Where sovereign Nature dictated the tasks
And occupations which her beauty adorned,
And Shepherds were the men that pleased me first;
Not such as Saturn ruled 'mid Latian wilds,
With arts and laws so tempered, that their lives
Left, even to us toiling in this late day,

A bright tradition of the golden age;
Not such as, 'mid Arcadian fastnesses
Sequestered, handed down among themselves
Felicity, in Grecian song renowned;
Nor such as—when an adverse fate had driven,
From house and home, the courtly band whose fortunes
Entered, with Shakespeare's genius, the wild woods
Of Arden—amid sunshine or in shade
Culled the best fruits of Time's uncounted hours,
Ere Phoebe sighed for the false Ganymede;
Or there where Perdita and Florizel
Together danced, Queen of the feast, and King;
Nor such as Spenser fabled. True it is.
That I had heard (what he perhaps had seen)
Of maids at sunrise bringing in from far
Their May-bush, and along the street in flocks
Parading with a song of taunting rhymes,
Aimed at the laggards slumbering within doors;
Had also heard, from those who yet remembered,
Tales of the May-pole dance, and wreaths that decked
Porch, door-way, or kirk-pillar; and of youths,
Each with his maid, before the sun was up,
By annual custom, issuing forth in troops,
To drink the waters of some sainted well,
And hang it round with garlands. Love survives;
But, for such purpose, flowers no longer grow:
The times, too sage, perhaps too proud, have dropped
These lighter graces; and the rural ways
And manners which my childhood looked upon
Were the unluxuriant produce of a life
Intent on little but substantial needs,
Yet rich in beauty, beauty that was felt.
But images of danger and distress,
Man suffering among awful Powers and Forms;
Of this I heard, and saw enough to make
Imagination restless; nor was free
Myself from frequent perils; nor were tales
Wanting,—the tragedies of former times,
Hazards and strange escapes, of which the rocks
Immutable, and everflowing streams,
Where'er I roamed, were speaking monuments.

Smooth life had flock and shepherd in old time,
Long springs and tepid winters, on the banks
Of delicate Galesus; and no less
Those scattered along Adria's myrtle shores:
Smooth life had herdsman, and his snow-white herd
To triumphs and to sacrificial rites

Devoted, on the inviolable stream
Of rich Clitumnus; and the goat-herd lived
As calmly, underneath the pleasant brows
Of cool Lucretilis, where the pipe was heard
Of Pan, Invisible God, thrilling the rocks
With tutelary music, from all harm
The fold protecting. I myself, mature
In manhood then, have seen a pastoral tract
Like one of these, where Fancy might run wild,
Though under skies less generous, less serene:
There, for her own delight had Nature framed
A pleasure-ground, diffused a fair expanse
Of level pasture, islanded with groves
And banked with woody risings; but the Plain
Endless, here opening widely out, and there
Shut up in lesser lakes or beds of lawn
And intricate recesses, creek or bay
Sheltered within a shelter, where at large
The shepherd strays, a rolling hut his home.
Thither he comes with spring-time, there abides
All summer, and at sunrise ye may hear
His flageolet to liquid notes of love
Attuned, or sprightly fife resounding far.
Nook is there none, nor tract of that vast space
Where passage opens, but the same shall have
In turn its visitant, telling there his hours
In unlaborious pleasure, with no task
More toilsome than to carve a beechen bowl
For spring or fountain, which the traveller finds,
When through the region he pursues at will
His devious course. A glimpse of such sweet life
I saw when, from the melancholy walls
Of Goslar, once imperial, I renewed
My daily walk along that wide champaign,
That, reaching to her gates, spreads east and west,
And northwards, from beneath the mountainous verge
Of the Hercynian forest. Yet, hail to you
Moors, mountains, headlands, and ye hollow vales,
Ye long deep channels for the Atlantic's voice,
Powers of my native region! ye that seize
The heart with firmer grasp! Your snows and streams
Ungovernable, and your terrifying winds,
That howl so dismally for him who treads
Companionless your awful solitudes!
There, 'tis the shepherd's task the winter long
To wait upon the storms: of their approach
Sagacious, into sheltering coves he drives
His flock, and thither from the homestead bears

A toilsome burden up the craggy ways,
And deals it out, their regular nourishment
Strewn on the frozen snow. And when the spring
Looks out, and all the pastures dance with lambs,
And when the flock, with warmer weather, climbs
Higher and higher, him his office leads
To watch their goings, whatsoever track
The wanderers choose. For this he quits his home
At day-spring, and no sooner doth the sun
Begin to strike him with a fire-like heat,
Than he lies down upon some shining rock,
And breakfasts with his dog. When they have stolen,
As is their wont, a pittance from strict time,
For rest not needed or exchange of love,
Then from his couch he starts; and now his feet
Crush out a livelier fragrance from the flowers
Of lowly thyme, by Nature's skill enwrought
In the wild turf: the lingering dews of morn
Smoke round him, as from hill to hill he hies,
His staff protending like a hunter's spear,
Or by its aid leaping from crag to crag,
And o'er the brawling beds of unbridged streams.
Philosophy, methinks, at Fancy's call,
Might deign to follow him through what he does
Or sees in his day's march; himself he feels,
In those vast regions where his service lies,
A freeman, wedded to his life of hope
And hazard, and hard labour interchanged
With that majestic indolence so dear
To native man. A rambling schoolboy, thus
I felt his presence in his own domain,
As of a lord and master, or a power,
Or genius, under Nature, under God,
Presiding; and severest solitude
Had more commanding looks when he was there.
When up the lonely brooks on rainy days
Angling I went, or trod the trackless hills
By mists bewildered, suddenly mine eyes
Have glanced upon him distant a few steps,
In size a giant, stalking through thick fog,
His sheep like Greenland bears; or, as he stepped
Beyond the boundary line of some hill-shadow,
His form hath flashed upon me, glorified
By the deep radiance of the setting sun:
Or him have I descried in distant sky,
A solitary object and sublime,
Above all height! like an aerial cross
Stationed alone upon a spiry rock

Of the Chartreuse, for worship. Thus was man
Ennobled outwardly before my sight,
And thus my heart was early introduced
To an unconscious love and reverence
Of human nature; hence the human form
To me became an index of delight,
Of grace and honour, power and worthiness.
Meanwhile this creature—spiritual almost
As those of books, but more exalted far;
Far more of an imaginative form
Than the gay Corin of the groves, who lives
For his own fancies, or to dance by the hour,
In coronal, with Phyllis in the midst—
Was, for the purpose of kind, a man
With the most common; husband, father; learned,
Could teach, admonish; suffered with the rest
From vice and folly, wretchedness and fear;
Of this I little saw, cared less for it,
But something must have felt.

Call ye these appearances—
Which I beheld of shepherds in my youth,
This sanctity of Nature given to man—
A shadow, a delusion, ye who pore
On the dead letter, miss the spirit of things;
Whose truth is not a motion or a shape
Instinct with vital functions, but a block
Or waxen image which yourselves have made,
And ye adore! But blessèd be the God
Of Nature and of Man that this was so;
That men before my inexperienced eyes
Did first present themselves thus purified,
Removed, and to a distance that was fit:
And so we all of us in some degree
Are led to knowledge, wheresoever led,
And howsoever; were it otherwise,
And we found evil fast as we find good
In our first years, or think that it is found,
How could the innocent heart bear up and live!
But doubly fortunate my lot; not here
Alone, that something of a better life
Perhaps was round me than it is the privilege
Of most to move in, but that first I looked
At man through objects that were great or fair;
First communed with him by their help. And thus
Was founded a sure safeguard and defence
Against the weight of meanness, selfish cares,

Coarse, manners, vulgar passions, that beat in
On all sides from the ordinary world
In which we traffic. Starting from this point
I had my face turned toward the truth, began
With an advantage furnished by that kind
Of prepossession, without which the soul
Receives no knowledge that can bring forth good,
No genuine insight ever comes to her.
From the restraint of over-watchful eyes
Preserved, I moved about, year after year,
Happy, and now most thankful that my walk
Was guarded from too early intercourse
With the deformities of crowded life,
And those ensuing laughters and contempts,
Self-pleasing, which, if we would wish to think
With a due reverence on earth's rightful lord,
Here placed to be the inheritor of heaven,
Will not permit us; but pursue the mind,
That to devotion willingly would rise,
Into the temple and the temple's heart.

Yet deem not, Friend! that human kind with me
Thus early took a place pre-eminent;
Nature herself was, at this unripe time,
But secondary to my own pursuits
And animal activities, and all
Their trivial pleasures; and when these had drooped
And gradually expired, and Nature, prized
For her own sake, became my joy, even then—
And upwards through late youth, until not less
Than two-and-twenty summers had been told—
Was Man in my affections and regards
Subordinate to her, her visible forms
And viewless agencies: a passion, she,
A rapture often, and immediate love
Ever at hand; he, only a delight
Occasional, an accidental grace,
His hour being not yet come. Far less had then
The inferior creatures, beast or bird, attuned
My spirit to that gentleness of love
(Though they had long been carefully observed),
Won from me those minute obeisances
Of tenderness, which I may number now
With my first blessings. Nevertheless, on these
The light of beauty did not fall in vain,
Or grandeur circumfuse them to no end.

But when that first poetic faculty
Of plain Imagination and severe,

No longer a mute influence of the soul,
Ventured, at some rash Muse's earnest call,
To try her strength among harmonious words;
And to book-notions and the rules of art
Did knowingly conform itself; there came
Among the simple shapes of human life
A wilfulness of fancy and conceit:
And Nature and her objects beautified
These fictions, as in some sort, in their turn,
They burnished her. From touch of this new power
Nothing was safe: the elder-tree that grew
Beside the well-known charnel-house had then
A dismal look; the yew-tree had its ghost,
That took his station there for ornament:
The dignities of plain occurrence then
Were tasteless, and truth's golden mean, a point
Where no sufficient pleasure could be found.
Then, if a widow, staggering with the blow
Of her distress, was known to have turned her steps
To the cold grave in which her husband slept,
One night, or haply more than one, through pain
Or half-insensate impotence of mind,
The fact was caught at greedily, and there
She must be visitant the whole year through,
Wetting the turf with never-ending tears.

Through quaint obliquities I might pursue
These cravings; when the foxglove, one by one,
Upwards through every stage of the tall stem,
Had shed beside the public way its bells,
And stood of all dismantled, save the last
Left at the tapering ladder's top, that seemed
To bend as doth a slender blade of grass
Tipped with a rain-drop, Fancy loved to seat,
Beneath the plant despoiled, but crested still
With this last relic, soon itself to fall,
Some vagrant mother, whose arch little ones,
All unconcerned by her dejected plight,
Laughed as with rival eagerness their hands
Gathered the purple cups that round them lay,
Strewing the turf's green slope.
A diamond light
(Whene'er the summer sun, declining, smote
A smooth rock wet with constant springs) was seen
Sparkling from out a copse-clad bank that rose
Fronting our cottage. Oft beside the hearth
Seated, with open door, often and long
Upon this restless lustre have I gazed,

That made my fancy restless as itself.
'Twas now for me a burnished silver shield
Suspended over a knight's tomb, who lay
Inglorious, buried in the dusky wood:
An entrance now into some magic cave
Or palace built by fairies of the rock;
Nor could I have been bribed to disenchant
The spectacle, by visiting the spot.
Thus wilful Fancy, in no hurtful mood,
Engrafted far-fetched shapes on feelings bred
By pure Imagination: busy Power
She was, and with her ready pupil turned
Instinctively to human passions, then
Least understood. Yet, 'mid the fervent swarm
Of these vagaries, with an eye so rich
As mine was through the bounty of a grand
And lovely region, I had forms distinct
To steady me: each airy thought revolved
Round a substantial centre, which at once
Incited it to motion, and controlled.
I did not pine like one in cities bred,
As was thy melancholy lot, dear Friend!
Great Spirit as thou art, in endless dreams
Of sickliness, disjoining, joining, things
Without the light of knowledge. Where the harm,
If, when the woodman languished with disease
Induced by sleeping nightly on the ground
Within his sod-built cabin, Indian-wise,
I called the pangs of disappointed love,
And all the sad etcetera of the wrong,
To help him to his grave? Meanwhile the man,
If not already from the woods retired
To die at home, was haply as I knew,
Withering by slow degrees, 'mid gentle airs,
Birds, running streams, and hills so beautiful
On golden evenings, while the charcoal pile
Breathed up its smoke, an image of his ghost
Or spirit that full soon must take her flight.
Nor shall we not be tending towards that point
Of sound humanity to which our Tale
Leads, though by sinuous ways, if here I show
How Fancy, in a season when she wove
Those slender cords, to guide the unconscious Boy
For the Man's sake, could feed at Nature's call
Some pensive musings which might well beseem
Maturer years.

A grove there is whose boughs
Stretch from the western marge of Thurston-mere,

With length of shade so thick, that whoso glides
Along the line of low-roofed water, moves
As in a cloister. Once—while, in that shade
Loitering, I watched the golden beams of light
Flung from the setting sun, as they reposed
In silent beauty on the naked ridge
Of a high eastern hill—thus flowed my thoughts
In a pure stream of words fresh from the heart:
Dear native Regions, whereso'er shall close
My mortal course, there will I think on you;
Dying, will cast on you a backward look;
Even as this setting sun (albeit the Vale
Is no where touched by one memorial gleam)
Doth with the fond remains of his last power
Still linger, and a farewell lustre sheds
On the dear mountain-tops where first he rose.

Enough of humble arguments; recall,
My Song! those high emotions which thy voice
Has heretofore made known; that bursting forth
Of sympathy, inspiring and inspired,
When everywhere a vital pulse was felt,
And all the several frames of things, like stars,
Through every magnitude distinguishable,
Shone mutually indebted, or half lost
Each in the other's blaze, a galaxy
Of life and glory. In the midst stood Man,
Outwardly, inwardly contemplated,
As, of all visible natures, crown, though born
Of dust, and kindred to the worm; a Being,
Both in perception and discernment, first
In every capability of rapture,
Through the divine effect of power and love;
As, more than anything we know, instinct
With godhead, and, by reason and by will,
Acknowledging dependency sublime.

Ere long, the lonely mountains left, I moved,
Begirt, from day to day, with temporal shapes
Of vice and folly thrust upon my view,
Objects of sport, and ridicule, and scorn,
Manners and characters discriminate,
And little bustling passions that eclipse,
As well they might, the impersonated thought,
The idea, or abstraction of the kind.

An Idler among academic bowers,
Such was my new condition, as at large

Has been set forth; yet here the vulgar light
Of present, actual, superficial life,
Gleaming through colouring of other times,
Old usages and local privilege,
Was welcome, softened, if not solemnised.
This notwithstanding, being brought more near
To vice and guilt, forerunning wretchedness,
I trembled,—thought, at times, of human life
With an indefinite terror and dismay,
Such as the storms and angry elements
Had bred in me; but gloomier far, a dim
Analogy to uproar and misrule,
Disquiet, danger, and obscurity.

It might be told (but wherefore speak of things
Common to all?) that, seeing, I was led
Gravely to ponder—judging between good
And evil, not as for the mind's delight
But for her guidance—one who was to *act*,
As sometimes to the best of feeble means
I did, by human sympathy impelled;
And, through dislike and most offensive pain,
Was to the truth conducted; of this faith
Never forsaken, that, by acting well,
And understanding, I should learn to love
The end of life, and everything we know.

Grave Teacher, stern Preceptress! for at times
Thou canst put on an aspect most severe;
London, to thee I willingly return.
Erewhile my verse played idly with the flowers
Enwrought upon thy mantle; satisfied
With that amusement, and a simple look
Of child-like inquisition now and then
Cast upwards on thy countenance, to detect
Some inner meanings which might harbour there.
But how could I in mood so light indulge,
Keeping such fresh remembrance of the day,
When, having thridded the long labyrinth
Of the suburban villages, I first
Entered thy vast dominion? On the roof
Of an itinerant vehicle I sate,
With vulgar men about me, trivial forms
Of houses, pavement, streets, of men and things,—
Mean shapes on every side: but, at the instant,
When to myself it fairly might be said,
The threshold now is overpast, (how strange
That aught external to the living mind

Should have such mighty sway? yet so it was),
A weight of ages did at once descend
Upon my heart; no thought embodied, no
Distinct remembrances, but weight and power,—
Power growing under weight: alas! I feel
That I am trifling: 'twas a moment's pause,—
All that took place within me came and went
As in a moment; yet with Time it dwells,
And grateful memory, as a thing divine.

The curious traveller, who, from open day,
Hath passed with torches into some huge cave,
The Grotto of Antiparos, or the Den
In old time haunted by that Danish Witch,
Yordas; he looks around and sees the vault
Widening on all sides; sees, or thinks he sees,
Erelong, the massy roof above his head,
That instantly unsettles and recedes,—
Substance and shadow, light and darkness, all
Commingled, making up a canopy
Of shapes and forms and tendencies to shape
That shift and vanish, change and interchange
Like spectres,—ferment silent and sublime!
That after a short space works less and less,
Till, every effort, every motion gone,
The scene before him stands in perfect view
Exposed, and lifeless as a written book!—
But let him pause awhile, and look again,
And a new quickening shall succeed, at first
Beginning timidly, then creeping fast,
Till the whole cave, so late a senseless mass,
Busies the eye with images and forms
Boldly assembled,—here is shadowed forth
From the projections, wrinkles, cavities,
A variegated landscape,—there the shape
Of some gigantic warrier clad in mail,
The ghostly semblance of a hooded monk,
Veiled nun, or pilgrim resting on his staff:
Strange congregation! yet not slow to meet
Eyes that perceive through minds that can inspire.

Even in such sort had I at first been moved,
Nor otherwise continued to be moved,
As I explored the vast metropolis,
Fount of my country's destiny and the world's;
That great emporium, chronicle at once
And burial-place of passions, and their home
Imperial, their chief living residence.

With strong sensations teeming as it did
Of past and present, such a place must needs
Have pleased me, seeking knowledge at that time
Far less than craving power; yet knowledge came,
Sought or unsought, and influxes of power
Came, of themselves, or at her call derived
In fits of kindliest apprehensiveness,
From all sides, when whate'er was in itself
Capacious found, or seemed to find, in me
A correspondent amplitude of mind;
Such is the strength and glory of our youth!
The human nature unto which I felt
That I belonged, and reverenced with love,
Was not a punctual presence, but a spirit
Diffused through the time and space, with love,
Was not punctual presence, but a spirit
Diffused through time and space, with aid derived
Of evidence from monuments, erect,
Prostrate, or leaning towards their common rest
In earth, the widely scattered wreck sublime
Of vanished nations, or more clearly drawn
From books and what they picture and record.

'Tis true, the history of our native land,
With those of Greece compared and popular Rome,
And in our high-wrought modern narratives
Stript of their harmonising soul, the life
Of manners and familiar incidents,
Had never much delighted me. And less
Than other intellects had mine been used
To learn upon extrinsic circumstance
Of record or tradition; but a sense
Of what in the Great City had been done
And suffered, and was doing, suffering, still,
Weighed with me, could support the test of thought;
And, in despite of all that had gone by,
Or was departing never to return,
There I conversed with majesty and power
Like independent natures. Hence the place
Was thronged with impregnations like the Wilds
In which my early feelings had been nursed—
Bare hills and valleys, full of caverns, rocks,
And audible seclusions, dashing lakes,
Echoes and waterfalls, and pointed crags
That into music touch the passing wind.
Here then my young imagination found
No uncongenial element; could here
Among new objects serve or give command,

Even as the heart's occasions might require,
To forward reason's else too scrupulous march.
The effect was, still more elevated views
Of human nature. Neither vice nor guilt,
Debasement undergone by body or mind,
Nor all the misery forced upon my sight,
Misery not lightly passed, but sometimes scanned
Most feelingly, could overthrow my trust
In what we *may* become; induce belief
That I was ignorant, had been falsely taught,
A solitary who with vain conceits
Had been inspired, and walked about in dreams.
From those sad scenes when meditation turned,
Lo! everything that was indeed divine
Retained its purity inviolate,
Nay brighter shone, by this portentous gloom
Set off; such opposition as aroused
The mind of Adam, yet in Paradise
Though fallen from bliss, when in the East he saw
Darkness ere day's mid course, and morning light
More orient in the western cloud, that drew
O'er the blue firmament a radiant white,
Descending slow with something heavenly fraught.

Add also, that among the multitudes
Of that huge city, oftentimes was seen
Affectingly set forth, more than elsewhere
Is possible, the unity of man,
One spirit over ignorance and vice
Predominant in good and evil hearts;
One sense for moral judgments, as one eye
For the sun's light. The soul when smitten thus
By a sublime *idea*, whencesoe'er
Vouchsafed for union or communion, feeds
On the pure bliss, and takes her rest with God.

Thus from a very early age, O Friend!
My thoughts by slow gradations had been drawn
To human-kind, and to the good and ill
Of human life: Nature had led me on;
And oft amid the "busy hum" I seemed
To travel independent of her help,
As if I had forgotten her; but no,
The world of human-kind outweighed not hers
In my habitual thoughts; the scale of love,
Though filling daily, still was light, compared
With that in which *her* mighty objects lay.

Dorothy Wordsworth
1771-1855

The sister of William Wordsworth and close friend of Samuel Taylor Coleridge, Dorothy Wordsworth was an important nature writer in her own right. She shared her brother's love of rural scenes, residing with or near him for most of her life and directly stimulating his production of poetry. Her own nature writing took the form of prose journals in which she recorded the details of her rural environments with almost uncanny accuracy and clarity.

Possessing an unusually inquisitive, gentle mind, she conveys in her journals a sensitivity to the behavior of animals and the colors and shapes of vegetation, especially the subtle changes wrought upon a scene by changing moods of weather. The feelings that natural objects evoked in her are marked by a great empathy with living things. Yet emotional reactions never replace the exquisite descriptions of landscapes and creatures; rather, the literal accuracy of her eye and ear is more than sufficient to imply emotions that the reader easily shares.

Dorothy wrote journals at Alfoxden, Grasmere, and on several walking tours. The journals are personal, obviously not intended for publication, but most readers are struck by the poetic qualities of her prose: brevity, directness, and most of all, fine description. Indeed, scholars have shown that many of her descriptions served as the basis for some of her brother's most successful poems.

Her life was, in the main, uneventful. She had little direct contact with the political persons or events that occupied William and Coleridge. On the other hand, she did lead a style of life relatively unbound by the conventions of the day. Reunited with her beloved brother twelve years after their father's death had separated them, she shared with him the spontaneous joys of woods and waters. Often they lived with little money and with no servant, renting inexpensive country houses while gardening and gathering wild fruit. She accompanied William and Coleridge on their walking tours of the countryside at a time when young ladies were not expected to behave in such a manner.

It was, in fact, her ability to embrace and love the world as she found it that characterizes Dorothy Wordsworth's nature writing. Throughout her journals she displays a quick receptiveness to natural detail that startles readers and challenges them to sharpen their own senses.

from THE ALFOXDEN JOURNAL (1798)*

February 1st. About two hours before dinner, set forward towards Mr. Bartholemew's. The wind blew so keen in our faces that we felt ourselves inclined to seek the covert of the wood. There we had a warm shelter, gathered a burthen of large rotten boughs blown down by the wind of the preceding night. The sun shone clear, but all at once a heavy blackness hung over the sea. The trees almost *roared,* and the ground seemed in motion with the multitudes of dancing leaves, which made a rustling sound, distinct from that of the trees. Still the asses pastured in quietness under the hollies, undisturbed by these forerunners of the storm. The wind beat furiously against us as we returned. Full moon. She rose in uncommon majesty over the sea, slowly ascending through the clouds. Sat with the window open an hour in the moonlight.

February 2nd. Walked through the wood, and on to the Downs before dinner; a warm pleasant air. The sun shone, but was often obscured by straggling clouds. The redbreasts made a ceaseless song in the woods. The wind rose very high in the evening. The room smoked so that we were obliged to quit it. Young lambs in a green pasture in the Coombe, thick legs, large heads, black staring eyes.

February 3rd. A mild morning, the windows open at breakfast, the redbreasts singing in the garden. Walked with Coleridge over the hills. The sea at first obscured by vapour; that vapour afterwards slid in one mighty mass along the seashore; the islands and one point of land clear beyond it. The distant country (which was purple in the clear dull air), overhung by straggling clouds that sailed over it, appeared like the darker clouds, which are often seen at a great distance apparently motionless, while the nearer ones pass quickly over them, driven by the lower winds. I never saw such a union of earth, sky, and sea. The clouds beneath our feet spread themselves to the water, and the clouds of the sky almost joined them. Gathered sticks in the wood; a perfect stillness. The redbreasts sang upon the leafless boughs. Of a great number of sheep in the field, only one standing. Returned to dinner at five o'clock. The moonlight still and warm as a summer's night at nine o'clock.

February 4th. Walked a great part of the way to Stowey with Coleridge. The morning warm and sunny. The young lasses seen on the hill-tops, in the

* This and the following selections by Dorothy Wordsworth are from *The Journals of Dorothy Wordsworth,* ed. William Knight (New York: McMillan & Co., 1925).

villages and roads, in their summer holiday clothes—pink petticoats and blue. Mothers with their children in arms, and the little ones that could just walk, tottering by their side. Midges or small flies spinning in the sunshine; the songs of the lark and redbreast; daisies upon the turf; the hazels in blossom; honeysuckles budding. I saw one solitary strawberry flower under a hedge. The furze gay with blossom. The moss rubbed from the pailings by the sheep, that leave locks of wool, and the red marks with which they are spotted, upon the wood.

February 5th. Walked to Stowey with Coleridge, returned by Woodlands; a very warm day. In the continued singing of birds distinguished the notes of a blackbird or thrush. The sea overshadowed by a thick dark mist, the land in sunshine. The sheltered oaks and beeches still retaining their brown leaves. Observed some trees putting out red shoots. Query: What trees are they?

. . .

February 8th. Went up the Park, and over the tops of the hills, till we came to a new and very delicious pathway, which conducted us to the Coombe. Sat a considerable time upon the heath. Its surface restless and glittering with the motion of the scattered piles of withered grass, and the waving of the spiders' threads. On our return the mist still hanging over the sea, but the opposite coast clear, and the rocky cliffs distinguishable. In the deep Coombe, as we stood upon the sunless hill, we saw miles of grass, light and glittering, and the insects passing.

. . .

February 13th. Walked with Coleridge through the wood. A mild and pleasant morning, the near prospect clear. The ridges of the hills fringed with wood, showing the sea through them like the white sky, and still beyond the dim horizon of the distant hills, hanging as it were in one undetermined line between sea and sky.

February 14th. Gathered sticks with William in the wood, he being unwell and not able to go further. The young birch trees of a bright red, through which gleams a shade of purple. Sat down in a thick part of the wood. The near trees still, even to their topmost boughs, but a perpetual motion in those that skirt the wood. The breeze rose gently; its path distinctly marked, till it came to the very spot where we were.

. . .

February 17th. A deep snow upon the ground. Wm. and Coleridge walked to Mr. Bartholemew's, and to Stowey. Wm. returned, and we walked through the wood into the Coombe to fetch some eggs. The sun shone bright and clear. A deep stillness in the thickest part of the wood, undisturbed except by the occasional dropping of the snow from the holly boughs; no other sound but that of the water, and the slender notes of a redbreast, which sang at intervals on the outskirts of the southern side of the wood. There the bright green moss was bare at the roots of the trees, and the little birds were upon it. The whole appearance of the wood was enchanting; and each tree, taken singly, was beautiful. The branches of the hollies pendent with their white burden, but still showing their bright red berries, and their glossy green leaves. The bare branches of the oaks thickened by the snow.

February 18th. Walked after dinner beyond Woodlands. A sharp and very cold evening; first observed the crescent moon, a silvery line, a thready bow, attended by Jupiter and Venus in their palest hues.

. . .

February 24th. Went to the hill-top. Sat a considerable time overlooking the country towards the sea. The air blew pleasantly round us. The landscape mildly interesting. The Welsh hills capped by a huge range of tumultuous white clouds. The sea, spotted with white, of a bluish grey in general, and streaked with darker lines. The near shores clear; scattered farm houses, half-concealed by green mossy orchards, fresh straw lying at the doors; hay-stacks in the fields. Brown fallows, the springing wheat, like a shade of green over the brown earth, and the choice meadow plots, full of sheep and lambs, of a soft and vivid green; a few wreaths of blue smoke, spreading along the ground; the oaks and beeches in the hedges retaining their yellow leaves; the distant prospect on the land side, islanded with sunshine; the sea, like a basin full to the margin; the dark fresh-ploughed fields; the turnips of a lively rough green. Returned through the wood.

. . .

February 27. I walked to Stowey in the evening. Wm. and Basil went with me through the wood. The prospect bright, yet *mildly* beautiful. The sea big and white, swelled to the very shores, but round and high in the middle. Coleridge returned with me, as far as the wood. A very bright moonlight night. Venus almost like another moon. Lost to us at Alfoxden long before she goes down the large white sea.

. . .

March 1st. We rose early. A thick fog obscured the distant prospect entirely, but the shapes of the nearer trees and the dome of the wood dimly seen and dilated. It cleared away between ten and eleven. The shapes of the mist, slowly moving along, exquisitely beautiful; passing over the sheep they almost seemed to have more of life than those quiet creatures. The unseen birds singing in the mist.

. . .

March 7th. William and I drank tea at Coleridge's. A cloudy sky. Observed nothing particularly interesting—the distant prospect obscured. One only leaf upon the top of a tree—the sole remaining leaf—danced round and round like a rag blown by the wind.

. . .

March 18th. The Coleridges left us. A cold, windy morning. Walked with them half way. On our return, sheltered under the hollies, during a hail-shower. The withered leaves danced with the hailstones. William wrote a description of the storm.

March 19th. Wm. and Basil and I walked to the hill-tops, a very cold bleak day. We were met on our return by a severe hailstorm. William wrote some lines describing a stunted thorn.

March 20th. Coleridge dined with us. We went more than half way home with him in the evening. A very cold evening, but clear. The spring seemingly very little advanced. No green trees, only the hedges are budding, and looking very lovely.

March 21st. We drank tea at Coleridge's. A quiet shower of snow was in the air during more than half our walk. At our return the sky partially shaded with clouds. The horned moon was set. Startled two night birds from the great elm tree.

March 22nd. I spent the morning in starching and hanging out linen; walked *through* the wood in the evening, very cold.

March 23rd. Coleridge dined with us. He brought his ballad finished. We walked with him to the Miner's house. A beautiful evening, very starry, the horned moon.

March 24th. Coleridge, the Chesters, and Ellen Cruikshank called. We walked with them through the wood. Went in the evening into the Coombe to get eggs; returned through the wood, and walked in the park. A duller night than last night: a sort of white shade over the blue sky. The stars dim. The spring continues to advance very slowly, no green trees, the hedges leafless; nothing green but the brambles that still retain their old leaves, the evergreens, and the palms, which indeed are not absolutely green. Some brambles I observed to-day budding afresh, and those have shed their old leaves. The crooked arm of the old oak tree points upwards to the moon.

. . .

April 2nd. A very high wind. Coleridge came to avoid the smoke; stayed all night. We walked in the wood, and sat under the trees. The half of the wood perfectly still, while the wind was making a loud noise behind us. The still trees only gently bowed their heads, as if listening to the wind. The hollies in the thick wood unshaken by the blast; only, when it came with a greater force, shaken by the rain drops falling from the bare oaks above.

. . .

April 15th. Set forward after breakfast to Crookham, and returned to dinner at three o'clock. A fine cloudy morning. Walked about the squire's grounds. Quaint waterfalls about, about which Nature was very successfully striving to make beautiful what art had deformed—ruins, hermitages, etc. etc. In spite of all these things, the dell romantic and beautiful, though everywhere planted with unnaturalised trees. Happily we cannot shape the huge hills, or carve out the valleys according to our fancy.

from THE GRASMERE JOURNAL (1800–1803)

I. May 14th to December 22nd, 1800

May 14th, 1800[*Wednesday*]. Wm. and John set off into Yorkshire after dinner at ½ past 2 o'clock, cold pork in their pockets. I left them at the turning of the Lowwood bay under the trees. My heart was so full that I could hardly speak to W. when I gave him a farewell kiss. I sate a long time upon a stone at the margin of the lake, and after a flood of tears my heart was easier. The lake looked to me, I knew not why, dull and melancholy, and the weltering on the shores seemed a heavy sound. I walked as long as I could amongst the stones of the shore. The wood rich in flowers; a beautiful yellow, palish yellow, flower, that looked thick, round, and double, and smelt very sweet—I supposed it was a ranunculus. Crowfoot, the grassy-leaved rabbit-toothed white flower, strawberries, geranium, scentless violets, anemones two kinds, orchises, primroses. The heckberry very beautiful, the crab coming out as a low shrub. Met a blind man, driving a very large beautiful Bull, and a cow—he walked with two sticks. Came home by Clappersgate. The valley very green; many sweet views up to Rydale head, when I could juggle away the fine houses; but they disturbed me, even more than when I have been happier; one beautiful view of the Bridge, without Sir Michael's. Sate down very often, though it was cold. I resolved to write a journal of the time till W. and J. return, and I set about keeping my resolve, because I will not quarrel with myself, and because I shall give Wm. pleasure by it when he comes home again. At Rydale, a woman of the village, stout and well dressed, begged a half-penny; she had never she said done it before, but these hard times! Arrived at home with a bad headach, set some slips of privett, the evening cold, had a sire, my face now flame-coloured. It is nine o'clock. I shall soon go to bed. A young woman begged at the door—she had come from Manchester on Sunday morn. with two shillings and a slip of paper which she supposed a Bank note—it was a cheat. She had buried her husband and three children within a year and a half—all in one grave—burying very dear—paupers all put in one place—20 shillings paid for as much ground as will bury a man—a stone to be put over it or the right will be lost—11/6 each time the ground is opened. Oh! that I had a letter from William!

May 15th, Thursday. A coldish dull morning—hoed the first row of peas, weeded etc. etc., sat hard to mending till evening. The rain which had threatened all day came on just when I was going to walk.

[*May 16th,*] *Friday morning.* Warm and mild, after a fine night of rain. Transplanted radishes after breakfast, walked to Mr. Gell's with the books, gathered mosses and plants. The woods extremely beautiful with all autumnal variety and softness. I carried a basket for mosses, and gathered some wild plants. Oh! that we had a book of botany. All flowers now are gay and deliciously sweet. The primrose still pre-eminent among the later flowers of the spring. Foxgloves very tall, with their heads budding. I went forward round the lake at the foot of Loughrigg Fell. I was much amused with the business of a pair of stone-chats; their restless voices as they skimmed along the water following each other, their shadows under them, and their returning back to the stones on the shore, chirping with the same unwearied voice. Could not cross the water, so I went round by the stepping-stones. The morning clear but cloudy, that is the hills were not overhung by mists. After dinner Aggy weeded onions and carrots. I helped for a little—wrote to Mary Hutchinson—washed my head—worked. After tea went to Ambleside—a pleasant cool but not cold evening. Rydale was very beautiful, with spear-shaped streaks of polished steel. No letters!—only one newspaper. I returned by Clappersgate. Grasmere was very solemn in the last glimpse of twilight; it calls home the heart to quietness. I had been very melancholy in my walk back. I had many of my saddest thoughts, and I could not keep the tears within me. But when I came to Grasmere I felt that it did me good. I finished my letter to M.H. Ate hasty pudding and went to bed. As I was going out in the morning I met a half crazy old man. He shewed me a pincushion and begged a pin, afterwards a half-penny. He began in a kind of indistinct voice in this manner: "Matthew Jobson's lost a cow. Tom Nichol has two good horses strayed. Jim Jones's cow's brokken her horn, etc. etc." He went into Aggy's and persuaded her to give him some whey, and let him boil some porridge. She declares he ate two quarts.

[*May 17th,*] *Saturday*. Incessant rain from morning till night. T. Ashburner brought us coals. Worked hard, and read *Midsummer Night's Dream,* [and] Ballads—sauntered a little in the garden. The Skobby sate quiety in its nest, rocked by the wind, and beaten by the rain.

[*May*] *18th, Sunday.* Went to church, slight showers, a cold air. The mountains from this window look much greener, and I think the valley is more green than ever. The corn begins to shew itself. The ashes are still bare, went part of the way home with Miss Simpson. A little girl from Coniston came to beg. She had lain out all night—her step-mother had turned her out of doors. Her father could not stay at home "she flights so". Walked to Ambleside in the evening round the lake, the prospect exceedingly beautiful from Loughrigg Fell. It was so green that no eye could be weary of reposing upon it. The most beautiful situation for a house in the field next to Mr. Benson's. It threatened rain all the evening but was mild and pleasant. I was overtaken by 2 Cumberland people on the other side of Rydale who complimented me upon my walking. They were going to sell cloth, and odd things which they make themselves, in Hawkshead and the neighbourhood. The post was not arrived, so I walked thro' the town, past Mrs. Taylor's, and met him. Letters from Coleridge and Cottle. John Fisher overtook me on the other side of Rydale. He talked much about the alteration in the times, and observed that in a short time there would be only two ranks of people, the very rich and the very poor, "for those who have small estates", says he, "are forced to sell, and all the land goes into one hand". Did not reach home till 10 o'clock.

[*May 19th,*] *Monday*. Sauntered a good deal in the garden, bound carpets, mended old clothes. Read *Timon of Athens*. Dried linen. Molly weeded the turnips, John stuck the peas. We had not much sunshine or wind, but no rain till about 7 o'clock, when we had a slight shower just after I had set out upon my walk. I did not return but walked up into the Black Quarter. I sauntered a long time among the rocks above the church. The most delightful situation possible for a cottage, commanding two distinct views of the vale and of the lake, is among those rocks. I strolled on, gathered mosses etc. The quietness and still seclusion of the valley affected me even to producing the deepest melancholy. I forced myself from it. The wind rose before I went to bed. No rain—Dodwell and Wilkinson called in my absence.

[*May 20th,*] *Tuesday Morning.* A fine mild rain. After breakfast the sky cleared and before the clouds passed from the hills I went to Ambleside. It was a sweet morning. Everything green and overflowing with life, and the streams making a perpetual song, with the thrushes and all little birds, not forgetting the stone-chats. The post was not come in. I walked as far as Windermere, and met him there. No letters! no papers. Came home by Clappersgate. I was sadly tired, ate a hasty dinner and had a bad headach—went to bed and slept at least 2 hours. Rain came on in the evening—Molly washing.

[*May 21st,*] *Wednesday*. Went often to spread the linen which was bleaching—a rainy day and very wet night.

[*May 22nd,*] *Thursday*. A very fine day with showers—dried the linen and starched. Drank tea at Mr. Simpson's. Brought down Batchelor's Buttons (Rock Ranunculus) and other plants—went part of the way back, a showery mild evening—all the peas up.

. . .

[*May*] *27th, Tuesday*. I walked to Ambleside with letters—met the post before I reached Mr. Partridge's, one paper, only a letter for Coleridge. I expected a letter from Wm. It was a sweet morning, the ashes in the valley nearly in full leaf, but still to be distinguished, quite bare on the higher ground. I was warm in returning, and becoming cold with sitting in the house I had a bad headach—went to bed after dinner, and lay till after 5. Not well after tea. I worked in the garden, but did not walk further. A delightful evening before the sun set, but afterwards it grew colder—mended stockings etc.

. . .

[*May 30th,*] *Friday*. In the morning went to Ambleside, forgetting that the post does not come till the evening. How was I grieved when I was so informed. I walked back, resolving to go again in the evening. It rained very mildly and sweetly in the morning as I came home, but came on a wet afternoon and evening, but chilly. I caught Mr. Olliff's lad as he was going for letters, he brought me one from Wm. and 12 papers. I planted London Pride upon the well, and many things on the borders. John sodded the wall. As I came past Rydale in the morning, I saw a Heron swimming with only its neck out of water; it beat and struggled amongst the water, when it flew away, and was long in getting loose.

. . .

June 1st, Sunday. Rain in the night—a sweet mild morning. Read Ballads; went to church. Singers from Wytheburn, went part of the way home with Miss Simpson. Walked upon the hill above the house till dinner time—went again to church—Christening and singing which kept us very late. The pewside came down with me. Walked with Mr. Simpson nearly home. After tea, went to Ambleside, round the lakes—a very fine warm evening. I lay upon the steep of Loughrigg, my heart dissolved in what I saw, when I was not startled but re-called from my reverie by a noise as of a child paddling without shoes. I looked up and saw a lamb close to me. It approached nearer and nearer, as if to examine me, and stood a long time. I did not move. At last it ran past me, and went bleating along the pathway, seeming to be seeking its mother. I saw a hare on the high road. The post was not come in; waited in the road till John's apprentice came with a letter from Coleridge and 3 papers. The moon shone upon the water—reached home at 10 o'clock, went to bed immediately. Molly brought daisies etc. which we planted.

Samuel Taylor Coleridge
1772-1834

Coleridge's writings on politics, philosophy and literary criticism have earned him a lasting reputation, but his greatest achievement lies in his poetry, and some of his best poems deal intimately and brilliantly with the world of nature. Intimacy is the key to his famed "conversation poems," such as "The Lime-tree Bower My Prison," which reveals seemingly spontaneous reflections about the ability of the human mind to appreciate natural beauty even when reconstructing its details from memory. Brilliance is the key to his even more famous poems "The Rime of the Ancient Mariner" and "Kubla Khan," which carry us to those boundaries of human imagination where concrete natural events become miraculous.

Both brilliance and the need for intimacy provide keys to understanding Coleridge's life. He was born in the country village of St. Mary's on the River Otter, the youngest of fourteen children. As an unusually intelligent child, his father's favorite, he became isolated from other children. His private joys were reading—often very deep reading—and dreaming about the ideas he gathered.

When Coleridge was eight years old, his father died, and the boy was sent to Christ's Hospital, a school for orphans in busy London. There loneliness and separation from rural scenes increased his intellectual activity, which already included writing poetry. His accomplishments won him acceptance to Cambridge University at a time when excitement over revolutionary France was reaching a high point. After initial academic success at Cambridge, he succumbed to the distractions of youth and politics, quit school, and joined the army—until his brother George rescued him.

In 1795 he married, largely in order to be part of a Utopian commune that he and his friends planned to create in America. The scheme, which offered an escape from personal failure and from disenchantment with the French Revolution, failed early on, leaving Coleridge with bitter feelings and an unhappy marriage. Despite his disappointments, some of his finest conversation poems were composed during this period, when idealistic plans gave way to gardening, reading, and lecturing.

The most fruitful period of his life began when he became close to William Wordsworth in 1797. Like Coleridge, Wordsworth was disillusioned with politics. The two shared a great love for natural scenes and found inspiration in each other's poetry. While they resided near one another, first at Nether Stowey, near the ocean, and then in the Lake District, they read and criticized each other's work with enthusiasm, generating a whole new idea of the function of poetry. The literary fruit of their relationship was the *Lyrical Ballads* (1798), which contains Coleridge's "Rime of the Ancient Mariner."

Coleridge's loneliness and visionary intellect were complicated by his addiction to opium, which began in 1800 as a treatment for rheumatism. Whether opium enhanced or destroyed Coleridge's literary talent, his production of poetry began to decline after the turn of this century, when he turned his intellectual energies to criticism and philosophy. Nevertheless, he enriched the tradition of nature writing with his familiar, thoughtful voice and a "visionary power" that yielded the lesson: "He prayeth best, who loveth best/All things both great and small."

THE RIME OF THE ANCIENT MARINER*

Part 1

It is an ancient Mariner,
And he stoppeth one of three.
'By thy long grey beard and glittering eye,
Now wherefore stopp'st thou me?

The Bridegroom's doors are opened wide,
And I am next of kin;
The guests are met, the feast is set:
May'st hear the merry din.'

He holds him with his skinny hand,
'There was a ship,' quoth he.
'Hold off! unhand me, grey-beard loon!'
Eftsoons his hand dropt he.

He holds him with his glittering eye—
The Wedding-Guest stood still,
And listens like a three years' child:
The Mariner hath his will.

The Wedding-Guest sat on a stone:
He cannot choose but hear;

This and the following poems by Samuel Taylor Coleridge are from *Coleridge, Poetical Works,* ed. Ernest Hartley Coleridge (London: Oxford University Press, 1912). Courtesy of Oxford University Press.

And thus spake on that ancient man,
The bright-eyed Mariner.

'The ship was cheered, the harbour cleared,
Merrily did we drop
Below the kirk, below the hill,
Below the lighthouse top.

The Sun came up upon the left,
Out of the sea came he!
And he shone bright, and on the right
Went down into the sea.

Higher and higher every day,
Till over the mast at noon—'
The Wedding-Guest here beat his breast,
For he heard the loud bassoon.

The bride hath paced into the hall,
Red as a rose is she;
Nodding their heads before her goes
The merry minstrelsy.

The Wedding-Guest he beat his breast,
Yet he cannot choose but hear;
And thus spake on that ancient man,
The bright-eyed Mariner.

'And now the STORM-BLAST came, and he
Was tyrannous and strong:
He struck with his o'ertaking wings,
And chased us south along.

With sloping masts and dipping prow,
As who pursued with yell and blow
Still treads the shadow of his foe,
And forward bends his head,
The ship drove fast, loud roared the blast,
And southward aye we fled.

And now there came both mist and snow,
And it grew wondrous cold:
And ice, mast-high, came floating by,
As green as emerald.

And through the drifts the snowy cliffs
Did send a dismal sheen:
Nor shapes of men nor beasts we ken—
The ice was all between.

The ice was here, the ice was there,
The ice was all around:
It cracked and growled, and roared and howled,
Like noises in a swound!

At length did cross an Albatross,
Thorough the fog it came;
As if it had been a Christian soul,
We hailed it in God's name.

It ate the food it ne'er had eat,
And round and round it flew.
The ice did split with a thunder-fit;
The helmsman steered us through!

And a good south wind sprung up behind;
The Albatross did follow,
And every day, for food or play,
Came to the mariner's hollo!

In mist or cloud, on mast or shroud,
It perched for vespers nine;
Whiles all the night, through fog-smoke white,
Glimmered the white Moon-shine.'

'God save thee, ancient Mariner!
From the fiends, that plague thee thus!—
Why look'st thou so?'—With my cross-bow
I shot the ALBATROSS.

Part II

The Sun now rose upon the right:
Out of the sea came he,
Still hid in mist, and on the left
Went down into the sea.

And the good south wind still blew behind,
But no sweet bird did follow,
Nor any day for food or play
Came to the mariners' hollo!

And I had done a hellish thing,
And it would work 'em woe:
For all averred, I had killed the bird
That made the breeze to blow.
Ah wretch! said they, the bird to slay,
That made the breeze to blow!

Nor dim nor red, like God's own head,
The glorious Sun uprist:
Then all averred, I had killed the bird
That brought the fog and mist.
'Twas right, said they, such birds to slay,
That bring the fog and mist.

The fair breeze blew, the white foam flew,

The furrow followed free;
We were the first that ever burst
Into that silent sea.

Down dropt the breeze, the sails dropt down,
'Twas sad as sad could be;
And we did speak only to break
The silence of the sea!

All in a hot and copper sky,
The bloody Sun, at noon,
Right up above the mast did stand,
No bigger than the Moon.

Day after day, day after day
We stuck, nor breath nor motion;
As idle as a painted ship
Upon a painted ocean.

Water, water every where,
And all the boards did shrink;
Water, water every where
Nor any drop to drink.

The very deep did rot: O Christ!
That ever this should be!
Yea, slimy things did crawl with legs
Upon the slimy sea.

About, about, in reel and rout
The death-fires danced at night;
The water, like a witch's oils,
Burnt green, and blue and white.

And some in dreams assuréd were
Of the Spirit that plagued us so;
Nine fathom deep he had followed us
From the land of mist and snow.

And every tongue, through utter drought,
Was withered at the root;
We could not speak, no more than if
We had been choked with soot.

Ah! well a-day! what evil looks
Had I from old and young!
Instead of the cross, the Albatross
About my neck was hung.

Part III

There passed a weary time. Each throat
Was parched, and glazed each eye.
A weary time! a weary time!

How glazed each weary eye,
When looking westward, I beheld
A something in the sky.

At first it seemed a little speck,
And then it seemed a mist;
It moved and moved, and took at last
A certain shape, I wist.

A speck, a mist, a shape, I wist!
And still it neared and neared:
As if it dodged a water-sprite,
It plunged and tacked and veered.

With throats unslaked, with black lips baked,
We could nor laugh nor wail;
Through utter drought all dumb we stool!
I bit my arm, I sucked the blood,
And cried, A sail! a sail!

With throats unslaked, with black lips baked,
Agape they heard me call:
Gramercy! they for joy did grin,
And all at once their breath drew in,
As they were drinking all.

See! see! (I cried) she tacks no more!
Hither to work us weal;
Without a breeze, without a tide,
She steadies with upright keel!

The western wave was all a-flame.
The day was well nigh done!
Almost upon the western wave
Rested the broad bright Sun;
When that strange shape drove suddenly
Betwixt us and the Sun.

And straight the Sun was flecked with bars,
(Heaven's Mother send us grace!)
As if through a dungeon-grate he peered
With broad and burning face.

Alas! (thought I, and my heart beat loud)
How fast she nears and nears!
Are those *her* sails that glance in the Sun,
Like restless gossameres?

Are those *her* ribs through which the Sun
Did peer, as through a grate?
And is that Woman all her crew?
Is that a DEATH? and are there two?
Is DEATH that woman's mate?

Her lips were red, *her* looks were free,
Her locks were yellow as gold:
Her skin was as white as leprosy,
The Night-mare LIFE-IN-DEATH was she,
Who thicks man's blood with cold.

The naked hulk alongside came,
And the twain were casting dice;
'The game is done! I've won! I've won!'
Quoth she, and whistles thrice.

The Sun's rim dips; the stars rush out:
At one stride comes the dark;
With far-heard whisper, o'er the sea,
Off shot the spectre-bark.

We listened and looked sideways up!
Fear at my heart, as at a cup,
My life-blood seemed to sip!
The Stars were dim, and thick the night,
The steersman's face by his lamp gleamed white;
From the sails the dew did drip—
Till clomb above the eastern bar
The hornéd Moon, with one bright star
Within the nether tip.

One after one, by the star-dogged Moon,
Too quick for groan or sigh,
Each turned his face with a ghastly pang,
And cursed me with his eye.

Four times fifty living men,
(And I heard nor sigh nor groan)
With heavy thump, a lifeless lump,
They dropped down one by one.

The souls did from their bodies fly,—
They fled to bliss or woe!
And every soul, it passed me by,
Like the whizz of my cross-bow!

Part IV

'I fear thee, ancient Mariner!
I fear thy skinny hand!
And thou art long, and lank, and brown,
As is the ribbed sea-sand.

I fear thee and thy glittering eye,
And thy skinny hand, so brown.'—
Fear not, fear not, thou Wedding-Guest!
This body dropt not down.

Alone, alone, all, all alone,
Alone on a wide wide sea!
And never a saint took pity on
My soul in agony.

The many men, so beautiful!
And they all dead did lie:
And a thousand thousand slimy things
Lived on; and so did I.

I looked upon the rotting sea,
And drew my eyes away;
I looked upon the rotting deck,
And there the dead men lay.

I looked to heaven, and tried to pray;
But or ever a prayer had gusht,
A wicked whisper came, and made
My heart as dry as dust.

I closed my lids, and kept them close,
And the balls like pulses beat;
For the sky and the sea, and the sea and the sky
Lay like a load on my weary eye,
And the dead were at my feet.

The cold sweat melted from their limbs,
Nor rot nor reek did they:
The look with which they looked on me
Had never passed away.

An orphan's curse would drag to hell
A spirit from on high;
But oh! more horrible than that
Is the curse in a dead man's eye!
Seven days, seven nights, I saw that curse,
And yet I could not die.

The moving Moon went up the sky,
And no where did abide:
Softly she was going up,
And a star or two beside—

Her beams bemocked the sultry main,
Like April hoar-frost spread;
But where the ship's huge shadow lay,
The charméd water burnt alway
A still and awful red.

Beyond the shadow of the ship,
I watched the water-snakes:
They moved in tracks of shining white,
And when they reared, the elfish light
Fell off in hoary flakes.

Within the shadow of the ship
I watched their rich attire:
Blue, glossy green, and velvet black,
They coiled and swam; and every track
Was a flash of golden fire.

O happy living things! no tongue
Their beauty might declare:
A spring of love gushed from my heart,
And I blessed them unaware:
Sure my kind saint took pity on me,
And I blessed them unaware.

The self-same moment I could pray;
And from my neck so free
The Albatross fell off, and sank
Like lead into the sea.

Part V

Oh sleep! it is a gentle thing,
Beloved from pole to pole!
To Mary Queen the praise be given!
She sent the gentle sleep from Heaven,
That slid into my soul.

The silly buckets on the deck,
That had so long remained,
I dreamt that they were filled with dew;
And when I awoke, it rained.

My lips were wet, my throat was cold.
My garments all were dank;
Sure I had drunken in my dreams,
And still my body drank.

I moved, and could not feel my limbs:
I was so light—almost
I thought that I had died in sleep,
And was a blesséd ghost.

And soon I heard a roaring wind:
It did not come anear;
But with its sound it shook the sails,
That were so thin and sere.

The upper air burst into life!
And a hundred fire-flags sheen,
To and fro they were hurried about!
And to and fro, and in and out,
The wan stars danced between.

And the coming wind did roar more loud,
And the sails did sigh like sedge;
And the rain poured down from one black
cloud;
The Moon was at its edge.

The thick black cloud was cleft, and still
The Moon was at its side:
Like waters shot from some high crag,
The lightning fell with never a jag,
A river steep and wide.

The loud wind never reached the ship,
Yet now the ship moved on!
Beneath the lightning and the Moon
The dead men gave a groan.

They groaned, they stirred, they all uprose,
Nor spake, nor moved their eyes;
It had been strange, even in a dream,
To have seen those dead men rise.

The helmsman steered, the ship moved on;
Yet never a breeze up-blew;
The mariners all 'gan work the ropes,
Where they were wont to do;
They raised their limbs like lifeless tools—
We were a ghastly crew.

The body of my brother's son
Stood by me, knee to knee:
The body and I pulled at one rope,
But he said nought to me.

'I fear thee, ancient Mariner!'
Be calm, thou Wedding-Guest!
'Twas not those souls that fled in pain,
Which to their corses came again,
But a troop of spirits blest:

For when it dawned—they dropped their arms,
And clustered round the mast;
Sweet sounds rose slowly through their mouths,
And from their bodies passed.

Around, around, flew each sweet sound
Then darted to the Sun;

Slowly the sounds came back again,
Now mixed, now one by one.

Sometimes a-dropping from the sky
I heard the sky-lark sing;
Sometimes all little birds that are,
How they seemed to fill the sea and air
With their sweet jargoning!

And now 'twas like all instruments,
Now like a lonely flute;
And now it is an angel's song,
That makes the heavens be mute.

It ceased; yet still the sails made on
A pleasant noise till noon,
A noise like of a hidden brook
In the leafy month of June,
That to the sleeping woods all night
Singeth a quiet tune.

Till noon we quietly sailed on,
Yet never a breeze did breathe:
Slowly and smoothly went the ship,
Moved onward from beneath.

Under the keel nine fathom deep,
From the land of mist and snow,
The spirit slid: and it was he
That made the ship to go.
The sails at noon left off their tune,
And the ship stood still also.

The Sun, right up above the mast,
Had fixed her to the ocean:
But in a minute she 'gan stir,
With a short uneasy motion—
Backwards and forwards half her length
With a short uneasy motion.

Then like a pawing horse let go,
She made a sudden bound:
It flung the blood into my head,
And I fell down in a swound.

How long in that same fit I lay,
I have not to declare;
But ere my living life returned,
I heard and in my soul discerned
Two voices in the air.

'Is it he?' quoth one, 'Is this the man?
By him who died on cross,

With his cruel bow he laid full low
The harmless Albatross.

The spirit who bideth by himself
In the land of mist and snow,
He loved the bird that loved the man
Who shot him with his bow.'

The other was a softer voice,
As soft as honey-dew:
Quoth he, 'The man hath penance done,
And penance more will do.'

Part VI

FIRST VOICE

'But tell me, tell me! speak again,
Thy soft response renewing—
What makes that ship drive on so fast?
What is the ocean doing?'

SECOND VOICE

'Still as a slave before his lord,
The ocean hath no blast;
His great bright eye most silently
Up to the Moon is cast—

If he may know which way to go;
For she guides him smooth or grim.
See, brother, see! how graciously
She looketh down on him.'

FIRST VOICE

'But why drives on that ship so fast.
Without or wave or wind?'

SECOND VOICE

'The air is cut away before,
And closes from behind.

Fly, brother, fly! more high, more high!
Or we shall be belated:
For slow and slow that ship will go,
When the Mariner's trance is abated.'

I woke, and we were sailing on
As in a gentle weather:
'Twas night, calm night, the moon was high;
The dead men stood together.

All stood together on the deck,
For a charnel-dungeon fitter:
All fixed on me their stony eyes,
That in the Moon did glitter.

The pang, the curse, with which they died,
Had never passed away:
I could not draw my eyes from theirs,
Nor turn them up to pray.

And now this spell was snapt: once more
I viewed the ocean green,
And looked far forth, yet little saw
Of what had else been seen—

Like one, that on a lonesome road
Doth walk in fear and dread,
And having once turned round walks on,
And turns no more his head;
Because he knows, a frightful fiend
Doth close behind him tread.

But soon there breathed a wind on me,
Nor sound nor motion made:
Its path was not upon the sea,
In ripple or in shade.

It raised my hair, it fanned my cheek
Like a meadow-gale of spring—
It mingled strangely with my fears,
Yet it felt like a welcoming.

Swiftly, swiftly flew the ship,
Yet she sailed softly too:
Sweetly, sweetly blew the breeze—
On me alone it blew.

Oh! dream of joy! is this indeed
The light-house top I see?
Is this the hill? is this the kirk?
Is this mine own countree?

We drifted o'er the harbour-bar,
And I with sobs did pray—
O let me be awake, my God!
Or let me sleep alway.

The harbour-bay was clear as glass,
So smoothly it was strewn!
And on the bay the moonlight lay,
And the shadow of the Moon.

The rock shone bright, the kirk no less,
That stands above the rock:
The moonlight steeped in silentness
The steady weathercock.

And the bay was white with silent light,

Till rising from the same,
Full many shapes, that shadows were,
In crimson colours came.

A little distance from the prow
Those crimson shadows were:
I turned my eyes upon the deck—
Oh, Christ! what saw I there!

Each corse lay flat, lifeless and flat,
And, by the holy rood!
A man all light, a seraph-man,
On every corse there stood.

This seraph-band, each waved his hand:
It was a heavenly sight!
They stood as signals to the land,
Each one a lovely light;

This seraph-band, each waved his hand,
No voice did they impart—
No voice; but oh! the silence sank
Like music on my heart.

But soon I heard the dash of oars,
I heard the Pilot's cheer;
My head was turned perforce away
And I saw a boat appear.

The Pilot and the Pilot's boy,
I heard them coming fast:
Dear Lord in Heaven! it was a joy
The dead men could not blast.

I saw a third—I heard his voice:
It is the Hermit good!
He singeth loud his godly hymns
That he makes in the wood.
He'll shrieve my soul, he'll wash away
The Ablatross's blood.

Part VII

This Hermit good lives in that wood
Which slopes down to the sea.
How loudly his sweet voice he rears!
He loves to talk with marineres
That come from a far countree.

He kneels at morn, and noon, and eve—
He hath a cushion plump:
It is the moss that wholly hides
The rotted old oak-stump.

The skiff-boat neared: I heard them talk,
'Why, this is strange, I trow!
Where are those lights so many and fair,
That signal made but now?'

'Strange, by my faith!' the Hermit said—
'And they answered not our cheer!
The planks looked warped! and see those sails,
How thin they are and sere!
I never saw aught like to them,
Unless perchance it were

Brown skeletons of leaves that lag
My forest-brook along;
When the ivy-tod is heavy with snow,
And the owlet whoops to the wolf below,
That eats the she-wolf's young.'

'Dear Lord! it hath a fiendish look—
(The Pilot made reply)
I am a-feared'—'Push on, push on!'
Said the Hermit cheerily.

The boat came closer to the ship,
But I nor spake nor stirred;
The boat came close beneath the ship,
And straight a sound was heard.

Under the water it rumbled on,
Still louder and more dread:
It reached the ship, it split the bay;
The ship went down like lead.

Stunned by that loud and dreadful sound,
Which sky and ocean smote,
Like one that hath been seven days drowned
My body lay afloat;
But swift as dreams, myself I found
Within the Pilot's boat.

Upon the whirl, where sank the ship,
The boat spun round and round;
And all was still, save that the hill
Was telling of the sound.

I moved my lips—the Pilot shrieked
And fell down in a fit;
The holy Hermit raised his eyes,
And prayed where he did sit.

I took the oars: the Pilot's boy,
Who now doth crazy go,

Laughed loud and long, and all the while
His eyes went to and fro.
'Ha! ha!' quoth he, 'full plain I see,
The Devil knows how to row.'

And now, all in my own countree,
I stood on the firm land!
The Hermit stepped forth from the boat,
And scarcely he could stand.

'O shrieve me, shrieve me, holy man!'
The Hermit crossed his brow.
'Say quick,' quoth he, 'I bid thee say—
What manner of man art thou?'

Forthwith this frame of mine was wrenched
With a woful agony,
Which forced me to begin my tale;
And then it left me free.

Since then, at an uncertain hour,
That agony returns:
And till my ghastly tale is told,
This heart within me burns.

I pass, like night, from land to land;
I have strange power of speech;
That moment that his face I see,
I know the man that must hear me:
To him my tale I teach.

What loud uproar bursts from that door!
The wedding-guests are there:
But in the garden-bower the bride
And bride-maids singing are:
And hark the little vesper bell,
Which biddeth me to prayer!

O Wedding-Guest! this soul hath been
Alone on a wide wide sea:
So lonely 'twas, that God himself
Scarce seeméd there to be.

O sweeter than the marriage-feast,
'Tis sweeter far to me,
To walk together to the kirk
With a goodly company!—

To walk together to the kirk,
And all together pray,
While each to his great Father bends,
Old men, and babes, and loving friends
And youths and maidens gay!

Farewell, farewell! but this I tell
To thee, thou Wedding-Guest!
He prayeth well, who loveth well
Both man and bird and beast.

He prayeth best, who loveth best
All things both great and small;
For the dear God who loveth us,
He made and loveth all.

The mariner, whose eye is bright,
Whose beard with age is hoar,
Is gone: and now the Wedding-Guest
Turned from the bridegroom's door.

He went like one that hath been stunned,
And is of sense forlorn:
A sadder and a wiser man,
He rose the morrow morn.

THE EOLIAN HARP

My pensive Sara! thy soft cheek reclined
Thus on mine arm, most soothing sweet it is
To sit beside our Cot, our Cot o'ergrown
With white-flower'd Jasmin, and the broad-leav'd Myrtle,
(Meet emblems they of Innocence and Love!)
And watch the clouds, that late were rich with light,
Slow saddening round, and mark the star of eve
Serenely brilliant (such should Wisdom be)
Shine opposite! How exquisite the scents
Snatch'd from yon bean-field! and the world *so* hush'd!
The stilly murmur of the distant Sea
Tells us of silence.
And that simplest Lute,
Placed length-ways in the clasping casement, hark!
How by the desultory breeze caress'd,
Like some coy maid half yielding to her lover,
It pours such sweet upbraiding, as must needs
Tempt to repeat the wrong! And now, its strings
Boldlier swept, the long sequacious notes
Over delicious surges sink and rise,
Such a soft floating witchery of sound
As twilight Elfins make, when they at eve
Voyage on gentle gales from Fairy-Land,
Where Melodies round honey-dropping flowers,
Footless and wild, like birds of Paradise,
Nor pause, nor perch, hovering on untam'd wing!
O! the one Life within us and abroad,
Which meets all motion and becomes its soul,

A light in sound, a sound-like power in light,
Rhythm in all thought, and joyance every where—
Methinks, it should have been impossible
Not to love all things in a world so fill'd;
Where the breeze warbles, and the mute still air
Is Music slumbering on her instrument.

And thus, my Love! as on the midway slope
Of yonder hill I stretch my limbs at noon,
Whilst through my half-clos'd eye-lids I behold
The sunbeams dance, like diamonds, on the main,
And tranquil muse upon tranquillity;
Full many a thought uncall'd and undetain'd,
And many idle flitting phantasies,
Traverse my indolent and passive brain,
As wild and various as the random gales
That swell and flutter on this subject Lute!
And what if all of animated nature
Be but organic Harps diversely fram'd,
That tremble into thought, as o'er them sweeps
Plastic and vast, one intellectual breeze,
At once the Soul of each, and God of all?
But thy more serious eye a mild reproof
Darts, O belovéd Woman! nor such thoughts
Dim and unhallow'd dost thou not reject,
And biddest me walk humbly with my God.
Meek Daughter in the family of Christ!
Well hast thou said and holily disprais'd
These shapings of the unregenerate mind;
Bubbles that glitter as they rise and break
On vain Philosophy's aye-babbling spring.
For never guiltless may I speak of him,
The Incomprehensible! save when with awe
I praise him, and with Faith that inly *feels*;
Who with his saving mercies healed me,
A sinful and most miserable man,
Wilder'd and dark, and gave me to possess
Peace, and this Cot, and thee, heart-honour'd Maid!

FROST AT MIDNIGHT

The frost performs its secret ministry,
Unhelped by any wind. The owlet's cry
Came loud—and hark, again! loud as before.
The inmates of my cottage, all at rest,
Have left me to that solitude, which suits
Abstruser musings: save that at my side
My cradled infant slumbers peacefully.

'Tis calm indeed! so calm, that it disturbs
And vexes meditation with its strange
And extreme silentness. Sea, hill, and wood,
This populous village! Sea, and hill, and wood,
With all the numberless goings-on of life,
Inaudible as dreams! the thin blue flame
Lies on my low-burnt fire, and quivers not;
Only that film, which fluttered on the grate,
Still flutters there, the sole unquiet thing.
Methinks, its motion in this hush of nature
Gives it dim sympathies with me who live,
Making it a companionable form,
Whose puny flaps and freaks the idling Spirit
By its own moods interprets, every where
Echo or mirror seeking of itself,
And makes a toy of Thought.

But O! how oft,
How oft, at school, with most believing mind,
Presageful, have I gazed upon the bars,
To watch that fluttering *stranger*! and as oft
With unclosed lids, already had I dreamt
Of my sweet birth-place, and the old church-tower,
Whose bells, the poor man's only music, rang
From morn to evening, all the hot Fair-day,
So sweetly, that they stirred and haunted me
With a wild pleasure, falling on mine ear
Most like articulate sounds of things to come!
So gazed I, till the soothing things, I dreamt,
Lulled me to sleep, and sleep prolonged my dreams!
And so I brooded all the following morn,
Awed by the stern preceptor's face, mine eye
Fixed with mock study on my swimming book:
Save if the door half opened, and I snatched
A hasty glance, and still my heart leaped up,
For still I hoped to see the *stranger's* face,
Townsman, or aunt, or sister more beloved,
My play-mate when we both were clothed alike!

Dear Babe, that sleepest cradled by my side,
Whose gentle breathings, heard in this deep calm,
Fill up the interspersèd vacancies
And momentary pauses of the thought!
My babe so beautiful! it thrills my heart
With tender gladness, thus to look at thee,
And think that thou shalt learn far other lore,
And in far other scenes! For I was reared
In the great city, pent 'mid cloisters dim,

And saw nought lovely but the sky and stars.
But *thou*, my babe! shalt wander like a breeze
By lakes and sandy shores, beneath the crags
Of ancient mountain, and beneath the clouds,
Which image in their bulk both lakes and shores
And mountain crags: so shalt thou see and hear
The lovely shapes and sounds intelligible
Of that eternal language, which thy God
Utters, who from eternity doth teach
Himself in all, and all things in himself.
Great universal Teacher! he shall mould
Thy spirit, and by giving make it ask.

Therefore all seasons shall be sweet to thee,
Whether the summer clothe the general earth
With greenness, or the redbreast sit and sing
Betwixt the tufts of snow on the bare branch
Of mossy apple-tree, while the nigh thatch
Smokes in the sun-thaw; whether the eave-drops fall
Heard only in the trances of the blast,
Or if the secret ministry of frost
Shall hang them up in silent icicles,
Quietly shining to the quiet Moon.

THIS LIME-TREE BOWER MY PRISON

Well, they are gone, and here must I remain,
This lime-tree bower my prison! I have lost
Beauties and feelings, such as would have been
Most sweet to my remembrance even when age
Had dimm'd mine eyes to blindness! They, meanwhile,
Friends, whom I never more may meet again,
On springy heath, along the hill-top edge,
Wander in gladness, and wind down, perchance,
To that still roaring dell, of which I told;
The roaring dell, o'erwooded, narrow, deep,
And only speckled by the mid-day sun;
Where its slim trunk the ash from rock to rock
Flings arching like a bridge;—that branchless ash,
Unsunn'd and damp, whose few poor yellow leaves
Ne'er tremble in the gale, yet tremble still,
Fann'd by the water-fall! and there my friends
Behold the dark green file of long lank weeds,
That all at once (a most fantastic sight!)
Still nod and drip beneath the dripping edge
Of the blue clay-stone.

Now, my friends emerge
Beneath the wide wide Heaven—and view again

The many-steepled tract magnificent
Of hilly fields and meadows, and the sea,
With some fair bark, perhaps, whose sails light up
The slip of smooth clear blue betwixt two Isles
Of purple shadow! Yes! they wander on
In gladness all; but thou, methinks, most glad,
My gentle-hearted Charles! for thou hast pined
And hunger'd after Nature, many a year,
In the great City pent, winning thy way
With sad yet patient soul, through evil and pain
And strange calamity! Ah! slowly sink
Behind the western ridge, thou glorious Sun!
Shine in the slant beams of the sinking orb,
Ye purple heath-flowers! richlier burn, ye clouds!
Live in the yellow light, ye distant groves!
And kindle, thou blue Ocean! So my friend
Struck with deep joy may stand, as I have stood,
Silent with swimming sense; yes, gazing round
On the wide landscape, gaze till all doth seem
Less gross than bodily; and of such hues
As veil the Almighty Spirit, when yet he makes
Spirits perceive his presence.

A delight
Comes sudden on my heart, and I am glad
As I myself were there! Nor in this bower,
This little lime-tree bower, have I not mark'd
Much that has sooth'd me. Pale beneath the blaze
Hung the transparent foliage; and I watch'd
Some broad and sunny leaf, and lov'd to see
The shadow of the leaf and stem above
Dappling its sunshine! And that walnut-tree
Was richly ting'd, and a deep radiance lay
Full on the ancient ivy, which usurps
Those fronting elms, and now, with blackest mass
Makes their dark branches gleam a lighter hue
Through the late twilight: and though now the bat
Wheels silent by, and not a swallow twitters,
Yet still the solitary humble-bee
Sings in the bean-flower! Henceforth I shall know
That Nature ne'er deserts the wise and pure;
No plot so narrow, be but Nature there,
No waste so vacant, but may well employ
Each faculty of sense, and keep the heart
Awake to Love and Beauty! and sometimes
'Tis well to be bereft of promis'd good,
That we may lift the soul, and contemplate
With lively joy the joys we cannot share.

My gentle-hearted Charles! when the last rook
Beat its straight path along the dusky air
Homewards, I blest it! deeming its black wing
(Now a dim speck, now vanishing in light)
Had cross'd the mighty Orb's dilated glory,
While thou stood'st gazing; or, when all was still,
Flew creeking o'er thy head, and had a charm
For thee, my gentle-hearted Charles, to whom
No sound is dissonant which tells of Life.

John Keats 1795-1821

Of the great nature writers, John Keats writes the most sensuous poetry. Enriched by concrete diction and vivid imagery, his poems capture the sights and sounds of natural scenes with almost startling realism. Keats's special talent is to describe a commonly named mood by presenting apt physical details that not only stimulate the senses but also evoke a particular feeling in the reader. His "Ode to Melancholy," for example, advises the reader not to seek death when melancholy strikes, but rather to feast the eyes on beauty:

. . . neither twist
Wolf's-bane, tight-rooted, for its poisonous wine;
Nor suffer thy pale forehead to be kiss'd
By nightshade, ruby grape of Proserpine;
Make not your rosary of yew-berries,
Nor let the beetle, nor the death-moth be
Your mournful Psyche, nor the downy owl
A partner in your sorrow's mysteries;
For shade to shade will come too drowsily,
And drown the wakeful anguish of the soul.

But when the melancholy fit shall fall
Sudden from heaven like a weeping cloud,
That fosters the droop-headed flowers all,
And hides the green hill in an April shroud;

Then glut thy sorrow on a morning rose,
Or on the rainbow of the salt sand-wave,
Or on the wealth of globed peonies . . .

Keats seems tuned to the smallest detail of a natural scene, such as the "wailful choir the small gnats sing" in his famous poem "To Autumn." Much of the success of his work lies in his skillful use of a wealth of concrete specifics.

Unlike Shelley, Keats reveled in the actual world. In fact, finding joy in concrete things became a major theme in his first attempt at a "great" poem, *Endymion*, the story of a Greek prince who falls in love with the moon goddess. He can approach such distant, ideal beauty only by developing his human affections for the mundane, actual items of his life. With Keats, we learn of the ideal and the abstract only by coming to terms with the objects that face us here and now.

Keats's biography reads like the romantic stereotype of a poet's life. Two facts dominate the story: his impoverishment and his early death at the age of twenty-five. He died just as his poetic talent was growing into maturity and promising great works for the future; nonetheless, he left a body of poems that rank him with the greatest poets in the English language.

He was born in London, the son of a stable hand who married his employer's daughter. When Keats was six, his father died; at fourteen, his mother died, leaving him and his brothers and sister to the care of their grandmother. After her death, a guardian swindled their inheritance and discouraged their education. Keats left the school where his initial preoccupation with fighting had been replaced with an interest in the poetry of Spenser and Shakespeare. He became an apprentice to a surgeon, then more a trade than a profession, and later studied medicine at Guy's Hospital. But he gave up that career when he found himself more interested in poetry and the life of the imagination than in the techniques of surgery. For the next five years Keats wrote poetry and searched for money enough to survive. While nursing his brother Tom, he contracted tuberculosis and slowly died of the disease.

Despite his lack of formal education, Keats early on formed a deep admiration for the classic English poets: Chaucer, Spenser, Milton, and Shakespeare. Later he came to include Wordsworth in that revered group. He was also strongly attached to classic Greek mythology, rooted as it is in physical phenomena. Throughout his short life, Keats's poetic search for ideal beauty enriched the tradition of nature writing with the energy and vividness of youth and the accuracy of maturity.

from ENDYMION: Book 1*

A thing of beauty is a joy for ever;
Its loveliness increases; it will never
Pass into nothingness; but still will keep
A bower quiet for us, and a sleep
Full of sweet dreams, and health, and quiet breathing.
Therefore, on every morrow, are we wreathing
A flowery band to bind us to the earth
Spite of despondence, of the inhuman dearth
Of noble natures, of the gloomy days,

*This and the following poems are from *John Keats and Percy Bysshe Shelley, Complete Works,* eds. Bennett A. Cerf and Donald S. Klopfer (New York: The Modern Library). Courtesy of Random House, Inc.

Of all the unhealthy and o'er-darkened ways
Made for our searching: yes, in spite of all,
Some shape of beauty moves away the pall
From our dark spirits. Such the sun, the moon,
Trees old, and young, sprouting a shady boon
For simple sheep; and such are daffodils
With the green world they live in; and clear rills
That for themselves a cooling covert make
'Gainst the hot season; the mid forest brake,
Rich with a sprinkling of fair musk-rose blooms:
And such too is the grandeur of the dooms
We have imagined for the mighty dead;
All lovely tales that we have heard or read:
An endless fountain of immortal drink,
Pouring unto us from the heaven's brink.

Nor do we merely feel these essences
For one short hour; no, even as the trees
That whisper round a temple become soon
Dear as the temple's self, so does the moon,
The passion poesy, glories infinite,
Haunt us till they become a cheering light
Unto our souls, and bound to us so fast,
That, whether there be shine, or gloom o'ercast,
They always must be with us, or we die.

Therefore, 'tis with full happiness that I
Will trace the story of Endymion.
The very music of the name has gone
Into my being, and each pleasant scene
Is growing fresh before me as the green
Of our own vallies; so I will begin
Now while I cannot hear the city's din;
Now while the early budders are just new,
And run in mazes of the youngest hue
About old forests; while the willow trails
Its delicate amber; and the dairy pails
Bring home increase of milk. And, as the year
Grows lush in juicy stalks, I'll smoothly steer
My little boat, for many quiet hours,
With streams that deepen freshly into bowers.
Many and many a verse I hope to write,
Before the daisies, vermeil rimm'd and white,
Hide in deep herbage; and ere yet the bees
Hum about globes of clover and sweet peas,
I must be near the middle of my story.
O may no wintry season, bare and hoary,
See it half finish'd: but let Autumn bold,
With universal tinge of sober gold,

Be all about me when I make an end.
And now at once, adventuresome, I send
My herald thought into a wilderness:
There let its trumpet blow, and quickly dress
My uncertain path with green, that I may speed
Easily onward, thorough flowers and weed.

Upon the sides of Latmos was outspread
A mighty forest; for the moist earth fed
So plenteously all weed-hidden roots
Into o'er-hanging boughs, and precious fruits.
And it had gloomy shades, sequestered deep,
Where no man went; and if from shepherd's keep
A lamb stray'd far a-down those inmost glens,
Never again saw he the happy pens
Whither his brethren, bleating with content,
Over the hills at every nightfall went.
Among the shepherds, 'twas believed ever,
That not one fleecy lamb which thus did sever
From the white flock, but pass'd unworried
By angry wolf, or pard with prying head,
Until it came to some unfooted plains
Where fed the herds of Pan: aye great his gains
Who thus one lamb did lose. Paths there were many,
Winding through palmy fern, and rushes fenny,
And ivy banks; all leading pleasantly
To a wide lawn, whence one could only see
Stems thronging all around between the swell
Of turf and slanting branches: who could tell
The freshness of the space of heaven above,
Edg'd round with dark tree tops? through which a dove
Would often beat its wings, and often too
A little cloud would move across the blue.

Full in the middle of this pleasantness
There stood a marble altar, with a tress
Of flowers budded newly; and the dew
Had taken fairy phantasies to strew
Daisies upon the sacred sward last eve,
And so the dawned light in pomp receive.
For 'twas the morn: Apollo's upward fire
Made every eastern cloud a silvery pyre
Of brightness so unsullied, that therein
A melancholy spirit well might win
Oblivion, and melt out his essence fine
Into the winds: rain-scented eglantine
Gave temperate sweets to that well-wooing sun;
The lark was lost in him; cold springs had run

To warm their chilliest bubbles in the grass;
Man's voice was on the mountains; and the mass
Of nature's lives and wonders puls'd tenfold,
To feel this sun-rise and its glories old.

Now while the silent workings of the dawn
Were busiest, into that self-same lawn
All suddenly, with joyful cries, there sped
A troop of little children garlanded;
Who gathering round the altar, seem'd to pry
Earnestly round as wishing to espy
Some folk of holiday: nor had they waited
For many moments, ere their ears were sated
With a faint breath of music, which ev'n then
Fill'd out its voice, and died away again.
Within a little space again it gave
Its airy swellings, with a gentle wave,
To light-hung leaves, in smoothest echoes breaking
Through copse-clad vallies,—ere their death, o'ertaking
The surgy murmurs of the lonely sea.

And now, as deep into the wood as we
Might mark a lynx's eye, there glimmered light
Fair faces and a rush of garments white,
Plainer and plainer showing, till at last
Into the widest alley they all past,
Making directly for the woodland altar.
O kindly muse! let not my weak tongue faulter
In telling of this goodly company,
Of their old piety, and of their glee:
But let a portion of ethereal dew
Fall on my head, and presently unmew
My soul; that I may dare, in wayfaring,
To stammer where old Chaucer us'd to sing.

Leading the way, young damsels danced along,
Bearing the burden of a shepherd song;
Each having a white wicker over brimm'd
With April's tender younglings: next, well trimm'd,
A crowd of shepherds with as sunburnt looks
As may be read of in Arcadian books;
Such as sat listening round Apollo's pipe,
When the great deity, for earth too ripe,
Let his divinity o'erflowing die
In music, through the vales of Thessaly:
Some idly trail'd their sheep-hooks on the ground,
And some kept up a shrilly mellow sound
With ebon-tipped flutes: close after these,

Now coming from beneath the forest trees,
A venerable priest full soberly,
Begirt with ministring looks: alway his eye
Stedfast upon the matted turf he kept,
And after him his sacred vestments swept.
From his right hand there swung a vase, milk-white,
Of mingled wine, out-sparkling generous light;
And in his left he held a basket full
Of all sweet herbs that searching eye could cull:
Wild thyme, and valley-lillies whiter still
Than Leda's love, and cresses from the rill.
His aged head, crowned with beechen wreath,
Seem'd like a poll of ivy in the teeth
Of winter hoar. Then came another crowd
Of shepherds, lifting in due time aloud
Their share of the ditty. After them appear'd,
Up-followed by a multitude that rear'd
Their voices to the clouds, a fair wrought car
Easily rolling so as scarce to mar
The freedom of three steeds of dapple brown:
Who stood therein did seem of great renown
Among the throng. His youth was fully blown,
Showing like Ganymede to manhood grown;
And, for those simple times, his garments were
A chieftain king's: beneath his breast, half bare,
Was hung a silver bugle, and between
His nervy knees there lay a boar-spear keen.
A smile was on his countenance; he seem'd,
To common lookers on, like one who dream'd
Of idleness in groves Elysian:
But there were some who feelingly could scan
A lurking trouble in his nether lip,
And see that oftentimes the reins would slip
Through his forgotten hands: then would they sigh,
And think of yellow leaves, of owlets' cry,
Of logs piled solemnly.—Ah, well-a-day,
Why should our young Endymion pine away!

. . .

ODE TO AUTUMN

Season of mists and mellow fruitfulness,
Close bosom-friend of the maturing sun;
Conspiring with him how to load and bless
With fruit the vines that round the thatch-eaves run;
To bend with apples the moss'd cottage-trees,
And fill all fruit with ripeness to the core;

To swell the gourd, and plump the hazel shells
With a sweet kernel; to set budding more,
And still more, later flowers for the bees,
Until they think warm days will never cease;
For Summer has o'erbrimm'd their clammy cells.

Who hath not seen thee oft amid thy store?
Sometimes whoever seeks abroad may find
Thee sitting careless on a granary floor,
Thy hair soft-lifted by the winnowing wind;
Or on a half-reap'd furrow sound asleep,
Drowsed with the fume of poppies, while thy hook
Spares the next swath and all its twinéd flowers:
And sometimes like a gleaner thou dost keep
Steady thy laden head across a brook:
Or by a cyder-press, with patient look,
Thou watchest the last oozings, hours by hours.

Where are the songs of Spring? Ay, where are they?
Think not of them, thou hast thy music too,—
While barréd clouds bloom the soft-dying day—
And touch the stubble-plains with rosy hue;
Then in a wailful choir the small gnats mourn
Among the river sallows, borne aloft
Or sinking as the light wind lives or dies;
And full-grown lambs loud bleat from hilly bourn;
Hedge-crickets sing; and now with treble soft
The red-breast whistles from a garden-croft;
And gathering swallows twitter in the skies.

ODE TO A NIGHTINGALE

My heart aches, and a drowsy numbness pains
My sense, as though of hemlock I had drunk,
Or emptied some dull opiate to the drains
One minute past, and Lethe-wards had sunk:
'Tis not through envy of thy happy lot,
But being too happy in thine happiness,—
That thou, light-winged Dryad of the trees
In some melodious plot
Of beechen green, and shadows numberless,
Singest of summer in full-throated ease.

O, for a draught of vintage! that hath been
Cool'd a long age in the deep-delvéd earth,
Tasting of Flora and the country green,
Dance, and Provencal song, sunburnt mirth!

O for a beaker full of the warm South,
Full of the true, the blushful Hippocrene,
With beaded bubbles winking at the brim,
And purple-stainéd mouth;
That I might drink, and leave the world unseen,
And with thee fade away into the forest dim:

Fade far away, dissolve, and quite forget
What thou among the leaves hast never known,
The weariness, the fever, and the fret
Here, where men sit and hear each other groan;
Where palsy shakes a few, sad, last grey hairs,
Where youth grows pale, and spectre-thin, and dies;
Where but to think is to be full of sorrow
And leaden-eyed despairs;
Where Beauty cannot keep her lustrous eyes,
Or new Love pine at them beyond to-morrow.

Away! away! for I will fly to thee,
Not charioted by Bacchus and his pards,
But on the viewless wings of Poesy,
Though the dull brain perplexes and retards:
Already with thee! tender is the night,
And haply the Queen-Moon is on her throne,
Cluster'd around by all her starry Fays;
But here there is no light,
Save what from heaven is with the breezes blown
Through verdurous glooms and winding mossy ways.

I cannot see what flowers are at my feet,
Nor what soft incense hangs upon the boughs,
But, in embalmèd darkness, guess each sweet
Wherewith the seasonable month endows
The grass, the thicket, and the fruit-tree wild;
White hawthorn, and the pastoral eglantine;
Fast fading violets cover'd up in leaves;
And mid-May's eldest child,
The coming musk-rose, full of dewy wine,
The murmurous haunt of flies on summer eves.

Darkling I listen; and for many a time
I have been half in love with easeful Death,
Call'd him soft names in many muséd rhyme,
To take into the air my quiet breath;
Now more than ever seems it rich to die,
To cease upon the midnight with no pain,
While thou art pouring forth thy soul abroad
In such an ecstacy!
Still wouldst thou sing, and I have ears in vain—
To thy high requiem become a sod.

Thou wast not born for death, immortal Bird!
No hungry generations tread thee down;
The voice I hear this passing night was heard
In ancient days by emperor and clown:
Perhaps the self-same song that found a path
Through the sad heart of Ruth, when, sick for home,
She stood in tears amid the alien corn;
The same that oft-times hath
Charm'd magic casements, opening on the foam
Of perilous seas, in faery lands forlorn.

Forlorn! the very word is like a bell
To toll me back from thee to my sole self!
Adieu! the fancy cannot cheat so well
As she is famed to do, deceiving elf.
Adieu! adieu! thy plaintive anthem fades
Past the near meadows, over the still stream,
Up the hill-side; and now 'tis buried deep
In the next valley-glades:
Was it a vision, or a waking dream?
Fled is that music:—do I wake or sleep?

TO ONE WHO HAS BEEN LONG IN CITY PENT

To one who has been long in city pent,
'Tis very sweet to look into the fair
And open face of heaven,—to breathe a prayer
Full in the smile of the blue firmament.
Who is more happy, when, with heart's content,
Fatigued he sinks into some pleasant lair
Of wavy grass, and reads a debonair
And gentle tale of love and languishment?
Returning home at evening, with an ear
Catching the notes of Philomel,—an eye
Watching the sailing cloudlet's bright career,
He mourns that day so soon has glided by:
E'en like the passage of an angel's tear
That falls through the clear ether silently.

John Clare
1793-1864

John Clare was not only a poet of nature but also a "natural poet." The son of a farm laborer, he worked in the fields from the time he was a boy and received little formal education. Physically weak and emotionally sensitive, Clare wrote poems about what he saw at work. He described animal behavior, especially as it included human interaction, in poems like "The Vixen" and "The Badger." The emotional experience of viewing a rural scene in solitude was another favorite topic. His peasant background not only provided for realistic, "unprettied" detail, it also gave his descriptions a sense of sincerity, a feeling that the author knew the countryside and was not simply striking an attitude while passing through. In "Winter Walk," for example, Clare's presentation of unexpected physical detail renders his description most believable:

> And in the bitterest day that ever blew
> The walk will find some places still and warm
> Where dead leaves rustle sweet and give alarm
> To little birds that flint and start away.

Initially Clare wrote for his own pleasure, but in 1820 he published *Poems Descriptive of Rural Life*. The book became popular very quickly and won its author introductions to established poets. Subsequently, his writing came to show the influence of nature poets like Wordsworth and Coleridge, especially in poems such as "Eternity of Nature":

All nature has a feeling: woods, fields, brooks
Are life eternal; and in silence they
Speak happiness beyond the reach of books;
There's nothing mortal in them; their decay
Is the green life of change; to pass away
And come again in blooms revivified.

The books Clare published after his first were poorly received and failed to sell. Clare found himself in debt, and in 1836 he had a nervous breakdown. He entered an institution where he remained for all but a few months of the rest of his life. His sickness included a fantasy of a long lost love, which adds a hauntingly poignant note to some of his later descriptions of natural scenes.

PASTORAL POESY*

True poesy is not in words,
But images that thoughts express,
By which the simplest hearts are stirred
To elevated happiness.

Mere books would be but useless things
Where none had taste or mind to read,
Like unknown lands where beauty springs
And none are there to heed.

But poesy is a language meet,
And fields are every one's employ;
The wild flower 'neath the shepherd's feet
Looks up and gives him joy;

A language that is ever green,
That feelings unto all impart,
As hawthorn blossoms, soon as seen,
Give May to every heart.

An image to the mind is brought,
Where happiness enjoys
An easy thoughtlessness of thought
And meets excess of joys.

And such is poesy; its power
May varied lights employ,
Yet to all minds it gives the dower
Of self-creating joy.

And whether it be hill or moor,
I feel where'er I go

*This and the following poems by John Clare are from *The Poems of John Clare*, ed. J.W. Tibble (London: J.M. Dent & Sons Ltd, 1935). Courtesy of J.M. Dent & Sons, Ltd.

A silence that discourses more
That any tongue can do.

Unruffled quietness hath made
A peace in every place,
And woods are resting in their shade
Of social loneliness.

The storm, from which the shepherd turns
To pull his beaver down,
While he upon the heath sojourns,
Which autumn pleaches brown,

Is music, ay, and more indeed
To those of musing mind
Who through the yellow woods proceed
And listen to the wind.

The poet in his fitful glee
And fancy's many moods
Meets it as some strange melody,
A poem of the woods,

And now a harp that flings around
The music of the wind;
The poet often hears the sound
When beauty fills the mind.

So would I my own mind employ,
And my own heart impress,
That poesy's self's a dwelling joy
Of humble quietness.

THE ETERNITY OF NATURE

Leaves from eternity are simple things
To the world's gaze—whereto a spirit clings
Sublime and lasting. Trampled under foot,
The daisy lives, and strikes its little root
Into the lap of time: centuries may come,
And pass away into the silent tomb,
And still the child, hid in the womb of time,
Shall smile and pluck them when this simple rhyme
Shall be forgotten, like a churchyard stone,
Or lingering lie unnoticed and alone.
When eighteen hundred years, our common date,
Grow many thousands in their marching state,
Ay, still the child, with pleasure in his eye,
Shall cry—the daisy! a familiar cry—

And run to pluck it, in the self-same state
As when Time found it in his infant date;
And, like a child himself, when all was new,
Might smile with wonder, and take notice too,
Its little golden bosom, frilled with snow,
Might win e'en Eve to stoop adown, and show
Her partner, Adam, in the silky grass
This little gem that smiled where pleasure was,
And loving Eve, from Eden followed ill,
And bloomed with sorrow, and lives smiling still,
As once in Eden under heaven's breath,
So now on earth, and on the lap of death
It smiles for ever.—Cowslips of gold bloom,
That in the pasture and the meadow come,
Shall come when kings and empires fade and die;
And in the closen, as Time's partners, lie
As fresh two thousand years to come as now,
With those five crimson spots upon their brow.
The little brooks that hum a simple lay
In green unnoticed spots, from praise away,
Shall sing when poets in time's darkness hid
Shall lie like memory in a pyramid,
Forgetting yet not all forgot, though lost
Like a thread's end in ravelled windings crost.
The little humble-bee shall hum as long
As nightingales, for Time protects the song;
And Nature is their soul, to whom all clings
Of fair or beautiful in lasting things.
The little robin in the quiet glen,
Hidden from fame and all the strife of men,
Sings unto Time a pastoral, and gives
A music that lives on and ever lives.
Spring and autumnal years shall bloom, and fade,
Longer than songs that poets ever made.
Think ye not these, Time's playthings, pass proud skill?
Time loves them like a child, and ever will;
And so I seek them in each bushy spot,
And sing with them when all else notice not,
And feel the music of their mirth agree
With that sooth quiet that bestirs in me.
And if I touch aright that quiet tone,
That soothing truth that shadows forth their own,
Then many a year to come, in after-days,
Shall still find hearts to love my quiet lays.
Thus cheering mirth with thoughts sung not for fame,
But for the joy that with their utterance came,
That inward breath of rapture urged not loud—
Birds, singing lone, fly silent past a crowd—

In these same pastoral spots, which childish time
Makes dear to me, I wander out and rhyme;
What hour the dewy morning's infancy
Hangs on each blade of grass and every tree,
And sprents the red thighs of the humble-bee,
Who 'gins betimes unwearied minstrelsy;
Who breakfasts, dines, and most divinely sups,
With every flower save golden buttercups—
On whose proud bosoms he will never go,
But passes by with scarcely 'How do ye do?'
Since in their showy, shining, gaudy cells
Haply the summer's honey never dwells.
All nature's ways are mysteries! Endless youth
Lives in them all, unchangeable as truth.
With the odd number five, her curious laws
Play many freaks, nor once mistake the cause;
For in the cowslip-peeps this very day
Five spots appear, which Time wears not away,
Nor once mistakes in counting—look within
Each peep, and five, nor more nor less, are seen.
So trailing bindweed, with its pinky cup,
Five leaves of paler hue go streaking up;
And many a bird, too, keeps the rule alive,
Laying five eggs, nor more nor less than five.
But flowers, how many own that mystic power,
With five leaves ever making up the flower!
The five-leaved grass, mantling its golden cup
Of flowers—five leaves make all for which I stoop.
The bryony, in the hedge, that now adorns
The tree to which it clings, and now the thorns,
Owns five-starred pointed leaves of dingy white;
Count which I will, all make the number right.
The spreading goose-grass, trailing all abroad
In leaves of silver green about the road—
Five leaves make every blossom all along.
I stoop for many, none are counted wrong.
'Tis Nature's wonder, and her Maker's will,
Who bade earth be, and order owns him still,
As that superior Power, who keeps the key
Of wisdom and of might through all eternity.

PASTORAL FANCIES

Sweet pastime here my mind so entertains,
    Abiding pleasaunce and heart-feeding joys,
To meet this blithesome day, these painted plains,
    Those singing maids and chubby laughing boys,
    Which hay-time and the summer here employs—

My rod and line doth all neglected lie;
        A higher joy my former sport destroys:
Nature this day doth bait the hook, and I
The glad fish am, that's to be caught thereby.

This silken grass, these pleasant flowers in bloom,
        Among these tasty mole-hills that do lie
Like summer cushions for all guests that come,
        Those little feathered folk, that sing and fly
        Above these trees, in that so gentle sky,
Where not a cloud dares soil its heavenly light,
        And this smooth river softly grieving by—
All fill mine eyes with so divine a sight
As makes me sigh that it should e'er be night.

In sooth, methinks the choice I most should prize
        Were in these meadows of delight to dwell,
To share the joyaunce heaven elsewhere denies,
        The calmness that doth relish passing well
        The quiet conscience, that aye bears the bell,
And happy musings nature would supply,
        Leaving no room for troubles to rebel:
Here would I think all day, at night would lie,
The hay my bed, my coverlid the sky.

THE VIXEN

Among the taller wood with ivy hung,
The old fox plays and dances round her young.
She snuffs and barks if any passes by
And swings her tail and turns prepared to fly.
The horseman hurries by, she bolts to see,
And turns agen, from danger never free.
If any stands she runs among the poles
And barks and snaps and drives them in the holes.
The shepherd sees them and the boy goes by
And gets a stick and progs the hole to try.
They get all still and lie in safety sure,
And out again when everything's secure,
And start and snap at blackbirds bouncing by
To fight and catch the great white butterfly.

TURKEYS

The turkeys wade the close to catch the bees
In the old border full of maple trees,
And often lay away and breed and come
And bring a brood of chelping chickens home.
The turkey gobbles loud and drops his rag

And struts and sprunts his tail and then lets drag
His wing on ground and makes a huzzing noise,
Nauntles at passer-by and drives the boys
And bounces up and flies at passer-by.
The old dog snaps and grins, nor ventures nigh.
He gobbles loud and drives the boys from play;
They throw their sticks and kick and run away.

RECOLLECTIONS AFTER A RAMBLE

The rosy day was sweet and young,
    The clod-brown lark that hail'd the morn
Had just his summer anthem sung,
    And trembling dropped in the corn;
The dew-rais'd flower was perk and proud,
    The butterfly around it play'd;
The skies blew clear, save woolly cloud
    That pass'd the sun without a shade.

On the pismire's castle hill,
    While the burnet-buttons quak'd,
While beside the stone-pav'd rill
    Cowslip bunches nodding shak'd,
Bees in every peep did try,
    Great had been the honey shower,
Soon their load was on their thigh,
    Yellow dust as fine as flour.

Brazen magpies, fond of clack,
    Full of insolence and pride,
Chattering on the donkey's back
    Percht, and pull'd his shaggy hide;
Odd crows settled on the pad,
    Dames from milking trotting home
Said no sign was half so sad,
    And shook their heads at ills to come.

While cows restless from the ground
    Plung'd into the stream and drank,
And the rings went whirling round,
    Till they toucht the flaggy bank,
On the arch's wall I knelt,
    Curious, as I often did,
To see the words the sculpture spelt,
    But the moss its letters hid.

Labour sought the water cool,
    And stretching took a hearty sup,
The fish were playing in the pool,

And turn'd their milk-white bellies up;
Clothes laid down behind a bush,
Boys were wading near the pad,
Deeply did the maiden blush
As she pass'd each naked lad.

Some with lines the fish to catch,
Quirking boys let loose from school,
Others 'side the hedgerow watch,
Where the linnet took the wool:
'Tending Hodge had slept too fast,
While his cattle stray'd abroad,
Swift the freed horse gallop'd past,
Pattering down the stony road.

The gipsies' tune was loud and strong,
As round the camp they danc'd a jig,
And much I lov'd the brown girl's song,
While list'ning on the wooden brig;
The shepherd, he was on his rounds,
The dog stopt short to lap the stream,
And jingling in the fallow grounds
The ploughman urg'd his reeking team.

Often did I stop to gaze
On each spot once dear to me,
Known 'mong those remember'd days
Of banish'd, happy infancy:
Often did I view the shade
Where once a nest my eyes did fill,
And often mark'd the place I play'd
At 'roly-poly' down the hill.

In the wood's deep shade did stand,
As I pass'd, the sticking-troop;
And Goody begg'd a helping hand
To heave her rotten faggot up:
The riding-gate, sharp jerking round,
Follow'd fast my heels again,
While echo mockt the clapping sound,
And 'clap, clap,' sang the woods amain.

The wood is sweet—I love it well,
In spending there my leisure hours,
To seek the snail its painted shell,
And look about for curious flowers;
Or 'neath the hazel's leafy thatch,
On a stulp or mossy ground,

Little squirrel's gambols watch,
    Dancing oak trees round and round.

Green was the shade—I love the woods,
    When autumn's wind is mourning loud,
To see the leaves float on the floods,
    Dead within their yellow shroud:
The wood was then in glory spread—
    I love the browning bough to see
That litters autumn's dying bed—
    Her latest sigh is dear to me.

'Neath a spreading shady oak
    For a while to muse I lay;
From its grains a bough I broke,
    To fan the teasing flies away:
Then I sought the woodland side,
    Cool the breeze my face did meet,
And the shade the sun did hide;
    Though 'twas hot, it seemed sweet.

And as while I clomb the hill,
    Many a distant charm I found,
Pausing on the lagging mill,
    That scarcely mov'd its sails around,
Hanging o'er a gate or stile,
    Till my curious eye did tire,
Leisure was employ'd awhile,
    Counting many a peeping spire.

While the hot sun 'gan to wane,
    Cooling glooms fast deep'ning still,
Refreshing greenness spread the plain,
    As black clouds crept the southern hill;
Labour sought a sheltering place,
    'Neath some thick wood-woven bower,
While odd rain-drops dampt his face,
    Heralds of the coming shower.

Where the oak-plank cross'd the stream,
    Which the early-rising lass
Climbs with milk-pail gathering cream,
    Crook'd paths tracking through the grass:
There, where willows hing their boughs,
    Briers and blackthorns form'd a bower
Stunted thick by sheep and cows—
    There I stood to shun the shower.

Sweet it was to feel the breeze
Blowing cool without the sun,
Bumming gad-flies ceas'd to tease,
All seem'd glad the shower to shun:
Sweet it was to mark the flower,
Rain-drops glist'ning on its head,
Perking up beneath the bower,
As if rising from the dead.

And full sweet it was to look,
How clouds misted o'er the hill,
Rain-drops how they dimpt the brook,
Falling fast and faster still;
While the gudgeons sturting by
Cring'd 'neath water-grasses' shade,
Startling as each nimble eye
Saw the rings the dropples made.

And upon the dripping ground,
As the shower had ceas'd again,
As the eye was wandering round,
Trifling troubles caus'd a pain;
Overtaken in the shower,
Bumble-bees I wander'd by,
Clinging to the drowking flower,
Left without the power to fly:

And full often, drowning wet,
Scampering beetles rac'd away,
Safer shelter glad to get,
Drownded out from whence they lay:
While the moth, for night's reprief,
Waited safe and snug withal
'Neath the plantain's bowery leaf,
Where not e'en a drop could fall.

Then the clouds dispers'd again,
And full sweet it was to view
Sunbeams, trembling long in vain,
Now they 'gan to glimmer through:
And as labour strength regains
From ale's booning bounty given,
So reviv'd the fresh'ning plains
From the smiling showers of heaven.

Sweet the birds did chant their songs,
Blackbird, linnet, lark, and thrush;
Music from a many tongues

Melted from each dripping bush:
Deafen'd echo, on the plain,
As the sunbeams broke the cloud,
Scarce could help repeat the strain,
Nature's anthem flow'd so loud.

What a fresh'ning feeling came,
As the sun's smile gleam'd again;
Sultry summer wa'n't the same,
Such a mildness swept the plain;
Breezes, such as one would seek,
Cooling infants of the shower,
Fanning sweet the burning cheek,
Trembled through the bramble-bower.

Insects of mysterious birth
Sudden struck my wondering sight,
Doubtless brought by moisture forth,
Hid in knots of spittle white;
Backs of leaves the burthen bear,
Where the sunbeams cannot stray,
'Wood-seers' call'd, that wet declare,
So the knowing shepherds say.

As the cart-rut rippled down
With the burden of the rain,
Boys came drabbling from the town,
Glad to meet their sports again;
Stopping up the mimic rills,
Till they forc'd their frothy bound,
Then the keck-made water-mills
In the current whisk'd around.

Once again did memory pain
O'er the life she once had led;
Once did manhood wish again
Childish joys had never fled:
'Could I lay these woes aside
Which I long have murmur'd o'er,
Mix a boy with boys,' I sigh'd,
'Fate should then be teas'd no more.'

Hot the sun in summer warms,
Quick the roads dry o'er the plain:
Girls, with baskets on their arms,
Soon renew'd their sports again;
O'er the green they sought their play,
Where the cowslip-bunches grew,

Quick the rush-bent fann'd away,
        As they danc'd and bounded through.

Some went searching by the wood,
        Peeping 'neath the weaving thorn,
Where the pouch-lipp'd cuckoo-bud
        From its snug retreat was torn;
Where the ragged-robin grew
        With its pip'd stem streak'd with jet,
And the crow-flower's golden hue
        Careless plenty easier met.

Some, with many an anxious pain
        Childish wishes to pursue,
From the pond-head gaz'd in vain
        On the flag-flower's yellow hue,
Smiling in its safety there,
        Sleeping o'er its shadow'd blow,
While the flood's triumphing care
        Crimpled round its root below.

Then I stood to pause again;
        Retrospection sigh'd and smil'd,
Musing, 'tween a joy and pain,
        How I acted when a child;
When by clearing brooks I've been,
        Where the painted sky was given,
Thinking, if I tumbled in,
        I should fall direct to heaven.

Many an hour had come and gone
        Since the town last met my eye,
Where, huge baskets mauling on,
        Maids hung out their clothes to dry;
Granny there was on the bench,
        Coolly sitting in the swale,
Stopping oft a love-sick wench,
        To pinch her snuff, and hear her tale.

Be the journey e'er so mean,
        Passing by a cot or tree,
In the route there's something seen
        Which the curious love to see;
In each ramble, taste's warm souls
        More of wisdom's self can view
Than blind ignorance beholds
        All life's seven stages through.

Percy Bysshe Shelley
1792-1822

Percy Bysshe Shelley began his brief life exactly one generation after the birth of William Wordsworth. His work shows the strong influence of the older poet, especially in its exploration of the power that nature works upon human intellect. "The everlasting universe of things," he writes in the opening lines of "Mont Blanc,"

> Flows through the mind, and rolls its rapid waves,
> Now dark—now glittering—now reflecting gloom—
> Now lending splendour, where from secret springs
> The source of human thought its tribute brings . . .

Shelley's interest in "the everlasting universe of things" had a scientific as well as a poetic bent. As a teenager Shelley was fascinated by experimental science at a time when it was not taught in the universities and was understood by only a small minority, even among the educated. While he attended school at Eton, his foul-smelling chemistry experiments earned him the reputation of a witch. His unhappiness over the cruel exercise of authority at Eton fed his childhood habit of dreaming about an ideal world where injustice and imperfection did not exist.

Shelley read widely among scientific studies, and absorbed empirical philosophy so deeply that in his first year at Oxford University he wrote a tract called *The Necessity of Atheism*, in which he argued that humans had no scientific knowledge of God and thus ought not to assume His existence. He was expelled for his efforts only six months after being admitted to college. This shocked his wealthy, conservative family and fixed Shelley's own resolve to oppose the tyranny of conventions imposed by religion and society. He subsequently married the daughter of an innkeeper to prevent her father from oppressing her, then left her behind when he fell in love with another woman, since he felt it would be immoral to go on living with someone he didn't love. When his forsaken wife committed suicide a few years later, Shelley fled England for Italy as a self-imposed exile.

There his own life was cut short by a tragic sailing accident, but only after he had written his greatest poetry. In it he fused his interest in natural science with his interest in the ideal realm taught by the philosopher Plato. His nature poetry often explores deep personal emotion, sometimes using it as a springboard to questions about meaning and order in life. Nature, he felt, could provide a liberating experience for the individual. Yet, as evidenced by "Mont Blanc," Shelley's great strength was his ability to relate his abstract thought to vivid depictions of natural scenes.

MONT BLANC*

LINES WRITTEN IN THE VALE OF CHAMOUNI

I

The everlasting universe of things
Flows through the mind, and rolls its rapid waves,
Now dark—now glittering—now reflecting gloom—
Now lending splendour, where from secret springs
The source of human thought its tribute brings
Of waters,—with a sound but half its own,
Such as a feeble brook will oft assume
In the wild woods, among the mountains lone,
Where waterfalls around it leap for ever,
Where woods and winds contend, and a vast river
Over its rocks ceaselessly bursts and raves.

II

Thus thou, Ravine of Arve—dark, deep Ravine—
Thou many-coloured, many-voicèd vale,
Over whose pines, and crags, and caverns sail
Fast cloud-shadows and sunbeams: awful scene,
Where Power in likeness of the Arve comes down
From the ice-gulfs that gird his secret throne,
Bursting through these dark mountains like the flame
Of lightning through the tempest;—thou dost lie,
Thy giant brood of pines around thee clinging,
Children of elder time, in whose devotion
The chainless winds still come and ever came

*This and the following poems by Percy Bysshe Shelley are from *John Keats* and *Percy Bysshe Shelley, Complete Works*, eds. Bennet A. Cerf and Donald S. Klopfer (New York: The Modern Library). Courtesy of Random House, Inc.

To drink their odours, and their mighty swinging
To hear—an old and solemn harmony;
Thine earthly rainbows stretched across the sweep
Of the aethereal waterfall, whose veil
Robes some unsculptured image; the strange sleep
Which when the voices of the desert fail
Wraps all in its own deep eternity;—
Thy caverns echoing to the Arve's commotion,
A loud, lone sound no other sound can tame;
Thou art pervaded with that ceaseless motion,
Thou art the path of that unresting sound—
Dizzy Ravine! and when I gaze on thee
I seem as in a trance sublime and strange
To muse on my own separate fantasy,
My own, my human mind, which passively
Now renders and receives fast influencings,
Holding an unremitting interchange
With the clear universe of things around;
One legion of wild thoughts, whose wandering wings
Now float above thy darkness, and now rest
Where that or thou art no unbidden guest,
In the still cave of the witch Poesy,
Seeking among the shadows that pass by
Ghosts of all things that are, some shade of thee,
Some phantom, some faint image; till the breast
From which they fled recalls them, thou art there!

III

Some say that gleams of a remoter world
Visit the soul in sleep,—that death is slumber,
And that its shapes the busy thoughts outnumber
Of those who wake and live.—I look on high;
Has some unknown omnipotence unfurled
The veil of life and death? or do I lie
In dream, and does the mightier world of sleep
Spread far around and inaccessibly
Its circles? For the very spirit fails,
Driven like a homeless cloud from steep to steep
That vanishes among the viewless gales!
Far, far above, piercing the infinite sky,
Mont Blanc appears,—still, snowy, and serene—
Its subject mountains their unearthly forms
Pile around it, ice and rock; broad vales between
Of frozen floods, unfathomable deeps,
Blue as the overhanging heaven, that spread
And wind among the accumulated steeps;
A desert peopled by the storms alone,

Save when the eagle brings some hunter's bone,
And the wolf tracks her there—how hideously
Its shapes are heaped around! rude, bare, and high,
Ghastly, and scarred, and riven.—Is this the scene
Where the old Earthquake-daemon taught her young
Ruin? Were these their toys? or did a sea
Of fire envelop once this silent snow?
None can reply—all seems eternal now.
The wilderness has a mysterious tongue
Which teaches awful doubt, or faith so mild,
So solemn, so serene, that man may be
But for such faith, with nature reconciled;
Thou hast a voice, great Mountain, to repeal
Large codes of fraud and woe; not understood
By all, but which the wise, and great, and good
Interpret, or make felt, or deeply feel.

IV

The fields, the lakes, the forests, and the streams,
Ocean, and all the living things that dwell
Within the daedal earth; lightning, and rain,
Earthquake, and fiery flood, and hurricane,
The torpor of the year when feeble dreams
Visit the hidden buds, or dreamless sleep
Holds every future leaf and flower;—the bound
With which from that detested trance they leap;
The works and ways of man, their death and birth,
And that of him and all that his may be
All things that move and breathe with toil and sound
Are born and die; revolve, subside, and swell.
Power dwells apart in its tranquillity,
Remote, serene, and inaccessible:
And *this*, the naked countenance of earth,
On which I gaze, even these primaeval mountains
Teach the adverting mind. The glaciers creep
Like snakes that watch their prey, from their far fountains,
Slow rolling on; there, many a precipice,
Frost and the Sun in scorn of mortal power
Have piled: dome, pyramid, and pinnacle,
A city of death, distinct with many a tower
And wall impregnable of beaming ice.
Yet not a city, but a flood of ruin
Is there, that from the boundaries of the sky
Rolls its perpetual stream; vast pines are strewing
Its destined path, or in the mangled soil
Branchless and shattered stand; the rocks, drawn down
From yon remotest waste, have overthrown

The limits of the dead and living world,
Never to be reclaimed. The dwelling-place
Of insects, beasts, and birds, becomes its spoil
Their food and their retreat for ever gone,
So much of life and joy is lost. The race
Of man flies far in dread; his work and dwelling
Vanish, like smoke before the tempest's stream,
And their place is not known. Below, vast caves
Shine in the rushing torrents' restless gleam,
Which from those secret chasms in tumult welling
Meet in the vale, and one majestic River,
The breath and blood of distant lands, for ever
Rolls its loud waters to the ocean-waves,
Breathes its swift vapours to the circling air.

V

Mont Blanc yet gleams on high:—the power is there,
The still and solemn power of many sights,
And many sounds, and much of life and death.
In the calm darkness of the moonless nights,
In the lone glare of day, the snows descend
Upon that Mountain; none beholds them there,
Nor when the flakes burn in the sinking sun,
Or the star-beams dart through them:—Winds contend
Silently there, and heap the snow with breath
Rapid and strong, but silently! Its home
The voiceless lightning in these solitudes
Keeps innocently, and like vapour broods
Over the snow. The secret Strength of things
Which governs thought, and to the infinite dome
Of Heaven is as a law, inhabits thee!
And what were thou, and earth, and stars, and sea,
If to the human mind's imaginings
Silence and solitude were vacancy?

July 23, 1816.

ODE TO THE WEST WIND

I

O wild West Wind, thou breath of Autumn's being,
Thou, from whose unseen presence the leaves dead
Are driven, like ghosts from an enchanter fleeing,

Yellow, and black, and pale, and hectic red,
Pestilence-stricken multitudes: O thou,
Who chariotest to their dark wintry bed

The wingèd seeds, where they lie cold and low,
Each like a corpse within its grave, until
Thine azure sister of the Spring shall blow

Her clarion o'er the dreaming earth, and fill
(Driving sweet buds like flocks to feed in air)
With living hues and odours plain and hill:

Wild Spirit, which art moving everywhere;
Destroyer and preserver; hear, oh, hear!

II

Thou on whose stream, mid the steep sky's commotion,
Loose clouds like earth's decaying leaves are shed,
Shook from the tangled boughs of Heaven and Ocean,

Angels of rain and lightning: there are spread
On the blue surface of thine aery surge,
Like the bright hair uplifted from the head

Of some fierce Maenad, even from the dim verge
Of the horizon to the zenith's height,
The locks of the approaching storm. Thou dirge

Of the dying year, to which this closing night
Will be the dome of a vast sepulchre,
Vaulted with all thy congregated might

Of vapours, from whose solid atmosphere
Black rain, and fire, and hail will burst: oh, hear!

III

Thou who didst waken from his summer dreams
The blue Mediterranean, where he lay,
Lulled by the coil of his crystalline streams,

Beside a pumice isle in Baiae's bay,
And saw in sleep old palaces and towers
Quivering within the wave's intenser day,

All overgrown with azure moss and flowers
So sweet, the sense faints picturing them! Thou
For whose path the Atlantic's level powers

Cleave themselves into chasms, while far below
The sea-blooms and the oozy woods which wear
The sapless foliage of the ocean, know

Thy voice, and suddenly grow gray with fear,
And tremble and despoil themselves: oh, hear!

IV

If I were a dead leaf thou mightest bear;
If I were a swift cloud to fly with thee;
A wave to pant beneath thy power, and share

The impulse of thy strength, only less free
Than thou, O uncontrollable! If even
I were as in my boyhood, and could be

The comrade of thy wanderings over Heaven,
As then, when to outstrip thy skiey speed
Scarce seemed a vision; I would ne'er have striven

As thus with thee in prayer in my sore need.
Oh, lift me as a wave, a leaf, a cloud!
I fall upon the thorns of life! I bleed!

A heavy weight of hours has chained and bowed
One too like thee: tameless, and swift, and proud.

V

Make me thy lyre, even as the forest is:
What if my leaves are falling like its own!
The tumult of thy mighty harmonies

Will take from both a deep, autumnal tone,
Sweet though in sadness. Be thou, Spirit fierce,
My spirit! Be thou me, impetuous one!

Drive my dead thoughts over the universe
Like withered leaves to quicken a new birth!
And, by the incantation of this verse,

Scatter, as from an unextinguished hearth
Ashes and sparks, my words among mankind!
Be through my lips to unawakened earth

The trumpet of a prophecy! Oh, Wind,
If Winter comes, can Spring be far behind?

THE CLOUD

I bring fresh showers for the thirsting flowers,
From the seas and the streams;
I bear light shade for the leaves when laid
In their noonday dreams.
From my wings are shaken the dews that waken
The sweet buds every one,
When rocked to rest on their mother's breast,
As she dances about the sun.
I wield the flail of the lashing hail,
And whiten the green plains under,
And then again I dissolve it in rain,
And laugh as I pass in thunder.

I sift the snow on the mountains below,
And their great pines groan aghast;
And all the night 'tis my pillow white,
While I sleep in the arms of the blast.
Sublime on the towers of my skiey bowers,
Lightning my pilot sits;
In a cavern under is fettered the thunder,
It struggles and howls at fits;

Over earth and ocean, with gentle motion,
This pilot is guiding me,
Lured by the love of the genii that move
In the depths of the purple sea;
Over the rills, and the crags, and the hills,
Over the lakes and the plains,
Wherever he dream, under mountain or stream,
The Spirit he loves remains;
And I all the while bask in Heaven's blue smile,
Whilst he is dissolving in rains.

The sanguine Sunrise, with his meteor eyes,
And his burning plumes outspread,
Leaps on the back of my sailing rack,
When the morning star shines dead;

As on the jag of a mountain crag,
        Which an earthquake rocks and swings,
An eagle alit one moment may sit
        In the light of its golden wings.
And when Sunset may breathe, from the lit sea beneath,
        Its ardours of rest and of love,
And the crimson pall of eve may fall
        From the depth of Heaven above,
With wings folded I rest, on mine aëry nest,
        As still as a brooding dove.

That orbèd maiden with white fire laden,
        Whom mortals call the Moon,
Glides glimmering o'er my fleece-like floor,
        By the midnight breezes strewn;
And wherever the beat of her unseen feet,
        Which only the angels hear,
May have broken the woof of my tent's thin roof,
        The stars peep behind her and peer;
And I laugh to see them whirl and flee,
        Like a swarm of golden bees,
When I widen the rent in my wind-built tent,
        Till the calm rivers, lakes, and seas,
Like strips of the sky fallen through me on high,
        Are each paved with the moon and these.

I bind the Sun's throne with a burning zone,
        And the Moon's with a girdle of pearl;
The volcanoes are dim, and the stars reel and swim,
        When the whirlwinds my banner unfurl.
From cape to cape, with a bridge-like shape,
        Over a torrent sea,
Sunbeam-proof, I hang like a roof,—
        The mountains its columns be.

The triumphal arch thoughts which I march
        With hurricane, fire, and snow,
When the Powers of the air are chained to my chair,
        Is the million-coloured bow;
The sphere-fire above its soft colours wove,
        While the moist Earth was laughing below.

I am the daughter of Earth and Water,
        And the nursling of the Sky;
I pass through the pores of the ocean and shores;
        I change, but I cannot die.
For after the rain when with never a stain
        The pavilion of Heaven is bare,

And the winds and sunbeams with their convex gleams
Build up the blue dome of air,
I silently laugh at my own cenotaph,
And out of the caverns of rain,
Like a child from the womb, like a ghost from the tomb,
I arise and unbuild it again.

TO A SKYLARK

Hail to thee, blithe Spirit!
Bird thou never wert,
That from Heaven, or near it,
Pourest thy full heart
In profuse strains of unpremeditated art.

Higher still and higher
From the earth thou springest
Like a cloud of fire;
The blue deep thou wingest,
And singing still dost soar, and soaring ever singest.

In the golden lightning
Of the sunken sun,
O'er which clouds are bright'ning,
Thou dost float and run;
Like an unbodied joy whose race is just begun.

The pale purple even
Melts around thy flight;
Like a star of Heaven,
In the broad daylight
Thou art unseen, but yet I hear thy shrill delight,

Keen as are the arrows
Of that silver sphere,
Whose intense lamp narrows
In the white dawn clear
Until we hardly see—we feel that it is there.

All the earth and air
With thy voice is loud,
As, when night is bare,
From one lonely cloud
The moon rains out her beams, and Heaven is overflowed.

What thou art we know not;
What is most like thee?

From rainbow clouds there flow not
  Drops so bright to see
As from thy presence showers a rain of melody.

Like a Poet hidden
  In the light of thought,
Singing hymns unbidden,
  Till the world is wrought
To sympathy with hopes and fears it heeded not:

Like a high-born maiden
  In a palace-tower,
Soothing her love-laden
  Soul in secret hour
With music sweet as love, which overflows her bower:

Lilke a glow-worm golden
  In a dell of dew,
Scattering unbeholden
  Its aereal hue
Among the flowers and grass, which screen it from the view!

Like a rose embowered
  In its own green leaves,
By warm winds deflowered,
  Till the scent it gives
Makes faint with too much sweet those heavy-wingèd thieves:

Sound of vernal showers
  On the twinkling grass,
Rain-awakened flowers,
  All that ever was
Joyous, and clear, and fresh, thy music doth surpass:

Teach us, Sprite or Bird,
  What sweet thoughts are thine:
I have never heard
  Praise of love or wine
That panted forth a flood of rapture so divine.

Chorus Hymeneal,
  Or triumphal chant,
Matched with thine would be all
  But an empty vaunt,
A thing wherein we feel there is some hidden want.

What objects are the fountains
  Of thy happy strain?

What fields, or waves, or mountains?
What shapes of sky or plain?
What love of thine own kind? what ignorance of pain?

With thy clear keen joyance
Languor cannot be:
Shadow of annoyance
Never came near thee:
Thou lovest—but ne'er knew love's sad satiety.

Waking or asleep,
Thou of death must deem
Things more true and deep
Than we mortals dream,
Or how could thy notes flow in such a crystal stream?

We look before and after,
And pine for what is not:
Our sincerest laughter
With some pain is fraught;
Our sweetest songs are those that tell of saddest thought.

Yet if we could scorn
Hate, and pride, and fear;
If we were things born
Not to shed a tear,
I know not how thy joy we ever should come near.

Better than all measures
Of delightful sound,
Better than all treasures
That in books are found,
Thy skill to poet were, thou scorner of the ground!

Teach me half the gladness
That thy brain must know,
Such harmonious madness
From my lips would flow
The world should listen then—as I am listening now.

SONG OF PROSERPINE

WHILE GATHERING FLOWERS ON THE PLAIN OF ENNA

I

Sacred Goddess, Mother Earth,
        Thou from whose immortal bosom
Gods, and men, and beasts have birth,
        Leaf and blade, and bud and blossom,
Breathe thine influence most divine
On thine own child, Proserpine.

II

If with mists of evening dew
        Thou dost nourish these young flowers
Till they grow, in scent and hue,
        Fairest children of the Hours,
Breathe thine influence most divine
On thine own child, Proserpine.

HYMN OF APOLLO

I

The sleepless Hours who watch me as I lie,
        Curtained with star-inwoven tapestries
From the broad moonlight of the sky,
        Fanning the busy dreams from my dim eyes,—
Waken me when their Mother, the gray Dawn,
Tells them that dreams and that the moon is gone.

II

Then I arise, and climbing Heaven's blue dome,
        I walk over the mountains and the waves,
Leaving my robe upon the ocean foam;
        My footsteps pave the clouds with fire; the caves
Are filled with my bright presence, and the air
Leaves the green Earth to my embraces bare.

III

The sunbeams are my shafts, with which I kill
Deceit, that loves the night and fears the day;
All men who do or even imagine ill
Fly me, and from the glory of my ray
Good minds and open actions take new might,
Until diminished by the reign of Night.

IV

I feed the clouds, the rainbows and the flowers
With their aethereal colours; the moon's globe
And the pure stars in their eternal bowers
Are cinctured with my power as with a robe;
Whatever lamps on Earth or Heaven may shine
Are portions of one power, which is mine.

V

I stand at noon upon the peak of Heaven,
Then with unwilling steps I wander down
Into the clouds of the Atlantic even;
For grief that I depart they weep and frown:
What look is more delightful than the smile
With which I soothe them from the western isle?

VI

I am the eye with which the Universe
Beholds itself and knows itself divine;
All harmony of instrument or verse,
All prophecy, all medicine is mine,
All light of art or nature;—to my song
Victory and praise in its own right belong.

MUTABILITY

We are as clouds that veil the midnight moon;
How restlessly they speed, and gleam, and quiver,
Streaking the darkness radiantly!—yet soon
Night closes round, and they are lost for ever:

Or like forgotten lyres, whose dissonant strings
Give various response to each varying blast,

To whose frail frame no second motion brings
    One mood or modulation like the last.

We rest.—A dream has power to poison sleep;
    We rise.—One wandering thought pollutes the day;
We feel, conceive or reason, laugh or weep;
    Embrace fond woe, or cast our cares away:

It is the same!—For, be it joy or sorrow,
    The path of its departure still is free:
Man's yesterday may ne'er be like his morrow;
    Nought may endure but Mutability.

Alfred Lord Tennyson
1809-1892

More than any other figure in the tradition of nature writing, Tennyson achieved popularity in his lifetime: he was named poet laureate in 1850, and in 1884 became Lord Tennyson, a peer of the realm. His early books of poetry, after about twenty years of neglect, began to gather critical and financial success that mounted for the remainder of his life.

His success was due partly to the fact that he addressed a wide variety of themes important to the English people: personal liberty, loyalty, money, contemporary political issues, and England's history as well as her future national destiny. He developed great skill as a narrative poet whose stories describe the emotions of ordinary English people toward their lovers and their land.

Although Tennyson lived through a period of great physical change in England, the consequence of industrial development, the land about which he wrote with affection was rural England, the land of his youth. He grew up in a country village where his father was clergyman, and from his youth developed a great love for rural scenes, his social contacts outside his family having been quite limited. After he entered college at Cambridge he became heavily influenced by the poetry of John Keats, whose production of lush yet realistic description of natural scenes was interrupted by premature death. Many of Tennyson's early poems, such as "The Kraken" and "The Hesperides," show striking resemblances of Keats's work, not only in descriptive force but also in the integration of mythical devices with direct natural description. Tennyson became expert in describing a setting—usually rooted in the land—in order to define a character, as he does in "Mariana."

"Mariana" shows a certain "romantic" decadence in its preoccupation with death. Such preoccupation was fashionable in the age, partly because of the rediscovery of the worth of Keats and Shelley, both of whom had died prematurely.

But a much more powerful preoccupation of death for Tennyson developed after 1833 when his intimate friend Arthur Hallam died unexpectedly. Tennyson's bereavement lasted, in effect, for the duration of his life. Henceforth his poetry changed direction: although still exploring emotion, it tended less to recreate emotion for its own sake, and tended more to give it social meaning. His masterpiece, "In Memoriam, A. H. H.," was an attempt to "make sense" out of his private grief so as to share it with the larger society. He treated the nature writing themes less in the fashion of Keats and more in the fashion of Vergil, the Roman poet who found in the natural world a sense of hopeful order.

Both Hallam's death and the ongoing changes in vast growth of scientific thought provided Tennyson with a group of related themes. Throughout his career he explored questions about the nature and even the existence of God and the dignity of human life, as well as the implications of scientific thought upon older defined relationships between mankind and the natural world. Geologic discoveries about the age of the earth and the Darwinian hypothesis of the evolution of species were topics that intrigued the age, and as a poet Tennyson treated them thoughtfully, giving answers both unique and personal, grounded in feeling. The violence inherent in natural selection, for example, prompted his famous line "nature red in tooth and claw," a simple statement of the need to review the conception of nature.

Pictorial descriptions of rural England characterize much of Tennyson's famous work, including the *Idylls of the King*, but the greatest nature writing in the latter part of his career celebrated rural life in pastorals such as "The Progress of Spring" and in sketches of rural characters, such as "Enoch Arden."

MARIANA*

With blackest moss the flower-pots
Were thickly crusted, one and all;
The rusted nails fell from the knots
That held the pear to the gable-wall.
The broken sheds look'd sad and strange:
Unlifted was the clinking latch;
Weeded and worn the ancient thatch
Upon the lonely moated grange.
She only said, 'My life is dreary,
He cometh not,' she said;
She said, 'I am aweary, aweary,
I would that I were dead!'

Her tears fell with the dews at even;
Her tears fell ere the dews were dried;
She could not look on the sweet heaven,
Either at morn or eventide.
After the flitting of the bats,
When thickest dark did trance the sky,

*This and the following poems by Alfred Lord Tennyson are from *The Poems and Plays of Alfred Lord Tennyson* (New York: Random House, 1938).

She drew her casement-curtain by,
And glanced athwart the glooming flats,
She only said, 'The night is dreary,
He cometh not,' she said;
She said, 'I am aweary, aweary,
I would that I were dead!'

Upon the middle of the night,
Waking she heard the night-fowl crow;
The cock sung out an hour ere light;
From the dark fen the oxen's low
Came to her; without hope of change,
In sleep she seem'd to walk forlorn,
Till cold winds woke the gray-eyed morn
About the lonely moated grange.
She only said, 'The day is dreary,
He cometh not,' she said;
She said, 'I am aweary, aweary,
I would that I were dead!'
About a stone-cast from the wall
A sluice with blacken'd waters slept,
And o'er it many, round and small,
The cluster'd marish-mosses crept.
Hard by a poplar shook alway,
All silver-green with gnarled bark:
For leagues no other tree did mark
The level waste, the rounding gray.
She only said, 'My life is dreary,
He cometh not,' she said;
She said, 'I am aweary, aweary,
I would that I were dead!'

And ever when the moon was low,
And the shrill winds were up and away,
In the white curtain, to and fro,
She saw the gusty shadow sway.
But when the moon was very low,
And wild winds bound within their cell,
The shadow of the poplar fell
Upon her bed, across her brow.
She only said, 'The night is dreary,
He cometh not,' she said;
She said, 'I am aweary, aweary,
I would that I were dead!'

All day within the dreamy house,
The doors upon their hinges creak'd;
The blue fly sung in the pane; the mouse

Behind the mouldering wainscot shriek'd,
Or from the crevice peer'd about.
Old faces glimmer'd thro' the doors,
Old footsteps trod the upper floors,
Old voices called her from without.
She only said, 'My life is dreary,
He cometh not,' she said;
She said, 'I am aweary, aweary,
I would that I were dead!'

The sparrow's chirrup on the roof,
The slow clock ticking, and the sound
Which to the wooing wind aloof
The poplar made, did all confound
Her sense; but most she loathed the hour
When the thick-moted sunbeam lay
Athwart the chambers, and the day
Was sloping toward his western bower.
Then said she, 'I am very dreary,
He will not come,' she said;
She wept, 'I am aweary, aweary,
O God, that I were dead!'

THE PROGRESS OF SPRING

I

The ground-flame of the crocus breaks the mould
Fair Spring slides hither o'er the Southern sea,
Wavers on her thin stem the snow-drop cold
That trembles not to kisses of the bee.
Come, Spring, for now from all the dripping eaves
The spear of ice has wept itself away,
And hour by hour unfolding woodbine leaves
O'er his uncertain shadow droops the day.
She comes! The loosen'd rivulets run;
The frost-bead melts upon her golden hair;
Her mantel, slowly greening in the Sun,
Now wraps her close, now arching leaves her bare
To breaths of balmier air;

II

Up leaps the lark, gone wild to welcome her,
About her dance the tits, and shriek the jays,
Before her skims the jubliant woodpecker,
The linnet's bosom blushes at her gaze,

While round her brows a woodland culver flits,
Watching her large light eyes and gracious looks,
And in her open palm a halcyon sits
Patient—the secret splendor of the brooks.
Come, Spring! She comes on waste and wood,
On farm and field; but enter also here,
Diffuse thyself at will thro' all my blood,
And, tho' thy violet sicken into sere,
Lodge with me all the year!

III

Once more a downy drift against the brakes,
Self-darken'd in the sky, descending slow!
But gladly see I thro' the wavering flakes
Yon blanching apricot like snow in snow.
These will thine eyes not brook in forest-paths,
On their perpetual pine, nor round the beech;
They fuse themselves to little spicy baths,
Solved in the tender blushes of the peach;
They lose themselves and die
On that new life that gems the hawthorn line;
Thy gay lent-lilies wave and put them by,
And out once more in varnish'd glory shine
Thy stars of celandine.

IV

She floats across the hamlet. Heaven lours,
But in the tearful splendor of her smiles
I see the slowly-thickening chestnut towers
Fill out the spaces by the barren tiles.
Now past her feet the swallow circling flies,
A clamorous cuckoo stoops to meet her hand;
Her light makes rainbows in my closing eyes,
I hear a charm of song thro' all the land.
Come, Spring! She comes, and Earth is glad
To roll her North below thy deepening dome,
But ere thy maiden birk be wholly clad,
And these low bushes dip their twigs in foam,
Make all true hearths thy home.

V

Across my garden! and the thicket stirs,
The fountain pulses high in sunnier jets,
The blackcap warbles, and the turtle purrs,
The starling claps his tiny castanets.

Still round her forehead wheels the woodland dove,
And scatters on her throat the sparks of dew,
The kingcup fills her footprint, and above
Broaden the glowing isles of vernal blue.
Hail, ample presence of a Queen,
Bountiful, beautiful, apparell'd gay,
Whose mantle, every shade of glancing green,
Flies back in fragrant breezes to display
A tunic white as May!

VI

She whispers, 'From the South I bring you balm,
For on a tropic mountain was I born,
While some dark dweller by the cocopalm
Watch'd my far meadow zoned with airy morn;
From under rose a muffled moan of floods;
I sat beneath a solitude of snow;
There no one came, the turf was fresh, the woods
Plunged gulf on gulf thro' all their vales below.
I saw beyond their silent tops
The streaming marshes of the scarlet cranes,
The slant seas leaning on the mangrove copse,
And summer basking in the sultry plains
About a land of cranes.

VII

'Then from my vapor-girdle soaring forth
I scaled the buoyant highway of the birds
And drank the dews and drizzle of the North,
That I might mix with men, and hear their words
On pathway'd plains; for—while my hand exults
Within the bloodless heart of lowly flowers
To work old laws of Love to fresh results,
Thro' manifold effect of simple powers—
I too would teach the man
Beyond the darker hour to see the bright,
That his fresh life may close as it began,
The still-fulfilling promise of a light
Narrowing the bounds of night.'

VIII

So wed thee with my soul, that I may mark
The coming year's great good and varied ills,
And new developments, whatever spark

Be struck from out the clash of warring wills;
Or whether, since our nature cannot rest,
The smoke of war's volcano burst again
From hoary deeps that belt the changeful West,
Old Empires, dwellings of the kings of men;
Or should those fail that hold the helm,
While the long day of knowledge grows and warms,
And in the heart of this most ancient realm
A hateful voice be utter'd, and alarms
Sounding 'To arms! to arms!'

IX

A simpler, saner lesson might he learn
Who reads thy gradual process, Holy Spring.
Thy leaves possess the season in their turn,
And in their time thy warblers rise on wing.
How surely glidest thou from March to May,
And changest, breathing it, the sullen wind,
Thy scope of operation, day by day,
Larger and fuller, like the human mind!
Thy warmths from bud to bud
Accomplish that blind model in the seed,
And men have hopes, which race the restless blood,
That after many changes may succeed
Life which is Life indeed.

THE KRAKEN

Below the thunders of the upper deep,
Far, far beneath in the abysmal sea,
His ancient, dreamless, uninvaded sleep
The Kraken sleepeth: faintest sunlights flee
About his shadowy sides; above him swell
Huge sponges of millennial growth and height;
And far away into the sickly light,
From many a wondrous grot and secret cell
Unnumber'd and enormous polypi
Winnow with giant arms the slumbering green.
There hath he lain for ages, and will lie
Battening upon huge sea-worms in his sleep,
Until the latter fire shall heat the deep;
Then once by man and angels to be seen,
In roaring he shall rise and on the surface die.

NOTHING WILL DIE

When will the stream be aweary of flowing
Under my eye?
When will the wind be aweary of blowing
Over the sky?
When will the clouds be aweary of fleeting?
When will the heart be aweary of beating?
And nature die?
Never, O, never, nothing will die;
The stream flows,
The wind blows,
The cloud fleets,
The heart beats,
Nothing will die.

Nothing will die;
All things will change
Thro' eternity.
'T is the world's winter;
Autumn and summer
Are gone long ago;
Earth is dry to the centre,
But spring, a new comer,
A spring rich and strange,
Shall make the winds blow
Round and round,
Thro' and thro',
Here and there,
Till the air
And the ground
Shall be fill'd with life anew.

The world was never made;
It will change, but it will not fade.
So let the wind range;
For even and morn
Ever will be
Thro' eternity.
Nothing was born;
Nothing will die;
All things will change.

THE EAGLE

FRAGMENT

He clasps the crag with crooked hands;
Close to the sun in lonely lands,
Ring'd with the azure world, he stands.

The wrinkled sea beneath him crawls;
He watches from his mountain walls,
And like a thunderbolt he falls.

THE BROOK

'Here by this brook we parted, I to the East
And he for Italy—too late—too late:
One whom the strong sons of the world despise;
For lucky rhymes to him were scrip and share,
And mellow metres more than cent for cent.
Nor could he understand how money breeds,
Thought it a dead thing; yet himself could make
The thing that is not as the thing that is.
O, had he lived! In our schoolbooks we say
Of those that held their heads above the crowd,
They flourish'd then or then; but life in him
Could scarce be said to flourish, only touch'd
On such a time as goes before the leaf,
When all the wood stands in a mist of green,
And nothing perfect. Yet the brook he loved,
For which, in branding summers of Bengal,
Or even the sweet half-English Neilgherry air,
I panted, seems, as I re-listen to it,
Prattling the primrose fancies of the boy
To me that loved him; for "O brook," he says,
"O babbling brook," says Edmund in his rhyme,
"Whence come you?" and the brook—why not?—replies:

I come from haunts of coot and hern,
  I make a sudden sally,
And sparkle out among the fern,
  To bicker down a valley.

By thirty hills I hurry down,
  Or slip between the ridges,
By twenty thorps, a little town,
  And half a hundred bridges.

Till last by Philip's farm I flow
To join the brimming river,
For men may come and men may go,
But I go on for ever.

'Poor lad, he died at Florence, quite worn out,
Travelling to Naples. There is Darnley bridge,
It has more ivy; there the river; and there
Stands Philip's farm where brook and river meet.

I chatter over stony ways,
In little sharps and trebles,
I bubble into eddying bays,
I babble on the pebbles.

With many a curve my banks I fret
By many a field and fallow,
And many a fairy foreland set
With willow-weed and mallow.

I chatter, chatter, as I flow
To join the brimming river,
For men may come and men may go,
But I go on for ever.

'But Philip chatter'd more than brook or bird,
Old Philip; all about the fields you caught
His weary daylong chirping, like the dry
High-elbow'd grigs that leap in summer grass.

I wind about, and in and out,
With here a blossom sailing,
And here and there a lusty trout,
And here and there a grayling,

And here and there a foamy flake
Upon me, as I travel
With many a silvery water-break
Above the golden gravel,

And draw them all along, and flow
To join the brimming river,
For men may come and men may go,
But I go on for ever.

'O darling Katie Willows, his one child!
A maiden of our century, yet most meek;
A daughter of our meadows, yet not coarse;
Straight, but as lissome as hazel wand;
Her eyes a bashful azure, and her hair

In gloss and hue the chestnut, when the shell
Divides threefold to show the fruit within.

'Sweet Katie, once I did her a good turn,
Her and her far-off cousin and betrothed,
James Willows, of one name and heart with her.
For here I came, twenty years back—the week
Before I parted with poor Edmund—crost
By that old bridge which, half in ruins then,
Still makes a hoary eyebrow for the gleam
Beyond it, where the waters marry—crost,
Whistling a random bar of Bonny Doon,
And push'd at Philip's garden-gate. The gate,
Half-parted from a weak and scolding hinge,
Stuck; and he clamor'd from a casement, "Run,"
To Katie somewhere in the walks below,
"Run, Katie!" Katie never ran; she moved
To meet me, winding under woodbine bowers,
A little flutter'd, with her eyelids down,
Fresh apple-blossom, blushing for a boon.

'What was it? less of sentiment than sense
Had Katie; not illiterate, nor of those
Who dabbling in the fount of fictive tears,
And nursed by mealy-mouth'd philanthropies,
Divorce the Feeling from her mate the Deed.

'She told me. She and James had quarrell'd. Why?
What cause of quarrel? None, she said, no cause;
James had no cause: but when I prest the cause,
I learnt that James had flickering jealousies
Which anger'd her. Who anger'd James? I said.
But Katie snatch'd her eyes at once from mine,
And sketching with her slender pointed foot
Some figure like a wizard pentagram
On garden gravel, let my query pass
Unclaim'd, in flushing silence, till I ask'd
If James were coming. "Coming every day,"
She answer'd, ever longing to explain,
But evermore her father came across
With some long-winded tale, and broke him short;
And James departed vext with him and her,"
How could I help her? "Would I—was it wrong?"—
Claspt hands and that petitionary grace
Of sweet seventeen subdued me ere she spoke—
"O, would I take her father for one hour,
For one half-hour, and let him talk to me!"
And even while she spoke, I saw where James

Made toward us, like a wader in the surf,
Beyond the brook, waist-deep in meadow-sweet.

'O Katie, what I suffer'd for your sake!
For in I went, and call'd old Philip out
To show the farm. Full willingly he rose;
He led me thro' the short sweet-smelling lanes
Of his wheat-suburb, babbling as he went.
He praised his land, his horses, his machines;
He praised his ploughs, his cows, his hogs, his dogs;
He praised his hens, his geese, his guinea-hens,
His pigeons, who in session on their roofs
Approved him, bowing at their own deserts,
Then from the plaintive mother's teat he took
Her blind and shuddering puppies, naming each,
And naming those, his friends, for whom they were;
Then crost the common into Darnley chase
To show Sir Arthur's deer. In copse and fern
Twinkled the innumerable ear and tail.
Then, seated on a serpent-rooted beech,
He pointed out a pasturing colt, and said,
"That was the four-year-old I sold the Squire."
And there he told a long, long-winded tale
Of how the Squire had seen the colt at grass,
And how it was the thing his daughter wish'd,
And how he sent the bailiff to the farm
To learn the price, and what the price he ask'd,
And how the bailiff swore that he was mad,
But he stood firm, and so the matter hung;
He gave them line; and five days after that
He met the bailiff at the Golden Fleece,
Who then and there had offer'd something more,
But he stood firm, and so the matter hung;
He knew the man, the colt would fetch its price;
He gave them line; and how by chance at last—
It might be May or April, he forgot,
The last of April or the first of May—
He found the bailiff riding by the farm,
And, talking from the point, he drew him in,
And there he mellow'd all his heart with ale,
Until they closed a bargain, hand in hand.

'Then, while I breathed in sight of haven, he—
Poor fellow, could he help it?—recommenced,
And ran thro' all the coltish chronicle,
Wild Will, Black Bess, Tantivy, Tallyho,
Reform, White Rose, Bellerophon, the Jilt,
Arbaces, and Phenomenon, and the rest,

Till, not to die a listener, I arose,
And with me Philip, talking still; and so
We turn'd our foreheads from the falling sun,
And following our own shadows thrice as long
As when they follow'd us from Philip's door,
Arrived, and found the sun of sweet content
Re-risen in Katie's eyes, and all things well.

I steal by lawns and grassy plots,
  I slide by hazel covers;
I move the sweet forget-me-nots
  That grow for happy lovers.

I slip, I slide, I gloom, I glance,
  Among my skimming swallows;
I make the netted sunbeam dance
  Against my sandy shallows.

I murmur under moon and stars
  In brambly wildernesses;
I linger by my shingly bars,
  I loiter round my cresses;

And out again I curve and flow
  To join the brimming river
For men may come and men may go,
  But I go on for ever.

Yes, men may come and go; and these are gone,
All gone. My dearest brother, Edmund, sleeps,
Not by the well-known stream and rustic spire,
But unfamiliar Arno, and the dome
Of Brunelleschi, sleeps in peace; and he,
Poor Philip, of all his lavish waste of words
Remains the lean P. W. on his tomb;
I scraped the lichen from it. Katie walks
By the long wash of Australasian seas
Far off, and holds her head to other stars,
And breathes in April-autumns. All are gone.'

So Lawrence Aylmer; seated on a stile
In the long hedge, and rolling in his mind
Old waifs of rhyme, and bowing o'er the brook
A tonsured head in middle age forlorn,
Mused, and was mute. On a sudden a low breath
Of tender air made tremble in the hedge
The fragile bindweed-bells and briony rings;
And he look'd up. There stood a maiden near,
Waiting to pass. In much amaze he stared

On eyes a bashful azure, and on hair
In gloss and hue the chestnut, when the shell
Divides threefold to show the fruit within;
Then, wondering, ask'd her, 'Are you from the farm?'
'Yes,' answer'd she. 'Pray stay a little; 'pardon me,
What do they call you?' 'Katie.' 'That were strange.
What surname?' 'Willows.' 'No!' 'That is my name.'
'Indeed!' and here he look'd so self-perplext,
That Katie laugh'd, and laughing blush'd, till he
Laugh'd also, but as one before he wakes,
Who feels a glimmering strangeness in his dream.
Then looking at her: 'Too happy, fresh and fair,
Too fresh and fair in our sad world's best bloom,
To be the ghost of one who bore your name
About these meadows, twenty years ago.'

'Have you not heard?' said Katie, 'we came back.
We bought the farm we tenanted before.
Am I so like her? so they said on board.
Sir, if you knew her in her English days,
My mother, as it seems you did, the days
That most she loves to talk of, come with me.
My brother James is in the harvest-field;
But she—you will be welcome—O, come in!'

BREAK, BREAK, BREAK

Break, break, break,
  On thy cold gray stones, O Sea!
And I would that my tongue could utter
  The thoughts that arise in me.

O, well for the fisherman's boy,
  That he shouts with his sister at play!
O, well for the sailor lad,
  That he sings in his boat on the bay!

And the stately ships go on
  To their haven under the hill;
But O for the touch of a vanish'd hand,
  And the sound of a voice that is still!

Break, break, break,
  At the foot of thy crags, O Sea!
But the tender grace of a day that is dead
  Will never come back to me.

Charles Darwin
1809-1882

The grandson of Erasmus Darwin, the poet-naturalist who wrote *The Loves of the Plants,* Charles Darwin became the author of a world-shaking new explanation of the natural world. He first published his theory of the evolution of species in 1859 in an essay called *On the Origin of Species by Means of Natural Selection.* He argued that species whose traits help them adapt to an environment, especially a changing environment, tend to continue, while other species tend to become extinct.

Darwin gathered the primary evidence of his theory when he served as chief Naturalist on a scientific expedition round South America aboard the H.M.S. *Beagle.* In isolated regions he compared differences among related species that inhabited neighboring locales with differing climactic conditions. Darwin's scientific observations depended upon his curious interest in animal behavior and his careful perception of detail.

Even after the close of his college career Darwin had been undecided about the choice of a career. He had received a liberal education at Oxford; as part of his scientific research for *The Origin of Species* he read widely in a variety of disciplines. *The Essay on Population* by Thomas Malthus, for example, was instrumental to his thought.

Thus Darwin's own education as well as his careful observations allowed him to publish *The Voyage of the Beagle,* a diary of his observations that possesses sensitivity, vitality, and art sufficient to qualify it as nature writing. The following excerpt is taken from the famous chapter on the Galapagos Islands.

from "Galapagos Archipelago"*
(in THE VOYAGE OF THE BEAGLE)

The natural history of these islands is eminently curious, and well deserves attention. Most of the organic productions are aboriginal creations, found nowhere else; there is even a difference between the inhabitants of the different islands; yet all show a marked relationship with those of America, though separated from that continent by an open space of ocean, between 500 and 600 miles in width. The archipelago is a little world within itself, or rather a satellite attached to America, whence it has derived a few stray colonists, and has received the general character of its indigenous productions. Considering the small size of the islands, we feel the more astonished at the number of their aboriginal beings, and at their confined range. Seeing every height crowned with its crater, and the boundaries of most of the lava-streams still distinct, we are led to believe that within a period geologically recent the unbroken ocean was here spread out. Hence, both in space and time, we seem to be brought somewhat near to that great fact—that mystery of mysteries—the first appearance of new beings on this earth.

Of terrestrial mammals, there is only one which must be considered as indigenous, namely, a mouse (Mus Galapagoensis), and this is confined, as far as I could ascertain, to Chatham Island, the most easterly island of the group. It belongs, as I am informed by Mr. Waterhouse, to a division of the family of mice characteristic of America. At James Island, there is a rat sufficiently distinct from the common kind to have been named and described by Mr. Waterhouse; but as it belongs to the old-world division of the family, and as this island has been frequented by ships for the last hundred and fifty years, I can hardly doubt that this rat is merely a variety produced by the new and peculiar climate, food, and soil, to which it has been subjected. Although no one has a right to speculate without distinct facts, yet even with respect to the Chatham Island mouse, it should be borne in mind, that it may possibly be an American species imported here; for I have seen, in a most unfrequented part of the Pampas, a native mouse living in the roof of a newly built hovel, and therefore its transportation in a vessel is not improbable: analogous facts have been observed by Dr. Richardson in North America.

. . .

We will now turn to the order of reptiles, which gives the most striking character to the zoology of these islands. The species are not numerous, but the numbers of individuals of each species are extraordinarily great. There is one small lizard belonging to a South American genus, and two species (and probably more) of the Amblyrhynchus—a genus confined to the Galapagos Islands. There is one snake which is numerous; it is identical, as I am informed by M. Bibron, with the Psammophis Temminckii from Chile. Of sea-turtle I believe there are more than one species; and of tortoises there are, as we shall presently show, two or three

*From *The Voyage of the Beagle*. Ed. Charles W. Eliot. New York: P.F. Collier & Son, 1909.

species or races. Of toads and frogs there are none: I was surprised at this, considering how well suited for them the temperature and damp upper woods appeared to be. It recalled to my mind the remark made by Bory St. Vincent, namely, that none of this family are found on any of the volcanic islands in the great oceans. As far as I can ascertain from various works, this seems to hold good throughout the Pacific, and even in the large islands of the Sandwich archipelago. Mauritius offers an apparent exception, where I saw the Rana Mascariensis in abundance: this frog is said now to inhabit the Seychelles, Madagascar, and Bourbon; but on the other hand, Du Bois, in his voyage in 1669, states that there were no reptiles in Bourbon except tortoises; and the Office du Roi asserts that before 1768 it had been attempted, without success, to introduce frogs into Mauritius—I presume for the purpose of eating: hence it may be well doubted whether this frog is an aboriginal of these islands. The absence of the frog family in the oceanic islands is the more remarkable, when contrasted with the case of lizards, which swarm on most of the smallest islands. May this difference not be caused, by the greater facility with which the eggs of lizards, protected by calcareous shells, might be transported through salt-water, than could the slimy spawn of frogs?

I will first describe the habits of the tortoise (Testudo aigra, formerly called Indica), which has been so frequently alluded to. These animals are found, I believe, on all the islands of the archipelago; certainly on the greater number. They frequent in preference the high damp parts, but they likewise live in the lower and arid districts. I have already shown, from the numbers which have been caught in a single day, how very numerous they must be. Some grow to an immense size: Mr. Lawson, an Englishman, and vice-governor of the colony, told us that he had seen several so large, that it required six or eight men to lift them from the ground; and that some had afforded as much as two hundred pounds of meat. The old males are the largest, the females rarely growing to so great a size: the male can readily be distinguished from the female by the greater length of its tail. The tortoises which live on those islands where there is no water, or in the lower and arid parts of the others, feed chiefly on the succulent cactus. Those which frequent the higher and damp regions, eat the leaves of various trees, a kind of berry (called guayavita) which is acid and austere, and likewise a pale green filamentous lichen (Usnera plicata), that hangs from the boughs of the trees.

The tortoise is very fond of water, drinking large quantities, and wallowing in the mud. The larger islands alone possess springs, and these are always situated towards the central parts, and at a considerable height. The tortoises, therefore, which frequent the lower districts, when thirsty, are obliged to travel from a long distance. Hence broad and well-beaten paths branch off in every direction from the wells down to the sea-coast; and the Spaniards by following them up, first discovered the watering-places. When I landed at Chatham Island, I could not imagine what animal travelled so methodically along well chosen tracks. Near the springs it was a curious spectacle to behold many of these huge creatures, one set eagerly travelling onwards with outstretched necks, and another set returning, after having drunk their fill. When the tortoise arrives at the spring, quite regardless of any spectator, he buries his head in the water above his eyes, and greedily swallows great mouthfuls, at the rate of about ten in a minute. The inhabitants say each animal stays three or four days in the neighbourhood of the water, and then returns to the lower country; but they differed respecting the frequency of these visits. The animal probably regulates them according to the nature of the food on which it has lived. It is, however, certain, that tortoises can subsist even on these islands where there is no other water than what falls during a few rainy days in the year.

I believe it is well ascertained, that the bladder of the frog acts as a reservoir for the moisture necessary to its existence: such seems to be the case with the tortoise. For some time after a visit to the springs, their urinary bladders are distended with fluid, which is said gradually to decrease in volume, and to become less pure. The inhabitants, when walking in the lower district, and overcome with thirst, often take advantage of this circumstance, and drink the contents of the bladder if full: in one I saw killed, the fluid was quite limpid, and had only a very slightly bitter taste. The inhabitants, however, always first drink the water in the pericardium, which is described as being best.

The tortoises, when purposely moving towards any point, travel by night and day, and arrive at their journey's end much sooner than would be expected. The inhabitants, from observing marked individuals, consider that they travel a distance of about eight miles in two or three days. One large tortoise, which I watched, walked at the rate of sixty yards in ten minutes, that is 360 yards in the hour, or four miles a day,—allowing a little time for it to eat on the road. During the breeding season, when the male and female are together, the male utters a hoarse roar or bellowing, which, it is said, can be heard at the distance of more than a hundred yards. The female never uses her voice, and the male only at these times; so that when the people hear this noise they know that the two are together. They were at this time (October) laying their eggs. The female, where the soil is sandy, deposits them together, and covers them up with sand; but where the ground is rocky she drops them indiscriminately in any hole: Mr. Bynoe found seven placed in a fissure. The egg is white and spherical; one which I measured was seven inches and three-eights in circumference, and therefore larger than a hen's egg. The young tortoises, as soon as they are hatched, fall a prey in great numbers to the carrion-feeding buzzard. The old ones seem generally to die from accidents, as from falling down precipices: at least, several of the inhabitants told me, that they never found one dead without some evident cause.

The inhabitants believe that these animals are absolutely deaf; certainly they do not overhear a person walking close behind them. I was always amused when overtaking one of these great monsters, as it was quietly pacing along, to see how suddenly, the instant I passed, it would draw in its head and legs, and uttering a deep hiss fall to the ground with a heavy sound, as if struck dead. I frequently got on their backs, and then giving a few raps on the hinder part of their shells, they would rise up and walk away;—but I found it very difficult to keep my balance. The flesh of this animal is largely employed, both fresh and salted; and a beautifully clear oil is prepared from the fat. When a tortoise is caught, the man makes a slit in the skin near its tail, so as to see inside its body, whether the fat under the dorsal plate is thick. If it is not, the animal is liberated and it is said to recover soon from this strange operation. In order to secure the tortoise, it is not sufficient to turn them like turtle, for they are often able to get on their legs again.

There can be little doubt that this tortoise is an aboriginal inhabitant of the Galapagoes; for it is found on all, or nearly all, the islands, even on some of the smaller ones where there is no water; had it been an imported species, this would hardly have been the case in a group which has been so little frequented. Moreover, the old Bucaniers found this tortoise in greater numbers even than at present: Wood and Rogers also, in 1708, say that it is the opinion of the Spaniards, that it is found nowhere else in this quarter of the world. It is now widely distributed; but it may be questioned whether it is in any other place an aboriginal. The bones of a tortoise at Mauritius, associated with those of the extinct Dodo, have generally been considered as belonging to this tortoise; if this had been so, undoubtedly it must have been there indigenous; but M. Bibron informs me that he believes that it was distinct, as the species now living there certainly is.

The Amblyrhynchus, a remarkable genus of lizards, is confined to this archipelago; there are two species, resembling each other in general form, one being terrestrial and the other aquatic. This latter species (A. cristatus) was first characterized by Mr. Bell, who well foresaw, from its short, broad head, and strong claws of equal length, that its habits of life would turn out very peculiar, and different from those of its nearest ally, the Iguana. It is extremely common on all the islands throughout the group, and lives exclusively on the rocky sea-beaches, being never found, at least I never saw one, even ten yards in-shore. It is a hideous-looking creature, of a dirty black colour, stupid, and sluggish in its movements. The usual length of a full-grown one is about a yard, but there are some even four feet long; a large one weighed twenty pounds: on the island of Albemarle they seem to grow to a greater size than elsewhere. Their tails are flattened sideways, and all four feet partially webbed. They are occasionally seen some hundred yards from the shore, swimming about; and Captain Collnett, in his Voyage says, "They go to sea in herds a-fishing, and sun themselves on the rocks; and may be called alligators in miniature." It must not, however, be supposed that they live on fish. When in the water this lizard swims with perfect ease and quickness, by a serpentine movement of its body and flattened tail—the legs being motionless and closely collapsed on its sides. A seaman on board sank one, with a heavy weight attached to it, thinking thus to kill it directly; but when, an hour afterwards, he drew up the line, it was quite active. Their limbs and strong claws are admirably adapted for crawling over the rugged and fissured masses of lava, which everywhere form the coast. In such situations, a group of six or seven of these hideous reptiles may oftentimes be seen on the black rocks, a few feet above the surf, basking in the sun with outstretched legs.

. . .

from "The Traveller Returned"

Let us now look at the brighter side of the past time. The pleasure derived from beholding the scenery and general aspect of the various countries we have visited, has decidedly been the most constant and highest source of enjoyment. It is probable that the picturesque beauty of many parts of Europe far exceeds anything we have beheld. But there is a growing pleasure in comparing the character of scenery in different countries, which to a certain degree is distinct from merely admiring their beauty. It more depends on an acquaintance with the individual parts of each view: I am strongly induced to believe that, as in music the person who understands every note, will, if he also has true taste, more thoroughly enjoy the whole, so he who examines each part of a fine view, may also thoroughly comprehend the full and combined effect. Hence a traveller should be a botanist, for in all views plants form the chief embellishment. Group masses of naked rocks, even in the wildest forms—for a time they may afford a sublime spectacle, but they will soon grow monotonous; paint them with bright and varied colours—they will become fantastic; clothe them with vegetation—they must form at least a decent, if not a most beautiful picture.

When I said that the scenery of Europe was probably superior to anything which we have beheld, I must except, as a class by itself, that of the intertropical regions. The two cannot be compared together; but I have already too often enlarged on the grandeur of these latter climates. As the force of impression frequently depends upon preconceived ideas, I may add that all mine were taken from the vivid descriptions in the *Personal Narrative* (of Alexander von Humboldt) which far exceed in merit anything I have ever read on the subject. Yet with these high-wrought ideas, my feelings were very remote from partaking of a tinge of disappointment on first landing on the coast of Brazil.

Amongst the scenes which are deeply impressed on my mind, none exceed in sublimity the primeval forests, undefaced by the hand of man, whether those of Brazil, where the powers of life are predominant, or those of Tierra del Fuego, where death and decay prevail. Both are temples filled with the varied productions of the God of Nature. No one can stand unmoved in these solitudes, without feeling that there is more in man than the mere breath of his body. In calling up images of the past, I find the plains of Patagonia most frequently cross before my eyes. Yet these plains are pronounced by all most wretched and useless. They are only characterised by negative possessions: without habitations, without water, without trees, without mountains, they support merely a few dwarf plants. Why then, and the case is not peculiar to myself, do these arid wastes take so firm possession of the memory? Why have not the still more level green and fertile pampas, which are serviceable to mankind, produced an equal impression? I can scarcely analyse these feelings, but it must be partly owing to the free scope given to the imagination. They are boundless, for they are scarcely practicable, and hence unknown: they bear the stamp of having thus lasted for ages, and there appears no limit to their duration through future time. If, as the ancients supposed, the flat earth was surrounded by an impassable breadth of water, or by deserts heated to an intolerable excess, who would not look at these last boundaries to man's knowledge with deep, but ill defined sensations?

Lastly, of natural scenery, the views from lofty mountains, though certainly in one sense not beautiful, are very memorable. I remember looking down from the crest of the highest Cordillera. The mind undisturbed by minute details, was filled by the stupendous dimensions of the surrounding masses.

Of individual objects, perhaps no one is more sure to create astonishment than the first sight in his native haunt of a real barbarian—of man in his lowest and most savage state. One's mind hurries back over past centuries, and then asks, could our progenitors be such as these? Men—whose very signs and expressions are less intelligible to us than those of the domesticated animals; who do not possess the instinct of those animals, nor yet appear to boast of human reason, or at least of arts consequent on that reason. I do not believe it is possible to describe or paint the difference of savage and civilised man. It is the difference between a wild and tame animal: and part of the interest in beholding a savage is the same which would lead every one to desire to see the lion in his desert, the tiger tearing his prey in the jungle, the rhinoceros on the wide plain, or the hippopotamus wallowing in the mud of some African river.

Amongst the other most remarkable spectacles which we have beheld, may be ranked the stars of the Southern hemisphere; the water-spout; the glacier leading its blue stream of ice in a bold precipice overhanging the sea; a lagoon island, raised by the coral-forming animalcule; an active volcano; the overwhelming effects of a violent earthquake. These latter phenomena perhaps possess for me a higher interest, from their intimate connection with the geological structure of the world. The earthquake must, however, be to everyone a most impressive event. The solid earth, considered from our earliest childhood as the very type of solidity, has oscillated like a thin crust beneath our feet and in seeing the most beautiful and laboured works of man in a moment overthrown, we feel the insignificance of his boasted power.

It has been said that the love of the chase is an inherent delight in man—a relic of an instinctive passion. If so, I am sure the pleasure of living in the open air, with the sky for a roof and the ground for a table, is part of the same feeling. It is the savage returning to his wild and native habits. I always look back to our boat cruises and my land journeys, when through unfrequented countries, with a kind of extreme delight, which no scenes of civilisation could create. I do not doubt every traveller must remember the glowing sense of happiness from the simple consciousness of breathing in a foreign clime where the civilised man has seldom or never trod.

. . .

Gerard Manley Hopkins
1844-1889

Hopkins was a devout Catholic, a Jesuit priest who refused to publish his poems. He saw the beauty and vitality of the natural world as a glimpse of divine majesty; more important to the tradition of nature writing, Hopins saw natural details with incredible vividness and accuracy, and his poetry communicated the intense joy he felt. His accuracy of description is well evidenced in "Spring":

> Nothing is so beautiful as spring—
> When weeds, in wheels shoot long and lovely and lush;
> Thrush's eggs look like low heavens, and thrush
> Through the echoing timber does so rinse and wring
> The ear, it strikes like lightnings to hear him sing;

Hopkins' joy in the natural world was reinforced by his reading of Wordsworth and Shelley and Keats, but his means for communicating that joy followed from his originality as a poet. Literary critics consider Hopkins a modern poet because of several innovations he employed: the use of a word in a startlingly unique way; the use of puns; a new idea for creating rhythm; and most important, his concept of "inscape." "Inscape" meant the valuing of individual things precisely for their uniqueness. For Hopkins as priest, the perception of uniqueness in a flower or an afternoon was the perception of the infinite variety in God's creation. For Hopkins the poet, fascination with the specialness of natural things infused his descriptions with great power. In "Pied Beauty," for example, Hopkins raises a prayer for "dappled things" and presents pictures of them that allow the reader to see "trout that swim" as he might not ever have considered viewing them.

The sacredness that Hopkins associated with creation spurred him occasionally to prophetic cries of protest against cruelties performed upon the environment:

> If we but knew what we do
> When we delve or hew—
> Hack and rack the growing green!

The first published edition of Hopkins poetry did not emerge until 1918, twenty-nine years after his death. His technical achievements made him a model for twentieth-century poets, including many who, like Dylan Thomas, would continue the tradition of nature writing.

GOD'S GRANDEUR*

The world is charged with the grandeur of God.
It will flame out, like shining from shook foil;
It gathers to a greatness, like the ooze of oil
Crushed. Why do men then now not reck his rod?
Generations have trod, have trod, have trod;
And all is seared with trade; bleared, smeared with toil;
And wears man's smudge and shares man's smell: the soil
Is bare now, nor can foot feel, being shod.

And for all this, nature is never spent;
There lives the dearest freshness deep down things;
And though the last lights off the black West went
Oh, morning, at the brown brink eastward, springs—
Because the Holy Ghost over the bent
World broods with warm breast and with ah! bright wings.

THE STARLIGHT NIGHT

Look at the stars! look, look up at the skies!
O look at all the fire-folk sitting in the air!
The bright boroughs, the circle-citadels there!
Down in dim woods the diamond delves! the elves'-eyes!
The grey lawns cold where gold, where quickgold lies!
Wind-beat whitebeam! airy abeles set on a flare!
Flake-doves sent floating forth at a farmyard scare!—
Ah well! it is all a purchase, all is a prize.

*This and the following poems by Gerard Manley Hopkins are from *Poems of Gerald Manley Hopkins*, ed. Robert Bridges (London: Oxford Univ. Press, 1938).

Buy then! bid then!—What?—Prayer, patience, alms, vows.
Look, look: a May-mess, like on orchard boughs!
Look! March-bloom, like on mealed-with-yellow sallows!
These are indeed the barn; withindoors house
The shocks. This piece-bright paling shuts the spouse
Christ home, Christ and his mother and all his hallows.

PIED BEAUTY

Glory be to God for dappled things—
For skies of couple-colour as a brinded cow;
For rose-moles all in stipple upon trout that swim;
Fresh-firecoal chestnut-falls; finches' wings;
Landscape plotted and pieced—fold, fallow, and plough;
And áll trádes, their gear and tackle and trim.

All things counter, original, spare, strange;
Whatever is fickle, freckled (who knows how?)
With swift, slow; sweet, sour; adazzle, dim;
He fathers-forth whose beauty is past change:
Praise him.

HURRAHING IN HARVEST

Summer ends now; now, barbarous in beauty, the stooks arise
Around; up above, what wind-walks! what lovely behaviour
Of silk-sack clouds! has wilder, wilful-wavier
Meal-drift moulded ever and melted across skies?

I walk, I lift up, I lift up heart, eyes,
Down all that glory in the heavens to glean our Saviour;
And, eyes, heart, what looks, what lips yet gave you a
Rapturous love's greeting of realer, of rounder replies?

BINSEY POPLARS

felled 1879

My aspens dear, whose airy cages quelled,
Quelled or quenched in leaves the leaping sun,
All felled, felled, are all felled;
Of a fresh and following folded rank

Not spared, not one
That dandled a sandalled
Shadow that swam or sank
On meadow and river and wind-wandering weed-winding bank.

O if we but knew what we do
When we delve or hew—
Hack and rack the growing green!
Since country is so tender
To touch, her being so slender,
That, like this sleek and seeing ball
But a prick will make no eye at all,
Where we, even where we mean
To mend her we end her,
When we hew or delve:
After-comers cannot guess the beauty been.
Ten or twelve, only ten or twelve
Strokes of havoc unselve
The sweet especial scene,
Rural scene, a rural scene,
Sweet especial rural scene.

INVERSNAID

This darksome burn, horseback brown,
His rollrock highroad roaring down,
In coop and in comb the fleece of his foam
Flutes and low to the lake falls home.

A windpuff-bonnet of fáwn-fróth
Turns and twindles over the broth
Of a pool so pitchblack, féll-frówning,
It rounds and rounds Despair to drowning.

Degged with dew, dappled with dew
Are the groins of the braes that the brook treads through,
Wiry heathpacks, flitches of fern,
And the beadbonny ash that sits over the burn.

What would the world be, once bereft
Of wet and of wildness? Let them be left,
O let them be left, wildness and wet;
Long live the weeds and the wilderness yet.

RIBBLESDALE

Earth, sweet Earth, sweet landscape, with leaves throng
And louched low grass, heaven that dost appeal
To, with no tongue to plead, no heart to feel;
That canst but only be, but dost that long—

Thou canst but be, but that thou well dost; strong
Thy plea with him who dealt, nay does now deal,
Thy lovely dale down thus and thus bids reel
Thy river, and o'er gives all to rack or wrong.

THE WINDHOVER:

TO CHRIST OUR LORD

I caught this morning morning's minion, king-
  dom of daylight's dauphin, dapple-dawn-drawn Falcon, in his riding
    Of the rolling level underneath him steady air, and striding
High there, how he rung upon the rein of a wimpling wing
In his ecstacy! then off, off forth on swing,
    As a skate's heel sweeps smooth on a bow-bend: the hurl and gliding
    Rebuffed the big wind. My heart in hiding
Stirred for a bird,—the achieve of, the mastery of the thing!

Brute beauty and valour and act, oh, air, pride, plume, here
    Buckle! And the fire that breaks from thee then, a billion
Times told lovelier, more dangerous, O my chevalier!

    No winder of it: shéer plód makes plough down sillion
Shine, and blue-bleak embers, ah my dear,
    Fall, gall themselves, and gash gold-vermilion.

WINTER WITH THE GULF STREAM

The boughs, the boughs are bare enough
But earth has never felt the snow.
Frost-furred our ivies are and rough

With bills of rime the brambles shew.
The hoarse leaves crawl on hissing ground
Because the sighing wind is low.

But if the rain-blasts be unbound
And from dark feathers wring the drops
The clogged brook runs with choking sound

Kneading the mounded mire that stops
His channel under damming coats
Of foliage fallen in the copse.

A simple passage of weak notes
Is all the winter bird dare try
The bugle moon by daylight floats

So glassy white about the sky,
So like a berg of hyaline,
And penciled blue so daintily,

I never saw her so divine.
But through black branches, rarely drest
In scarves of silky shot and shine.

The webbed and the watery west
Where yonder crimson fireball sits
Looks laid for feasting and for rest.

I see long reefs of violets
In beryl-covered fens so dim,
A gold-water Pactolus frets

Its brindled wharves and yellow brim,
The waxen colours weep and run,
And slendering to his burning rim

Into the flat blue mist the sun
Drops out and all our day is done.

SPRING

Nothing is so beautiful as spring—
  When weeds, in wheels, shoot long and lovely and lush;
  Thrush's eggs look little low heavens, and thrush
Through the echoing timber does so rinse and wring
The ear, it strikes like lightnings to hear him sing;
  The glassy peartree leaves and blooms, they brush
  The descending blue; that blue is all in a rush
With richness; the racing lambs too have fair their fling.

What is all this juice and all this joy?
   A strain of the earth's sweet being in the beginning
In Eden garden.—Have, get, before it cloy,
   Before it cloud, Christ, lord; and sour with sinning,
Innocent mind and Mayday in girl and boy,
   Most, O maid's child, thy choice and worthy the winning.

Nature in America: Colonial Times Through the Era of Conservation

During the successful settlement of New England in the early seventeenth century, those who came to the New World seeking religious freedom and economic opportunity seemed to have two approaches to the wilderness they found there, the utilitarian and the theological. The utilitarian approach was sounded even before the Pilgrims' *Mayflower* landed in 1620 by Captain John Smith in his *Description of New England* (1616), where he promised a natural bounty that might be wrested from the land by hard work and practical know-how. And much later, as their era came to a close, Cotton Mather summed up the Puritans' utilitarianism when he said, "What is not useful is viscious."

During the transformation of the New England landscape from wilderness to settlement, the Puritan writer and (as we might call him today) "civil engineer" Edward Johnson catalogued the labor and machinery of successful landscape transformation in his *Wonder-Working Providence of Sions Saviour in New England* (1653). Johnson's work is a paean to the actual and imagined machinery that would change the natural environment. Through the draining of swamps and the use of saw, corn, iron, and fulling mills, the Puritans succeeded in creating something close to the ordered civilized commonwealth that they had hoped to establish in the New World. In doing so, they believed themselves fulfilling God's injunction to man in *Genesis* to subdue the earth and hold dominion over it.

"Remake the World!" Such was the theme of Johnson's book as he looked proudly upon the accomplishments of the Puritan Laborers and their Machinery:

> This remote, rocky, barren, bushy, wild-wood wilderness, a receptacle for Lions, Wolves, Bears, Foxes, Rockoones . . . Bevers, Otters, and all kind of wild creatures, a place that never afforded the Natives better than the flesh of a few wild creatures and parch't Indian corn incht out with Chestnuts and bitter Acorns, now through the mercy of Christ become a second England for fertilness. In so short a space [roughly ten years], that it is indeed the wonder of the world.

To the Puritans, the machine, or technology, was the instrument to create the Garden, not, as the machine later would be viewed by some, the instrument that destroyed the Garden. The roots of what we might call today's technological "superfaith" grew here. Hard work and utilitarianism—the human control of the natural environment—were not only part of the Judeo-Christian heritage of the Puritans, but also necessary attributes for a people whose survival was, after all, threatened by the strange wilderness they encountered.

The second approach to the wilderness embodied in the Puritans—the theological—also arose out of their biblical heritage and the realities of surviving in the wild. The Puritans viewed wilderness as a horrifying arena of millennial battle. The evils of the landscape for the Puritans are typified by the famous lines of the Puritan poet Micheal Wigglesworth, who in 1662, described New England as a "waste and howling wilderness/Where none inhabited/But hellish fiends, and brutish men/That Devils worshipped." Puritan distinctions between good and evil were based on ancient Scriptual injunctions to tame and control wild landscapes, and by doing so to assert chosen status. As Cecelia Tichi has recently argued in *New World, New Earth*, the Puritans themselves did not represent so much blind and destroying arrogance as the aspiration to "reform" the landscape. Such reform was the means to, and the testimony of, the reform of political and spiritual life that began with the Protestant Reformation in Europe. We would suggest, however, that if this legacy of radical landscape reform led to three centuries of arrogant destruction long after the land was settled for humanity's balanced use, the destruction comes to the same thing—biblical roots or not.

Conceiving of the world as the battleground of Good and Evil, the Puritans in New England fought the forests and swamps just as the British Puritans fought "the King's men" and other sinners. One hears even medieval echoes in the Puritan approach to nature—in their military metaphors, their recourse to Genesis and Revelations, their struggles against forest devils, and in their hope for establishing a Christian Millennium in New England. Indeed, Cotton Mather believed that his people were God's instrument, the means of casting out Heathens (the Indians) to make room for those saints who would create the New Canaan and build God's Garden anew. For Mather, the Indians were soulless animals or, worse, satanic agents who proved their damnation by their lack of technical skills in mining, shipping, building, and economics. In the wild land of savages there lived, according to Mather, dragons, flying serpents, monsters, witches, and devils. Reform of the landscape was the noblest cause of all: the divinely inspired reformation of the world.

In his *Wilderness and the American Mind,* Roderick Nash connects the early Americans' fear of wilderness and the consequent subjugation of it not only to Puritanical religious and utilitarian principles, but also to the "primordial dread of wilderness" that modern humanity has only recently begun to overcome. The dangerous, embattled condition of mankind in a wild state for hundreds of thousands of years has left, Nash argues, evolutionary imprints that are not easily eradicated from the race, imprints that in numerous civilizations have led to all kinds of social and religious rationales for destruction. The Puritans indeed carried a full legacy of intellectual imprints from the Old World: the "bias against wilderness" in the Old Testament, in prescientific folklore, in the classical pastoral tradition, and in the cultivated garden—at once idyllic and practical—of the Renaissance. The medieval vision of wilderness in *Beowulf,* a wilderness harboring man-eating monstrosities, looks back to the wilderness of humanity's primordial fears. Nash makes the interesting if puzzling point that such is the legacy of Western culture until well into the nineteenth century, and only in the East has wilderness been more consistently venerated as the symbol and essence of diety through the religious systems of Buddhism, Hinduism, and, most clearly, in Japanese "nature worship" called Shintoism. Nash sees the new twentieth-century attitude of favoring and protecting wilderness as a radical transformation in the human organism. But to follow his logic we would have to say that transformation is perhaps of the human organism as it happened to express itself through Western culture. Such transformation is, of course, far from complete, for even after World War II, many argue that humanity still faces "the eternal problem of subduing the earth." William Cronan, in *Changes in the Land,* emphasizes the influence of European capitalism on the colonists' view of ecosystems as composed of extractable units for use as commodities. Cronan argues that New England ecology was blighted before the end of the colonial era.

There were, of course, exceptions in early America. The eighteenth-century Puritan theologian Johnathan Edwards is often cited as one who deeply felt the beauty of and divine presence in nature. South of New England, William Byrd (1674–1744), a Virginian gentleman, took pleasure in his experiences of the Appalachian wilderness. His *History of the Dividing Line,* filled with a naturalist's data and description, recognizes not only the beauty of swamps, but their ecological usefulness. The *History* is the first full-length work in American literature to show such positive feelings toward the American wilderness. Byrd is, at the same time, aware of the practical uses of natural resources, and he never hides the trials and real dangers of wilderness travel.

John Bartram (1699–1777), another explorer and early naturalist who saw the wilderness as a natural laboratory, was the foremost botanist of his day in America. He trained his son William (1739–1823) to appreciate, explore, and know the American wilds, most notably through the 1765 botanical trip father and son took up the St. Johns River. William Bartram's *Travels* (1791) is a classic of wilderness literature and a portentous point in the American vision of the landscape. William's scientific interest in plants and animals did not exclude a reverence for wilderness. In England he was read by Coleridge, Wordsworth, and Carlyle, and he likewise influenced a later generation of American Romantic writers and painters who found in America's nature both sublimity and the creative power of God. The Bartrams and more especially Byrd were influenced in their own turn by the

European literary *avant garde*. That rising enthusiasm for the exotic, mysterious, and solitary in early Romanticism, and the early Romantic resurgence of "primitivism" (the vision of civilization as a hindrance to the best in humanity), were currents from the Europe of Montaigne, Rousseau, and Chateaubriand that formed the vision of these and other educated, early American gentlemen. Another naturalist, John James Audubon (1785–1851) traveled in the middle and southern American frontier and between 1827–1897 published *Birds of America,* the *Ornithological Biography*, and the *Missouri River Journals*. Audubon was a complicated man who could combine minute observation and the tall tale, could shoot specimens yet feel compassion for the suffering of animals, could appreciate animals' behavior and beauty as well as their dangers to man.

These naturalist-explorers and the settlers south of New England lacked the religious fervor and ideology of the Puritan approach to nature. Indeed, the southern settlers viewed America more mildly through a tradition of pastoralism. What might be called the "Edenic" tradition led to a southern agrarianism that shaped American political and environmental thought in the early years of the Republic. Even in the south, however, realities often frustrated dreams. The first excursions to and settlements in Jamestown, for example, failed because dreams of gold and Eden gave way beneath the sheer weight of the struggle for survival against wilderness, Indians, and disease. Such settlers had come to America on the wave of European promotional literature that, like Captain Arthur Barlow's 1584 account of Virginia, depicted the New World during the Renaissance as an established Eden, an Arcadian world beyond the need for reform, and the "only paradise," as Michael Drayton called it in his "To the Virginian Voyage" in 1606. After all, Sir Thomas More's *Utopia* was set in the Americas, as was Shakespeare's *The Tempest*, both based on travel accounts of the Americas as a pastoral land where humanity might regain a lost innocence.

Despite the real hardships, this pastoral impulse blossomed into the agrarian ideal in American social thought that was best expressed by Thomas Jefferson and St. Jean de Crèvecoeur. Briefly, agrarianism is the faith, deeply rooted in the Western pastoral tradition, that social and political stability are best obtained by the agricultural life and economy. Independence, self-sufficiency, and living with the land in harmonious productivity are all agrarian ideals.

The years 1781–1804 mark the first transitional period in the move away from the Puritanical attitude toward nature. Between those years Jefferson's *Notes on the State of Virginia* (1781) became the classic statement of agrarian thought, and Alexander Wilson's "The Foresters, Description of a Pedestrian Tour to the Fall of the Niagra in the Autumn of 1804," an epic poem celebrating the American wilds, announced the nineteenth-century Romantic appreciation for wilderness in America.

Jefferson's book established him as an authority on natural history, as one whose philosophical drift was toward reconciling Edmund Burke and European Romanticism with the contemporary currents of science, exploration, and philosophy through his own experience of the American landscape. As a scientist, Jefferson—influenced by the rational religion, or Deism, of his day that saw in nature the work of God—advised going to nature and her laws for the means of easing mankind's hardships. Like Francis Bacon before him—who advised studying nature to glorify God and help mankind—and like his contemporary Ben Franklin, Jefferson had a strong utilitarian strain himself. He did more than anyone else in his day to advance agricultural techniques through developments in machinery, stock breeding, and agricultural societies. As an agrarian, he spoke a basic premise upon which the early Republic was founded: "Those who labor in the earth are the chosen people of God. . .whose breast he has made his particular deposit for substantial virtue." Jefferson may have preferred human artifice to wilderness in man's social condition, but such artifice allowed room for wilderness and was used in harmony with nature.

The opposing and extreme utilitarianism of the time was no longer purely Puritanical, but, perhaps borrowing something from the early New Englanders, became more mercantile and materialistic. James Madison, who said that instead of "poetry" we want "something more substantial, more durable, more profitable," was one spokesman for the materialistic approach to life and nature. Yet what De Crevecoeur, Alexander Wilson, William Cullen Bryant, and Timothy Dwight, among many others, were offering in the nineteenth century was the prose and poetry of Romantic nature writing and agrarian thought.

During the nineteenth century, Romanticism in literature and the later rise of Conservationism in politics gradually reshaped the way the American people viewed the natural world. The new vision would culminate after the turn of the century in the administration of President Theodore Roosevelt. One approach to nature in America during the nineteenth century began with Jefferson's explorers Lewis and Clark recording both the horrifying and sublime sides of the natural environment and hinting that the wilderness held the lessons of endurance. But it was the Frenchman Alexis de Tocqueville who clarified the American people's general approach to their landscape and warned of a dangerous rejection of the agrarian ideal as early as 1831, when he visited the United States and observed it as an outsider. The American pioneer, said De Tocqueville, prizes only man's work, not nature's.

> In Europe people talk a great deal of the wilds of America, but the Americans themselves never think about them; they are insensible to the wonders of inanimate nature and they may be said not to perceive the mighty forests that surround them until they fall beneath the hatchet. Their eyes are fixed upon another sight, the . . . march across these wilds, draining swamps, turning the course of rivers, peopling solitudes, and subduing nature.

Some recent feminist scholarship has echoed De Toqueville. Annette Kolodny, for example, explored those male fantasies that governed Euro-American relations with the landscape in *The Lay of the Land: Metaphor as Experience and History in American Life and Letters* (1975). And in *The Land Before Her: Fantasy and Experience of the American Frontiers, 1630-1860* (1984), Kolodny explored the imagery women used to express their own sense of, and relation to, the American wilderness. Kolodny views the landscape as a symbolic realm—a place upon which men and women project their innermost desires. "Our actions in the world," she writes, "are shaped by the paradigms in our head." The value in understanding our fantasies, Kolodny argues, is that we may then choose from among our deepest attitudes those that are life-affirming against those that are life-denying. Kolodny discovered a fundamental contrast between male and female fantasies through a succession of westward-moving frontiers. Men have expressed a desire to possess the virgin continent by force, by competition that demands a willingness to violate the primal garden and human relations for the accumulation of capital wealth. Women, on the other hand, have expressed the desire to create in the wilderness a cultivated garden or sanctuary for idealized domestic life, have emphasized the gratification of home and family relations.

De Tocqueville doubtless spoke of the prevailing American vision, represented then by such men as Colorado Governor William Gilpin who argued that American's Manifest Destiny was "providential ordinance" because, after all, "Progress is God." In fact, Gilpin could be speaking for the majority voice today, just as de Tocqueville might have been describing twentieth-century America and independent farming when he said that "the cultivation of the ground promises an almost certain result to his [the farmer's] exertions, but a slow one; men are not enriched by it without patience and toil . . . Thus democracy not only swells the number of working men, but it leads men to prefer one kind of labor to another; and whilst it diverts them from agriculture, it encourages their taste for commerce and manufactures."

Almost as if in answer to de Tocqueville, the American Romantic Movement in literature was about to become a considerable force against the merely utilitarian approach to nature and the merely mercantile drive for rapid monetary profit, just as in our century the environmental movement has become a force against merely utilitarian and mercantile values. In the nineteenth century it was the American poet William Cullen Bryant (1794–1878) and the novelist James Fenimore Cooper (1789–1851) who ushered in the age of Romantic nature writing and forged the first principles of conservation. An influential editor and liberal, Bryant could be called the first major American poet to return to the wilderness. Just as William Bartram influenced the Lake Poets, so in turn did the Lake Poets, along with Byron and Scott, influence Bryant and his contemporaries throughout the nineteenth century. Bryant and Alexander Wilson shaped the way a new generation of Americans would come to view nature, as attested by the rising tide of magazines devoted to explorations and landscape between 1801–1827. In Bryant's "Forest Hymn" (1825), woods are God's temples, healers of humanity's soul. "The Prairies" (1833) celebrates the isolation and vastness of the American plains as much as it foresees the coming of the white man's civilization.

Cooper's *The Pioneers* (1823) made him a literary hero in his day and began the famous Leatherstocking series with its frontiersman-hero Natty Bumpo. Bumpo was an early spokesman for conservation and ecological consciousness. He demonstrated Cooper's belief that wilderness had an important moral influence on human conduct. It was the waste of natural resources and creatures that troubled Cooper most. "Use, but don't waste," is the way Bumpo put it. The theme of using the wilderness respectfully, not wastefully, was sounded here and rang through the next century down to our own day. In the famous pigeon-shooting scene in *Pioneers*, Natty speaks of the wasteful slaughter this way: "the Lord won't see waste of his creatures for nothing, and right will be done to the pigeons, as well as others, by and by." Even on his deathbed, Natty ponders "how much has the beauty of the wilderness been deformed in two short lives."

Cooper was an eminently civilized man himself who was not blindly arguing for keeping America in a wilderness state nor her people in primitive conditions. But he was concerned over the white man's ability to balance his civilization with the natural environment, and it was the act of striking a balance that, for Cooper, would be fundamentally moral. In this regard, Cooper himself was an agrarian. In *The American Democrat* (1838), where he argues for individual property ownership as the sole basis for establishing a vital agrarian economy that can supply not only the necessities, but the "elegancies, refinements, or mental pleasures" of life, Cooper established a principle of continuing importance to conservationists: you can not do absolutely anything you want to with property you own. At the point where your actions hurt another or endanger the larger community, law must restrict what your own moral judgment neglects.

During the early years of Cooper's and Bryant's influence another phenomenon in America shaped the way Americans would view nature in the nineteenth century—landscape painting. Oddly enough, it was English painters who introduced Americans to the wonders of the American wilderness as landscape painting moved in the eighteenth and nineteenth centuries from naive and formalized art to increasingly romantic and realistic art. In the early 1800's Thomas Cole and Washington Allston introduced Romantic landscape painting, and Cole founded what came to be known as the Hudson River School of landscape painting. Cole (1801–48) and Bryant were fellow artists and friends. Cole's school developed the concept—initiated by Bartram and Audubon and retained by Bryant—that nature for its own sake is a fit subject for art, and that, moreover, the artist learns from nature. This artistic approach to nature would be followed by such painters as Asher Durand, Worthington Whitteredge, George Inness, and Winslow Homer, and by such writers as Thoreau, John Burroughs, and John Muir. When Cole went to the American wilderness to paint in 1823, he went, as he said, to capture the "wild and great features that know not man." His paintings of the Catskills after 1825—"Mountain Sunrise," "Landscape with Tree Trunks," "View Near Ticonderoga"—lend religious as well as aesthetic importance to nature, as did his paintings of the White Mountains after 1828. Indeed, the Hudson River painters became known for their belief that a painting should make the viewer feel the presence of God's work, not man's. By 1866 Asher Durand (1796–1886) had called for a wilderness art. His student Frederic Church (1826–1900) took up the challenge and started the long line of wilderness art that led from Albert Bierstadt's Rocky Mountain paintings in the 1850's to Thomas Moran's western paintings of the Tetons and Sierras during the next two decades and, finally, to the work of William H. Jackson, the father of landscape photography, in the last years of the nineteenth century.

With her artists in the vanguard, America's people followed. As the urban and industrial centers of America arose in the second half of the nineteenth century, the interest in landscape art, outdoor sports and activites, and urban parks increased. A whole literature of travel arose to stimulate the fantasies of both armchair adventurers and urban renegades who searched for the picturesque in nature. By the 1850's, the railroads, capitalizing on a good thing, carried hordes of tourists to the West, the White Mountains, and the natural wonders throughout America that had been painted and described. White Mountain painters like Edward Hill (1843–1923) made their living painting natural scenes for tourists. Washington Irving's *A Tour of the Praries* (1835) was followed by George Catlin's *Letters and Notes on the Manners, Customs and Conditions of the North American Indians* (1842), where Catlin makes the first recorded appeal for wilderness protection through national parks. Catlin's work was followed by John C. Fremont's *Report of the Exploring Expedition to the Rocky Mountains . . . and California* (1845), which was universally popular, and by historian Francis Parkman's *The California and Oregon Trail* (1839), which Parkman himself called part of his great "history of the American Forest," and by Clarence King's *Mountaineering in the Sierra Nevada* (1872), to name but a few of the most important. Along with such books a veritable industry of scenery magazines arose from the 1830's to 50's, capped by Irving's collection *The Home Book of the Picturesque American Scenery, Art, and Literature* (1852) and Bryant's edition of *Picturesque America* (1852).

From the 1830's to 60's in New England, the Transcendentalists found in nature a scientific edification as well as a transcendent—or religious—experience. Against what were becoming shopworn concepts of "sublimity" and "the picturesque," Ralph Waldo Emerson (1803–82) spoke of nature as a link between God and humanity. Turning completely from the Puritan view, Emerson connected nature with morality, or the spiritual growth of the individual, and pitted the creative force and inspiration of nature against the restrictions of society. His friend and follower Henry David Thoreau (1817–62) provided the concrete observation through which Emerson's principles might live. Following the influence of these two men and their colleagues, including George Ripley (who founded Brook Farm in 1841), Margaret Fuller, and the scientist Louis Agassiz, Americans with any awareness of their cultural heritage could never again naively view nature as demonic wilderness or as a collection of inanimate resources depending solely on man's exploitation for their proper use.

With their deep concern for the quality of life in America and for spiritual and ethical issues as old as the classical pastoral and as far-reaching as the ancient religion of the East, the Transcendentalists turned their force against the entire weight of that increasingly materialistic, industrial, and commercial civilization whose birth de Tocqueville had witnessed. They were the progenitors of the primitive, mystic strain in American literature that lives in our own time through such poets as Alan Ginsburg, Kenneth Rexroth, Gary Snyder, Robert Bly, and Galway Kinnell. Focusing America's attention on the issues of individualism, self-reliance, the "divinity" in mankind and nature, and the value of other life forms, the Transcendentalists exacerbated the conflict that remains with us today between wilderness and agrarian values, on the one hand, and industrial and technocratic values, on the other.

After Emerson and Thoreau came a host of American essayists, poets, and novelists of nature that included James Russell Lowell's editorship of the *Atlantic Monthly*, Henry Ward Beecher's *Star Papers* (1855), Susan Fenimore Cooper's *Rhyme and Reason of Country Life* (1855), Wilson Flag's *Studies in Field and Forest* (1857), Thomas Starr King's *The White Hills* (1860), George P. Marsh's *Man and Nature* (1864)—a classic revised in 1874 under the title *The Earth as Modified by Human Action*—Walt Whitman's ever-developing vision in the nine editions of *Leaves of Grass* (1855–92), John Greenleaf Whitter's *Among the Hills* (1867), and Emily Dickinson's private poetry. This tide of nature literature crested toward and after the end of the century with the two towering American nature essayists of the time—John Burroughs and John Muir. These two men, though their writings, speeches, and consultantships, overshadowed all others in having the greatest impact on the modern American conservation movement.

The history of the conservation movement can be briefly outlined, with the help of Hans Huth's *Nature and the American* (1957), from President Lincoln's signing of a

Congressional Bill in 1864 that protected recreational wilderness areas in California, including the Yosemite Valley and the Mariposa Big Trees. The landscape and parks architect Fredrick Law Olmstead, who built city parks throughout the nation, was instrumental in preparing the way for such legislation. In 1875 the American Forestry Association was established to ensure that the use and preservation of the remaining American forest would be based on scientific principles, and by 1886 the Federal government had established its own protective Division of Forestry under the guiding hand of Gifford Pinchot, a scientific forester. In 1891 Congress gave the President authority to set aside national forest reserves. By 1902 John Muir had established the Sierra Club and by 1903 Muir and President Theodore Roosevelt had toured the Sierras and Burroughs had taken the President to Yellowstone. Muir and Burroughs greatly influenced Roosevelt, who established the Grand Canyon National Monument in 1908. From 1873–1913 *Century Magazine* was in the forefront of the national conservation cause and did much to awaken the public to the problem of depleted natural resources. The Sierra Club, President Roosevelt, the American Scenic and Historic Preservation Society (1895), and Gifford Pinchot all worked together in a massive effort that combined the ethical, economic, and national security grounds for conservation. By 1916 there were thirty-seven national parks. But perhaps the most significant and successful event of this crucial transitional period was the 1908 Conference of Governors held by Roosevelt at the White House to lay the foundation for America's future conservation policy. J. Horace McFarland, President of the American Civic Association, presented the opening speech at the conference, a speech that suggests how great a distance from the Puritan vision and de Tocqueville's America many Americans had come. It would, from this point on, be up to future generations to preserve that distance and continue the fight.

The true glory of the United States," McFarland argued, "must rest, and has rested, upon a deeper foundation than that of her purely material resources. It is the love of country that lights . . . the holy fire of patriotism. And this love is excited primarily by the beauty of the country." McFarland frankly scourged his countrymen for the too-frequent presence of "careless commercial filth." And he went on to look toward a brighter future if only Americans wanted it. "We have for a century . . . stood actually, if not ostensibly, for an uglier America; let us here and now resolve, for every patriotic and economic reason, to stand openly and solidly for a more beautiful and therefore a more prosperous America."

William Byrd
1674-1774

Son of a wealthy Virginian, educated in England, member of the British Royal Society at twenty-two, William Byrd became an important public figure in America after returning from England to his native Virginia. There he inherited 26,000 acres after his father's death, was elected to the House of Burgess, and founded the city of Richmond. On his plantation he exemplified the Virginian gentleman, the early type of the tolerant southern patrician who would later play so great a role in the American Revolution. His library was one of the largest in colonial America, and his *Secret Diaries* (1709-1712 and 1739-1741), not published until the twentieth century, established his learning, his humanity, and his literary standing in American literature for future generations. But it is his *History of the Dividing Line Run in the Year 1728,* written for his own record and amusement, that most concerns us here. It is one of the earliest classics of American "wilderness literature."

As Chief Virginia Commissioner, Byrd was appointed in 1728 to join a party charged with settling the boundary dispute between Virginia and North Carolina. He wrote of his travels on the commission and drew sharp pictures of early life in the frontier, of Indians, and of the natural world he found in the wilderness. Like the more observant, if rare, of his contemporaries, Byrd sympathized with the already displaced Indians, but he refused to make "noble savages" of them and deny what he had observed of their, to him, barbaric and unhygienic practices. A practical man who was as at home with the urban sophisticates of London as with plain settlers and Indians, Byrd was not beyond arguing that a swamp be drained for its agricultural potential while fully aware of the natural uses of swamps and the beauties of mountains and primitive forests.

from THE HISTORY OF THE DIVIDING LINE*

October 1, 1728. At a small distance from our camp we crossed Great creek, and about seven miles further Nut-bush creek, so called from the many hazel-trees growing upon it. By good luck many branches of these creeks were full of reeds, to the great comfort of our horses. Near five miles from thence we encamped on a branch that runs into Nut-bush creek, where those reeds flourished more than ordinary. The land we marched over was for the most part broken and stony, and in some places covered over with thickets almost impenetrable. At night the surveyors, taking advantge of a clear sky, made a third trial of the variation, and found it still something less than three degrees, so that it did not diminish by advancing towards the west, or by approaching the mountains, nor yet by increasing our distance from the sea; but remained much the same we found it at Coratuck inlet. One of our Indians killed a large fawn, which was very welcome, though, like Hudibras' horse, it had hardly flesh enough to cover its bones. In the low grounds the Carolina gentlemen showed us another plant, which they said was used in their country to cure the bite of the rattlesnake. It put forth several leaves in figure like a heart, and was clouded so like the common Assa-rabacca, that I conceived it to be of that family.

2d. So soon as the horses could be found, we hurried away the surveyors, who advanced the line nine miles and two hundred and fifty-four poles. About three miles from the camp they crossed a large creek, which the Indians called Massamoni, signifying, in their language, Paint creek, because of the great quantity of red ocher found in its banks. This in every fresh tinges the water just as the same mineral did formerly, and to this day continues to tinge, the famous river Adonis, in Phoenicia, by which there hangs a celebrated fable. Three miles beyond that we passed another water with difficulty, called Yapatsco, or Beaver creek. Those industrious animals had dammed up the water so high, that we had much ado to get over. It is hardly credible how much work of this kind they will do in space of one night. They bite young saplings into proper lengths with their fore-teeth, which are exceeding strong and sharp, and afterwards drag them to the place where they intend to stop the water. Then they know how to join timber and earth together with so much skill, that their work is able to resist the most violent flood that can happen. In this they are qualified to instruct their betters, it being certain their dams will stand firm when the strongest that are made by men will be carried down the stream. We observed very broad low grounds upon this creek, with a growth of large trees, and all the other signs of fertility, but seemed subject to be everywhere overflowed in a fresh. The certain way to catch these sagacious animals is this: Squeeze all the juice out of the large pride of the beaver, and six drops out of the small pride. Powder the inward bark of sassafras, and mix it with this juice, then bait therewith a steel trap, and they will eagerly come to it, and be taken.

About three miles and a half further we came to the banks of another

*From *A Journey to the Land of Eden and Other Papers*, ed. Mark Van Doren (New York: Vanguard Press, 1928).

creek, called, in the Saponi language, Ohimpa-moni, signifying Jumping creek, from the frequent jumping of fish during the spring season.

Here we encamped, and by the time the horses were hobbled, our hunters brought us no less than a brace and a half of deer, which made great plenty, and consequently great content in our quarters. Some of our people had shot a great wild cat, which was that fatal moment making a comfortable meal upon a fox-squirrel, and an ambitious sportsman of our company claimed the merit of killing this monster after it was dead. The wild cat is as big again as any household cat, and much the fiercest inhabitant of the woods. Whenever it is disabled, it will tear its own flesh for madness. Although a panther will run away from a man, a wild cat will only make a surly retreat, and now and then facing about, if he be too closely pursued; and will even pursue in his turn, if he observe the least sign of fear or even of caution in those that pretend to follow him. The flesh of this beast, as well as of the panther, is as white as veal, and altogether as sweet and delicious.

3d. We got to work early this morning, and carried the line eight miles and a hundred and sixty poles. We forded several runs of excellent water, and afterwards traversed a large level of high land full of lofty walnut, poplar, and white oak trees, which are certain proofs of a fruitful soil. This level was near two miles in length, and of an unknown breadth, quite out of danger of being over-flowed, which is a misfortune most of the low grounds are liable to in those parts. As we marched along we saw many buffalo tracks, and abundance of their dung very fresh, but could not have the pleasure of seeing them. They either smelt us out, having that sense very quick, or else were alarmed at the noise that so many people must necessarily make in marching along. At the sight of a man they will snort and grunt, cock up their ridiculous short tails, and tear up the ground with a sort of timorous fury. These wild cattle hardly ever range alone, but herd together like those that are tame. They are seldom seen so far north as forty degrees of latitude, delighting much in canes and reeds, which grow generally more southerly.

We quartered on the banks of a creek that the inhabitants call Tewahominy, or Tuskarooda creek, because one of that nation had been killed thereabouts, and his body thrown into the creek.

Our people had the fortune to kill a brace of does, one of which we presented to the Carolina gentlemen, who were glad to partake of the bounty of Providence, at the same time that they sneered at us for depending upon it.

4th. We hurried away the surveyors about nine this morning, who extended the line seven miles and a hundred and sixty poles, notwithstanding the ground was exceedingly uneven. At the distance of five miles we forded a stream to which we gave the name of Bluewing creek, because of the great number of those fowls that then frequented it. About two and a half miles beyond that, we came upon Sugar-tree creek, so called from the many trees of that kind that grow upon it. By tapping this tree, in the first warm weather in February, one may get from twenty to forty gallons of liquor, very sweet to the taste and agreeable to the stomach. This may be boiled into molasses first, and afterwards into very good sugar, allowing about ten gallons of the liquor to make a pound. There is no doubt, too, that a very fine spirit may be distilled from the molasses, at least as good as rum. The sugar tree delights only in rich ground, where it grows very tall, and by the softness and sponginess of the wood should be a quick grower. Near this creek we discovered likewise several spice trees, the leaves of which are fragrant, and the berries they bear are black when dry, and of a hot taste, not much unlike pepper. The low grounds upon the creek are very wide, sometimes on one side, sometimes on the other; though most commonly upon the opposite shore the highland advances close to the bank, only on the north side of the line it spreads itself into a great breadth of rich low ground on both sides the creek for four miles together, as far as this stream runs into Hico river, whereof I shall presently make mention. One of our men spied three buffaloes, but his piece being loaded only with goose-shot, he was able to make no effectual impression on their thick hides; however, this disappointment was made up by a brace of bucks, and as many wild turkeys, killed by the rest of the company. Thus Providence was very bountiful to our endeavors, never disappointing those that faithfully rely upon it, and pray heartily for their daily bread,

. . .

7th. We had now no other drink but what Adam drank in Paradise, though to our comfort we found the water excellent, by the help of which we perceived our appetites to mend, our slumbers to sweeten, the stream of life to run cool and peaceably in our veins, and if ever we dreamed of women, they were kind. Our men killed a very fat buck and several turkeys. These two kinds of meat boiled together, with the addition of a little rice or French barley, made excellent soup, and what happens rarely in other good things, it never cloyed, no more than an engaging wife would do, by being a constant dish. Our Indian was very superstitious in this matter, and told us, with a face full of concern, that if we continued to boil venison and turkey together, we should for the future kill nothing, because the spirit that presided over the woods would drive all the game out of our sight. But we had the happiness to find this an idle superstition, and though his argument could not convince us, yet our repeated experience at last, with much ado, convinced him. We observed abundance of colt's foot and maiden-hair in many places, and no where a larger quantity than here. They are both excellent pectoral plants, and seem to have greater virtues much in this part of the world than in more northern climates; and I believe it may pass for a rule in botanics, that where any vegetable is planted by the hand of nature, it has more virtue than in places whereto it is transplanted by the curiosity of man.

8th. Notwithstanding we hurried away the surveyors very early, yet the underwoods embarrassed them so much that they could with difficulty advance the line four miles and twenty poles. Our clothes suffered extremely by the bushes, and it was really as much as both our hands could do to preserve our eyes in our heads. Our poor horses, too, could hardly drag their loads through the saplings, which stood so close together that it was necessary for them to draw and carry at the same time. We quartered near a spring of very fine water, as soft as oil and as cold as ice, to make us amends for the want of wine. And our Indian knocked down a very fat doe, just time enough to hinder us from going supperless to bed. The heavy baggage could not come up with us, because of the excessive badness of the ways. This gave us no small uneasiness, but it went worse with the poor men that guarded it. They had nothing in the world with them but dry bread, nor durst they eat any of that, for fear of inflamming their thirst, in a place where they could find no water to quench it. This was, however, the better to be endured, because it was the first fast any one had kept during the whole journey, and then, thanks to the gracious Guardian of the woods! there was no more than a single meal lost to a few of the company. We were entertained this night with the yell of a whole family of wolves, in which we could distinguish the treble, tenor and bass very clearly. These beasts of prey kept pretty much upon our track, being tempted by the garbage of the creatures we killed every day; for which we were serenaded with their shrill pipes almost every night. This beast is not so untameable as the panther, but the Indians know how to gentle their whelps, and use them about their cabins instead of dogs.

9th. The thickets were hereabouts so impenetrable, that we were obliged, at first setting off this morning, to order four pioneers to clear the way before the surveyors. But, after about two miles of these rough woods, we had the pleasure to meet with open grounds and not very uneven, by the help of which we were enabled to push the line about six miles. The baggage that lay short of our camp last night came up about noon, and the men made heavy complaints, that they had been half starved, like Tantalus, in the midst of plenty, for the reason above mentioned.

The soil we passed over this day was generally very good, being clothed with large trees, of popular, hickory and oak. But another certain token of its fertility was, that wild angelica grew plentifully upon it. The root of this plant, being very warm and aromatic, is coveted by woodsmen extremely as a dry dram, that is, when rum, that cordial for all distresses, is wanting. Several deer came into our view as we marched along, but none into the pot, which made it necessary for us to sup on the fragments we had been so provident as to carry along with us. This being but a temperate repast, made some of our hungry fellows call the place we lodged at that night, Bread and Water Camp.

A great flock of cranes flew over our quarters, that were exceeding clamorous in their flight. They seem to steer their course towards the south (being birds of passage) in quest of warmer weather. They only took this country in their way, being as rarely met with, in this part of the world, as a highwayman or a beggar. These birds travel generally in flocks, and when they roost they place sentinels upon some of the highest trees, which constantly stand upon one leg to keep themselves waking.*

Our Indian killed nothing all day but a mountain partridge, which a little resembled the common partridge in the plumage, but was near as large as a dunghill hen. These are very frequent towards the mountains, though we had the fortune to meet with very few. They are apt to be shy, and consequently the noise of so great a number of people might easily scare them away from our sight. We found what we conceived to be good limestone in several places, and a great quantity of blue slate.

10th. The day began very fortunately by killing a fat doe, and two brace of wild turkeys; so the plenty of the morning made amends for the short commons over night. One of the new men we brought out with us the last time was unfortunately heard to wish himself at home, and for that show of impatience was publicly reprimanded at the head of the men, who were all drawn up to witness his disgrace. He was asked how he came so soon to be tired of the company of so many brave fellows, and whether it was the danger or the fatigue of the journey that disheartened him? This public reproof from thenceforward put an effectual stop to all complaints, and not a man amongst us after that pretended so much as to wish himself in Paradise. A small distance from our camp we crossed a pleasant stream of water called Cocquade creek, and something more than a mile from thence our line intersected the south branch of Roanoke river the first time, which we called the Dan. It was about two hundred yards wide where we forded it, and when we came over to the west side, we found the banks lined with a forest of tall canes, that grew more than a furlong in depth. So that it cost us abundance of time and labor to cut a passage through them wide enough for our baggage. In the meantime we had leisure to take a full view of this charming river. The stream, which was perfectly clear, ran down about two knots, or two miles, an hour, when the water was at the lowest. The bottom was covered with a coarse gravel, spangled very thick with a shining substance, that almost dazzled the eye, and the sand upon either shore sparkled with the same splendid particles. At first sight, the sunbeams giving a yellow cast to these spangles made us fancy them to be gold dust, and consequently that all our fortunes were made. Such hopes as these were the less extravagant, because several rivers lying much about the same latitude with this have formerly abounded with fragments of that tempting metal. Witness the Tagus in Portugal, the Heber in Thrace, and the Pactolus in Lesser Asia; not to mention the rivers on the Gold Coast in Africa, which lie in a more southern climate. But we soon found ourselves mistaken, and our gold dust dwindled into small flakes of isinglass. However, though this did not make the river so rich as we could wish, yet it made it exceedingly

*Nor are these birds the only animals that appoint scouts to keep the main body from being surprised. For the baboons, whenever they go upon any mischievous expedition, such as robbing an orchard, place sentinels to look out towards every point of the compass, and give notice of any danger. Then ranking themselves in one file, that reaches from the mountain where they harbor, to the orchard they intend to rob, some of them toss the fruits from the trees to those that stand nearest, these throw them to the next, and so from one to the other, till the fruit is all secured in a few minutes out of harm's way. In the meantime, if any of the scouts should be careless at their posts, and suffer any surprise, they are torn to pieces without mercy. In case of danger these sentinels set up a fearful cry, upon which the rest take the alarm, and scour away to the mountains as fast as they can.

beautiful. We marched about two miles and a half beyond this river, as far as Cane creek, so called from a prodigious quantity of tall canes that fringed the banks of it. On the west side of this creek we marked out our quarters, and were glad to find our horses fond of the canes, though they scoured them smartly at first, and discolored their dung. This beautiful vegetable grows commonly from twelve to sixteen feet high, and some of them as thick as a man's wrist. Though these appeared large to us, yet they are no more than spires of grass, if compared to those which some curious travelers tell us grow in the East Indies, one joint of which will make a brace of canoes, if sawed in two in the middle. Ours continue green through all the seasons during the space of six years, and the seventh shed their seed, wither away and die. The spring following they begin to shoot again, and reach their former stature the second or third year after. They grow so thick, and their roots lace together so firmly, that they are the best guard that can be of the river bank, which would otherwise be washed away by the frequent inundations that happen in this part of the world. They would also serve excellently well to plant on the borders of fish-ponds and canals, to secure their sides from falling in; though I fear they would not grow kindly in a cold country, being seldom seen here so northerly as thirty-eight degrees of latitude.

11th. At the distance of four miles and sixty poles from the place where we encamped, we came upon the river Dan a second time; though it was not so wide in this place as where we crossed it first, being not above a hundred and fifty yards over. The west shore continued to be covered with the canes above mentioned, but not to so great a breadth as before, and it is remarkable that these canes are much more frequent on the west side of the river than on the east, where they grow generally very scattering. It was still a beautiful stream, rolling down its limpid and murmuring waters among the rocks, which lay scattered here and there, to make up the variety of the prospect. It was about two miles from this river to the end of our day's work, which led us mostly over broken grounds and troublesome underwoods. Hereabout, from one of the highest hills, we made the first discovery of the mountains, on the northwest of our course. They seemed to lie off at a vast distance, and looked like ranges of blue clouds rising one above another. We encamped about two miles beyond the river, where we made good cheer upon a very fat buck, that luckily fell in our way. The Indian likewise shot a wild turkey, but confessed he would not bring it us, lest we should continue to provoke the guardian of the forest, by cooking the beasts of the field and the birds of the air together in one vessel. This instance of Indian superstition, I confess, is countenanced in some measure by the Levitical law, which forbade the mixing things of a different nature together in the same field, or in the same garment, and why not then in the same kettle? But, after all, if the jumbling of two sorts of flesh together be a sin, how intolerable an offense must it be to make a Spanish olla, that is, a hotchpotch of every kind of thing that is eatable? And the good people of England would have a great deal to answer for, for beating up so many different ingredients into a pudding.

12th. We were so cruelly entangled with bushes and grapevines all day, that we could advance the line no farther than five miles and twenty-eight poles. The vines grow very thick in these woods, twining lovingly round the trees almost everywhere, especially to the saplings. This makes it evident how natural both the soil and climate of this country are to vines, though I believe most to our own vines. The grapes we commonly met with were black, though there be two or three kinds of white grapes that grow wild. The black are very sweet, but small, because the strength of the vine spends itself in wood; though without question a proper culture would make the same grapes both larger and sweeter. But, with all these disadvantages, I have drunk tolerable good wine pressed from them, though made without skill. There is then good reason to believe it might admit of great improvement, if rightly managed. Our Indian killed a bear, two years old, that was feasting on these grapes. He was very fat, as they generally are in that season of the year. In the fall, the flesh of this animal has a high relish, different from that of other creatures, though inclining nearest to that of pork, or rather of wild boar. A true woodsman prefers this sort of meat to that of the fattest venison, not only for the *haut gout,* but also because the fat of it is well tasted, and never rises in the stomach. Another proof of the goodness of this meat is, that it is less apt to corrupt than any other with which we are acquainted. As agreeable as such rich diet was to the men, yet we who were not accustomed to it, tasted it at first with some sort of squeamishness, that animal being of the dog kind; though a little use soon reconciled us to this American venison. And that its being of the dog kind might give us the less disgust, we had the example of that ancient and polite people, the Chinese, who reckon dog's flesh too good for any under the quality of a mandarin. This beast is in truth a very clean feeder, living, while the season lasts, upon acorns, chestnuts and chinquapins, wild honey and wild grapes. They are naturally not carnivorous, unless hunger constrain them to it, after the mast is all gone, and the product of the woods quite exhausted. They are not provident enough to lay up any hoard, like the squirrels, nor can they, after all, live very long upon licking their paws, as sir John Mandevil and some other travelers tell us, but are forced in the winter months to quit the mountains, and visit the inhabitants. Their errand is then to surprise a poor hog at a pinch to keep from starving. And to show that they are not flesh-eaters by trade, they devour their prey very awkwardly. They do not kill it right out, and feast upon its blood and entrails, like other ravenous beasts, but having, after a fair pursuit, seized it with their paws, they begin first upon the rump, and so devour one collop after another, till they come to the vitals, the poor animals crying all the while, for several minutes together. However, in so doing, Bruin acts a little imprudently, because the dismal outcry of the hog alarms the neighborhood, and it is odds but he pays the forfeit with his life, before he can secure his retreat. But bears soon grow weary of this unnatural diet, and about January, when there is nothing to be gotten in the woods, they retire into some cave or hollow tree, where they sleep away two or three months very comfortably. But then they quit their holes in March, when the fish begin to run up the rivers, on which they are forced to keep Lent, till some fruit or berry comes in season. But bears are fondest of chestnuts, which grow plentifully towards the mountains, upon very large trees, where the soil happens to be rich. We were curious to know how it happened that many of the outward branches of those trees came to be broken off in that solitary place, and were informed that the bears are so discreet as not to trust their unwieldly bodies on the smaller limbs of the tree, that would not bear their weight; but after venturing as far as is safe, which they can judge to an inch, they bit off the end of the branch, which falling down, they are content to finish their repast upon the ground. In the same cautious manner they secure the acorns that grow on the weaker limbs of the oak. And it must be allowed that, in these instances, a bear carries instinct a great way, and acts more reasonably than many of his betters, who indiscreetly venture upon frail projects that will not bear them.

13th. This being Sunday, we rested from our fatigue, and had leisure to reflect on the signal mercies of Providence.

The great plenty of meat wherewith Bearskin furnished us in these lonely woods made us once more shorten the men's allowance of bread, from five to four pounds of biscuit a week. This was the more necessary, because we knew not yet how long our business might require us to be out.

In the afternoon our hunters went forth, and returned triumphantly with three brace of wild turkeys. They told us they could see the mountains distinctly from every eminence, though the atmosphere was so thick with smoke that they appeared at a greater distance than they really were.

In the evening we examined our friend Bearskin, concerning the religion of his country, and he explained it to us, without any of that reserve to which his nation is subject. He told us he believed there was one supreme God, who had several subaltern deities under him. And that this master God made the world a long time ago. That he told the sun, the moon, and stars, their business in the beginning, which they, with good looking after, have faithfully performed ever since. That the same Power that made all things at first has taken care to keep them in the same method and motion ever since. He believed that God had formed many worlds before he formed this, but that those worlds either grew old and ruinous, or were destroyed for the dishonesty of the inhabitants. That God is very just and very good—ever well pleased with those men who possess those god-like qualities. That he takes good people into his safe protection, makes them very rich, fills their bellies plentifully, preserves them from sickness, and from being surprised or overcome by their enemies. But all such as tell lies, and cheat those they have dealings with, he never fails to punish with sickness, poverty and hunger, and, after all that, suffers them to be knocked on the head and scalped by those that fight against them. He believed that after death both good and bad people are conducted by a strong guard into a great road, in which departed souls travel together for some time, till at a certain distance this road forks into two paths, the one extremely level, and the other stony and mountainous. Here the good are parted from the bad by a flash of lightning, the first being hurried away to the right, the other to the left. The right hand road leads to a charming warm country, where the spring is everlasting, and every month is May; and as the year is always in its youth, so are the people, and particularly the women are bright as stars, and never scold. That in this happy climate there are deer, turkeys, elks, and buffaloes innumerable, perpetually fat and gentle, while the trees are loaded with delicious fruit quite throughout the four seasons. That the soil brings forth corn spontaneously, without the curse of labor, and so very wholesome, that none who have the happiness to eat of it are ever sick, grow old, or die. Near the entrance into this blessed land sits a venerable old man on a mat richly woven, who examines strictly all that are brought before him, and if they have behaved well, the guards are ordered to open the crystal gate, and let them enter into the land of delight. The left hand path is very rugged and uneven, leading to a dark and barren country, where it is always winter. The ground is the whole year round covered with snow, and nothing is to be seen upon the trees but icicles. All the people are hungry, yet have not a morsel of anything to eat, except a bitter kind of potato, that gives them the dry gripes, and fills their whole body with loathsome ulcers, that stink, and are insupportably painful. Here all the women are old and ugly, having claws like a panther, with which they fly upon the men that slight their passion. For it seems these haggard old furies are intolerably fond, and expect a vast deal of cherishing. They talk much, and exceedingly shrill, giving exquisite pain to the drum of the ear, which in that place of torment is so tender, that every sharp note wounds it to the quick. At the end of this path sits a dreadful old women on a monstrous toad-stool, whose head is covered with rattle-snakes instead of tresses, with glaring white eyes, that strike a terror unspeakable into all that behold her. This hag pronounces sentence of woe upon all the miserable wretches that hold up their hands at her tribunal. After this they are delivered over to huge turkey-buzzards, like harpies, that fly away with them to the place above mentioned. Here, after they have been tormented a certain number of years, according to their several degrees of guilt, they are again driven back into this world, to try if they will mend their manners, and merit a place the next time in the regions of bliss. This was the substance of Bearskin's religion, and was as much to the purpose as could be expected from a mere state of nature, without one glimpse of revelation or philosophy. It contained, however, the three great articles of natural religion: the belief of a God; the moral distinction betwixt good and evil; and the expectation of rewards and punishments in another world. Indeed, the Indian notion of a future happiness is a little gross and sensual, like Mahomet's paradise. But how can it be otherwise, in a people that are contented with Nature as they find her, and have no other lights but what they receive from purblind tradition?

. . .

25th. The air clearing up this morning, we were again agreeably surprised with a full prospect of the mountains. They discovered themselves both to the north and south of us, on either side, not distant above ten miles, according to our best computation. We could now see those to the north rise in four distinct ledges, one above another, but those to the south formed only a single ledge, and that broken and interrupted in many places; or rather they were only single mountains detached from each other. One of the southern mountains was so vastly high, it seemed to hide its head in the clouds, and the west end of it terminated in a horrible precipice, that we called the Despairing Lover's Leap. The next to it, towards the east, was lower, except at one end, where it heaved itself up in the form of a vast stack of chimneys. The course of the northern mountains seemed to tend west-southwest, and those to the southward very near west. We could descry other mountains ahead of us, exactly in the course of the line, though at a much greater distance. In this point of view, the ledges on the right and left both seemed to close, and form a natural amphitheater. Thus it was our fortune to be wedged in betwixt these two ranges of mountains, insomuch that if our line had run ten miles on either side, it had butted before this day either upon one or the other, both of them now stretching away plainly to the eastward of us. It had rained a little in the night, which dispersed the smoke and opened this romantic scene to us all at once, though it was again hid from our eyes as we moved forward, by the rough woods we had the misfortune to be engaged with. The bushes were so thick for near four miles together, that they tore the deer skins to pieces that guarded the bread bags. Though, as rough as the woods were, the soil was extremely good all the way, being washed down from the neighboring hills into the plain country. Notwithstanding all these difficulties, the surveyors drove on the line four miles and two hundred and five poles.

In the meantime we were so unlucky as to meet with no sort of game the whole day, so that the men were obliged to make a frugal distribution of what little they left in the morning. We encamped upon a small rill, where the horses came off as temperately as their masters. They were by this time grown so thin, by hard travel and spare feeding, that henceforth, in pure compassion, we chose to perform the greater part of the journey on foot. And as our baggage was by this time grown much lighter, we divided it, after the best manner, so that every horse's load might be proportioned to the strength he had left. Though, after all the prudent measures we could take, we perceived the hills began to rise upon us so fast in our front, that it would be impossible for us to proceed much farther.

We saw very few squirrels in the upper parts, because the wild cats devour them unmercifully. Of these there are four kinds: the fox squirrel, the gray, the flying, and the ground squirrel. These last resemble a rat in everything but the tail, and the black and russet streaks that run down the length of their little bodies.

. . .

Nov. 10th. In a dearth of provisions our chaplain pronounced it lawful to make bold with the sabbath, and send a party out a-hunting. They fired the dry leaves in a ring of five miles' circumference, which, burning inwards, drove all the game to the center, where they were easily killed. It is really a pitiful sight to see the extreme distress the poor deer are in, when they find themselves surrounded with this circle of fire; they weep and groan like a human creature, yet cannot move the compassion of those hard-hearted people, who are about to murder them. This unmerciful sport is called fire hunting, and is much practiced by the Indians and frontier inhabitants who sometimes, in the eagerness of their diversion, are punished for their cruelty, and are hurt by one another when they shoot across at the deer which are in the middle. What the Indians do now by a circle of fire, the ancient Persians performed formerly by a circle of men: and the same is practiced at this day in Germany upon extraordinary occasions, when any of the princes of the empire have a mind to make a general hunt, as they call it. At such times they order a vast number of people to surround a whole territory. Then marching inwards in close order, they at last force all the wild beasts into a narrow compass, that the prince and his company may have the diversion of slaughtering as many as they please with their own hands. Our hunters massacred two brace of deer after this unfair way, of which they brought us one brace whole, and only the primings of the rest.

So many were absent on this occasion, that we who remained excused the chaplain from the trouble of spending his spirits by preaching to so thin a congregation. One of the men, who had been an old Indian trader, brought me a stem of silk grass, which was about as big as my little finger. But, being so late in the year that the leaf was fallen off, I am not able to describe the plant. The Indians use it in all their little manufactures, twisting a thread of it that is prodigiously strong. Of this they make their baskets and the aprons which their women wear about their middles, for decency's sake. These are long enough to wrap quite round them and reach down to their knees, with a fringe on the under part by way of ornament. They put on this modest covering with so much art, that the most impertinent curiosity cannot in the negligentest of their motions or postures make the least discovery. As this species of silk grass is much stronger than hemp, I make no doubt but sail cloth and cordage might be made of it with considerable improvement.

11th. We had all been so refreshed by our day of rest, that we decamped earlier than ordinary, and passed the several fords of Hico river. The woods were thick great part of this day's journey, so that we were forced to scuffle hard to advance seven miles, being equal in fatigue to double that distance of clear and open grounds. We took up our quarters upon Sugar-tree creek, in the same camp we had lain in when we came up, and happened to be entertained at supper with a rarity we had never had the fortune to meet with before, during the whole expedition. A little wide of this creek, one of the men had the luck to meet with a young buffalo of two years old. It was a bull, which, notwithstanding he was no older, was as big as an ordinary ox. His legs were very thick and very short, and his hoofs exceeding broad. His back rose into a kind of bunch a little above the shoulders, which I believe contributes not a little to that creature's enormous strength. His body is vastly deep from the shoulders to the brisket, sometimes six feet in those that are full grown. The portly figure of this animal is disgraced by a shabby little tail, not above twelve inches long. This he cocks up on end whenever he is in a passion, and, instead of lowing or bellowing, grunts with no better grace than a hog. The hair growing on his head and neck is long and shagged, and so soft that it will spin into thread not unlike mohair, which might be wove into a sort of camlet. Some people have stockings knit of it, that would have served an Israelite during his forty years' march through the wilderness. Its horns are short and strong, of which the Indians make large spoons, which they say will split and fall to pieces whenever poison is put into them. Its color is a dirty brown, and its hide so thick that it is scarce penetrable. However, it makes very spongy sole leather by the ordinary method of tanning, though this fault might by good contrivance be mended. As thick as this poor beast's hide was, a bullet made shift to enter it and fetch him down. It was found all alone, though buffaloes seldom are. They usually range about in herds, like other cattle, and, though they differ something in figure, are certainly of the same species. There are two reasons for this opinion: the flesh of both has exactly the same taste, and the mixed breed betwixt both, they say, will generate. All the difference I could perceive between the flesh of buffalo and common beef was, that the flesh of the first was much yellower than that of the other, and the lean something tougher. The men were so delighted with this new diet, that the gridiron and frying-pan had no more rest all night, than a poor husband subject to curtain lectures. Buffaloes may be easily tamed when they are taken young. The best way to catch them is to carry a milch mare into the woods, and when you find a cow and calf, to kill the cow, and then having caught the calf, to suckle it upon the mare. After once or twice sucking her, it will follow her home, and become as gentle as another calf. If we could get into a breed of them, they might be made very useful, not only for the dairy, by giving an ocean of milk, but also for drawing vast and cumbersome weights by their prodigious strength. These, with the other advantages I mentioned before, would make this sort of cattle more profitable to the owner, than any other we are acquainted with, though they would need a world of provendor.

St. Jean de Crèvecoeur
1735-1813

As a soldier and surveyor a much-traveled and aristocratic young man, Michel-Guillaume St. Jean de Crèvecoeur knew the forest, the Indians, and the villages and farms in America. Arriving here from France by way of Canada about 1759, he became one of the greatest optimistic spokesmen for early American democracy and agricultural self-reliance at a time when ninety percent of Americans lived on the soil.

We see in Crèvecoeur a shift in American nature writing from wilderness to the rural and agrarian, to the depiction of men and women laboring together to provide food, clothing, and shelter for themselves and their children. Crèvecoeur remained closer to the realism of the georgic, however, than to the pastoral tradition and its tendency toward idealism and fantasy. His first book, *Letters from an American Farmer* (1782), shows that he had traveled in Nova Scotia, Martha's Vineyard, Massachusetts, Connecticut, Pennsylvania, and New York before settling in the Hudson Valley at "Pine Hill Farm" from 1765 until the Revolution. He married in 1769.

Letters was popular in Europe, and it is easy to see why. Using the popular device of presenting letters to an inquiring, if imagined, friend, the book combines close observations of animals and insects with observations of the transforming American frontier. The delights, details, and labors of early agricultural life still interest readers today. Although he himself farmed, Crèvecoeur's references to some events and family members in the *Letters* are not strictly autobiographical, but intended to flesh out a composite portrait of the American farmer living the good, if industrious and frugal, agrarian life.

Crèvecoeur joined the late eighteenth-century movement—led by the Connecticut clergyman Jared Eliot—that was devoted to the scientific improvement of agriculture. This movement drew the interest of men of stature such as Washington and Jefferson, and it did indeed help revolutionize farming practices. Crèvecoeur himself also helped establish the New Haven botanical gardens and eventually became a member of the French Academy of Science.

Despite his faith in colonial agrarianism and democracy, Crèvecoeur's aristocratic background lent his writings a tone of Royalist sympathy before the American Revolution. Pressured from both sides in the conflict, he and his son were driven from their home and on to France in 1780, where his literary reputation flourished. Upon his return to America as French Consul in 1783, he found his other children safe in Boston, but his wife dead and his farm destroyed by an Indian raid. He spent the last twenty years of his life back in France, devoting much time and energy to the French Revolution.

from LETTERS FROM AN AMERICAN FARMER*

LETTER II

ON THE SITUATION, FEELINGS, AND PLEASURES, OF AN AMERICAN FARMER

As you are the first enlightened European I have ever had the pleasure of being acquainted with, you will not be surprised that I should, according to your earnest desire and my promise, appear anxious of preserving your friendship and correspondence. By your accounts, I observe a material difference subsists between your husbandry, modes, and customs, and ours; everything is local; could we enjoy the advantages of the English farmer, we should be much happier, indeed, but this wish, like many others, implies a contradiction; and could the English farmer have some of those privileges we possess, they would be the first of their class in the world. Good and evil I see is to be found in all societies, and it is in vain to seek for any spot where those ingredients are not mixed. I therefore rest satisfied, and thank God that my lot is to be an American farmer, instead of a Russian boor, or an Hungarian peasant. I thank you kindly for the idea, however dreadful, which you have given me of their lot and condition; your observations have confirmed me in the justness of my ideas, and I am happier now than I thought myself before. It is strange that misery, when viewed in others, should become to us a sort of real good, though I am far from rejoicing to hear that there are in the world men so thoroughly wretched; they are no doubt as harmless, industrious, and willing to work as we are. Hard is their fate to be thus condemned to a slavery worse than that of our negroes. Yet when young I entertained some thoughts of selling my farm. I thought it afforded but a dull repetition of the same labours and pleasures. I thought the former tedious and heavy, the latter few and insipid; but when I came to consider myself as divested of my farm, I then found the world so wide, and every place so full, that I began to fear lest there would be no room for me. My farm, my house, my barn, presented to my imagination objects from which I adduced quite new ideas; they were more forcible than before. Why should not I find myself happy, said I, where my father was before? He left me no good books it is true, he gave me

*From *Letters from an American Farmer,* ed. Warren Barton Blake (New York: E. P. Dutton, 1912 & 26)

no other education than the art of reading and writing; but he left me a good farm, and his experience; he left me free from debts, and no kind of difficulties to struggle with. —I married, and this perfectly reconciled me to my situation; my wife rendered my house all at once cheerful and pleasing; it no longer appeared gloomy and solitary as before; when I went to work in my fields I worked with more alacrity and sprightliness; I felt that I did not work for myself alone, and this encouraged me much. My wife would often come with her knitting in her hand, and sit under the shady trees, praising the straightness of my furrows, and the docility of my horses; this swelled my heart and made everything light and pleasant, and I regretted that I had not married before.

I felt myself happy in my new situation, and where is that station which can confer a more substantial system of felicity than that of an American farmer, possessing freedom of action, freedom of thoughts, ruled by a mode of government which requires but little from us? I owe nothing, but a pepper corn to my country, a small tribute to my king, with loyalty and due respect; I know no other landlord than the lord of all land, to whom I owe the most sincere gratitude. My father left me three hundred and seventy-one acres of land, forty-seven of which are good timothy meadow, an excellent orchard, a good house, and a substantial barn. It is my duty to think how happy I am that he lived to build and to pay for all these improvements; what are the labours which I have to undergo, what are my fatigues when compared to his, who had everything to do, from the first tree he felled to the finishing of his house? Every year I kill from 1500 to 2000 weight of pork, 1200 of beef, half a dozen of good wethers in harvest: of fowls my wife has always a great stock: what can I wish more? My negroes are tolerably faithful and healthy; by a long series of industry and honest dealings, my father left behind him the name of a good man; I have but to tread his paths to be happy and a good man like him. I know enough of the law to regulate my little concerns with propriety, nor do I dread its power; these are the grand outlines of my situation, but as I can feel much more than I am able to express, I hardly know how to proceed.

When my first son was born, the whole train of my ideas were suddenly altered; never was there a charm that acted so quickly and powerfully; I ceased to ramble in imagination through the wide world; my excursions since have not exceeded the bounds of my farm, and all my principal pleasures are now centred within its scanty limits: but at the same time there is not an operation belonging to it in which I do not find some food for useful reflections. This is the reason, I suppose, that when you was here, you used, in your refined style, to denominate me the farmer of feelings; how rude must those feelings be in him who daily holds the axe or the plough, how much more refined on the contrary those of the European, whose mind is improved by education, example, books, and by every acquired advantage! Those feelings, however, I will delineate as well as I can, agreeably to your earnest request.

When I contemplate my wife, by my fire-side, while she either spins, knits, darns, or suckles our child, I cannot describe the various emotions of love, of gratitude, of conscious pride, which thrill in my heart and often overflow in involuntary tears. I feel the necessity, the sweet pleasure of acting my part, the part of an husband and father, with an attention and propriety which may entitle me to my good fortune. It is true these pleasing images vanish with the smoke of my pipe, but though they disappear from my mind, the impression they have made on my heart is indelible. When I play with the infant, my warm imagination runs forward, and eagerly anticipates his future temper and constitution. I would willingly open the book of fate, and know in which page his destiny is delineated; alas! where is the father who in those moments of paternal ecstasy can delineate one half of the thoughts which dilate his heart? I am sure I cannot; then again I fear for the health of those who are become so dear to me, and in their sicknesses I severely pay for the joys I experienced while they were well. Whenever I go abroad it is always involuntary. I never return home without feeling some pleasing emotion, which I often suppress as useless and foolish. The instant I enter on my own land, the bright idea of property, of exclusive right, of independence exalt my mind. Precious soil, I say to myself, by what singular custom of law is it that thou wast made to constitute the riches of the freeholder? What should we American farmers be without the distinct possession of that soil? It feeds, it clothes us, from it we draw even a great exuberancy, our best meat, our richest drink, the very honey of our bees comes from this privileged spot. No wonder we should thus cherish its possession, no wonder that so many Europeans who have never been able to say that such portion of land was theirs, cross the Atlantic to realise that happiness. This formerly rude soil has been converted by my father into a pleasant farm, and in return it has established all our rights; on it is founded our rank, our freedom, our power as citizens, our importance as inhabitants of such a district. These images I must confess I always behold with pleasure, and extend them as far as my imagination can reach: for this is what may be called the true and the only philosophy of an American farmer.

Pray do not laugh in thus seeing an artless countryman tracing himself through the simple modifications of his life; remember that you have required it, therefore with candour, though with diffidence, I endeavour to follow the thread of my feelings, but I cannot tell you all. Often when I plough my low ground, I place my little boy on a chair which screws to the beam of the plough—its motion and that of the horses please him, he is perfectly happy and begins to chat. As I lean over the handle, various are the thoughts which crowd into my mind. I am now doing for him, I say, what my father formerly did for me, may God enable him to live that he may perform the same operations for the same purposes when I am worn out and old! I relieve his mother of some trouble while I have him with me, the odoriferous furrow exhilarates his spirits, and seems to do the child a great deal of good, for he looks more blooming since I have adopted that practice; can more pleasure, more dignity be added to that primary occupation? The father thus ploughing with his child, and to feed his family, is inferior only to the emperor of China ploughing as an example to his kingdom. In the evening when I return home through my low grounds, I am astonished at the myriads of insects which I perceive dancing in the beams of the setting sun. I was before scarcely acquainted with their existence, they are so small that it is difficult to distinguish them; they are carefully improving this short evening space, not daring to expose themselves to the blaze of our meridian sun. I never see an egg brought on my table but I feel penetrated with the wonderful change it would have undergone but for my gluttony; it might have been a gentle useful hen leading her chickens with a care and vigilance which speaks shame to many women. A cock perhaps, arrayed with the most majestic plumes, tender to its mate, bold, courageous, endowed with an astonishing instinct, with thoughts, with memory, and every distinguishing characteristic of the reason of man. I never see my trees drop their leaves and their fruit in the autumn, and bud again in the spring, without wonder; the sagacity of those animals which have long been the tenants of my farm astonish me: some of them seem to surpass even men in memory and sagacity. I could tell you singular instances of that kind. What then is this instinct which we so debase, and of which we are taught to entertain so diminutive an idea? My bees, above any other tenants of my farm, attract my attention and respect; I am astonished to see that nothing exists but what has its enemy, one species pursue and live upon the other: unfortunately our kingbirds are the destroyers of those industrious insects; but on the other hand, these birds preserve our fields from the depredation of crows which they pursue on the wing with great vigilance and astonishing dexterity.

Thus divided by two interested motives, I have long resisted the desire I had to kill them, until last year, when I thought they increased too much, and my indulgence had been carried too far; it was at the time of swarming when they all came and fixed themselves on the neighbouring trees, from whence they catched those that returned loaded from the fields. This made me resolve to kill as many as I could, and I was just ready to fire, when a bunch of bees as big as my fist, issued from one of the hives, rushed on one of the birds, and probably stung him, for he instantly screamed, and flew, not as before, in an irregular manner, but in a direct line. He was followed by the same bold phalanx, at a considerable distance, which unfortunately becoming too sure of victory, quitted their military array and disbanded themselves. By this inconsiderate step they lost all that aggregate of force which had made the bird fly off. Perceiving their disorder he immediately returned and snapped as many as he wanted; nay, he had even the impudence to alight on the very twig from which the bees had drove him. I killed him and immediately opened his craw, from which I took 171 bees; I laid them all on a blanket in the sun, and to my great surprise 54 returned to life, licked themselves clean, and joyfully went back to the hive; where they probably informed their companions of such an adventure and escape, as I believe had never happened before to American bees! I draw a great fund of pleasure from the quails which inhabit my farm; they abundantly repay me, by their various notes and peculiar tameness, for the inviolable hospitality I constantly show them in the winter. Instead of perfidiously taking advantage of their great and affecting distress, when nature offers nothing but a barren universal bed of snow, when irresistible necessity forces them to my barn doors, I permit them to feed unmolested; and it is not the least agreeable spectable which that dreary season presents, when I see those beautiful birds, tamed by hunger, intermingling with all my cattle and sheep, seeking in security for the poor scanty grain which but for them would be useless and lost. Often in the angles of the fences where the motion of the wind prevents the snow from settling, I carry them both chaff and grain; the one to feed them, the other to prevent their tender feet from freezing fast to the earth as I have frequently observed them to do.

I do not know an instance in which the singular barbarity of man is so strongly delineated, as in the catching and murthering those harmless birds, at that cruel season of the year. Mr.____, one of the most famous and extraordinary farmers that has ever done honour to the province of Connecticut, by his timely and humane assistance in a hard winter, saved this species from being entirely destroyed. They perished all over the country, none of their delightful whistlings were heard the next spring, but upon this gentleman's farm; and to his humanity we owe the continuation of their music. When the severities of that season have dispirited all my cattle, no farmer ever attends them with more pleasure than I do; it is one of those duties which is sweetened with the most rational satisfaction. I amuse myself in beholding their different tempers, actions, and the various effects of their instinct now powerfully impelled by the force of hunger. I trace their various inclinations, and the different effects of their passions, which are exactly the same as among men; the law is to us precisely what I am in my barn yard, a bridle and check to prevent the strong and greedy from oppressing the timid and weak. Conscious of superiority, they always strive to encroach on their neighbours; unsatisfied with their portion, they eagerly swallow it in order to have an opportunity of taking what is given to others, except they are prevented. Some I chide, others, unmindful of my admonitions, receive some blows. Could victuals thus be given to men without the assistance of any language, I am sure they would not behave better to one another, nor more philosophically than my cattle do.

The same spirit prevails in the stable; but there I have to do with more generous animals, there my well-known voice has immediate influence, and soon restores peace and tranquility. Thus by superior knowledge I govern all my cattle as wise men are obliged to govern fools and the ignorant. A variety of other thoughts crowd on my mind at that peculiar instant, but they all vanish by the time I return home. If in a cold night I swiftly travel in my sledge, carried along at the rate of twelve miles an hour, many are the reflections excited by surrounding circumstances. I ask myself what sort of an agent is that which we call frost? Our minister compares it to needles, the points of which enter our pores. What is become of the heat of the summer; in what part of the world is it that the N.W. keeps these grand magazines of nitre? when I see in the morning a river over which I can travel, that in the evening before was liquid, I am astonished indeed! What is become of those millions of insects which played in our summer fields, and in our evening meadows; they were so puny and so delicate, the period of their existence was so short, that one cannot help wondering how they could learn, in that short space, the sublime art to hide themselves and their offspring in so perfect a manner as to baffle the rigour of the season, and preserve that precious embryo of life, that small portion of ethereal heat, which if once destroyed would destroy the species! Whence that irresistible propensity to sleep so common in all those who are severely attacked by the frost. Dreary as this season appears, yet it has like all others its miracles, it presents to man a variety of problems which he can never resolve; among the rest, we have here a set of small birds which never appear until the snow falls; contrary to all others, they dwell and appear to delight in that element.

It is my bees, however, which afford me the most pleasing and extensive themes; let me look at them when I will, their government, their industry, their quarrels, their passions, always present me with something new; for which reason, when weary with labour, my common place of rest is under my locust-tree, close by my bee-house. By their movements I can predict the weather, and can tell the day of their swarming; but the most difficult point is, when on the wing, to know whether they want to go to the woods or not. If they have previously pitched in some hollow trees, it is not the allurements of salt and water, of fennel, hickory leaves, etc., nor the finest box, that can induce them to stay; they will prefer those rude, rough habitations to the best polished mahogany hive. When that is the case with mine, I seldom thwart their inclinations; it is in freedom that they work: were I to confine them, they would dwindle away and quit their labour. In such excursions we only part for a while; I am generally sure to find them again the following fall. This elopement of theirs only adds to my recreations; I know how to deceive even their superlative instinct; nor do I fear losing them, though eighteen miles from my house, and lodged in the most lofty trees, in the most impervious of our forests. I once took you along with me in one of these rambles, and yet you insist on my repeating the detail of our operations: it brings back into my mind many of the useful and entertaining reflections with which you so happily beguiled our tedious hours.

After I have done sowing, by way of recreation, I prepare for a week's jaunt in the woods, not to hunt either the deer or the bears, as my neighbours do, but to catch the more harmless bees. I cannot boast that this chase is so noble, or so famous among men, but I find it less fatiguing, and full as profitable; and the last consideration is the only one that moves me. I take with me my dog, as a companion, for he is useless as to this game; my gun, for no man you know ought to enter the woods without one; my blanket, some provisions, some wax, vermilion, honey, and a small pocket compass. With these implements I proceed to such woods as are at a considerable distance from any settlements. I carefully examine whether they abound with large trees, if so, I make a small fire on some flat stones, in a convenient place; on the fire I put some wax; close by this fire, on another stone, I drop honey in distinct drops, which I surround with small quantities of vermilion, laid on the stone; and then I retire carefully to watch whether any bees appear. If there are any in that neighbourhood, I rest assured that the smell of the burnt wax will unavoidably attract them; they will soon find out the honey, for they are fond of preying on that which is not their own; and in their approach they will necessarily tinge themselves with some particles of vermilion, which will adhere long to their bodies. I next fix my compass, to find out their course, which they keep invariably straight, when they are returning home loaded. By the assistance of my watch, I observe how long those are returning which are marked with vermilion. Thus possessed of the course, and, in some measure, of the distance, which I can easily guess at, I follow the first, and seldom fail of coming to the tree where those republics are lodged. I then mark it; and thus, with patience, I have found out sometimes eleven swarms in a season; and it is inconceivable what a quantity of honey these trees will sometimes afford. It entirely depends on the size of the hollow, as the bees never rest nor swarm till it is all replenished; for like men, it is only the want of room that induces them to quit the maternal hive. Next I proceed to some of the nearest settlements, where I procure proper assistance to cut down the trees, get all my prey secured, and then return home with my prize. The first bees I ever procured were thus found in the woods, by mere accident; for at that time I had no kind of skill in this method of tracing them. The body of the tree being perfectly sound, they had lodged themselves in the hollow of one of its principal limbs, which I carefully sawed off and with a good deal of labour and industry brought it home, where I fixed it up again in the same position in which I found it growing. This was in April; I had five swarms that year, and they have been ever since very prosperous. This business generally takes up a week of my time every fall, and to me it is a week of solitary ease and relaxation.

The seed is by that time committed to the ground; there is nothing very material to do at home, and this additional quantity of honey enables me to be more generous to my home bees, and my wife to make a due quantity of mead. The reason, Sir, that you found mine better than that of others is, that she puts two gallons of brandy in each barrel, which ripens it, and takes off that sweet, luscious taste, which it is apt to retain a long time. If we find anywhere in the woods (no matter on whose land) what is called a bee-tree, we must mark it; in the fall of the year when we propose to cut it down, our duty is to inform the proprietor of the land, who is entitled to half the contents; if this is not complied with we are exposed to an action of trespass, as well as he who should go and cut down a bee-tree which he had neither found out nor marked.

We have twice a year the pleasure of catching pigeons, whose numbers are sometimes so astonishing as to obscure the sun in their flight. Where is it that they hatch? for such multitudes must require an immense quantity of food. I fancy they breed toward the plains of Ohio, and those about lake Michigan, which abound in wild oats; though I have never killed any that had that grain in their craws. In one of them, last year, I found some undigested rice. Now the nearest rice fields from where I live must be at least 560 miles; and either their digestion must be suspended while they are flying, or else they must fly with the celerity of the wind. We catch them with a net extended on the ground, to which they are allured by what we call *tame wild pigeons*, made blind, and fastened to a long string; his short flights, and his repeated calls, never fail to bring them down. The greatest number I ever catched was fourteen dozen, though much larger quantities have often been trapped. I have frequently seen them at the market so cheap, that for a penny you might have as many as you could carry away; and yet from the extreme cheapness you must not conclude, that they are but an ordinary food; on the contrary, I think they are excellent. Every farmer has a tame wild pigeon in a cage at his door all the year round, in order to be ready whenever the season comes for catching them.

The pleasure I receive from the warblings of the birds in the spring, is superior to my poor description, as the continual succession of their tuneful notes is for ever new to me. I generally rise from bed about that indistinct interval, which, properly speaking, is neither night or day; for this is the moment of the most universal vocal choir. Who can listen unmoved to the sweet love tales of our robins, told from tree to tree? or to the shrill cat birds? The sublime accents of the thrush from on high always retard my steps that I may listen to the delicious music. The variegated appearances of the dew drops, as they hang to the different objects, must present even to a clownish imagination, the most voluptuous ideas. The astonishing art which all birds display in the construction of their nests, ill provided as we may suppose them with proper tools, their neatness, their convenience, always make me ashamed of the slovenliness of our houses; their love to their dame, their incessant careful attention, and the peculiar songs they address to her while she tediously incubates their eggs, remind me of my duty could I ever forget it. Their affection to their helpless little ones, is a lively precept; and in short, the whole economy of what we proudly call the brute creation, is admirable in every circumstance; and vain man, though adorned with the additional gift of reason, might learn from the perfection of instinct, how to regulate the follies, and how to temper the errors which this second gift often makes him commit. This is a subject, on which I have often bestowed the most serious thoughts; I have often blushed within myself, and been greatly astonished, when I have compared the unerring path they all follow, all just, all proper, all wise, up to the necessary degree of perfection, with the coarse, the imperfect systems of men, not merely as governors and kings, but as masters, as husbands, as fathers, as citizens. But this is a sanctuary in which an ignorant farmer must not presume to enter.

If ever man was permitted to receive and enjoy some blessings that might alleviate the many sorrows to which he is exposed, it is certainly in the country, when he attentively considers those ravishing scenes with which he is everywhere surrounded. This is the only time of the year in which I am avaricious of every moment, I therefore lose none that can add to this simple and inoffensive happiness. I roam early throughout all my fields; not the least operation do I perform, which is not accompanied with the most pleasing observations; were I to extend them as far as I have carried them, I should become tedious; you would think me guilty of affectation, and I should perhaps represent many things as pleasurable from which you might not perhaps receive the least agreeable emotions. But, believe me, what I write is all true and real.

Some time ago, as I sat smoking a contemplative pipe in my piazza, I saw with amazement a remarkable instance of selfishness displayed in a very small bird, which I had hitherto respected for its inoffensiveness. Three nests were placed almost contiguous to each other in my piazza; that of a swallow was affixed in the corner next to the house, that of a phebe in the other, a wren possessed a little box which I had made on purpose, and hung between. Be not surprised at their tameness, all my family had long been taught to respect them as well as myself. The wren had shown before signs of dislike to the box which I had given it, but I knew not on what account; at last it resolved, small as it was, to drive the swallow from its own habitation, and to my very great surprise it succeeded. Impudence often gets the better of modesty, and this exploit was no sooner performed, than it removed every material to its own box with the most admirable dexterity; the signs of triumph appeared very visible, it fluttered its wings with uncommon velocity, an universal joy was perceivable in all its movements. Where did this little bird learn that spirit of injustice? It was not endowed with what we term reason! Here then is a proof that both those gifts border very near on one another; for we see the perfection of the one mixing with the errors of the other! The peaceable swallow, like the passive Quaker, meekly sat at a small distance and never offered the least resistance; but no sooner was the plunder carried away, than the injured bird went to work with unabated ardour, and in a few days the depredations were repaired. To prevent however a repetition of the same violence, I removed the wren's box to another part of the house.

In the middle of my new parlour I have, you may remember, a curious republic of industrious hornets; their nest hangs to the ceiling, by the same twig on which it was so admirably built and contrived in the woods. Its removal did not displease them, for they find in my house plenty of food; and I have left a hole open in one of the panes of the window, which answers all their purposes. By this kind usage they are become quite harmless; they live on the flies, which are very troublesome to us throughout the summer; they are constantly busy in catching them, even on the eyelids of my children. It is surprising how quickly they smear them with a sort of glue, lest they might escape, and when thus prepared, they carry them to their nests, as food for their young ones. These globular nests are most ingeniously divided into many stories, all provided with cells, and proper communications. The materials with which this fabric is built, they procure from the cottony furze, with which our oak rails are covered; this substance tempered with glue, produces a sort of pasteboard, which is very strong, and resists all the inclemencies of the weather. By their assistance, I am but little troubled with flies. All my family are so accustomed to their strong buzzing, that no one takes any notice of them; and though they are fierce and vindictive, yet kindness and hospitality has made them useful and harmless.

We have a great variety of wasps; most of them build their nests in mud, which they fix against the shingles of our roofs, as nigh the pitch as they can. These aggregates represent nothing, at first view, but coarse and irregular lumps, but if you break them, you will observe, that the inside of them contains a great number of oblong cells, in which they deposit their eggs, and in which they bury themselves in the fall of the year. Thus immured they securely pass through the severity of that season, and on the return of the sun are enabled to perforate their cells and to open themselves a passage from these recesses into the sunshine. The yellow wasps, which build under ground, in our meadows, are much more to be dreaded, for when the mower unwittingly passes his scythe over their holes they immediately sally forth with a fury and velocity superior even to the strength of man. They make the boldest fly, and the only remedy is to lie down and cover our heads with hay, for it is only at the head they aim their blows; nor is there any possibility of finishing that part of the work until, by means of fire and brimstone, they are all silenced. But though I have been obliged to execute this dreadful sentence in my own defence, I have often thought it a great pity, for the sake of a little hay, to lay waste so ingenious a subterranean town, furnished with every conveniency, and built with a most surprising mechanism.

I never should have done were I to recount the many objects which involuntarily strike my imagination in the midst of my work, and spontaneously afford me the most pleasing relief. These appear insignificant trifles to a person who has travelled through Europe and America, and is acquainted with books and with many sciences; but such simple objects of contemplation suffice me, who have no time to bestow on more extensive observations. Happily these require no study, they are obvious, they gild the moments I dedicate to them, and enliven the severe labours which I perform. At home my happiness springs from very different objects; the gradual unfolding of my children's reason, the study of their dawning tempers attract all my paternal attention. I have to contrive little punishments for their little faults, small encouragements for their good actions, and a variety of other expedients dictated by various occasions. But these are themes unworthy your perusal, and which ought not to be carried beyond the walls of my house, being domestic mysteries adapted only to the locality of the small sanctuary wherein my family resides. Sometimes I delight in inventing and executing machines which simplify my wife's labour. I have been tolerably successful that way; and these, Sir, are the narrow circles within which I constantly revolve, and what can I wish for beyond them? I bless God for all the good he has given me; I envy no man's prosperity, and with no other portion of happiness than that I may live to teach the same philosophy to my children; and give each of them a farm, show them how to cultivate it, and be like their father, good substantial independent American farmers—an appellation which will be the most fortunate one a man of my class can possess, so long as our civil government continues to shed blessings on our husbandry. Adieu.

William Bartram
1739-1823

Son of the greatest botanist in America of his day, William Bartram established himself through his writings as one of the first important naturalists and chroniclers of early American life and landscape. Trained by his father John Bartram—botanist to the king of Great Britain, Fellow in the Royal Society, founder of the first botanical garden in America—William accompanied his father on a botanical trip up the St. Johns River in 1765, and then, on his own, extensively explored the American Southeast from 1773-1778. His account of those explorations, entitled *Travels Through North & South Carolina, Georgia, East & West Florida...,* was published in Philadelphia in 1791 and, soon after, throughout Europe. Bartram's book is *the* great botanical and ethnological record of his day, influencing both Wordsworth and Coleridge, and being enjoyed by Carlyle. Coleridge drew images for "The Rime of the Ancient Mariner" and "Kubla Khan" from it, and echoes of Bartram can be heard in such Wordsworthian poems as "She Was a Phantom of Delight" and "Ruth."

Traveling at the request of Dr. Fothergill of London, Bartram searched the Floridas and parts of Carolina and Georgia "for the ...rare and useful productions of nature." But Bartram found himself "seduced by the sublime enchanting scenes of primitive nature" which stimulated him to write his *Travels.* "Whilst I was continually impelled by a restless spirit of curiosity in pursuit of new productions of nature," Bartram wrote, "my chief happiness consisted in tracing and admiring the infinite power, majesty, and perfection of the great Almighty Creator...." Eighteenth-century references to "the sublime" fill this work, the first work of American literature to use the phrase extensively. Still, careful observation is Bartram's hallmark. *Travels* includes the best picture we have of the Southeastern

Indian tribes of his time. And the entire final part of the book is devoted to Indian society and culture. He respected the Indians immensely, speaking, for example, of the Creek tribes "as moral men who certainly stand in no need of European civilization." Yet he did not romanticize Indians; he devoted four paragraphs in one section of *Travels,* for example, to the Indians' "vices, immoralities, and imperfections from my own observations."

from THE TRAVELS *

PART I, CHAPTER III

Being safely landed on the opposite bank, I mounted my horse, and followed the high road to the ferry on St. Ille, about sixty miles south of the Alatamaha, passing through an uninhabited wilderness. The sudden transition from rich cultivated settlements, to high pine forests, dark and grassy savannas, forms in my opinion no disagreeable contrast; and the new objects of observation in the works of nature soon reconcile the surprised imagination to the change. As soon as I had lost sight of the river, ascending some sand-hills, I observed a new and most beautiful species of Annona, having clusters of large white fragrant flowers, and a diminutive but elegant Kalmia. The stems are very small, feeble, and for the most part undivided, furnished with little ovate pointed leaves, and terminate with a simple racemi, or spike of flowers, salver formed, and of a deep rose red. The whole plant is ciliated. It grows in abundance all over the moist savannas, but more especially near ponds and bay-swamps. In similar situations, and commonly a near neighbour to this new Kalmia, is seen a very curious species of Annona. It is very dwarf, the stems seldom extending from the earth more than a foot or eighteen inches, and are weak and almost decumbent. The leaves are long, extremely narrow, almost lineal. However, small as they are, they retain the figure common to the species, that is, lanciolate, broadest at the upper end, and attenuating down to the petiole, which is very short; their leaves stand alternately, nearly erect, forming two series, or wings, on the arcuated stems. The flowers, both in size and colour, resemble those of the Antrilobe, and are single from the axillae of the leaves on incurved pedunculi, nodding downwards. I never saw the fruit. The dens, or caverns, dug in the sand-hills, by the great land-tortoise, called here Gopher,[1] present a very singular appearance; these vast caves are their castles and diurnal retreats, from whence they issue forth in the night, in search of prey. The little mounds, or hillocks of fresh earth, thrown up in great numbers in the night, have also a curious appearance.

In the evening I arrived at a cow-pen, where there was a habitation, and the peole received me very civilly. I staid here all night, and had for supper plenty of milk, butter, and very good cheese of their own make, which is a novelty in the maritime parts of Carolina and Georgia; the inhabitants being chiefly supplied with it from Europe and the northern states. The varied: high open forests of stately pines, flowery plains, and extensive

*Reprinted from the original text with permission from The American Antiquarian Society.

[1]Testudo Polyphemus.

next day's progress, in general, presented scenes similar to the preceding, though the land is lower, more level and humid, and the produce more green savannas, chequered with the incarnate Chironia, Pillcherima, and Assclepias fragrans, perfumed the air whilst they pleased the eye. I met with some troublesome cane swamps, saw herds of horned cattle, horses and deer, and took notice of a procumbent species of Hibiscus, the leaves palmated, the flowers large and expanded, pale yellow and white, having a deep crimson eye; the whole plant, except the corolla, armed with stiff hair. I also saw a beautiful species of Lupin, having pale green villous lingulate[2] leaves; the flowers are disposed in long erect spikes; some plants produce flowers of the finest celestial blue, others incarnate, and some milk white, and though they all three seem to be varieties of one species, yet they associate in separate communities, sometimes approaching near each other's border, or in sight at a distance. Their districts are situated on dry sandy heights, in open pine forests, which are naturally thin of undergrowth, and appear to great advantage; generally, where they are found, they occupy many acres of surface. The vegetative mould is composed of fine white sand, mixed, and coloured, with dissolved and calcined vegetable substances; but this stratum is not very deep, and covers one of a tenacious cinereous coloured clay, as we may observe by the earth adhering to the roots of trees, torn up by storms &c. and by the little chimnies, or air holes of cray-fish, which perforate the savannas. Turkeys, quails, and small birds, are here to be seen; but birds are not numerous in desert forests; they draw near to the habitations of men, as I have constantly observed in all my travels.

I arrived at St. Ille's in the evening, where I lodged, and next morning, having crossed over in a ferry boat, sat forward for St. Mary's. The situation of the territory, its soil and productions, between these two last rivers, are nearly similar to those which I had passed over, except that the savannas are more frequent and extensive.

It may be proper to observe, that I had now passed the utmost frontier of the white settlements on that border. It was drawing on towards the close of day, the skies serene and calm, the air temperately cool, and gentle zephyrs breathing through the fragrant pines; the prospect around enchantingly varied and beautiful; endless green savannas, chequered with coppices of fragrant shrubs, filled the air with the richest perfume. The gaily attired plants which enamelled the green had begun to imbibe the pearly dew of evening; nature seemed silent, and nothing appeared to ruffle the happy moments of evening contemplation: when, on a sudden, an Indian appeared crossing the path, at a considerable distance before me. On perceiving that he was armed with a rifle, the first sight of him startled me, and I endeavoured to elude his sight, by stopping my pace, and keeping large trees between us; but he espied me, and turning short about, sat spurs to his horse, and came up on full gallop. I never before this was afraid at the sight of an Indian, but at this time, I must own that my spirits were very much agitated: I saw at once, that being unarmed, I was in his power, and having now but a few moments to prepare, I resigned myself entirely to the

[2]Lupinus breunis, foliis integerimis oblongis villosis.

will of the Almighty, trusting to his mercies for my preservation; my mind then became tranquil, and I resolved to meet the dreaded foe with resolution and cheerful confidence. The intrepid Siminole stopped suddenly, three or four yards before me, and silently viewed me, his countenance angry and fierce, shifting his rifle from shoulder to shoulder, and looking about instantly on all sides. I advanced towards him, and with an air of confidence offered him my hand, hailing him, brother; at this he hastily jerked back his arm, with a look of malice, rage and disdain, seeming every way disconcerted; when again looking at me more attentively, he instantly spurred up to me, and, with dignity in his look and action, gave me his hand. Possibly the silent language of his soul, during the moment of suspense (for I believe his design was to kill me when he first came up) was after this manner: "White man, thou art my enemy, and thou and thy brethren may have killed mine; yet it may not be so, and even were that the case, thou art now alone, and in my power. Live; the Great Spirit forbids me to touch thy life; go to thy brethren, tell them thou sawest an Indian in the forests, who knew how to be humane and compassionate." In fine, we shook hands, and parted in a friendly manner, in the midst of a dreary wilderness; and he informed me of the course and distance to the trading-house, where I found he had been extremely ill-treated the day before.

I now sat forward again, and after eight or ten miles riding, arrived at the banks of St. Mary's, opposite the stores, and got safe over before dark. The river is here about one hundred yards across, has ten feet water, and, following its course, about sixty miles to the sea, though but about twenty miles by land. The trading company here received and treated me with great civility. On relating my adventures on the road, particularly the last with the Indian, the chief replied, and with a countenance that at once bespoke surprise and pleasure, "My friend, consider yourself a fortunate man: that fellow," said he, "is one of the greatest villians on earth, a noted murderer, and outlawed by his countrymen. Last evening he was here, we took his gun from him, broke it in pieces, and gave him a severe drubbing: he, however, made his escape, carrying off a new rifle gun, with which, he said, going off, he would kill the first white man he met."

On seriously contemplating the behaviour of this Indian towards me, so soon after his ill treatment, the following train of sentiments insensibly crowded in upon my mind.

Can it be denied, but that the moral principle, which directs the savages to virtuous and praiseworthy actions, is natural or innate? It is certain they have not the assistance of letters, or those means of education in the schools of philosophy, where the virtuous sentiments and actions of the most illustrious characters are recorded, and carefully laid before the youth of civilized nations: therefore this moral principle must be innate, or they must be under the immediate influence and guidance of a more divine and powerful preceptor, who, on these occasions, instantly inspires them, and as with a ray of divine light, points out to them at once the dignity, propriety, and beauty of virtue.

The land on, and adjacent to, this river, notwithstanding its arenaceous surface, appears naturally fertile. The peach trees are large, healthy, and fruitful; and Indian corn, rice, cotton, and indigo, thrive exceedingly. This sandy surface, one would suppose, from its loose texture, would possess a percolating quality, and suffer the rain-waters quickly to drain off; but it is quite the contrary, at least in these low maritime sandy countries of Carolina and Florida, beneath the mountains, for in the sands, even the heights, where the arenaceous stratum is perhaps five, eight, and ten feet above the clay, the earth, even in the longest droughts, is moist an inch or two under the surface; whereas, in the rich tenacious low lands, at such times, the ground is dry, and, as it were, baked many inches, and sometimes some feet deep, and the crops, as well as almost all vegetation, suffer in such soils and situations. The reason of this may be, that this kind of earth admits more freely of a transpiration of vapours, arising from intestine watery canals to the surface; and probably these vapours are impregnated with saline or nitrous principles, friendly and nutritive to vegetables; however, of these causes and secret operations of nature I am ignorant, and resume again my proper employment, that of discovering and collecting data for the exercise of more able physiologists.

The savannas about St. Mary's, at this season, display a very charming appearance of flowers and verdure; their more elevated borders are varied with beds of violets, lupins, Amaryllis atamasco, and plants of a new and very beautiful species of Mimosa sensitiva, which I think as admirable and more charming than the celebrated Humble plant, equally chaste and fearful of the hasty touch of the surprised admirer; the flower is larger, of a bright damask rose colour, and exceedingly fragrant: the whole plant is destitute of prickles, but hairy; it is precumbent, reclining itself upon the green turf, and from these trailing branches proceed an upright peduncle, six or eight inches high, supporting an oblong head of flowerets, which altogether, at a small distance, have the appearance of an exuberant field of clover; and, what is singular, and richly varies the scene, there are interspersed patches of the same species of plants, having flowers of the finest golden yellow, and others snow white; but the incarnate is most prevalent.

. . .

The evening was temperately cool and calm. The crocodiles began to roar and appear in uncommon numbers along the shores and in the river. I fixed my camp in an open plain, near the utmost projection of the promontory, under the shelter of a large live oak, which stood on the highest part of the ground and but a few yards from my boat. From this open, high situation, I had a free prospect of the river, which was a matter of no trivial consideration to me, having good reason to dread the subtle attacks of the alligators, who were crowding about my harbour. Having collected a good quantity of wood for the purpose of keeping up a light and smoke during the night, I began to think of preparing my supper, when, upon examining my stores, I found but a scanty provision; I thereupon determined, as the most expeditious way of supplying my necessities, to take my bob and try for some trout. About one hundred yards above my harbour began a cove or bay of the river, out of which opened a large lagoon. The mouth or entrance from the river to it was narrow, but the waters soon after spread and formed a little lake, extending into the marshes, its entrance and shores within I observed to be verged with floating lawns of the pistia and nymphea and other aquatic plants; these I knew were excellent haunts for trout.

The verges and islets of the lagoon were elegantly embellished with flowering plants and shrubs; the laughing coots with wings half spread were tripping over the little coves and hiding themselves in the tufts of grass; young broods of the painted summer teal, skimming the still surface of the waters, and following the watchful parent unconscious of danger, were frequently surprised by the voracious trout, and he in turn as often by the subtle, greedy alligator. Behold him rushing forth from the flags and reeds. His enormous body swells. His plaited tail brandished high, floats upon the lake. The waters like a cataract descend from his opening jaws. Clouds of smoke issue from his dilated nostrils. The earth trembles with his thunder. When immediately from the opposite coast of the lagoon, emerges from the deep his rival champion. They suddenly dart upon each other. The boiling surface of the lake marks their rapid course, and a terrific conflict commences. They now sink to the bottom folded together in horrid wreaths. The water becomes thick and discoloured. Again they rise, their jaws clap together, re-echoing through the deep surrounding forests. Again they sink, when the contest ends at the muddy bottom of the lake, and the vanquished makes a hazardous escape, hiding himself in the muddy turbulent waters and sedge on a distant shore. The proud victor exulting returns to the place of action. The shores and forests resound his dreadful roar, together with the triumphing shouts of the plaited tribes around, witnesses of the horrid combat.

My apprehensions were highly alarmed after being a spectator of so dreadful a battle; it was obvious that every delay would but tend to increase my dangers and difficulties, as the sun was near setting and the alligators gathered around my harbour from all quarters; from these considerations I concluded to be expeditious in my trip to the lagoon, in order to take some fish. Not thinking it prudent to take my fusee with me, lest I might lose it overboard in case of a battle, which I had every reason to dread before my return, I therefore furnished myself with a club for my defense, went on board, and penetrating the first line of those which surrounded my harbour, they gave way; but being pursued by several very large ones, I kept strictly on the watch, and paddled with all my might towards the entrance of the lagoon, hoping to be sheltered there from the multitude of my assailants; but ere I had half-way reached the place, I was attacked on all sides, several endeavouring to overset the canoe. My situation now became precarious to the last degree: two very large ones attacked me closely, at the same instant, rushing up with their heads and part of their bodies above the water, roaring terribly and belching floods of water over me. They struck their jaws together so close to my ears, as almost to stun me, and I expected every moment to be dragged out of the boat and instantly devoured, but I applied my weapons so effectually about me, though at random, that I was so successful as to beat them off a little; when, finding that they designed to renew the battle, I made for the shore, as the only means left me for my preservation, for, by keeping close to it, I should have my enemies on one side of me only, whereas I was before surrounded by them, and there was a probability, if pushed to the last extremity, of saving myself, by jumping out of the canoe on shore, as it is easy to outwalk them on land, although comparatively as swift as lightning in the water. I found this last expedient alone could fully answer my expectations, for as soon as I gained the shore they drew off and kept aloof. This was a happy relief, as my confidence was, in some degree, recovered by it. On recollecting myself, I discovered that I had almost reached the entrance of the lagoon, and determined to venture in, if possible to take a few fish and then return to my harbour, while day-light continued, for I could now, with caution and resolution, make my way with safety along shore; and indeed there was no other way to regain my camp, without leaving my boat and making my retreat through the marshes and reeds, which, if I could even effect, would have been in a manner throwing myself away, for then there would have been no hopes of ever recovering my bark, and returning in safety to any settlements of men. I accordingly proceeded and made good my entrance into the lagoon, though not without opposition from the alligators, who formed a line across the entrance, but did not pursue me into it, nor was I molested by any there, though there were some very large ones in a cove at the upper end. I soon caught more trout than I had present occasion for, and the air was too hot and sultry to admit of their being kept for many hours, even though salted or barbecued. I now prepared for my return to camp, which I succeeded in with but little trouble, by keeping close to the shore, yet I was opposed upon re-entering the river out of the lagoon, and pursued near to my landing (though not closely attacked) particularly by an old daring one, about twelve feet in length, who kept close after me, and when I stepped on shore and turned about, in order to draw up my canoe, he rushed up near my feet and lay there for some time, looking me in the face, his head and shoulders out of water; I resolved he should pay for his temerity, and having a heavy load in my fusee, I ran to my camp, and returning with my piece, found him with his foot on the gunwale of the boat, in search of fish. On my coming up he withdrew sullenly and slowly into the water, but soon returned and placed himself in his former position, looking at me and seeming neither fearful or any way disturbed. I soon dispatched him by lodging the contents of my gun in his head, and then proceeded to cleanse and prepare my fish for supper, and accordingly took them out of the boat, laid them down on the sand close to the water, and began to scale them, when, raising my head, I saw before me, through the clear water, the head and shoulders of a very large alligator, moving slowly towards me; I instantly stepped back, when, with a sweep of his tail, he brushed off several of my fish. It was certainly most providential that I looked up at that instant, as the monster would probably, in less than a minute, have seized and dragged me into the river. This incredible boldness of the animal disturbed me greatly, supposing there could now be no reasonable safety for me during the night, but by keeping continually on the watch; I therefore, as soon as I had prepared the fish, proceeded to secure myself and effects in the best manner I could: in the first place, I hauled my bark upon the shore, almost clear out of the water, to prevent their oversetting or sinking her; after this every moveable was taken out and carried to my camp, which was but a few yards off; then ranging some dry wood in such order as was the most convenient, cleared the ground round about it, that there might be no impediment in my way, in case of an attack in the night, either from the water or the land; for I discovered by this time, that this small isthmus, from its remote situation and fruitfulness, was resorted to by bears and wolves. Having prepared myself in the best manner I could, I charged my gun and proceeded to reconnoitre my camp and the adjacent grounds; when I discovered that the peninsula and grove, at the distance of about two hundred yards from my encampment, on the land side, were invested by a Cypress swamp, covered with water, which below was joined to the shore of the little lake, and above to the marshes surrounding the lagoon, so that I was confined to an islet exceedingly circumscribed, and I found there was no other retreat for me, in case of an attack, but by either ascending one of the large Oaks, or pushing off with my boat.

It was by this time dusk, and the alligators had nearly ceased their roar, when I was again alarmed by a tumultuous noise that seemed to be in my harbour, and therefore engaged my immediate attention. Returning to my camp I found it undisturbed, and then continued on to the extreme point of the promontory, where I saw a scene, new and surprising, which at first threw my sense into such a tumult, that it was some time before I could comprehend what was the matter; however, I soon accounted for the prodigious assemblage of crocodiles at this place, which exceeded every thing of the kind I had ever heard of.

How shall I express myself so as to convey an adequate idea of it to the reader, and at the same time avoid raising suspicions of my want of veracity? Should I say, that the river (in this place) from shore to shore, and perhaps near half a mile above and below me, appeared to be one solid bank of fish, of various kinds, pushing through this narrow pass of St. Juan's into the little lake, on their return down the river, and that the alligators were in such incredible numbers, and so close together from shore to shore, that it would have been easy to have walked across on their heads, had the animals been harmless. What expressions can sufficiently declare the shocking scene that for some minutes continued, whilst this mighty army of fish were forcing the pass? During this attempt, thousands, I may say hundreds of thousands of them were caught and swallowed by the devouring alligators. I have seen an alligator take up out of the water several great fish at a time, and just squeeze them betwixt his jaws, while the tails of the great trout flapped about his eyes and lips, ere he had swallowed them. The horrid noise of their closing jaws, their plunging amidst the broken banks of fish, and rising with their prey some feet upright above the water, the floods of water and blood rushing out of their mouths, and the clouds of vapour issuing from their wide nostrils, were truly frightful. This scene continued at intervals during the night, as the fish came to the pass. After this sight, shocking and tremendous as it was, I found myself somewhat easier and more reconciled to my situation, being convinced that their extraordinary assemblage here was owing to the annual feast of fish, and that they were so well employed in their own element, that I had little occasion to fear their paying me a visit.

It being now almost night, I returned to my camp, where I had left my fish broiling and my kettle of rice stewing; and having with me, oil, pepper, and salt, and excellent oranges hanging in abundance over my head (a valuable substitute for vinegar) I sat down and regaled myself cheerfully; having finished my repast, I re-kindled my fire for lights and whilst I was revising the notes of my past day's journey, I was suddenly roused with a noise behind me toward the main land; I sprang up on my feet, and listening, I distinctly heard some creature wading the water of the isthmus; I seized my gun and went cautiously from my camp, directing my steps towards the noise; when I had advanced about thiry yards, I halted behind a coppice of Orange trees, and soon perceived two very large bears, which had made their way through the water, and had landed in the grove, about one hundred yards distance from me, and were advancing towards me. I waited until they were within thirty yards of me, they there began to snuff and look towards my camp, I snapped my piece, but it flashed, on which they both turned about and galloped off, plunging through the water and swamp, never halting as I suppose, until they reached fast land, as I could hear them leaping and plunging a long time; they did not presume to return again, nor was I molested by any other creature, except being occasionally awakened by the whooping of owls, screaming of bitterns, or the wood-rats running amongst the leaves.

The wood-rat is a very curious animal, they are not half the size of the domestic rat; of a dark brown or black colour; their tail slender and shorter in proportion, and covered thinly with short hair; they are singular with respect to their ingenuity and great labour in the construction of their habitations, which are conical pyramids about three or four feet high, constructed with dry branches, which they collect with great labour and perseverance, and pile up without any apparent order; yet they are so interwoven with one another, that it would take a bear or wild-cat some time to pull one of these castles to pieces, and allow the animals sufficient time to secure a retreat with their young.

The noise of the crocodiles kept me awake the greater part of the night, but when I arose in the morning, contrary to my expectations, there was perfect peace; very few of them to be seen, and those were asleep on the shore, yet I was not able to suppress my fears and apprehensions of being attacked by them in future; and indeed yesterday's combat with them, notwithstanding I came off in a manner victorious, or at least made a safe retreat, had left sufficient impression on my mind to damp my courage, and it seemed too much for one of my strength, being alone in a very small boat to encounter such collected danger. To pursue my voyage up the river, and be obliged every evening to pass such dangerous defiles, appeared to me as perilous as running the gauntlet betwixt two rows of Indians armed with knives and firebrands; I however resolved to continue my voyage one day longer, if I possibly could with safety, and then return down the river, should I find the like difficulties to oppose. Accordingly I got every thing on board, charged my gun, and set sail cautiously along shore; as I passed by Battle lagoon, I began to tremble and keep a good look out, when suddenly a huge alligator rushed out of the reeds, and with a tremendous roar, came up, and darted as swift as an arrow under my boat, emerging upright on my lee quarter, with open jaws, and belching water and smoke that fell upon me like rain in a hurricane; I laid soundly about his head with my club and beat him off, and after plunging and darting about my boat, he went off on a straight line through the water, seemingly with the rapidity of lightning, and entered the cape of the lagoon; I now employed my time to the very best advantage in paddling close along shore, but could not forbear looking now and then behind me, and presently perceived one of them coming up again; the water of the river hereabouts, was shoal and very clear, the monster came up with the usual roar and menaces, and passed close by the side of my boat, when I could distinctly see a young brood of alligators to the number of one hundred or more, following after her in a long train, they kept close together in a column without straggling off to the one side or the other, the young appeared to be of an equal size, about fifteen inches in length, almost black, with pale yellow transverse waved clouds or blotches, much like rattlesnakes in colour. I now lost sight of my enemy again.

Still keeping close along shore; on turning a point or projection of the river bank, at once I beheld a great number of hillocks or small pyramids, resembling hay-cocks, ranged like an encampment along the banks, they stood fifteen or twenty yards distant from the water, on a high marsh, about four feet perpendicular above the water; I knew them to be the nests of the crocodile, having had a description of them before, and now expected a furious and general attack, as I saw several large crocodiles swimming abreast of these buildings. These nests being so great a curiosity to me, I was determined at all events immediately to land and examine them. Accordingly I ran my bark on shore at one of their landing places, which was a sort of nick or little dock, from which ascended a sloping path or road up to the edge of the meadow, where their nests were, most of them were deserted, and the great thick whitish egg-shells lay broken and scattered upon the ground round about them.

The nests or hillocks are of the form of an obtuse cone, four feet high and four or five feet in diameter at their bases; they are constructed with mud, grass and herbage: at first they lay a floor of this kind of tempered mortar on the ground, upon which they deposit a layer of eggs, and upon this a stratum of mortar seven or eight inches in thickness, and then another layer of eggs, and in this manner one stratum upon another, nearly to the top: I believe they commonly lay from one to two hundred eggs in a nest: these are hatched I suppose by the heat of the sun; and perhaps the vegetable substances mixed with the earth, being acted upon by the sun, may cause a small degree of fermentation, and so increase the heat in those hillocks. The ground for several acres about these nests shewed evident marks of a continual resort of alligators; the grass was every where beaten down, hardly a blade or straw was left standing; whereas, all about, at a distance, it was five or six feet high, and as thick as it could grow together. The female, as I imagine, carefully watches her own nest of eggs until they are all hatched, or perhaps while she is attending her own brood, she takes under her care and protection as many as she can get at one time, either from her own particular nest or others: but certain it is, that the young are not left to shift for themselves, having had frequent opportunities of seeing the female alligator, leading about the shores her train of young ones, just like a hen does her brood of chickens; and she is equally assiduous and courageous in defending the young, which are under their care, and providing for their subsistence; and when she is basking upon the warm banks, with her brood around her, you may hear the young ones continually whining and barking, like young puppies. I believe but few of a brood live to the years of full growth and magnitude, as the old feed on the young as long as they can make prey of them.

The alligator when full grown is a very large and terrible creature, and of prodigious strength, activity and swiftness in the water. I have seen them twenty feet in length, and some are supposed to be twenty-two or twenty-three feet; their body is as large as that of a horse; their shape exactly resembles that of a lizard, except their tail, which is flat or cuniform, being compressed on each side, and gradually diminishing from the abdomen to the extremity, which, with the whole body is covered with horny plates or squammae, impenetrable when on the body of the live animal, even to a rifle ball, except about their head and just behind their fore-legs or arms, where it is said they are only vulnerable. The head of a full grown one is about three feet, and the mouth open nearly the same length, the eyes are small in proportion and seem sunk deep in the head, by means of the prominency of the brows; the nostrils are large, inflated and prominent on the top, so that the head in the water resembles, at a distance, a great chunk of wood floating about. Only the upper jaw moves, which they raise almost perpendicular, so as to form a right angle with the lower one. In the fore part of the upper jaw, on each side, just under the nostrils, are two very large, thick, strong teeth or tusks, not very sharp, but rather the shape of a cone, these are as white as the finest polished ivory, and are not covered by any skin or lips, and always in sight, which gives the creature a frightful appearance; in the lower jaw are holes opposite to these teeth, to receive them; when they clap their jaws together it causes a surprising noise, like that which is made by forcing a heavy plank with violence upon the ground, and may be heard at a great distance.

But what is yet more surprising to a stranger, is the incredible loud and terrifying roar, which they are capable of making, especially in the spring season, their breeding time; it most resembles very heavy distant thunder, not only shaking the air and waters, but causing the earth to tremble; and when hundreds and thousands are roaring at the same time, you can scarcely be persuaded, but that the whole globe is violently and dangerously agitated.

An old champion, who is perhaps absolute sovereign of a little lake or lagoon (when fifty less than himself are obliged to content themselves with swelling and roaring in little coves round about) darts forth from the reedy coverts all at once, on the surface of the waters, in a right line; at first seemingly as rapid as lightning, but gradually more slowly until he arrives at the center of the lake, when he stops; he now swells himself by drawing in wind and water through his mouth, which causes a loud sonorous rattling in the throat for near a minute, but it is immediately forced out again through is mouth and nostrils, with a loud noise, brandishing his tail in the air, and the vapour ascending from his nostrils like smoke. At other times, when swollen to an extent ready to burst, his head and tail lifted up, he spins or twirls round on the surface of the water. He acts his part like an Indian chief when rehearsing his feats of war, and then retiring, the exhibition is continued by others who dare to step forth, and strive to excel each other, to gain the attention of the favourite female.

. . .

from PART II, CHAPTER X

But let us again resume the subject of the rattle snake; a wonderful creature, when we consider his form, nature and disposition, it is certain that he is capable by a puncture or scratch of one of his fangs, not only to kill the largest animal in America, and that in a few minutes time, but to turn the whole body into corruption; but such is the nature of this dreadful reptile, that he cannot run or creep faster than a man or child can walk, and he is never known to strike until he is first assaulted or fears himself in danger, and even then always gives the earliest warning by the rattles at the extremity of the tail. I have in the course of my travels in the Southern states (where they are the largest, most numerous and supposed to be the most venomous and vindictive) stept unknowingly so close as almost to touch one of them with my feet, and when I perceived him he was already drawn up in circular coils ready for a blow. But however incredible it may appear, the generous, I may say magnanimous creature lay as still and motionless as if inanimate, his head crouched in, his eyes almost shut. I precipitately withdrew, unless when I have been so shocked with surprise and horror as to be in a manner rivetted to the spot, for a short time not having strength to go away, when he often slowly extends himself and quiety moves off in a direct line, unless pursued when he erects his tail as far as the rattles extend, and gives the warning alarm by intervals, but if you pursue and overtake him with a show of enmity, he instantly throws himself into the spiral coil, his tail by the rapidity of its motion appears like a vapour, making a quick tremulous sound, his whole body swells through rage, continually rising and falling as a bellows; his beautiful parti-coloured skin becomes speckled and rough by dilatation, his head and neck are flattened, his cheeks swollen and his lips constricted, discovering his mortal fangs; his eyes red as burning coals, and his brandishing forked tongue of the colour of the hottest flame, continually menances death and destruction, yet never strikes unless sure of his mark.

The rattle snake is the largest serpent yet known to exist in North America, I have heard of their having been seen formerly, at the first settling of Georgia, seven, eight and even ten feet in length, and six or eight inches diameter, but there are none of that size now to be seen, yet I have seen them above six feet in length, and about six inches in thickness, or as large as a man's leg, but their general size is four, five and six feet in length. They are supposed to have the power of fascination in an eminent degree, so as to inthrall their prey. It is generally believed that they charm birds, rabbits, squirrels and other animals, and by steadfastly looking at them possess them with infatuation; be the cause what it may, the misierable creatures undoubtedly strive by every possible means to escape, but alas! their endeavours are in vain, they at last lose the power of resistance, and flutter or move slowly, but reluctantly towards the yawning jaws of their devourers, and creep into their mouths or lay down and suffer themselves to be taken and swallowed.

Since, within the circle of my acquaintance, I am known to be an advocate or vindicator of the benevolent and peaceable disposition of animal creation in general, not only towards mankind, whom they seem to venerate, but always towards one another, except where hunger or the rational and necessary provocations of the sensual appetite interfere, I shall mention a few instances, amongst many, which I have had an opportunity of remarking during my travels, particularly with regard to the animal I have been treating of, I shall strictly confine myself to facts.

When on the sea coast of Georgia, I consented, with a few friends, to make a party of amusement at fishing and fowling on Sapello, one of the sea coast islands; we accordingly descended the Alatamaha, crossed the sound and landed on the North end of the island, near the inlet, fixing our encampment at a pleasant situation, under the shade of a grove of Live Oaks, and Laurels,[1] on the high banks of a creek which we ascended, winding through a salt marsh, which had its source from a swamp and savanna in the island: our situation elevated and open, commanded a comprehensive landscape; the great ocean, the foaming surf breaking on the sandy beach, the snowy breakers on the bar, the endless chain of islands, checkered sound and high continent all appearing before us. The diverting toils of the day were not fruitless, affording us opportunities of furnishing ourselves plentifully with a variety of game, fish and oysters for our supper.

About two hundred yards from our camp was a cool spring, amidst a grove of the odoriferous Myrica; the winding path to this salubrious fountain led through a grassy savanna; I visited the spring several times in the night, but little did I know, or any of my careless drowsy companions, that every time we visited the fountain we were in imminent danger, as I am going to relate. Early in the morning, excited by unconquerable thirst, I arose and went to the spring, and having, thoughtless of harm or danger, nearly half past the dewy vale, along the serpentine foot path, my hasty steps were suddenly stopped by the sight of a hideous serpent, the formidable rattle snake, in a high spiral coil, forming a circular mound half the height of my knees, within six inches of the narrow path; as soon as I recovered my senses and strength from so sudden a surprise, I started back out of his reach, where I stood to view him; he lay quiet whilst I surveyed

[1]Magnolia grandiflora, called by the inhabitants the Laurel.

him, appearing no way surprised or disturbed, but kept his half-shut eyes fixed on me; my imagination and spirits were in a tumult, almost equally divided betwixt thanksgiving to the Supreme Creator and preserver, and the dignified nature of the generous though terrible creature, who had suffered us all to pass many times by him during the night, without injuring us in the least, although we must have touched him, or our steps guided therefrom by a supreme guardian spirit: I hastened back to acquaint my associates, but with a determination to protect the life of the generous serpent; I presently brought my companions to the place, who were, beyond expression, surprised and terrified at the sight of the animal, and in a moment acknowledged their escape from destruction to be miraculous; and I am proud to assert, that all of us, except one person, agreed to let him lay undisturbed, and that person was at length prevailed upon to suffer him to escape.

Again, when in my youth, attending my father on a journey to the Catskill Mountains, in the government of New-York; having nearly ascended the peak of Giliad, being youthful and vigorous in the pursuit of botanical and novel objects, I had gained the summit of a steep rocky precipice, a-head of our guide, when, just entering a shady vale, I saw at the root of a small shrub, a singular and beautiful appearance, which I remember to have instantly apprehended to be a large kind of Fungus which we call Jews ears, and was just drawing back my foot to kick it over, when at the instant, my father being near, cried out, a rattle snake my son, and jerked me back, which probably saved my life; I had never before seen one, this was of the kind which our guide called a yellow one, it was very beautiful, speckled and clouded. My father plead for his life, but our guide was inexorable, saying he never spared the life of a rattle snake, and killed him; my father took his skin and fangs.

Some years after this, when again in company with my father on a journey into East Florida, on the banks of St. Juan, at Fort Picolata, attending the congress at a treaty between that government and the Creek Nation, for obtaining a territory from that people to annex to the new government. After the Indians and a detachment from the garrison of St. Augustine had arrived and encamped separately, near the fort, some days elapsed before the business of the treaty came on, waiting the arrival of a vessel from St. Augustine, on board of which were the presents for the Indians. My father employed this time of leisure in little excursions round about the fort; and one morning, being the day the treaty commenced, I attended him on a botanical excursion, some time after we had been rambling in a swamp about a quarter of a mile from the camp, I being a-head a few paces, my father bid me observe the rattle snake before and just at my feet, I stopped and saw the monster formed in a high spiral coil, not half his length from my feet, another step forward would have put my life in his power, as I must have touched if not stumbled over him; the fright and perturbation of my spirits at once excited resentment, at that time I was entirely insensible to gratitude or mercy; I instantly cut off a little sapling, and soon dispatched him: this serpent was about six feet in length, and as thick as an ordinary man's leg. The rencounter deterred us from proceeding on our researches for that day. So I cut off a long tough withe or vine, which fastening round the neck of the slain serpent I dragged him after me, his scaly body sounding over the ground, and entering the camp with him in triumph, was soon surrounded by the amazed multitude, both Indians and my countrymen. The adventure soon reached the ears of the commander, who sent an officer to request that, if the snake had not bit himself, he might have him served up for his dinner; I readily delivered up the body of the snake to the cooks, and being that day invited to dine at the governor's table, saw the snake served up in several dishes; governor Grant being fond of the flesh of the rattle snake; I tasted of it but could not swallow it. I, however, was sorry after killing the serpent when cooly recollecting every circumstance, he certainly had it in his power to kill me almost instantly, and I make no doubt but that he was conscious of it. I promised myself that I would never again be accessary to the death of a rattle snake, which promise I have invariably kept to. This dreaded animal is easily killed, a stick no thicker than a man's thumb is sufficient to kill the largest at one stroke, if well directed either on the head or across the back, nor can they make their escape by running off, nor indeed do they attempt it when attacked.

The moccasin snake is a large and horrid serpent to all appearance, and there are very terrifying stories related of him by the inhabitants of the Southern states, where they greatly abound, particularly in East Florida: that their bite is always incurable, the flesh for a considerable space about the wound rotting to the bone, which then becomes carious and a general mortification ensues, which infallibly destroys the patient; the members of the body rotting and dying by piecemeal, and that there is no remedy to prevent a lingering miserable death but by immediately cutting away the flesh to the bone, for some distance round about the wound. In shape and proportion of parts they much resemble the rattle snake, and are marked or clouded much after the same manner, but their colours more dull and obscure; and in their disposition seem to agree with that dreadful reptile, being slow of progression, and throw themselves in a spiral coil ready for a blow when attacked. They have one peculiar quality, which is this, when discovered, and observing their enemy to take notice of them, after throwing themselves in a coil, they gradually raise their upper mandible or jaw until it falls back nearly touching their neck, at the same time slowly vibrating their long purple forked tongue, their crooked poisonous fangs directed right at you, gives the creature a most terrifying appearance. They are from three to four and even five feet in length, and as thick as a man's leg; they are not numerous, yet too common, and a sufficient terror to the miserable naked slaves, who are compelled to labour in the swamps and low lands where they only abound.

I never could find any that knew an instance of any person's losing their life from the bite of them, only by hearsay. Yet I am convinced it is highly prudent for every person to be on their guard against them. They appear to be of the viper tribe, from their swelling of their body and flattening their neck when provoked, and from their large poisonous fangs; their head, mouth and eyes are remarkably large.

There is another snake in Carolina and Florida called the moccasin, very different from this, which is a very beautiful creature, and I believe not of a destructive or vindictive nature; these when grown to their greatest size are about five feet in length, and near as thick as a man's arm; their skin scaly but smooth and shining, of a pale grey and sky colour ground, uniformly marked with transverse undulatory ringlets or blotches of a deep nut brown, edged with red or bright Spanish brown; they appear innocent, very active and swift, endeavouring to escape from one; they have no poisonous fangs. These are seen in high forest lands, about rotten logs or decayed fallen limbs of trees, and they harbour about old log buildings. They seem to be a species, if not the very same snake which in Pennsylvania and Virginia, are called the wampum snake, but here in warmer Southern climes they grow to a much larger size, and from the same accident their colour may be more variable and deeper. They are by the inhabitants asserted to be dangerously venomous, their bite incurable, &c. But as I could never learn an instance of their bite being mortal or attended with any dangerous consequence, and having had frequent opportunities of observing their nature and disposition, I am inclined to pronounce them an innocent creature, with respect to mankind.

The bastard rattle snake, by some called ground rattle snake, is a dangerous little creature; their bite is certainly mortal if present medical relief is not administered: they seem to be much of the nature of the asp or adder of the old world.

This little viper is in form and colour much like the rattle snake, but not so bright and uniformly marked; their head is broader and shorter in proportion with the other parts of their body; their nose prominent and turned upwards; their tail becomes suddenly small from the vent to the extremity, which terminates with three minute articulations, resembling rattles; when irritated they turn up their tail which vibrates so quick as to appear like a mist or vapour, but causes little or no sound or noise, yet it is the common report of the inhabitants, that they cause that remarkable vehement noise, so frequently observed in forests in the heat of summer and autumn, very terrifying to strangers, which is, probably, caused by a very sable, small insect of the genus cicadae, or which are called locusts in America, yet it is possible I may be mistaken in this conjecture. This dangerous viper is from eight to ten inches in length, and of proportionable thickness; they are a spiteful, snappish creature, throwing themselves into a little coil, swell and flatten themselves, continually darting out their head, and they seem capable of springing beyond their length. They seem destitute of the pacific disposition and magnanimity of the rattle snake, and are unworthy of an alliance with him; no man ever saves their lives, yet they remain too numerous, even in the oldest settled parts of the country.

The green snake is a beautiful innocent creature; they are from two to three feet in length, but not so thick as a person's little finger, of the finest green colour. They are very abundant, commonly seen on the limbs of trees and shrubs: they prey upon insects and reptiles, particularly the little green chameleon; and the forked tailed hawk or kite feeds on both of them, snatching them off the boughs of the trees.

The ribband snake is another very beautiful innocent serpent; they are eighteen inches in length, and about the thickness of a man's little finger; the head is very small; the ground colour of a full, clear vermillion, variegated with transverse bars or zones of a dark brown, which people fancy represents a ribband wound round the creature's body: they are altogether inoffensive to man, and are in a manner domestic, frequenting old wooden buildings, open grounds and plantations.

The chicken snake is a large, strong and swift serpent, six or seven feet in length, but scarcely so thick as a man's wrist; they are of a cinerious, earthy colour, and striped longitudinally with broad lines or lists, of a dusky or blackish colour. They are a domestic snake, haunting about houses and plantations, and would be useful to man if tamed and properly tutored, being great devourers of rats, but they are apt to disturb hen roosts and prey upon chickens. They are as innocent as a worm with respect to venom, are easily tamed and soon become very familiar.

The pine or bull snake is very large and inoffensive with respect to mankind, but devour squirrels, birds, rabbits and every other creature they can take as food. They are the largest snake yet known in North America, except the rattle snake, and perhaps exceed him in length; they are pied black and white; they utter a terrible loud hissing noise, sounding very hollow and like distant thunder, when irritated, or at the time of incubation, when the males contend with each other for the desired female. These serpents are also called horn snakes, from their tail terminating with a hard, horny spur, which they vibrate very quick when disturbed, but they never attempt to strike with it; they have dens in the earth, whither they retreat precipitately when apprehensive of danger.

. . .

This exalted peak I named mount Magnolia[1], from a new and beautiful species of that celebrated family of flowering trees, which here, at the cascades of Falling Creek, grows in a high degree of perfection, for although I had noticed this curious tree several times before, particularly on the high ridges betwixt Sinica and Keowe, and on ascending the first mountain after leaving Keowe, when I observed it in flower, but here it flourishes and commands our attention.

This tree, or perhaps rather a shrub, rises eighteen to thirty feet in height, there are usually many stems from a root or source, which lean a little, or slightly diverge from each other, in this respect imitating the Magnolia tripetala; the crooked wreathing branches arising and subdividing from the main stem without order or uniformity, their extremities turn upwards, producing a very large rosaceous, perfectly white, double or polypetalous flower, which is of a most fragrant scent; this fine flower sits in the center of a radices of very large leaves, which are of a singular figure, somewhat lanciolate, but broad towards their extremities, terminating with an acuminated point, and backwards they attenuate and become very narrow towards their bases, terminating that way with two long, narrow ears or lappets, one on each side of the insertion of the petiole; the leaves have only

[1]Magnolia auriculata.

short footstalks, sitting very near each other, at the extremities of the floriferous branches, from whence they spread themselves after a regular order, like the spokes of a wheel, their margins touching or lightly lapping upon each other, form an expansive umbrella superbly crowned or crested with the fragrant flower, representing a white plume; the blossom is succeeded by a very large crimson cone or strobile, containing a great number of scarlet berries, which, when ripe, spring from their cells and are for a time suspended by a white silky web or thread. The leaves of these trees which grow in a rich, light, humid soil, when fully expanded and at maturity, are frequently above two feet in length and six or eight inches where broadest. I discovered in the maritime parts of Georgia, particularly on the banks of the Alatamaha, another new species of Magnolia, whose leaves were nearly of the figure of those of this tree, but they were much less in size, not more than six or seven inches in length, and the strobile very small, oblong, sharp pointed, and of a fine deep crimson colour, but I never saw the flower. These trees grow straight and erect, thirty feet or more in height, and of a sharp conical form, much resembling the Cucumber tree (Mag. acuminata) in figure.

The day being remarkably warm and sultry, which, together with the labour and fatigue of ascending the mountains, made me very thirsty and in some degree sunk my spirits. Now past mid-day, I sought a cool shaded retreat, where was water for refreshment and grazing for my horse, my faithful slave and only companion. After proceeding a little farther, descending the other side of the mountain, I perceived at some distance before me, on my right hand, a level plain supporting a grand high forest and groves: the nearer I approach my steps are the more accelerated from the flattering prospect opening to view; I now enter upon the verge of the dark forest, charming solitude! as I advanced through the animating shades, observed on the farther grassy verge a shady grove; thither I directed my steps; on approaching these shades, between the stately columns of the superb forest trees, presented to view, rushing from rocky precipices under the shade of the pensile hills, the unparalleled cascade of Falling Creek, rolling and leaping off the rocks, which uniting below, spread a broad, glittering sheet of chrystal waters, over a vast convex elevation of plain, smooth rocks, and are immediately received by a spacious basin, where, trembling in the centre through hurry and agitation, they gently subside, encircling the painted still verge, from whence gliding swiftly, they soon form a delightful little river, which continuing to flow more moderately, is restrained for a moment, gently undulating in a little lake, they then pass on rapidly to a high perpendicular steep of rocks, from whence these delightful waters are hurried down with irresistible rapidity. I here seated myself on the moss clad rocks, under the shade of spreading trees and floriferous fragrant shrubs, in full view of the cascades.

At this rural retirement were assembled a charming circle of mountain vegetable beauties, Magnolia auriculata, Rhododendron ferrugineum, Kalmia latifolia, Robinia montana, Azalea flammula, Rosa paniculata, Calycanthus Floridus, Philadelphus inodorus, perfumed Convalaria majalis, Anemone thalictroides, Anemone hepatica, Erythronium maculatum, Leontice thalictroides, Trillium sessile, Trillium cesnum, Cypripedium, Arethusa, Ophrys, Sanguinaria, Viola uvul ria, Epigea, Mitchella repens, Stewartia, Halesia, Styrax, Lonicera, &c. Some of these roving beauties are strolling over the mossy, shelving, humid rocks, or from off the expansive wavy boughs of trees, bending over the floods, salute their delusive shades, playing on the surface, some plunge their perfumed heads and bathe their flexile limbs in the silver stream, whilst others by the mountain breezes are tossed about, their blooming tufts bespangled with pearly and chrystaline dew-drops collected from the falling mists, glisten in the rainbow arch. Having collected some valuable specimens at this friendly retreat, I continued my lonesome pilgrimage. My road for a considerable time led me winding and turning about the steep rockly hills; the descent of some of which were very rough and troublesome, by means of fragments of rocks, slippery clay and talc; but after this I entered a spacious forest, the land having gradually acquired a more level surface; a pretty grassy vale appears on my right, through which my wandering path led me, close by the banks of a delightful creek, which sometimes falling over steps of rocks, glides gently with serpentine meanders through the meadows.

After crossing this delightful brook and mead, the land rises again with sublime magnificence, and I am led over hills and vales, groves and high forests, vocal with the melody of the feathered songsters, the snow-white cascades glittering on the sides of the distant hills.

It was now afternoon; I approached a charming vale, amidst sublimely high forests, awful shades! Darkness gathers around, far distant thunder rolls over the trembling hills; the black clouds with august majesty and power, move slowly forwards, shading regions of towering hills, and threatening all the destructions of a thunder storm; all around is now still as death, not a whisper is heard, but a total inactivity and silence seem to pervade the earth; the birds afraid to utter a chirrup, and in low tremulous voices take leave of each other, seeking covert and safety; every insect is silenced, and nothing heard but the roaring of the approaching hurricane; the mighty cloud now expands its sable wings, extending from North to South, and is driven irresistibly on by the tumultuous winds, spreading his livid wings around the gloomy concave, armed with terrors of thunder and fiery shafts of lightning; now the lofty forests bend low beneath its fury, their limbs and wavy boughs are tossed about and catch hold of each other; the mountains tremble and seem to reel about, and the ancient hills to be shaken to their foundations: the furious storm sweeps along, smoaking through the vale and over the resounding hills; the face of the earth is obscured by the deluge descending from the firmament, and I am deafened by the din of the thunder; the tempestuous scene damps my spirits, and my horse sinks under me at the tremendous peals, as I hasten on for the plain.

The storm abating, I saw an Indian hunting cabin on the side of a hill, a very agreeable prospect, especially in my present condition; I made up to it and took quiet possession, there being no one to dispute it with me except a few bats and whip-poor-wills, who had repaired thither for shelter from the violence of the hurricane.

Having turned out my horse in the sweet meadows adjoining, and finding some dry wood under shelter of the old cabin, I struck up a fire, dried my clothes and comforted myself with a frugal repast of biscuit and dried beef, which was all the food my viaticum afforded me by this time, excepting a small piece of cheese which I had furnished myself with at Charleston and kept till this time.

The night was clear, calm and cool, and I rested quietly. Next morning at day break I was awakened and summoned to resume my daily task, by the shrill cries of the social night hawk and active merry mock-bird. By the time the rising sun had gilded the tops of the towering hills, the mountains and vales rang with the harmonious shouts of the pious and cheerful tenants of the groves and meads.

I observed growing in great abundance in these mountain meadows, Sanguisorba Canadensis and Heracleum maximum, the latter exhibiting a fine show, being rendered conspicious even at a great distance, by its great height and spread, vast pennatifid leaves and expansive umbels of snow-white flowers; the swelling bases of the surrounding hills fronting the meadows, present, for my acceptance, the fragrant red strawberry in painted beds of many acres surface, indeed I may safely say many hundreds.

After passing through this meadow, the road led me over the bases of a ridge of hills, which as a bold promontory dividing the fields I had just passed, form expansive green lawns. On these towering hills appeared the ruins of the ancient famous town of Sticoe. Here was a vast Indian mount or tumulus and great terrace, on which stood the council-house, with banks encompassing their circus; here were also old Peach and Plumb orchards, some of the trees appeared yet thriving and fruitful; presently after leaving these ruins, the vale and fields are divided by means of a spur of the mountains pushing forward; here likewise the road forked, the left-hand path continued up the mountain to the Overhill towns; I followed the vale to the right hand, and soon began again to ascend the hills, riding several miles over very rough, stony land, yielding the like vegetable productions as heretofore; and descending again gradually, by a dubious winding path, leading into a narrow vale and lawn, through which rolled on before me a delightful brook, water of the Tanase; I crossed it and continued a mile or two down the meadows, when the high mountains on each side suddenly receding, discovered the opening of the extensive and fruitful vale of Cowe, through which meanders the head branch of the Tanase, almost from its source, sixty miles, following its course down to Cowe.

I left the stream for a little while, passing swiftly and foaming over its rocky bed, lashing the steep craggy banks, and then suddenly sunk from my sight, murmuring hollow and deep under the rocky surface of the ground: on my right hand the vale expands, receiving a pretty silvery brook of water, which came hastily down from the adjacent hills, and entered the river a little distance before me; I now turn from the heights on my left, the road leading into the level lawns, to avoid the hollow rocky grounds, full of holes and cavities, arching over the river, through which the waters are seen gliding along, but the river is soon liberated from these solitary and gloomy recesses, and appears waving through the green plain before me. I continued several miles, pursuing my serpentine path, through and over the meadows and green fields, and crossing the river, which is here incredibly increased in size, by the continual accession of brooks flowing in from the hills on each side, dividing their green turfy beds, forming them into parterres, vistas and verdant swelling knolls, profusely productive of flowers and fragrant strawberries, their rich juice dying my horse's feet and ancles.

These swelling hills, the prolific beds on which the towering mountains repose, seem to have been the common situations of the towns of the ancients, as appears from the remaining ruins of them yet to be seen; and the level rich vale and meadows in front, their planting grounds.

Continuing yet ten or twelve miles down the vale, my road leading at times close to the banks of the river, the Azalea, Kalmia, Rhododendron, Philadelphus, &c. beautifying his now elevated shores, and painting the cove with a rich and cheerful scenery, continually unfolding new prospects as I traverse the shores; towering mountains seem continually in motion as I pass along, pompously raising their superb crests towards the lofty skies, traversing the far distant horizon.

The Tanase is now greatly increased from the conflux of the multitude of rivulets and brooks, descending from the hills on either side, generously contributing to establish his future fame, already a spacious river.

The mountains recede, the vale expands, two beautiful rivulets stream down through lateral vales, gliding in serpentine mazes over the green turfy knolls, and enter the Tanase nearly opposite to each other. Straight forward the expansive green vale seems yet infinite: now on the right hand a lofty pyramidal hill terminates a spur of the adjacent mountain, and advances almost into the river; but immediately after doubling this promontory, an expanded wing of the vale spreads on my right, down which came precipitately a very beautiful creek, which flowed into the river just before me; but now behold, high upon the side of a distant mountain overlooking the vale, the fountain of this brisk flowing creek; the unparalleled waterfall appears as a vast edifice with chrystal front, or a field of ice lying on the bosom of the hill.

I now approach the river at the fording place, which was greatly swollen by the floods of rain that fell the day before, and ran with foaming rapidity, but observing that it had fell several feet perpendicular, and perceiving the bottom or bed of the river to be level, and covered evenly with pebbles, I ventured to cross over, however I was obliged to swim two or three yards at the deepest channel of it, and landed safely on the banks of a fine meadow, which lay on the opposite shore, where I immediately alighted and spread aboard on the turf my linen, books and specimens of plants, &c to dry, turned out my steed to graze and then advanced into the strawberry plains to regale on the fragrant, delicious fruit, welcomed by communities of the splendid meleagris, the capricious roe-buck, and all the free and happy tribes which possess and inhabit those prolific fields, who appeared to invite and joined with me in the participation of the bountiful repast presented to us from the lap of nature.

I mounted again and followed the trading path about a quarter of a mile through the fields, then gently ascended the green beds of the hills, and entered the forests, being a point of a chain of hills projecting into the green vale or low lands of the rivers; this forest continued about a mile, the surface of the land level but rought, being covered with stones or fragments of rocks, and very large, smooth pebbles of various shapes and sizes, some of ten or fifteen pounds weight: I observed on each side of the road many vast heaps of these stones, Indian graves undoubtedly.*

After I left the graves,the ample vale soon offered on my right hand, through the tall forest trees, charming views, and which exhibited a pleasing contrast, immediately out of the gloomy shades and scenes of death, into expansive, lucid, green, flowery fields, expanding between retiring hills, and turfy eminences, the rapid Tanase gliding through a vast serpent rushing after his prey.

My winding path now leads me again over the green fields into the meadows, sometimes visiting the decorated banks of the river, as it meanders through the meadows, or boldly sweeps along the bases of the mountains, its surface receiving the images reflected from the flowery banks above.

Thus was my agreeable progress for about fifteen miles, since I came upon the sources of the Tanase, at the head of this charming vale; in the evening espying a human habitation at the foot of the sloping green hills, beneath lofty forests of the mountains on the left hand, and at the same time observing a man crossing the river from the opposite shore in a canoe and coming towards me, I waited his approach, who hailing me, I answered I was for Cowe; he entreated me very civilly to call at his house, adding that he would presently come to me.

I was received and entertained here until next day with the most perfect civility. After I had dined, towards evening, a company of Indian girls, inhabitants of a village in the hills at a small distance, called, having baskets of strawberries; and this man, who kept here a trading-house, and being married to a Cherokee woman of family, was indulged to keep a stock of cattle, and his helpmate being an excellent house-wife and a very agreeable good woman, treated us with cream and strawberries.

. . .

Having paid our attention to this useful part of the creation, who, if they are under our dominion, have consequently a right to our protection and favour. We returned to our trusty servants that were regaling themselves in the exuberant sweet pastures and strawberry fields in sight, and mounted again; proceeding on our return to town, continued through part of this high forest skirting on the meadows; began to ascend the hills of a ridge which we were under the necessity of crossing, and having gained its

*At this place was fought a bloody and decisive battle between these Indians and the Carolinians, under the conduct of general Middleton, when a great number of Cherokee warriors were slain, which shook their power, terrified and humbled them, insomuch that they deserted most of their settlements in the low countries, and betook themselves to the mountains as less accessible to the regular forces of the white people.

summit, enjoyed a most enchanting view, a vast expanse of green meadows and strawberry fields; a meandering river gliding through, saluting in its various turnings the swelling, green, turfy knolls, embellished with parterres of flowers and fruitful strawberry beds; flocks of turkies strolling about them; herds of deer prancing in the meads or bounding over the hills; companies of young, innocent Cherokee virgins, some busily gathering the rich fragrant fruit, others having already filled their baskets, lay reclined under the shade of floriferous and fragrant native bowers of Magnolia, Azalea, Philadelphus, perfumed Calycanthus, sweet Yellow Jessamine and cerulean Glycine frutescens, disclosing their beauties to the fluttering breeze, and bathing their limbs in the cool fleeting streams; whilst other parties, more gay and libertine, were yet collecting strawberries or wantonly chasing their companions, tantalising them, staining their lips and cheeks with the rich fruit.

This sylvan scene of primitive innocence was enchanting, and perhaps too enticing for hearty young men long to continue idle spectators.

In fine, nature prevailing over reason, we wished at least to have a more active part in their delicious sports. Thus precipitately resolving, we cautiously made our approaches, yet undiscovered, almost to the joyous scene of action. Now, although we meant no other than an innocent frolic with this gay assembly of hamadryades, we shall leave it to the person of feeling and sensibility to form an idea to what lengths our passions might have hurried us, thus warmed and excited, had it not been for the vigilance and care of some envious matrons who lay in ambush, and espying us gave the alarm, time enough for the nymphs to rally and assemble together; we however pursued and gained ground on a group of them, who had incautiously strolled to a greater distance from their guardians, and finding their retreat now like to be cut off, took shelter under cover of a little grove, but on perceiving themselves to be discovered by us, kept their station, peeping through the bushes; when observing our approaches, they confidently discovered themselves and decently advanced to meet us, half unveiling their blooming faces, incarnated with the modest maiden blush, and with native innocence and cheerfulness, presented their little baskets, merrily telling us their fruit was ripe and sound.

We accepted a basket, sat down and regaled ourselves on the delicious fruit, encircled by the whole assembly of the innocent jocose sylvan nymphs; by this time the several parties, under the conduct of the elder matrons, had disposed themselves in companies on the green, turfy banks.

My young companion, the trader, by concessions and suitable apologies for the bold intrusion, having compromised the matter with them, engaged them to bring their collection to his house at a stipulated price, we parted friendly.

And now taking leave of these Elysian fields, we again mounted the hills, which we crossed, and traversing obliquely their flowery beds, arrived in town in the cool of the evening.

Thomas Jefferson
1743-1826

Statesman, scientist, musician, agriculturalist, lawyer, educator, inventor, philologist, and geographer, Thomas Jefferson wrote only one book, *Notes on the State of Virginia* (1784–85), during his busy life. He left, however, nearly fifty volumes of papers and letters that reflect the quality of his mind and the diversity of his interests. *Notes,* written in response to questions about Virginia posed by the French Secretary, is of interest because it demonstrates one man's intellectual discovery of his own country, a country represented by the sprawling Virginia of his day. Here we see the eighteenth-century scientist studying nature (as well as economics, religion, law, and ethnology), yet expressing at times romantic feelings for the grandeur of the American environment. Natural history was always the main field of Jefferson's scientific study. And in America, Jefferson found evidence—contrary to that of such natural historians as Buffon—that the aboriginal people and animal species of America were not decaying but were strong, diverse, and healthy.

The history of Jefferson's statesmanship, beginning in 1774 when the coming Revolution forced him to abandon his law practice, is well enough known. But his interest and influence in the American tradition of agrarianism and wilderness use is perhaps less obvious. Jefferson, for instance, was responsible for developing the nation's first land law, the Ordinance of 1784, which created a series of territories in expanding America bounded by lines of longitude and latitude. The ordinance provided the impetus for new and free states to arise out of the American frontier as it was being developed by settlers moving west. His architectural and landscaping achievement, Monticello, embodied his ideal of the agrarian life—beautiful, simple, and logical. The buildings expressed the "sententious brevity" of style that Jefferson learned from his Roman masters.

His writings are full of moral earnestness, born of the Enlightenment, of Bacon, Newton, Locke, and the British rationalists, and reflecting his ideal that philosophy, art, and architecture were meant not to *reflect* the world, but—revolutionary that he was—to *change* it. Beyond bigotry and superstition, he sought the truths of nature and of this new American earth in the service of respectful mankind.

Somehow in Jefferson's mind were combined the ideals of commercial freedom, agrarianism, and the democratic revolution at home and abroad; this combined ideal, he believed, might serve as a bulwark against elitist, centralized, and privileged politics. His public activity on behalf of his ideals, despite his desire to return to his "farm, family, and books," is the mark of the man. He could function, because it was necessary, as cosmopolite and urban sophisticate when he served five years as America's Minister to France, when he was secretary of state under Washington in 1789, when he was Vice President in 1797, and when he was President for two terms (1801–1809) while serving also as President of the American Philosophical Society. His final retirement to his "potatoes and garden" and books, as the "Sage of Monticello," came in 1809. His fascination with the scientific exploration of wilderness was carried into his Presidency by the Lewis and Clark Expedition, following the purchase of the 82,000-square-mile Louisiana Territory in 1803.

Jefferson's report for the French Secretary Marquis de Barbe-Marbois aroused such curiosity among scientists in Philadelphia that he continued his investigations and revised them from 1782–84, when they were printed privately in Paris in two hundred copies as *Notes on Virginia*. The book established his reputation as a natural historian and scientist.

from NOTES ON THE STATE OF VIRGINIA*
Query II

. . . The *Mississippi* will be one of the principal channels of future commerce for the country westward of the Alleghany. From the mouth of this river to where it receives the Ohio, is 1,000 miles by water, but only 500 by land, passing through the Chickasaw country. From the mouth of the Ohio to that of the Missouri, is 230 miles by water, and 140 by land. From thence to the mouth of the Illinois river, is always muddy, and abounding with sand bars, which frequently change their places. However, it carries 15 feet water to the mouth of the Ohio, to which place it is from one and a half to two miles wide, and thence to Kaskaskia from one mile to a mile and a quarter wide. Its current is so rapid, that it never can be stemmed by the force of the wind alone, acting on sails. Any vessel, however, navigated with oars, may come up at any time, and receive much aid from the wind. A batteau passes from the mouth of Ohio to the mouth of Mississippi in three weeks, and is from two to three months getting up again. During its floods, which are periodical as those of the Nile, the largest vessels may pass down it, if their steerage can be insured. These floods begin in April, and the river returns into its banks early in August. The inundation extends further on the western than eastern side, covering the lands in some places for 50 miles

*Reprinted with permission from The American Antiquarian Society, Early American Imprints.

from its banks. Above the mouth of the Missouri, it becomes much such a river as the Ohio, like it clear, and gentle in its current, not quite so wide, the period of its floods nearly the same, but not rising to so great a height. The streets of the village at Cohoes are not more than 10 feet above the ordinary level of the water, and yet were never overflowed. Its bed deepens every year. Cohoes, in the memory of many people now living, was insulated by every flood of the river. What was the eastern channel has now become a lake, 9 miles in length and one in width, into which the river at this day never flows. This river yields turtle of a peculiar kind, perch, trout, gar, pike, mullets, herrings, carp, spatula-fish of 50 lb. weight, cat-fish of 100 lb. weight, buffalo fish, and sturgeon. Alligators or crocodiles have been seen as high up as the Acansas. It also abounds in herons, cranes, ducks, brant, geese, and swans. Its passage is commanded by a fort established by this State, five miles below the mouth of Ohio, and ten miles above the Carolina boundary.

The Missouri, since the treaty of Paris, the Illinois and northern branches of the Ohio, since the cession to Congress, are no longer within our limits. Yet having been so heretofore, and still opening to us channels of extensive communications with the western and north-western country, they shall be noted in their order.

The *Missouri* is, in fact, the principal river, contributing more to the common stream than does the Mississippi, even after its junction with the Illinois. It is remarkably cold, muddy and rapid. Its overflowings are considerable. They happen during the months of June and July. Their commencement being so much later than those of the Mississippi, would induce a belief that the sources of the Missouri are northward of those of the Mississippi, unless we suppose that the cold increases again with the ascent of the land from the Mississippi westwardly. That this ascent is great, is proved by the rapidity of the river. Six miles above the mouth it is brought within the compass of a quarter of a mile's width: yet the Spanish merchants at Pancore, or St. Louis, say they go two thousand miles up it. It heads far westward of Rio Norte, or North River. There is, in the villages of Kaskaskia, Cohoes and St. Vincennes, no inconsiderable quantity of plate, said to have been plundered during the last war by the Indians from the churches and private houses of Santa Fé, on the North river, and brought to these villages for sale. From the mouth of Ohio to Santa Fé are forty days journey, or about 1,000 miles. What is the shortest distance between the navigable waters of the Missouri, and those of the North river, or how far this is navigable above Santa Fé, I could never learn. From Santa Fé to its mouth in the Gulf of Mexico is about 1,200 miles. The road from New Orleans to Mexico crosses this river at the post of Rio Norte, 800 miles below Santa Fé, and from this post to New Orleans is about 1,200 miles; thus making 2,000 miles betwen Santa Fé and New Orleans, passing down the North river, Red river and Mississippi; whereas it is 2,230 through the Missouri and Mississippi. From the same post of Rio Norte, passing near the mines of La Sierra and Laiguana, which are between the North river and the river Salina to Sartilla, is 375 miles; and from thence, passing the mines of Charcas, Zaccatecas and Potosi, to the city of Mexico is 375 miles; in all,

1,550 miles from Santa Fé to the city of Mexico. From New Orleans to the city of Mexico is about 1,950 miles: the roads, after setting out from the Red river, near Natchitoches, keeping generally parallel with the coast, and about two hundred miles from it, till it enters the city of Mexico.

The *Illinois* is a fine river, clear, gentle, and without rapids; insomuch that it is navigable for batteaux to its source. From thence is a portage of two miles only to the Chickago, which affords a batteau navigation of 16 miles to its entrance into lake Michigan. The Illinois, about 10 miles above its mouth, is 300 yards wide.

The *Kaskaskia* is 100 yards wide at its entrance into the Mississippi, and preserves that breadth to the Buffalo plains, 70 miles above. So far also it is navigable for loaded batteaux, and perhaps much further. It is not rapid.

The *Ohio* is the most beautiful river on earth. Its current gentle, waters clear, and bosom smooth and unbroken by rocks and rapids, a single instance only excepted.

It is ¼ of a mile wide at Fort Pitt:

500 yards at the mouth of the Great Kanhaway:

1 mile and 25 poles at Louisville:

¼ of a mile on the rapids, three or four miles below Louisville:

½ a mile where the low country begins, which is 20 miles above Green river.

1¼ at the receipt of the Tanissee:

And a mile wide at the mouth.

. . .

Query IV

A NOTICE *of its Mountains*

For the particular geography of our mountains I must refer to Fry and Jefferson's map of Virginia; and to Evans's analysis of his map of America for a more philosophical view of them than is to be found in any other work. It is worthy of notice, that our mountains are not solitary and scattered confusedly over the face of the country; but that they commence at about 150 miles from the sea-coast, are disposed in ridges one behind another, running nearly parallel with the sea-coast, though rather approaching it as they advance north-eastwardly. To the south-west, as the tract of country between the sea-coast and the Mississippi becomes narrower, the mountains converge into a single ridge, which, as it approaches the Gulf of Mexico, subsides into plain country, and gives rise to some of the waters of that Gulf, and particularly to a river called the Apalachicola, probably from the Apalachies, an Indian nation formerly residing on it. Hence the mountains giving rise to that river, and seen from its various parts, were called the Apalachian mountains, being in fact the end or termination only of the great ridges passing through the continent. European geographers however extended the name northwardly as far as the mountains extended; some giving it, after their separation into different ridges, to the Blue Ridge, others to the North Mountain, others to the Alleghaney, others to the Laurel Ridge, as may be seen in their different maps. But the fact I believe is, that none of these ridges were ever known by that name to the inhabitants, either native or emigrant, but as they saw them so called in European maps. In the same direction generally are the veins of lime-stone, coal and other minerals hitherto discovered; and so range the falls of our great rivers. But the courses of the great rivers are at right angles with these. James and Patowmac penetrate through all the ridges of mountains eastward of the Alleghaney, that is broken by no water course. It is in fact the spine of the country between the Atlantic on one side, and the Mississippi and St. Lawrence on the other. The passage of the Patowmac through the Blue Ridge is perhaps one of the most stupendous scenes in nature. You stand on a very high point of land. On your right comes up the Shenandoah, having ranged along the foot of the mountain an hundred miles to seek a vent. On your left approaches the Patowmac, in quest of a passage also. In the moment of their junction they rush together against the mountain, rend it asunder, and pass off to the sea. The first glance of this scene hurries our senses into the opinion, that this earth has been created in time, that the mountains were formed first, that the rivers began to flow afterwards, that in this place particularly they have been dammed up by the Blue Ridge of mountains, and have formed an ocean which filled the whole valley; that continuing to rise they have at length broken over at this spot, and have torn the mountain down from its summit to its base. The piles of rock on each hand, but particularly on the Shenandoah, the evident marks of their disruptive and avulsion from their beds by the most powerful agents of nature, corroborate the impression. But the distant finishing which nature has given to the picture is of a very different character. It is a true contrast to the foreground. It is as placid and delightful, as that is wild and tremendous. For the mountain being cloven asunder, she presents to your eye, through the cleft, a small catch of smooth blue horizon, at an infinite distance in the plain country, inviting you, as it were, from the riot and tumult roaring around, to pass through the breach and participate of the calm below. Here the eye ultimately composes itself; and that way too the road happens actually to lead. You cross the Patowmac above the junction, pass along its side through the base of the mountain for three miles, its terrible precipices hanging fragments over you, and within about 20 miles reach Frederick town and the fine country round that. This scene is worth a voyage across the Atlantic. Yet here, as in the neighborhood of the natural bridge, are people who have passed their lives within half a dozen miles, and have never been to survey these monuments of a war between rivers and mountains, which must have shaken the earth itself to its centre. (2)—The height of our mountains has not yet been estimated with any degree of exactness. The Alleghaney being the great ridge which divides the waters of the Atlantic from those of the Mississippi, its summit is doubtless more elevated above the ocean than that of any other mountain. But its relative height, compared with the base on which it stands, is not so great as that of some others, the country rising behind the successive ridges like the steps of stairs. The mountains of the Blue Ridge, and of these the Peaks of Otter, are thought to be of a greater height, measured from their base, than any others in our country, and perhaps in North America. From data, which may found a tolerable conjecture, we suppose the highest peak to be about 4,000 feet perpendicular, which is not a fifth part of the height of the mountains of South America, nor one-third of the height which would be necessary in our latitude to preserve ice in the open air unmelted through the year. The ridge of mountains next beyond the Blue Ridge, called by us the North Mountain, is of the greatest extent; for which reason they were named by the Indians the Endless Mountains.

A substance supposed to be pumice, found floating on the Mississippi, has induced a conjecture, that there is a volcano on some of its waters: and as these are mostly known to their sources, except the Missouri, our expectations of verifying the conjecture would of course be led to the mountains which divide the waters of the Mexican Gulf from those of the South Sea; but no volcano having ever yet been known at such a distance from the sea, we must rather suppose that this floating substance has been erroneously deemed pumice.

Query V

ITS *Cascades and Caverns*

The only remarkable cascade in this country is that of the Falling Spring in Augusta. It is a water of James river, where it is called Jackson's river, rising in the Warm Spring mountains about twenty miles South West of the Warm Spring, and flowing into that valley. About three-quarters of a mile from its source, it falls over a rock 200 feet into the valley below. The sheet of water is broken in its breadth by the rock in two or three places, but not at all in its height. Between the sheet and the rock, at the bottom, you may walk across dry. This cataract will bear no comparison with that of Niagara, as to the quantity of water composing it; the sheet being only 12 or 15 feet wide above, and somewhat more spread below; but it is half as high again, the latter being only 156 feet, according to the mensuration made by order of M. Vaudreuil, Governor of Canada, and 130 according to a more recent account.

In the lime-stone country, there are many caverns of very considerable extent. The most noted is called Madison's Cave, and is on the North side of the Blue ridge, near the intersection of the Rockingham and Augusta line with the south fork of the southern river of Shenandoah. It is in a hill of about 200 feet perpendicular height, the ascent of which, on one side, is so steep, that you may pitch a biscuit from its summit into the river which washes its base. The entrance of the cave is, in this side, about two thirds of the way up. It extends into the earth about 300 feet, branching into subordinate caverns, sometimes ascending a little, but more generally descending, and at length terminates, in two different places, at basons of water of unknown extent, and which I should judge to be nearly on a level with the water of the river; however, I do not think they are formed by refluent water from that, because they are never turbid; because they do not rise and fall in correspondence with that in times of flood, or of drought; and because the water is always cool. It is probably one of the many reservoirs with which the interior parts of the earth are supposed to abound, and which yield supplies to the fountains of water, distinguished from others only by its being accessible. The vault of this cave is of solid lime-stone, from 20 to 40 or 50 feet high, through which water is continually percolating. This, trickling down the sides of the cave, has incrusted them over in the form of elegant drapery; and dripping from the top of the vault generates on that, and on the base below, stalactites of a conical form, some of which have met and formed massive columns.

Another of these caves is near the North mountain, in the country of Frederick, on the lands of Mr. Zane. The entrance into this is on the top of an extensive ridge. You descend 30 or 40 feet, as into a well, from whence the cave then extends, nearly horizontally, 400 feet into the earth, preserving a breadth of from 20 to 50 feet, and a height of from 5 to 12 feet. After entering this cave a few feet, the mercury, which in the open air was 50°, rose to 57° of Fahrenheit's thermometer, answering to 11° of Reaumur's, and it continued at that to the remotest parts of the cave. The uniform temperature of the cellars of the observatory of Paris, which are 90 feet deep, and of all subterranean cavities of any depth, where no chemical agents may be supposed to produce a factitious heat, has been found to be 10° of Reaumur, equal to 54½° of Fahrenheit. The temperature of the cave above mentioned so nearly corresponds with this, that the difference may be ascribed to a difference of instruments.

At the Panther gap, in the ridge which divides the waters of the Cow and the Calf pasture is what is called the *Blowing cave.* It is in the side of a hill, is of about 100 feet diameter, and emits constantly a current of air of such force, as to keep the weeds prostrate to the distance of twenty yards before it. This current is strongest in dry frosty weather, and in long spells of rain weakest. Regular inspirations and expirations of air, by caverns and fissures, have been probably enough accounted for, by supposing them combined with intermitting fountains; as they must of course inhale air while their reservoirs are emptying themselves, and again emit it while they are filling. But a constant issue of air, only varying in its force as the weather is drier or damper, will require a new hypothesis. There is another blowing cave in the Cumberland mountain, about a mile from where it crosses the Carolina line. All we know of this is, that it is not constant, and that a fountain of water issues from it.

The *Natural bridge*, the most sublime of nature's works, though not comprehended under the present head, must not be pretermitted. It is on the ascent of a hill, which seems to have been cloven through its length by some great convulsion. The fissure, just at the bridge, is, by some admeasurements, 270 feet deep, by others only 205. It is about 45 feet wide at the bottom, and 90 feet at the top; this of course determines the length of the bridge, and its height from the water. Its breadth in the middle, is about

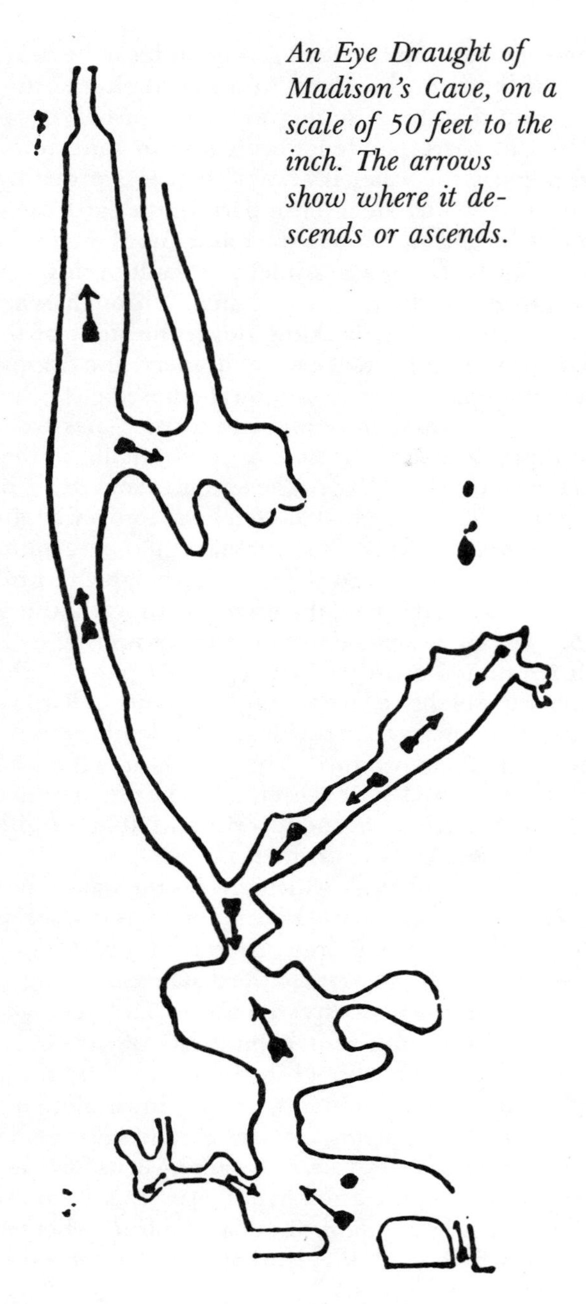

An Eye Draught of Madison's Cave, on a scale of 50 feet to the inch. The arrows show where it descends or ascends.

60 feet, but more at the ends, and the thickness of the mass at the summit of the arch, about 40 feet. A part of this thickness is constituted by a coat of earth, which gives growth to many large trees. The residue, with the hill on both sides, is one solid rock of lime-stone. The arch approaches the semi-elliptical form; but the larger axis of the ellipsis, which would be the cord of the arch, is many times longer than the transverse. Though the sides of this bridge are provided in some parts with a parapet of fixed rocks, yet few men

have resolution to walk to them and look over into the abyss. You involuntarily fall on your hands and feet, creep to the parapet and peep over it. Looking down from this height about a minute, gave me a violent head-ache. If the view from the top be painful and intolerable, that from below is delightful in an equal extreme. It is impossible for the emotions arising from the sublime, to be felt beyond what they are here: so beautiful an arch, so elevated, so light, and springing as it were up to heaven, the rapture of the spectator is really indescribable! The fissure continuing narrow, deep, and straight for a considerable distance above and below the bridge, opens a short but very pleasing view of the North mountain on one side, and Blue Ridge on the other, at the distance each of them of about five miles. This bridge is in the country of Rockbridge, to which it has given name, and affords a public and commodious passage over a valley, which cannot be crossed elsewhere for a considerable distance. The stream passing under it is called Cedear creek. It is a water of James river, and sufficient in the driest seasons to turn a grist-mill, though its fountain is not more than two miles above.[1]

[1]Don Ulloa mentions a break, similar to this, in the province of Angaraez, in South America. It is from sixteen to twenty-two feet wide, one hundred and eleven feet deep, and of 1.3 miles continuance, English measure. Its breadth at top is not sensibly greater than at bottom. But the following fact is remarkable, and will furnish some light for conjecturing the probable origin of our natural bridge. . . . Don Ulloa inclines to the opinion that this channel has been effected by the wearing of the water which runs through it, rather than that the mountain should have been broken open by any convulsion of nature. But if it had been worn by the running of water, would not the rocks which form the sides, have been worn plain? or if, meeting in some parts with veins of harder stone, the wtaer had left prominences on the side, would not the same cause have sometimes, or perhaps generally, occasioned prominences o the other side also? Yet Don Ulloa tells us, that on the other side there are always corresponding cavities, and that these tally with the prominences so perfectly, that, were the two sides to come together they would fit in all their indentures, without leaving any void. I think that this does not resemble the effect of running water, but looks rather as if the two sides had parted asunder. The sides of the break, over which is the natural bridge of Virginia, consisting of a veiny rock which yields to time, the correspondence between the salient and re-entering inequalities, if it existed at all, has now disappeared. This break has the advantage of the one described by Don Ulloa in its finest circumstance: no portion in that instance having held together, during the separation of the other parts, so as to form a bridge over the abyss.—T.J.

John James Audubon
1785-1851

John J. Audubon, whose name in our time is synonymous with the protection of birds and animals, was born in Haiti of a French sea captain father and a Haitian mother who died shortly after his birth in a slave rebellion. He began living in America, on a farm his father had purchased during his service in the American Revolution, only in 1803 at the age of 18. His father sent him from France to complete his education and find himself a career. Although young Audubon had lived in France from the age of three under the care of his foster mother, he made, or so his father believed, insufficient progress in his education whether through expensive tutoring or through entering the French Navy and studying for officer exams. Audubon's father believed that education was the one thing of value a man could have, so between his son's failures to apply himself and the wars in France toward the end of the century, he believed his son might have his best chance for a future in America at his "Mill Grove" farm in Pennsylvania.

Neither a pedant nor a caricature of the military leader, Audubon's father taught his son to appreciate the ways and beauties of nature. But it was nature only, from the first, that seemed to interest the son as an object of study and observation. Observing and drawing birds, hunting, fishing, art and music were his delights. "I pursued my simple and agreeable studies in Pennsylvania," he said, looking back on his youth from age, "with as little concern about the future as if the world had been made for me."

Even after his marriage, Audubon preferred to follow the call of the American wilderness rather than tend to the economies of running a family business in Kentucky. As a result he became a far greater woodsman and artist than businessman and husband. Like so many people of his age, he had both scientific and artistic inclinations. Even while a youth at Mill Grove, he performed on phoebes what were probably the first bird-banding experiments. He also dissected and studied dead bird specimens to learn the true anatomy of birds. The dual approach to nature's creatures always remained a conflict for him: "The moment a bird was dead," he wrote, "no matter how beautiful it had been in life, the pleasure of possession became blunted for me. I wished to possess all the productions of nature, but I wished to see *life* in them, as fresh from the hands of their Maker."

Audubon's journals are remarkable for depicting scenes of a frontier and wilderness that, as Audubon knew, were already slipping away in his time. His efforts to publish his work were part of a long and frustrating struggle for recognition, but even in his time there were some devotees. The greatest Shakespearean actress of her day, Fanny Kemble was known, for example, to recite Audubon's description of Niagara Falls in literary salons of Boston. His great work is *Birds of America* (1827-1838), a four-volume presentation of 1,065 life-sized colored plates of his paintings.

Unlike Byrd and Bartram, and very unlike the other Western explorer George Catlin, Audubon had not much sympathy with his Indian contacts in the West. "Several great warriors have condescended to shake my hand," he was capable of writing; "their very touch is disgusting—it will indeed be a deliverance to get rid of all this 'Indian poetry.' "

The sketches that follow are from *The Missouri River Journals* (1897) based on Audubon's 1843 trip, at nearly the age of sixty, aboard a fur-company boat to the Upper Missouri and the Yellowstone, and from "Episodes" of his *Ornithological Biography* that was published along with *Birds of America.*

from THE MISSOURI RIVER JOURNALS*

July 26, Wednesday. We were all on foot before day-break and had our breakfast by an early hour, and left on our trip for Buffalo cows. The wagon was sent across by hauling it through the east channel, which is now quite low, and across the sand-bars, which now reach seven-eighths of the distance across the river. We crossed in the skiff, and walked to the ferry-boat—I barefooted, as well as Mr. Culbertson; others wore boots or moccasins, but my feet have been tender of late, and this is the best cure. Whilst looking about for sticks to support our mosquito bars, I saw a Rabbit standing before me, within a few steps, but I was loaded with balls, and should have torn the poor thing so badly that it would have been useless as a specimen, so let it live. We left the ferry before six, and went on as usual. We saw two Antelopes on entering the bottom prairie, but they had the wind of us, and scampered off to the hills. We saw two Grouse, one of which Bell killed, and we found it very good this evening for our supper. Twelve bulls were seen, but we paid no attention to them. We saw a fine large Hawk, apparently the size of a Red-tailed Hawk, but with the whole head white. It had alighted on a clay hill or bank, but, on being approached, flew off to another, was pursued and again flew away, so that we could not procure it, but I have no doubt that it is a species not yet described. We now crossed Blackfoot River, and saw great numbers of Antelopes. Their play

*These selections are from *Audubon and His Journals*, II (New York: Charles Scribner's Sons, 1897).

and tricks are curious; I watched many of the groups a long time, and will not soon forget them. At last, seeing we should have no meat for supper, and being a party of nine, it was determined that the first animal seen should be run down and killed. We soon saw a bull, and all agreed to give every chance possible to Squires. Mr. C., Owen, and Squires started, and Harris followed without a gun, to see the chase. The bull was wounded twice by Squires, but no blood came from the mouth, and now all three shot at it, but the bull was not apparently hurt seriously; he became more and more furious, and began charging upon them. Unfortunately, Squires ran between the bull and a ravine quite close to the animal, and it suddenly turned on him; his horse became frightened and jumped into the ravine, the bull followed, and now Squires lost his balance; however, he threw his gun down, and fortunately clung to the mane of his horse and recovered his seat. The horse got away and saved his life, for, from what Mr. C. told me, had he fallen, the bull would have killed him in a few minutes, and no assistance could be afforded him, as Mr. C. and Owen had, at that moment, empty guns. Squires told us all; he had never been so bewildered and terrified before. The bull kept on running, and was shot at perhaps twenty times, for when he fell he had *twelve balls* in his side, and had been shot twice in the head. Another bull was now seen close by us, and Owen killed it after four shots. Whilst we were cutting up this one, La Fleur and some one else went to the other, which was found to be very poor, and, at this season smelling very rank and disagreeable. A few of the best pieces were cut away, and, as usual, the hunters ate the liver and fat quite raw, like Wolves, and we were now on the move again. Presently we saw seven animals coming towards us, and with the glass discovered there were six bulls and one cow. The hunters mounted in quick time, and away after the cow, which Owen killed very soon. To my surprise the bulls did not leave her, but stood about one hundred yards from the hunters, who were cutting her in pieces; the best parts were taken for dried meat. Had we not been so many, the bulls would, in all probability, have charged upon the butchers, but after a time they went off at a slow canter. At this moment Harris and I were going towards the party thus engaged, when a Swift Fox started from a hole under the feet of Harris' horse. I was loaded with balls, and he also; he gave chase and gained upon the beautiful animal with remarkable quickness. Bell saw this, and joined Harris, whilst I walked towards the butchering party. The Fox was overtaken by Harris, who took aim at it several times, but could not get sight on him, and the little fellow doubled and cut about in such a manner that it escaped into a ravine, and was seen no more. Now who will tell me that no animal can compete with this Fox in speed, when Harris, mounted on an Indian horse, overtook it in a few minutes? We were now in sight of a large band of cows and bulls, but the sun was low, and we left them to make our way to the camping-place, which we reached just before the setting of the sun. We found plenty of water, and a delightful spot, where we were all soon at work unsaddling our horses and mules, bringing wood for fires, and picking service-berries, which we found in great quantities and very good. We were thirty miles from Fort Union, close to the three Mamelles, but must have travelled near fifty, searching for and running down the game. All slept well, some outside and others inside the tent, after our good supper. We had a clear, bright day, with the wind from the westward.

July 27, Thursday. This morning was beautiful, the birds singing all around us, and after our early breakfast, Harris, with La Fleur and Mr. Culbertson, walked to the top of the highest of the three Mamelles; Bell went to skinning the birds shot yesterday, among which was a large Titmouse of the Eastern States, while I walked off a short distance, and made a sketch of the camp and the three Mamelles. I hope to see a fair picture from this, painted by Victor, this next winter, God willing. During the night the bulls were heard bellowing, and the Wolves howling, all around us. Bell had seen evidences of Grizzly Bears close by, but we saw none of the animals. An Antelope was heard snorting early this morning, and seen for a while, but La Fleur could not get it. The snorting of the Antelope is more like a whistling, sneezing sound, than like the long, clear snorting of our common Deer, and it is also very frequently repeated, say every few minutes, when in sight of an object of which the animal does not yet know the nature; for the moment it is assured of danger, it bounds three or four times like a sheep, and then either trots off or gallops like a horse. On the return of the gentlemen from the eminence, from which they had seen nothing but a Hawk, and heard the notes of the Rock Wren, the horses were gathered, and preparations made to go in search of cows. I took my gun and walked off ahead, and on ascending the first hill saw an Antelope, which, at first sight, I thought was an Indian. It stood still, gazing at me about five hundred yards off; I never stirred, and presently it walked towards me; I lay down and lowered my rifle; the animal could not now see my body; I showed it my feet a few times, at intervals. Presently I saw it coming full trot towards me; I cocked my gun, loaded with buck-shot in one barrel and ball in the other. He came within thirty yards of me and stopped suddenly, then turned broadside towards me. I could see his very eyes, his beautiful form, and his fine horns, for it was a buck. I pulled one trigger—it snapped, the animal moved not; I pulled the other, snapped again, and away the Antelope bounded, and ran swiftly from me. I put on fresh caps, and saw it stop after going a few hundred yards, and presently it came towards me again, but not within one hundred and fifty yards, when seeing that it would not come nearer I pulled the trigger with the ball; off it went, and so did the Antelope, which this time went quite out of my sight. I returned to camp and found all ready for a move. Owen went up a hill to reconnoitre for Antelopes and cows; seeing one of the former he crept after it. Bell followed, and at this moment a Hare leaped from the path before us, and stopped within twenty paces. Harris was not loaded with shot, and I only with buck-shot; however, I fired and killed it; it proved to be a large female, and after measuring, we skinned it, and I put on a label "Townsend's Hare, killed a few miles from the three Mamelles, July 27, 1843." After traveling for a good while, Owen, who kept ahead of us, made signs from the top of a high hill that Buffaloes were in sight. This signal is made by walking the rider's horse backwards and forwards several times. We hurried on towards him, and when we reached the place, he pointed to the spot where he had seen them, and said they were travelling fast, being a band of both cows and bulls. The hunters were mounted at once, and on account of Squires' soreness I begged him not to run; so he drove me in the wagon as fast as possible over hills, through plains and ravines of all descriptions, at a pace beyond belief. From time to time we saw the hunters, and once or twice the Buffaloes, which were going towards the fort. At last we reached an eminence from which we saw both the game and the hunters approaching the cattle, preparatory to beginning the chase. It seems there is no etiquette among Buffalo hunters, and this proved a great disappointment to friend Harris, who was as anxious to kill a cow, as he had been to kill a bull. Off went the whole group, but the country was not as advantageous to the pursuers, as to the pursued. The cows separated from the bulls, the latter making their way towards us, and six of them passed within one hundred yards of where I stood; we let them pass, knowing well how savage they are at these times, and turned our eyes again to the hunters. I saw Mr. C. pursuing one cow, Owen another, and Bell a third. Owen shot one and mortally wounded it; it walked up on a hill and stood there for some minutes before falling. Owen killed a second close by the one Mr. C. had now killed, Bell's dropped dead in quite another direction, nearly one mile off. Two bulls we saw coming directly towards us, so La Fleur and I went under cover of the hill to await their approach, and they came within sixty yards of us. I gave La Fleur the choice of shooting first, as he had a rifle; he shot and missed; they turned and ran in an opposite direction, so that I, who had gone some little distance beyond La Fleur, had no chance, and I was sorry enough for my politeness. Owen had shot a third cow, which went part way up a hill, fell, and kicked violently; she, however, rose and again fell, and kept kicking with all her legs in the air. Squires now drove to her, and I walked, followed by Moncrévier, a hunter; seeing Mr. C. and Harris on the bottom below we made signs for them to come up, and they fortunately did, and by galloping to Squires probably saved that young man from more danger; for though I cried to him at the top of my voice, the wind prevented him from hearing me; he now stopped, however, not far from a badly broken piece of ground over which had he driven at his usual speed, which I doubt not he would have attempted, some accident must have befallen him. Harris and Mr. C. rode up to the cow, which expired at that moment. The cow Mr. C. had killed was much the largest, and we left a cart and two men to cut up this, and the first two Owen had killed, and went to the place where the first lay, to have it skinned for me. Bell joined us soon, bringing a tongue with him, and he immediately began operations on the cow, which proved a fine one, and I have the measurements as follows: "Buffalo Cow, killed by Mr. Alexander Culbertson, July 27, 1843. Nose to root of tail, 96 inches. Height at shoulder, 60; at rump, 55½. Length of tail vertebrae, 13; to end of hair, 25; from brisket to bottom of feet, 21½; nose to anterior canthus, 10½; between horns at root, 11⅜; between tops of ditto, 17⅛; between nostrils, 2¼; length of ditto, 2½; height of nose, 3⅛; nose to opening of ear, 20; ear from opening to tip, 5; longest hair on head, 14 inches; from angle of mouth to end of under lip, 3½." Whilst we were at this, Owen and Pike were hacking at their cow. After awhile all was ready for departure, and we made for the "coupe" at two o'clock, and expected to have found water to enable us to water our horses, for we had yet some gallons of the Missouri water for our own use. We found the road to the "coupe," which was seen for many, many miles. The same general appearance of country shows throughout the whole of these dreary prairies; up one hill and down on the other side, then across a plain with ravines of more or less depth. About two miles west of the "coupe," Owen and others went in search of water, but in vain; and we have had to cross the "coupe" and travel fully two miles east of it, when we came to a mere puddle, sufficient however, for the night, and we stopped. The carts with the meat, and our effects, arrived after a while; the meat was spread on the grass, the horses and mules hoppled and let go, to drink and feed. All hands collected Buffalo dung for fuel, for not a bush was in sight, and we soon had a large fire. In the winter season this prairie fuel is too wet to burn, and oftentimes the hunters have to eat their meat raw, or go without their supper. Ours was cooked however; I made mine chiefly from the liver, as did Harris; others ate boiled or roasted meat as they preferred. The tent was pitched, and I made a bed for Mr. C. and myself, and guns, etc., were all under cover; the evening was cool, the wind fresh, and no mosquitoes. We had seen plenty of Antelopes; I shot at one twenty yards from the wagon with small shot. Harris killed a Wolf, but we have seen very few, and now I will wish you all good-night; God bless you!

July 28, Friday. This morning was cold enough for a frost, but we all slept soundly until daylight, and about half-past three we were called for breakfast. The horses had all gone but four, and, as usual, Owen was despatched for them. The horses were brought back, our coffee swallowed, and we were off, Mr. C. and I, in the wagon. We saw few Antelopes, no Buffalo, and reached the ferry opposite the fort at half-past seven. We found all well, and about eleven Assiniboins, all young men, headed by the son of a great chief called "Le mangeur d'hommes" (the man-eater). The poor wretched Indian whom Harris had worked over, died yesterday morning, and was buried at once. I had actually felt chilly riding in the wagon, and much enjoyed a breakfast Mrs. Culbertson had kindly provided for me. We had passed over some very rough roads, and at breakneck speed, but I did not feel stiff as I expected, though somewhat sore, and a good night's rest is all I need. This afternoon the cow's skin and head, and the Hare arrived, and have been preserved.

. . .

August 9, Wednesday. The weather is cool and we are looking for rain. Squires, Provost, and La Fleur went off this morning after an early breakfast, across the river for Bighorns with orders not to return without some of these wild animals, which reside in the most inaccessible portions of the broken and lofty clay hills and stones that exist in this region of the country; they never resort to the low lands except when moving from one spot to another; they swim rivers well, as do Antelopes. I have scarcely done anything but write this day, and my memorandum books are now crowded with sketches, measurements, and descriptions. We have nine Indians, all

Assiniboins, among whom *five* are chiefs. These nine Indians fed for three days on the flesh of only a single Swan; they saw no Buffaloes, though they report large herds about their village, fully two hundred miles from here. This evening I caught about one dozen catfish, and shot a *Spermophilus hoodii*, an old female, which had her pouches distended and filled with the seeds of the wild sunflower of this region. I am going to follow one of their holes and describe the same.

August 10, Thursday. Bell and I took a walk after Rabbits, but saw none. The nine Indians, having received their presents, went off with apparent reluctance, for when you begin to give them, the more they seem to demand. The horseguards brought in another *Spermophilus hoodii*; after dinner we are going to examine one of their burrows. We have been, and have returned; the three burrows which we dug were as follows: straight downward for three or four inches, and gradually becoming deeper in an oblique slant, to the depths of eight or nine inches, but not more, and none of these holes extended more than six or seven feet beyond this. I was disappointed at not finding nests, or rooms for stores. Although I have said much about Buffalo running, and butchering in general, I have not given the particular manner in which the latter is performed by the hunters of this country,—I mean the white hunters,—and I will now try to do so. The moment that the Buffalo is dead, three or four hunters, their faces and hands often covered with gunpowder, and with pipes lighted, place the animal on its belly, and by drawing out each fore and hind leg, fix the body so that it cannot fall down again; an incision is made near the root of the tail, immediately above the root in fact, and the skin cut to the neck, and taken off in the roughest manner imaginable, downwards and on both sides at the same time. The knives are going in all directions, and many wounds occur to the hands and fingers, but are rarely attended to at this time. The pipe of one man has perhaps given out, and with his bloody hands he takes the one of his nearest companion, who has his own hands equally bloody. Now one breaks in the skull of the bull, and with bloody fingers draws out the hot brains and swallows them with peculiar zest; another has now reached the liver, and is gobbling down enormous pieces of it; whilst, perhaps, a third, who has come to the paunch, is feeding luxuriously on some—to me—disgusting-looking offal. But the main business proceeds. The flesh is taken off from the sides of the boss, or hump bones, from where these bones begin to the very neck, and the hump itself is thus destroyed. The hunters give the name of "hump" to the mere bones when slightly covered by flesh; and it is cooked, and very good when fat, young, and well broiled. The pieces of flesh taken from the sides of these bones are called *filets*, and are the best portion of the animal when properly cooked. The fore-quarters, or shoulders, are taken off, as well as the hind ones, and the sides, covered by a thin portion of flesh called the *depouille*, are taken out. Then the ribs are broken off at the vertebrae, as well as the boss bones. The marrow-bones, which are those of the fore and hind legs only, are cut out last. The feet usually remain attached to these; the paunch is stripped of its covering of layers of fat, the head and the backbone are left to the Wolves, the pipes are all emptied, the hands, faces, and clothes all bloody, and now a glass of grog is often enjoyed, as the stripping off the skins and flesh of three or four animals is truly very hard work. In some cases when no water was near, our supper was cooked without our being washed, and it was not until we had traveled several miles the next morning that we had any opportunity of cleaning ourselves; and yet, despite everything, we are all hungry, eat heartily, and sleep soundly. When the wind is high and the Buffaloes run towards it, the hunter's guns very often snap, and it is during their exertions to replenish their pans, that the powder flies and sticks to the moisture every moment accumulating on their faces; but nothing stops these daring and usually powerful men, who the moment the chase is ended, leap from their horses, let them graze, and begin their butcher-like work.

August 11, Friday. The weather has been cold and windy, and the day has passed in comparative idleness with me. Squires returned this afternoon alone, having left Provost and La Fleur behind. They have seen only two Bighorns, a female and her young. It was concluded that, if our boat was finished by Tuesday next, we would leave on Wednesday morning, but I am by no means assured of this, and Harris was quite startled at the very idea. Our boat, though forty feet long, is, I fear, too small. *Nous verrons!* Some few preparations for packing have been made, but Owen, Harris, and Bell are going out early to-morrow morning to hunt Buffaloes, and when they return we will talk matters over. The activity of Buffaloes is almost beyond belief; they can climb the steep defiles of the Mauvaises Terres in hundreds of places where men cannot follow them, and it is a fine sight to see a large gang of them proceeding along these defiles four or five hundred feet above the level of the bottoms, and from which pathway if one of the number makes a mis-step or accidentally slips, he goes down rolling over and over, and breaks his neck ere the level ground is reached. Bell and Owen saw a bull about three years old that leaped a ravine filled with mud and water, at least twenty feet wide; it reached the middle at the first bound, and at the second was mounted on the opposite bank, from which it kept on bounding, till it gained the top of quite a high hill. Mr. Culbertson tells me that these animals can endure hunger in a most extraordinary manner. He says that a large bull was seen on a spot half way down a precipice, where it had slid, and from which it could not climb upwards, and either could not or would not descend; at any rate, it did not leave the position in which it found itself. The party who saw it returned to the fort, and, on their way back on the *twenty-fifth* day after, they passed the hill, and saw the bull standing there. The thing that troubles them most is crossing rivers on the ice; their hoofs slip from side to side, they become frightened, and stretch their four legs apart to support the body, and in such situations the Indians and white hunters easily approach, and stab them to the heart, or cut the hamstrings, when they become an easy prey. When in large gangs those in the centre are supported by those on the outposts, and if the stream is not large, reach the shore and readily escape. Indians of different tribes hunt the Buffalo in different ways; some hunt on horseback, and use arrows altogether; they are rarely expert in reloading the gun in the close race. Others hunt on foot, using guns, arrows, or both. Others follow with patient perseverance, and kill them also. But I will give you the manner pursued by the Mandans.

Twenty to fifty men start, as the occasion suits, each provided with two horses, one of which is a pack-horse, the other fit for the chase. They have quivers with from twenty to fifty arrows, according to the wealth of the hunter. They ride the pack horse bareback, and travel on, till they see the game, when they leave the pack-horse, and leap on the hunter, and start at full speed and soon find themselves amid the Buffaloes, on the flanks of the herd, and on both sides. When within a few yards the arrow is sent, they shoot at a Buffalo somewhat ahead of them, and send the arrow in an oblique manner, so as to pass through the lights. If the blood rushes out of the nose and mouth the animal is fatally wounded, and they shoot at it no more; if not, a second, and perhaps a third arrow, is sent before this happens. The Buffaloes on starting carry the tail close in between the legs, but when wounded they switch it about, especially if they wish to fight, and then the hunter's horse shies off and lets the mad animal breathe awhile. If shot through the heart, they occasionally fall dead on the instant; sometimes, if not hit in the right place, a dozen arrows will not stop them. When wounded and mad they turn suddenly round upon the hunter and rush upon him in such a quick and furious manner that if horse and rider are not both on the alert, the former is overtaken, hooked and overthrown, the hunter pitched off, trampled and gored to death. Although the Buffalo is such a large animal, and to all appearance a clumsy one, it can turn with the quickness of thought, and when once enraged, will rarely give up the chase until avenged for the wound it has received. If, however, the hunter is expert, and the horse fleet, they outrun the bull, and it returns to the herd. Usually the greater number of the gang is killed, but it very rarely happens that some of them do not escape. This however, is not the case when the animal is pounded, especially by the Gros Ventres, Black Feet, and Assiniboins. These pounds are called "parks," and the Buffaloes are made to enter them in the following manner: The park is sometimes round and sometimes square, this depending much on the ground where it is put up; at the end of the park is what is called a *precipice* of some fifteen feet or less, as may be found. It is approached by a funnel-shaped passage, which like the park itself is strongly built of logs, brushwood, and pickets, and when all is ready a young man, very swift of foot, starts at daylight covered over with a Buffalo robe and wearing a Buffalo head-dress. The moment he sees the herd to be taken, he bellows like a young calf, and makes his way slowly towards the contracted part of the funnel, imitating the cry of the calf, at frequent intervals. The Buffaloes advance after the decoy; about a dozen mounted hunters are yelling and galloping behind them, and along both flanks of the herd, forcing them by these means to enter the mouth of the funnel. Women and children are placed behind the fences of the funnel to frighten the cattle, and as soon as the young man who acts as decoy feels assured that the game is in a fair way to follow to the bank or "precipice," he runs or leaps down the bank, over the barricade, and either rests, or joins in the fray. The poor Buffaloes, usually headed by a large bull, proceed, leap down the bank in haste and confusion, the Indians all yelling and pursuing till every bull, cow, and calf is impounded. Although this is done at all seasons, it is more general in October or November, when the hides are good and salable. Now the warriors are all assembled by the pen, calumets are lighted, and the chief smokes to the Great Spirit, the four points of the compass, and lastly to the Buffaloes. The pipe is passed from mouth to mouth in succession, and as soon as this ceremony is ended, the destruction commences. Guns shoot, arrows fly in all directions, and the hunters being on the outside of the enclosure, destroy the whole gang, before they jump over to clean and skin the murdered herd. Even the children shoot small, short arrows to assist in the destruction. It happens sometimes however, that the leader of the herd will be restless at the sight of the precipices, and if the fence is weak will break through it, and all his fellows follow him, and escape. The same thing sometimes takes place in the pen, for so full does this become occasionally that the animals touch each other, and as they cannot move, the very weight against the fence of the pen is quite enough to break it through; the smallest aperture is sufficient, for in a few minutes it becomes wide, and all the beasts are seen scampering over the prairies, leaving the poor Indians starving and discomfited. Mr. Kipp told me that while traveling from Lake Travers to the Mandans, in the month of August, he rode in a heavily laden cart for six successive days through masses of Buffaloes, which divided for the cart, allowing it to pass without opposition. He has seen the immense prairie back of Fort Clark look black to the tops of the hills, though the ground was covered with snow, so crowded was it with these animals; and the masses probably extended much further. In fact it is *impossible to describe or even conceive* the vast multitudes of these animals that exist even now, and feed on these ocean-like prairies.

August 12, Saturday. Harris, Bell, and Owen went after Buffaloes; killed six cows and brought them home. Weather cloudy, and rainy at times. Provost returned with La Fleur this afternoon, had nothing, but had seen a Grizzly Bear. The "Union" was launched this evening and packing, etc., is going on. I gave a memorandum to Jean Baptiste Moncrévier of the animals I wish him to procure for me.

August 13, Sunday. A most beautiful day. About dinner time I had a young Badger brought to me dead; I bought it, and gave in payment two pounds of sugar. The body of these animals is broader than high, the neck is powerfully strong, as well as the fore-arms, and strongly clawed fore-feet. It weighed 8½ lbs. Its measurements were all taken. When the pursuer gets between a Badger and its hole, the animal's hair rises, and it at once shows fight. A half-breed hunter told Provost, who has just returned from Fort Mortimer, that he was anxious to go down the river with me, but I know the man and hardly care to have him. If I decide to take him Mr. Culbertson, to whom I spoke of the matter, told me my only plan was to pay him by the piece for what he killed and brought on board, and that in case he did not turn out well between this place and Fort Clark, to leave him there; so I have sent word to him to this effect by Provost this afternoon. Bell is skinning the Badger, Sprague finishing the map of the river made by Squires, and the latter is writing. The half-breed has been here, and the following is our agreement: "It is understood that Francois Détaillé will go with me, John J. Audubon, and to secure for me the following quadrupeds—if possible—

for which he will receive the prices here mentioned, payable at Fort Union, Fort Clark or Fort Pierre, as may best suit him.

For each Bighorn male	$10.00
For a large Grizzly bear	20.00
For a large male Elk	6.00
For a Black-tailed Deer, male or female	6.00
For Red Foxes	3.00
For small Gray Foxes	3.00
For Badgers	2.00
For large Porcupine	2.00

Independent of which I agree to furnish him with his passage and food, he to work as a hand on board. Whatever he kills for food will be settled when he leaves us, or, as he says, when he meets the Opposition boat coming up to Fort Mortimer." He will also accompany us in our hunt after Bighorns, which I shall undertake, notwithstanding Mr. Culbertson and Squires, who have been to the Mauvaises Terres, both try to dissuade me from what they fear will prove over-fatiguing; but though my strength is not what it was twenty years ago, I am yet equal to much, and my eyesight far keener than that of many a younger man, though that too tells me I am no longer a youth. . . .

The only idea I can give in *writing* of what are called the "Mauvaises Terres" would be to place some thousands of loaves of sugar of different sizes, from quite small and low, to large and high, all irregularly truncated at top, and placed somewhat apart from each other. No one who has not seen these places can form any idea of these resorts of the Rocky Mountain Rams, or the difficulty of approaching them, putting aside their extreme wildness and their marvellous activity. They form paths around these broken-headed cones (that are from three to fifteen hundred feet high), and run round them at full speed on a track that, to the eye of the hunter, does not appear to be more than a few inches wide, but which is, in fact, from a foot to eighteen inches in width. In some places there are piles of earth from eight to ten feet high, or even more, the tops of which form platforms of a hard and shelly rocky substance where the Bighorn is often seen looking on the hunter far below, and standing immovable, as if a statue. No one can imagine how they reach these places, and that too with their young, even when the latter are quite small. Hunters say that the young are usually born in such places, the mothers going there to save the helpless little one from the Wolves, which, after men, seem to be their greatest destroyers. The Mauvaises Terres are mostly formed of grayish white clay, very sparsely covered with small patches of thin grass, on which the Bighorns feed, but which, to all appearance, is a very scanty supply, and there, and there only, they feed, as not one has ever been seen on the bottom or prairie land further than the foot of these most extraordinary hills. In wet weather, no man can climb any of them, and at such times they are greasy, muddy, sliding grounds. Oftentimes when a Bighorn is seen on a hill-top, the hunter has to ramble about for three or four miles before he can approach within gunshot of the game, and if the Bighorn ever sees his enemy, pursuit is useless. The tops of some of these hills, and in some cases whole hills about thirty feet high, are composed of a conglomerated mass of stones, sand, and clay, with earth of various sorts, fused together, and having a brick-like appearance. In this mass pumice-stone of various shapes and sizes is to be found. The whole is evidently the effect of volcanic action. The bases of some of these hills cover an area of twenty acres or more, and the hills rise to the height of three or four hundred feet, sometimes even to eight hundred or a thousand; so high can the hunter ascend that the surrounding country is far, far beneath him. The strata are of different colored clays, coal, etc., and an earth impregnated with a salt which appears to have been formed by internal fire or heat, the earth or stones of which I have first spoken in this account, lava, sulphur, salts of various kinds, oxides and sulphates of iron; and in the sand at the tops of some of the highest hills I have found marine shells, but so soft and crumbling as to fall apart the instant they were exposed to the air. I spent some time over various lumps of sand, hoping to find some perfect ones that would be hard enough to carry back to St. Louis; but 'twas "love's labor lost," and I regretted exceedingly that only a few fragments could be gathered. I found globular and oval shaped stones, very heavy, apparently composed mostly of iron, weighing from fifteen to twenty pounds; numbers of petrified stumps from one to three feet in diameter; the Mauvaises Terres abound with them; they are to be found in all parts from the valleys to the tops of the hills, and appear to be principally of cedar. On the sides of the hills, at various heights, are shelves of rock or stone projecting out from two to six, eight, or even ten feet, and generally square, or nearly so; these are the favorite resorts of the Bighorns during the heat of the day, and either here or on the tops of the highest hills they are to be found. Between the hills there is generally quite a growth of cedar, but mostly stunted and crowded close together, with very large stumps, and between the stumps quite a good display of grass; on the summits, in some *few* places, there are table-lands, varying from an area of one to ten or fifteen acres; these are covered with a short, dry, wiry grass, and immense quantities of flat leaved cactus, the spines of which often warn the hunter of their proximity, and the hostility existing between them and his feet. These plains are not more easily travelled then the hillsides, as every step may lead the hunter into a bed of these pests of the prairies. In the valleys between the hills are ravines, some of which are not more than ten or fifteen feet wide, while their depth is beyond the reach of the eye. Others vary in depth from ten to fifty feet, while some make one giddy to look in; they are also of various widths, the widest perhaps a hundred feet. The edges, at times, are lined with bushes, mostly wild cherry; occasionally Buffaloes make paths across them, but this is rare. The only safe way to pass is to follow the ravine to the head, which is usually at the foot of some hill, and go round. These ravines are mostly between every two hills, although like every general rule there are variations and occasionally places where three or more hills make only one ravine. These small ravines all connect with some larger one, the size of which is in proportion to its tributaries. The large one runs to the river, or the water is carried off by a subterranean channel. In these valleys, and sometimes on the tops of the hills, are holes, called "sink holes;" these are formed by the water running in a small hole and working away the earth beneath the surface, leaving a crust incapable of supporting the weight of a man; and if an unfortunate steps on this crust, he soon finds himself in rather an unpleasant predicament. This is one of the dangers that attend the hunter in these lands; these holes eventually form a ravine such as I have before spoken of. Through these hills it is almost impossible to travel with a horse, though it is sometimes done by careful management, and a correct knowledge of the country. The sides of the hills are very steep, covered with the earth and stones of which I have spoken, all of which are quite loose on the surface; occasionally a bunch of wormwood here and there seems to assist the daring hunter; for it is no light task to follow the Bighorns through these lands, and the pursuit is attended with much danger, as the least slip at times would send one headlong into the ravines below. On the sides of these high hills the water has washed away the earth, leaving caves of various sizes; and, in fact, in some places all manner of fantastic forms are made by the same process. Occasionally in the valleys are found isolated cones or domes, destitute of vegetation, naked and barren. Throughout the Mauvaises Terres there are springs of water impregnated with salt, sulphur, magnesia, and many other salts of all kinds. Such is the water the hunter is compelled to drink, and were it not that it is as cold as ice it would be almost impossible to swallow it. As it is, many of these waters operate as cathartics or emetics; this is one of the most disagreeable attendants of hunting in these lands. Moreover, venomous snakes of many kinds are also found here. I saw myself only one copperhead, and a common garter-snake. Notwithstanding the rough nature of the country, the Buffaloes have paths running in all directions, and leading from the prairies to the river. The hunter sometimes, after toiling for an hour or two up the side of one of these hills trying to reach the top in hopes that when there he will have for a short distance at least, either a level place or good path to walk on, finds to his disappointment that he has secured a point that only affords a place scarcely large enough to stand on, and he has the trouble of descending, perhaps to renew his disappointment in the same way, again and again, such is the deceptive character of the country. I was thus deceived time and again, while in search of Bighorns. If the hill does not terminate in a point it is connected with another hill, by a ridge so narrow that nothing but a Bighorn can walk on it. This is the country that the Mountain Ram inhabits, and if, from this imperfect description, any information can be derived, I shall be more than repaid for the trouble I have had in these tiresome hills. Whether my theory be correct or incorrect, it is this: These hills were at first composed of the clays that I have mentioned, mingled with an immense quantity of combustible material, such as coal, sulphur, bitumen, etc.; these have been destroyed by fire, or (at least the greater part) by volcanic action, as to this day, on the Black Hills and in the hills near where I have been, fire still exists; and from the immense quantities of pumice-stone and melted ores found among the hills, even were there no fire now to be seen, no one could doubt that it had, at some date or other, been there; as soon as this process had ceased, the rains washed out the loose material, and carried it to the rivers, leaving the more solid parts as we now find them; the action of water to this day continues. As I have said, the Bighorns are very fond of resorting to the shelves, or ledges, on the sides of the hills, during the heat of the day, when these places are shaded; here they lie, but are aroused instantly upon the least appearance of danger, and, as soon as they have discovered the cause of alarm, away they go, over hill and ravine, occasionally stopping to look round, and when ascending the steepest hill, there is no apparent diminution of their speed. They will ascend and descend places, when thus alarmed, so inaccessible that it is almost impossible to conceive how, and where, they find a foothold. When observed before they see the hunter, or while they are looking about when first alarmed, are the only opportunities the hunter has to shoot them; for, as soon as they start there is no hope, as to follow and find them is a task not easily accomplished, for where or how far they go when thus on the alert, heaven only knows, as but few hunters have ever attempted a chase. At all times they have to be approached with the greatest caution, as the least thing renders them on the *qui vive*. When not found on these shelves, they are seen on the tops of the most inaccessible and highest hills, looking down on the hunters, apparently conscious of their securitiy, or else lying down tranquilly in some sunny spot quite out of reach. As I have observed before, the only times that these animals can be shot are when on these ledges, or when moving from one point to another. Sometimes they move only a few hundred yards, but it will take the hunter several hours to approach near enough for a shot, so long are the *détours* he is compelled to make. I have been thus baffled two or three times. The less difficult hills are found cut up by paths made by these animals; these are generally about eighteen inches wide. These animals appear to be quite as agile as the European Chamois, leaping down precipices, across ravines, and running up and down almost perpendicular hills. The only places I could find that seemed to afford food for them, was between the cedars, as I have before mentioned; but the places where they are most frequently found are barren, and without the least vestige of vegetation. From the character of the lands where these animals are found, their own shyness, watchfulness, and agility, it is readily seen what the hunter must endure, and what difficulties he must undergo to near these "Wild Goats." It is one constant time of toil, anxiety, fatigue, and danger. Such the country! Such the animal! Such the hunting!

. . .

from EPISODES

THE HURRICANE

Various portions of our country have at different periods suffered severely from the influence of violent storms of wind, some of which have been known to traverse nearly the whole extent of the United States, and to leave such deep impressions in their wake as will not easily be forgotten. Having witnessed one of these awful phenomena, in all its grandeur, I shall attempt to describe it for your sake, kind reader, and for your sake only; the recollection of that astonishing revolution of the ethereal element even now bringing with it so disagreeable a sensation that I feel as if about to be affected by a sudden stoppage of the circulation of my blood.

I had left the village of Shawanne, situated on the banks of Ohio, on my return from Henderson, which is also situated on the banks of the same beautiful stream. The weather was pleasant, and I thought not warmer than usual at that season. My horse was jogging quietly along, and my thoughts were, for once at least in the course of my life, entirely engaged in commercial speculations. I had forded Highland Creek, and was on the eve of entering a tract of bottom land or valley that lay between it and Canoe Creek, when on a sudden I remarked a great difference in the aspect of the heavens. A hazy thickness had overspread the country, and I for some time expected an earthquake; but my horse exhibited no propensity to stop and prepare for such an occurrence. I had nearly arrived at the verge of the valley, when I thought fit to stop near a brook, and dismounted to quench the thirst which had come upon me.

I was leaning on my knees, with my lips about to touch the water, when, from my proximity to the earth, I heard a distant murmuring sound of an extraordinary nature. I drank, however, and as I rose on my feet, looked towards the southwest, where I observed a yellowish oval spot, the appearance of which was quite new to me. Little time was left me for consideration, as the next moment a smart breeze began to agitate the taller trees. It increased to an unexpected height, and already the smaller branches and twigs were seen falling in a slanting direction towards the ground. Two minutes had scarcely elapsed, when the whole forest before me was in fearful motion. Here and there, where one tree pressed against another, a creaking noise was produced, similar to that occasioned by the violent gusts which sometimes sweep over the country. Turning instinctively towards the direction from which the wind blew, I saw to my great astonishment that the noblest trees of the forest bent their lofty heads for a while, and, unable to stand against the blast, were falling into pieces. First the branches were broken off with a crackling noise; then went the upper parts of the massy trunks; and in many places whole trees of gigantic size were falling entire to the ground. So rapid was the progress of the storm that before I could think of taking measures to insure my safety the hurricane was passing opposite the place where I stood. Never can I forget the scene which at that moment presented itself. The tops of the trees were seen moving in the strangest manner, in the central current of the tempest, which carried along with it a mingled mass of twigs and foliage that completely obscured the view. Some of the largest trees were seen bending and writhing under the gale; others suddenly snapped across; and many, after a momentary resistance, fell uprooted to the earth. The mass of branches, twigs, foliage, and dust that moved through the air was whirled onwards like a cloud of feathers, and on passing disclosed a wide space filled with fallen trees, naked stumps, and heaps of shapeless ruins which marked the path of the tempest. This space was about a fourth of a mile in breadth, and to my imagination resembled the dried up bed of the Mississippi, with its thousands of planters and sawyers strewed in the sand

and inclined in various degrees. The horrible noise resembled that of the great cataracts of Niagara, and, as it howled along in the track of the desolating tempest, produced a feeling in my mind which it were impossible to describe.

The principal force of the hurricane was now over, although millions of twigs and small branches that had been brought from a great distance were seen following the blast, as if drawn onwards by some mysterious power. They even floated in the air for some hours after, as if supported by the thick mass of dust that rose high above the ground. The sky had now a greenish lurid hue, and an extremely disagreeable sulphurous odor was diffused in the atmosphere. I waited in amazement, having sustained no material injury, until nature at length resumed her wonted aspect. For some moments I felt undetermined whether I should return to Morgantown, or attempt to force my way through the wrecks of the tempest. My business, however, being of an urgent nature, I ventured into the path of the storm, and after encountering innumerable difficulties, succeeded in crossing it. I was obliged to lead my horse by the bridle, to enable him to leap over the fallen trees, whilst I scrambled over or under them in the best way I could, at times so hemmed in by the broken tops and tangled branches as almost to become desperate. On arriving at my house, I gave an account of what I had seen, when, to my astonishment, I was told there had been very little wind in the neighborhood, although in the streets and gardens many branches and twigs had fallen in a manner which excited great surprise.

Many wondrous accounts of the devastating effects of this hurricane were circulated in the country after its occurrence. Some log houses, we were told, had been over-turned and their inmates destroyed. One person informed me that a wire sifter had been conveyed by the gust to a distance of many miles. Another had found a cow lodged in the fork of a large half-broken tree. But, as I am disposed to relate only what I have myself seen, I shall not lead you into the region of romance, but shall content myself with saying that much damage was done by this awful visitation. The valley is yet a desolate place, over-grown with briers and bushes, thickly entangled amidst the tops and trunks of the fallen trees, and is the resort of ravenous animals, to which they betake themselves when pursued by man, or after they have committed their depredations on the farms of the surrounding district. I have crossed the path of the storm at a distance of a hundred miles from the spot where I witnessed its fury, and again, four hundred miles farther off, in the State of Ohio. Lastly, I observed traces of its ravages on the summits of the mountains connected with the Great Pine Forest of Pennsylvania, three hundred miles beyond the place last mentioned. In all these different parts it appeared to me not to have exceeded a quarter of a mile in breadth.

. . .

THE BURNING OF THE FORESTS

With what pleasure have I seated myself by the blazing fire of some lonely cabin, when, faint with fatigue, and chilled with the piercing blast, I had forced my way to it through the drifted snows that covered the face of the country as with a mantle. The affectionate mother is hushing her dear babe to repose, while a group of sturdy children surround their father, who has just returned from the chase, and deposited on the rough flooring of his hut the varied game which he has procured. The great back-log, that with some difficulty has been rolled into the ample chimney, urged, as it were, by lighted pieces of pine, sends forth a blaze of light over the happy family. The dogs of the hunter are already licking away the trickling waters of the thawing icicles that sparkle over their shaggy coats, and the comfort-loving cat is busied in passing her furry paws over each ear, or with her rough tongue smoothing her glossy coat.

How delightful to me has it been when, kindly received and hospitably treated under such a roof, by persons whose means were as scanty as their generosity was great, I have entered into conversation with them respecting subjects of interest to me, and received gratifying information. When the humble but plentiful repast was ended, the mother would take from the shelf the Book of books, and mildly request the attention of her family, while the father read aloud a chapter. Then to Heaven would ascend their humble prayers, and a good-night would be bidden to all friends far and near. How comfortably have I laid my wearied frame on the Buffalo hide, and covered me with the furry skin of some huge Bear! How pleasing have been my dreams of home and happiness, as I there lay, secure from danger and sheltered from the inclemency of the weather.

I recollect that once while in the State of Maine, I passed such a night as I have described. Next morning the face of nature was obscured by the heavy rains that fell in torrents, and my generous host begged me to remain, in such pressing terms that I was well content to accept his offer. Breakfast over, the business of the day commenced; the spinning-wheels went round, and the boys employed themselves, one in searching for knowledge, another in attempting to solve some ticklish arithmetical problem. In a corner lay the dogs, dreaming of plunder, while close to the ashes stood grimalkin, seriously purring in concert with the wheels. The hunter and I seated outselves each on a stool, while the matron looked after her domestic arrangements.

"Puss," quoth the dame, "get away; you told me last night of this day's rain, and I fear you may now give us worse news with tricky paws." Puss accordingly went off, leaped on a bed, and rolling herself in a ball, composed herself for a comfortable nap. I asked the husband what his wife meant by what she had just said. "The good woman," said he, "has some curious notions at times, and she believes, I think, in the ways of animals of all kinds. Now, her talk to the cat refers to the fires of the woods around us, and although they have happened long ago, she fears them quite as much as ever, and, indeed, she and I and all of us have good reason to dread them, as they have brought us many calamities." Having read of the great fires to which my host alluded, and frequently observed with sorrow the mournful state of the forests, I felt anxious to know something of the causes by which these direful effects had been produced. I therefore requested him to give me an account of the events resulting from those fires which he had witnessed. Willingly he at once went on, nearly as follows:—

"About twenty-five years ago the larch, or hackmatack, trees were nearly all killed by insects. This took place in what hereabouts is called the 'black soft growth' land, that is, the spruce, pine, and all other firs. The destruction of the trees was effected by the insects cutting the leaves, and you must know that, although other trees are not killed by the loss of their leaves, the evergreens always are. Some few years after this destruction of the larch, the same insects attacked the spruces, pines, and other firs, in such a manner that, before half a dozen years were over, they began to fall, and, tumbling in all directions, they covered the whole country with matted masses. You may suppose that when partially dried or seasoned, they would prove capital fuel, as well as supplies for the devouring flames, which accidentally, or perhaps by intention, afterwards raged over the country, and continued burning at intervals for years, in many places stopping all communication by the roads; the resinous nature of the firs being of course best fitted to insure and keep up the burning of the deep beds of dry leaves or of the other trees." Here I begged him to give me some idea of the form of the insects which had caused such havoc.

"The insects," said he, "were, in their caterpillar form, about three quarters of an inch in length, and as green as the leaves of the trees they fed on, when they committed their ravages. I must tell you also that, in most of the places over which the fire passed, a new growth of wood has already sprung up, of what we lumberers call hard wood, which consists of all other sorts but pine or fir; and I have always remarked that wherever the first natural growth of a forest is destroyed, either by the axe, the hurricane, or the fire, there springs up spontaneously another of quite a different kind." I again stopped my host to inquire if he knew the method or nature of the first kindling of the fires.

"Why, sir," said he, "there are different opinions about this. Many believe that the Indians did it, either to be the better able to kill the game, or to punish their enemies the Pale-faces. My opinion, however, is different; and I derive it from my experience in the woods as a lumberer. I have always thought that the fires began by the accidental fall of a dry trunk against another, when their rubbing together, especially as many of them are covered with resin, would produce fire. The dry leaves on the ground are at once kindled, next the twigs and branches, when nothing but the intervention of the Almighty could stop the progress of the fire.

"In some instances, owing to the wind, the destructive element approached the dwellings of the inhabitants of the woods so rapidly that it was difficult for them to escape. In some parts, indeed, hundreds of families were obliged to flee from their homes, leaving all they had behind them, and here and there some of the affrighted fugitives were burnt alive."

At this moment a rush of wind came down the chimney, blowing the blaze of fire towards the room. The wife and daughter, imagining for a moment that the woods were again on fire, made for the door, but the husband explaining the cause of their terror, they resumed their work.

"Poor things," said the lumberer, "I dare say that what I have told you brings sad recollections to the minds of my wife and eldest daughter, who, with myself, had to fly from our home, at the time of the great fires." I felt so interested in his reaction of the causes of the burnings that I asked him to describe to me the particulars of his misfortunes at the time. "If Prudence and Polly," said he, looking towards his wife and daughter, "will promise to sit still should another puff of smoke come down the chimney, I will do so." The good-natured smile with which he made this remark elicited a return from the women and he proceeded:—

"It is a difficult thing, sir, to describe, but I will do my best to make your time pass pleasantly. We were sound asleep one night in a cabin about a hundred miles from this, when, about two hours before day, the snorting of the horses and lowing of the cattle which I had ranging in the woods suddenly awakened us. I took yon rifle and went to the door, to see what beast had caused the hubbub, when I was struck by the glare of light reflected on all the trees before me, as far as I could see through the woods. My horses were leaping about, snorting loudly, and the cattle ran among them with their tails raised straight over their backs. On going to the back of the house, I plainly heard the crackling made by the burning brushwood, and saw the flames coming towards us in a far extended line. I ran to the house, told my wife to dress herself and the child as quick as possible, and take the little money we had, while I managed to catch and saddle the two best horses. All this was done in a very short time, for I guessed that every moment was precious to me.

"We then mounted, and made off from the fire. My wife, who is an excellent rider, stuck close to me; my daughter, who was then a small child, I took in one arm. When making off as I said, I looked back and saw that the frightful blaze was close upon us, and had already laid hold of the house. By good luck, there was a horn attached to my hunting-clothes, and I blew it, to bring after us, if possible, the remainder of my live stock, as well as the dogs. The cattle followed for a while; but, before an hour had elapsed, they all ran as if mad through the woods, and that, sir, was the last of them. My dogs, too, although at other times extremely tractable, ran after the Deer that in bodies sprung before us, as if fully aware of the death that was so rapidly approaching.

"We heard blasts from the horns of our neighbors as we proceeded, and knew that they were in the same predicament. Intent on striving to the utmost to preserve our lives, I thought of a large lake some miles off, which might possibly check the flames; and, urging my wife to whip up her horse, we set off at full speed, making the best way we could over the fallen trees and brush-heaps, which lay like so many articles placed on purpose to keep up the terrific fires that advanced with a broad front upon us.

"By this time we could feel the heat; and we were afraid that our horses would drop every instant. A singular kind of breeze was passing over our heads, and the glare of the atmosphere shone over the daylight. I was sensible of a slight faintness, and my wife looked pale. The heat had produced such a flush in the child's face that when she turned towards either of us, our grief and perplexity were greatly increased. Ten miles, you know, are soon gone over on swift horses; but, notwithstanding this, when we reached the borders of the lake, covered with sweat and quite exhausted, our hearts failed us. The heat of the smoke was insufferable, and sheets of blazing fire flew over us in a manner beyond belief. We reached the shores, however, coasted the lake for a while, and got round to the lee side. There we gave up our horses, which we never saw again. Down among the rushes we plunged by the edge of the water, and laid ourselves flat, to wait the chance of escaping from being burnt or devoured. The water refreshed us, and we enjoyed the coolness.

"On went the fire, rushing and crashing through the woods. Such a sight may we never see! The heavens, themselves, I thought were frightened, for all above us was a red glare mixed with clouds of smoke, rolling and sweeping away. Our bodies were cool enough, but our heads were scorching, and the child, who now seemed to understand the matter, cried so as nearly to break our hearts.

"The day passed on, and we became hungry. Many wild beasts came plunging into the water beside us, and others swam across to our side and stood still. Although faint and weary, I managed to shoot a Porcupine, and we all tasted its flesh. The night passed, I cannot tell you how. Smouldering fires covered the ground, and trees stood like pillars of fire, or fell across each other. The stifling and sickening smoke still rushed over us, and the burnt cinders and ashes fell thick about us. How we got through that night I really cannot tell, for about some of it I remember nothing." Here the hunter paused, and took breath. The recital of his adventure seemed to have exhausted him. His wife proposed that we should have a bowl of milk, and the daughter having handed it to us, we each took a draught.

"Now," said he, "I will proceed. Towards morning, although the heat did not abate, the smoke became less, and blasts of fresh air sometimes made their way to us. When morning came, all was calm, but a dismal smoke still filled the air, and the smell seemed worse than ever. We were now cooled enough, and shivered as if in an ague fit; so we removed from the water, and went up to a burning log, where we warmed ourselves. What was to become of us, I did not know. My wife hugged the child to her breast, and wept bitterly; but God had preserved us through the worst of the danger, and the flames had gone past, so I thought it would be both ungrateful to him and unmanly to despair now. Hunger once more pressed upon us, but this was easily remedied. Several Deer were still standing in the water, up the head, and I shot one of them. Some of its flesh was soon roasted; and after eating it we felt wonderfully strengthened.

"By this time the blaze of the fire was beyond our sight, although the ground was still burning in many places, and it was dangerous to go among the burnt trees. After resting awhile, and trimming ourselves, we prepared to commence our march. Taking up the child, I led the way over the hot ground and rocks; and, after two weary days and nights, during which we shifted in the best manner we could, we at last reached the 'hard woods' which had been free of the fire. Soon after we came to a house, where we were kindly treated for a while. Since then, sir, I have worked hard and constantly as a lumberer; but, thanks be to God, here we are safe, sound, and happy!"

. . .

MY STYLE OF DRAWING BIRDS

When, as a little lad, I first began my attempts at representing birds on paper, I was far from possessing much knowledge of their nature, and, like hundreds of others, when I had laid the effort aside, I was under the impression that it was a finished picture of a bird because it possessed some sort of a head and tail, and two sticks in lieu of legs; I never troubled myself with the thought that abutments were requisite to prevent it from falling either backward or forward, and oh! what bills and claws I did draw, to say nothing of a perfectly straight line for a back, and a tail stuck in anyhow, like an unshipped rudder.

Many persons besides my father saw my miserable attempts, and so many praised them to the skies that perhaps no one was ever nearer being completely wrecked than I by these mistaken, though affectionate words. My father, however, spoke very differently to me; he constantly impressed upon me that nothing in the world possessing life and animation was easy to imitate, and that as I grew older he hoped I would become more and more alive to this. He was so kind to me, and so deeply interested in my improvement that to have listened carelessly to his serious words would have been highly ungrateful. I listened less to others, more to him, and his words became my law.

The first collection of drawings I made were from European specimens, procured by my father or myself, and I still have them in my possession.[1] They were all represented *strictly ornithologically*, which means neither more nor less than in stiff, unmeaning profiles, such as are found in most works published to the present day. My next set was begun in America, and there, without my honored mentor, I betook myself to the drawing of specimens hung by a string tied to one foot, having a desire to show every portion, as the wings lay loosely spread, as well as the tail. In this manner I made some pretty fair signs for poulterers.

One day, while watching the habits of a pair of Pewees at Mill Grove, I looked so intently at their graceful attitudes that a thought struck my mind like a flash of light, that nothing, after all, could ever answer my enthusiastic desires to represent nature, except to copy her in her own way, alive and moving! Then I began again. On I went, forming, literally, hundreds of outlines of my favorites, the Pewees; how good or bad I cannot tell, but I fancied I had mounted a step on the high pinnacle before me. I continued for months together, simply outlining birds as I observed them, either alighted or on the wing, but could finish none of my sketches. I procured many individuals of different species, and laying them on the table or on the ground, tried to place them in such attitudes as I had sketched. But, alas! they were *dead*, to all intents and purposes, and neither wing, leg, nor tail could I place according to my wishes. A second thought came to my assistance; by means of threads I raised or lowered a head, wing, or tail, and by fastening the threads securely, I had something like life before me; yet much was wanting. When I saw the living birds, I felt the blood rush to my temples, and almost in despair spent about a month without drawing, but in deep thought, and daily in the company of the feathered inhabitants of dear Mill Grove.

I had drawn from the "manikin" whilst under David, and had obtained tolerable figures of our species through this means, so I cogitated how far a manikin of a bird would answer. I labored with wood cork, and wires, and formed a grotesque figure, which I cannot describe in any other words than by saying that when set up it was a tolerable-looking Dodo. A friend roused my ire by laughing at it immoderately, and assuring me that if I wished to represent a tame gander it might do. I gave it a kick, broke it to atoms, walked off, and thought again.

Young as I was, my impatience to obtain my desire filled my brains with many plans. I not infrequently dreamed that I had made a new discovery; and long before day, one morning, I leaped out of bed fully persuaded that I had obtained my object. I ordered a horse to be saddled, mounted, and went off at a gallop towards the little village of Norristown, distant about five miles. When I arrived there not a door was open, for it was not yet daylight. Therefore I went to the river, took a bath, and, returning to the town, entered the first opened shop, inquired for wire of different sizes, bought some, leaped on my steed, and was soon again at Mill Grove. The wife of my tenant, I really believe, thought that I was mad, as, on offering me breakfast, I told her I only wanted my gun. I was off to the creek, and shot the first Kingfisher I met. I picked the bird up, carried it home by the bill, sent for the miller, and bade him bring me a piece of board of soft wood. When he returned he found me filing sharp points to some pieces of wire, and I proceeded to show him what I meant to do. I pierced the body of the fishing bird, and fixed it on the board; another wire passed above his upper mandible held the head in a pretty fair attitude, smaller ones fixed the feet according to my notions, and even common pins came to my assistance. The last wire proved a delightful elevator to the bird's tail, and at last—there stood before me the *real* Kingfisher.

Think not that my lack of breakfast was at all in my way. No, indeed! I outlined the bird, aided by compasses and my eyes, colored it, finished it, without a thought of hunger. My honest miller stood by the while, and was delighted to see me pleased. This was what I shall call my first drawing actually from nature, for even the eye of the Kingfisher was as if full of life whenever I pressed the lids aside with my finger.

In those happy days of my youth I was extremely fond of reading what I still call the delightful fables of La Fontaine. I had frequently perused the one entitled "*L'hirondelle et les petits oiseaux*," and thought much of the meaning imparted in the first line, which, if I now recollect rightly, goes on to say that "*Quiconque a beaucoup vu, peut avoir beaucoup retenu*." To me this meant that to study Nature was to ramble through her domains late and early, and if I observed all as I should, that the memory of what I saw would at least be of service to me.

"Early to bed, and early to rise," was another adage which I thought, and still think, of much value; 't is a pity that instead of being merely an adage it has not become a general law; I have followed it ever since I was a child, and am ever grateful for the hint it conveyed.

As I wandered, mostly bent on the study of birds, and with a wish to represent all those found in our woods, to the best of my powers, I gradually became acquainted with their forms and habits, and the use of my wires was improved by constant practice. Whenever I produced a better representation of any species the preceding one was destroyed, and after a time I laid down what I was pleased to call a constitution of my manner of drawing birds, formed upon natural principles, which I will try to put briefly before you.

The gradual knowledge of the forms and habits of the birds of our country impressed me with the idea that each part of a family must possess a certain degree of affinity, distinguishable at sight in any one of them. The Pewees, which I knew by experience were positively Flycatchers, led me to the discovery that every bird truly of that genus, when standing, was usually in a passive attitude; that they sat uprightly, now and then glancing their eyes upwards or sideways, to watch the approach of their insect prey; that if in pursuit of this prey their movements through the air were, in each and all of that tribe, the same, etc., etc.

Gallinaceous birds I saw were possessed of movements and positions peculiar to them. Amongst the waterbirds also I found characteristic manners. I observed that the Herons walked with elegance and stateliness, that, in fact, every family had some mark by which it could be known; and, after having collected many ideas and much material of this kind, I fairly began, in greater earnest than ever, the very collection of Birds of America, which is now being published.

The better I understood my subjects, the better I became able to represent them in what I hoped were natural positions. The bird once fixed with wires on squares, I studied as a lay figure before me, its nature, previously known to me as far as habits went, and its general form having been frequently observed. Now I could examine more thoroughly the bill, nostrils, eyes, legs, and claws, as well as the structure of the wings and tail; the very tongue was of importance to me, and I thought the more I understood all these particulars, the better representations I made of the originals.

My drawings at first were made altogether in water-colors, but they wanted softness and a great deal of finish. For a long time I was much dispirited at this, particularly when vainly endeavoring to imitate birds of soft and downy plumage, such as that of most Owls, Pigeons, Hawks, and Herons. How this could be remedied required a new train of thought, or some so-called accident, and the latter came to my aid.

One day, after having finished a miniature portrait of the one dearest to me in all the world, a portion of the face was injured by a drop of water, which dried where it fell; and although I labored a great deal to repair the damage, the blur still remained. Recollecting that, when a pupil of David, I had drawn heads and figures in different colored chalks, I resorted to a piece of that material of the tint required for the part, applied the pigment, rubbed the place with a cork stump, and at once produced the desired effect.

My drawings of Owls and other birds of similar plumage were much improved by such applications; indeed, after a few years of patience, some of my attempts began almost to please me, and I have continued the same style ever since, and that now is for more than thirty years.

Whilst travelling in Europe as well as America, many persons have evinced the desire to draw birds in my manner, and I have always felt much pleasure in showing it to any one by whom I hoped ornithological delineations or portraitures would be improved.

William Cullen Bryant
1794-1878

Bryant is often called the "father of American poetry." The size and influence of his poetic work has the stature one normally associates with major poets, and his poetry treats the large theme of the American landscape with consistency and originality. Moreover, Bryant led an active and influential public life. Long-time editor of America's first major newspaper, the New York *Evening Post,* he was also the editor of collections of landscape writings, a friend and mentor to the Hudson River School of painters, and an activist liberal during America's greatest period of expansion. From the time of President Jackson to the Civil War was Bryant's heyday, and few writers better express the idealism and optimism of America's people during that time.

As literary critic, he encouraged writers to turn to America for their themes. His own poetry is known for its love and careful observation of the natural American environment, for reconciling the poles of European past and American present and future, and for combining classical restraint with romantic taste for the past, for nature, for death, and for freedom. Typical of the poetry of his day, Bryant's poems also work toward universal themes or truths (often made explicit) from the concrete details of natural phenomena.

Upon reading Wordsworth's and Coleridge's *Lyrical Ballads* in his youth, Bryant felt "a thousand springs . . . gush up at once into my heart, and the face of nature, of a sudden, to change into a strange freshness." In turn, Bryant revealed nature anew and established the importance of the nature theme for a generation of writers that followed him, as well as for his many readers across the land.

INSCRIPTION FOR THE ENTRANCE TO A WOOD*

Stranger, if thou hast learned a truth which needs
No school of long experience, that the world
Is full of guilt and misery, and hast seen
Enough of all its sorrows, crimes, and cares,
To tire thee of it, enter this wild wood
And view the haunts of Nature. The calm shade
Shall bring a kindred calm, and the sweet breeze
That makes the green leaves dance, shall waft a balm
To thy sick heart. Thou wilt find nothing here
Of all that pained thee in the haunts of men,
And made thee loathe thy life. The primal curse
Fell, it is true, upon the unsinning earth,
But not in vengeance. God hath yoked to guilt
Her pale tormentor, misery. Hence, these shades
Are still the abodes of gladness; the thick roof
Of green and stirring branches is alive
And musical with birds, that sing and sport
In wantonness of spirit; while below
The squirrel, with raised paws and form erect,
Chirps merrily. Throngs of insects in the shade
Try their thin wings and dance in the warm beam
That waked them into life. Even the green trees
Partake the deep contentment; as they bend
To the soft winds, the sun from the blue sky
Looks in and sheds a blessing on the scene.
Scarce less the cleft-born wild-flower seems to enjoy
Existence than the wingèd plunderer
That sucks its sweets. The mossy rocks themselves,
And the old and ponderous trunks of prostrate trees
That lead from knoll to knoll a causey rude
Or bridge the sunken brook, and their dark roots,
With all their earth upon them, twisting high,
Breathe fixed tranquillity. The rivulet
Sends forth glad sounds, and tripping o'er its bed
Of pebbly sands, or leaping down the rocks,
Seems, with continuous laughter, to rejoice
In its own being. Softly tread the marge,
Lest from her midway perch thou scare the wren
That dips her bill in water. The cool wind,
That stirs the stream in play, shall come to thee,
Like one that loves thee nor will let thee pass
Ungreeted, and shall give its light embrace.

*These poetic selections are from *The Life and Works of William Cullen Bryant*, ed. Parke Godwin, III (New York: D. Appleton & Co., 1883).

TO A WATERFOWL

Whither, midst falling dew,
While glow the heavens with the last steps of day,
Far, through their rosy depths, dost thou pursue
Thy solitary way?

Vainly the fowler's eye
Might mark thy distant flight to do thee wrong,
As, darkly painted on the crimson sky,
Thy figure floats along,

Seek'st thou the plashy brink
Of weedy lake, or marge of river wide,
Or where the rocking billows rise and sink
On the chafed ocean-side?

There is a Power whose care
Teaches thy way along that pathless coast—
The desert and illimitable air—
Lone wandering, but not lost.

All day thy wings have fanned,
At that far height, the cold, thin atmosphere,
Yet stoop not, weary, to the welcome land,
Though the dark night is near.

And soon that toil shall end;
Soon shalt thou find a summer home, and rest,
And scream among thy fellows; reeds shall bend,
Soon, o'er thy sheltered nest.

Thou'rt gone, the abyss of heaven
Hath swallowed up thy form; yet, on my heart
Deeply has sunk the lesson thou hast given,
And shall not soon depart,

He who, from zone to zone,
Guides through the boundless sky thy certain flight,
In the long way that I must tread alone,
Will lead my steps aright.

A FOREST HYMN*

The groves were God's first temples. Ere man learned
To hew the shaft, and lay the architrave,
And spread the roof above them—ere he framed

*This is the last poem Bryant wrote during his life in the country before moving to New York. It is an appropriate expression of what he felt about the world he was leaving behind as he was about to enter public, urban life.

The lofty vault, to gather and roll back
The sound of anthems; in the darkling wood,
Amid the cool and silence, he knelt down,
And offered to the Mightiest solemn thanks
And supplication. For his simple heart
Might not resist the sacred influence
Which, from the stilly twilight of the place,
And from the gray old trunks that high in heaven
Mingled their mossy boughs, and from the sound
Of the invisible breath that swayed at once
All their green tops, stole over him, and bowed
His spirit with the thought of boundless power
And inaccessible majesty. Ah, why
Should we, in the world's riper years, neglect
God's ancient sanctuaries, and adore
Only among the crowd, and under roofs
That our frail hands have raised? Let me, at least,
Here, in the shadow of this aged wood,
Offer one hymn—thrice happy, if it find
Acceptance in His ear.

Father, thy hand
Hath reared these venerable columns, thou
Didst weave this verdant roof. Thou didst look down
Upon the naked earth, and, forthwith, rose
All these fair ranks of trees. They, in thy sun,
Budded, and shook their green leaves in thy breeze,
And shot toward heaven. The century-living crow
Whose birth was in their tops, grew old and died
Among their branches, till, at last, they stood,
As now they stand, massy, and tall, and dark,
Fit shrine for humble worshipper to hold
Communion with his Maker. These dim vaults,
These winding aisles, of human pomp or pride
Report not. No fantastic carvings show
The boast of our vain race to change the form
Of thy fair works. But thou art here—thou fill'st
The solitude. Thou art in the soft winds
That run along the summit of these trees
In music; thou art in the cooler breath
That from the inmost darkness of the place
Comes, scarcely felt; the barky trunks, the ground,
The fresh moist ground, are all instinct with thee.
Here is continual worship;—Nature, here,
In the tranquillity that thou dost love,
Enjoys thy presence. Noiselessly, around,
From perch to perch, the solitary bird
Passes; and yon clear spring, that, midst its herbs,

Wells softly forth and wandering steeps the roots
Of half the mighty forest, tells no tale
Of all the good it does. Thou hast not left
Thyself without a witness, in the shades,
Of thy perfections. Grandeur, strength, and grace
Are here to speak of thee. This mighty oak—
By whose immovable stem I stand and seem
Almost annihilated—not a prince,
In all that proud old world beyond the deep,
E'er wore his crown as loftily as he
Wears the green coronal of leaves with which
Thy hand has graced him. Nestled at his root
Is beauty, such as blooms not in the glare
Of the broad sun. That delicate forest flower,
With scented breath and look so like a smile,
Seems, as it issues from the shapeless mould,
An emanation of the indwelling Life,
A visible token of the upholding Love,
That are the soul of this great universe.

My heart is awed within me when I think
Of the great miracle that still goes on,
In silence, round me—the perpetual work
Of thy creation, finished, yet renewed
Forever. Written on thy works I read
The lesson of thy own eternity.
Lo! all grow old and die—but see again,
How on the faltering footsteps of decay
Youth presses—ever gay and beautiful youth
In all its beautiful forms. These lofty trees
Wave not less proudly that their ancestors
Moulder beneath them. Oh, there is not lost
One of earth's charms: upon her bosom yet,
After the flight of untold centuries,
The freshness of her far beginning lies
And yet shall lie. Life mocks the idle hate
Of his arch-enemy Death—yea, seats himself
Upon the tryant's throne—the sepulchre,
And of the triumphs of his ghastly foe
Makes his own nourishment. For he came forth
From thine own bosom, and shall have no end.

There have been holy men who hid themselves
Deep in the woody wilderness, and gave
Their lives to thought and prayer, till they outlived
The generation born with them, nor seemed
Less aged than the hoary trees and rocks
Around them;—and there have been holy men

Who deemed it were not well to pass life thus.
But let me often to these solitudes
Retire, and in thy presence reassure
My feeble virtue. Here its enemies,
The passions, at thy plainer footsteps shrink
And tremble and are still. O God! when thou
Dost scare the world with tempests, set on fire
The heavens with falling thunderbolts, or fill,
With all the waters of the firmament,
The swift dark whirlwind that uproots the woods
And drowns the villages; when, at thy call,
Uprises the great deep and throws himself
Upon the continent, and overwhelms
Its cities—who forgets not, at the sight
Of these tremendous tokens of thy power,
His pride, and lays his strifes and follies by?
Oh, from these sterner aspects of thy face
Spare me and mine, nor let us need the wrath
Of the mad unchained elements to teach
Who rules them. Be it ours to meditate,
In these calm shades, thy milder majesty,
And to the beautiful order of thy works
Learn to conform the order of our lives.

TO COLE, THE PAINTER, DEPARTING FOR EUROPE

Thine eyes shall see the light of distant skies;
Yet, COLE! thy heart shall bear to Europe's strand
A living image of our own bright land,
Such as upon thy glorious canvas lies;
Lone lakes—savannas where the bison roves—
Rocks rich with summer garlands—solemn streams—
Skies, where the desert eagle wheels and screams—
Spring bloom and autumn blaze of boundless groves.
Fair scenes shall greet thee where thou goest—fair,
But different—everywhere the trace of men,
Paths, homes, graves, ruins, from the lowest glen
To where life shrinks from the fierce Alpine air.
Gaze on them, till the tears shall dim thy sight,
But keep that earlier, wilder image bright.

THE PRAIRIES*

These are the gardens of the Desert, these
The unshorn fields, boundless and beautiful,
For which the speech of England has no name—
The Prairies. I behold them for the first,

*Bryant first saw this part of America in 1832 while visiting his brothers, who were among the early settlers of Illinois.

And my heart swells, while the dilated sight
Takes in the encircling vastness. Lo! they stretch,
In airy undulations, far away,
As if the ocean, in his gentlest swell,
Stood still, with all his rounded billows fixed,
And motionless forever.—Motionless?—
No—they are all unchained again. The clouds
Sweep over with their shadows, and, beneath,
The surface rolls and fluctuates to the eye;
Dark hollows seem to glide along and chase
The sunny ridges. Breezes of the South!
Who toss the golden and the flame-like flowers,
And pass the prairie-hawk that, poised on high,
Flaps his broad wings, yet moves not—ye have played
Among the palms of Mexico and vines
Of Texas, and have crisped the limpid brooks
That from the fountains of Sonora glide
Into the calm Pacific—have ye fanned
A nobler or a lovelier scene than this?
Man hath no power in all this glorious work:
The hand that built the firmament hath heaved
And smoothed these verdant swells, and sown their slopes
With herbage, planted them with island groves,
And hedged them round with forests. Fitting floor
For this magnificent temple of the sky—
With flowers whose glory and whose multitude
Rival the constellations! The great heavens
Seem to stoop down upon the scene in love,—
A nearer vault, and of a tenderer blue,
Than that which bends above our eastern hills.

As o'er the verdant waste I guide my steed,
Among the high rank grass that sweeps his sides
The hollow beating of his footstep seems
A sacrilegious sound. I think of those
Upon whose rest he tramples. Are they here—
The dead of other days?—and did the dust
Of these fair solitudes once stir with life
And burn with passion? Let the mighty mounds
That overlook the rivers, or that rise
In the dim forest crowded with old oaks,
Answer. A race, that long has passed away,
Built them;—a disciplined and populous race
Heaped, with long toil, the earth, while yet the Greek
Was hewing the Pentelicus to forms
Of symmetry, and rearing on its rock
The glittering Parthenon. These ample fields
Nourished their harvests, here their herds were fed,

When haply by their stalls the bison lowed,
And bowed his manèd shoulder to the yoke.
All day this desert murmured with their toils,
Till twilight blushed, and lovers walked, and wooed
In a forgotten language, and old tunes,
From instruments of unremembered form,
Gave the soft winds a voice. The red man came—
The roaming hunter tribes, warlike and fierce,
And the mound-builders vanished from the earth.
The solitude of centuries untold
Has settled where they dwelt. The prairie-wolf
Hunts in their meadows, and his fresh-dug den
Yawns by my path. The gopher mines the ground
Where stood their swarming cities. All is gone;
All—save the piles of earth that hold their bones,
The platforms where they worshipped unknown gods,
The barriers which they builded from the soil
To keep the foe at bay—till o'er the walls
The wild beleaguerers broke, and, one by one,
The strongholds of the plain were forced, and heaped
With corpses. The brown vultures of the wood
Flocked to those vast uncovered sepulchres,
And sat unscared and silent at their feast.
Haply some solitary fugitive,
Lurking in marsh and forest, till the sense
Of desolation and of fear became
Bitterer than death, yielded himself to die.
Man's better nature triumphed then. Kind words
Welcomed and soothed him; the rude conquerors
Seated the captive with their chiefs; he chose
A bride among their maidens, and at length
Seemed to forget—yet ne'er forgot—the wife
Of his first love, and her sweet little ones,
Butchered, amid their shrieks, with all his race.

Thus change the forms of being. Thus arise
Races of living things, glorious in strength,
And perish, as the quickening breath of God
Fills them, or is withdrawn. The red man, too,
Has left the blooming wilds he ranged so long,
And, nearer to the Rocky Mountains, sought
A wilder hunting-ground. The beaver builds
No longer by these streams, but far away,
On waters whose blue surface ne'er gave back
The white man's face—among Missouri's springs,
And pools whose issues swell the Oregon—
He rears his little Venice. In these plains
The bison feeds no more. Twice twenty leagues

Beyond remotest smoke of hunter's camp,
Roams the majestic brute, in herds that shake
The earth with thundering steps—yet here I meet
His ancient footprints stamped beside the pool.

Still this great solitude is quick with life,
Myriads of insects, gaudy as the flowers
They flutter over, gentle quadrupeds,
And birds, that scarce have learned the fear of man,
Are here, and sliding reptiles of the ground,
Startlingly beautiful. The graceful deer
Bounds to the wood at my approach. The bee,
A more adventurous colonist than man,
With whom he came across the eastern deep,
Fills the savannas with his murmurings,
And hides his sweets, as in the golden age,
Within the hollow oak. I listen long
To his domestic hum, and think I hear
The sound of that advancing multitude
Which soon shall fill these deserts. From the ground
Comes up the laugh of children, the soft voice
Of maidens, and the sweet and solemn hymn
Of Sabbath worshippers. The low of herds
Blends with the rustling of the heavy grain
Over the dark brown furrows. All at once
A fresher wind sweeps by, and breaks my dream,
And I am in the wilderness alone.

Thomas Cole
1801-1848

One of the greatest and most influential of nineteenth-century American painters, Thomas Cole was an Englishman by birth. His family moved to America in 1818 when Cole was seventeen. After moving about, they finally settled in Ohio for a time. As an artist, Cole is unusual in being entirely self-taught (for a time he lived as an itinerant painter who did portraits for food, lodging, and support of his travels) and in being recognized early in his life as an original genius whose many successes and whose notoriety followed him through the rest of his life.

By the age of twenty-four he had moved on, through Philadelphia, to New York, where his father had resettled. Shortly afterwards he made his famous trip up the Hudson River. In many ways this trip was the real beginning of his creative life. The power of the great river and the spectacle of the Catskill Mountains struck him like a revelation when he was twenty-five. The landscape gave him a sense of purpose, hope, and life, and it gave him his theme—the majesty of God in nature, and particularly in the American landscape, which as a painter he "discovered" for Americans. Three paintings based on this trip sold quickly and almost immediately established his reputation. His success continued until he was one of the most popular and critically acclaimed artists in America. Out of his art and public recognition developed a growing friendship with William C. Bryant. For both men, nature in America represented not only divine but moral force. For Cole as painter, the many painstaking details of his art revealed the miraculous power he felt in the details of the natural world.

From 1829-32 he made the first of his trips to Europe, was influenced by classical art and the more "realistic" of modern masters, and returned to America at the age of thirty-one to begin his series of didactic and moralizing pictures, one of the most notable of which is *The Course of Empire* (1836) depicting the Romantic theory of the decay of civilizations. He did not stop painting landscapes, yet his allegorical work remained second rate in comparison to his landscapes.

When Cole died at the age of forty-seven, Bryant delivered the funeral oration, saying of Cole's paintings that they "are of that nature that it hardly transcends the proper use of language to call them acts of religion." Asher Durand, Cole's friend, early supporter, and fellow artist in the "Hudson River School" of painters, as Cole's followers came to be called, painted the commemorative and now famous *Kindred Spirits,* a picture showing Cole and Bryant standing over a Catskill valley and observing the landscape. Cole's "Essay on American Scenery" remains a classic statement of the American discovery of the spirit and beauty of the American earth in the nineteenth century.

ESSAY ON AMERICAN SCENERY*

The Essay, which is here offered, is a mere sketch of an almost illimitable subject—American Scenery; and in selecting the theme the writer placed more confidence in its overflowing richness, than in his own capacity for treating it in a manner worthy of its vastness and importance.

It is a subject that to every American ought to be of surpassing interest; for, whether he beholds the Hudson mingling waters with the Atlantic—explores the central wilds of this vast continent, or stands on the margin of the distant Oregon, he is still in the midst of American scenery—it is his own land; its beauty, its magnificence, its sublimity—all are his; and how undeserving of such a birthright, if he can turn towards it an unobserving eye, an unaffected heart!

Before entering into the proposed subject, in which I shall treat more particularly of the scenery of the Northern and Eastern States, I shall be excused for saying a few words on the advantages of cultivating a taste for scenery, and for exclaiming against the apathy with which the beauties of external nature are regarded by the great mass, even of our refined community.

It is generally admitted that the liberal arts tend to soften our manners; but they do more—they carry with them the power to mend our hearts.

Poetry and Painting sublime and purify thought, by grasping the past, the present, and the future—they give the mind a foretaste of its immortality, and thus prepare it for performing an exalted part amid the realities of life. And *rural nature* is full of the same quickening spirit—it is, in fact, the exhaustless mine from which the poet and the painter have brought such wondrous treasures—an unfailing fountain of intellectual enjoyment, where all may drink, and be awakened to a deeper feeling of the works of genius, and a keener perception of the beauty of our existence. For those whose days are all consumed in the low pursuits of avarice, or the

*From *American Art 1700-1960: Sources and Documents,* ed. John W. McCoubrey (Englewood Cliffs, NJ: Prentice-Hall, 1965).

gaudy frivolities of fashion, unobservant of nature's loveliness, are unconscious of the harmony of creation—

> Heaven's roof to them
> Is but a painted ceiling hung with lamps;
> No more—that lights them to their purposes—
> They wander 'loose about;' they nothing see,
> Themselves except, and creatures like themselves,
> Short lived, short sighted.

What to them is the page of the poet where he describes or personifies the skies, the mountains, or the streams, if those objects themselves have never awakened observation or excited pleasure? What to them is the wild Salvator Rosa, or the aerial Claude Lorrain?

There is in the human mind an almost inseparable connection between the beautiful and the good, so that if we contemplate the one the other seems present; and an excellent author has said, "it is difficult to look at any objects with pleasure—unless where it arises from brutal and tumultuous emotions—without feeling that disposition of mind which tends towards kindness and benevolence; and surely, whatever creates such a disposition, by increasing our pleasures and enjoyments, cannot be too much cultivated."

It would seem unnecessary to those who can see and feel, for me to expatiate on the loveliness of verdant fields, the sublimity of lofty mountains, or the varied magnificence of the sky; but that the number of those who *seek* enjoyment in such sources is comparatively small. From the indifference with which the multitude regard the beauties of nature, it might be inferred that she had been unnecessarily lavish in adorning this world for beings who take no pleasure in its adornment. Who in grovelling pursuits forget their glorious heritage. Why was the earth made so beautiful, or the sun so clad in glory at his rising and setting, when *all* might be unrobed of beauty without affecting the insensate multitude, so they can be "lighted to their purposes?"

It *has not* been in vain—the good, the enlightened of all ages and nations, have found pleasure and consolation in the beauty of the rural earth. Prophets of old retired into the solitudes of nature to wait the inspiration of heaven. It was on Mount Horeb that Elijah witnessed the mightly wind, the earthquake, and the fire; and heard the "still small voice"—that voice is YET heard among the mountains! St. John preached in the desert;—the wilderness is YET a fitting place to speak of God. The solitary Anchorites of Syria and Egypt, though ignorant that the busy world is man's noblest sphere of usefulness, well knew how congenial to religious musings are the pathless solitudes.

He who looks on nature with a "loving eye," cannot move from his dwelling without the salutation of beauty; even in the city the deep blue sky and the drifting clouds appeal to him. And if to escape its turmoil—if only to obtain a free horizon, land and water in the play of light and shadow yields delight—let him be transported to those favored regions, where the features of the earth are more varied, or yet add the sunset, that wreath of glory daily bound around the world, and he, indeed, drinks from pleasure's purest cup. The delight such a man experiences is not merely sensual, or selfish, that passes with the occasion leaving no trace behind; but in gazing on the pure creations of the Almighty, he feels a calm religious tone steal through his mind, and when he has turned to mingle with his fellow men, the chords which have been struck in that sweet communion cease not to vibrate.

In what has been said I have alluded to wild and uncultivated scenery; but the cultivated must not be forgotten, for it is still more important to man in his social capacity—necessarily bringing him in contact with the cultured; it encompasses our homes, and, though devoid of the stern sublimity of the wild, its quieter spirit steals tenderly into our bosoms mingled with a thousand domestic affections and heart-touching associations—human hands have wrought, and human deeds hallowed all around.

And it is here that taste, which is the perception of the beautiful, and the knowledge of the principles on which nature works, can be applied, and our dwelling-places made fitting for refined and intellectual beings.

If, then, it is indeed true that the contemplation of scenery can be so abundant a source of delight and improvement, a taste for it is certainly worthy of particular cultivation; for the capacity for enjoyment increases with the knowledge of the true means of obtaining it.

In this age, when a meager utilitarianism seems ready to absorb every feeling and sentiment, and what is sometimes called improvement in its march makes us fear that the bright and tender flowers of the imagination shall all be crushed beneath its iron tramp, it would be well to cultivate the oasis that yet remains to us, and thus preserve the germs of a future and a purer system. And now, when the sway of fashion is extending widely over society—poisoning the healthful streams of true refinement, and turning men from the love of simplicity and beauty, to a senseless idolatry of their own follies—to lead them gently into the pleasant paths of Taste would be an object worthy of the highest efforts of genius and benevolence. The spirit of our society is to contrive but not to enjoy—toiling to produce more toil—accumulating in order to aggrandize. The pleasures of the imagination, among which the love of scenery holds a conspicuous place, will alone temper the harshness of such a state; and, like the atmosphere that softens the most rugged forms of the landscape, cast a veil of tender beauty over the asperities of life.

Did our limits permit I would endeavor more fully to show how necessary to the complete appreciation of the Fine Arts is the study of scenery, and how conducive to our happiness and well-being is that study and those arts; but I must now proceed to the proposed subject of this essay—American Scenery!

There are those who through ignorance or prejudice strive to maintain that American scenery possesses little that is interesting or truly beautiful—that it is rude without picturesqueness, and monotonous without sublimity—that being destitute of those vestiges of antiquity, whose associations so strongly affect the mind, it may not be compared with European scenery. But from whom do these opinions come? From those who have read of European scenery, of Grecian mountains, and Italian skies, and never troubled themselves to look at their own; and from those traveled ones whose eyes were never opened to the beauties of nature until they beheld foreign lands, and when those lands faded from the sight were again closed and forever; disdaining to destroy their trans-atlantic impressions by the observation of the less fashionable and unfamed American scenery. Let such persons shut themselves up in their narrow shell of prejudice—I hope they are few,—and the community increasing in intelligence, will know better how to appreciate the treasures of their own country.

I am by no means desirous of lessening in your estimation the glorious scenes of the old world—that ground which has been the great theater of human events—those mountains, woods, and streams, made sacred in our minds by heroic deeds and immortal song—over which time and genius have suspended an imperishable halo. No! But I would have it remembered that nature has shed over *this* land beauty and magnificence, and although the character of its scenery may differ from the old world's, yet inferiority must not therefore be inferred; for though American scenery is destitute of many of those circumstances that give value to the European, still it has features, and glorious ones, unknown to Europe.

A very few generations have passed away since this vast tract of the American continent, now the United States, rested in the shadow of primaeval forests, whose gloom was peopled by savage beasts, and scarcely less savage men; or lay in those wide grassy plains called prairies—

> The Gardens of the Desert, these
> The unshorn fields, boundless and beautiful.

And, although an enlightened and increasing people have broken in upon the solitude, and with activity and power wrought changes that seem magical, yet the most distinctive, and perhaps the most impressive, characteristic of American scenery is its wildness.

It is the most distinctive, because in civilized Europe the primitive features of scenery have long since been destroyed or modified—the extensive forests that once overshadowed a great part of it have been felled—rugged mountains have been smoothed, and impetuous rivers turned from their courses to accommodate the tastes and necessities of a dense population—the once tangled wood is now a grassy lawn; the turbulent brook a navigable stream—crags that could not be removed have been crowned with towers, and the rudest valleys tamed by the plough.

And to this cultivated state our western world is fast approaching; but nature is still predominant, and there are those who regret that with the improvements of cultivation the sublimity of the wilderness should pass away: for those scenes of solitude from which the hand of nature has never been lifted, affect the mind with a more deep toned emotion than aught which the hand of man has touched. Amid them the consequent associations are of God the creator—they are his undefiled works, and the mind is cast into the contemplation of eternal things.

As mountains are the most conspicuous objects in landscape, they will take the precedence in what I may say on the elements of American scenery.

It is true that in the eastern part of this continent there are no mountains that vie in altitude with the snow-crowned Alps—that the Alleghanies and the Catskills are in no point higher than five thousand feet; but this is no inconsiderable height; Snowdon in Wales, and Ben-Nevis in Scotland, are not more lofty; and in New Hampshire, which has been called the Switzerland of the United States, the White Mountains almost pierce the region of perpetual snow. The Alleghanies are in general heavy in form; but the Catskills, although not broken into abrupt angles like the most picturesque mountains of Italy, have varied, undulating, and exceedingly beautiful outlines—they heave from the valley of the Hudson like the subsiding billows of the ocean after a storm.

American mountains are generally clothed to the summit by dense forests, while those of Europe are mostly bare, or merely tinted by grass or heath. It may be that the mountains of Europe are on this account more picturesque in form, and there is a grandeur in their nakedness; but in the gorgeous garb of the American mountains there is more than an equivalent; and when the woods "have put their glory on," as an American poet has beautifully said, the purple heath and yellow furze of Europe's mountains are in comparison but as the faint secondary rainbow to the primal one.

But in the mountains of New Hampshire there is a union of the picturesque, the sublime, and the magnificent; there the bare peaks of granite, broken and desolate, cradle the clouds; while the vallies and broad bases of the mountains rest under the shadow of noble and varied forests; and the traveller who passes the Sandwich range on his way to the White Mountains, of which it is a spur, cannot but acknowledge, that although in some regions of the globe nature has wrought on a more stupendous scale, yet she has nowhere so completely married together grandeur and loveliness—there he sees the sublime melting into the beautiful, the savage tempered by the magnificent.

I will now speak of another component of scenery, without which every landscape is defective—it is water. Like the eye in the human countenance, it is a most expressive feature: in the unrippled lake, which mirrors all surrounding objects, we have the expression of tranquillity and peace—in the rapid stream, the headlong cataract, that of turbulence and impetuosity.

In this great element of scenery, what land is so rich? I would not speak of the Great Lakes, which are in fact inland seas—possessing some of the attributes of the ocean, though destitute of its sublimity; but of those smaller lakes, such as Lake George, Champlain, Winnipisiogee, Otsego, Seneca, and a hundred others, that stud like gems the bosom of this country. There is one delightful quality in nearly all these lakes—the purity and transparency of the water. In speaking of scenery it might seem unnecessary to mention this; but independent of the pleasure that we all have in beholding pure water, it is a circumstance which contributes greatly to the beauty of landscape; for the reflections of surrounding objects, trees, mountains, sky, are most perfect in the clearest water; and the most perfect is the most beautiful.

I would rather persuade you to visit the "Holy Lake," the beautiful "Horican," than attempt to describe its scenery—to behold you rambling on its storied shores, where its southern expanse is spread, begemmed with isles of emerald, and curtained by green receding hills—or to see you gliding over its bosom, where the steep and rugged mountains approach from either side, shadowing with black precipices the innumerable islets—some of which bearing a solitary tree, others a group of two or three, or a "goodly company," seem to have been sprinkled over the smiling deep in Nature's frolic hour. These scenes are classic—History and Genius have hallowed them. War's shrill clarion once waked the echoes from these now silent hills—the pen of a living master has portrayed them in the pages of romance—and they are worthy of the admiration of the enlightened and the graphic hand of Genius.

Though differing from Lake George, Winnipisiogee resembles it in multitudinous and uncounted islands. Its mountains do not stoop to the water's edge, but through varied screens of forest may be seen ascending the sky softened by the blue haze of distance—on the one hand rise the Gunstock Mountains; on the other the dark Ossipees, while above and far beyond, rear the "cloud capt" peaks of the Sandwich and White Mountains.

I will not fatigue with a vain attempt to describe the lakes that I have named; but would turn your attention to those exquisitely beautiful lakes that are so numerous in the Northern States, and particularly in New Hampshire. In character they are truly and peculiarly American. I know nothing in Europe which they resemble; the famous lakes of Albano and Nemi, and the small and exceedingly picturesque lakes of Great Britain may be compared in size, but are dissimilar in almost every other respect. Embosomed in the primitive forest, and sometimes overshadowed by huge mountains, they are the chosen places of tranquility; and when the deer issues from the surrounding woods to drink the cool waters, he beholds his own image as in a polished mirror,—the flight of the eagle can be seen in the lower sky; and if a leaf falls, the circling undulations chase each other to the shores unvexed by contending tides.

There are two lakes of this description, situated in a wild mountain gorge called the Franconia Notch, in New Hampshire. They lie within a few hundred feet of each other, but are remarkable as having no communication—one being the source of the wild Amonoosuck, the other of the Pemigiwasset. Shut in by stupendous mountains which rest on crags that tower more than a thousand feet above the water, whose rugged brows and shadowy breaks are clothed by dark and tangled woods, they have such an aspect of deep seclusion, of utter and unbroken solitude, that, when standing on their brink a lonely traveller. I was overwhelmed with an emotion of the sublime, such as I have rarely felt. It was not that the jagged precipices were lofty, that the encircling woods were of the dimmest shade, or that the waters were profoundly deep; but that over all, rocks, wood, and water brooded the spirit of repose, and the silent energy of nature stirred the soul to its inmost depths.

I would not be understood that these lakes are always tranquil; but that tranquillity is their great characteristic. There are times when they take a far different expression; but in scenes like these the richest chords are those struck by the gentler hand of nature.

And now I must turn to another of the beautifiers of the earth—the Waterfall; which in the same object at once presents to the mind the beautiful, but apparently incongruous idea, of fixedness and motion—a single existence in which we perceive unceasing change and everlasting duration. The waterfall may be called the voice of the landscape, for, unlike the rocks and woods which utter sounds as the passive instruments played on by the elements, the waterfall strikes its own chords, and rocks and mountains re-echo in rich unison. And this is a land abounding in cataracts; in these Northern States where shall we turn and not find them? Have we not Kaaterskill, Trenton, the Flume, the Genesee, stupendous Niagara, and a hundred other named and nameless ones, whose exceeding beauty must be acknowledged when the hand of taste shall point them out?

In the Kaaterskill we have a stream, diminutive indeed, but throwing itself headlong over a fearful precipice into a deep gorge of the densely wooded mountains—and possessing a singular feature in the vast arched cave that extends beneath and behind the cataract. At Trenton there is a chain of waterfalls of remarkable beauty, where the foaming waters, shadowed by steep cliffs, break over rocks of architectural formation, and tangled and picturesque trees mantle abrupt precipices, which it would be easy to imagine crumbling and "time disparting towers."

And Niagara! that wonder of the world!—where the sublime and beautiful are bound together in an indissoluble chain. In gazing on it we feel as though a great void had been filled in our minds—our conceptions expand—we become a part of what we behold! At our feet the floods of a thousand rivers are poured out—the contents of vast inland seas. In its volume we conceive immensity; in its course, everlasting duration; in its impetuosity, uncontrollable power. These are the elements of its sublimity. Its beauty is garlanded around in the varied hues of the water, in the spray that ascends the sky, and in that unrivalled bow which forms a complete cincture round the unresting floods.

The river scenery of the United States is a rich and boundless theme. The Hudson for natural magnificence is unsurpassed. What can be more beautiful than the lake-like expanses of Tapaan and Haverstraw, as seen from the rich orchards of the surrounding hills? hills that have a legend, which has been so sweetly and admirably told that it shall not perish but with the language of the land. What can be more imposing than the precipitous Highlands; whose dark foundations have been rent to make a passage for the deep-flowing river? And, ascending still, where can be found scenes more enchanting? The lofty Catskills stand afar off—the green hills gently rising from the flood, recede like steps by which we may ascend to a great temple, whose pillars are those everlasting hills, and whose dome is the blue boundless vault of heaven.

The Rhine has its castled crags, its vine-clad hills, and ancient villages; the Hudson has its wooded mountains, its rugged precipices, its green undulating shores—a natural majesty, and an unbounded capacity for improvement by art. Its shores are not besprinkled with venerated ruins, or the palaces of princes; but there are flourishing towns, and neat villas, and the hand of taste has already been at work. Without any great stretch of the imagination we may anticipate the time when the ample waters shall reflect temple, and tower, and dome, in every variety of picturesqueness and magnificence.

In the Connecticut we behold a river that differs widely from the Hudson. Its sources are amid the wild mountains of New Hampshire; but it soon breaks into a luxuriant valley, and flows for more than a hundred miles, sometimes beneath the shadow of wooded hills, and sometimes glancing through the green expanse of elm-besprinkled meadows. Whether we see it at Haverhill, Northampton, or Hartford, it still possesses that gentle aspect; and the imagination can scarcely conceive Arcadian vales more lovely or more peaceful than the valley of the Connecticut—its villages are rural places where trees overspread every dwelling, and the fields upon its margin have the richest verdure.

Nor ought the Ohio, the Susquehannah, the Potomac, with their tributaries, and a thousand others, be omitted in the rich list of the American rivers—they are a glorious brotherhood; but volumes would be insufficient for their description.

In the Forest scenery of the United States we have that which occupies the greatest space, and is not the least remarkable; being primitive, it differs widely from the European. In the American forest we find trees in every stage of vegetable life and decay—the slender sapling rises in the shadow of the lofty tree, and the giant in his prime stands by the hoary patriarch of the wood—on the ground lie prostrate decaying ranks that once waved their verdant heads in the sun and wind. These are circumstances productive of great variety and picturesqueness—green umbrageous masses—lofty and scathed trunks—contorted branches thrust athwart the sky—the mouldering dead below, shrouded in moss of every hue and texture, from richer combinations than can be found in the trimmed and planted grove. It is true that the thinned and cultivated wood offers less obstruction to the feet, and the trees throw out their branches more horizontally, and are consequently more umbrageous when taken singly; but the true lover of the picturesque is seldom fatigued—and trees that grow widely apart are often heavy in form, and resemble each other too much for picturesqueness. Trees are like men, differing widely in character; in sheltered spots, or under the influence of culture, they show few contrasting points; peculiarities are pruned and trained away, until there is a general resemblance. But in exposed situations, wild and uncultivated, battling with the elements and with one another for the possession of a morsel of soil, or a favoring rock to which they may cling—they exhibit striking peculiarities, and sometimes grand originality.

For variety, the American forest is unrivalled: in some districts are found oaks, elms, birches, beeches, planes, pines, hemlocks, and many other kinds of trees, commingled—clothing the hills with every tint of green, and every variety of light and shade.

There is a peculiarity observable in some mountainous regions, where trees of a genus band together—there often may be seen a mountain whose foot is clothed with deciduous trees, while on its brow is a sable crown of pines; and sometimes belts of dark green encircle a mountain horizontally, or are stretched in well-defined lines from the summit to the base. The nature of the soil, or the courses of rivulets, are the causes of this variety;—and it is a beautiful instance of the exhaustlessness of nature; often where we would expect unvarying monotony, we behold a charming diversity. Time will not permit me to speak of the American forest trees individually; but I must notice the elm, that paragon of beauty and shade; the maple, with its rainbow hues; and the hemlock, the sublime of trees, which rises from the gloom of the forest like a dark and ivy-mantled tower.

There is one season when the American forest surpasses all the world in gorgeousness—that is the autumnal;—then every hill and dale is riant in the luxury of color—every hue is there, from the liveliest green to deepest purple—from the most golden yellow to the intensest crimson. The artist looks despairingly upon the glowing landscape, and in the old world his truest imitations of the American forest, at this season, are called falsely bright, and scenes in Fairy Land.

The sky will next demand our attention. The soul of all scenery, in it are the fountains of light, and shade, and color. Whatever expression the sky takes, the features of the landscape are affected in unison, whether it be the serenity of the summer's blue, or the dark tumult of the storm. It is the sky that makes the earth so lovely at sunrise, and so splendid at sunset. In the one it breathes over the earth the crystal-like ether, in the other the liquid gold. The climate of a great part of the United States is subject to great vicissitudes, and we complain; but nature offers a compensation. These very vicissitudes are the abundant sources of beauty—as we have the temperature of every clime, so have we the skies—we have the blue unsearchable depths of the northern sky—we have the upheaped thunder-clouds of the Torrid Zone, fraught with gorgeousness and sublimity—we have the silver haze of England, and the golden atmosphere of Italy. And if he who has traveled and observed the skies of other climes will spend a few months on the banks of the Hudson, he must be constrained to acknowledge that for variety and magnificence American skies are unsurpassed. Italian skies have been lauded by every tongue, and sung by every poet, and who will deny their wonderful beauty? At sunset the serene arch is filled with alchemy that transmutes mountains, and streams, and temples, into living gold.

But the American summer never passes without many sunsets that might vie with the Italian, and many still more gorgeous—that seem peculiar to this clime.

Look at the heavens when the thunder shower has passed, and the sun stoops behind the western mountains—there the low purple clouds hang in festoons around the steeps—in the higher heaven are crimson bands interwoven with feathers of gold, fit for the wings of angels—and still above is spread that interminable field of ether, whose color is too beautiful to have a name.

It is not in the summer only that American skies are beautiful; for the winter evening often comes robed in purple and gold, and in the westering sun the iced groves glitter as beneath a shower of diamonds—and through the twilight heaven innumerable stars shine with a purer light than summer ever knows.

I will now venture a few remarks on what has been considered a grand defect in American scenery—the want of associations, such as arise amid the scenes of the old world.

We have many a spot as umbrageous as Vallombrosa, and as picturesque as the solitudes of Vaucluse; but Milton and Petrarch have not hallowed them by their footsteps and immortal verse. He who stands on Mont Albano and looks down on ancient Rome, has his mind peopled with the gigantic associations of the storied past; but he who stands on the mounds of the West, the most venerable remains of American antiquity, *may* experience the emotion of the sublime, but it is the sublimity of a shoreless ocean un-islanded by the recorded deeds of man.

Yet American scenes are not destitute of historical and legendary associations—the great struggle for freedom has sanctified many a spot, and many a mountain, stream, and rock has its legend, worthy of poet's pen or the painter's pencil. But American associations are not so much of the past as of the present and the future. Seated on a pleasant knoll, look down into the bosom of that secluded valley, begirt with wooded hills—through those enamelled meadows and wide waving fields of grain, a silver stream winds lingeringly along—here, seeking the green shade of trees—there, glancing in the sunshine: on its banks are rural dwellings shaded by elms and garlanded by flowers—from yonder dark mass of foliage the village spire beams like a star. You see no ruined tower to tell of outrage—no gorgeous temple to speak of ostentation; but freedom's offspring—peace, security, and happiness, dwell there, the spirits of the scene. On the margin of that gentle river the village girls may ramble unmolested—and the glad school-boy, with hook and line, pass his bright holiday—those neat dwellings, unpretending to magnificence, are the abodes of plenty, virtue, and refinement. And in looking over the yet uncultivated scene, the mind's eye may see far into futurity. Where the wolf roams, the plough shall glisten; on the gray crag shall rise temple and tower—mighty deeds shall be done in the now pathless wilderness; and poets yet unborn shall sanctify the soil.

It was my intention to attempt a description of several districts remarkable for their picturesqueness and truly American character; but I fear to trespass longer on your time and patience. Yet I cannot but express my sorrow that the beauty of such landscapes are quickly passing away—the ravages of the axe are daily increasing—the most noble scenes are made desolate, and oftentimes with a wantonness and barbarism scarcely credible in a civilized nation. The way-side is becoming shadeless, and another generation will behold spots, now rife with beauty, desecrated by what is called improvement; which, as yet, generally destroys Nature's beauty without substituting that of Art. This is a regret rather than a complaint; such is the road society has to travel; it may lead to refinement in the end, but the traveler who sees the place of rest close at hand, dislikes the road that has so many unnecessary windings.

I will now conclude, in the hope that, though feebly urged, the importance of cultivating a taste for scenery will not be forgotten. Nature has spread for us a rich and delightful banquet. Shall we turn from it? We are still in Eden; the wall that shuts us out of the garden is our own ignorance and folly. We should not allow the poet's words to be applicable to us—

> Deep in rich pasture do thy flocks complain?
> Not so; but to their master is denied
> To share the sweet serene.

May we at times turn from the ordinary pursuits of life to the pure enjoyment of rural nature; which is in the soul like a fountain of cool waters to the way-worn traveller; and let us

> Learn
> The laws by which the Eternal doth sublime
> And sanctify his works, that we may see
> The hidden glory veiled from vulgar eyes.

George Perkins Marsh
1801-1882

In our century, the writer and social critic Lewis Mumford called Marsh's book *Man and Nature, or Physical Geography Modified by Human Action* (1864)—later thoroughly revised as *The Earth As Modified by Human Action* (1874)—"the fountainhead of the conservation movement." Certainly Marsh's work had a worldwide impact on the modern trend toward conservation and preservation. And it is appropriate that his influence should be so great, for Marsh was an "international citizen," a man of many languages and professional interests.

By training, Marsh was a philologist and a lawyer. Born in Woodstock, Vermont, the bookish boy was looked upon as the most brilliant of his Dartmouth class of 1820. And as early as 1835 the state governor, recognizing Marsh's brilliance as a businessman, lawyer, and scholar, appointed him to the Vermont Executive Council. Thus began the long public career of this scion of the New England intellectual aristocracy who had studied law in his father's office. He was elected to the U.S. Congress in 1842, served as Minister to Turkey from 1849–53, and as Minister to Italy, under President Lincoln, from 1861 until his death in 1882. He wrote books on the history of the English language and literature and lectured at the Lowell Institute and Columbia University on philology and etymology as an established authority in his field.

But Marsh was also a geographer and amateur zoologist; he collected reptiles for the Smithsonian Institution, and he wrote the masterwork of physiogeography and ecology that Mumford admired. These selections from *The Earth* suggest his wide acquaintance with world history and geography as well as the prophetic originality, for his day, of his vision of the order of nature.

from THE EARTH AS MODIFIED BY HUMAN ACTION*

Natural Advantages of the Territory of the Roman Empire.

The Roman Empire, at the period of its greatest expansion, comprised the regions of the earth most distinguished by a happy combination of physical conditions. The provinces bordering on the principal and the secondary basins of the Mediterranean enjoyed, in healthfulness and equability of climate, in fertility of soil, in variety of vegetable and mineral products, and in natural facilities for the transportation and distribution of exchangeable commodities, advantages which have not been possessed in an equal degree by any territory of like extent in the Old World or the New. The abundance of the land and of the waters adequately supplied every material want, ministered liberally to every sensuous enjoyment. Gold and silver, indeed, were not found in the profusion which has proved so baneful to the industry of lands richer in veins of the precious metals; but mines and river beds yielded them in the spare measure most favorable to stability of value in the medium of exchange, and, consequently, to the regularity of commercial transactions. The ornaments of the barbaric pride of the East, the pearl, the ruby, the sapphire, and the diamond—though not unknown to the luxury of a people whose conquests and whose wealth commanded whatever the habitable world could contribute to augment the material splendor of their social life—were scarcely native to the territory of the empire; but the comparative rarity of these gems in Europe at somewhat earlier periods, was, perhaps, the very circumstance that led the cunning artists of classic antiquity to enrich softer stones with engravings that invest the common onyx and cornealian with a worth surpassing, in cultivated eyes, the lustre of the most brilliant oriental jewels.

Of these manifold blessings the temperature of the air, the distribution of the rains, the relative disposition of land and water, the plenty of the sea, the composition of the soil, and the raw material of the primitive arts, were wholly gratuitous gifts. Yet the spontaneous nature of Europe, of Western Asia, of Libya, neither fed nor clothed the civilized inhabitants of those provinces. The luxuriant harvests of cereals that waved on every field from the shores of the Rhine to the banks of the Nile, the vines that festooned the hillsides of Syria, of Italy and of Greece, the olives of Spain, the fruits of the gardens of the Hesperides, the domestic quadrupeds and fowls known in ancient rural husbandry—all these were original products of foreign climes, naturalized in new homes, and gradually ennobled by the art of man, while centuries of persevering labor were expelling the wild vegetation, and fitting the earth for the production of more generous growths. Every loaf was eaten in the sweat of the brow. All must be earned by toil. But toil was nowhere else rewarded by so generous wages; for nowhere would a given amount of intelligent labor produce so abundant, and, at the same time, so varied returns of the good things of material existence.

*From George Perkins Marsh, *The Earth as Modified by Human Action* (New York: Charles Scribner's Son, 1898).

Physical Decay of the Territory of the Roman Empire.

If we compare the present physical condition of the countries of which I am speaking, with the descriptions that ancient historians and geographers have given of their fertility and general capability of ministering to human uses, we shall find that more than one-half their whole extent—not excluding the provinces most celebrated for the profusion and variety of their spontaneous and their cultivated products, and for the wealth and social advancement of their inhabitants—is either deserted by civilized man and surrendered to hopeless desolation, or at least greatly reduced in both productiveness and population. Vast forests have disappeared from mountain spurs and ridges; the vegetable earth accumulated beneath the trees by the decay of leaves and of fallen trunks, the soil of the alpine pastures which skirted and indented the woods, and the mould of the upland fields, are washed away; meadows, once fertilized by irrigation, are waste and unproductive, because the cisterns and reservoirs that supplied the ancient canals are broken, or the springs that fed them dried up; rivers famous in history and song have shrunk to humble brooklets; the willows that ornamented and protected the banks of the lesser watercourses are gone, and the rivulets have ceased to exist as perennial currents, because the little water that finds its way into their old channels is evaporated by the droughts of summer, or absorbed by the parched earth before it reaches the lowlands; the beds of the brooks have widened into broad expanses of pebbles and gravel, over which, though in the hot season passed dryshod, in winter sealike torrents thunder; the entrances of navigable streams are obstructed by sandbars; and harbors, once marts of an extensive commerce, are shoaled by the deposits of the rivers at whose mouths they lie; the elevation of the beds of estuaries, and the consequently diminished velocity and increased lateral spread of the streams which flow into them, have converted thousands of leagues of shallow sea and fertile lowland into unproductive and miasmatic morasses.

Besides the direct testimony of history to the ancient fertility of the now exhausted regions to which I refer—Northern Africa, the greater Arabian peninsula, Syria, Mesopotamia, Armenia and many other provinces of Asia Minor, Greece, Sicily, and parts of even Italy and Spain—the multitude and extent of yet remaining architectural ruins, and of decayed works of internal improvement, show that at former epochs a dense population inhabited those now lonely districts. Such a population could have been sustained only by a productiveness of soil of which we at present discover but slender traces; and the abundance derived from that fertility serves to explain how large armies, like those of the ancient Persians, and of the Crusaders and the Tartars in later ages, could, without an organized commissariat, secure adequate supplies in long marches through territories which, in our times, would scarcely afford forage for a single regiment.

It appears, then, that the fairest and fruitfulest provinces of the Roman Empire, precisely that portion of terrestrial surface, in short, which, about the commencement of the Christian era, was endowed with the greatest superiority of soil, climate, and position, which had been carried to the highest pitch of physical improvement, and which thus combined the natural and artificial conditions best fitting it for the habitation and enjoyment of a dense and highly refined and cultivated population, are now completely exhausted of their fertility, or so diminished in productiveness, as, with the exception of a few favored oases that have escaped the general ruin, to be no longer capable of affording sustenance to civilized man. If to this realm of desolation we add the now wasted and solitary soils of Persia and the remoter East that once fed their millions with milk and honey, we shall see that a territory larger than all Europe, the abundance of which sustained in bygone centuries a population scarcely inferior to that of the whole Christian world at the present day, has been entirely withdrawn from human use, or, at best, is thinly inhabited by tribes too few in numbers, too poor in superfluous products, and too little advanced in culture and the social arts, to contribute anything to the general moral or material interests of the great commonwealth of man.

Causes of this Decay.

The decay of these once flourishing countries is partly due, no doubt, to that class of geological causes whose action we can neither resist nor guide, and partly also to the direct violence of hostile human force; but it is, in a far greater proportion, either the result of man's ignorant disregard of the laws of nature, or an incidental consequence of war and civil and ecclesiastical tyranny and misrule. Next to ignorance of these laws, the primitive source, the *causa causarum*, of the acts and neglects which have blasted with sterility and physical decrepitude the noblest half of the empire of the Caesars, is, first, the brutal and exhausting despotism which Rome herself exercised over her conquered kingdoms and even over her Italian territory; then, the host of temporal and spiritual tyrannies which she left as her dying curse to all her wide dominion, and which, in some form of violence or of fraud, still brood over almost every soil subdued by the Roman legions.* Man cannot

---

*In the Middle Ages, feudalism, and a nominal Christianity whose corruptions had converted the most beneficent of religions into the most baneful of superstitions, perpetuated every abuse of Roman tyranny, and added new oppressions and new methods of extortion to those invented by older despotisms. The burdens in question fell most heavily on the provinces that had been longest colonized by the Latin race, and these are the portions of Europe which have suffered the greatest physical degradation. "Feudalism," says Blanqui, "was a concentration of scourges. The peasant, stripped of the inheritance of his fathers, became the property of inflexible, ignorant, indolent masters; he was obliged to travel fifty leagues with their carts whenever they required it; he labored for them three days in the week, and surrendered to them half the product of his earnings during the other three; without their consent he could not change his residence, or marry. And why, indeed, should he wish to marry, when he could scarcely save enough to maintain himself? The Abbot Alcuin had twenty thousand slaves, called *serfs*, who were forever attached to the soil. This is the great cause of the rapid depopulation observed in the Middle Ages, and of the prodigious multitude of monasteries which sprang up on every side. It was doubtless a relief to such miserable men to find in the cloisters a retreat from oppression; but the human race never suffered a more cruel outrage, industry never received a wound better calculated to plunge the world again into the darkness of the rudest antiquity. It suffices to say that the prediction of the approaching end of the world, industriously spread by the rapacious monks at this time, was received without terror."—*Resume de l'Histoire du Commerce*, p. 156. See also Michelet, *Histoire de France*, Vol. V., pp. 216, 217.

The abbey of Saint-Germain-des Pres, which in the time of Charlemagne had possessed a million of acres, was, down to the Revolution, still so wealthy that the personal income of the abbot was 300,000 livres. The abbey of Saint-Denis was nearly as rich as that of Saint-Germain-des-Pres.—Lavergne, *Economie Rurale de la France,* p. 104.

struggle at once against human oppression and the destructive forces of inorganic nature. When both are combined against him, he succumbs after a shorter or longer struggle, and the fields he has won from the primeval wood relapse into their original state of wild and luxuriant, but unprofitable, forest growth, or fall into that of a dry and barren wilderness.

Rome imposed on the products of agricultural labor, in the rural districts, taxes which the sale of the entire harvest would scarcely discharge; she drained them of their population by military conscription; she impoverished the peasantry by forced and unpaid labor on public works; she hampered industry and both foreign and internal commerce by absurd restrictions and unwise regulations.* Hence, large tracts of land were left uncultivated, or altogether deserted, and exposed to all the destructive forces which act with such energy on the surface of the earth when it is deprived of those protections by which nature originally guarded it, and for which, in well-ordered husbandry, human ingenuity has contrived more or less efficient substitutes.* Similar abuses have tended to perpetuate and extend these evils in later ages, and it is but recently that, even in the most populous parts of Europe, public attention has been half awakened to the necessity of restoring the disturbed harmonies of nature, whose well-balanced influences are so propitious to all her organic offspring, and of

---

Paul Louis Courier quotes from La Bruyere the following striking picture of the condition of the French peasantry in his time: "One sees certain dark, livid, naked, sunburnt, wild animals, male and female, scattered over the country and attached to the soil, which they root and turn over with indomitable perseverance. They have, as it were, an articulate voice, and when they rise to their feet, they show a human face. They are, in fact, men; they creep at night into dens, where they live on black bread, water, and roots. They spare other men the labor of ploughing, sowing and harvesting, and therefore deserve some small share of the bread they have grown." "These are his own words," adds Courier, "and he is speaking of the *fortunate* peasants, of those who had work and bread, and they were then the few."—*Petition a la Chambre des Deputes pour les Villageois que l'on empeche de danser.*

Arthur young, who traveled in France from 1787 to 1789, gives, in the twenty-first chapter of his *Travels*, a fruitful account of the burdens of the rural population even at that late period. Besides the regular governmental taxes and a multitude of heavy fines imposed for trifling offences, he enumerates about thirty seignorial rights, the very origin and nature of some of which are now unknown, while those of some others are as repulsive to humanity and morality as the worst abuses ever practised by heathen despotism. But Young underrates the number of these oppressive impositions. Moreau de Jonnes, a higher authority, asserts that in a brief examination he had discovered upwards of three hundred distinct rights of the feudatory over the person or the property of his vassal. See *Etat Economique et Social de la France*, Paris, 1870, p. 389. Most of these, indeed, had been commuted for money payments, and were levied on the peasantry as pecuniary imposts for the benefit of prelates and lay lords, who, by virtue of their nobility, were exempt from taxation. The collection of the taxes was enforced, with unrelenting severity. On one occasion, in the reign of Louis XIV., the troops sent out against the recreant peasants made more than 3,000 prisoners, of whom 400 were condemned to the galleys for life, and a number so large that the government did not dare to disclose it, were hung on trees or broken on the wheel.—Moreau de Jonnes, *Etat Ecoomique et Social de la France* p. 420. Who can wonder at the hostility of the French plebeian classes towards the aristocracy in the days of the Revolution?

*Commerce, in common with all gainful occupations except agriculture, was despised by the Romans, and the exercise of it was forbidden to the higher ranks. Cicero, however, admits that though retail trade, which could only prosper by lying and knavery, was contemptible, yet wholesale commerce was not altogether to be condemned, and might even be laudable, provided the merchant retired early from trade and invested his gains in farm lands.—*De Officiis,* lib. i., 42.

*The temporary depopulation of an exhausted soil may be, in some cases, a physical, though, like fallows in agriculture, a dear-bought advantage. Under favorable circumstances, the withdrawal of man and his flocks allows the earth to clothe itself again with forests, and in a few generations to recover its ancient productiveness. In the Middle Ages, worn-out fields were depopulated, in many parts of the Continent, by civil and ecclesiastical tyrannies which insisted on the surrender of the half of a loaf already too small to sustain its producer. Thus abandoned, these lands often relapsed into the forest state, and, some centuries later, were again brought under cultivation with renovated fertility.

repaying to our great mother the debt which the prodigality and the thriftlessness of former generations have imposed upon their successors—thus fulfilling the command of religion and of practical wisdom, to use this world as not abusing it.

. . .

Destructiveness of Man

Man has too long forgotten that the earth was given to him for usufruct alone, not for consumption, still less for profligate waste. Nature has provided against the absolute destruction of any of her elementary matter, the raw material of her works; the thunderbolt and the tornado, the most convulsive throes of even the volcano and the earthquake, being only phenomena of decomposition and recomposition. But she has left it within the power of man irreparably to derange the combinations of inorganic matter and of organic life, which through the night of aeons she had been proportioning and balancing, to prepare the earth for his habitation, when in the fulness of time his Creator should call him forth to enter into its possession.

Apart from the hostile influence of man, the organic and the inorganic world are, as I have remarked, bound together by such mutual relations and adaptations as secure, if not the absolute permanence and equilibrium of both, a long continuance of the established conditions of each at any given time and place, or at least, a very slow and gradual succession of changes in those conditions. But man is everywhere a disturbing agent. Wherever he plants his foot, the harmonies of nature are turned to discords. The proportions and accommodations which insured the stability of existing arrangements are overthrown. Indigenous vegetable and animal species are extirpated, and supplanted by others of foreign origin, spontaneous production is forbidden or restricted, and the face of the earth is either laid bare or covered with a new and reluctant growth of vegetable forms and with alien tribes of animal life. These intentional changes and substitutions constitute, indeed, great revolutions; but vast as is their magnitude and importance, they are, as we shall see, insignificant in comparison with the contingent and unsought results which have flowed from them.

The fact that, of all organic beings, man alone is to be regarded as essentially a destructive power, and that he wields energies to resist which Nature—that nature whom all material life and all inorganic substance obey—is wholly impotent, tends to prove that, though living in physical nature, he is not of her, that he is of more exalted parentage, and belongs to a higher order of existences, than those which are born of her womb and live in blind submission to her dictates.

There are, indeed, brute destroyers, beasts and birds and insects of prey—all animal life feeds upon, and, of course, destroys other life,—but this destruction is balanced by compensations. It is, in fact, the very means by which the existence of one tribe of animals or of vegetables is secured against being smothered by the encroachments of another; and the reproductive powers of species which serve as the food of others are always proportioned to the demand they are destined to supply. Man pursues his victims with reckless destructiveness; and while the sacrifice of life by the lower animals is limited by the cravings of appetite, he unsparingly persecutes, even to extirpation, thousands of organic forms which he can not consume.*

---

*The terrible destructiveness of man is remarkably exemplified in the chase of large mammalia and birds, for single products, attended with the entire waste of enormous quantities of flesh and of other parts of the animal which are capable of valuable uses. The wild cattle of South America are slaughtered by millions, for their hides and horns; the buffalo of North America, for his skin or his tongue; the elephant, the walrus, and the narwhal, for their tusks; the cetacea, and some other marine animals, for their whalebone and oil; the ostrich and other large birds, for their plumage. Within a few years, sheep have been killed in New England, by whole flocks, for their pelts and suet alone, the flesh being thrown away; and it is even said that the bodies of the same quadrupeds have been used in Australia as fuel for limekilns. What a vast amount of human nutriment, of bone, and of other animal products valuable in the arts, is thus recklessly squandered! In nearly all these cases, the part which constitutes the motive for this wholesale destruction, and is alone saved, is essentially for insignificant value as compared with what is thrown away. The horns and hide of an ox are not economically worth a tenth part as much as the entire carcass. During the present year, large quantities of Indian corn have been used as domestic fuel, and even for burning lime, in Iowa and other Western States. Corn at from fifteen to eighteen cents per bushel is found cheaper than wood at from five to seven dollars per cord, or coal at six or seven dollars per ton.—*Rep. Agric. Dept.,* Nov. and Dec., 1872, p. 487.

One of the greatest benefits to be expected from the improvements of civilization is, that increased facilities of communication will render it possible to transport to places of consumption much valuable material that is now wasted because the price at the nearest market will not pay freight. The cattle slaughtered in South America for their hides would feed millions of the starving population of the Old World, if their flesh could be economically preserved and transported across the ocean. This indeed is already done, but on a scale which, though absolutely considerable, is relatively insignificant. South America sends to Europe a certain quantity of nutriment in the form of meat extracts, Liebig's and others; and preserved flesh from Australia is beginning to figure in the English market.

[Since the above paragraph was written the transportation of *fresh* meat from distant countries to England has been attended with remarkable success. A single ship is said on good authority to have brought from New Zealand to England, in the spring of 1882, the flesh of 5,000 sheep in perfectly good condition. The course of this vessel necessarily lay across the tropics, and her delicate freight sustained no injury whatever from the great heat to which she was exposed. By means of a refrigerating apparatus the meat was kept at a temperature near or at the freezing point.]

A very important recent economy is the utilization of those portions of certain agricultural products that were formerly treated as mere refuse. The cotton-growing States in America produce annually about three million tons of cotton seed. This until very recently has been thrown away as a useless incumbrance, but it is now valued at from ten to twelve dollars per ton for the cotton fibre which adheres to it, for the oil extracted from it, and for the feed which it afterwards furnishes to cattle. The oil—which may be described as neutral—is used very largely for mixing with other oils, many of which bear a large proportion of it without injury to their special properties. The *sansa*, or pulp of the olive remaining after the oil has been expressed, until very recently considered worthless except as manure, is now found to be capable of yielding, by a different treatment, a considerable quantity of oil and some other valuable products. Even the waste from silk manufactories, and the shreds and fragments from the shops of modistes, formerly thrown away as useless, are now carefully saved. A long series of costly experiments has led to the invention of processes for reducing all this material to a fibrous condition, and for re-spinning and weaving it into every possible tissue. The operation is carried on in England on a scale of really great industrial importance.

The substitution of expensive machinery for manual labor, even in agriculture—not to speak of older and more familiar applications—besides being highly remunerative, has better secured the harvests, and it is computed that the 230,000 threshing machines used in the United States in 1870 obtained five per cent, more grain from the sheaves which passed through them than could have been secured by the use of the flail.

We are also beginning to learn a better economy in dealing with the inorganic world. The utilization—or, as the Germans more happily call it, the Verwerthung, the *beworthing*—of waste from metallurgical, chemical and manufacturing establishments, is among the most important results of the application of science to industrial purposes. The incidental products from the laboratories of manufacturing chemists often become more valuable than those for the preparation of which they were erected. The slags from silver refineries, and even from smelting houses of the coarser metals, have not unfrequently yielded to a second operator a better return than the first had derived from dealing with the natural ore; and the saving of lead carried off in the smoke of furnaces has, of itself, given a large profit on the capital invested in the works. According to *Ure's Dictionary of Arts*, see vol. ii, p. 832, an English miner has constructed flues five miles in length for the condensation of the smoke from his lead-works, and makes thereby an annual saving of metal to the value of ten thousand pounds sterling. A few years ago, an officer of an American mint was charged with embezzling gold committed to him for coinage. He insisted, in his defense, that much of the metal was volatilized and lost in refining and melting, and upon scraping the chimneys of the melting furnaces and the roofs of the adjacent houses, gold enough was found in the soot to account for no small part of the deficiency.

The earth was not, in its natural condition, completely adapted to the use of man, but only to the sustenance of wild animals and wild vegetation. These live, multiply their kind in just proportion, and attain their perfect measure of strength and beauty, without producing or requiring any important change in the natural arrangements of surface or in each other's spontaneous tendencies, except such mutual repression of excessive increase as may prevent the extirpation of one species by the encroachments of another. In short, without man, lower animal and spontaneous vegetable life would have been practically constant in type, distribution and proportion, and the physical geography of the earth would have remained undisturbed for indefinite periods, and been subject to revolution only from slow development, from possible unknown cosmical causes, or from geological action.

But man, the domestic animals that serve him, the field and garden plants the products of which supply him with food and clothing, can not subsist and rise to the full development of their higher properties, unless brute and unconscious nature be effectually combated, and, in a great degree, vanquished by human art. Hence, a certain measure of transformation of terrestrial surface, of suppression of natural, and stimulation of artificially modified productivity becomes necessary. This measure man has unfortunately exceeded. He has felled the forests whose network of fibrous roots bound the mould to the rocky skeleton of the earth; but had he allowed here and there a belt of woodland to reproduce itself by spontaneous propagation, most of the mischiefs which his reckless destruction of the natural protection of the soil has occasioned would have been averted. He has broken up the mountain reservoirs, the percolation of whose waters through unseen channels supplied the fountains that refreshed his cattle and fertilized his fields; but he has neglected to maintain the cisterns and the canals of irrigation which a wise antiquity had constructed to neutralize the consequences of its own imprudence. While he has torn the thin glebe which confined the light earth of extensive plains, and has destroyed the fringe of semi-aquatic plants which skirted the coast and checked the drifting of the sea sand, he has failed to prevent the spreading of the dunes by clothing them with artificially propagated vegetation. He has ruthlessly warred on all the tribes of animated nature whose spoil he could convert to his own uses, and he has not protected the birds which prey on the insects most destructive to his own harvests.

It is familiarly known that the sweepings of gold and silver smiths' shops have a regular market value. It is worth noticing that the "sweep" of the British mint in 1878 yielded L. 2,995, 8, 3.

There are still, however, cases of enormous waste in many mineral and mechanical industries. Thus, while in many European countries common salt is a government monopoly, and consequently so dear that the poor do not use as much of it as health requires, in others, as in Transylvania, where it is quarried like stone, the large blocks only are saved, the fragments, to the amount of millions of hundredweights, being thrown away.—Boner, *Transylvania*, p. 455, 6.

One of the most interesting and important branches of economy at the present day is the recovery of agents such as ammonia and others which had been utilized in chemical manufactures, and re-employed them indefinitely afterwards in repeating the same process.

Among the supplemental exhibitions which will be formed in connection with the Vienna Universal Exhibition is to be one showing what steps have been taken since 1851 (the date of the first London Exhibition) in the utilization of substances previously regarded as waste. On the one hand will be shown the waste products in all the industrial processes included in the forthcoming Exhibition; on the other hand, the useful products which have been obtained from such wastes since 1851. This is intended to serve as an incentive to further researches in the same important direction.

Purely untutored humanity, it is true, interferes comparatively little with the arrangements of nature,* and the destructive agency of man becomes

---

*It is an interesting and not hitherto sufficiently noticed fact, that the domestications of the organic world, so far as it has yet been achieved, belongs, not indeed to the savage state, but to the earliest dawn of civilization; the conquest of inorganic nature, almost as exclusively to the most advanced stages of artificial culture. Civilization has added little to the number of vegetable or animal species grown in our fields or bred in our folds—the cranberry and the wild grape being almost the only plants which the Anglo-American has reclaimed out of our vast native flora and added to his harvests—while, on the contrary, the subjugation of the inorganic forces, and the consequent extension of man's sway over, not the annual products of the earth only, but her substance and her springs of action, is almost entirely the work of highly refined and cultivated ages. The employment of the elasticity of wood and of horn, as a projectile power in the bow, is nearly universal among the rudest savages. The application of compressed air to the same purpose in the blowpipe is more restricted, and the use of the mechanical powers, the inclined plane, the wheel and axle, and even the wedge and lever, seems almost unknown except to civilized man. I have myself seen European peasants to whom one of the simplest applications of this latter power was a revelation.

It is familiarly known to all who have occupied themselves with the psychology and habits of the ruder races, and of persons with imperfectly developed intellects in civilized life, that although these humble tribes and individuals sacrifice, without scruple, the lives of the lower animals to the gratification of their appetites and the supply of their other physical wants, yet they nevertheless seem to cherish with brutes, and even with vegetable life, sympathies which are much more feebly felt by civilized men. May we not ascribe to this sympathy the fact that Homer does not refer to the ass as a type of stupidity, nor to the swine as an example of uncleanness? The father of Ulysses is called the *god-like swineherd*. The popular traditions of the simpler peoples recognize a certain community of nature between man, brute animals, and even plants; and this serves to explain why the apologue or fable, which ascribes the power of speech and the faculty of reason to birds, quadrupeds, insects, flowers and trees, is one of the earliest forms of literary composition.

In almost every wild tribe, some particular quadruped or bird, though persecuted as a destroyer of other animals more useful to man, or hunted for food, is regarded with peculiar respect, one might almost say, affection. The Ainos, after killing a bear, sit round the body in great solemnity, as if worshipping, and offer it food and drink. Some of the North American aboriginal nations celebrate a propitiatory feast to the manes of the intended victim before they commence a bear-hunt; and the Norwegian peasantry have not only retained an old proverb which ascribes to the same animal "*ti Moends Styrke og tolv Moends Vid*," *ten men's strength and twelve men's cunning*, but they still pay to him something of the reverence with which ancient superstition invested him. The student of Icelandic literature will find in the saga of *Finnbogi hinn rami* a curious illustration of this feeling, in an account of a dialogue between a Norwegian bear and an Icelandic champion—dumb show on the part of Bruin, and chivalric words on that of Finnbogi—followed by a duel, in which the latter, who had thrown away his arms and armor in order that the combatants might meet on equal terms, was victorious. See also FRIIS, *Lappisk Mythologi*, Christiania, 1871, S 37, and the earlier authors there cited. Drummond Hay's very interesting work on Morocco contains many amusing notices of a similar feeling entertained by the Moors towards the redoubtable enemy of their flocks—the lion.

This sympathy helps us to understand how it is that most if not all the domestic animals—if indeed they ever existed in a wild state—were appropriated, reclaimed and trained before men had been gathered into organized and fixed communities, that almost every known esculent plant had acquired substantially its present artificial character, and that the properties of nearly all vegetable drugs and poisons were known at the remotest period to which historical records reach. Did nature bestow upon primitive man some instinct akin to that by which she has been supposed to teach the brute to select the nutritious and to reject the noxious vegetables indiscriminately mixed in forest and pasture?

This instinct, it must be admitted, is far from infallible, and, as has been hundreds of times remarked by naturalists, it is in many cases not an original faculty but an acquired and transmitted habit. It is a fact familiar to persons engaged in sheep husbandry in New England—and I have seen it confirmed by personal observation—that sheep bred where the common laurel, as it is called, *Kalmia angustifolia*, abounds, almost always avoid browsing upon the leaves of that plant, while those brought from districts where laurel is unknown, and turned into pastures where it grows, very often feed upon it and are poisoned by it. A curious acquired and hereditary instinct, of a different character, may not improperly be noticed here. I refer to that by which horses bred in provinces where quicksands are common avoid their dangers or extricate themselves from them. See Bremontier, *Memoire sur les Dunes, Annales des Ponts et Chaussees,* 1833: *premier semestre*, pp. 155–157.

It is commonly said in New England, and I believe with reason, that the crows of this generation are wiser than their ancestors. Scarecrows which were effectual fifty years ago are no longer respected by the plunderers of the cornfield, and new terrors must from time to time be invented for its protection.

Schroeder van der Kolk, in *Het Verschil tusschen den Psychischen Aanleg van het Dier en van den Mensch*, cites many interesting facts respecting instincts lost, or newly developed and become hereditary, in the lower animals, and he quotes Aristotle and Pliny as evidence that the common quadrupeds and fowls of our fields and our poultry yards were much less perfectly domesticated in their times than long, long ages of servitude have now made them.

Among other instances of obliterated instincts, this author states that in Holland, where, for centuries, the young of the cow has been usually taken from the dam at birth and fed by hand, calves, even if left with the mother, make no attempt to suck; while in England, where calves are not weaned until several weeks old, they resort to the udder as naturally as the young of wild quadrupeds.—*Ziel en Ligchaam*, p. 128, *n*.

Perhaps the half-wild character ascribed by P. Laestadius and other Swedish writers to the reindeer of more and more energetic and unsparing as he advances in civilization, until the impoverishment, with which his exhaustion of the natural resources of the soil is threatening him, at last awakens him to the necessity of preserving what is left, if not of restoring what has been wantonly wasted. The wandering savage grows no cultivated vegetable, fells no forest, and extirpates no useful plant, no noxious weed. If his skill in the chase enables him to entrap numbers of the animals on which he feeds, he compensates this loss by destroying also the lion, the tiger, the wolf, the otter, the seal, and the eagle, thus indirectly protecting the feebler quadrupeds and fish and fowls, which would otherwise become the booty of beasts and birds of prey. But with stationary life, or at latest with the pastoral state, man at once commences an almost indiscriminate warfare upon all the forms of animal and vegetable existence around him, and as he advances in civilization, he gradually eradicates or transforms every spontaneous product of the soil he occupies.*

Human and Brute Action Compared.

It is maintained by authorities as high as any known to modern science, that the action of man upon nature, though greater in *degree*, does not differ in *kind* from that of wild animals. It is perhaps impossible to establish a radical distinction *in genere* between the two classes of effects, but there is an essential difference between the motive of action which calls out the energies of civilized man and the mere appetite which controls the life of the beast. The action of man, indeed, is frequently followed by unforeseen and undesired results, yet it is nevertheless guided by a self-conscious will aiming as often at secondary and remote as at immediate objects. The wild animal, on the other hand, acts instinctively, and, so far as we are able to perceive, always with a view to single and direct purposes. The backwoodsman and the beaver alike fell trees; the man, that he may convert the forest into an olive grove that will mature its fruit only for a succeeding generation; the beaver, that he may feed upon the bark of the trees or use them in the construction of his habitation. The action of brutes upon the material world is slow and gradual, and usually limited, in any given case, to a narrow extent of territory. Nature is allowed time and opportunity to set her restorative powers at work, and the destructive animal has hardly retired from the field of his ravages before nature has repaired the damages occasioned by his operations. In fact, he is expelled from the scene by the

Lapland, may be in some degree due to the comparative shortness of the period during which he has been partially tamed. The domestic swine bred in the woods of Hungary, and the buffalo of Southern Italy, are so wild and savage as to be very dangerous to all but their keepers. The former have relapsed into their original condition, the latter, perhaps, have never been fully reclaimed from it.

*The difference between the relations of savage life and of incipient civilization to nature, is well seen in that part of the valley of the Mississippi which was once occupied by the mound builders and afterwards by the far less developed Indian tribes. When the tillers of the fields which must have been cultivated to sustain the large population that once inhabited those regions, perished or were driven out, the soil fell back to the normal forest state, and the savages who succeeded the more advanced race interfered very little, if at all, with the ordinary course of spontaneous nature.

very efforts which she makes for the restoration of her dominion. Man, on the contrary, extends his action over vast spaces, his revolutions are swift and radical, and his devastations are, for an almost incalculable time after he has withdrawn the arm that gave the blow, irreparable.

The form of geographical surface, and very probably the climate, of a given country, depend much on the character of the vegetable life belonging to it. Man has, by domestication, greatly, changed the habits and properties of the plants he rears; he has, by voluntary selection, immensely modified the forms and qualities of the animated creatures that serve him; and he has, at the same time, completely rooted out many forms of animal if not of vegetable being.* What is there in the influence of brute life that corresponds to this? We have no reason to believe that, in that portion of the American continent which, though peopled by many tribes of quadruped and fowl, remained uninhabited by man or only thinly occupied by purely savage tribes, any sensible geographical change had occurred within twenty centuries before the epoch of discovery and colonization, while, during the same period, man had changed millions of square miles, in the fairest and most fertile regions of the Old World, into the barrenest deserts.

The ravages committed by man subvert the relations and destroy the balance which nature had established between her organized and her inorganic creations, and she avenges herself upon the intruder, by letting loose upon her defaced provinces destructive energies hitherto kept in check by organic forces destined to be his best auxiliaries, but which he has unwisely dispersed and driven from the field of action. When the forest is gone, the great reservoir of moisture stored up in its vegetable mould is evaporated, and returns only in deluges of rain to wash away the parched dust into which that mould has been converted. The well-wooded and humid hills are turned to ridges of dry rock, which encumber the low grounds and choke the watercourses with their debris, and—except in countries favored with an equable distribution of rain through the seasons, and a moderate and regular inclination of surface—the whole earth, unless rescued by human art from the physical degradation to which it tends, becomes an assemblage of bald mountains, of barren, turfless hills, and of swampy and malarious plains. There are parts of Asia Minor, of Northern Africa, of Greece, and even of Alpine Europe, where the operation of causes set in action by man has brought the face of the earth to a desolation almost as complete as that of the moon; and though, within that brief space of time which we we call "the historical period," they are known to have been covered with luxuriant woods, verdant pastures, and fertile meadows, they are now too far deteriorated to be reclaimable by man, nor can they

---

*Whatever may be thought of the modification of organic species by natural selection, there is certainly no evidence that animals have exerted upon any form of life an influence analogous to that of domestication upon plants, quadrupeds and birds reared artificially by man; and this is as true of unforeseen as of purposely effected improvements accomplished by voluntary selection of breeding animals.

It is true that nature employs birds and quadrupeds for the dissemination of vegetable and even of animal species. But when the bird drops the seed of a fruit it has swallowed, and when the sheep transports in its fleece the seed-vessel of a burdock from the plain to the mountain, its action is purely mechanical and unconscious, and does not differ from that of the wind in producing the same effect.

become again fitted for human use, except through great geological changes, or other mysterious influences or agencies of which we have no present knowledge and over which we have no prospective control. The earth is fast becoming an unfit home for its noblest inhabitant, and another era of equal human crime and human improvidence, and of like duration with that through which traces of that crime and that improvidence extend, would reduce it to such a condition of impoverished productiveness, of shattered surface, of climatic excess, as to threaten the depravation, barbarism and perhaps even extinction of the species.*

Physical Improvement.

True, there is a partial reverse to this picture. On narrow theatres, new forests have been planted; inundations of flowing streams restrained by heavy walls of masonry and other constructions; torrents compelled to aid, by depositing the slime with which they are charged, in filling up lowlands, and raising the level of morasses which their own overflows had created; ground submerged by the encroachments of the ocean, or exposed to be covered by its tides, has been rescued from its dominion by diking; swamps and even lakes have been drained, and their beds brought within the domain of agricultural industry; drifting coast dunes have been checked and made productive by plantation; seas and inland waters have been repeopled with fish, and even the sands of the Sahara have been fertilized by artesian fountains. These achievements are more glorious than the proudest triumphs of war, but, thus far, they give but faint hope that we shall yet make full atonement for our spendthrift waste of the bounties of nature.*

Limits of Human Power.

It is, on the one hand, rash and unphilosophical to attempt to set limits to the ultimate power of man over inorganic nature, and it is unprofitable, on the other, to speculate on what may be accomplished by the discovery of now unknown and unimagined natural forces, or even by the invention of new arts and new processes. But since we have seen aerostation, the motive

*—"And it may be remarked that, as the world has passed through these several stages of strife to produce a Christendom, so by relaxing in the enterprises it has learnt, does it tend downwards, through inverted steps, to wildness and the waste again. Let a people give up their contest with moral evil; disregard the injustice, the ignorance, the greediness, that may prevail among them, and part more and more with the Christian element of their civilization; and in declining this battle with sin, they will inevitably get embroiled with men. Threats of war and revolution punish their unfaithfulness; and if then, instead of retracing their steps, they yield again, and are driven before the storm, the very arts they had created, the structures they had raised, the usages they had established, are swept away; 'in that very day their thoughts perish.' The portion they had reclaimed from the young earth's ruggedness is lost; and failing to stand fast against man, they finally get embroiled with nature, and are thrust down beneath her ever-living hand."—Martineau's *Sermon*, "*The Good Soldier of Jesus Christ.*"

*The wonderful success which has attended the measures for subduing torrents and preventing inundations employed in Southern France since 1865, and described in Chapter III., *post*, ought to be here noticed as a splendid and most encouraging example of well-directed effort in the way of physical restoration.

power of elastic vapors, the wonders of modern telegraphy, the destructive explosiveness of gunpowder, of nitro-glycerine, and even of a substance so harmless, unresisting and inert as cotton, there is little in the way of mechanical achievement which seems hopelessly impossible, and it is hard to restrain the imagination from wandering forward a couple of generations to an epoch when our descendants shall have advanced as far beyond us in physical conquest, as we have marched beyond the trophies erected by our grandfathers. There are, nevertheless, in actual practice, limits to the efficiency of the forces which we are now able to bring into the field, and we must admit that, for the present, the agencies known to man and controlled by him are inadequate to the reducing of great Alpine precipices to such slopes as would enable them to support a vegetable clothing, or to the covering of large extents of denuded rock with earth, and planting upon them a forest growth. Yet among the mysteries which science is hereafter to reveal, there may be still undiscovered methods of accomplishing even grander wonders than these. Mechanical philosophers have suggested the possibility of accumulating and treasuring up for human use some of the greater natural forces, which the action of the elements puts forth with such astonishing energy.* Could we gather, and bind, and make subservient to our control, the power which a West Indian hurricane exerts through a small area in one continuous blast, or the momentum expended by the waves, in a tempestuous winter, upon the breakwater at Cherbourg, †or the lifting power of the tide, for a month, at the head of the Bay of Fundy, or the pressure of a square mile of sea water at the depth of five thousand fathoms, or a moment of the might of an earthquake or a volcano, our age—which moves no mountains and casts them into the sea by faith

---

*Some well-known experiments show that it is quite possible to accumulate the solar heat by a simple apparatus, and thus to obtain a temperature which might be economically important even in the climate of a Switzerland. Saussure, by receiving the sun's rays in a nest of boxes blackened within and covered with glass, raised a thermometer enclosed in the inner box to the boiling point; and under the more powerful sun of the Cape of Good Hope, Sir John Herschel cooked the materials for a family dinner by a similar process, using, however, but a single box, surrounded with dry sand and covered with two glasses. Why should not so easy a method of economizing fuel be restored to in Italy, in Spain, and even in more northerly climates?

The unfortunate John Davidson records in his journal that he saved fuel in Morocco by exposing his tea-kettle to the sun on the roof of his house, where the water rose to the temperature of one hundred and forty degrees, and, of course, needed little fire to bring it to boil. But this was the direct and simple, not the concentrated or accumulated, heat of the sun.

On the utilizing of the solar heat, simply as heat, see the work of Mouchot, *La Chaleur solaire et ses applications industrielles.* Paris, 1869.

The reciprocal convertibility of the natural forces has suggested the possibility of advantageously converting the heat of the sun into mechanical power. Ericsson calculates that in all latitudes between the equator and 45°, a hundred square feet of surface exposed to the solar rays develop continuously, for nine hours a day on an average, eight and one-fifth horse power.

I do not know that any attempts have been made to accumulate and store up for use at pleasure, force derived from this powerful source.

†In heavy storms, the force of the waves as they strike against a sea-wall is from one and a half to two tons to the square foot, and Stevenson, in one instance at Skerryvore and in another at the Bell Rock lighthouse, found this force equal to nearly three tons per foot.

The seaward front of the breakwater at Cherbourg exposes a surface of about 2,500,000 square feet. In rough weather the waves beat against this whole face, though, at the depth of twenty-two yards, which is the height of the breakwater, they exert a very much less violent motive force than at and near the surface of the sea, because this force diminishes in geometrical, as the distance below the surface increases in arithmetical, proportion. The shock of the waves is received several thousand times in the course of twenty-four hours, and hence the sum of impulse which the breakwater resists in one stormy day amounts to many thousands of millions of tons. The breakwater is entirely an artificial construction. If then man could accumulate and control the forces which he is able effectually to resist, he might be said to be, physically speaking, omnipotent.

alone—might hope to scarp the rugged walls of the Alps and Pyrenees and Mount Taurus, robe them once more in a vegetation as rich as that of their pristine woods, and turn their wasting torrents into refreshing streams.

The recent discoveries of, if not new laws, but least of new relations between electrical energy and other natural forces and objects, and the various inventions for rendering this energy available for human uses, open a prospect of vast addition to the powers hitherto wielded by man. It is too soon even to conjecture by what limits these powers are conditioned, but it would seem that there is every reason to expect that man's most splendid achievements hitherto, in the conquest of Nature, will soon be eclipsed by new and more brilliant victories of mind over matter.

Could this old world, which man has overthrown, be rebuilded, could human cunning rescue its wasted hillsides and its deserted plains from solitude or mere nomade occupation, from barrenness, from nakedness, and from insalubrity, and restore the ancient fertility and healthfulness of the Etruscan sea coast, the Campagna and the Pontine marshes, of Calabria, of Sicily, of the Peloponnesus and insular and continental Greece, of Asia Minor of the slopes of Lebanon and Hermon, of Palestine, of the Syrian desert, of Mesopotamia and the delta of the Euphrates, of the Cyrenaica, of Africa proper, Numidia and Mauritania, the thronging millions of Europe might still find room on the Eastern continent, and the main current of emigration be turned towards the rising instead of the setting sun.

But changes like these must await not only great political and moral revolutions in the governments and peoples by whom those regions are now possessed, but, especially, a command of pecuinary and of mechanical means not at present enjoyed by those nations, and a more advanced and generally diffused knowledge of the processes by which the amelioration of soil and climate is possible than now anywhere exists. Until such circumstances shall conspire to favor the work of geographical regeneration, the countries I have mentioned, with here and there a local exception, will continue to sink into yet deeper desolation, and in the meantime the American continent, Southern Africa, Australia, New Zealand, and the smaller oceanic islands, will be almost the only theatres where man is engaged, on a great scale, in transforming the face of nature.

Importance of Physical Conservation and Restoration.

Comparatively short as is the period through which the colonization of foreign lands by European emigrants extends, great and, it is to be feared, sometimes irreparable injury has already been done in the various process by which man seeks to subjugate the virgin earth; and many provinces, first trodden by the *homo sapiens Europoe* within the last two centuries, begin to show signs of that melancholy dilapidation which is now driving so many of the peasantry of Europe from their native hearths. It is evidently a matter of great moment, not only to the population of the states where these symptoms are manifesting themselves, but to the general interests of humanity, that this decay should be arrested, and that the future operations of rural husbandry and of forest industry, in districts yet remaining substantially in their native condition, should be so conducted as to prevent the widespread mischiefs which have been elsewhere produced by thoughtless or wanton destruction of the natural safeguards of the soil. This can be done only by the diffusion of knowledge on this subject among the classes that, in earlier days, subdued and tilled ground in which they had no vested rights, but who, in our time, own their woods, their pastures, and their ploughlands as a perpetual possession for them and theirs, and have, therefore, a strong interest in the protection of their domain against deterioration. . . .

Ralph Waldo Emerson
1803-1882

Because Emerson turned to nature, and especially to the transcendent experience in nature, in his writings, speeches, and sermons, and because in the process he became one of the most influential writers and thinkers America has produced, he is an especially important figure in the history of nature writing. With his friend and protégé Henry Thoreau, he connected nature to human morality, conscience, and spiritual growth. As with Wordsworth and Coleridge in England, Emerson and Thoreau would deeply affect or change the approaches to nature taken by later writers. Even if one did not agree with them, their views demanded consideration and reaction in taking nature as one's theme.

There have been few greater spokesmen for individualism and self-reliance in America. And in Emerson's plea for ever-greater individual freedom, growth, and opportunity, all of which he believed to be based on man's connection to nature, he was a prophet for his time and ours. He saw coming even in the nineteenth century the mass society of industralism and technocracy, and warned us of the ways in which the world we were building would diminish us as human beings, as divinely inspired creatures. In his own life the radical nature of his public addresses, his resignation in 1832 from a ministry that seemed to stifle his belief in the general divinity of man and in self-reliance, and his devotion to the life of ideas and natural observations at a time when all his countrymen were turning to mercantilism suggest that here was the kind of man who followed his own advice and lived his own life. Perhaps the single greatest influence upon Thoreau was Emerson's essay "Self-Reliance," the epigraph of which is: "Do not seek answers outside of yourself." "Society everywhere," Emerson wrote, "is in conspiracy against the manhood of everyone of its members. Society is a joint-stock company in which the members agree, for the better securing of his bread to each shareholder, to surrender the liberty and culture of the eater. The virtue in most request is conformity. Self-reliance is its aversion .... Nothing is at last sacred but the integrity of your own mind."

In the early 1830's Emerson traveled to Europe and Great Britain, and he met and was influenced by the Lake Poets and Carlyle—the most influential Romantics and nature writers of their day. He was in turn the center of the informal Transcendental Club in America (a group of writers and thinkers including Bronson Alcott, Thoreau, and Margret Fuller) and the second editor of the Club's organ, *The Dial* magazine.

Emerson's life was a quest for unity, for the divine presence that animated all human, plant, and animal life. His seminal book *Nature* (1836) made deep impressions on American writers like Thoreau and Whitman. Emerson himself considered it "an entering wedge for something more significant"—those writers who would develop his vision of unity and divinity. The book, excerpted below, is the first fully expressed vision of American Transcendentalism and one of the most important statements of humanity's relationship to nature that American culture has produced.

from NATURE*

"Nature is but an image or imitation of wisdom,
the last thing of the soul; nature being a thing
which doth only do, but not know."

—PLOTINUS
(Motto of 1836)

A subtle chain of countless rings
The next unto the farthest brings;
The eye reads omens where it goes,
And speaks all languages the rose;
And, striving to be man, the worm
Mounts through all the spires of form.

(Motto of 1849)

INTRODUCTION

Our age is retrospective. It builds the sepulchres of the fathers. It writes biographies, histories, and criticism. The foregoing generations beheld God and nature face to face; we, through their eyes. Why should not we also enjoy an original relation to the universe? Why should not we have a poetry and philosophy of insight and not of tradition, and a religion by revelation to us, and not the history of theirs? Embosomed for a season in nature, whose floods of life stream around and through us, and invite us, by the powers they supply, to action proportiond to nature, why should we grope among the dry bones of the past, or put the living generation into masquerage out of its faded wardrobe? The sun shines today also. There is more wool and flax in the fields. There are new lands, new men, new thoughts. Let us demand our own works and laws and worship.

Undoubtedly we have no questions to ask which are unanswerable. We must trust the perfection of the creation so far as to believe that whatever

*From *Selections From Ralph Waldo Emerson,* edited by Stephen E. Whicher. Riverside Edition A13, copyright© 1957 by Stephen E. Whicher. Reprinted by permission of Houghton Mifflin Company.

curiosity the order of things has awakened in our minds, the order of things can satisfy. Every man's condition is a solution in hieroglyphic to those inquiries he would put. He acts it as life, before he apprehends it as truth. In like manner, nature is already, in its forms and tendencies, describing its own design. Let us interrogate the great apparition that shines so peacefully around us. Let us inquire, to what end is nature?

All science has one aim, namely, to find a theory of nature. We have theories of races and of functions, but scarcely yet a remote approach to an idea of creation. We are now so far from the road to truth, that religious teachers dispute and hate each other, and speculative men are esteemed unsound and frivolous. But to a sound judgment, the most abstract truth is the most practical. Whenever a true theory appears, it will be its own evidence. Its test is, that it will explain all phenomena. Now many are thought not only unexplained but inexplicable; as language, sleep, madness, dreams, beasts, sex.

Philosophically considered, the universe is composed of Nature and the Soul. Strictly speaking, therefore, all that is separate from us, all which Philosophy distinguishes as the NOT ME, that is, both nature and art, all other men and my own body, must be ranked under this name, NATURE. In enumerating the values of nature and casting up their sum, I shall use the word in both senses;—in its common and in its philosophical import. In inquiries so general as our present one, the inaccuracy is not material; no confusion of thought will occur. *Nature,* in the common sense, refers to essences unchanged by man; space, the air, the river, the leaf. *Art* is applied to the mixture of his will with the same things, as in a house, a canal, a statue, a picture. But his operations taken together are so insignificant, a little chipping, baking, patching, and washing, that in an impression so grand as that of the world on the human mind, they do not vary the result.

I. NATURE

To go into solitude, a man needs to retire as much from his chamber as from society. I am not solitary whilst I read and write, though nobody is with me. But if a man would be alone, let him look at the stars. The rays that come from those heavenly worlds will separate between him and what he touches. One might think the atmosphere was made transparent with this design, to give man, in the heavenly bodies, the perpetual presence of the sublime. Seen in the streets of cities, how great they are! If the stars should appear one night in a thousand years, how would men believe and adore; and preserve for many generations the remembrance of the city of God which had been shown! But every night come out these envoys of beauty, and light the universe with their admonishing smile.

The stars awaken a certain reverence, because though always present, they are inaccessible; but all natural objects make a kindred impression, when the mind is open to their influence. Nature never wears a mean appearance. Neither does the wisest man extort her secret, and lose his curiosity by finding out all her perfection. Nature never became a toy to a wise spirit. The flowers, the animals, the mountains, reflected the wisdom of his best hour, as much as they had delighted the simplicity of his childhood.

When we speak of nature in this manner, we have a distinct but most poetical sense in the mind. We mean the integrity of impression made by manifold natural objects. It is this which distinguishes the stick of timber of the wood-cutter from the tree of the poet. The charming landscape which I saw this morning is indubitably made up of some twenty or thirty farms. Miller owns this field, Locke that, and Manning the woodland beyond. But none of them owns the landscape. There is a property in the horizon which no man has but he whose eye can integrate all the parts, that is, the poet. This is the best part of these men's farms, yet to this their warranty-deeds give no title.

To speak truly, few adult persons can see nature. Most persons do not see the sun. At least they have a very superficial seeing. The sun illuminates only the eye of the man, but shines into the eye and the heart of the child. The lover of nature is he whose inward and outward senses are still truly adjusted to each other; who has retained the spirit of infancy even into the era of manhood. His intercourse with heaven and earth becomes part of his daily food. In the presence of nature a wild delight runs through the man, in spite of real sorrows. Nature says,—he is my creature, and maugre all his impertinent griefs, he shall be glad with me. Not the sun or the summer alone, but every hour and season yields its tribute of delight; for every hour and change corresponds to and authorizes a different state of the mind, from breathless noon to grimmest midnight. Nature is a setting that fits equally well a comic or a mourning piece. In good health, the air is a cordial of incredible virtue. Crossing a bare common, in snow puddles, at twilight, under a clouded sky, without having in my thoughts any occurrence of special good fortune, I have enjoyed a perfect exhilaration. I am glad to the brink of fear. In the woods, too, a man casts off his years, as the snake his slough, and at what period soever of life is always a child. In the woods is perpetual youth. Within these plantations of God, a decorum and sanctity reign, a perennial festival is dressed, and the guest sees not how he should tire of them in a thousand years. In the woods, we return to reason and faith. There I feel that nothing can befall me in life,—no disgrace, no calamity (leaving me my eyes), which nature cannot repair. Standing on the bare ground—my head bathed by the blithe air and uplifted into infinite space,—all mean egotism vanishes. I become a transparent eyeball; I am nothing; I see all; the currents of the Universal Being circulate through me; I am part of parcel of God. The name of the nearest friend sounds then foreign and accidental: to be brothers, to be acquaintances, master or servant, is then a trifle and a disturbance. I am the lover of uncontained and immortal beauty. In the wilderness, I find something more dear and connate than in streets or villages. In the tranquil landscape, and especially in the distant line of the horizon, man beholds somewhat as beautiful as his own nature.

The greatest delight which the fields and woods minister is the suggestion of an occult relation between man and the vegetable. I am not alone and unacknowledged. They nod to me, and I to them. The waving of the boughs in the storm is new to me and old. It takes me by surprise, and yet is not unknown. Its effect is like that of a higher thought or a better emotion coming over me, when I deemed I was thinking justly or doing right.

Yet it is certain that the power to produce this delight does not reside in nature, but in man, or in a harmony of both. It is necessary to use these pleasures with great temperance. For nature is not always tricked in holiday attire, but the same scene which yesterday breathed perfume and glittered as for the frolic of the nymphs is overspread with melancholy today. Nature always wears the colors of the spirit. To a man laboring under calamity, the heat of his own fire hath sadness in it. Then there is a kind of contempt of the landscape felt by him who has just lost by death a dear friend. The sky is less grand as it shuts down over less worth in the population.

II. COMMODITY

Whoever considers the final cause of the world will discern a multitude of uses that enter as parts into that result. They all admit of being thrown into one of the following classes: Commodity; Beauty; Language; and Discipline.

Under the general name of commodity, I rank all those advantages which our senses owe to nature. This, of course, is a benefit which is temporary and mediate, not ultimate, like its service to the soul. Yet although low, it is perfect in its kind, and is the only use of nature which all men apprehend. The misery of man appears like childish petulance, when we explore the steady and prodigal provision that has been made for his support and delight on this green ball which floats him through the heavens. What angels invented these splendid ornaments, these rich conveniences, this ocean of air above, this ocean of water beneath, this firmament of earth between? this zodiac of lights, this tent of dropping clouds, this striped coat of climates, this fourfold year? Beasts, fire, water, stones, and corn serve him. The field is at once his floor, his work-yard, his play-ground, his garden, and his bed.

"More servants wait on man
Than he'll take notice of."

Nature, in its ministry to man, is not only the material, but is also the process and the result. All the parts incessantly work into each other's hands for the profit of man. The wind sows the seed; the sun evaporates the sea; the wind blows the vapor to the field; the ice, on the other side of the planet, condenses rain on this; the rain feeds the plant; the plant feeds the animal; and thus the endless circulations of the divine charity nourish man.

The useful arts are reproductions or new combinations by the wit of man, of the same natural benefactors. He no longer waits for favoring gales, but by means of steam, he realizes the fable of Aeolus's bag, and carries the two and thirty winds in the boiler of his boat. To diminish friction, he paves the road with iron bars, and, mounting a coach with a ship-load of men, animals, and merchandise behind him, he darts through the country, from town to town, like an eagle or a swallow through the air. By the aggregate of these aids, how is the face of the world changed, from the era of Noah to that of Napoleon! The private poor man hath cities, ships, canals, bridges, built for him. He goes to the post-office, and the human race run on his errands; to the book-shop, and the human race read and write of all that happens, for him; to the court-house, and nations repair his wrongs. He sets his house upon the road, and the human race go forth every morning, and shovel out the snow, and cut a path for him.

But there is no need of specifying particulars in this class of uses. The catalogue is endless, and the examples so obvious, that I shall leave them to the reader's reflection, with the general remark, that this mercenary benefit is one which has respect to a farther good. A man is fed, not that he may be fed, but that he may work.

III. BEAUTY

A nobler want of man is served by nature, namely, the love of Beauty.

The ancient Greeks called the world *Κο'σμος*, beauty. Such is the constitution of all things, or such the plastic power of the human eye, that the primary forms, as the sky, the mountain, the tree, the animal, give us a delight *in and for themselves;* a pleasure arising from outline, color, motion, and grouping. This seems partly owing to the eye itself. The eye is the best of artists. By the mutual action of its structure and of the laws of light, perspective is produced, which integrates every mass of objects, of what character soever, into a well colored and shaded globe, so that where the particular objects are mean and unaffecting, the landscape which they compose is round and symmetrical. And as the eye is the best composer, so light is the first of painters. There is no object so foul that intense light will not make beautiful. And the stimulus it affords to the sense, and a sort of infinitude which it hath, like space and time, make all matter gay. Even the corpse has its own beauty. But besides this general grace diffused over nature, almost all the individual forms are agreeable to the eye, as is proved by our endless imitations of some of them, as the acorn, the grape, the pine-cone, the wheat-ear, the egg, the wings and forms of most birds, the lion's claw, the serpent, the butterfly, sea-shells, flames, clouds, buds, leaves, and the forms of many trees, as the palm.

For better consideration, we may distribute the aspects of Beauty in a threefold manner.

1. First, the simple perception of natural forms is a delight. The influence of the forms and actions in nature is so needful to man, that, in its lowest functions, it seems to lie on the confines of commodity and beauty. To the body and mind which have been cramped by noxious work or company, nature is medicinal and restores their tone. The tradesman, the attorney comes out of the din and craft of the street and sees the sky and the woods, and is a man again. In their eternal calm, he finds himself. The health of the eye seems to demand a horizon. We are never tired, so long as we can see far enough.

But in other hours, Nature satisfies by its loveliness, and without any mixture of corporeal benefit. I see the spectacle of morning from the hilltop over against my house, from daybreak to sunrise, with emotions which an angel might share. The long slender bars of cloud float like fishes in the sea of crimson light. From the earth, as a shore, I look out into that silent sea. I seem to partake its rapid transformations; the active enchantment reaches my dust, and I dilate and conspire with the morning wind. How does Nature deify us with a few and cheap elements! Give me health and a day, and I will make the pomp of emperors ridiculous. The dawn is my Assyria; the sunset and moonrise my Paphos, and unimaginable realms of faerie; broad noon shall be my England of the senses and the understanding; the night shall be my Germany of mystic philosophy and dreams.

Not less excellent, except for our less susceptibility in the afternoon, was the charm, last evening, of a January sunset. The western clouds divided and subdivided themselves into pink flakes modulated with tints of unspeakable softness, and the air had so much life and sweetness that it was a pain to come within doors. What was it that nature would say? Was there no meaning in the live repose of the valley behind the mill, and which Homer or Shakespeare could not re-form for me in words? The leafless trees become spires of flame in the sunset, with the blue east for their background, and the stars of the dead calices of flowers, and every withered stem and stubble rimed with frost, contribute something to the mute music.

The inhabitants of cities suppose that the country landscape is pleasant only half the year. I please myself with the graces of the winter scenery, and believe that we are as much touched by it as by the genial influences of summer. To the attentive eye, each moment of the year has its own beauty, and in the same field, it beholds, every hour, a picture which was never seen before, and which shall never be seen again. The heavens change every moment, and reflect their glory or gloom on the plains beneath. The state of the crop in the surrounding farms alters the expression of the earth from week to week. The succession of native plants in the pastures and roadsides, which makes the silent clock by which time tells the summer hours, will make even the divisions of the day sensible to a keen observer. The tribes of birds and insects, like the plants punctual to their time, follow each other, and the year has room for all. By watercourses, the variety is greater. In July, the blue pontederia or pickerelweed blooms in large beds in the shallow parts of our pleasant river, and swarms with yellow butterflies in continual motion. Art cannot rival this pomp of purple and gold. Indeed the river is a perpetual gala, and boasts each month a new ornament.

But this beauty of Nature which is seen and felt as beauty, is the least part. The shows of day, the dewy morning, the rainbow, mountains, orchards in blossom, stars, moonlight, shadows in still water, and the like, if too eagerly hunted, become shows merely, and mock us with their unreality. Go out of the house to see the moon, and 'tis mere tinsel; it will not please as when its light shines upon your necessary journey. The beauty that shimmers in the yellow afternoons of October, who ever could clutch it? Go forth to find it, and it is gone; 'tis only a mirage as you look from the windows of diligence.

2. The presence of a higher, namely, of the spiritual element is essential to its perfection. The high and divine beauty which can be loved without effeminacy, is that which is found in combination with the human will. Beauty is the mark God sets upon virtue. Every natural action is graceful. Every heroic act is also decent, and causes the place and the bystanders to shine. We are taught by great actions that the universe is the property of every individual in it. Every rational creature has all nature for his dowry and estate. It is his, if he will. He may divest himself of it; he may creep into a corner, and abdicate his kingdom, as most men do, but he is entitled to the world

by his constitution. In proportion to the energy of his thought and will, he takes up the world into himself. "All those things for which men plough, build, or sail, obey virtue," said Sallust. "The winds and waves," said Gibbon, "are always on the side of the ablest navigators." So are the sun and moon and all the stars of heaven. When a noble act is done,—perchance in a scene of great natural beauty; when Leonidas and his three hundred martyrs consume one day in dying, and the sun and moon come each and look at them once in the steep defile of Thermopylae; when Arnold Winkelried, in the high Alps, under the shadow of the avalanche, gathers in his side a sheaf of Austrian spears to break the line for his comrades; are not these heroes entitled to add the beauty of the scene to the beauty of the deed? When the bark of Columbus nears the shore of America;—before it the beach lined with savages, fleeing out of all their huts of cane; the sea behind; and the purple mountains of the Indian Archipelago around, can we separate the man from the living picture? Does not the New World clothe his form with her palm-groves and savannahs as fit drapery? Ever does natural beauty steal in like air, and envelope great actions. When Sir Harry Vane was dragged up the Tower-hill, sitting on a sled, to suffer death as the champion of the English laws, one of the multitude cried out to him, "You never sate on so glorious a seat!" Charles II, to intimidate the citizens of London, caused the patriot Lord Russell to be drawn in an open coach through the principal streets of the city on his way to the scaffold. "But," his biographer says, "the multitude imagined they saw liberty and virtue sitting by his side." In private places, among sordid objects, an act of truth or heroism seems at once to draw to itself the sky as its temple, the sun as its candle. Nature stretches out her arms to embrace man, only let his thoughts be of equal greatness. Willingly does she follow his steps with the rose and the violet, and bend her lines of grandeur and grace to the decoration of her darling child. Only let his thoughts be of equal scope, and the frame will suit the picture. A virtuous man is in unison with her works, and makes the central figure of the visible sphere. Homer, Pindar, Socrates, Phocion, associate themselves fitly in our memory with the geography and climate of Greece. The visible heavens and earth sympathize with Jesus. And in common life whosoever has seen a person of powerful character and happy genius, will have remarked how easily he took all things along with him,—the persons, the opinions, and the day, and nature become ancillary to a man.

3. There is still another aspect under which the beauty of the world may be viewed, namely, as it becomes an object of the intellect. Beside the relation of things to virtue, they have a relation to thought. The intellect searches out the absolute order of things as they stand in the mind of God, and without the colors of affection. The intellectual and the active powers seem to succeed each other, and the exclusive activity of the one generates the exclusive activity of the other. There is something unfriendly in each to the other, but they are like the alternate periods of feeding and working in animals; each prepares and will be followed by the other. Therefore does beauty, which, in relation to actions, as we have seen, comes unsought, and comes because it is unsought, remain for the apprehension and pursuit of the intellect; and

then again, in its turn, of the active power. Nothing divine dies. All good is eternally reproductive. The beauty of nature re-forms itself in the mind, and not for barren contemplation, but for new creation.

All men are in some degree impressed by the face of the world; some men even to delight. This love of beauty is Taste. Others have the same love in such excess, that, not content with admiring, they seek to embody it in new forms. The creation of beauty is Art.

The production of a work of art throws a light upon the mystery of humanity. A work of art is an abstract or epitome of the world. It is the result or expression of nature, in miniature. For although the works of nature are innumerable and all different, the result or the expression of them all is similar and single. Nature is a sea of forms radically alike and even unique. A leaf, a sunbeam, a landscape, the ocean, make an analogous impression on the mind. What is common to them all,—that perfectness and harmoy, is beauty. The standard of beauty is the entire circuit of natural forms,—the totality of nature; which the Italians expressed by defining beauty "il più nell' uno." Nothing is quite beautiful alone; nothing but is beautiful in the whole. A single object is only so far beautiful as it suggests this universal grace. The poet, the painter, the sculptor, the musician, the architect, seek each to concentrate this radiance of the world on one point, and each in his several work to satisfy the love of beauty which stimulates him to produce. Thus is Art a nature passed through the alembic of man. Thus in art does Nature work through the will of a man filled with the beauty of her first works.

The world thus exists to the soul to satisfy the desire of beauty. This element I call an ultimate end. No reason can be asked or given why the soul seeks beauty. Beauty, in its largest and profoundest sense, is one expression for the universe. God is the all-fair. Truth, and goodness, and beauty, are but different faces of the same All. But beauty in nature is not ultimate. It is the herald of inward and eternal beauty, and is not alone a solid and satisfactory good. It must stand as a part, and not as yet the last or highest expression of the final cause of Nature.

. . .

V. DISCIPLINE

In view of the significance of nature, we arrive at once at a new fact, that nature is a discipline. This use of the world includes the preceding uses, as parts of itself.

Space, time, society, labor, climate, food, locomotion, the animals, the mechanical forces, give us sincerest lessons, day by day, whose meaning is unlimited. They educate both the Understanding and the Reason. Every property of matter is a school for the understanding,—its solidity or resistance, its inertia, its extension, its figure, its divisibility. The understanding adds, divides, combines, measures, and finds nutriment and room for its activity in this worthy scene. Meantime, Reason transfers all these lessons into its own world of thought, by perceiving the analogy that marries Matter and Mind.

1. Nature is a discipline of the understanding in intellectual truths. Our dealing with sensible objects is a constant exercise in the necessary lessons of difference, of likeness, of order, of being and seeming, of progressive arrangement; of ascent from particular to general; of combination to one end of manifold forces. Proportioned to the importance of the organ to be formed, is the extreme care with which its tuition is provided,—a care pretermitted in no single case. What tedious training, day after day, year after year, never ending, to form the common sense; what continual reproduction of annoyances, inconveniences, dilemmas; what rejoicing over us of little men; what disputing of prices, what reckonings of interest,—and all to form the Hand of the mind;—to instruct us that "good thoughts are no better than good dreams, unless they be executed!"

The same good office is performed by Property and its filial systems of debt and credit. Debt, grinding debt, whose iron face the widow, the orphan, and the sons of genius fear and hate;— debt, which consumes so much time, which so cripples and disheartens a great spirit with cares that seem so base, is a preceptor whose lessons cannot be foregone, and is needed most by those who suffer from it most. Moreover, property, which has been well compared to snow,—"if it fall level today, it will be blown into drifts tomorrow,"—is the surface action of internal machinery, like the index on the face of a clock. Whilst now it is the gymnastics of the understanding, it is hiving, in the foresight of the spirit, experience in profounder laws.

The whole character and fortune of the individual are affected by the least inequalities in the culture of the understanding; for example, in the perception of differences. Therefore is Space, and therefore Time, that man may know that things are not huddled and lumped, but sundered and individual. A bell and a plough have each their use, and neither can do the office of the other. Water is good to drink, coal to burn, wool to wear; but wool cannot be drunk, nor water spun, nor coal eaten. The wise man shows his wisdom in separation, in gradation, and his scale of creatures and of merits is as wide as nature. The foolish have no range in their scale, but suppose every man is as every other man. What is not good they call the worst, and what is not hateful, they call the best.

In like manner, what good heed Nature forms in us!. She pardons no mistakes. Her yea is yea, and her nay, nay.

The first steps in Agriculture, Astronomy, Zoölogy (those first steps which the farmer, the hunter, and the sailor take), teach that Nature's dice are always loaded; that in her heaps and rubbish are concealed sure and useful results.

How calmly and genially the mind apprehends one after another the laws of physics! What noble emotions dilate the mortal as he enters into the councils of the creation, and feels by knowledge the privilege to Be! His insight refines him. The beauty of nature shines in his own breast. Man is greater that he can see this, and the universe less, because Time and Space relations vanish as laws are known.

Here again we are impressed and even daunted by the immense Universe to be explored. "What we know is a point to what we do not know." Open any recent journal of science, and weigh the problems suggested concerning Light, Heat, Electricity, Magnetism, Physiology, Geology, and judge whether the interest of natural science is likely to be soon exhausted.

Passing by many particulars of the discipline of nature, we must not omit to specify two.

The exercise of the Will, or the lesson of power, is taught in every event. From the child's successive possession of his several senses up to the hour when he saith, "Thy will be done!" he is learning the secret that he can reduce under his will not only particular events but great classes, nay, the whole series of events, and so conform all facts to his character. Nature is thoroughly mediate. It is made to serve. It receives the dominion of man as meekly as the ass on which the Saviour rode. It offers all its kingdoms to man as the raw material which he may mold into what is useful. Man is never weary of working it up. He forges the subtile and delicate air into wise and melodious words, and gives them wing as angels of persuasion and command. One after another his victorious thought comes up with and reduces all things, until the world becomes at last only a realized will,—the double of the man.

2. Sensible objects conform to the premonitions of Reason and reflect the conscience. All things are moral; and in their boundless changes have an unceasing reference to spiritual nature. Therefore is nature glorious with form, color, and motion; that every globe in the remotest heaven, every chemical change from the rudest crystal up to the laws of life, every change of vegetation from the first principle of growth in the eye of a leaf, to the tropical forest and antediluvian coal-mine, every animal function from the sponge up to Hercules, shall hint or thunder to man the laws of right and wrong, and echo the Ten Commandmants. Therefore is Nature ever the ally of Religion: lends all her pomp and riches to the religious sentiment. Prophet and priest, David, Isaiah, Jesus, have drawn deeply from this source. This ethical character so penetrates the bone and marrow of nature, as to seem the end for which it was made. Whatever private purpose is answered by any member or part, this is its public and universal function, and is never omitted. Nothing in nature is exhausted in its first use. When a thing has served an end to the uttermost, it is wholly new for an ulterior service. In God, every end is converted into a new means. Thus the use of commodity, regarded by itself, is mean and squalid. But it is to the mind an education in the doctrine of Use, namely, that a thing is good only so far as it serves; that a conspiring of parts and efforts to the production of an end is essential to any being. The first and gross manifestation of this truth is our inevitable and hated training in values and wants, in corn and meat.

It has already been illustrated, that every natural process is a version of a moral sentence. The moral law lies at the center of nature and radiates to the circumference. It is the pith and marrow of every substance, every relation, and every process. All things with which we deal, preach to us. What is a farm but a mute gospel? The chaff and the wheat, weeds and plants, blight, rain insects, sun,—it is a sacred emblem from the first furrow of spring to the last stack which the snow of winter overtakes in the fields. But the sailor, the shepherd, the miner, the merchant, in their several resorts, have each an experience precisely parallel, and leading to the same conclusion: because all organizations are radically alike. Nor can it be doubted that this moral sentiment which thus scents the air, grows in the grain, and impregnates the waters of the world, is caught by man and sinks into his soul. The moral influence of nature upon every individual is that amount of truth which it illustrates to him. Who can estimate this? Who can guess how much firmness the sea-beaten rock has taught the fisherman? how much tranquillity has been reflected to man from the azure sky, over whose unspotted deeps the winds forevermore drive flocks of stormy clouds, and leave no wrinkle or stain? how much industry and providence and affection we have caught from the pantomine of brutes? What a searching preacher of self-command is the varying phenomenon of Health!

Herein is especially apprehended the unity of Nature,—the unity in variety,—which meets us everywhere. All the endless variety of things make an identical impression. Xenophanes complained in his old age, that, look where he would, all things hastened back to Unity. He was weary of seeing the same entity in the tedious variety of forms. The fable of Proteus has a cordial truth. A leaf, a drop, a crystal, a moment of time, is related to the whole and partakes of the perfection of the whole. Each particle is a microcosm, and faithfully renders the likeness of the world.

Not only resemblances exist in things whose analogy is obvious, as when we detect the type of the human hand in the flipper of the fossil saurus, but also in objects wherein there is great superficial unlikeness. Thus architecture is called "frozen music," by De Staël and Goethe. Vitruvius thought an architect should be a musician. "A Gothic church," said Coleridge, "is a petrified religion." Michael Angelo maintained, that, to an architect, a knowledge of anatomy is essential. In Haydn's oratorios, the notes present to the imagination not only motions, as of the snake, the stag, and the elephant, but colors also; as the green grass. The law of harmonic sounds reappears in the harmonic colors. The granite is differenced in its laws only by the more or less of heat from the river that wears it away. The river, as it flows, resembles the air that flows over it; the air resembles the light which traverses it with more subtile currents; the light resembles the heat which rides with it through Space. Each creature is only a modification of the other; the likeness in them is more than the difference, and their radical law is one and the same. A rule of one art, or a law of one organization, holds true throughout nature. So intimate is this Unity, that, it is easily seen, it lies under the undermost garment of Nature, and betrays its source in Universal Spirit. For it pervades Thought also. Every universal truth which we express in words, implies or supposes every other truth. *Omne verum vero consonat.* It is like a great circle on a sphere, comprising all possible circles; which, however, may be drawn and comprise it in like manner. Every such truth is the absolute Ens seen from one side. But is has innumerable sides.

The central Unity is still more conspicuous in actions. Words are finite organs of the infinite mind. They cannot cover the dimensions of what is in truth. They break, chop, and impoverish it. An action is the perfection and publication of thought. A right action seems to fill the eye, and to be related to all nature. "The wise man, in doing one thing, does all; or, in the one thing he does rightly, he sees the likeness of all which is done rightly,"

Words and actions are not the attributes of brute nature. They introduce us to the human form, of which all other organizations appear to be degradations. When this appears among so many that surround it, the spirit prefers it to all others. It says, "From such as this have I drawn joy and knowledge; in such as this have I found and beheld myself; I will speak to it; it can speak again; it can yield me thought already formed and alive." In fact, the eye,—the mind,—is always accompanied by these forms, male and female; and these are incomparably the richest informations of the power and order that lie at the heart of things. Unfortunately every one of them bears the marks as of some injury; is marred and superficially defective. Nevertheless, far different from the deaf and dumb nature around them, these all rest like fountain-pipes on the unfathomed sea of thought and virtue whereto they alone, of all organizations, are the entrances.

. . .

VII. SPIRIT

It is essential to a true theory of nature and of man, that it should contain somewhat progressive. Uses that are exhausted or that may be, and facts that end in the statement, cannot be all that is true of this brave lodging wherein man is harbored, and wherein all his faculties find appropriate and endless exercise. And all the uses of nature admit of being summed in one, which yields the activity of man an infinite scope. Through all its kingdoms, to the suburbs and outskirts of things, it is faithful to the cause whence it had its origin. It always speaks of Spirit. It suggests the absolute. It is a perpetual effect. It is a great shadow pointing always to the sun behind us.

The aspect of Nature is devout. Like the figure of Jesus, she stands with bended head, and hands folded upon the breast. The happiest man is he who learns from nature the lesson of worship.

Of that ineffable essence which we call Spirit, he that thinks most, will say least. We can foresee God in the coarse, and, as it were, distant phenomena of matter; but when we try to define and describe himself, both language and thought desert us, and we are as helpless as fools and savages. That essence refuses to be recorded in propositions, but when man has worshipped him intellectually, the noblest ministry of nature is to stand as the apparition of God. It is the organ through which the universal spirit speaks to the individual, and strives to lead back the individual to it.

When we consider Spirit, we see that the views already presented do not include the whole circumference of man. We must add some related thoughts.

Three problems are put by nature to the mind: What is matter? Whence is it? and Whereto? The first of these questions only, the ideal theory answers. Idealism saith; matter is a phenomenon, not a substance. Idealism acquaints us with the total disparity between the evidence of our own being and the evidence of the world's being. The one is perfect; the other, incapable of any assurance; the mind is a part of the nature of things; the world is a divine dream, from which we may presently awake to the glories and certainties of day. Idealism is a hypothesis to account for nature by other principles than those of carpentry and chemistry. Yet, if it only deny the existance of matter, it does not satisfy the demands of the spirit. It leaves God out of me. It leaves me in the splendid labyrinth of my perceptions, to wander without end. Then the heart resists it, because it balks the affections in denying substantive being to men and women. Nature is so pervaded with human life that there is something of humanity in all and in every particular. But this theory makes nature foreign to me, and does not account for that consanguinity which we acknowledge to it.

Let it stand then, in the present state of our knowledge, merely as a useful introductory hypothesis, serving to apprize us of the eternal distinction between the soul and the world.

But when, following the invisible steps of thought, we come to inquire, Whence is matter? and Whereto? many truths arise to us out of the recesses of consciousness. We learn that the highest is present to the soul of man; that the dread universal essence, which is not wisdom, or love, or beauty, or power, but all in one, and each entirely, is that for which all things exist, and that by which they are; that spirit creates; that behind nature, throughout nature, spirit is present; one and not compound it does not act upon us from without, that is, in space and time, but spiritually, or through ourselves: therefore, that spirit, that is, the Supreme Being, does not build up nature around us, but puts it forth through us, as the life of the tree puts forth new branches and leaves through the pores of the old. As a plant upon the earth, so a man rests upon the bosom of God; he is nourished by unfailing fountains, and draws at his need inexhaustible power. Who can set bounds to the possibilities of man? Once inhale the upper air, being admitted to behold the absolute natures of justice and truth, and we learn that man has access to the entire mind of the Creator, is himself the creator in the finite. This view, which admonishes me where the sources of wisdom and power lie, and points to virtue as to

"The golden key
Which opes the palace of eternity,"

carries upon its face the highest certificate of truth, because it animates me to create my own world through the purification of my soul.

The world proceeds from the same spirit as the body of man. It is a remoter and inferior incarnation of God, a projection of God in the unconscious. But it differs from the body in one important respect. It is not, like that, now subjected to the human will. Its serene order is inviolable by us. It is, therefore, to us, the present expositor of the divine mind. It is a fixed point whereby we may measure our departure. As we degenerate, the contrast between us and our house is more evident. We are as much strangers in nature as we are aliens from God. We do not understand the notes of birds. The fox and the deer run away from us; the bear and tiger rend us. We do not know the uses of more than a few plants, as corn and the apple, the potato and the vine. Is not the landscape, every glimpse of which hath a grandeur, a face of him? Yet this may show us what discord is between man and nature, for you cannot freely admire a noble landscape if laborers are digging in the field hard by. The poet finds something ridiculous in his delight until he is out of the sight of men.

VIII. PROSPECTS

In inquiries respecting the laws of the world and the frame of things, the highest reason is always the truest. That which seems faintly possible, it is so refined, is often faint and dim because it is deepest seated in the mind among the eternal verities. Empirical science is apt to cloud the sight, and by the very knowledge of functions and processes to bereave the student of the manly contemplation of the whole. The savant becomes unpoetic. But the best read naturalist who lends an entire and devout attention to truth, will see that there remains much to learn of his relation to the world, and that it is not to be learned by any addition or subtraction or other comparison of known quantities, but is arrived at by untaught sallies of the spirit, by a continual self-recovery, and by entire humility. He will perceive that there are far more excellent qualities in the student than preciseness and infallibility; that a guess is often more fruitful than an indisputable affirmation, and that a dream may let us deeper into the secret of nature than a hundred concerted experiments.

For the problems to be solved are precisely those which the physiologist and the naturalist omit to state. It is not so pertinent to man to know all the individuals of the animal kingdom, as it is to know whence and whereto is this tyrannizing unity in his constitution, which evermore separates and classifies things, endeavoring to reduce the most diverse to one form. When I behold a rich landscape, it is less to my purpose to recite correctly the order and superposition of the strata, than to know why all thought of multitude is lost in a tranquil sense of unity. I cannot greatly honor minuteness in details, so long as there is no hint to explain the relation between things and thoughts; no ray upon the *metaphysics* of conchology, of botany, of the arts, to show the relation of the forms of flowers, shells, animals, architecture, to the mind, and build science upon ideas. In a cabinet of natural history, we become sensible of a certain occult recognition and sympathy in regard to the most unwieldly and eccentric forms of beast, fish, and insect. The American who has been confined, in his own country, to the sight of buildings designed after foreign models, is surprised on entering York Minster or St. Peter's at Rome, by the feeling that these structures are imitations also,—faint copies of an invisible archetype. Nor has science sufficient humanity, so long as the naturalist overlooks that wonderful congruity which subsists between man and the world; of which he is lord, not because he is the most subtile inhabitant, but because he is its head and heart, and finds something of himself in every great and small thing, in every mountain stratum, in every new law of color, fact of astronomy, or atmospheric influence which observation or analysis lays open. A perception of this mystery inspires the muse of George Herbert, the beautiful psalmist of the seventeenth century. The following lines are part of his little poem on Man.

> "Man is all symmetry,
> Full of proportions, one limb to another,
> And all to all the world besides.
> Each part may call the farthest, brother;
> For head with foot hath private amity,
> And both with moons and tides.
>
> "Nothing hath got so far
> But man hath caught and kept it as his prey;
> His eyes dismount the highest star:
> He is in little all the sphere.
> Herbs gladly cure our flesh, because that they
> Find their acquaintance there.
>
> "For us, the winds do blow,
> The earth doth rest, heaven move, and fountains flow;
> Nothing we see, but means our good,
> As our delight, or as our treasure;
> The whole is either our cupboard of food,
> Or cabinet of pleasure.
>
> "The stars have us to bed:
> Night draws the curtain; which the sun withdraws.
> Music and light attend our head.
> All things unto our flesh are kind,
> In their descent and being; to our mind,
> In their ascent and cause.
>
> "More servants wait on man
> Than he'll take notice of. In every path,
> He treads down that which doth befriend him
> When sickness makes him pale and wan.
> Oh mighty love! Man is one world, and hath
> Another to attend him."

The perception of this class of truths makes the attraction which draws men to science, but the end is lost sight of in attention to the means. In view of this half-sight of science, we accept the sentence of Plato, that "poetry comes nearer to vital truth than history." Every surmise and vaticination of the mind is entitled to a certain respect, and we learn to prefer imperfect theories, and sentences which contain glimpses of truth, to digested systems which have no one valuable suggestion. A wise writer will feel that the ends of study and composition are best answered by announcing undiscovered regions of thought, and so communicating, through hope, new activity to the torpid spirit.

I shall therefore conclude this essay with some traditions of man and nature, which a certain poet sang to me; and which, as they have always been in the world, and perhaps reappear to every bard, may be both history and prophecy.

"The foundations of man are not in matter, but in spirit. But the element of spirit is eternity. To it, therefore, the longest series of events, the oldest chronologies are young and recent. In the cycle of the universal man, from whom the known individuals proceed, centuries are points, and all history is but the epoch of one degradation.

"We distrust and deny inwardly our sympathy with nature. We own and disown our relation to it, by turns. We are like Nebuchadnezzar, dethroned, bereft of reason, and eating grass like an ox. But who can set limits to the remedial force of spirit?

"A man is a god in ruins. When men are innocent, life shall be longer, and shall pass into the immortal as gently as we awake from dreams. Now, the world would be insane and rabid, if these disorganizations should last for hundreds of years. It is kept in check by death and infancy. Infancy is the perpetual Messiah, which comes into the arms of fallen men, and pleads with them to return to paradise.

"Man is the dwarf of himself. Once he was permeated and dissolved by spirit. He filled nature with his overflowing currents. Out from him sprang the sun and moon; from man the sun, from woman the moon. The laws of his mind, the periods of his actions externized themselves into day and night, into the year and the seasons. But, having made for himself this huge shell, his waters retired; he no longer fills the veins and veinlets; he is shrunk to a drop. He sees that the structure still fits him, but fits him colossally. Say, rather, once it fitted him, now it corresponds to him from far and on high. He adores timidly his own work. Now is man the follower of the sun, and woman the follower of the moon. Yet sometimes he starts in his slumber, and wonders at himself and his house, and muses strangely at the resemblance betwixt him and it. He perceives that if his law is still paramount, if still he have elemental power, if his word is sterling yet in nature, it is not conscious power, it is not inferior but superior to his will. It is instinct." Thus my Orphic poet sang.

At present, man applies to nature but half his force. He works on the world with his understanding alone. He lives in it and masters it by a penny-wisdom; and he that works most in it is but a half-man, and whilst his arms are strong and his digestion good, his mind is imbruted, and he is a selfish savage. His relation to nature, his power over it, is through the understanding, as by manure; the economic use of fire, wind, water, and the mariner's needle; steam, coal, chemical agriculture; the repairs of the human body by the dentist and the surgeon. This is such a resumption of power as if a banished king should buy his territories inch by inch, instead of vaulting at once into his throne. Meantime, in the thick darkness, there are not wanting gleams of a better light,—occasional examples of the action of man upon nature with his entire force,—with reason as well as understanding. Such examples are, the traditions of miracles in the earliest antiquity of all nations; the history of Jesus Christ; the achievements of a principle, as in religious and political revolutions, and in the abolition of the slave-trade; the miracles of enthusiasm, as those reported of Swedenborg, Hohenlohe, and the Shakers; many obscure and yet contested facts, now arranged under the name of Animal Magnetism; prayer; eloquence; self-healing; and the wisdom of children. These are examples of Reason's momentary grasp of the scepter; the exertions of a power which exists not in time or space, but an instantaneous in-streaming causing power. The difference between the actual and the ideal force of man is happily figured by the schoolmen, in saying, that the knowledge of man is an evening knowledge, *vespertina cognitio,* but that of God is a morning knowledge, *matutina cognitio.*

The problem of restoring to the world original and eternal beauty is solved by the redemption of the soul. The ruin or the blank that we see when we look at nature, is in our own eye. The axis of vision is not coincident with the axis of things, and so they appear not transparent but opaque. The reason why the world lacks unity, and lies broken and in heaps, is because man is disunited with himself. He cannot be a naturalist until he satisfies all the demands of the spirit. Love is as much its demand as perception. Indeed, neither can be perfect without the other. In the uttermost meaning of the words, thought is devout, and devotion is thought. Deep calls unto deep. But in actual life, the marriage is not celebrated. There are innocent men who worship God after the tradition of their fathers, but their sense of duty has not yet extended to the use of all their faculties. And there are patient naturalists, but they freeze their subject under the wintry light of the understanding. Is not prayer also a study of truth,—a sally of the soul into the unfound infinite? No man ever prayed heartily without learning something. But when a faithful thinker, resolute to detach every object from personal relations and see it in the light of thought, shall, at the same time, kindle science with the fire of the holiest affections, then will God go forth anew into the creation.

It will not need, when the mind is prepared for study to search for objects. The invariable mark of wisdom is to see the miraculous in the common. What is a day? What is a year? What is summer? What is woman? What is a child? What is sleep? To our blindness, these things seem unaffecting. We make fables to hide the baldness of the fact and conform it, as we say, to the higher law of the mind. But when the fact is seen under the light of an idea, the gaudy fable fades and shrivels. We behold the real higher law. To the wise, therefore, a fact is true poetry, and the most beautiful of fables. These wonders are brought to our own door. You also are a man. Man and woman and their social life, poverty, labor, sleep, fear, fortune, are known to you. Learn that none of these things is superficial, but that each phenomenon has its roots in the faculties and affections of the mind. Whilst the abstract question occupies your intellect, nature brings it in the concrete to be solved by your hands. It were a wise inquiry for the closet, to compare, point by point, especially at remarkable crises in life, our daily history with the rise and progress of ideas in the mind.

So shall we come to look at the world with new eyes. It shall answer the endless inquiry of the intellect,—What is truth? and of the affections,—What is good? by yielding itself passive to the educated Will. Then shall come to pass what my poet said: "Nature is not fixed but fluid. Spirit alters, molds, makes it. The immobility or bruteness of nature is the absence of spirit; to pure spirit it is fluid, it is volatile, it is obedient. Every spirit builds itself a house, and beyond its house a world, and beyond its world a heaven. Know then that the world exists for you. For you is the phenomenon perfect. What we are, that only can we see. All that Adam had, all that Caesar could, you have and can do. Adam called his house, heaven and earth; Caesar called his house, Rome; you perhaps call yours, a cobbler's trade; a hundred acres of ploughed land; or a scholar's garret. Yet line for line and point for point your dominion is as great as theirs, though without fine names. Build therefore your own world. As fast as you conform your life to the pure idea in your mind, that will unfold its great proportions. A correspondent revolution in things will attend the influx of the spirit. So fast will disagreeable appearances, swine, spiders, snakes, pests, madhouses, prisons, enemies, vanish; they are temporary and shall be no more seen. The sordor and filths of nature, the sun shall dry up and the wind exhale. As when the summer comes from the south the snow-banks melt and the face of the earth becomes green before it, so shall the advancing spirit create its ornaments along its path, and carry with it the beauty it visits and the song which enchants it; it shall draw beautiful faces, warm hearts, wise discourse, and heroic acts, around its way, until evil is no more seen. The kingdom of man over nature, which cometh not with observation,—a dominion such as now is beyond his dream of God,—he shall enter without more wonder than the blind man feels who is gradually restored to perfect sight."

THE RHODORA

On Being Asked, Whence Is the Flower?

In May, when sea-winds pierced our solitudes,
I found the fresh Rhodora in the woods,
Spreading its leafless blooms in a damp nook,
To please the desert and the sluggish brook.
The purple petals, fallen in the pool,
Made the black water with their beauty gay;
Here might the red-bird come his plumes to cool,
And court the flower that cheapens his array.
Rhodora! if the sages ask thee why
This charm is wasted on the earth and sky,
Tell them, dear, that if eyes were made for seeing,
Then Beauty is its own excuse for being:
Why thou wert there, O rival of the rose!
I never thought to ask, I never knew:
But, in my simple ignorance, suppose
The self-same Power that brought me there brought you.

THE SNOW-STORM

Announced by all the trumpets of the sky,
Arrives the snow, and, driving o'er the fields,
Seems nowhere to alight: the whited air
Hides hills and woods, the river, and the heaven,
And veils the farm-house at the garden's end.
The sled and traveler stopped, the courier's feet
Delayed, all friends shut out, the housemates sit
Around the radiant fireplace, enclosed
In a tumultuous privacy of storm.

Come see the north wind's masonry.
Out of an unseen quarry evermore
Furnished with tile, the fierce artificer
Curves his white bastions with projected roof
Round every windward stake, or tree, or door.
Speeding, the myriad-handed, his wild work
So fanciful, so savage, nought cares he
For number or proportion. Mockingly,
On coop or kennel he hangs Parian wreaths;
A swan-like form invests the hidden thorn;
Fills up the farmer's lane from wall to wall,
Maugre the farmer's sighs; and at the gate
A tapering turret overtops the work.
And when his hours are numbered, and the world
Is all his own, retiring, as he were not,
Leaves, when the sun appears, astonished Art

To mimic in slow structures, stone by stone,
Built in an age, the mad wind's night-work,
The frolic architecture of the snow.

from WOODNOTES, I

2

And such I knew, a forest seer,
A minstrel of the natural year,
Foreteller of the vernal ides,
Wise harbinger of spheres and tides,
A lover true, who knew by heart
Each joy the mountain dales impart;
It seemed that Nature could not raise
A plant in any secret place,
In quaking bog, on snowy hill,
Beneath the grass that shades the rill,
Under the snow, between the rocks,
In damp fields known to bird and fox,
But he would come in the very hour
It opened in its virgin bower,
As if a sunbeam showed the place,
And tell its long-descended race.
It seemed as if the breezes brought him;
It seemed as if the sparrows taught him;
As if by secret sight he knew
Where, in far fields, the orchis grew.
Many haps fall in the field
Seldom seen by wishful eyes,
But all her shows did Nature yield,
To please and win this pilgrim wise.
He saw the partridge drum in the woods;
He heard the woodcock's evening hymn;
He found the tawny thrushes' broods;
And the shy hawk did wait for him;
What others did at distance hear,
And guessed within the thicket's gloom,
Was shown to this philosopher,
And at his bidding seemed to come.

HAMATREYA

Bulkeley, Hunt, Willard, Hosmer, Meriam, Flint,
Possessed the land which rendered to their toil
Hay, corn, roots, hemp, flax, apples, wool and wood.
Each of these landlords walked amidst his farm,
Saying, " 'Tis mine, my children's and my name's.
How sweet the west wind sounds in my own trees!

How graceful climb those shadows on my hill!
I fancy these pure waters and the flags
Know me, as does my dog: we sympathize;
And, I affirm, my actions smack of the soil."
Where are these men? Asleep beneath their grounds:
And strangers, fond as they, their furrows plough.
Earth laughs in flowers, to see her boastful boys
Earth-proud, proud of the earth which is not theirs;
Who steer the plough, but cannot steer their feet
Clear of the grave.
They added ridge to valley, brook to pond,
And sighed for all that bounded their domain;
"This suits me for a pasture; that's my park;
We must have clay, lime, gravel, granite-ledge,
And misty lowland, where to go for peat.
The land is well,—lies fairly to the south.
'Tis good, when you have crossed the sea and back,
To find the sitfast acres where you left them."
Ah! the hot owner see not Death, who adds
Him to his land, a lump of mold the more.
Hear what the Earth says:

EARTH-SONG

"Mine and yours;
Mine, not yours.
Earth endures;
Stars abide—
Shine down in the old sea;
Old are the shores;
But where are old men?
I who have seen much,
Such have I never seen.

"The lawyer's deed
Ran sure,
In tail,
To them, and to their heirs
Who shall succeed,
Without fail,
Forevermore.

"Here is the land,
Shaggy with wood,
With its old valley,
Mound and flood.

But the heritors?—
Fled like the flood's foam.

The lawyer, and the laws,
And the kingdom,
Clean swept herefrom.

"They called me theirs,
Who so controlled me;
Yet every one
Wished to stay, and is gone,
How am I theirs,
If they cannot hold me,
But I hold them?"

When I heard the Earth-song
I was no longer brave;
My avarice cooled
Like lust in the chill of the grave.

THE HUMBLE-BEE

Burly, dozing humble-bee,
Where thou art is clime for me.
Let them sail for Porto Rique,
Far-off heats through seas to seek;
I will follow thee alone,
Thou animated torrid-zone!
Zigzag steerer, desert cheerer,
Let me chase thy waving lines;
Keep me nearer, me thy hearer,
Singing over shrubs and vines.

Insect lover of the sun,
Joy of thy dominion!
Sailor of the atmosphere;
Swimmer through the waves of air;
Voyager of light and noon;
Epicurean of June;
Wait, I prithee, till I come
Within earshot of thy hum,—
All without is martyrdom.

When the south wind, in May days,
With a net of shining haze
Silvers the horizon wall,
And with softness touching all,
Tints the human countenance
With a color of romance,
And infusing subtle heats,
Turns the sod to violets,

Thou, in sunny solitudes,
Rover of the underwoods,
The green silence dost displace
With thy mellow, breezy bass.

Hot midsummer's petted crone,
Sweet to me thy drowsy tone
Tells of countless sunny hours,
Long days, and solid banks of flowers;
Of gulfs of sweetness without bound
In Indian wildernesses found;
Of Syrian peace, immortal leisure,
Firmest cheer, and bird-like pleasure.

Aught unsavory or unclean
Hath my insect never seen;
But violets and bilberry bells,
Maple-sap and daffodels,
Grass with green flag half-mast high,
Succory to match the sky,
Columbine with horn of honey,
Scented fern, and agrimony,
Clover, catchfly, adder's-tongue
And brier-roses, dwelt among;
All beside was unknown waste,
All was picture as he passed.

Wiser far then human seer,
Yellow-breeched philosopher!
Seeing only what is fair,
Sipping only what is sweet,
Thou dost mock at fate and care,
Leave the chaff, and take the wheat.
When the fierce northwestern blast
Cools sea and land so far and fast,
Thou already slumberest deep;
Woe and want thou canst outsleep;
Want and woe, which torture us,
Thy sleep makes ridiculous.

WALDEINSAMKEIT*

I do not cound the hours I spend
In wandering by the sea;
The forest is my loyal friend,
Like God it useth me.

*Forest solitude.

In plains that room for shadows make
Of skirting hills to lie,
Bound in by streams which give and take
Their colors from the sky;

Or on the mountain-crest sublime,
Or down the oaken glade,
O what have I to do with time?
For this the day was made.

Cities of mortals woe-begone
Fantastic care derides,
But in the serious landscape lone
Stern benefit abides.

Sheen will tarnish, honey cloy,
And merry is only a mask of sad,
But, sober on a fund of joy,
The woods at heart are glad.

There the great Planter plants
Of fruitful worlds the grain,
And with a million spells enchants
The souls that walk in pain.

Still on the seeds of all he made
The rose of beauty burns;
Through times that wear and forms that fade,
Immortal youth returns.

The black ducks mounting from the lake,
The pigeon in the pines,
The bittern's boom, a desert make
Which no false art refines.

Down in yon watery nook,
Where bearded mists divide,
The gray old gods whom Chaos knew,
The sires of Nature, hide.

Aloft, in secret veins of air,
Blows the sweet breath of song,
O, few to scale those uplands dare,
Though they to all belong!

See thou bring not to field or stone
The fancies found in books;

Leave authors' eyes, and fetch your own,
To brave the landscape's looks.

Oblivion here thy wisdom is,
Thy thrift, the sleep of cares;
For a proud idleness like this
Crowns all thy mean affairs.

Henry David Thoreau
1817-1862

Readers of Thoreau quickly recognize the remarkable integrity of this man who lived according to his own words and ideals. He was above all a man of principles, discipline, and self-reliance—traits learned and reaffirmed through his close observations of nature. Like Emerson, he boldly criticized, often in good humor, the foibles and hypocrisies of the emerging American industrial civilization of his day. "We have need to be as sturdy pioneers still as Miles Standish, or Church, or Lovewell," Thoreau wrote. "We are to follow on another trail, it is true, but one as convenient for ambushes. What if the Indians are exterminated; are not savages as grim prowling about the clearings today?" The savages, of course, are in ourselves, savages worse than the Indians ever were.

His observations are scrupulous, detailed, like those of a scientist or engineer. He sought the greatest of realities through the details of nature, because nature offered so much, was so sincere in her lessons, and spoke to humanity of the One beneath the many and the ephemeral. A civilization lived, for Thoreau, to the extent that it was united with nature. His lifelong fascination with the American Indian was based on the Indian's direct connection to nature, his enviable status as inhabitant rather than guest. It was the white man who had separated himself from nature, who could not wear nature gracefully as the Indian could. "Nature does not cast pearls before swine. There is just as much beauty visible to us in the landscape as we are prepared to appreciate—not a grain more."

Thoreau was only forty-four when he died, having published relatively little of his writing. Yet *Walden* now stands as a classic of American and world literature, published through more than one hundred and fifty editions and twenty languages.

Although life itself and writing were Thoreau's chief concerns, he supported himself through numerous odd jobs, ranging from teaching school after his graduation from Harvard, to manufacturing pencils in his father's business, to land surveying and carpentry. Always, however, he was recording his inner life in the *Journals.* And from Bangor to Philadelphia he lectured, perhaps with less skill than Emerson, in what came to be known as the Lyceum (or public education) Movement of the day.

His concern, his speaking, and his activism in the great social issues of his time, such as abolition, were secondary only to his feeling for and study of nature. His famous essay "Civil Disobedience," an enormously influential work down to our time, is the best gathering of Thoreau's activist views of the place and duty of the individual in society.

A Week on the Concord and Merrimack Rivers (1849) and *Walden* (1854) were published during his lifetime to, at best, mixed receptions. *Cape Cod* (1865) grew out of his walking tour of Cape Cod, and *A Yankee in Canada* (1866) was inspired by a trip to Canada with William Ellery Channing in 1850.

The following selections from *Cape Cod* and *The Maine Woods* (1864) barely touch the full quality and richness of Thoreau's mind and character. As much as anyone included in this anthology, Thoreau is best approached with supplementary readings from whole works.

from CAPE COD*

I

THE SHIPWRECK

Wishing to get a better view than I had yet had of the ocean, which, we are told, covers more than two thirds of the globe, but of which a man who lives a few miles inland may never see any trace, more than of another world, I made a visit to Cape Cod in October, 1849, another the succeeding June, and another to Truro in July, 1855; the first and last time with a single companion, the second time alone. I have spent, in all, about three weeks on the Cape; walked from Eastham to Provincetown twice on the Atlantic side, and once on the Bay side also, excepting four or five miles, and crossed the Cape half a dozen times on my way; but having come so fresh to the sea, I have got but little salted. My readers must expect only so much saltness as the land breeze acquires from blowing over an arm of the sea, or is tasted on the windows and the bark of trees twenty miles inland, after September gales. I have been accustomed to make excursions to the ponds within ten miles of Concord, but latterly I have extended my excursions to the seashore.

I did not see why I might not make a book on Cape Cod, as well as my neighbor on "Human Culture." It is but another name for the same thing, and hardly a sandier phase of it. As for my title, I suppose that the word

*From *The Writings of Henry David Thoreau.* Vol. IV (Boston: Houghton, Mifflin Co., 1893).

Cape is from the French *cap*; which is from the Latin *caput*, a head; which is, perhaps, from the verb *capere*, to take,—that being the part by which we take hold of a thing:—Take Time by the forelock. It is also the safest part to take a serpent by. And as for Cod, that was derived directly from that "great store of cod-fish" which Captain Bartholomew Gosnold caught there in 1602; which fish appears to have been so called from the Saxon word *codde*, "a case in which seeds are lodged," either from the form of the fish, or the quantity of spawn it contains; whence also, perhaps, *codling* ("*pomum coctile*"?) and coddle,—to cook green like peas. (V. Dic.)

Cape Cod is the bared and bended arm of Massachusetts: the shoulder is at Buzzard's Bay; the elbow, or crazy-bone, at Cape Mallebarre; the wrist at Truro; and the sandy fist at Provincetown,—behind which the state stands on her guard, with her back to the Green Mountains, and her feet planted on the floor of the ocean, like an athlete protecting her Bay,—boxing with northeast storms, and, ever and anon, having up her Atlantic adversary from the lap of earth,—ready to thrust forward her other fist, which keeps guard the while upon her breast at Cape Ann.

On studying the map, I saw that there must be an uninterrupted beach on the east or outside of the forearm of the Cape, more than thirty miles from the general line of the coast, which would afford a good sea view, but that, on account of an opening in the beach, forming the entrance to Nauset Harbor, in Orleans, I must strike it in Eastham, if I approached it by land, and probably I could walk thence straight to Race Point, about twenty-eight miles, and not meet with any obstruction.

We left Concord, Massachusetts, on Tuesday, October 9, 1849. On reaching Boston, we found that the Provincetown steamer, which should have got in the day before, had not yet arrived, on account of a violent storm; and, as we noticed in the streets a handbill headed, "Death! one hundred and forty-five lives lost at Cohasset," we decided to go by way of Cohasset. We found many Irish in the cars, going to identify bodies and to sympathize with the survivors, and also to attend the funeral which was to take place in the afternoon;—and when we arrived at Cohasset, it appeared that nearly all the passengers were bound for the beach, which was about a mile distant, and many other persons were flocking in from the neighboring country. There were several hundreds of them streaming off over Cohasset common in that direction, some on foot and some in wagons,—and among them were some sportsmen in their hunting-jackets, with their guns, and game-bags, and dogs. As we passed the graveyard we saw a large hole, like a cellar, freshly dug there, and, just before reaching the shore, by a pleasantly winding and rocky road, we met several hay-riggings and farm-wagons coming away toward the meeting-house, each loaded with three large, rough deal boxes. We did not need to ask what was in them. The owners of the wagons were made the undertakers. Many horses in carriages were fastened to the fences near the shore, and, for a mile or more, up and down, the beach was covered with people looking out for bodies, and examining the fragments of the wreck. There was a small island called Brook Island, with a hut on it, lying just off the shore. This is said to be the rockiest shore in Massachusetts, from Nantasket to Scituate,—hard sienitic rocks, which the waves have laid bare, but have not been able to crumble. It has been the scene of many a shipwreck.

The brig St. John, from Galway, Ireland, laden with emigrants, was wrecked on Sunday morning; it was now Tuesday morning, and the sea was still breaking violently on the rocks. There were eighteen or twenty of the same large boxes that I have mentioned, lying on a green hillside, a few rods from the water, and surrounded by a crowd. The bodies which had been recovered, twenty-seven or eight in all, had been collected there. Some were rapidly nailing down the lids, others were carting the boxes away, and others were lifting the lids, which were yet loose, and peeping under the cloths, for each body, with such rags as still adhered to it, was covered loosely with a white sheet. I witnessed no signs of grief, but there was a sober dispatch of business which was affecting. One man was seeking to identify a particular body, and one undertaker or carpenter was calling to another to know in what box a certain child was put. I saw many marble feet and matted heads as the cloths were raised, and one livid, swollen, and mangled body of a drowned girl,—who probably had intended to go out to service in some American family,—to which some rags still adhered, with a string, half concealed by the flesh, about its swollen neck; the coiled-up wreck of a human hulk, gashed by the rocks or fishes, so that the bones and muscle were exposed, but quite bloodless,—merely red and white,—with wide-open and staring eyes, yet lustreless, deadlights; or like the cabin windows of a stranded vessel, filled with sand. Sometimes there were two or more children, or a parent and child, in the same box, and on the lid would perhaps be written with red chalk, "Bridget such-a-one, and sister's child." The surrounding sward was covered with bits of sails and clothing. I have since heard, from one who lives by this beach, that a woman who had come over before, but had left her infant behind for her sister to bring, came and looked into these boxes, and saw in one—probably the same whose superscription I have quoted—her child in her sister's arms, as if the sister had meant to be found thus; and within three days after, the mother died from the effect of that sight.

We turned from this and walked along the rocky shore. In the first cove were strewn what seemed the fragments of a vessel, in small pieces mixed with sand and seaweed, and great quantities of feathers; but it looked so old and rusty, that I at first took it to be some old wreck which had lain there many years. I even thought of Captain Kidd, and that the feathers were those which sea-fowl had cast there; and perhaps there might be some tradition about it in the neighborhood. I asked a sailor if that was the St. John. He said it was. I asked him where she struck. He pointed to a rock in front of us, a mile from the shore, called the Grampus Rock, and added,—

"You can see a part of her now sticking up; it looks like a small boat."

I saw it. It was thought to be held by the chain-cables and the anchors. I asked if the bodies which I saw were all that were drowned.

"Not a quarter of them," said he.

"Where are the rest?"

"Most of them right underneath that piece you see."

It appeared to us that there was enough rubbish to make the wreck of a large vessel in this cove alone, and that it would take many days to cart it off. It was several feet deep, and here and there was a bonnet or a jacket on it. In the very midst of the crowd about this wreck, there were men with carts busily collecting the seaweed which the storm had cast up, and conveying it beyond the reach of the tide, though they were often obliged to separate fragments of clothing from it, and they might at any moment have found a human body under it. Drown who might, they did not forget that this weed was a valuable manure. This shipwreck had not produced a visible vibration in the fabric of society.

About a mile south we could see, rising above the rocks, the masts of the British brig which the St. John had endeavored to follow, which had slipped her cables, and, by good luck, run into the mouth of Cohasset Harbor. A little further along the shore we saw a man's clothes on a rock; further, a woman's scarf, a gown, a straw bonnet, the brig's caboose, and one of her masts high and dry, broken into several pieces. In another rocky cove, several rods from the water, and behind rocks twenty feet high, lay a part of one side of the vessel, still hanging together. It was, perhaps, forty feet long, by fourteen wide. I was even more surprised at the power of the waves, exhibited on this shattered fragment, than I had been at the sight of the smaller fragments before. The largest timbers and iron braces were broken superfluously, and I saw that no material could withstand the power of the waves; that iron must go to pieces in such a case, and an iron vessel would be cracked up like an egg-shell on the rocks. Some of these timbers, however, were so rotten that I could almost thrust my umbrella through them. They told us that some were saved on this piece, and also showed where the sea had heaved it into this cove which was now dry. When I saw where it had come in, and in what condition, I wondered that any had been saved on it. A little further on a crowd of men was collected around the mate of the St. John, who was telling his story. He was a slim-looking youth, who spoke of the captain as the master, and seemed a little excited. He was saying that when they jumped into the boat, she filled, and, the vessel lurching, the weight of the water in the boat caused the painter to break, and so they were separated. Whereat one man came away, saying,—

"Well, I don't see but he tells a straight story enough. You see, the weight of the water in the boat broke the painter. A boat full of water is very heavy,"—and so on, in a loud and impertinently earnest tone, as if he had a bet depending on it, but had no humane interest in the matter.

Another, a large man, stood near by upon a rock, gazing into the sea, and chewing large quids of tobacco, as if that habit were forever confirmed with him.

"Come," says another to his companion, "let's be off. We've seen the whole of it. It's no use to stay to the funeral."

Further, we saw one standing upon a rock, who, we were told, was one that was saved. He was a sober-looking man, dressed in a jacket and gray pantaloons, with his hands in the pockets. I asked him a few questions, which he answered; but he seemed unwilling to talk about it, and soon walked away. By his side stood one of the life-boat men, in an oilcloth jacket, who told us how they went to the relief of the British brig, thinking that the boat of the St. John, which they passed on the way, held all her crew,—for the waves prevented their seeing those who were on the vessel, though they might have saved some had they known there were any there. A little further was the flag of the St. John spread on a rock to dry, and held down by stones at the corners. This frail, but essential and significant portion of the vessel, which had so long been the sport of the winds, was sure to reach the shore. There were one or two houses visible from these rocks, in which were some of the survivors recovering from the shock which their bodies and minds had sustained. One was not expected to live.

We kept on down the shore as far as a promontory called Whitehead, that we might see more of the Cohasset Rocks. In a little cove, within half a mile, there were an old man and his son collecting, with their team, the seaweed which that fatal storm had cast up, as serenely employed as if there had never been a wreck in the world, though they were within sight of the Grampus Rock, on which the St. John had struck. The old man had heard that there was a wreck and knew most of the particulars, but he said that he had not been up there since it happened. It was the wrecked weed that concerned him most, rock-weed, kelp, and seaweed, as he named them, which he carted to his barnyard; and those bodies were to him but other weeds which the tide cast up, but which were of no use to him. We afterwards came to the life-boat in its harbor, waiting for another emergency,—and in the afternoon we saw the funeral procession at a distance, at the head of which walked the captain with the other survivors.

On the whole, it was not so impressive a scene as I might have expected. If I had found one body cast upon the beach in some lonely place, it would have-affected me more. I sympathized rather with the winds and waves, as if to toss and mangle these poor human bodies was the order of the day. If this was the law of Nature, why waste any time in awe or pity? If the last day were come, we should not think so much about the separation of friends or the blighted prospects of individuals. I saw that corpses might be multiplied, as on the field of battle, till they no longer affected us in any degree, as exceptions to the common lot of humanity. Take all the graveyards together, they are always the majority. It is the individual and private that demands our sympathy. A man can attend but one funeral in the course of his life, can behold but one corpse. Yet I saw that the inhabitants of the shore would be not a little affected by this event. They would watch there many days and nights for the sea to give up its dead, and their imaginations and sympathies would supply the place of mourners far away, who as yet knew not of the wreck. Many days after this, something white was seen floating on the water by one who was sauntering on the beach. It was approached in a boat, and found to be the body of a woman, which had risen in an upright position, whose white cap was blown back with the wind. I saw that the beauty of the shore itself was wrecked for many a lonely walker there, until he could perceive, at last, how its beauty was enhanced by wrecks like this, and it acquired thus a rarer and sublimer beauty still.

Why care for these dead bodies? They really have no friends but the worms or fishes. Their owners were coming to the New World, as

Columbus and the Pilgrims did,—they were within a mile of its shores; but, before they could reach it, they emigrated to a newer world than ever Columbus dreamed of, yet one of whose existence we believe that there is far more universal and convincing evidence—though it has not yet been discovered by science—than Columbus had of this: not merely mariners' tales and some paltry drift-wood and seaweed, but a continual drift and instinct to all our shores. I saw their empty hulks that came to land; but they themselves, meanwhile, were cast upon some shore yet further west, toward which we are all tending, and which we shall reach at last, it may be through storm and darkness, as they did. No doubt, we have reason to thank God that they have not been "shipwrecked into life again." The mariner who makes the safest port in Heaven, perchance, seems to his friends on earth to be shipwrecked, for they deem Boston Harbor the better place; though perhaps invisible to them, a skillful pilot comes to meet him, and the fairest and balmiest gales blow off that coast, his good ship makes the land in halcyon days, and he kisses the shore in rapture there, while his old hulk tosses in the surf here. It is hard to part with one's body, but, no doubt, it is easy enough to do without it when once it is gone. All their plans and hopes burst like a bubble! Infants by the score dashed on the rocks by the enraged Atlantic Ocean! No, no! If the St. John did not make her port here, she has been telegraphed there. The strongest wind cannot stagger a Spirit; it is a Spirit's breath. A just man's purpose cannot be split on any Grampus or material rock, but itself will split rocks till it succeeds.

The verses addressed to Columbus, dying, may, with slight alterations, be applied to the passengers of the St. John,—

"Soon with them will all be over,
Soon the voyage will be begun
That shall bear them to discover,
Far away, a land unknown.

"Land that each, alone, must visit,
But no tidings bring to men;
For no sailor, once departed,
Ever hath returned again.

"No carved wood, no broken branches
Ever drift from that far wild;
He who on that ocean launches
Meets no corse of angel child.

"Undismayed, my noble sailors,
Spread, then spread your canvas out;
Spirits! on a sea of ether
Soon shall ye serenely float!

"Where the deep no plummet soundeth,
Fear no hidden breakers there,
And the fanning wing of angels
Shall your bark right onward bear.

"Quit, now, full of heart and comfort,
These rude shores, they are of earth;
Where the rosy clouds are parting,
There the blessed isles loom forth."

One summer day, since this, I came this way, on foot, along the shore from Boston. It was so warm, that some horses had climbed to the very top of the ramparts of the old fort at Hull, where there was hardly room to turn round, for the sake of the breeze. The *Datura stramonium*, or thorn-apple, was in full bloom along the beach; and, at sight of this cosmopolite,—this Captain Cook among plants,—carried in ballast all over the world, I felt as if I were on the highway of nations. Say, rather, this Viking, king of the Bays, for it is not an innocent plant; it suggests not merely commerce, but its attendant vices, as if its fibres were the stuff of which pirates spin their yarns. I heard the voices of men shouting aboard a vessel, half a mile from the shore, which sounded as if they were in a barn in the country, they being between the sails. It was a purely rural sound. As I looked over the water, I saw the isles rapidly wasting away, the sea nibbling voraciously at the continent, the springing arch of a hill suddenly interrupted, as at Point Allerton,—what botanists might call premorse,—showing, by its curve against the sky, how much space it must have occupied, where now was water only. On the other hand, these wrecks of isles were being fancifully arranged into new shores, as at Hog Island, inside of Hull, where everything seemed to be gently lapsing into futurity. This isle had got the very form of a ripple,—and I thought that the inhabitants should bear a ripple for device on their shields, a wave passing over them, with the *datura*, which is said to produce mental alienation of long duration without affecting the bodily health,[1] springing from its edge. The most interesting thing which I heard of, in this township of Hull, was an unfailing spring, whose locality was pointed out to me, on the side of a distant hill, as I was panting along the shore, though I did not visit it. Perhaps, if I should go through Rome, it would be some spring on the Capitoline Hill I should remember the longest. It is true, I was somewhat interested in the well at the old French fort, which was said to be ninety feet deep, with a cannon at the bottom of it. On Nantasket beach I counted a dozen chaises from the

[1]The Jamestown weed (or thorn-apple). "This, being an early plant, was gathered very young for a boiled salad, by some of the soldiers sent thither [i.e., to Virginia] to quell the rebellion of Bacon; and some of them ate plentifully of it, the effect of which was a very pleasant comedy, for they turned natural fools upon it for several days: one would blow up a feather in the air; another would dart straws at it with much fury; and another, stark naked, was sitting up in a corner like a monkey, grinning and making mows at them; a fourth would fondly kiss and paw his companions, and sneer in their faces, with a countenance more antic than any in a Dutch droll. In this frantic condition they were confined, lest they should, in their folly, destroy themselves,—though it was observed that all their actions were full of innocence and good nature. Indeed, they were not very cleanly. A thousand such simple tricks they played, and after eleven days returned to themselves again, not remembering anything that had passed."—Beverly's *History of Virginia*, p. 120.

public-house. From time to time the riders turned their horses toward the sea, standing in the water for the coolness,—and I saw the value of beaches to cities for the sea breeze and the bath.

At Jerusalem village the inhabitants were collecting in haste, before a thunder-shower now approaching, the Irish moss which they had spread to dry. The shower passed on one side, and gave me a few drops only, which did not cool the air. I merely felt a puff upon my cheek, though, within sight, a vessel was capsized in the bay, and several others dragged their anchors, and were near going ashore. The sea-bathing at Cohasset Rocks was perfect. The water was purer and more transparent than any I had ever seen. There was not a particle of mud or slime about it. The bottom being sandy, I could see the sea-perch swimming about. The smooth and fantastically worn rocks, and the perfectly clean and tress-like rock-weeds falling over you, and attached so firmly to the rocks that you could pull yourself up by them, greatly enhanced the luxury of the bath. The stripe of barnacles just above the weeds reminded me of some vegetable growth,—the buds, and petals, and seed-vessels of flowers. They lay along the seams of the rock like buttons on a waistcoat. It was one of the hottest days in the year, yet I found the water so icy cold that I could swim but a stroke or two, and thought that, in case of shipwreck, there would be more danger of being chilled to death than simply drowned. One immersion was enough to make you forget the dog-days utterly. Though you were sweltering before, it will take you half an hour now to remember that it was ever warm. There were the tawny rocks, like lions couchant, defying the ocean, whose waves incessantly dashed against and scoured them with vast quantities of gravel. The water held in their little hollows, on the receding of the tide, was so crystalline that I could not believe it salt, but wished to drink it; and higher up were basins of fresh water left by the rain,—all which, being also of different depths and temperature, were convenient for different kinds of baths. Also, the larger hollows in the smoothed rocks formed the most convenient of seats and dressing-rooms. In these respects it was the most perfect seashore that I had seen. . . .

from THE MAINE WOODS*

KTAADN

On the 31st of August, 1846, I left Concord in Massachusetts for Bangor and the backwoods of Maine, by way of the railroad and steamboat, intending to accompany a relative of mine, engaged in the lumber trade in Bangor, as far as a dam on the west branch of the Penobscot, in which property he was interested. From this place, which is about one hundred miles by the river above Bangor, thirty miles from the Houlton military road, and five miles beyond the last log-hut, I proposed to make excursions to Mount Ktaadn, the second highest mountain in New England, about

*From Henry David Thoreau. *The Maine Woods* (Boston & NY: Houghton, Mifflin Co., 1892).

thirty miles distant, and to some of the lakes of the Penobscot, either alone or with such company as I might pick up there. It is unusual to find a camp so far in the woods at that season, when lumbering operations have ceased, and I was glad to avail myself of the circumstance of a gang of men being employed there at that time in repairing the injuries caused by the great freshet in the spring. The mountain may be approached more easily and directly on horseback and on foot from the northeast side, by the Aroostook road, and the Wassataquoik River; but in that case you see much less of the wilderness, none of the glorious river and lake scenery, and have no experience of the batteau and the boatman's life. I was fortunate also in the season of the year, for in the summer myriads of black flies, mosquitoes, and midges, or, as the Indians call them, "no-see-ems," make traveling in the woods almost impossible; but now their reign was nearly over.

Ktaadn, whose name is an Indian word signifying highest land, was first ascended by white men in 1804. It was visited by Professor J.W. Bailey of West Point in 1836; by Dr. Charles T. Jackson, the State Geologist, in 1837; and by two young men from Boston in 1845. All these have given accounts of their expeditions. Since I was there, two or three other parties have made the excursion, and told their stories. Besides these, very few, even among backwoodsmen and hunters, have ever climbed it, and it will be a long time before the tide of fashionable travel sets that way. The mountainous region of the State of Maine stretches from near the White Mountains, northeasterly one hundred and sixty miles, to the head of the Aroostook River, and is about sixty miles wide. The wild or unsettled portion is far more extensive. So that some hours only of travel in this direction will carry the curious to the verge of a primitive forest, more interesting, perhaps, on all accounts, than they would reach by going a thousand miles westward.

The next forenoon, Tuesday, September 1, I started with my companion in a buggy from Bangor for "up river," expecting to be overtaken the next day night at Mattawamkeag Point, some sixty miles off, by two more Bangoreans, who had decided to join us in a trip to the mountain. We had each a knapsack or bag filled with such clothing and articles as were indispensable, and my companion carried his gun.

Within a dozen miles of Bangor we passed through the villages of Stillwater and Oldtown, built at the falls of the Penobscot, which furnish the principal power by which the Maine woods are converted into lumber. The mills are built directly over and across the river. Here is a close jam, a hard rub, at all seasons; and then the once green tree, long since white, I need not say as the driven snow, but as a driven log, becomes lumber merely. Here your inch, your two and your three inch stuff begin to be, and Mr. Sawyer marks off those spaces which decide the destiny of so many prostrate forests. Through this steel riddle, more or less coarse, is the arrowy Maine forest, from Ktaadn and Chesuncook, and the head-waters of the St. John, relentlessly sifted, till it comes out boards, clapboards, laths, and shingles such as the wind can take, still, perchance to be slit and slit again, till men get a size that will suit. Think how stood the white-pine tree on the shore of Chesuncook, its branches soughing with the four winds, and every individual needle trembling in the sunlight,—think how it stands with it now,—sold, perchance, to the New England Friction-Match Company! There were in 1937, as I read, two hundred and fifty saw-mills on the Penobscot and its tributaries above Bangor, the greater part of them in this immediate neighborhood, and they sawed two hundred millions of feet of boards annually. To this is to be added the lumber of the Kennebec, Androscoggin, Saco, Passamaquoddy, and other streams. No wonder that we hear so often of vessels which are becalmed off our coast, being surrounded a week at a time by floating lumber from the Maine woods. The mission of men there seems to be, like so many busy demons, to drive the forest all out of the country, from every solitary beaver-swamp and mountain-side, as soon as possible.

At Oldtown, we walked into a batteau-manufactory. The making of batteaux is quite a business here for the supply of the Penobscot River. We examined some on the stocks. They are light and shapely vessels, calculated for rapid and rocky streams, and to be carried over long portages on men's shoulders, from twenty to thirty feet long, and only four or four and a half wide, sharp at both ends like a canoe, though broadest forward on the bottom, and reaching seven or eight feet over the water, in order that they may slip over rocks as gently as possible. They are made very slight, only two boards to a side, commonly secured to a few light maple or other hard-wood knees, but inward are of the clearest and widest white-pine stuff, of which there is a great waste on account of their form, for the bottom is left perfectly flat, not only from side to side, but from end to end. Sometimes they become "hogging" even, after long use, and the boatmen then turn them over and straighten them by a weight at each end. They told us that one wore out in two years, or often in a single trip, on the rocks, and sold for from fourteen to sixteen dollars. There was something refreshing and wildly musical to my ears in the very name of the white man's canoe, reminding me of Charlevoix and Canadian Voyageurs. The batteau is a sort of mongrel between the canoe and the boat, a fur-trader's boat.

The ferry here took us past the Indian island. As we left the shore, I observed a short, shabby, washerwoman-looking Indian—they commonly have the woebegone look of the girl that cried for spilt milk,—just from "up river,"—land on the Oldtown side near a grocery, and, drawing up his canoe, take out a bundle of skins in one hand, and an empty keg or half-barrel in the other, and scramble up the bank with them. This picture will do to put before the Indian's history, that is, the history of his extinction. In 1837 there were three hundred and sixty-two souls left of this tribe. The island seemed deserted to-day, yet I observed some new houses among the weather-stained ones, as if the tribe had still a design upon life; but generally they have a very shabby, forlorn, and cheerless look, being all back side and woodshed, not homesteads, even Indian homesteads, but instead of home or abroad-steads, for their life is *domi aut militiae,* at home or at war, or now rather *venatus*, that is, a hunting, and most of the latter. The church is the only trim-looking building, but that is not Abenaki, that was Rome's doings. Good Canadian it may be, but it is poor Indian. These were once a powerful tribe. Politics are all the rage with them now. I even thought that a row of wigwams, with a dance of powwows, and a prisoner tortured at the stake, would be more respectable than this.

We landed in Milford, and rode along on the east side of the Penobscot, having a more or less constant view of the river, and the Indian islands in it, for they retain all the islands as far up as Nicketow, at the mouth of the East Branch. They are generally well-timbered, and are said to be better soil than the neighboring shores. The river seemed shallow and rocky, and interrupted by rapids, rippling and gleaming in the sun. We paused a moment to see a fish-hawk dive for a fish down straight as an arrow, from a great height, but he missed his prey this time. It was the Houlton road on which we were now traveling, over which some troops were marched once towards Mars' Hill, though not to Mars' *field*, as it proved. It is the main, almost the only, road in these parts, as straight and well made, and kept in as good repair as almost any you will find anywhere. Everywhere we saw signs of the great freshet,—this house standing awry, and that where it was not founded, but where it was found, at any rate, the next day; and that other with a waterlogged look, as if it were still airing and drying its basement, and logs with everybody's marks upon them, and sometimes the marks of their having served as bridges, strewn along the road. We crossed the Sunkhaze, a summery Indian name, the Olemmon, Passadumkeag, and other streams, which make a greater show on the map than they now did on the road. At Passadumkeag we found anything but what the name implies,—earnest politicians, to wit,—white ones, I mean,—on the alert to know how the election was likely to go; men who talked rapidly, with subdued voice, and a sort of factitious earnestness you could not help believing, hardly waiting for an introduction, one on each side of your buggy, endeavoring to say much in little, for they see you hold the whip impatiently, but always saying little in much. Caucuses they have had, it seems, and caucuses they are to have again,—victory and defeat. Somebody may be elected, somebody may not. One man, a total stranger, who stood by our carriage in the dusk, actually frightened the horse with his asseverations, growing more solemnly positive as there was less in him to be positive about. So Passadumkeag did not look on the map. At sundown, leaving the river road awhile for shortness, we went by way of Enfield, where we stopped for the night. This, like most of the localities bearing names on this road, was a place to name which, in the midst of the unnamed and unincorporated wilderness, was to make a distinction without a difference, it seemed to me. Here, however, I noticed quite an orchard of healthy and well-grown apple-trees, in a bearing state, it being the oldest settler's house in this region, but all natural fruit and comparatively worthless for want of a grafter. And so it is generally, lower down the river. It would be a good speculation, as well as a favor conferred on the settlers, for a Massachusetts boy to go down there with a trunk full of choice scions, and his grafting apparatus, in the spring.

The next morning we drove along through a high and hilly country, in view of Cold-Stream Pond, a beautiful lake four or five miles long, and came into the Houlton road again, here called the military road, at Lincoln, forty-five miles from Bangor, where there is quite a village for this country,—the principal one above Oldtown. Learning that there were several wigwams here, on one of the Indian islands, we left our horse and wagon, and walked through the forest half a mile to the river, to procure a guide to the mountain. It was not till after considerable search that we discovered their habitations,—small huts, in a retired place, where the scenery was unusually soft and beautiful, and the shore skirted with pleasant meadows and graceful elms. We paddled ourselves across to the island side in a canoe, which we found on the shore. Near where we landed sat an Indian girl, ten or twelve years old, on a rock in the water, in the sun, washing, and humming or moaning a song meanwhile. It was an aboriginal strain. A salmon-spear, made wholly of wood, lay on the shore, such as they might have used before white men came. It had an elastic piece of wood fastened to one side of its point, which slipped over and closed upon the fish, somewhat like the contrivance for holding a bucket at the end of a well-pole. As we walked up to the nearest house, we were met by a sally of a dozen wolfish-looking dogs, which may have been lineal descendants from the ancient Indian dogs, which the first voyageurs describe as "their wolves." I suppose they were. The occupant soon appeared, with a long pole in his hand, with which he beat off the dogs, while he parleyed with us. A stalwart, but dull and greasy-looking fellow, who told us, in his sluggish way, in answer to our questions, as if it were the first serious business he had to do that day, that there *were* Indians going "up river"—he and one other—to-day, before noon. And who was the other? Louis Neptune, who lives in the next house. Well, let us go over and see Louis together. The same doggish reception, and Louis Neptune makes his appearance,—a small, wiry man, with puckered and wrinkled face, yet he seemed the chief man of the two; the same, as I remembered, who had accompanied Jackson to the mountain in '37. The same questions were put to Louis, and the same information obtained, while the other Indian stood by. It appeared that they were going to start by noon, with two canoes, to go up to Chesuncook to hunt moose,—to be gone a month. "Well, Louis, suppose you get to the Point (to the Five Islands, just below Mattawamkeag) to camp, we walk on up the West Branch to-morrow,—four of us,—and wait for you at the dam, or this side. You overtake us to-morrow or next day, and take us into your canoes. We stop for you, you stop for us. We pay you for your trouble." "Ye!" replied Louis, "may be you carry some provision for all,—some pork,—some bread,—and so pay." He said, "Me sure get some moose;" and when I asked if he thought Pomola would let us go up, he answered that we must plant one bottle of rum on the top; he had planted good many; and when he looked again, the rum was all gone. He had been up two or three times; he had planted letter,—English, German, French, etc. These men were slightly clad in shirt and pantaloons, like laborers with us in warm weather. They did not invite us into their houses, but met us outside. So we left the Indians, thinking ourselves lucky to have secured such guides and companions.

There were very few houses along the road, yet they did not altogether fail, as if the law by which men are dispersed over the globe were a very stringent one, and not to be resisted with impunity or for slight reasons.

There were even the germs of one or two villages just beginning to expand. The beauty of the road itself was remarkable. The various evergreens, many of which are rare with us,—delicate and beautiful specimens of the larch, arbor-vitae, ball-spruce, and fir-balsam, from a few inches to many feet in height,—lined its sides, in some places like a long, front yard, springing up from the smooth grass-plots which uninterruptedly border it, and are made fertile by its wash; while it was but a step on either hand to the grim, untrodden wilderness, whose tangled labyrinth of living, fallen, and decaying trees only the deer and moose, the bear and wolf can easily penetrate. More perfect specimens than any front-yard plot can show grew there to grace the passage of the Houlton teams.

About noon we reached the Mattawamkeag, fifty-six miles from Bangor by the way we had come, and put up at a frequented house still on the Houlton road, where the Houlton stage stops. Here was a substantial covered bridge over the Mattawamkeag, built, I think they said, some seventeen years before. We had dinner,—where, by the way, and even at breakfast, as well as supper, at the public-houses on this road, the front rank is composed of various kinds of "sweet cakes," in a continuous line from one end of the table to the other. I think I may safely say that there was a row of ten or a dozen plates of this kind set before us two here. To account for which, they say that, when the lumberers come out of the woods, they have a craving for cakes and pies, and such sweet things, which there are almost unknown, and this is the *supply* to satisfy that *demand.* The supply is always equal to the demand, and these hungry men think a good deal of getting their money's worth. No doubt the balance of victuals is restored by the time they reach Bangor,—Mattawamkeag takes off the raw edge. Well, over this front rank, I say, you, coming from the "sweet cake" side, with a cheap philosophic indifference though it may be, have to assault what there is behind, which I do not by any means mean to insinuate is insufficient in quantity or quality to supply that other demand, of men, not from the woods, but from the towns, for venison and strong country fare. After dinner we strolled down to the "Point," formed by the junction of the two rivers, which is said to be the scene of an ancient battle between the Eastern Indians and the Mohawks, and searched there carefully for relics, though the men at the bar-room had never heard of such things; but we found only some flakes of arrow-head stone, some points of arrow-heads, one small leaden bullet, and some colored beads, the last to be referred, perhaps, to early fur-trader days. The Mattawamkeag, though wide, was a mere river's bed, full of rocks and shallows at this time, so that you could cross it almost dry-shod in boots; and I could hardly believe my companion, when he told me that he had been fifty or sixty miles up it in a batteau, through distant and still uncut forests. A batteau could hardly find a harbor now at its mouth. Deer and caribou, or reindeer, are taken here in the winter, in sight of the house.

Before our companions arrived, we rode on up the Houlton road seven miles to Molunkus, where the Aroostook road comes into it, and where there is a spacious public house in the woods, called the "Molunkus House," kept by one Libbey, which looked as if it had its hall for dancing and for military drills. There was no other evidence of man but this huge shingle palace in this part of the world; but sometimes even this is filled with travelers. I looked off the piazza round the corner of the house up the Aroostook road, on which there was no clearing in sight. There was a man just adventuring upon it this evening in a rude, original, what you may call Aroostook wagon,—a mere seat, with a wagon swung under it, a few bags on it, and a dog asleep to watch them. He offered to carry a message for us to anybody in that country, cheerfully. I suspect that, if you should go to the end of the world, you would find somebody there going farther, as if just starting for home at sundown, and having a last word before he drove off. Here, too, was a small trader, whom I did not see at first, who kept a store,—but no great store, certainly,—in a small box over the way, behind the Molunkus signpost. It looked like the balance-box of a patent hay-scales. As for his house, we could only conjecture where that was; he may have been a boarder in the Molunkus House. I saw him standing in his shop-door,—his shop was so small, that, if a traveler should make demonstrations of entering in, *he* would have to go out by the back way, and confer with his customer through a window, about his goods in the cellar, or, more probably, bespoken, and yet on the way. I should have gone in, for I felt a real impulse to trade, if I had not stopped to consider what would become of him. The day before, we had walked into a shop, over against an inn where we stopped, the puny beginning of trade, which would grow at last into a firm copartnership in the future town or city,—indeed, it was already "Somebody & Co.," I forget who. The woman came forward from the penetralia of the attached house, for "Somebody & Co." was in the burning, and she sold us percussion-caps, canalès and smooth, and knew their prices and qualities, and which the hunters preferred. Here was a little of everything in a small compass to satisfy the wants and the ambition of the woods,—a stock selected with what pains and care, and brought home in the wagon-box, or a corner of the Houlton team; but there seemed to me, as usual, a preponderance of children's toys,—dogs to bark, and cats to mew, and trumpets to blow, where natives there hardly are yet. As if a child, born into the Maine woods, among the pine-cones and cedar-berries, could not do without such a sugar-man or skipping-jack as the young Rothschild has.

I think that there was not more than one house on the road to Molunkus, or for seven miles. At that place we got over the fence into a new field, planted with potatoes, where the logs were still burning between the hills; and, pulling up the vines, found good-sized potatoes, nearly ripe, growing like weeds, and turnips mixed with them. The mode of clearing and planting is to fell the trees, and burn once what will burn, then cut them up into suitable lengths, roll into heaps, and burn again; then, with a hoe, plant potatoes where you can come at the ground between the stumps and charred logs; for a first crop the ashes sufficing for manure, and no hoeing being necessary the first year. In the fall, cut, roll, and burn again, and so on, till the land is cleared; and soon it is ready for grain, and to be laid down. Let those talk of poverty and hard times who will in the towns and cities; cannot the emigrant who can pay his fare to New York or Boston pay five dollars more to get here,—I paid three, all told, for my passage from Boston to Bangor, two hundred and fifty miles,—and be as rich as he pleases, where land virtually costs nothing, and houses only the labor of building, and he may begin life as Adam did? If he will still remember the distinction of poor and rich, let him bespeak him a narrower house forthwith.

When we returned to the Mattawamkeag, the Houlton stage had already put up there; and a Province man was betraying his greenness to the Yankees by his questions. Why Province money won't pass here at par, when States' money is good at Fredericton,—though this, perhaps, was sensible enough. From what I saw then, it appears that the Province man was now the only real Jonathan, or raw country bumpkin, left so far behind by his enterprising neighbors that he didn't know enough to put a question to them. No people can long continue provincial in character who have the propensity for politics and whittling, and rapid traveling, which the Yankees have, and who are leaving the mother country behind in the variety of their notions and inventions. The possession and exercise of practical talent merely are a sure and rapid means of intellectual culture and independence.

The last edition of Greenleaf's Map of Maine hung on the wall here, and, as we had no pocket-map, we resolved to trace a map of the lake country. So, dipping a wad of tow into the lamp, we oiled a sheet of paper on the oiled table-cloth, and, in good faith, traced what we afterwards ascertained to be a labyrinth of errors, carefully following the outlines of the imaginary lakes which the map contains. The Map of the Public Lands of Maine and Massachusetts is the only one I have seen that at all deserves the name. It was while we were engaged in this operation that our companions arrived. They had seen the Indians' fire on the Five Islands, and so we concluded that all was right.

Early the next morning we had mounted our packs, and prepared for a tramp up the West Branch, my companion having turned his horse out to pasture for a week or ten days, thinking that a bite of fresh grass, and a taste of running water would do him as much good as backwoods fare and new country influences his master. Leaping over a fence, we began to follow an obscure trail up the northern bank of the Penobscot. There was now no road further, the river being the only highway, and but half a dozen log-huts confined to its banks, to be met with for thirty miles. On either hand, and beyond, was a wholly uninhabited wilderness, stretching to Canada. Neither horse nor cow, nor vehicle of any kind, had ever passed over this ground; the cattle, and the few bulky articles which the loggers use, being got up in the winter on the ice, and down again before it breaks up. The evergreen woods had a decidedly sweet and bracing fragrance; the air was a sort of diet-drink, and we walked on buoyantly in Indian file, stretching our legs. Occasionally there was a small opening on the bank, made for the purpose of log-rolling, where we got a sight of the river,—always a rocky and rippling stream. The roar of the rapids, the note of a whistler-duck on the river, of the jay and chickadee around us, and of the pigeon-woodpecker in the openings, were the sounds that we heard. This was what you might call a bran-new country; the only roads were of Nature's making, and the few houses were camps. Here, then, one could no longer accuse institutions and society, but must front the true source of evil.

There are three classes of inhabitants who either frequent or inhabit the country which we had now entered;—first, the loggers, who, for a part of the year, the winter and spring, are far the most numerous, but in the summer, except a few explorers for timber, completely desert it; second, the few settlers I have named, the only permanent inhabitants, who live on the verge of it, and help raise supplies for the former; third, the hunters, mostly Indians, who range over it in their season.

At the end of three miles we came to the Mattaseunk stream and mill, where there was even a rude wooden railroad running down to the Penobscot, the last railroad we were to see. We crossed one tract, on the bank of the river, of more than a hundred acres of heavy timber, which had just been felled and burnt over, and was still smoking. Our trail lay through the midst of it, and was wellnigh blotted out. The trees lay at full length, four or five feet deep, and crossing each other in all directions, all black as charcoal, but perfectly sound within, still good for fuel or for timber; soon they would be cut into lengths and burnt again. Here were thousands of cords, enough to keep the poor of Boston and New York amply warm for a winter, which only cumbered the ground and were in the settler's way. And the whole of that solid and interminable forest is doomed to be gradually devoured thus by fire, like shavings, and no man be warmed by it. At Crocker's log-hut, at the mouth of Salmon River, seven miles from the Point, one of the party commenced distributing a store of small, cent picture-books among the children, to teach them to read, and also newspapers, more or less recent, among the parents, than which nothing can be more acceptable to a backwoods people. It was really an important item in our outfit, and, at times, the only currency that would circulate. I walked through Salmon River with my shoes on, it being low water, but not without wetting my feet. A few miles farther we came to "Marm Howard's," at the end of an extensive clearing, where there were two or three log-huts in sight at once, one on the opposite side of the river, and a few graves, even surrounded by a wooden paling, where already the rude forefathers of *a* hamlet lie, and a thousand years hence, perchance, some poet will write his "Elegy in a Country Churchyard." The "Village Hampdens," the "mute, inglorious Miltons," and Cromwells, "guiltless of" their "country's blood," were yet unborn.

> "Perchance in this *wild* spot *there will be* laid
> Some heart once pregnant with celestial fire;
> Hands that the rod of empire might have swayed,
> Or waked to ecstasy the living lyre."

The next house was Fisk's, ten miles from the Point at the mouth of the East Branch, opposite to the island Nicketow, or the Forks, the last of the Indian islands. I am particular to give the names of the settlers and the distances, since every log-hut in these woods is a public house, and such information is of no little consequence to those who may have occasion to travel this way. Our course here crossed the Penobscot, and followed the southern bank. One of the party, who entered the house in search of some one to set us over, reported a very neat dwelling, with plenty of books, and a new wife, just imported from Boston, wholly new to the woods. We found the East Branch a large and rapid stream at its mouth, and much deeper than it appeared. Having with some difficulty discovered the trail again, we kept up the south side of the West Branch, or main river, passing by some rapids called Rock-Ebeeme, the roar of which we heard through the woods, and, shortly after, in the thickest of the wood, some empty loggers' camps, still new, which were occupied the previous winter. Though we saw a few more afterwards, I will make one account serve for all. These were such houses as the lumberers of Maine spend the winter in, in the wilderness. There were the camps and the hovels for the cattle, hardly distinguishable, except that the latter had no chimney. These camps were about twenty feet long by fifteen wide, built of logs,—hemlock, cedar, spruce or yellow birch,—one kind alone, or all together, with the bark on; two or three large ones first, one directly above another, and notched together at the ends, to the height of tree or four feet, then of smaller logs resting upon transverse ones at the ends, each of the last successively shorter than the other, to form the roof. The chimney was an oblong square hole in the middle, three or four feet in diameter, with a fence of logs as high as the ridge. The interstices were filled with moss, and the roof wsa shingled with long and handsome splints of cedar, or spruce, or pine, rifted with a sledge and cleaver. The fire-place, the most important place of all, was in shape and size like the chimney, and directly under it, defined by a log fence or fender on the ground, and a heap of ashes, a foot or two deep within, with solid benches of split logs running round it. Here the fire usually melts the snow, and dries the rain before it can descend to quench it. The faded beds of arborvitae leaves extended under the eaves on either hand. There was the place for the water-pail, pork-barrel, and wash-basin, and generally a dingy pack of cards left on a log. Usually a good deal of whittling was expended on the latch, which was made of wood, in the form of an iron one. These houses are made comfortable by the huge fires, which can be afforded night and day. Usually the scenery about them is drear and savage enough; and the loggers' camp is as completely in the woods as a fungus at the foot of a pine in a swamp; no outlook but to the sky overhead; no more clearing than is made by cutting down the trees of which it is built, and those which are necessary for fuel. If only it be well sheltered and convenient to his work, and near a spring, he wastes no thought on the prospect. They are very proper forest houses, the stems of the trees collected together and piled up around a man to keep out wind and rain,—made of living green logs, hanging with moss and lichen, and with the curls and fringes of the yellow-birch bark, and dripping with resin, fresh and moist, and redolent of swampy odors, with that sort of vigor and perennialness even about them that toadstools suggest.[1] The logger's fare consists of tea, molasses, flour, pork (sometimes beef), and beans. A great proportion of the beans raised in Massachusetts find their market here. On expeditions it is only hard bread and pork, often raw, slice upon slice, with tea or water, as the case may be.

The primitive wood is always and everywhere damp and mossy, so that I traveled constantly with the impression that I was in a swamp; and only when it was remarked that this or that tract, judging from the quality of the timber on it, would make a profitable clearing, was I reminded, that if the sun were let in it would make a dry field, like the few I had seen, at once. The best shod for the most part travel with wet feet. If the ground was so wet and spongy at this, the dryest part of a dry season, what must it be in the spring? The woods hereabouts abounded in beech and yellow birch, of which last there were some very large specimens; also spruce, cedar, fir, and hemlock; but we saw only the stumps of the white-pine here, some of them of great size, these having been already culled out, being the only tree much sought after, even as low down as this. Only a little spruce and hemlock beside had been logged here. The Eastern wood which is sold for fuel in Massachusetts all comes from below Bangor. It was the pine alone, chiefly the white-pine, that had tempted any but the hunter to precede us on this route.

Waite's farm, thirteen miles from the Point, is an extensive and elevated clearing, from which we got a fine view of the river, rippling and gleaming far beneath us. My companions had formerly had a good view of Ktaadn and the other mountains here, but to-day it was so smoky that we could see nothing of them. We could overlook an immense country of uninterrupted forest, stretching away up the East Branch toward Canada on the north and northwest, and toward the Aroostook valley on the northeast; and imagine what wild life was stirring in its midst. Here was quite a field of corn for this region, whose peculiar dry scent we perceived a third of a mile off, before we saw it.

Eighteen miles from the Point brought us in sight of McCauslin's, or "Uncle George's," as he was familiarly called by my companions, to whom he was well known, where we intended to break our long fast. His house was in the midst of an extensive clearing of intervale, at the mouth of the Little Schoodic River, on the opposite or north bank of the Penobscot. So we collected on a point of the shore, that we might be seen, and fired our gun as a signal, which brought out his dogs forthwith, and thereafter their master, who in due time took us across in his batteau. This clearing was bounded abruptly, on all sides but the river, by the naked stems of the forest, as if you were to cut only a few feet square in the midst of a thousand acres of mowing, and set down a thimble therein. He had a whole heaven and horizon to himself, and the sun seemed to be journeying over his clearing only the livelong day. Here we concluded to spend the night, and wait for

[1]Springer, in his *Forest Life* (1851), says that they first remove the leaves and turf from the spot where they intend to build a camp, for fear of fire; also, that "the spruce-tree is generally selected for camp-building, it being light, straight, and quite free from sap;" that "the root is finally covered with the boughs of the fir, spruce, and hemlock, so that when the snow falls upon the whole, the warmth of the camp is preserved in the coldest weather;" and that they make the log seat before the fire, called the "Deacon's Seat," of a spruce or fir split in halves, with three or four stout limbs left on one side for legs, which are not likely to get loose.

the Indians, as there was no stopping-place so convenient above. He had seen no Indians pass, and this did not often happen without his knowledge. He thought that his dogs sometimes gave notice of the approach of Indians half an hour before they arrived.

McCauslin was a Kennebec man, of Scotch descent, who had been a waterman twenty-two years, and had driven on the lakes and head-waters of the Penobscot five or six springs in succession, but was now settled here to raise supplies for the lumberers and for himself. He entertained us a day or two with true Scotch hospitality, and would accept no recompense for it. A man of a dry wit and shrewdness, and a general intelligence which I had not looked for in the backwoods. In fact, the deeper you penetrate into the woods, the more intelligent, and, in one sense, less countrified do you find the inhabitants; for always the pioneer has been a traveler, and, to some extent, a man of the world; and, as the distances with which he is familiar are greater, so is his information more general and far reaching than the villagers. If I were to look for a narrow, uninformed, and countrified mind, as opposed to the intelligence and refinement which are thought to emanate from cities, it would be among the rusty inhabitants of an old-settled country, on farms all run out and gone to seed with life-everlasting, in the towns about Boston, even on the high-road in Concord, and not in the backwoods of Maine.

Supper was got before our eyes in the ample kitchen, by a fire which would have roasted an ox; many whole logs, four feet long, were consumed to boil our tea-kettle,—birch, or beech, or maple, the same summer and winter; and the dishes were soon smoking on the table, late the arm-chair, against the wall, from which one of the party was expelled. The arms of the chair formed the frame on which the table rested; and, when the round top was turned up against the wall, it formed the back of the chair, and was no more in the way than the wall itself. This, we noticed, was the prevailing fashion in these log-houses, in order to economize in room. There were piping-hot wheaten cakes, the flour having been brought up the river in batteaux,—no Indian bread, for the upper part of Maine, it will be remembered, is a wheat country,—and ham, eggs, and potatoes, and milk and cheese, the produce of the farm; and also shad and salmon, tea sweetened with molasses, and sweet cakes, in contradistinction to the hot cakes not sweetened, the one white, the other yellow, to wind up with. Such we found was the prevailing fare, ordinary and extraordinary, along this river. Mountain cranberries (*Vaccinium Vitis-Idaea*), stewed and sweetened, were the common dessert. Everything here was in profusion, and the best of its kind. Butter was in such plenty that it was commonly used, before it was salted, to grease boots with.

In the night we were entertained by the sound of rain-drops on the cedar-splints which covered the roof, and awaked the next morning with a drop or two in our eyes. It had set in for a storm, and we made up our minds not to forsake such comfortable quarters with this prospect, but wait for Indians and fair weather. It rained and drizzled and gleamed by turns, the livelong day. What we did there, how we killed the time would perhaps be idle to tell; how many times we buttered our boots, and how often a drowsy one was seen to sidle off to the bedroom. When it held up, I strolled up and down the bank, and gathered the harebell and cedar-berries, which grew there; or else we tried by turns the long-handled axe on the logs before the door. The axe-helves here were made to chop standing on the log,—a primitive log of course,—and were, therefore, nearly a foot longer than with us. One while we walked over the farm and visited his well-filled barns with McCauslin. There were one other man and two women only here. He kept horses, cows, oxen, and sheep. I think he said that he was the first to bring a plough and a cow so far; and he might have added the last, with only two exceptions. The potato-rot had found him out here, too, the previous year, and got half or two thirds of his crop, though the seed was of his own raising. Oats, grass, and potatoes were his staples; but he raised also, a few carrots and turnips, and "a little corn for the hens," for this was all that he dared risk, for fear that it would not ripen. Melons, squashes, sweet-corn, beans, tomatoes, and many other vegetables, could not be ripened there.

The very few settlers along this stream were obviously tempted by the cheapness of the land mainly. When I asked McCauslin why more settlers did not come in, he answered, that one reason was, they could not buy the land, it belonged to individuals or companies who were afraid that their wild lands would be settled, and so incorporated into towns, and they be taxed for them; but to settling on the States' land there was no such hindrance. For his own part, he wanted no neighbors,—he didn't wish to see any road by his house. Neighbors, even the best, were a trouble and expense, especially on the score of cattle and fences. They might live across the river, perhaps, but not on the same side.

The chickens here were protected by the dogs. As McCauslin said, "The old one took it up first, and she taught the pup, and now they had got it into their heads that it wouldn't do to have anything of the bird kind on the premises." A hawk hovering over was not allowed to alight, but barked off by the dogs circling underneath; and a pigeon, or a "yellow-hammer," as they called the pigeon-woodpecker, on a dead limb or stump, was instantly expelled. It was the main business of their day, and kept them constantly coming and going. One would rush out of the house on the least alarm given by the other.

When it rained hardest, we returned to the house, and took down a tract from the shelf. There was the "Wandering Jew," cheap edition, and fine print, the "Criminal Calendar," and "Parish's Geography," and flash novels two or three. Under the pressure of circumstances, we read a little in these. With such aid, the press is not so feeble an engine, after all. This house, which was a fair specimen of those on this river, was built of huge logs, which peeped out everywhere, and were chinked with clay and moss. It contained four or five rooms. There were no sawed boards, or shingles, or clapboards, about it; and scarcely any tool but the axe had been used in its construction. The partitions were made of long clapboard-like splints, of spruce or cedar, turned to a delicate salmon color by the smoke. The roof and sides were covered with the same, instead of shingles and clapboards, and some of a much thicker and larger size were used for the floor. These were all so straight and smooth, that they answered the purpose admirably, and a careless observer would not have suspected that they were not sawed and planed. The chimney and hearth were of vast size, and made of stone. The broom was a few twigs of arborvitae tied to a stick; and a pole was suspended over the hearth, close to the ceilings, to dry stockings and clothes on. I noticed that the floor was full of small, dingy holes, as if made with a gimlet, but which were, in fact, made by the spikes, nearly an inch long, which the lumberers wear in their boots to prevent their slipping on wet logs. Just above McCauslin's, there is a rocky rapid, where logs jam in the spring; and many "drivers" are there collected, who frequent his house for supplies; these were their tracks which I saw.

At sundown McCauslin pointed away over the forest, across the river, to signs of fair weather amid the clouds,—some evening redness there. For even there the points of compass held; and there was a quarter of the heavens appropriated to sunrise and another to sunset.

The next morning, the weather proving fair enough for our purpose, we prepared to start, and, the Indians having failed us, persuaded McCauslin, who was not unwilling to revisit the scenes of his driving, to accompany us in their stead, intending to engage one other boatman on the way. A strip of cotton cloth for a tent, a couple of blankets, which would suffice for the whole party, fifteen pounds of hard bread, ten pounds of "clear" pork, and a little tea, made up "Uncle George's" pack. The last three articles were calculated to be provision enough for six men for a week, with what we might pick up. A tea-kettle, a frying-pan, and an axe, to be obtained at the last house, would complete our outfit.

We were soon out of McCauslin's clearing, and in the ever green woods again. The obscure trail made by the two settlers above, which even the woodman is sometimes puzzled to discern, erelong crossed a narrow, open strip in the woods overrun with weeds, called the Burnt Land, where a fire had raged formerly, stretching northward nine or ten miles, to Millinocket Lake. At the end of three miles, we reached Shad Pond, or Noliseemack, an expansion of the river. Hodge, the Assistant State Geologist, who passed through this on the 25th of June, 1837, says, "We pushed our boat through an acre or more of buck-beans, which had taken root at the bottom, and bloomed above the surface in the greatest profusion and beauty." Thomas Fowler's house is four miles from McCauslin's, on the shore of the pond, at the mouth of the Millinocket River, and eight miles from the lake of the same name, on the latter stream. This lake affords a more direct course to Ktaadn, but we preferred to follow the Penobscot and the Pamadumcook lakes. Fowler was just completing a new log-hut, and was sawing out a window through the logs, nearly two feet thick, when we arrived. He had begun to paper his house with spruce-bark, turned inside out, which had a good effect, and was in keeping with the circumstances. Instead of water we got here a draught of beer, which, it was allowed, would be better; clear and thin, but strong and stringent as the cedar-sap. It was as if we sucked at the very teats of Nature's pine-clad bosom in these parts,—the sap of all Millinocket botany commingled,—the topmost, most fantastic, and spiciest sprays of the primitive wood, and whatever invigorating and stringent gum or essence it afforded steeped and dissolved in it,—a lumberer's drink, which would acclimate and naturalize a man at once,—which would make him see green, and, if he slept, dream that he heard the wind sough among the pines. Here was a fife, praying to be played on, through which we breathed a few tuneful strains,—brought hither to tame wild beasts. As we stood upon the pile of chips by the door, fish-hawks were sailing overhead; and here, over Shad Pond, might daily be witnessed the tyranny of the bald-eagle over that bird. Tom pointed away over the lake to a bald-eagle's nest, which was plainly visible more than a mile off, on a pine, high above the surrounding forest, and was frequented from year to year by the same pair, and held sacred by him. There were these two houses only there, his low hut and the eagles' airy cart-load of fagots. Thomas Fowler, too, was persuaded to join us, for two men were necessary to manage the batteau, which was soon to be our carriage, and these men needed to be cool and skillful for the navigation of the Penobscot. Tom's pack was soon made, for he had not far to look for his waterman's boots, and a red flannel shirt. This is the favorite color with lumbermen; and red flannel is reputed to possess some mysterious virtues, to be most healthful and convenient in respect to perspiration. In every gang there will be a large proportion of red birds. We took here a poor and leaky batteau, and began to pole up the Millinocket two miles, to the elder Fowler's, in order to avoid the Grand Falls of the Penobscot, intending to exchange our batteau there for a better. The Millinocket is a small, shallow, and sandy stream, full of what I took to be lamprey-eels' or suckers' nests, and lined with musquash cabins, but free from rapids, according to Fowler, excepting at its outlet from the lake. He was at this time engaged in cutting the native grass—rush-grass and meadow-clover, as he called it—on the meadows and small, low islands of this stream. We noticed flattened places in the grass on either side, where, he said, a moose had laid down the night before, adding, that there were thousands in these meadows.

Old Fowler's, on the Millinocket, six miles from McCauslin's, and twenty-four from the Point, is the last house. Gibson's, on the Sowadnehunk, is the only clearing above, but that had proved a failure, and was long since deserted. Fowler is the oldest inhabitant of these woods. He formerly lived a few miles from here, on the south side of the West Branch, where he built his house sixteen years ago, the first house built above the Five Islands. Here our new batteau was to be carried over the first portage of two miles, round the Grand Falls of the Penobscot, on a horse-sled made of saplings, to jump the numerous rocks in the way; but we had to wait a couple of hours for them to catch the horses, which were pastured at a distance, amid the stumps, and had wandered still farther off. The last of the salmon for this season had just been caught, and were still fresh in pickle, from which enough was extracted to fill our empty kettle, and so graduate our introduction to simpler forest fare. The week before they had lost nine sheep here out of their first flock, by the wolves. The surviving sheep came round the house, and seemed frightened, which induced them to go and look for the rest, when they found seven dead and lacerated, and two still alive. These last they carried to the house, and, as Mrs. Fowler said, they were merely scratched in the throat, and had no more visible wound than would be produced by the prick of a pin. She sheared off the wool from their throats, and washed them, and put on some salve, and turned them out, but in a few moments they were missing, and had not been found since. In fact, they were all poisoned, and those that were found swelled up at once, so that they saved neither skin nor wool. This realized the old fables of the wolves and the sheep, and convinced me that that ancient hostility still existed. Verily, the shepherd-boy did not need to sound a false alarm this time. There were steel traps by the door, of various sizes, for wolves, otter, and bears, with large claws instead of teeth, to catch in their sinews. Wolves are frequently killed with poisoned bait.

At length, after we had dined here on the usual backwoods fare, the horses arrived, and we hauled our batteau out of the water, and lashed it to its wicker carriage, and, throwing in our packs, walked on before, leaving the boatmen and driver, who was Tom's brother, to manage the concern. The route, which led through the wild pasture where the sheep were killed, was in some places the roughest ever traveled by horses, over rocky hills, where the sled bounced and slid along, like a vessel pitching in a storm; and one man was as necessary to stand at the stern, to prevent the boat from being wrecked, as a helmsman in the roughest sea. The philosophy of our progress was something like this: when the runners struck a rock three or four feet high, the sled bounced back and upwards at the same time; but, as the horses never ceased pulling, it came down on the top of the rock, and so we got over. This portage probably followed the trail of an ancient Indian carry round these falls. By two o'clock we, who had walked on before, reached the river above the falls, not far from the outlet of Quakish Lake, and waited for the batteau to come up. We had been here but a short time, when a thunder-shower was seen coming up from the west, over the still invisible lakes, and that pleasant wilderness which we were so eager to become acquainted with; and soon the heavy drops began to patter on the leaves around us. I had just selected the prostrate trunk of a huge pine, five or six feet in diameter, and was crawling under it, when, luckily, the boat arrived. It would have amused a sheltered man to witness the manner in which it was unlashed, and whirled over, while the first water-spout burst upon us. It was no sooner in the hands of the eager company than it was abandoned to the first revolutionary impulse, and to gravity, to adjust it; and they might have been seen all stooping to its shelter, and wriggling under like so many eels, before it was fairly deposited on the ground. When all were under, we propped up the lee side, and busied ourselves there whittling thole-pins for rowing, when we should reach the lakes; and made the woods ring, between the claps of thunder, with such boat-songs as we could remember. The horses stood sleek and shining with the rain, all drooping and crestfallen, while deluge after deluge washed over us; but the bottom of a boat may be relied on for a tight roof. At length, after two hours' delay at this place, a streak of fair weather appeared in the northwest, whither our course now lay, promising a serene evening for our voyage; and the driver returned with his horses, while we made haste to launch our boat, and commence our voyage in good earnest.

There were six of us, including the two boatmen. With our packs heaped up near the bows, and ourselves disposed as baggage to trim the boat, with instructions not to move in case we should strike a rock, more than so many barrels of pork, we pushed out into the first rapid, a slight specimen of the stream we had to navigate. With Uncle George in the stern, and Tom in the bows, each using a spruce pole about twelve feet long, pointed with iron,[1] and poling on the same side, we shot up the rapids like a salmon, the water rushing and roaring around, so that only a practiced eye could distinguish a safe course, or tell what was deep water and what rocks, frequently grazing the latter on one or both sides, with a hundred as narrow escapes as ever the Argo had in passing through the Symplegades. I, who had had some experience in boating, had never experienced any half so exhilarating before. We were lucky to have exchanged our Indians, whom we did not know, for these men, who, together with Tom's brother, were reputed the best boatmen on the river, and were at once indispensable pilots and pleasant companions. The canoe is smaller, more easily upset, and sooner worn out; and the Indian is said not to be so skillful in the management of the batteau. He is, for the most part, less to be relied on, and more disposed to sulks and whims. The utmost familiarity with dead streams, or with the ocean, would not prepare a man for this peculiar navigation; and the most skillful boatman anywhere else would here be obliged to take out his boat and carry round a hundred times, still with great risk, as well as delay, where the practiced batteau-man poles up with comparative ease and safety. The hardy "voyageur'" pushes with incredible perseverance and success quite up to the foot of the falls, and then only carries round some perpendicular ledge, and launches again in

> "The torrent's smoothness, ere it dash below,"

to struggle with the boiling rapids above. The Indians say that the river once ran both ways, one half up and the other down, but that, since the white man came, it all runs down, and now they must laboriously pole their canoes against the stream, and carry them over numerous portages. In the summer, all stores—the grindstone and the plough of the pioneer, flour, pork, and utensils for the explorer,—must be conveyed up the river in batteaux; and many a cargo and many a boatman is lost in these waters. In the winter, however, which is very equable and long, the ice is the great highway, and the loggers' team penetrates to Chesuncook Lake, and still higher up, even two hundred miles above Bangor. Imagine the solitary sled-track running far up into the snowy and ever-green wilderness, hemmed in closely for a hundred miles by the forest, and again stretching straight across the broad surfaces of concealed lakes!

We were soon in the smooth water of the Quakish Lake, and took our turns at rowing and paddling across it. It is a small, irregular, but handsome lake, shut in on all sides by the forest, and showing no traces of man but some low boom in a distant cove, reserved for spring use. The spruce and cedar on its shores, hung with gray lichens, looked at a distance

[1] The Canadians call it *picquer de fond.*

like the ghosts of trees. Ducks were sailing here and there on its surface, and a solitary loon, like a more living wave,—a vital spot on the lake's surface,—laughed and frolicked, and showed its straight leg, for our amusement. Joe Merry Mountain appeared in the northwest, as if it were looking down on this lake especially; and we had our first but a partial view of Ktaadn, its summit veiled in clouds, like a dark isthmus in that quarter, connecting the heavens with the earth. After two miles of smooth rowing across this lake, we found ourselves in the river again, which was a continuous rapid for one mile, to the dam requiring all the strength and skill of our boatmen to pole up it.

This dam is a quite important and expensive work for this country, whither cattle and horses cannot penetrate in the summer, raising the whole river ten feet, and flooding, as they said, some sixty square miles by means of the innumerable lakes with which the river connects. It is a lofty and solid structure, with sloping piers, some distance above, made of frames of logs filled with stones, to break the ice.[1] Here every log pays toll as it passes through the sluices.

We filed into the rude loggers' camp at this place, such as I have described, without ceremony, and the cook, at that moment the sole occupant, at once set about preparing tea for his visitors. His fireplace, which the rain had converted into a mud-puddle, was soon blazing again, and we sat down on the log benches around it to dry us. On the well-flattened and somewhat faded beds of arbor-vitae leaves, which stretched on either hand under the eaves behind us, lay an odd leaf of the Bible, some genealogical chapter out of the Old Testament; and, half buried by the leaves, we found Emerson's Address on West India Emancipation, which had been left here formerly by one of our company, and *had made two converts to the Liberty party here*, as I was told; also, an odd number of the Westminster Review, for 1834, and a pamphlet entitled History of the Erection of the Monument on the grave of Myron Holly. This was the readable or reading matter in a lumberer's camp in the Maine woods, thirty miles form a road, which would be given up to the bears in a fortnight. These things were well thumbed and soiled. This gang was headed by one John Morrison, a good specimen of a Yankee; and was necessarily composed of men not bred to the business of dam-building, but who were Jacks-at-all-trades, handy with the axe, and other simple implements, and well skilled in wood and water craft. We had hot cakes for our supper even here, white as snowballs, but without butter, and the never-failing sweet cakes, with which we filled our pockets, foreseeing that we should not soon meet with the like again. Such delicate puff-balls seemed a singular diet for backwoodsmen. There was also tea without milk, sweetened with molasses. And so, exchanging a word with John Morrison and his gang when we had returned to the shore, and also exchanging our batteau for a better still, we made haste to improve the little daylight that remained. This camp, exactly twenty-nine miles from Mattawamkeag Point by the way we had come, and

[1]Even the Jesuit missionaires, accustomed to the St. Lawrence and other rivers of Canada, in their first expeditions to the Abenaquinois, speak of rivers *ferrees de rochers*, shod with rocks.

about one hundred from Bangor by the river, was the last human habitation of any kind in this direction. Beyond, there was no trail, and the river and lakes, by batteaux and canoes, was considered the only practicable route. We were about thirty miles by the river from the summit of Ktaadn, which was in sight, though not more than twenty, perhaps, in a straight line.

It being about the full of the moon, and a warm and pleasant evening, we decided to row five miles by moonlight to the head of the North Twin Lake, lest the wind should rise on the morrow. After one mile of river, or what the boatmen call "thoroughfare,"—for the river becomes at length only the connecting link between the lakes,—and some slight rapid which had been mostly made smooth water by the dam, we entered the North Twin Lake just after sundown, and steered across for the river "thoroughfare," four miles distant. This is a noble sheet of water, where one may get the impression which a new country and a "lake of the woods" are fitted to create. There was the smoke of no log-hut nor camp of any kind to greet us, still less was any lover of nature or musing traveler watching our batteau from the distant hills; not even the Indian hunter was there, for he rarely climbs them, but hugs the river like ourselves. No face welcomed us but the fine fantastic sprays of free and happy evergreen trees, waving one above another in their ancient home. At first the red clouds hung over the western shore as gorgeously as if over a city, and the lake lay open to the light with even a civilized aspect, as if expecting trade and commerce, and towns and villas. We could distinguish the inlet to the South Twin, which is said to be the larger, where the shore was misty and blue, and it was worth the while to look thus through a narrow opening across the entire expanse of a concealed lake to its own yet more dim and distant shore. The shores rose gently to ranges of low hills covered with forests; and though, in fact, the most valuable white-pine timber, even about this lake, had been culled out, this would never have been suspected by the voyager. The impression, which indeed corresponded with the fact, was, as if we were upon a high table-land between the States and Canada, the northern side of which is drained by the St. John and Chaudière, the southern by the Penobscot and Kennebec. There was no bold mountainous shore, as we might have expected, but only isolated hills and mountains rising here and there from the plateau. The country is an archipelago of lakes,—the lake-country of New England. Their levels vary but a few feet, and the boatmen, by short portages, or by none at all, pass easily from one to another. They say that at very high water the Penobscot and the Kennebec flow into each other, or at any rate, that you may lie with your face in the one and your toes in the other. Even the Penobscot and St. John have been connected by a canal, so that the lumber of the Allegash, instead of going down the St. John, comes down the Penobscot; and the Indian's tradition, that the Penobscot once ran both ways for his convenience, is, in one sense, partially realized to-day.

None of our party but McCauslin had been above this lake, so we trusted to him to pilot us, and we could not but confess the importance of a pilot on these waters. While it is river, you will not easily forget which way is up stream; but when you enter a lake, the river is completely lost, and you scan the distant shores in vain to find where it comes in. A stranger is, for the time at least, lost, and must set about a voyage of discovery first of all to find the river. To follow the windings of the shore when the lake is ten miles, or even more, in length, and of an irregularity which will not soon be mapped, is a wearisome voyage, and will spend his time and his provisions. They tell a story of a gang of experienced woodmen sent to a location on this stream, who were thus lost in the wilderness of lakes. They cut their way through thickets, and carried their baggage and their boats over from lake to lake, sometimes several miles. They carried into Millinocket Lake, which is on another stream, and is ten miles square, and contains a hundred islands. They explored its shores thoroughly, and then carried into another, and another, and it was a week of toil and anxiety before they found the Penobscot River again, and then their provisions were exhausted, and they were obliged to return.

While Uncle George steered for a small island near the head of the lake, now just visible, like a speck on the water, we rowed by turns swiftly over its surface, singing such boat-songs as we could remember. The shores seemed at an indefinite distance in the moon-light. Occasionally we paused in our singing and rested on our oars, while we listened to hear if the wolves howled, for this is a common serenade, and my companions affirmed that it was the most dismal and unearthly of sounds; but we heard none this time. If we did not *hear*, however, we did *listen*, not without a reasonable expectation; that at least I have to tell,—only some utterly uncivilized, big-throated owl hooted loud and dismally in the drear and boughy wilderness, plainly not nervous about his solitary life, nor afraid to hear the echoes of his voice there. We remembered also that possibly moose were silently watching us from the distant coves, or some surly bear or timid caribou had been startled by our singing. It was with new emphasis that we sang there the Canadian boat-song,—

> "Row, brothers, row, the stream runs fast,
> The Rapids are near and the daylight's past!"—

which describes precisely our own adventure, and was inspired by the experience of a similar kind of life,—for the rapids were ever near, and the daylight long past; the woods on shore looked dim, and many an Utawas' tide here emptied into the lake.

> "Why should we yet our sail unfurl?
> There is not a breath the blue wave to curl!
> But, when the wind blows off the shore,
> Oh, sweetly we'll rest our weary oar."

> "Utawas' tide! this trembling moon
> Shall see us float o'er thy surges soon."

At last we glided past the "green isle," which had been our landmark, all joining in the chorus; as if by the watery links of rivers and of lakes we were about to float over unmeasured zones of earth, bound on unimaginable adventures,—

> "Saint of this green isle! hear our prayers,
> Oh, grant us cool heavens and favoring airs!"

About nine o'clock we reached the river, and ran our boat into a natural haven between some rocks, and drew her out on the sand. This camping-ground McCauslin had been familiar with in his lumbering days, and he now struck it unerringly in the moonlight, and we heard the sound of the rill which would supply us with cool water emptying into the lake. The first business was to make a fire, an operation which was a little delayed by the wetness of the fuel and the ground, owing to the heavy showers of the afternoon. The fire is the main comfort of the camp, whether in summer or winter, and is about as ample at one season as at another. It is as well for cheerfulness as for warmth and dryness. It forms one side of the camp; one bright side at any rate. Some were dispersed to fetch in dead trees and boughs, while Uncle George felled the birches and beeches which stood convenient, and soon we had a fire some ten feet long by three our four high, which rapidly dried the sand before it. This was calculated to burn all night. We next proceeded to pitch our tent; which operation was performed by sticking our two spike-poles into the ground in a slanting direction, about ten feet apart, for rafters, and then drawing our cotton cloth over them, and tying it down at the ends, leaving it open in front, shed-fashion. But this evening the wind carried the sparks on to the tent and burned it. So we hastily drew up the batteau just within the edge of the woods before the fire, and propping up one side three or four feet high, spread the tent on the ground to lie on; and with the corner of a blanket, or what more or less we could get to put over us, lay down with our heads and bodies under the boat, and our feet and legs on the sand toward the fire. At first we lay awake, talking of our course, and finding ourselves in so convenient a posture for studying the heavens, with the moon and stars shining in our faces, our conversation naturally turned upon astronomy, and we recounted by turns the most interesting discoveries in that science. But at length we composed ourselves seriously to sleep. It was interesting, when awakened at midnight, to watch the grotesque and fiend-like forms and motions of some one of the party, who, not being able to sleep, had got up silently to arouse the fire, and add fresh fuel, for a change; now stealthily lugging a dead tree from out the dark, and heaving it on, now stirring up the embers with his fork, or tiptoeing about to observe the stars, watched, perchance, by half the prostrate party in breathless silence; so much the more intense because they were awake, while each supposed his neighbor sound asleep. Thus aroused, I, too, brought fresh fuel to the fire, and then rambled along the sandy shore in the moonlight, hoping to meet a moose come down to drink, or else a wolf. The little rill tinkled the louder, and peopled all the wilderness for me; and the glassy smoothness of the sleeping lake, laving the shores of a new world, with the dark, fantastic rocks rising here and there from its surface, made a scene not easily described. It has left such an impression of stern, yet gentle, wildness on my memory as will not soon be effaced. Not far from midnight we were one after another awakened by rain falling on our extremities; and as each was made aware of the fact by cold or wet, he drew a long sigh and then drew up his legs, until gradually we had all sidled round from lying at right angles with the boat, till our bodies formed an acute angle with it, and were wholly protected. When next we awoke, the moon and stars were shining again, and there were signs of dawn in the east. I have been thus particular in order to convey some idea of a night in the woods.

We had soon launched and loaded our boat, and, leaving our fire blazing, were off again before breakfast. The lumberers rarely trouble themselves to put out their fires, such is the dampness of the primitive forest; and this is one cause, no doubt, of the frequent fires in Maine, of which we hear so much on smoky days in Massachusetts. The forests are held cheap after the white-pine has been culled out; and the explorers and hunters pray for rain only to clear the atmosphere of smoke. The woods were so wet to-day, however, that there was no danger of our fire spreading. After poling up half a mile of river, or thoroughfare, we rowed a mile across the foot of Pamadumcook Lake, which is the name given on the map to this whole chain of lakes, as if there was but one, though they are, in each instance,distinctly separated by a reach of the river, with its narrow and rocky channel and its rapids. This lake, which is one of the largest, stretched northwest ten miles, to hills and mountains in the distance. McCauslin pointed to some distant, and as yet inaccessible, forests of white-pine, on the sides of a mountain in that direction. The Joe Merry Lakes, which lay between us and Moosehead, on the west, were recently, if they are not still, "surrounded by some of the best timbered land in the State." By another thoroughfare we passed into Deep Cove, a part of the same lake, which makes up two miles, toward the northeast, and rowing two miles across this, by another short thoroughfare, entered Ambejijis Lake.

At the entrance to a lake we sometimes observed what is technically called "fencing stuff," or the unhewn timbers of which booms are formed, either secured together in the water, or laid up on the rocks and lashed to trees, for spring use. But it was always startling to discover so plain a trail of civilized man there. I remember that I was strangely affected, when we were returning, by the sight of a ring-bolt well drilled into a rock, and fastened with lead, at the head of this solitary Ambejijis Lake.

It was easy to see that driving logs must be an exciting as well as arduous and dangerous business. All winter long the logger goes on piling up the trees which he has trimmed and hauled in some dry ravine at the head of a stream, and then in the spring he stands on the bank and whistles for Rain and Thaw, ready to wring the perspiration out of his shirt to swell the tide, till suddenly, with a whoop and halloo from him, shutting his eyes, as if to bid farewell to the existing state of things, a fair proportion of his winter's work goes scrambling down the country, followed by his faithful dogs, Thaw and Rain and Freshet and Wind, the whole pack in full cry, toward the

Orono Mills. Every log is marked with the owner's name, cut in the sapwood with an axe or bored with an auger, so deep as not to be worn off in the driving, and yet not so as to injure the timber; and it requires considerable ingenuity to invent new and simple marks where there are so many owners. They have quite an alphabet of their own, which only the practised can read. One of my companions read off from his memorandum book some marks of his own logs, among which there were crosses, belts, crow's feet, girdles, etc., as, "Y—girdle—crow-foot," and various other devices. When the logs have run the gauntlet of innumerable rapids and falls, each on its own account, with more or less jamming and bruising, those bearing various owners' marks being mixed up together,—since all must take advantage of the same freshet,—they are collected together at the heads of the lakes, and surrounded by a boom fence of floating logs, to prevent their being dispersed by the wind, and are thus towed all together, like a flock of sheep, across the lake, where there is no current, by a windlass, or boom-head, such as we sometimes saw standing on an island or headland, and, if circumstances permit, with the aid of sails and oars. Sometimes, notwithstanding, the logs are dispersed over many miles of lake surface in a few hours by winds and freshets, and thrown up on distant shroes, where the driver can pick up only one or two at a time, and return with them to the thoroughfare; and before he gets his flock well through Ambejijis or Pamadumcook, he makes many a wet and uncomfortable camp on the shore. He must be able to navigate a log as if it were a canoe, and be as indifferent to cold and wet as a muskrat. He uses a few efficient tools,—a lever commonly of rock-maple, six or seven feet long, with a stout spike in it, strongly ferruled on, and a long spike-pole, with a screw at the end of the spike to make it hold. The boys along shore learn to walk on floating logs as city boys on sidewalks. Sometimes the logs are thrown up on rocks in such positions as to be irrecoverable but by another freshet as high, or they jam together at rapids and falls, and accumulate in vast piles, which the driver must start at the risk of his life. Such is the lumber business, which depends on many accidents, as the early freezing of the rivers, that the teams may get up in season, a sufficient freshet in the spring, to fetch the logs down, and many others.[1] I quote Michaux on Lumbering on the Kennebec, then the sources of the best white-pine lumber carried to England. "The persons engaged in this branch of industry are generally emigrants from New Hampshire. . . .In the summer they unite in small companies, and traverse these vast solitudes in every direction, to ascertain the places in which the pines abound. After cutting the grass and converting it into hay for the nourishment of the cattle to be employed in their labor, they return home. In the beginning of the winter they enter the forests again, establish themselves in huts covered with the bark of the canoe-birch, or the arbor-vitae; and, though the cold is so intense that the mercury sometimes remains for several weeks from 40° to 50° [Fahr.] below

[1]"A steady current or pitch of water is preferable to one either rising or diminishing; as, when rising rapidly, the water at the middle of the river is considerably higher than at the shores,—so much so as to be distinctly perceived by the eye of a spectator on the banks, presenting an appearance like a turnpike road. The lumber, therefore, is always sure to incline from the centre of the channel toward either shore."—Springer.

the point of congelation, they persevere, with unabated courage, in their work." According to Springer, the company consists of choppers, swampers,—who make roads,—barker and loader, teamster, and cook. "When the trees are felled, they cut them into logs from fourteen to eighteen feet long, and, by means of their cattle, which they employ with great dexterity, drag them to the river, and, after stamping on them a mark of property, roll them on its frozen bosom. At the breaking of the ice, in the spring, they float down with the current. . . .The logs that are not drawn the first year," adds Michaux, "are attacked by large worms, which form holes about two lines in diameter, in every direction; but, if stripped of their bark, they will remain uninjured for thirty years."

Ambejijis, this quiet Sunday morning, struck me as the most beautiful lake we had seen. It is said to be one of the deepest. We had the fairest view of Joe Merry, Double Top, and Ktaadn, from its surface. The summit of the latter had a singularly flat, table-land appearance, like a short highway, where a demigod might be let down to take a turn or two in an afternoon, to settle his dinner. We rowed a mile and a half to near the head of the lake, and, pushing through a field of lily-pads, landed, to cook our breakfast, by the side of a large rock, known to McCauslin. Our breakfast consisted of tea, with hardbread and pork, and fried salmon, which we ate with forks neatly whittled from alder-twigs, which grew there, off strips of birch-bark for plates. The tea was black tea, without milk to color or sugar to sweeten it, and two tin dippers were our teacups. This beverage is as indispensable to the loggers as to any gossiping old women in the land, and they, no doubt, derive great comfort from it. Here was the site of an old logger's camp, remembered by McCauslin, now over-grown with weeds and bushes. In the midst of a dense underwood we noticed a whole brick, on a rock, in a small run, clean and red and square as in a brick-yard, which had been brought thus far formerly for tamping. Some of us afterward regretted that we had not carried this on with us to the top of the mountain, to be left there for our mark. It would certainly have been a simple evidence of civilized man. McCauslin said that large wooden crosses, made of oak, still sound, were sometimes found standing in this wilderness, which were set up by the first Catholic missionaries who came through to the Kennebec.

In the next nine miles, which were the extent of our voyage, and which it took us the rest of the day to get over, we rowed across several small lakes, poled up numerous rapids and thoroughfares, and carried over four portages. I will give the names and distances, for the benefit of future tourists. First, after leaving Ambejijis Lake, we had a quarter of a mile of rapids to the portage, or carry of ninety rods around Ambejijis Falls; then a mile and a half through Passamagamet Lake, which is narrow and river-like, to the falls of the same name,—Ambejijis stream coming in on the right; then two miles through Katepskonegan Lake to the portage of ninety rods around Katepskonegan Falls, which name signifies "carrying-place,"—Passamagamet stream coming in on the left; then three miles through Pockwockomus Lake, a slight expansion of the river, to the portage of forty rods around the falls of the same name,—Katepskonegan stream coming in on the left; then three quarters of a mile through Aboljacarmegus Lake, similar to the last, to the portage of forty rods around the falls of the same name; then half a mile of rapid water to the Sowadnehunk dead-water, and the Aboljacknagesic stream.

This is generally the order of names as you ascend the river: First, the lake, or, if there is no expansion, the dead-water; then the falls; then the stream emptying into the lake, or river above, all of the same name. First we came to Passamagamet Lake, then to Passamagamet Falls, then to Passamagamet stream, emptying in. This order and identity of names, it will be perceived, is quite philosophical, since the dead-water or lake is always at least partially produced by the stream emptying in above; and the first fall below, which is the outlet of that lake, and where that tributary water makes its first plunge, also naturally bears the same name.

At the portage around Ambejijis Falls I observed a pork-barrel on the shore, with a hole eight or nine inches square cut in one side, which was set against an upright rock; but the bears, without turning or upsetting the barrel, had gnawed a hole in the opposite side, which looked exactly like an enormous rat-hole, big enough to put their heads in; and at the bottom of the barrel were still left a few mangled and slabbered slices of pork. It is usual for the lumberers to leave such supplies as they cannot conveniently carry along with them at carries or camps, to which the next comers do not scruple to help themselves, they being the property, commonly, not of an individual, but a company, who can afford to deal liberally.

I will describe particularly how we got over some of these portages and rapids, in order that the reader may get an idea of the boatman's life. At Ambejijis Falls, for instance, there was the roughest path imaginable cut through the woods; at first up hill, at an angle of nearly forty-five degrees, over rocks and logs without end. This was the manner of the portage. We first carried over our baggage, and deposited it on the shore at the other end; then, returning to the batteau, we dragged it up the hill by the painter, and onward, with frequent pauses, over half the portage. But this was a bungling way, and would soon have worn out the boat. Commonly, three men walk over with a batteau weighing from three to five or six hundred pounds on their heads and shoulders, the tallest standing under the middle of the boat, which is turned over, and one at each end, or else there are two at the bows. More cannot well take hold at once. But this requires some practice, as well as strength, and is in any case extremely laborious, and wearing to the constitution, to follow. We were, on the whole, rather an invalid party, and could render our boatmen but little assistance. Our two men at length took the batteau upon their shoulders, and, while two of us steadied it, to prevent it from rocking and wearing into their shoulders, on which they placed their hats folded, walked bravely over the remaining distance, with two or three pauses. In the same manner they accomplished the other portages. With this crushing weight they must climb and stumble along over fallen trees and slippery rocks of all sizes, where those who walked by the sides were continually brushed off, such was the narrowness of the path. But we were fortunate not to have to cut our path in the first place. Before we launched our boat, we scraped the bottom smooth again, with our knives, where it had rubbed on the rocks, to save friction.

To avoid the difficulties of the portage, our men determined to "warp up" the Passamagamet Falls; so while the rest walked over the portage with the baggage, I remained in the batteau, to assist in warping up. We were soon in the midst of the rapids, which were more swift and tumultuous than any we had poled up, and had turned to the side of the stream for the purpose of warping, when the boatmen, who felt some pride in their skill, and were ambitious to do something more than usual, for my benefit, as I surmised, took one more view of the rapids, or rather the falls; and, in answer to our question, whether we couldn't get up there, the other answered that he guessed he'd try it. So we pushed again into the midst of the stream, and began to struggle with the current. I sat in the middle of the boat to trim it, moving slightly to the right or left as it grazed a rock. With an uncertain and wavering motion we wound and bolted our way up, until the bow was actually raised two feet above the stern at the steepest pitch; and then, when everything depended upon his exertions, the bowman's pole snapped in two; but before he had time to take the spare one, which I reached him, he had saved himself with the fragment upon a rock; and so we got up by a hair's breadth; and Uncle George exclaimed that that was never done before, and he had not tried it if he had not known whom he had got in the bow, nor he in the bow, if he had not known him in the stern. At this place there was a regular portage cut through the woods, and our boatmen had never known a batteau to ascend the falls. As near as I can remember, there was a perpendicular fall here, at the worst place of the whole Penobscot River, two or three feet at least. I could not sufficiently admire the skill and coolness with which they performed this feat, never speaking to each other. The bowman, not looking behind, but knowing exactly what the other is about, works as if he worked alone. Now sounding in vain for a bottom in fifteen feet of water, while the boat falls back several rods, held straight only with the greatest skill and exertion; or, while the sternman obstinately holds his ground, like a turtle, the bowman springs from side to side with wonderful suppleness and dexterity, scanning the rapids and the rocks with a thousand eyes; and now, having got a bite at last, with a lusty shove, which makes his pole bend and quiver, and the whole boat tremble, he gains a few feet upon the river. To add to the danger, the poles are liable at any time to be caught between the rocks, and wrenched out of their hands, leaving them at the mercy of the rapids,—the rocks, as it were, lying in wait, like so many alligators, to catch them in their teeth, and jerk them from your hands, before you have stolen an effectual shove against their palates. The pole is set close to the boat, and the prow is made to overshoot, and just turn the corners of the rocks, in the very teeth of the rapids. Nothing but the length and lightness, and the slight draught of the batteau, enables them to make any headway. The bowman must quickly choose his course; there is no time to deliberate. Frequently the boat is shoved between rocks where both sides touch, and the waters on either hand are a perfect maelstrom.

Half a mile above this two of us tried our hands at poling up a slight rapid; and we were just surmounting the last difficulty, when an unlucky rock confounded our calculations; and while the batteau was sweeping round irrecoverably amid the whirlpool, we were obliged to resign the poles to more skillful hands.

Katepskonegan is one of the shallowest and weediest of the lakes, and looked as if it might abound in pickerel. The falls of the same name, where we stopped to dine, are considerable and quite picturesque. Here Uncle George had seen trout caught by the barrelful; but they would not rise to our bait at this hour. Half-way over this carry, thus far in the Maine wilderness on its way to the Provinces, we noticed a large, flaming, Oak Hall hand-bill, about two feet long, wrapped round the trunk of a pine, from which the bark had been stripped, and to which it was fast glued by the pitch. This should be recorded among the advantages of this mode of advertising, that so, possibly, even the bears and wolves, moose, deer, otter, and beaver, not to mention the Indian, may learn where they can fit themselves according to the latest fashion, or, at least, recover some of their own lost garments. We christened this the Oak Hall carry.

The forenoon was as serene and placid on this wild stream in the woods, as we are apt to imagine that Sunday in summer usually is in Massachusetts. We were occasionally startled by the scream of a bald-eagle, sailing over the stream in front of our batteau; or of the fish-hawks, on whom he levies his contributions. There were, at intervals, small meadows of a few acres on the sides of the stream, waving with uncut grass, which attracted the attention of our boatmen, who regretted that they were not nearer to their clearings, and calculated how many stacks they might cut. Two or three men sometimes spend the summer by themselves, cutting the grass in these meadows, to sell to the loggers in the winter, since it will fetch a higher price on the spot than in any market in the State. On a small isle, covered with this kind of rush, or cut grass, on which we landed to consult about our further course, we noticed the recent track of a moose, a large, roundish hole in the soft, wet ground, evincing the great size and weight of the animal that made it. They are fond of the water, and visit all these island-meadows, swimming as easily from island to island as they make their way through the thickets on land. Now and then we passed what McCauslin called a pokelogan, an Indian term for what the drivers might have reason to call a poke-logs-in, an inlet that leads nowhere. If you get in, you have got to get out again the same way. These, and the frequent "run-rounds" which come into the river again, would embarrass an inexperienced voyager not a little.

The carry around Pockwockomus Falls was exceedingly rough and rocky, the batteau having to be lifted directly from the water up four or five feet on to a rock, and launched again down a similar bank. The rocks on this portage were covered with the *dents* made by the spikes in the lumberers' boots while staggering over under the weight of their batteaux; and you could see where the surface of some large rocks on which they had rested their batteaux was worn quite smooth with use. As it was, we had carried over but half the usual portage at this place for this stage of the water, and launched our boat in the smooth wave just curving to the fall, prepared to struggle with the most violent rapid we had to encounter. The rest of the party walked over the remainder of the portage, while I remained with the boatmen to assist in warping up. One had to hold the boat while the others got in to prevent if from going over the falls. When we had pushed up the rapids as far as possible, keeping close to the shore, Tom seized the painter and leaped out upon a rock just visible in the water, but he lost his footing, notwithstanding his spiked boots, and was instantly amid the rapids; but recovering himself by good luck, and reaching another rock, he passed the painter to me, who had followed him, and took his place again in the bows. Leaping from rock to rock in the shoal water, close to the shore, and now and then getting a bite with the rope round an upright one, I held the boat while one reset his pole, and then all three forced it upward against any rapid. This was "warping up." When a part of us walked round at such a place, we generally took the precaution to take out the most valuable part of the baggage for fear of being swamped.

As we poled up a swift rapid for half a mile above Aboljacarmegus Falls, some of the party read their own marks on the huge logs which lay piled up high and dry on the rocks on either hand, the relics probably of a jam which had taken place here in the Great Freshet in the spring. Many of these would have to wait for another great freshet, perchance, if they lasted so long, before they could be got off. It was singular enough to meet with property of theirs which they had never seen, and where they had never been before, thus detained by freshets and rocks when on its way to them. Methinks that must be where all my property lies, cast up on the rocks on some distant and unexplored stream, and waiting for an unheard-of freshnet to fetch it down. O make haste, ye gods, with your winds and rains, and start the jam before it rots!

The last half mile carried us to the Sowadnehunk dead-water, so called from the stream of the same name, signifying "running between mountains," an important tributary which comes in a mile above. Here we decided to camp, about twenty miles from the Dam, at the mouth of Murch Brook and the Aboljacknagesic, mountain streams, broad off from Ktaadn, and about a dozen miles from its summit, having made fifteen miles this day.

We had been told by McCauslin that we should here find trout enough; so, while some prepared the camp, the rest fell to fishing. Seizing the birch poles which some party of Indians, or white hunters, had left on the shore, and baiting our hooks with pork, and with trout, as soon as they were caught, we cast our lines into the mouth of the Aboljacknagesic, a clear, swift, shallow stream, which came in from Ktaadn. Instantly, a shoal of white chivin (*Leucisci pulchelli*), silvery roaches, cousin-trout, or what not, large and small, prowling thereabouts, fell upon our bait, and one after another were landed amidst the bushes. Anon their cousins, the true trout, took their turn, and alternately the speckled trout, and the silvery roaches, swallowed the bait as fast as we could throw in; and the finest specimens of both that I have ever seen, the largest one weighing three pounds, were heaved upon the shore, though at first in vain, to wriggle down into the water again, for we stood in the boat; but soon we learned to remedy this evil; for one, who had lost his hook, stood on shore to catch them as they fell in a perfect shower around him,—sometimes, wet and slippery, full in his face and bosom, as his arms were outstretched to receive them. While yet alive, before their tints had faded, they glistened like the fairest flowers, the product of primitive rivers; and he could hardly trust his senses, as he stood over them, that these jewels should have swam away in that Abol-jacknagesic water for so long, so many dark ages;—these bright fluviatile flowers, seen of Indians only, made beautiful, the Lord only knows why, to swim there! I could understand better for this, the truth of mythology, the fables of Proteus, and all those beautiful sea-monsters,—how all history, indeed, put to a terrestrial use, is mere history; but put to a celestial, is mythology always.

But there is the rough voice of Uncle George, who commands at the frying-pan, to send over what you've got, and then you may stay till morning. The pork sizzles and cries for fish. Luckily for the foolish race, and this particularly foolish generation of trout, the night shut down at last, not a little deepened by the dark side of Ktaadn, which, like a permanent shadow, reared itself from the eastern bank. Lescarbot, writing in 1609, tells us that the Sieur Champdoré, who, with one of the people of the Sieur de Monts, ascended some fifty leagues up the St. John in 1608, found the fish so plenty, "qu'en mettant la chaudiere sur le feu ils en avoient pris suffisamment poor eux disner avant que l'eau fust chaude." Their descendants here are no less numerous. So we accompanied Tom into the woods to cut cedar-twigs for our bed. While he went ahead with the axe and lopped off the smallest twigs of the flat-leaved cedar, the arbor-vitae of the gardens, we gathered them up, and returned with them to the boat, until it was loaded. Our bed was made with as much care and skill as a roof is shingled; beginning at the foot, and laying the twig end of the cedar upward, we advanced to the head, a course at a time, thus successively covering the stub-ends, and producing a soft and level bed. For us six it was about ten feet long by six in breadth. This time we lay under our tent, having pitched it more prudently with reference to the wind and the flame, and the usual huge fire blazed in front. Supper was eaten off a large log, which some freshet had thrown up. This night we had a dish of arbor-vitae, or cedar-tea, which the lumberer sometimes uses when other herbs fail,—

> "A quart of arbor-vitae,
> To make him strong and mighty,"

but I had no wish to repeat the experiment. It had too medicinal a taste for my palate. There was the skeleton of a moose here, whose bones some Indian hunters had picked on this very spot.

In the night I dreamed of trout-fishing; and, when at length I awoke, it seemed a fable that this painted fish swam there so near my couch, and rose to our hooks the last evening, and I doubted if I had not dreamed it all. So I arose before dawn to test its truth, while my companions were still sleeping. There stood Ktaadn with distinct and cloudless outline in the moonlight; and the rippling of the rapids was the only sound to break the stillness. Standing on the shore, I once more cast my line into the stream, and found the dream to be real and the fable true. The speckled trout and silvery roach, like flying-fish, sped swiftly through the moonlight air, describing bright arcs on the dark side of Ktaadn, until moonlight, now fading into daylight, brought satiety to my mind, and the minds of my companions, who had joined me.

By six o'clock, having mounted our packs and a good blanketful of trout, ready dressed, and swung up such baggage and provision as we wished to leave behind upon the tops of saplings, to be out of the reach of bears, we started for the summit of the mountain, distant, as Uncle George said the boatmen called it, about four miles, but as I judged, and as it proved, nearer fourteen. He had never been any nearer the mountain than this, and there was not the slightest trace of man to guide us farther in this direction. At first, pushing a few rods up the Aboljacknagesic, or "open-land stream," we fastened our batteau to a tree, and traveled up the north side, through burnt lands, now partially overgrown with young aspens and other shrubbery; but soon, recrossing this stream, where it was about fifty or sixty feet wide, upon a jam of logs and rocks,—and you could cross it by this means almost anywhere,—we struck at once for the highest peak, over a mile or more of comparatively open land, still very gradually ascending the while. Here it fell to my lot, as the oldest mountain-climber, to take the lead. So, scanning the woody side of the mountain, which lay still at an indefinite distance, stretched out some seven or eight miles in length before us, we determined to steer directly for the base of the highest peak, leaving a large slide, by which, as I have since learned, some of our predecessors ascended, on our left. This course would lead us parallel to a dark seam in the forest, which marked the bed of a torrent, and over a slight spur, which extended southward from the main mountain, from whose bare summit we could get an outlook over the country, and climb directly up the peak, which would then be close at hand. Seen from this point, a bare ridge at the extremity of the open land, Ktaadn presented a different aspect from any mountain I have seen, there being a greater proportion of naked rock rising abruptly from the forest; and we looked up at this blue barrier as if it were some fragment of a wall which anciently bounded the earth in that direction. Setting the compass for a northeast course, which was the bearing of the southern base of the highest peak, we were soon buried in the woods.

We soon began to meet with traces of bears and moose, and those of rabbits were everywhere visible. The tracks of moose, more or less recent, to speak literally, covered every square rod on the sides of the mountain; and these animals are probably more numerous there now than ever before, being driven into this wilderness, from all sides, by the settlements. The track of a full-grown moose is like that of a cow, or larger, and of the young, like that of a calf. Sometimes we found ourselves traveling in faint paths, which they had made, like cow-paths in the woods, only far more indistinct, being rather openings, affording imperfect vistas through the dense underwood, than trodden paths; and everywhere the twigs had been browsed by them, clipped as smoothly as if by a knife. The bark of trees was stripped up by them to the height of eight or nine feet, in long, narrow strips, an inch wide, still showing the distinct marks of their teeth. We expected nothing less than to meet a herd of them every moment, and our Nimrod held his shooting-iron in readiness; but we did not go out of our way to look for them, and, though numerous, they are so wary that the unskillful hunter might range the forest a long time before he could get sight of one. They are sometimes dangerous to encounter, and will not turn out for the hunter, but furiously rush upon him and trample him to death, unless he is lucky enough to avoid them by dodging round a tree. The largest are nearly as large as a horse, and weigh sometimes one thousand pounds; and it is said that they can step over a five-foot gate in their ordinary walk. They are described as exceedingly awkward-looking animals, with their long legs and short bodies, making a ludicrous figure when in full run, but making great headway, nevertheless. It seemed a mystery to us how they could thread these woods, which it required all our suppleness to accomplish,—climbing, stooping, and winding, alternately. They are said to drop their long and branching horns, which usually spread five or six feet, on their backs, and make their way easily by the weight of their bodies. Our boatmen said, but I know not with how much truth, that their horns are apt to be gnawed away by vermin while they sleep. Their flesh, which is more like beef than venison, is common in Bangor market.

We had proceeded on thus seven or eight miles, till about noon, with frequent pauses to refresh the weary ones, crossing a considerable mountain stream, which we conjectured to be Murch Brook, at whose mouth we had camped, all the time in woods, without having once seen the summit, and rising very gradually, when the boatmen beginning to despair a little, and fearing that we were leaving the mountain on one side of us, for they had not entire faith in the compass, McCauslin climbed a tree, from the top of which he could see the peak, when it appeared that we had not swerved from a right line, the compass down below still ranging with his arm, which pointed to the summit. By the side of a cool mountain rill, amid the woods, where the water began to partake of the purity and transparency of the air, we stopped to cook some of our fishes, which we had brought thus far in order to save our hard bread and pork, in the use of which we had put ourselves on short allowance. We soon had a fire blazing, and stood around it, under the damp and sombre forest of firs and birches, each with a sharpened stick, three or four feet in length, upon which he had spitted his trout, or roach, previously well gashed and salted, our sticks radiating like the spokes of a wheel from one centre, and each crowding his particular fish into the most desirable exposure, not with the truest regard always to his neighbor's rights. Thus we regaled ourselves, drinking meanwhile at the spring, till one man's pack, at least, was considerably lightened, when we again took up our line of march.

At length we reached an elevation sufficiently bare to afford a view of the summit, still distant and blue, almost as if retreating from us. A torrent, which proved to be the same we had crossed, was seen tumbling down in front, literally from out of the clouds. But this glimpse at our whereabouts was soon lost, and we were buried in the woods again. The wood was chiefly yellow birch, spruce, fir, mountain-ash, or round-wood, as the Maine people call it, and moose-wood. It was the worst kind of traveling; sometimes like the densest scrub-oak patches with us. The cornel, or bunch-berries, were very abundant, as well as Solomon's seal and mooseberries. Blueberries were distributed along our whole route; and in one place the bushes were drooping with the weight of the fruit, still as fresh as ever. It was the 7th of September. Such pathces afforded a grateful repast, and served to bait the tired party forward. When any lagged behind, the cry of "blueberries" was most effectual to bring them up. Even at this elevation we passed through a moose-yard, formed by a large flat rock, four or five rods square, where they tread down the snow in winter. At length, fearing that if we held the direct course to the summit, we should not find any water near our camping-ground, we gradually swerved to the west, till, at four o'clock, we struck again the torrent which I have mentioned, and here, in view of the summit, the weary party decided to camp that night.

While my companions were seeking a suitable spot for this purpose, I improved the little daylight that was left in climbing the mountain alone. We were in a deep and narrow ravine, sloping up to the clouds, at an angle of nearly forty-five degrees, and hemmed in by walls of rock, which were at first covered with low trees, then with impenetrable thickets of scraggy birches and spruce-trees, and with moss, but at last bare of all vegetation but lichens, and almost continually draped in clouds. Following up the course of the torrent which occupied this,—and I mean to lay some emphasis on this word *up*,—pulling myself up by the side of perpendicular falls of twenty or thirty feet, by the roots of firs and birches, and then, perhaps, walking a level rod or two in the thin stream, for it took up the whole road, ascending by huge steps, as it were, a giant's stairway, down which a river flowed, I had soon cleared the trees, and paused on the successive shelves, to look back over the country. The torrent was from fifteen to thirty feet wide, without a tributary, and seemingly not diminishing in breadth as I advanced; but still it came rushing and roaring down, with a copious tide, over and amidst masses of bare rock, from the very clouds, as though a waterspout had just burst over the mountain. Leaving this at last, I began to work my way, scarcely less arduous than Satan's anciently through Chaos, up the nearest, though not the highest peak. At first scrambling on all fours over the tops of ancient black spruce-trees (*Abies nigra*), old as the flood, from two to ten or twelve feet in height, their tops flat and spreading, and their foliage blue, and nipped with cold, as if for centuries they had ceased growing upward against the bleak sky, the solid cold. I walked some good rods erect upon the tops of these trees, which were overgrown with moss and mountain-cranberries. It seemed that in the course of time they had filled up the intervals between the huge rocks, and the cold wind had uniformly leveled all over. Here the principle of vegetation was hard put to it. There was apparently a belt of this kind running quite round the mountain, though, perhaps, nowhere so remarkable as here. Once slumping through, I looked down ten feet, into a dark and cavernous region, and saw the stem of a spruce, on whose top I stood, as on a mass of coase basket-work, fully nine inches in diameter at the ground. These holes were bears' dens, and the bears were even then at home. This was the sort of garden I made my way *over*, for an eighth of a mile, at the risk, it is true, of treading on some of the plants, not seeing any path *through* it,—certainly the most treacherous and porous country I ever traveled.

> "Nigh foundered on he fares,
> Treading the crude consistence, half on foot,
> Half flying."

But nothing could exceed the toughness of the twigs,—not one snapped under my weight, for they had slowly grown. Having slumped, scrambled, rolled, bounced, and walked, by turns, over this scraggy country, I arrived upon a side-hill, or rather side-mountain, where rocks, gray, silent rocks, were the flocks and heards that pastured, chewing a rocky cud at sunset. They looked at me with hard gray eyes, without a bleat or a low. This brought me to the skirt of a cloud, and bounded my walk that night. But I had already seen that Maine country when I turned about, waving, flowing, rippling, down below.

When I returned to my companions, they had selected a camping-ground on the torrent's edge, and were resting on the ground; one was on the sick list, rolled in a blanket, on a damp shelf of rock. It was a savage and dreary scenery enough; so wildly rough, that they looked long to find a level and open space for the tent. We could not well camp higher, for want of fuel; and the trees here seemed so ever-green and sappy, that we almost doubted if they would acknowledge the influence of fire; but fire prevailed at last, and blazed here, too, like a good citizen of the world. Even at this height we met with frequent traces of moose, as well as of bears. As here was no cedar, we made our bed of coarser feathered spruce; but at any rate the feathers were plucked from the live tree. It was, perhaps, even a more grand and desolate place for a night's lodging than the summit would have been, being in the neighborhood of those wild trees, and of the torrent. Some more aerial and finer-spirited winds rushed and roared through the ravine all night, from time to time arousing our fire, and dispersing the embers about. It was as if we lay in the very nest of a young whirlwind. At midnight, one of my bed-fellows, being startled in his dreams by the sudden blazing up to its top of a fir-tree, whose green boughs were dried by the heat, sprang up, with a cry, from his bed, thinking the world on fire, and drew the whole camp after him.

In the morning, after whetting our appetite on some raw pork, a wafer of hard bread, and a dipper of condensed cloud or waterspout, we all together began to make our way up the falls, which I have described; this time choosing the right hand, or highest peak, which was not the one I had approached before. But soon my companions were lost to my sight behind the mountain ridge in my rear, which still seemed ever retreating before me, and I climbed alone over huge rocks, loosely poised, a mile or more, still edging toward the clouds; for though the day was clear elsewhere, the summit was concealed by mist. The mountain seemed a vast aggregation of loose rocks, as if some time it had rained rocks, and they lay as they fell on the mountain sides, nowhere fairly at rest, but leaning on each other, all rocking-stones, with cavities between, but scarcely any soil or smoother shelf. They were the raw materials of a planet dropped from an unseen quarry, which the vast chemistry of nature would anon work up, or work down, into the smiling and verdant plains and valleys of earth. This was an undone extremity of the globe; as in lignite, we see coal in the process of formation.

At length I entered within the skirts of the cloud which seemed forever drifting over the summit, and yet would never be gone, but was generated out of that pure air as fast as it flowed away; and when, a quarter of a mile farther, I reached the summit of the ridge, which those who have seen in clearer weather say is about five miles long, and contains a thousand acres of table-land, I was deep within the hostile ranks of clouds, and all objects were obscured by them. Now the wind would blow me out a yard of clear sunlight, wherein I stood; then a gray, dawning light was all it could accomplish, the cloud-line ever rising and falling with the wind's intensity. Sometimes it seemed as if the summit would be cleared in a few moments, and smile in sunshine; but what was gained on one side was lost on another. It was like sitting in a chimney and waiting for the smoke to blow away. It was, in fact, a cloud factory,—these were the cloud-works, and the wind turned them off done from the cool, bare rocks. Occasionally, when the windy columns broke in to me, I caught sight of a dark, damp crag to the right or left; the mist driving ceaselessly between it and me. It reminded me of the creations of the old epic and dramatic poets, of Atlas, Vulcan, the Cyclops, and Prometheus. Such was Caucasus and the rock where Prometheus was bound. Aeschylus had no doubt visited such scenery as this. It was vast, Titanic, and such as man never inhabits. Some part of the beholder, even some vital part, seems to escape through the loose grating of his ribs as he ascends. He is more lone than you can imagine. There is less of substantial thought and fair understanding in him than in the plains where men inhabit. His reason is dispersed and shadowy, more thin and subtile, like the air. Vast, Titanic, inhuman Nature has got him at disadvantage, caught him alone, and pilfers him of some of his divine faculty. She does not smile on him as in the plains. She seems to say sternly, Why came ye here before your time. This ground is not prepared for you. Is it not enough that I smile in the valleys? I have never made this soil for thy feet, this air for thy breathing, these rocks for thy neighbors. I cannot pity nor fondle thee here, but forever relentlessly drive thee hence to where I *am* kind. Why seek me where I have not called thee, and then complain because you find me but a stepmother? Shouldst thou freeze or starve, or shudder thy life away, here is no shrine, nor altar, nor any access to my ear.

> "Chaos and ancient Night, I come no spy
> With purpose to explore or to disturb
> The secrets of your realm, but . . .
> . . . . . as my way
> Lies through your spacious empire up to light."

The tops of mountains are among the unfinished parts of the globe, whither it is a slight insult to the gods to climb and pry into their secrets, and try their effect on our humanity. Only daring and insolent men, perchance, go there. Simple races, as savages do not climb mountains,—their tops are sacred and mysterious tracts never visited by them. Pomola is always angry with those who climb to the summit of Ktaadn.

According to Jackson, who, in his capacity of geological surveyor of the State, has accurately measured it,—the altitude of Ktaadn is 5300 feet, or a little more than one mile above the level of the sea,—and he adds, "It is then evidently the highest point in the State of Maine, and is the most abrupt granite mountain in New England." The peculiarities of that spacious table-land on which I was standing, as well as the remarkable semi-circular precipice or basin on the eastern side, were all concealed by the mist. I had brought my whole pack to the top, not knowing but I should have to make my descent to the river, and possibly to the settled portion of the State alone, and by some other route, and wishing to have a complete outfit with me. But at length, fearing that my companions would be anxious to reach the river before night, and knowing that the clouds might rest on the mountain for days, I was compelled to descend. Occasionally, as I came down, the wind would blow me a vista open, through which I could see the country eastward, boundless forests, and lakes, and streams, gleaming in the sun, some of them emptying into the East Branch. There were also new mountains in sight in that direction. Now and then some small bird of the sparrow family would flit away before me, unable to command its course, like a fragment of the gray rock blown off by the wind.

I found my companions where I had left them, on the side of the peak, gathering the mountain-cranberries, which filled every crevice between the rocks, together with blueberries, which had a spicier flavor the higher up they grew, but were not the less agreeable to our palates. When the country is settled, and roads are made, these cranberries will perhaps become an article of commerce. From this elevation, just on the skirts of the clouds, we could overlook the country, west and south, for a hundred miles. There it was, the State of Maine, which we had seen on the map, but not much like that,—immeasurable forest for the sun to shine on, that eastern *stuff* we hear of in Massachusetts. No clearing, no house. It did not look as if a solitary traveler had cut so much as a walking-stick there. Countless lakes,—Moosehead in the southwest, forty miles long by ten wide, like a gleaming silver platter at the end of the table; Chesuncook, eighteen long by three wide, without an island; Millinocket, on the south, with its hundred islands; and a hundred others without a name; and mountains, also, whose names, for the most part, are known only to the Indians. The forest looked like a firm grass sward, and the effect of these lakes in its midst has been well compared, by one who has since visited this same spot, to that of a "mirror broken into a thousand fragments, and wildly scattered over the grass, reflecting the full blaze of the sun." It was a large farm for somebody, when cleared. According to the Gazetteer, which was printed before the boundary question was settled, this single Penobscot county, in which we were, was larger than the whole State of Vermont, with its fourteen counties; and this was only a part of the wild lands of Maine. We are concerned now, however, about natural, not political limits. We were about eighty miles, as the bird flies, from Bangor, or one hundred and fifteen, as we had ridden, and walked, and paddled. We had to console ourselves with the reflection that this view was probably as good as that from the peak, as far as it went; and what were a mountain without its attendant clouds and mists? Like ourselves, neither Bailey nor Jackson had obtained a clear view from the summit.

Setting out on our return to the river, still at an early hour in the day, we decided to follow the course of the torrent, which we supposed to be Murch Brook, as long as it would not lead us too far out of our way. We thus traveled about four miles in the very torrent itself, continually crossing and recrossing it, leaping from rock to rock, and jumping with the stream down falls of seven or eight feet, or sometimes sliding down on our backs in a thin sheet of water. This ravine had been the scene of an extraordinary freshet in the spring, apparently accompanied by a slide from the mountain. It must have been filled with a stream of stones and water, at least twenty feet above the present level of the torrent. For a rod or two, on either side of its channel, the trees were barked and splintered up to their tops, the birches bent over, twisted, and sometimes finely split, like a stable-broom; some, a foot in diameter, snapped off, and whole clumps of trees bent over with the weight of rocks piled on them. In one place we noticed a rock, two or three feet in diameter, lodged nearly twenty feet high in the crotch of a tree. For the whole four miles, we saw but one rill emptying in, and the volume of water did not seem to be increased from the first. We traveled thus very rapidly with a downward impetus, and grew remarkably expert at leaping from rock to rock, for leap we must, and leap we did, whether there was any rock at the right distance or not. It was a pleasant picture whent he foremost turned about and looked up the winding ravine, walled in with rocks and the green forest, to see, at intervals of a rod or two, a red-shirted or green-jacketed mountaineer against the white torrent, leaping down the channel with his pack on his back, or pausing upon a convenient rock in the midst of the torrent to mend a rent in his clothes, or unstrap the dipper at his belt to take a draught of the water. At one place we were startled by seeing, on a little sandy shelf by the side of the stream, the fresh print of a man's foot, and for a moment realized how Robinson Crusoe felt in a similar case; but at last we remembered that we had struck this stream on our way up, though we could not have told where, and one had descended into the ravine for a drink. The cool air above and the continual bathing of our bodies in mountain water, alternate foot, sitz, douche, and plunge baths, made this walk exceedingly refreshing, and we had traveled only a mile or two, after leaving the torrent, before every thread of our clothes was as dry as usual, owing perhaps to a peculiar quality in the atmosphere.

After leaving the torrent, being in doubt about our course, Tom threw down his pack at the foot of the loftiest spruce-tree at hand, and shinned up the bare trunk some twenty feet, and then climbed through the green tower, lost to our sight, until he held the topmost spray in his hand.[1] McCauslin, in his younger days, had marched through the wilderness with a body of troops, under General Somebody, and with one other man did all the scouting and spying service. The General's word was, "Throw down the top of that tree," and there was no tree in the Maine woods so high that it did not lose its top in such a case. I have heard a story of two men being lost once in these woods, nearer to the settlements than this, who climbed the loftiest pine they could find, some six feet in diameter at the ground, from whose top they discovered a solitary clearing and its smoke. When at this height, some two hundred feet from the ground, one of them became dizzy, and fainted in his companion's arms, and the latter had to accomplish the descent with him, alternately fainting and reviving, as best he could. To Tom we cried, Where away does the summit bear? where the burnt lands? The last he could only conjecture; he descried, however, a little meadow and pond, lying probably in our course, which we concluded to steer for. On reaching this secluded meadow, we found fresh tracks of moose on the shore of the pond, and the water was still unsettled as if they had fled before us. A little farther, in a dense thicket, we seemed to be still on their trail. It was a small meadow, of a few acres, on the mountain side, concealed by the forest, and perhaps never seen by a white man before, where one would think that the moose might browse and bathe, and rest in peace. Pursuing this course, we soon reached the open land, which went sloping down some miles toward the Penobscot.

Perhaps I most fully realized that this was primeval, untamed, and forever untamable *Nature*, or whatever else men call it, while coming down this part of the mountain. We were passing over "Burnt Lands," burnt by lightning, perchance, though they showed no recent marks of fire, hardly so much as a charred stump, but looked rather like a natural pasture for the moose and deer, exceedingly wild and desolate, with occasional strips of timber crossing them, and low poplars springing up, and patches of blueberries here and there. I found myself traversing them familiarly, like some pasture run to waste, or partially reclaimed by man; but when I reflected what man, what brother or sister or kinsman of our race made it and claimed it, I expected the proprietor to rise up and dispute my passage. It is difficult to conceive of a region uninhabited by man. We habitually presume his presence and influence everywhere. And yet we have not seen pure Nature, unless we have seen her thus vast and drear and inhuman, though in the midst of cities. Nature was here something savage and awful, though beautiful. I looked with awe at the ground I trod on, to see what the Powers had made there, the form and fashion and material of their work. This was that Earth of which we have heard, made out of Chaos and Old Night. Here was no man's garden, but the unhandseled globe. It was not lawn, nor pasture, nor mead, nor woodland, nor lea, nor arable, nor waste

[1]"The spruce tree," says Springer in '51, "is generally selected, principally for the superior facilities which its numerous limbs afford the climber. To gain the first limbs of this tree, which are from twenty to forty feet from the ground, a smaller tree is undercut and lodged against it, clambering up which the top of the spruce is reached. In some cases, when a very elevated position is desired, the spruce-tree is lodged against the trunk of some lofty pine, up which we ascend to a height twice that of the surrounding forest."

To indicate the direction of pines, one throws down a branch, and a man on the ground takes the bearing.

land. It was the fresh and natural surface of the planet Earth, as it was made forever and ever,—to be the dwelling of man, we say,—so Nature made it, and man may use it if he can. Man was not to be associated with it. It was Matter, vast, terrific,—not his Mother Earth that we have heard of, not for him to tread on, or be buried in,—no, it were being too familiar even to let his bones lie there,—the home, this, of Necessity and Fate. There was clearly felt the presence of a force not bound to be kind to man. It was a place for heathenism and superstitious rites,—to be inhabited by men nearer of kin to the rocks and to wild animals than we. We walked over it with a certain awe, stopping from time to time, to pick the blueberries which grew there, and had a smart and spicy taste. Perchance where *our* wild pines stand, and leaves lie on their forest floor, in Concord, there were once reapers, and husbandmen planted grain; but here not even the surface had been scarred by man, but it was a specimen of what God saw fit to make this world. What is it to be admitted to a museum, to see a myriad of particular things, compared with being shown some star's surface, some hard matter in its home! I stand in awe of my body, this matter to which I am bound has become so strange to me. I fear not spirits, ghosts, of which I am one,—*that* my body might,—but I fear bodies, I tremble to meet them. What is this Titan that has possession of me? Talk of mysteries! Think of our life in nature,—daily to be shown matter, to come in contact with it,—rocks, trees, wind on our cheeks! the *solid* earth! the *actual* world! the *common sense! Contact! Contact! Who* are we? *where* are we?

Erelong we recognized some rocks and other features in the landscape which we had purposely impressed on our memories, and, quickening our pace, by two o'clock we reached the batteau.[1] Here we had expected to dine on trout, but in this glaring sunlight they were slow to take the bait, so we were compelled to make the most of the crumbs of our hard bread and our pork, which were both nearly exhausted. Meanwhile we deliberated whether we should go up the river a mile farther, to Gibson's clearing, on the Sowadnehunk, where there was a deserted log-hut, in order to get a half-inch auger, to mend one of our spike-poles with. There were young spruce-trees enough around us, and we had a spare spike, but nothing to make a hole with. But as it was uncertain whether we should find any tools left there, we patched up the broken pole, as well as we could, for the downward voyage, in which there would be but little use for it. Moreover, we were unwilling to lose any time in this expedition, lest the wind should rise before we reached the larger lakes, and detain us; for a moderate wind produces quite a sea on these waters, in which a batteau will not live for a moment; and on one occasion McCauslin had been delayed a week at the head of the North Twin, which is only four miles across. We were nearly out of provisions, and ill prepared in this respect for what might possibly prove a week's journey round by the shore, fording innumerable streams, and threading a trackless forest, should any accident happen to our boat.

It was with regret that we turned our backs on Chesuncook, which McCauslin had formerly logged on, and the Allegash lakes. There were still

[1]The bears had not touched things on our possessions. They sometimes tear a batteau to pieces for the sake of the tar with which it is besmeared.

longer rapids and portages above; among the last the Rippogenus Portage, which he described as the most difficult on the river, and three miles long. The whole length of the Penobscot is two hundred and seventy-five miles, and we are still nearly one hundred miles from its source. Hodge, the assistant State Geologist, passed up this river in 1837, and by a portage of only one mile and three quarters crossed over into the Allegash, and so went down that into the St. John, and up the Madawaska to the Grand Portage across to the St. Lawrence. His is the only account that I know of an expedition through to Canada in this direction. He thus describes his first sight of the latter river, which, to compare small things with great, is like Balboa's first sight of the Pacific from the mountains of the Isthmus of Darien. "When we first came in sight of the St. Lawrence," he says, "from the top of a high hill, the view was most striking, and much more interesting to me from having been shut up in the woods for the two previous months. Directly before us lay the broad river, extending across nine or ten miles, its surface broken by a few islands and reefs, and two ships riding at anchor near the shore. Beyond, extended ranges of uncultivated hills, parallel with the river. The sun was just going down behind them, and gilding the whole scene with its parting rays."

About four o'clock, the same afternoon, we commenced our return voyage, which would require but little if any poling. In shooting rapids the boatmen use large and broad paddles, instead of poles, to guide the boat with. Though we glided so swiftly, and often smoothly, down, where it had cost us no slight effort to get up, our present voyage was attended with far more danger; for if we once fairly struck one of the thousand rocks by which we were surrounded the boat would be swamped in an instant. When a boat is swamped under these circumstances, the boatmen commonly find no difficulty in keeping afloat at first, for the current keeps both them and their cargo up for a long way down the stream; and if they can swim, they have only to work their way gradually to the shore. The greatest danger is of being caught in an eddy behind some larger rock, where the water rushes up stream faster than elsewhere it does down, and being carried round and round under the surface till they are drowned. McCauslin pointed out some rocks which had been the scene of a fatal accident of this kind. Sometimes the body is not thrown out for several hours. He himself had performed such a circuit once, only his legs being visible to his companions; but he was fortunately thrown out in season to recover his breath.[1] In shooting the rapids, the boatman has this problem to solve: to choose a circuitous and safe course amid a thousand sunken rocks, scattered over a quarter or half a mile, at the same time that he is moving steadily on at the rate of fifteen miles an hour. Stop he cannot; the only question is, where will he go? The bowman chooses the course with all his eyes about him, striking broad off with his paddle, and drawing the boat by main force into her course. The sternman faithfully follows the bow.

We were soon at the Aboljacarmegus Falls. Anxious to avoid the delay, as

[1] I cut this from a newspaper. "On the 11th (instant?) [May, '49], on Rappogenes Falls. Mr. John Delantee, of Orono, Me., was drowned while running logs. He was a citizen of Orono, and was twenty-six years of age. His companions found his body, enclosed it in bark, and buried it in the solemn woods."

well as the labor, of the portage here, our boatmen went forward first to reconnoitre, and concluded to let the batteau down the falls, carrying the baggage only over the portage. Jumping from rock to rock until nearly in the middle of the stream, we were ready to receive the boat and let her down over the first fall, some six or seven feet perpendicular. The boatmen stand upon the edge of a shelf of rock, where the fall is perhaps nine or ten feet perpendicular, in from one to two feet of rapid water, one on each side of the boat, and let it slide gently over, till the bow is run out ten or twelve feet in the air; then, letting it drop squarely, while one holds the painter, the other leaps in, and his companion following, they are whirled down the rapids to a new fall, or to smooth water. In a very few minutes they had accomplished a passage in safety, which would be as foolhardy for the unskillful to attempt as the descent of Niagara itself. It seemed as if it needed only a little familiarity, and a little more skill, to navigate down such falls as Niagara itself with safety. At any rate, I should not despair of such men in the rapids above Table-Rock, until I saw them actually go over the falls, so cool, so collected, so fertile in resources are they. One might have thought that these were falls, and that falls were not to be waded through with impunity, like a mud-puddle. There was really danger of their losing their sublimity in losing their power to harm us. Familiarity breeds contempt. The boatman pauses, perchance, on some shelf beneath a table-rock under the fall, standing in some cove of back-water two feet deep, and you hear his rough voice come up through the spray, coolly giving directions how to launch the boat this time.

Having carried round Pockwockomus Falls, our oars soon brought us to the Katepskonegan, or Oak Hall carry, where we decided to camp half-way over, leaving our batteau to be carried over in the morning on fresh shoulders. One shoulder of each of the boatmen showed a red spot as large as one's hand, worn by the batteau on this expedition; and this shoulder, as it did all the work, was perceptibly lower than its fellow, from long service. Such toil soon wears out the strongest constitution. The drivers are accustomed to work in the cold water in the spring, rarely ever dry; and if one falls in all over he rarely changes his clothes till night, if then, even. One who takes this precaution is called by a particular nickname, or is turned off. None can lead this life who are not almost amphibious. McCauslin said soberly, what is at any rate a good story to tell, that he had seen where six men were wholly under water at once, at a jam, with their shoulders to handspikes. If the log did not start, then they had to put out their heads to breathe. The driver works as long as he can see, from dark to dark, and at night has not time to eat his supper and dry his clothes fairly, before he is asleep on his cedar bed. We lay that night on the very bed made by such a party, stretching our tent over the poles which were still standing, but re-shingling the damp and faded bed with fresh leaves.

In the morning we carried our boat over and launched it, making haste lest the wind should rise. The boatmen ran down Passamagamet, and soon after Ambejijis Falls, while we walked round with the baggage. We made a hasty breakfast at the head of Ambejijis Lake on the remainder of our pork, and were soon rowing across its smooth surface again, under a pleasant sky, the mountain being now clear of clouds in the northeast. Taking turns at the oars, we shot rapidly across Deep Cove, the foot of Pamadumcook, and the North Twin, at the rate of six miles an hour, the wind not being high enough to disturb us, and reached the Dam at noon. The boatmen went through one of the log sluices in the batteau, where the fall was ten feet at the bottom, and took us in below. Here was the longest rapid in our voyage, and perhaps the running this was as dangerous and arduous a task as any. Shooting down sometimes at the rate, as we judged, of fifteen miles an hour, if we struck a rock we were split from end to end in an instant. Now like a bait bobbing for some river monster, amid the eddies, now darting to this side of the stream, now to that, gliding swift and smooth near to our destruction, or striking broad off with the paddle and drawing the boat to right or left with all our might, in order to avoid a rock. I suppose that it was like running the rapids of the Sault Sainte Marie, at the outlet of Lake Superior, and our boatmen probably displayed no less dexterity than the Indians there do. We soon ran through this mile, and floated in Quakish Lake.

After such a voyage, the troubled and angry waters, which once had seemed terrible and not to be trifled with, appeared tamed and subdued; they had been bearded and worried in their channels, pricked and whipped into submission with the spike-pole and paddle, gone through and through with impunity, and all their spirit and their danger taken out of them, and the most swollen and impetuous rivers seemed but playthings henceforth. I began, at length, to understand the boatman's familiarity with, and contempt for, the rapids. "Those Fowler boys," said Mrs. McCauslin, "are perfect ducks for the water." They had run down to Lincoln, according to her, thirty or forty miles, in a batteau, in the night, for a doctor, when it was so dark that they could not see a rod before them, and the river was swollen so as to be almost a continuous rapid, so that the doctor *cried*, when they brought him up by daylight, "Why, Tom, how did you see to steer?" "We didn't steer much,—only kept her straight." And yet they met with no accident. It is true, the more difficult rapids are higher up than this.

When we reached the Millinocket opposite to Tom's house, and were waiting for his folks to set us over, for we had left our batteau above the Grand Falls, we discovered two canoes, with two men in each, turning up this stream from Shad Pond, one keeping the opposite side of a small island before us, while the other approached the side where we were standing, examining the banks carefully for muskrats as they came along. the last proved to be Louis Neptune and his companion, now, at last, on their way up to Chesuncook after moose; but they were so disguised that we hardly knew them. At a little distance they might have been taken for Quakers, with their broad-brimmed hats and overcoats with broad capes, the spoils of Bangor, seeking a settlement in this Sylvania,—or, nearer at hand, for fashionable gentlemen the morning after a spree. Met face to face, these Indians in their native woods looked like the sinister and slouching fellows whom you meet picking up strings and paper in the streets of a city. There is, in fact, a remarkable and unexpected resemblance between the degraded savage and the lowest classes in a great city. The one is no more a child of nature than the other. In the progress of degradation the distinction of races is soon lost. Neptune at first was only anxious to know what we "kill," seeing some partridges in the hands of one of the party, but we had assumed too much anger to permit of a reply. We thought Indians had some honor before. But—"Me been sick. Oh, me unwell now. You make bargain, then me go." They had in fact been delayed so long by a drunken frolic at the Five Islands, and they had not yet recovered from its effects. They had some young musquash in their canoes, which they dug out of the banks with a hoe, for food, not for their skins, for musquash are their principal food on these expeditions. So they went on up the Millinocket, and we kept down the bank of the Penobscot, after recruiting ourselves with a draught of Tom's beer, leaving Tom at his home.

Thus a man shall lead his life away here on the edge of the wilderness, on Indian Millinocket stream, in a new world, far in the dark of a continent, and have a flute to play at evening here, while his strains echo to the stars, amid the howling of wolves; shall live, as it were, in the primitive age of the world, a primitive man. Yet he shall spend a sunny day, and in this century be my contemporary; perchance shall read some scattered leaves of literature, and sometimes talk with me. Why read history, then, if the ages, and the generations are now? He lives three thousand years deep into time, an age not yet described by poets. Can you well go further back in history than this? Ay! ay!—for there turns up but now into the mouth of Millinocket stream a still more ancient and primitive man, whose history is not brought down even to the former. In a bark vessel sewn with the roots of the spruce, with hornbeam paddles, he dips his way along. He is but dim and misty to me, obscured by the aeons that lie between the bark canoe and the batteau. He builds no house of logs, but a wigwam of skins. He eats no hot bread and sweet cake, but musquash and moose meat and the fat of bears. He glides up the Millinocket and is lost to my sight, as a more distant and misty cloud is seen flitting by behind a nearer, and is lost in space. So he goes about his destiny, the red face of man.

After having passed the night, and buttered our boots for the last time, at Uncle George's, whose dogs almost devoured him for joy at his return, we kept on down the river the next day, about eight miles on foot, and then took a batteau, with a man to pole it, to Mattawamkeag, ten more. At the middle of that very night, to make a swift conclusion to a long story, we dropped our buggy over the half-finished bridge at Oldtown, where we heard the confused din and clink of a hundred saws, which never rest, and at six o'clock the next morning one of the party was steaming his way to Massachusetts.

What is most striking in the Maine wilderness is the continuousness of the forest, with fewer open intervals or glades than you had imagined. Except the few burnt lands, the narrow intervals on the rivers, the bare tops of the high mountains, and the lakes and streams, the forest is uninterrupted. It is even more grim and wild than you had anticipated, a damp and intricate wilderness, in the spring everywhere wet and miry. The aspect of the country, indeed, is universally stern and savage, excepting the distant views of the forest from hills, and the lake prospects, which are mild and civilizing in a degree. The lakes are something which you are unprepared for; they lie up so high, exposed to the light, and the forest is diminished to a fine fringe on their edges, with here and there a blue mountain, like amethyst jewels set around some jewel of the first water,—so anterior, so superior, to all the changes that are to take place on their shores, even now civil and refined, and fair as they can ever be. These are not the artificial forests of an English king,—a royal preserve merely. Here prevail no forest laws but those of nature. The aborigines have never been dispossessed, nor nature disforested.

It is a country full of evergreen trees, of mossy silver birches and watery maples, the ground dotted with insipid, small, red berries, and strewn with damp and moss-grown rocks,—a country diversified with innumerable lakes and rapid streams, peopled with trout and various species of *leucisci*, with salmon, shad, and pickerel, and other fishes; the forest resounding at rare intervals with the note of the chickadee, the blue-jay, and the woodpecker, the scream of the fish-hawk and the eagle, the laugh of the loon, and the whistle of ducks along the solitary streams; at night, with the hooting of owls and howling of wolves; in summer, swarming with myriads of black flies and mosquitoes, more formidable than wolves to the white man. Such is the home of the moose, the bear, the caribou, the wolf, the beaver, an the Indian. Who shall describe the inexpressible tenderness and immortal life of the grim forest, where Nature, though it be mid-winter, is ever in her spring, where the moss-grown and decaying trees are not old, but seem to enjoy a perpetual youth; and blissful, innocent Nature, like a serene infant, is too happy to make a noise, except by a few tinkling, lisping birds and trickling rills?

What a place to live, what a place to die and be buried in! There certainly men would live forever, and laugh at death, and the grave. There they could have no such thoughts as are associated with the village graveyard,—that make a grave out of one of those moist evergreen hummocks!

Die and be buried who will,
  I mean to live here still;
My nature grows ever more young
  The primitive pines among.

I am reminded by my journey how exceedingly new this country still is. You have only to travel for a few days into the interior and back parts even of many of the old States, to come to that very America which the Northmen, and Cabot, and Gosnold, and Smith, and Raleigh visited. If Columbus was the first to discover the islands, Americus Vespucius and Cabot, and the Puritans, and we their descendants, have discovered only the shores of America. While the republic has already acquired a history world-wide, America is still unsettled and unexplored. Like the English in New Holland, we live only on the shores of a continent even yet, and hardly know where the rivers come from which float our navy. The very timber and boards and shingles of which our houses are made grew but yesterday in a wilderness where the Indian still hunts and the moose runs wild. New York has her wilderness within her own borders; and though the sailors of Europe are familiar with the soundings of her Hudson, and Fulton long since invented the steamboat on its waters, an Indian is still necessary to guide her scientific men to its headwaters in the Adirondack country.

Have we even so much as discovered and settled the shores? Let a man travel on foot along the coast, from the Passamaquoddy to the Sabine, or to the Rio Bravo, or to wherever the end is now, if he is swift enough to overtake it, faithfully following the windings of every inlet and of every cape, and stepping to the music of the surf,—with a desolate fishing-town once a week, and a city's port once a month to cheer him, and putting up at the light-houses, when there are any,—and tell me if it looks like a discovered and settled country, and not rather, for the most part, like a desolate island, and No-Man's Land.

We have advanced by leaps to the Pacific, and left many a lesser Oregon and California unexplored behind us. Though the railroad and the telegraph have been established on the shores of Maine, the Indian still looks out from her interior mountains over all these to the sea. There stands the city of Bangor, fifty miles up the Penobscot, at the head of navigation for vessels of the largest class, the principal lumber depot on this continent, with a population of twelve thousand, like a star on the edge of night, still hewing at the forests of which it is built, already overflowing with the luxuries and refinement of Europe, and sending its vessels to Spain, to England, and to the West Indies for its groceries,—and yet only a few axe-men have gone "up river," into the howling wilderness which feeds it. The bear and deer are still found within its limits; and the moose, as he swims the Penobscot, is entangled amid its shipping, and taken by foreign sailors in its harbor. Twelve miles in the rear, twelve miles of railroad, are Orono and the Indian Island, the home of the Penobscot tribe, and then commence the batteau and the canoe, and the military road; and sixty miles above, the country is virtually unmapped and unexplored, and there still waves the virgin forest of the New World.

Walt Whitman
1819-1892

When reading selections from Whitman you will see a number of connections between Whitman and Ralph Waldo Emerson. Upon first publication of Whitman's *Leaves of Grass* (July 4, 1855), Emerson congratulated and backed the poet at a time when few others in America did. Whitman, like Emerson, expressed the optimism and idealism of the age of American expansion. Like the Transcendentalists, he sang the praises of American individualism. Yet, as in his prose work *Democratic Vistas* (1871), Whitman also expressed an awareness of the excesses, cruelties, and destructive potential of an America which was growing into the world's great commercial and political power.

Like the writing of Emily Dickinson, Whitman's poetry was radically original for his time. He believed that poetry should become "a new national declamatory expression" to "elevate, enlarge, deepen, and make happy the attributes of the body and soul of man." Through his use of the language of the "common man," his sometimes rhythmical, sometimes loose and incantatory verse, he liberated poetry from nineteenth-century categories of meter, rhyme, and diction. Above all he focused his genius on the landscape, the creatures, the people, and the cities he knew through direct experience. His influence on modern poetry was greater than any American poet before him and perhaps since.

Born on a farm in then rural Long Island, he knew—through his farmer-carpenter father and his own observations of sailors and fishermen—the cross section of American life he would write about. Journalist, teacher, editor, part-time carpenter, volunteer war nurse, traveler, government clerk, and poet, his wide experience enlivens his poetry and reinforces his claim that one life, through poetry, may come to represent all lives. Revolutionary as it was in content, frankness, and form, his magnum opus *Leaves of Grass,* published through seven ever-changing and growing editions, was not accepted by his compatriots with the enthusiasm it received from the critics and artists of Europe, and in this regard he represents the typical experiences of many American writers, artists, and musicians before and since. He died, as he had lived most of his life, near poverty.

Just as his poetry speaks of the tides of humanity, the forces of industry, and the cities of America, so does it also speak of the American landscape and its creatures, and of the forces of nature—the stars, moon, sun, and sea. It is his vision of nature that the following selections reveal. For additional reading, try Whitman's *Specimen Days* (1882)—his collection of prose essays and prefaces. This book, largely autobiographical, often describes the influence of nature in his early life and is good for understanding the role of nature in the making of the poet, whether it be the experience of Long Island shores and fields and waters, of nature's creatures, or the simple act of sun-bathing.

from The Preface to 1855 Edition of LEAVES OF GRASS*

. . . Of all nations the United States with veins full of poetical stuff most need poets and will doubtless have the greatest and use them the greatest. Their Presidents shall not be their common referee so much as their poets shall. Of all mankind the great poet is the equable man. Not in him but off from him things are grotesque or eccentric or fail of their sanity. Nothing out of its place is good and nothing in its place is bad. He bestows on every object or quality its fit proportions neither more nor less. He is the arbiter of the diverse and he is the key. He is the equalizer of his age and land . . . he supplies what wants supplying and checks what wants checking. If peace is the routine out of him speaks the spirit of peace, large, rich, thrifty, building vast and populous cities, encouraging agriculture and the arts and commerce—lighting the study of man, the soul, immortality—federal, state or municipal government, marriage, health, free trade, intertravel by land and sea . . . nothing too close, nothing too far off . . . the stars not too far off. In war he is the most deadly force of the war. Who recruits him recruits horse and foot . . . he fetches parks of artillery the best that engineer ever knew. If the time becomes slothful and heavy he knows how to arouse it . . . he can make every word he speaks draw blood. Whatever stagnates in the flat of custom or obedience or legislation he never stagnates. Obedience does not master him, he masters it. High up out of reach he stands turning a concentrated light . . . he turns the pivot with his finger . . . he baffles the swiftest runners as he stands and easily overtakes and envelops them. The time straying toward infidelity and confections and persiflage he withholds by his steady faith . . . he spreads out his dishes . . . he offers the sweet firmfibred meat that grows men and women. His brain is the ultimate brain. He is no arguer . . . he is judgment. He judges not as the judge judges but as the sun falling around a helpless thing. As he sees the farthest he has the most faith. His thoughts are the hymns of the praise of things. In the talk on the soul and eternity and God off of his equal plane he is silent. He sees eternity less like a play with a prologue and denouement . . . he sees

*From Walt Whitman, *Leaves of Grass*, ed. Emory Holloway (New York: Doubleday, Doran & Co., 1926).

eternity in men and women . . . he does not see men and women as dreams or dots. Faith is the antiseptic of the soul . . . it pervades the common people and preserves them . . . they never give up believing and expecting and trusting. There is that indescribable freshness and unconsciousness about an illiterate person that humbles and mocks the power of the noblest expressive genius. The poet sees for a certainty how one not a great artist may be just as sacred as the greatest artist . . . The power to destroy or remould is freely used by him but never the power of attack. What is past is past. If he does not expose superior models and prove himself by every step he takes he is not what is wanted. The presence of the greatest poet conquers . . . not parleying or struggling or any prepared attempts. Now he has passed that way see after him! there is not left any vestige of despair or misanthropy or cunning or exclusiveness or the ignominy of a nativity or color or delusion of hell or the necessity of hell . . . and no man thenceforward shall be degraded for ignorance or weakness or sin.

The greatest poet hardly knows pettiness or triviality. If he breathes into any thing that was before thought small it dilates with the grandeur and life of the universe. He is a seer . . . he is individual . . . he is complete in himself . . . the others are as good as he, only he sees it and they do not. He is not one of the chorus . . . he does not stop for any regulations . . . he is the president of regulation. What the eyesight does to the rest he does to the rest. Who knows the curious mystery of the eyesight? The other senses corroborate themselves, but this is removed from any proof but its own and foreruns the identities of the spiritual world. A single glance of it mocks all the investigations of man and all the instruments and books of the earth and all reasoning. What is marvelous? what is unlikely? what is impossible or baseless or vague? after you have once just opened the space of a peachpit and given audience to far and near and to the sunset and had all things enter with electric swiftness softly and duly without confusion or jostling or jam.

The land and sea, the animals fishes and birds, the sky of heaven and the orbs, the forests mountains and rivers, are not small themes . . . but folks expect of the poet to indicate more than the beauty and dignity which always attach to dumb real objects . . . they expect him to indicate the path between reality and their souls. Men and women perceive the beauty well enough . . . probably as well as he. The passionate tenacity of hunters, woodmen, early risers, cultivators of gardens and orchards and fields, the love of healthy women for the manly form, seafaring persons, drivers of horses, the passion for light and the open air, all is an old varied sign of the unfailing perception of beauty and of a residence of the poetic in outdoor people. They can never be assisted by poets to perceive . . . some may but they never can. The poetic quality is not marshalled in rhyme or uniformity or abstract addresses to things nor in melancholy complaints or good precepts, but is the life of these and much else and is in the soul. The profit of rhyme is that it drops seeds of a sweeter and more luxuriant rhyme, and of uniformity that it conveys itself into its own roots in the ground out of sight. The rhyme and uniformity of perfect poems show the free growth of metrical laws and bud from them as unerringly and loosely as lilacs or roses on a bush, and take shapes as compact as the shapes of chestnuts and oranges and melons and pears, and shed the perfume impalpable to form. The fluency and ornaments of the finest poems or music or orations or recitations are not independent but dependent. All beauty comes from beautiful blood and a beautiful brain. If the greatnesses are in conjunction in a man or woman it is enough . . . the fact will prevail through the universe . . . but the gaggery and gilt of a million years will not prevail. Who troubles himself about his ornaments or fluency is lost. This is what you shall do: Love the earth and sun and the animals, despise riches, give alms to every one that asks, stand up for the stupid and crazy, devote your income and labor to others, hate tyrants, argue not concerning God, have patience and indulgence toward the people, take off your hat to nothing known or unknown or to any man or number of men, go freely with powerful uneducated persons and with the young and with the mothers of families, read these leaves in the open air every season of every year of your life, re-examine all you have been told at school or church or in any book, dismiss whatever insults your own soul, and your very flesh shall be a great poem and have the richest fluency not only in its words but in the silent lines of its lips and face and between the lashes of your eyes and in every motion and joint of your body . . . . The poet shall not spend his time in unneeded work. He shall know that the ground is always ready [to be] plowed and manured . . . others may not know it but he shall. He shall go directly to the creation. His trust shall master the trust of everything he touches . . . and shall master all attachment.

The known universe has one complete lover and that is the greatest poet. He consumes an eternal passion and is indifferent which chance happens and which possible contingency of fortune or misfortune and persuades daily and hourly his delicious pay. What balks or breaks others is fuel for his burning progress to contact and amorous joy. Other proportions of the reception of pleasure dwindle to nothing to his proportions. All expected from heaven or from the highest he is rapport with in the sight of the daybreak or a scene of the winterwoods or the presence of children playing or with his arm round the neck of a man or woman. His love above all love has leisure and expanse . . . he leaves room ahead of himself. He is no irresolute or suspicious lover . . . he is sure . . . he scorns intervals. His experience and the showers and thrills are not for nothing. Nothing can jar him . . . suffering and darkness cannot—death and fear cannot. To him complaint and jealousy and envy are corpses buried and rotten in the earth . . . he saw them buried. The sea is not surer of the shore or the shore of the sea than he is of the fruition of his love and of all perfection and beauty.

The fruition of beauty is no chance of hit or miss . . . it is inevitable as life . . . it is exact and plumb as gravitation. From the eyesight proceeds another eyesight and from the hearing proceeds another hearing and from the voice proceeds another voice eternally curious of the harmony of things with man. To these respond perfections not only in the committees that were supposed to stand for the rest but in the rest themselves just the same. These understand the law of perfection in masses and floods . . . that its finish is to each for itself and onward from itself . . . that it is profuse and impartial . . . that there is not a minute of the light or dark nor an acre of the earth or sea without it—nor any direction of the sky nor any trade or employment nor any turn of events. This is the reason that about the proper expression of beauty there is precision and balance . . . one part does not need to be thrust above another. The best singer is not the one who has the most lithe and powerful organ . . . the pleasure of poems is not in them that take the handsomest measure and similes and sound.

Without effort and without exposing in the least how it is done the greatest poet brings the spirit of any or all events and passions and scenes and persons some more and some less to bear on your individual character as you hear or read. To do this well is to compete with the laws that pursue and follow time. What is the purpose must surely be there and the clue of it must be there . . . and the faintest indication is the indication of the best and then becomes the clearest indication. Past and present and future are not disjoined but joined. The greatest poet forms the consistence of what is to be from what has been and is. He drags the dead out of their coffins and stands them again on their feet . . . he says to the past, Rise and walk before me that I may realize you. He learns the lesson . . . he places himself where the future becomes present. The greatest poet does not only dazzle his rays over character and scenes and passions . . . he finally ascends and finishes all . . . he exhibits the pinnacles that no man can tell what they are for or what is beyond . . . he glows a moment on the extremest verge. He is most wonderful in his last half-hidden smile or frown . . . by that flash of the moment of parting the one that sees it shall be encouraged or terrified afterwards for many years. The greatest poet does not moralize or make applications of morals . . . he knows the soul. The soul has that measureless pride which consists in never acknowledging any lessons but its own. But it has sympathy as measureless as its pride and the one balances the other and neither can stretch too far while it stretches in company with the other. The inmost secrets of art sleep with the twain. The greatest poet has lain close betwixt both and they are vital in his style and thoughts.

The art of art, the glory of expression and the sunshine of the light of letters is simplicity. Nothing is better than simplicity . . . nothing can make up for excess or for the lack of definiteness. To carry on the heave of impulse and pierce intellectual depths and give all subjects their articulations are powers neither common nor very uncommon. But to speak in literature with the perfect rectitude and insousiance of the movements of animals and the unimpeachableness of the sentiment of trees in the woods and grass by the roadside is the flawless triumph of art. If you have looked on him who has achieved it you have looked on one of the masters of the artists of all nations and times. You shall not contemplate the flight of the graygull over the bay or the mettlesome action of the blood horse or the tall leaning of sunflowers on their stalk or the appearance of the sun journeying through heaven or the appearance of the moon afterward with any more satisfaction than you shall contemplate him. The greatest poet has less a marked style and is more the channel of thoughts and things without increase or diminution, and is the free channel of himself. He swears to his art, I will not be meddlesome, I will not have in my writing any elegance or effect or originality to hang in the way between me and the rest like curtains. I will have nothing hang in the way, not the richest curtains. What I tell I tell for precisely what it is. Let who may exalt or startle or fascinate or sooth I will have purposes as health or heat or snow has and be as regardless of observation. What I experience or portray shall go from my composition without a shred of my composition. You shall stand by my side and look in the mirror with me. . . .

Men and women and the earth and all upon it are simply to be taken as they are, and the investigation of their past and present and future shall be unintermitted and shall be done with perfect candor. Upon this basis philosophy speculates ever looking toward the poet, ever regarding the eternal tendencies of all toward happiness never inconsistent with what is clear to the senses and to the soul. For the eternal tendencies of all toward happiness make the only point of sane philosophy. Whatever comprehends less than that . . . whatever is less than the laws of light and of astronomical motion . . . or less than the laws that follow the thief the liar the glutton and the drunkard through this life and doubtless afterward . . . or less than vast stretches of time or the slow formation of density or the patient upheaving of strata—is of no account. Whatever would put God in a poem or system of philosophy as contending against some being or influence, is also of no account. Sanity and ensemble characterise the great master . . . spoilt in one principle all is spoilt. The great master has nothing to do with miracles. He sees health for himself in being one of the mass . . . he sees the hiatus in singular eminence. To the perfect shape comes common ground. To be under the general law is great for that is to correspond with it. The master knows that he is unspeakably great and that all are unspeakably great . . . that nothing for instance is greater than to conceive children and bring them up well . . . that to be is just as great as to perceive or tell. . . .

SONG OF MYSELF

1

I celebrate myself, and sing myself,
And what I assume you shall assume,
For every atom belonging to me as good belongs to you.

I loafe and invite my soul,
I lean and loafe at my ease observing a spear of summer grass.

My tongue, every atom of my blood, form'd from this soil, this air,
Born here of parents born here from parents the same, and their parents the same,
I, now thirty-seven years old in perfect health begin,
Hoping to cease not till death.

Creeds and schools in abeyance,
Retiring back a while sufficed at what they are, but never forgotten,

I harbor for good or bad, I permit to speak at every hazard,
Nature without check with original energy.

2

Houses and rooms are full of perfumes, the shelves are crowded with perfumes,
I breathe the fragrance myself and know it and like it,
The distillation would intoxicate me also, but I shall not let it.

The atmosphere is not a perfume, it has no taste of the distillation, it is odorless,
It is for my mouth forever, I am in love with it,
I will go to the bank by the wood and become undisguised and naked,
I am mad for it to be in contact with me.

The smoke of my own breath,
Echoes, ripples, buzz'd whispers, love-root, silk-thread, crotch and vine,
My respiration and inspiration, the beating of my heart, the passing of blood and
air through my lungs,
The sniff of green leaves and dry leaves, and of the shore and dark-color'd
sea-rocks, and of hay in the barn,
The sound of the belch'd words of my voice loos'd to the eddies of the wind,
A few light kisses, a few embraces, a reaching around of arms,
The play of shine and shade on the trees as the supple boughs wag,
The delight alone or in the rush of the streets, or along the fields and hill-sides,
The feeling of health, the full-noon trill, the song of me rising from bed and
meeting the sun.

Have you reckon'd a thousand acres much? have you reckon'd the earth much?
Have you practis'd so long to learn to read?
Have you felt so proud to get at the meaning of poems?

Stop this day and night with me and you shall possess the origin of all poems,
You shall possess the good of the earth and sun, (there are millions of suns left,)
You shall no longer take things at second or third hand, nor look through the eyes
of the dead, nor feed on the spectres in books,
You shall not look through my eyes either, nor take things from me,
You shall listen to all sides and filter them from your self.

. . .

6

A child said *What is the grass?* fetching it to me with full hands,
How could I answer the child? I do not know what it is any more than he.

I guess it must be the flag of my disposition, out of hopeful green stuff woven.

Or I guess it is the handkerchief of the Lord,
A scented gift and remembrancer designedly dropt,

Bearing the owner's name someway in the corners, that we may see
and remark, and say *Whose?*

Or I guess the grass is itself a child, the produced babe of the vegetation.

Or I guess it is a uniform hieroglyphic,
And it means, Sprouting alike in broad zones and narrow zones,
Growing among black folks as among white,
Kanuck, Tuckahoe, Congressman, Cuff, I give them the same, I
receive them the same.

And now it seems to me the beautiful uncut hair of graves.

Tenderly will I use you curling grass,
It may be you transpire from the breasts of young men,
It may be if I had known them I would have loved them,
It may be you are from old people, or from offspring taken soon out of
their mothers' laps,
And here you are the mothers' laps.

This grass is very dark to be from the white heads of old mothers,
Darker than the colorless beards of old men,
Dark to come from under the faint red roofs of mouths.
O I perceive after all so many uttering tongues,
And I perceive they do not come from the roofs of mouths for nothing.

I wish I could translate the hints about the dead young men and women,
And the hints about old men and mothers, and the offspring taken soon
out of their laps.

What do you think has become of the young and old men?
And what do you think has become of the women and children?

They are alive and well somewhere,
The smallest sprout shows there is really no death,
And if ever there was it led forward life, and does not wait at the end to arrest it,
And ceas'd the moment life appear'd.

All goes onward and outward, nothing collapses,
And to die is different from what any one supposed, and luckier.

. . .

31

I believe a leaf of grass is no less than the journey-work of the stars,
And the pismire is equally perfect, and a grain of sand, and the egg of the wren,
And the tree-toad is a chef-d'oeuvre for the highest,
And the running blackberry would adorn the parlors of heaven,

And the narrowest hinge in my hand puts to scorn all machinery,
And the cow crunching with depress'd head surpasses any statue,
And a mouse is miracle enough to stagger sextillions of infidels.

I find I incorporate gneiss, coal, long-threaded moss, fruits, grains, esculent roots,
And am stucco'd with quadrupeds and birds all over,
And have distanced what is behind me for good reasons,
But call any thing back again when I desire it.

In vain the speeding or shyness,
In vain the plutonic rocks send their old heat against my approach,
In vain the mastodon retreats beneath its own powder'd bones,
In vain objects stand leagues off and assume manifold shapes,
In vain the ocean settling in hollows and the great monsters lying low,
In vain the buzzard houses herself with the sky,
In vain the snake slides through the creepers and logs,
In vain the elk takes to the inner passes of the woods,
In vain the razor-bill'd auk sails far north to Labrador,
I follow quickly, I ascend to the nest in the fissure of the cliff.

32

I think I could turn and live with animals, they're so placid and self-contain'd,
I stand and look at them long and long.

They do not sweat and whine about their condition,
They do not lie awake in the dark and weep for their sins,
They do not make me sick discussing their duty to God,
Not one is dissatisfied, not one is demented with the mania of owning things,
Not one kneels to another, nor to his kind that lived thousands of years ago,
Not one is respectable or unhappy over the whole earth.

So they show their relations to me and I accept them,
They bring me tokens of myself, they evince them plainly in their possession.

I wonder where they get those tokens,
Did I pass that way huge times ago and negligently drop them?

Myself moving forward then and now and forever,
Gathering and showing more always and with velocity,
Infinite and omnigenous, and the like of these among them,
Not too exclusive toward the reachers of my remembrancers,
Picking out here one that I love, and now go with him on brotherly terms.

A gigantic beauty of a stallion, fresh and responsive to my caresses,
Head high in the forehead, wide between the ears,
Limbs glossy and supple, tail dusting the ground,
Eyes full of sparkling wickedness, ears finely cut, flexibly moving.

His nostrils dilate as my heels embrace him,
His well-built limbs tremble with pleasure as we race around and return.
I but use you a minute, then I resign you, stallion,
Why do I need your paces when I myself out-gallop them?
Even as I stand or sit passing faster than you.

. . .

SONG OF THE REDWOOD-TREE

1

A California song,
A prophecy and indirection, a thought impalpable to breathe as air,
A chorus of dryads, fading, departing, or hamadryads departing,
A murmuring, fateful, giant voice, out of the earth and sky,
Voice of a mighty dying tree in the redwood forest dense.

Farewell my brethren,
Farewell O earth and sky, farewell ye neighboring waters,
My time has ended, my term has come.

Along the northern coast,
Just back from the rock-bound shore and the caves,
In the saline air from the sea in the Mendocino country,
With the surge for base and accompaniment low and hoarse,
With crackling blows of axes sounding musically driven by strong arms,
Riven deep by the sharp tongues of the axes, there in the redwood forest dense,
I heard the mighty tree its death-chant chanting.

The choppers heard not, the camp shanties echoed not,
The quick-ear'd teamsters and chain and jack-screw men heard not,
As the wood-spirits came from their haunts of a thousand years to join the refrain,
But in my soul I plainly heard.

Murmuring out of its myriad leaves,
Down from its lofty top rising two hundred feet high,
Out of its stalwart trunk and limbs, out of its foot-thick bark,
That chant of the seasons and time, chant not of the past only but the future.

You untold life of me,
And all you venerable and innocent joys,
Perennial hardy life of me with joys 'mid rain and many a summer sun,
And the white snows and night and the wild winds;
O the great patient rugged joys, my soul's strong joys unreck'd by man,
(For know I bear the soul befitting me, I too have consciousness, identity,
And all the rocks and mountains have, and all the earth,)
Joys of the life befitting me and brothers mine,
Our time, our term has come.

Nor yield we mournfully majestic brothers,
We who have grandly fill'd our time;
With Nature's calm content, with tacit huge delight,
We welcome what we wrought for through the past,
And leave the field for them.
For them predicted long,
For a superber race, they too to grandly fill their time,
For them we abdicate, in them ourselves ye forest kings!
In them these skies and airs, these mountain peaks, Shasta, Nevadas,
These huge precipitous cliffs, this amplitude, these valleys, far Yosemite,
To be in them absorb'd, assimilated.

Then to a loftier strain,
Still prouder, more ecstatic rose the chant,
As if the heirs, the deities of the West,
Joining with master-tongue bore part.

Not wan from Asia's fetiches,
Nor red from Europe's old dynastic slaughter-house,
(Area of murder-plots of thrones, with scent left yet of wars and scaffolds everywhere,)
But come from Nature's long and harmless throes, peacefully builded thence,
These virgin lands, lands of the Western shore,
To the new culminating man, to you, the empire new,
You promis'd long, we pledge, we dedicate.

You occult deep volitions,
You average spiritual manhood, purpose of all, pois'd on yourself, giving not taking law,
You womanhood divine, mistress and source of all, whence life and love and
aught that comes from life and love,
You unseen moral essence of all the vast materials of America, (age upon
age working in death the same as life,)
You that, sometimes known, oftener unknown, really shape and mould the
New World, adjusting it to Time and Space,
You hidden national will lying in your abysms, conceal'd but ever alert,
You past and present purposes tenaciously pursued, may-be unconscious of yourselves,
Unswerv'd by all the passing errors, perturbations of the surface;
You vital, universal, deathless germs, beneath all creeds, arts, statutes, literatures,
Here build your homes for good, establish here, these areas entire, lands of the Western shore,
We pledge, we dedicate to you.

For man of you, your characteristic race,
Here may he hardy, sweet, gigantic grow, here tower proportionate to Nature,
Here climb the vast pure space unconfined, uncheck'd by wall or roof,
Here laugh with storm or sun, here joy, here patiently inure,
Here heed himself, unfold himself, (not others' formulas heed,) here fill his time,
To duly fall, to aid, unreck'd at last.
To disappear, to serve.

Thus on the northern coast,
In the echo of teamsters' calls and the clinking chains, and the music of
choppers' axes,
The falling trunk and limbs, the crash, the muffled shriek, the groan,
Such words combined from the redwood-tree, as of voices ecstatic,
ancient and rustling,
The century-lasting, unseen dryads, singing, withdrawing,
All their recesses of forests and mountains leaving,
From the Cascade range to the Wasatch, or Idaho far, or Utah,
To the deities of the modern henceforth yielding,
The chorus and indications, the vistas of coming humanity, the settlements,
features all,
In the Mendocino woods I caught.

2

The flashing and golden pageant of California,
The sudden and gorgeous drama, the sunny and ample lands,
The long and varied stretch from Puget sound to Colorado south,
Lands bathed in sweeter, rarer, healthier air, valleys and mountain cliffs,
The fields of Nature long prepared and fallow, the silent, cyclic chemistry,
The slow and steady ages plodding, the unoccupied surface ripening,
the rich ores forming beneath;
At last the New arriving, assuming, taking possession,
A swarming and busy race settling and organizing everywhere,
Ships coming in from the whole round world, and going out to the whole
world,
To India and China and Australia and the thousand island paradises of
the Pacific,
Populous cities, the latest inventions, the steamers on the rivers, the railroads,
with many a thrifty farm, with machinery,
And wool and wheat and the grape, and diggings of yellow gold.

3

But more in you than these, lands of the Western shore,
(These but the means, the implements, the standing-ground,)
I see in you, certain to come, the promise of thousands of years, till now deferr'd,
Promis'd to be fulfilled, our common kind, the race.

The new society at last, proportionate to Nature,
In man of you, more than your mountain peaks or stalwart trees imperial,
In woman more, far more, than all your gold or vines, or even vital air.

Fresh come, to a new world indeed, yet long prepared,
I see the genius of the modern, child of the real and ideal,
Clearing the ground for broad humanity, the true America, heir of the
past so grand,
To build a grander future.

SEA-DRIFT

OUT OF THE CRADLE ENDLESSLY ROCKING

Out of the cradle endlessly rocking,
Out of the mocking-bird's throat, the musical shuttle,
Out of the Ninth-month midnight,
Over the sterile sands and the fields beyond, where the child leaving his
bed wander'd alone, bareheaded, barefoot,
Down from the shower'd halo,
Up from the mystic play of shadows twining and twisting as if they were alive,
Out from the patches of briers and blackberries,
From the memories of the bird that chanted to me,
From your memories sad brother, from the fitful risings and fallings I heard,
From under that yellow half-moon late-risen and swollen as if with tears,
From those beginning notes of yearning and love there in the mist,
From the thousand responses of my heart never to cease,
From the myriad thence-arous'd words,
From the word stronger and more delicious than any,
From such as now they start the scene revisiting
As a flock, twittering, rising, or overhead passing,
Borne hither, ere all eludes me, hurriedly,
A man, yet by these tears a little boy again,
Throwing myself on the sand, confronting the waves,
I, chanter of pains and joys, uniter of here and hereafter,
Taking all hints to use them, but swiftly leaping beyond them,
A reminiscence sing.

Once Paumanok,
When the lilac-scent was in the air and Fifth-month grass was growing,
Up this seashore in some briers,
Two feather'd guests from Alabama, two together,
And their nest, and four light-green eggs spotted with brown,
And every day the he-bird to and fro near at hand,
And every day the she-bird crouch'd on her nest, silent, with bright eyes,
And every day I, a curious boy, never too close, never disturbing them,
Cautiously peering, absorbing, translating.

Shine! shine! shine!
Pour down your warmth, great sun!
While we bask, we two together,

Two together!
Winds blow south, or winds blow north,
Day come white, or night come black,
Home, or rivers and mountains from home,
Singing all time, minding no time,
While we two keep together.

Till of a sudden,
May-be kill'd, unknown to her mate,
One forenoon the she-bird crouch'd not on the nest,
Nor return'd that afternoon, nor the next,
Nor ever appear'd again.

And thenceforward all summer in the sound of the sea,
And at night under the full of the moon in calmer weather,
Over the hoarse surging of the sea,
Or flitting from brier to brier by day,
I saw, I heard at intervals the remaining one, the he-bird,
The solitary guest from Alabama.

Blow! blow! blow!
Blow up sea-winds along Paumanok's shore;
I wait and I wait till you blow my mate to me.

Yes, when the stars glisten'd,
All night long on the prong of a moss-scallop'd stake,
Down almost amid the slapping waves,
Set the lone singer wonderful causing tears.
He call'd on his mate,
He pour'd forth the meanings which I of all men know.

Yes my brother I know,
The rest might not, but I have treasur'd every note,
For more than once dimly down to the beach gliding,
Silent, avoiding the moonbeams, blending myself with the shadows,
Recalling now the obscure shapes, the echoes, the sounds and sights
after their sorts,
The white arms out in the breakers tirelessly tossing,
I, with bare feet, a child, the wind wafting my hair,
Listen'd long and long.

Listen'd to keep, to sing, now translating the notes,
Following you my brother.

Soothe! soothe! soothe!
Close on its wave soothes the wave behind,
And again another behind embracing and lapping, every one close,
But my love soothes not me, not me.

Low hangs the moon, it rose late,
It is lagging—O I think it is heavy with love, with love.

O madly the sea pushes upon the land,
With love, with love.

O night! do I not see my love fluttering out among the breakers?
What is that little black thing I see there in the white?

Loud! loud! loud!
Loud I call to you, my love!
High and clear I shoot my voice over the waves,
Surely you must know who is here, is here,
You must know who I am, my love.

Low-hanging moon!
What is that dusky spot in your brown yellow?
O it is the shape, the shape of my mate!
O moon do not keep her from me any longer.

Land! land! O land!
Whichever way I turn, O I think you could give me my mate back again if you only would,
For I am almost sure I see her dimly whichever way I look.

O rising stars!
Perhaps the one I want so much will rise, will rise with some of you.

O throat! O trembling throat!
Sound clearer through the atmosphere!
Pierce the woods, the earth,
Somewhere listening to catch you must be the one I want.

Shake out carols!
Solitary here, the night's carols!
Carols of lonesome love! death's carols!
Carols under that lagging, yellow, waning moon!
O under that moon where she droops almost down into the sea!
O reckless despairing carols.

But soft! sink low!
Soft! let me just murmur,
And do you wait a moment you husky-nois'd sea,
For somewhere I believe I heard my mate responding to me,
So faint, I must be still, be still to listen,
But not altogether still, for then she might not come immediately to me.

Hither my love!
Here I am! here!
With this just-sustain'd note I announce myself to you,
This gentle call is for you my love, for you.

Do not be decoy'd elsewhere,
That is the whistle of the wind, it is not my voice,
That is the fluttering, the fluttering of the spray,
Those are the shadows of leaves.

O darkness! O in vain!
O I am very sick and sorrowful.

O brown halo in the sky near the moon, drooping upon the sea!
O troubled reflection in the sea!
O throat! O throbbing heart!
And I singing uselessly, uselessly all the night.

O past! O happy life! O songs of joy!
In the air, in the woods, over fields,
Loved! loved! loved! loved! loved!
But my mate no more, no more with me!
We two together no more.

The aria sinking,
All else continuing, the stars shining,
The winds blowing, the notes of the bird continuous echoing,
With angry moans the fierce old mother incessantly moaning,
On the sands of Paumanok's shore gray and rustling,
The yellow half-moon enlarged, sagging down, drooping, the face of the
sea almost touching,
The boy ecstatic, with his bare feet the waves, with his hair the atmosphere dallying,
The love in the heart long pent, now loose, now at last tumultuously bursting,
The aria's meaning, the ears, the soul, swiftly depositing,
The strange tears down the cheeks coursing,
The colloquy there, the trio, each uttering,
The undertone, the savage old mother incessantly crying,
To the boy's soul's questions sullenly timing, some drown'd secret hissing,
To the outsetting bard.

Demon or bird! (said the boy's soul,)
Is it indeed toward your mate you sing? or is it really to me?
For I, that was a child, my tongue's use sleeping, now I have heard you,
Now in a moment I know what I am for, I awake,
And already a thousand singers, a thousand songs, clearer, louder and more
sorrowful than yours,
A thousand warbling echoes have started to life within me, never to die.

O you singer solitary, singing by yourself, projecting me,
O solitary me listening, never more shall I cease perpetuating you,
Never more shall I escape, never more the reverberations,
Never more the cries of unsatisfied love be absent from me,
Never again leave me to be the peaceful child I was before what there in the night,
By the sea under the yellow and sagging moon,
The messenger there arous'd, the fire, the sweet hell within,
The unknown want, the destiny of me.

O give me the clew! (it lurks in the night here somewhere,)
O if I am to have so much, let me have more!

A word then, (for I will conquer it,)
The word final, superior to all,
Subtle, sent up—what is it?—I listen;
Are you whispering it, and have been all the time, you sea waves?
Is that it from your liquid rims and wet sands?

Whereto answering, the sea,
Delaying not, hurrying not,
Whisper'd me through the night, and very plainly before daybreak,
Lisp'd to me the low and delicious word death,
And again death, death, death, death,
Hissing melodious, neither like the bird nor like my arous'd child's heart,
But edging near as privately for me rustling at my feet,
Creeping thence steadily up to my ears and laving me softly all over,
Death, death, death, death, death.

Which I do not forget,
But fuse the song of my dusky demon and brother,
That he sang to me in the moonlight on Paumanok's gray beach,
With the thousand responsive songs at random,
My own songs awaked from that hour,
And with them the key, the word up from the waves,
The word of the sweetest song and all songs,
That strong and delicious word which, creeping to my feet,
(Or like some old crone rocking the cradle, swathed in sweet garments,
bending aside,)
The sea whisper'd me.

THE WORLD BELOW THE BRINE

The world below the brine,
Forests at the bottom of the sea, the branches and leaves,
Sea-lettuce, vast lichens, strange flowers and seeds, the thick tangle,
openings, and pink turf,
Different colors, pale gray and green, purple, white, and gold, the play
of light through the water,
Dumb swimmers there among the rocks, coral, gluten, grass, rushes, and the
aliment of the swimmers,
Sluggish existences grazing there suspended, or slowly crawling close
to the bottom,
The sperm-whale at the surface blowing air and spray, or disporting with
his flukes,
The leaden-eyed shark, the walrus, the turtle, the hairy sea-leopard, and
the sting-ray,
Passions there, wars, pursuits, tribes, sight in those ocean-depths, breathing

that thick-breathing air, as so many do,
The change thence to the sight here, and to the subtle air breathed by
beings like us who walk this sphere,
The change onward from ours to that of beings who walk other spheres.

THE DALLIANCE OF THE EAGLES

Skirting the river road, (my forenoon walk, my rest,)
Skyward in air a sudden muffled sound, the dalliance of the eagles,
The rushing amorous contact high in space together,
The clinching interlocking claws, a living, fierce, gyrating wheel,
Four beating wings, two beaks, a swirling mass tight grappling,
In tumbling turning clustering loops, straight downward falling,
Till o'er the river pois'd, the twain yet one, a moment's lull,
A motionless still balance in the air, then parting, talons loosing,
Upward again on slow-firm pinions slanting, their separate diverse flight,
She hers, he his, pursuing.

THIS COMPOST

1

Something startles me where I thought I was safest,
I withdraw from the still woods I loved,
I will not go now on the pastures to walk,
I will not strip the clothes from my body to meet my lover the sea,
I will not touch my flesh to the earth as to other flesh to renew me.

O how can it be that the ground itself does not sicken?
How can you be alive you growths of spring?
How can you furnish health you blood of herbs, roots, orchards, grain?
Are they not continually putting distemper'd corpses within you?
Is not every continent work'd over and over with sour dead?

Where have you disposed of their carcasses?
Those drunkards and gluttons of so many generations?
Where have you drawn off all the foul liquid and meat?
I do not see any of it upon you to-day, or perhaps I am deceiv'd,
I will run a furrow with my plough, I will press my spade through the sod and
turn it up underneath,
I am sure I shall expose some of the foul meat.

2

Behold this compost! behold it well!
Perhaps every mite has once form'd part of a sick person—yet behold!
The grass of spring covers the prairies,
The bean bursts noiselessly through the mould in the garden,
The delicate spear of the onion pierces upward,
The apple-buds cluster together on the apple-branches,
The resurrection of the wheat appears with pale visage out of its graves,
The tinge awakes over the willow-tree and the mulberry-tree,
The he-birds carol mornings and evenings while the she-birds sit on their nests,
The young poultry break through the hatch'd eggs,
The new-born of animals appear, the calf is dropt from the cow,
the colt from the mare,
Out of its little hill faithfully rise the potato's dark green leaves,
Out of its hill rises the yellow maize-stalk, the lilacs bloom in the door-yards,
The summer growth is innocent and disdainful above all those strata
of sour dead.

What chemistry!
That the winds are really not infectious,
That this is no cheat, this transparent green-wash of the sea which is so
amorous after me,
That it is safe to allow it to lick my naked body all over with its tongues,
That it will not endanger me with the fevers that have deposited themselves in it,
That all is clean forever and forever,
That the cool drink from the well tastes so good,
That blackberries are so flavorous and juicy,
That the fruits of the apple-orchard and the orange-orchard, that
melons, grapes, peaches, plums, will none of them poison me,
That when I recline on the grass I do not catch any disease,
Though probably every spear of grass rises out of what was once a
catching disease.

Now I am terrified at the Earth, it is that calm and patient,
It grows such sweet things out of such corruptions,
It turns harmless and stainless on its axis, with such endless successions of
diseas'd corpses,
It distills such exquisite winds out of such infused fetor,
It renews with such unwitting looks its prodigal, annual, sumptuous crops,
It gives such divine materials to men, and accepts such leavings from them at last.

Emily Dickinson
1830-1886

Emily Dickinson, a recluse for most of her life, published only seven poems (anonymously) during her lifetime, yet she stands beside Walt Whitman as one of the revolutionary poets of her time. Both influenced twentieth-century poetry enormously, both found "ecstasy in living" (as Dickinson put it), both wrote outside of the conventions of the day, and both took nature as one of their major themes. Unlike Whitman, Dickinson's experience of life was mostly limited to her home and family in Amherst, Massachusetts, and to a few friends. Yet like Whitman she lived intensely.

After a year at Mount Holyoke Female Seminary, Emily returned home to live her days in Amherst, traveling briefly to Boston, Washington, and Philadelphia. Her editor and biographer Thomas Johnson writes that she had one love in her life—the married Philadelphia minister Charles Wadsworth—but that this experience of love "may well have been the single most important event in her life." Dickinson met Wadsworth briefly in 1860 in Amherst, but when Wadsworth left Philadelphia for San Francisco shortly afterwards, she became more reclusive than ever, dressing in her "bridal" white, haunting her father's grounds and gardens, writing—in a tremendously productive period of eight years—the bulk of her 1,775 poems. In fact, many of her poems are more readily understood by the reader who is aware of how close they were written to the powerful moment of love and the immediate loss of the loved one afterwards. She never married.

Emerson influenced her, as did the whole Romantic and Transcendental movement of the century. Yet she was perhaps equally influenced by the disciplines and denials of Puritan theology lingering in New England and in her family. A life of imagination and lyric poetry was how she struck her balance. For all its freedom and lack of convention, her poetry uses a biblical idiom and imagery and the rhythms of English hymns. Elliptical, clever, epigrammatic, full of irony and paradox and startling comparisons, her poems also have roots in the seventeenth-century English verse of Herrick, Donne, and the so-called "metaphysical" poets. If like the Transcendentalists and Romantics she took as her greatest theme the life of the spirit and imagination, she described that life through the commonplace things and events of domestic life and nature in New England.

THESE ARE THE DAYS WHEN BIRDS COME BACK*

These are the days when Birds come back—
A very few—a Bird or two—
To take a backward look.

These are the days when skies resume
The old—old sophistries of June—
A blue and gold mistake.

Oh fraud that cannot cheat the Bee—
Almost thy plausibility
Induces my belief.

Till ranks of seeds their witness bear—
And softly thro' the altered air
Hurries a timid leaf.

Oh Sacrament of summer days,
Oh Last Communion in the Haze—
Permit a child to join.

Thy sacred emblems to partake—
Thy consecrated bread to take
And thine immortal wine!

COME SLOWLY—EDEN

Come slowly—Eden!
Lips unused to Thee—
Bashful—sip thy Jessamines—
As the fainting Bee—

Reaching late his flower,
Round her chamber hums—
Counts his nectars—
Enters—and is lost in Balms.

I TASTE A LIQUOR NEVER BREWED

I taste a liquor never brewed—
From Tankards scooped in Pearl—
Not all the Vats upon the Rhine
Yield such an Alcohol!

Inebriate of Air—am I—
And Debauchee of Dew—
Reeling—thro endless summer days—
From inns of Molten Blue—

When "Landlords" turn the drunken Bee
Out of the Foxglove's door—
When Butterflies—renounce their "drams"—
I shall but drink the more!

Till Seraphs swing their snowy Hats—
And Saints—to windows run—
To see the little Tippler
Leaning against the—Sun—

THERE'S A CERTAIN SLANT OF LIGHT

There's a certain Slant of light,
Winter Afternoons—
That oppresses, like the Heft
Of Cathedral Tunes—

Heavenly Hurt, it gives us—
We can find no scar,
But internal difference
Where the Meanings, are—

None may teach it—Any—
'Tis the Seal Despair—
An imperial affliction
Sent us of the Air—

When it comes, the Landscape listens—
Shadows—hold their breath—
When it goes, 'tis like the Distance
On the look of Death—

THERE CAME A DAY AT SUMMER'S FULL

There came a Day at Summer's full,
Entirely for me—

I thought that such were for the Saints,
Where Resurrections—be—

The Sun, as common, went abroad,
The flowers, accustomed, blew,
As if no soul the solstice passed
That maketh all things new—

The time was scarce profaned, by speech—
The symbol of a word
Was needless, as at Sacrament,
The Wardrobe—of our Lord—

Each was to each The Sealed Church,
Permitted to commune this—time—
Lest we too awkward show
At Supper of the Lamb.

The Hours slid fast—as Hours will,
Clutched tight, by greedy hands—
So faces on two Decks, look back,
Bound to opposing lands—

And so when all the time had leaked,
Without external sound
Each bound the Other's Crucifix—
We gave no other Bond—

Sufficient troth, that we shall rise—
Deposed—at length, the Grave—
To that new Marriage,
Justified—through Calvaries of Love—

I DREADED THAT FIRST ROBIN SO

I dreaded that first Robin, so,
But He is mastered, now,
I'm some accustomed to Him grown,
He hurts a little, though—

I thought if I could only live
Till that first Shout got by—
Not all Pianos in the Woods
Had power to mangle me—

I dared not meet the Daffodils—
For fear their Yellow Gown
Would pierce me with a fashion
So foreign to my own—

I wished the Grass would hurry—
So—when 'twas time to see—
He'd be too tall, the tallest one
Could stretch—to look at me—

I could not bear the Bees should come,
I wished they'd stay away
In those dim countries where they go,
What word had they, for me?

They're here, though; not a creature failed—
No Blossom stayed away
In gentle deference to me—
The Queen of Calvary—

Each one salutes me, as he goes,
And I, my childish Plumes,
Lift, in bereaved acknowledgment
Of their unthinking Drums—

THIS IS MY LETTER TO THE WORLD

This is my letter to the World
That never wrote to Me—
The simple News that Nature told—
With tender Majesty

Her Message is committed
To Hands I cannot see—
For love of Her—Sweet—countrymen—
Judge tenderly—of Me

I STARTED EARLY—TOOK MY DOG

I started Early—Took my Dog—
And visited the Sea—
The Mermaids in the Basement
Came out to look at me—

And Frigates—in the Upper Floor
Extended Hempen Hands—
Presuming Me to be a Mouse—
Aground—upon the Sands—

But no Man moved Me—till the Tide
Went past my simple Shoe—
And past my Apron—and my Belt
And past my Bodice—too—

And made as He would eat me up—
As wholly as a Dew
Upon a Dandelion's Sleeve—
And then—I started—too—

And He—He followed—close behind—
I felt His Silver Heel
Upon my Ankle—Then my Shoes
Would overflow with Pearl—

Until We met the Solid Town—
No One He seemed to know—
And bowing—with a Mighty look—
At me—The Sea withdrew—

ESSENTIAL OILS—ARE WRUNG

Essential Oils—are wrung—
The Attar from the Rose
Be not expressed by Suns—alone—
It is the gift of Screws—

The General Rose—decay—
But this—in Lady's Drawer
Make Summer—When the Lady lie
In Ceaseless Rosemary—

NATURE—THE GENTLEST MOTHER IS

Nature—the Gentlest Mother is,
Impatient of no Child—
The feeblest—or the waywardest—
Her Admonition mild—

In Forest—and the Hill—
By Traveller—be heard—
Restraining Rampant Squirrel—
Or too impetuous Bird—

How fair Her Conversation—
A Summer Afternoon—
Her Household—Her Assembly—
And when the Sun go down—

Her Voice among the Aisles
Incite the timid prayer
Of the minutest Cricket—
The most unworthy Flower—

When all the Children sleep—
She turns as long away
As will suffice to light Her lamps—
Then bending from the Sky—

With infinite Affection—
And infiniter Care—
Her Golden finger on Her lip—
Wills Silence—Everywhere—

AT HALF PAST THREE, A SINGLE BIRD

At Half past Three, a single Bird
Unto a silent Sky
Propounded by a single term
Of cautious melody.

At Half past Four, Experiment
Had subjugated test
And lo, Her silver Principle
Supplanted all the rest.

At Half past Seven, Element
Nor Implement, be seen—
And Place was where the Presence was
Circumference between.

HOW FITS HIS UMBER COAT

How fits his Umber Coat
The Tailor of the Nut?
Combined without a seam
Like Raiment of a Dream—

Who spun the Auburn Cloth?
Computed how the girth?
The Chestnut aged grows
In those primeval Clothes—

We know that we are wise—
Accomplished in Surprise—
Yet by this Countryman—
This nature—how undone!

WHAT MYSTERY PERVADES A WELL!

What mystery pervades a well!
That water lives so far—

A neighbor from another world
Residing in a jar

Whose limit none have ever seen,
But just his lid of glass—
Like looking every time you please
In an abyss's face!

The grass does not appear afraid,
I often wonder he
Can stand so close and look so bold
At what is awe to me.

Related somehow they may be,
The sedge stands next the sea—
Where he is floorless
And does no timidity betray

But nature is a stranger yet;
The ones that cite her most
Have never passed her haunted house,
Nor simplified her ghost.

To pity those that know her not
Is helped by the regret
That those who know her, know her less
The nearer her they get.

THE BIRD HER PUNCTUAL MUSIC BRINGS

The Bird her punctual music brings
And lays it in its place—
Its place is in the Human Heart
And in the Heavenly Grace—
What respite from her thrilling toil
Did Beauty ever take—
But Work might be electric Rest
To those that Magic make—

John Burroughs
1837-1921

After the death of Thoreau in 1862, two writers divide between them the role of outstanding American prose writer about nature—John Burroughs and John Muir. Together they established, in America at least, a new literary genre, the nature essay. Burroughs, in association with Theodore Roosevelt and others, waged a campaign against the corruption of that genre which Burroughs had witnessed even in his own time. In "The Literary Treatment of Nature," Burroughs sniped at the so-called "Nature Fakers" and defined the "nature essayist" by distinguishing him from the scientific naturalists. The scientist, he wrote, records facts largely for other scientists and for experimentation, while the essayist gathers facts in the field and rearranges, synthesizes, and in turn generalizes them so as to appeal to the human feelings, to arouse interest, and to establish our rapport with nature. He attempts to show a living nature and a living natural thing—bird, tree, forest—in totality, not microscopically, not analyzed narrowly in part. Yet if the essayist sees himself in nature and in animals, he must see them without mawkish sentimentalilty or a silly attribution to animals of such human traits as sophisticated language or reason. What the nature essayist does see and establish for his readers is our kinship with organic matter, or life, our instinctual, struggling, racial selves.

Burroughs was born on an isolated dairy farm—300 acres of upland meadow and woods—in Roxbury, New York, in the Catskill Mountains. Here, as a boy, he learned to love nature, and here he would return later to devote himself to nature study. He read widely and was influenced by Wordsworth and Carlyle, but especially by Emerson. He wrote that he read the author of *Nature* "in a sort of ecstacy. I got him in my blood, and he colored my whole intellectual outlook." The other great influence upon his life was Whitman, not only as a writer but as a friend. After some years as a country school teacher and after initiating his literary career with a series of nature essays under the title "From the Back Country" in the *New York Leader,* Burroughs lived in Washington, D.C., and worked with Whitman as a clerk in the U.S. Treasury Department from 1863–73. It was the most important and expansive friendship of Burrough's life. His first book in 1867 was on Whitman as "a poet and a person." And in 1896 he published another, *Whitman, A Study.* "I owe more to him," Burroughs said, "than to any man in the world. He brooded me; gave me things to think of; he taught me generosity, breadth, and an all-embracing charity."

During this time also, his nature essays began to appear in the *Atlantic,* and along with his first nature book, *Wake-Robin* (1871), he became established enough to consider returning to his beloved Catskills for a life of retreat, study, and writing, with occasional travels elsewhere. Henry James captured the personal qualities of Burroughs as "a sort of reduced, but also more humorous, more available, more sociable Thoreau." Indeed, comparison to Thoreau is broader and quite common, for although Burroughs travelled from the tropics to Alaska, most of his writing focuses on his local, home ground. He is not the writer of the sublime and awesome panorama that John Muir is. Local nature provided wealth enough: "One has only to sit in the woods or by the shore of the river or lake, and nearly everything of interest will come round to him, the birds, the animals, the insects."

By 1873 Burroughs bought a house, which he called "Riverby," eighty miles up the Hudson River from New York. His ornithological books *Wake-Robin* and *Birds and Poets* (1877) came from his fascination with Audubon and with the birds of his native New York, but the books also represent a first stage in several changes in Burrough's approach to nature from the mid-nineteenth through the twentieth centuries.

In the early period Burroughs is his most poetic, appreciative, lyrical, and embracing in his approach to nature. But his growing fascination with scientific advances before and after the turn of the century captivated his imagination for many years. From *Locust and Wild Honey* (1879) through *Leaf and Tendril* (1908), his view of nature became more rationalistic, factual, scientific, and, some would say, mechanistic. In *The Light of Day* (1900), for example, Burroughs exalted the exact, objective knowledge of science over the subjectivity of poetry, religion, and metaphor; he believed, indeed, that science would properly replace literature and religion. But Burroughs changed again. The experience of a lifetime and wider reading, especially the French philosopher, poet, and scientist Henri Bergson, led Burroughs to adjust the balance of his vision in later years through such books as *Time and Change* (1912), *The Summit of the Years* (1914), *The Breath of Life* (1915), and *Under Apple Trees* (1916), where he acknowledged that the extreme mechanism of a purely scientific civilization is a kind of death. "Where there is no vision, no intuitive perception of the great fundamental truths of the inner spiritual world, science will not save us. In such a case our civilization is like an engine running without a headlight." During the First World War, Burroughs saw Germany as the epitome of the destructive power of the gods of science gone unchecked. If the intellect could discover and understand the *physical order* of the universe, only the intuition could discover the *vital order,* the unifying creative impulse that Emerson, Bergson, and finally Burroughs saw in all life.

from WAKE-ROBIN*

THE RETURN OF THE BIRDS

Spring in our northern climate may fairly be said to extend from the middle of March to the middle of June. At least, the vernal tide continues to rise until the latter date, and it is not till after the summer solstice that the shoots and twigs begin to harden and turn to wood, or the grass to lose any of its freshness and succulency.

It is this period that marks the return of the birds,—one or two of the more hardy or half-domesticated species, like the song-sparrow and the bluebird, usually arriving in March, while the rarer and more brilliant wood-birds bring up the procession in June. But each stage of the advancing season gives prominence to certain species, as to certain flowers. The dandelion tells me when to look for the swallow, the dog-toothed violet when to expect the wood-thrush, and when I have found the wake-robin in bloom I know the season is fairly inaugurated. With me this flower is associated, not merely with the awakening of Robin, for he has been awake some weeks, but with the universal awakening and rehabilitation of nature.

Yet the coming and going of the birds is more or less a mystery and a surprise. We go out in the morning, and no thrush or vireo is to be heard; we go out again, and every tree and grove is musical; yet again, and all is silent. Who saw them come? Who saw them depart?

This pert little winter-wren, for instance, darting in and out the fence, diving under the rubbish here and coming up yards away,—how does he manage with those little circular wings to compass degrees and zones, and arrive always in the nick of time? Last August I saw him in the remotest wilds of the Adirondacs, impatient and inquisitive as usual; a few weeks later, on the Potomac, I was greeted by the same hardy little busybody. Does he travel by easy stages from bush to bush and from wood to wood? or has that compact little body force and courage to brave the night and the upper air, and so achieve leagues at one pull?

And yonder bluebird with the earth tinge on his breast and the sky tinge on his back,—did he come down out of heaven on that bright March morning when he told us so softly and plaintively that if we pleased, spring had come? Indeed, there is nothing in the return of the birds more curious and suggestive than in the first appearance, or rumors of the appearance, of this little blue-coat. The bird at first seems a mere wandering voice in the air; one hears its call or carol on some bright March morning, but is uncertain of its source or direction; it falls like a drop of rain when no cloud is visible; one looks and listens, but to no purpose. The weather changes, perhaps a cold snap with snow comes on, and it may be a week before I hear the note again, and this time or the next perchance see the bird sitting on a stake in the fence lifting his wing as he calls cheerily to his mate. Its notes now become daily more frequent; the birds multiply, and, flitting from point to point, call and warble more confidently and gleefully. Their boldness increases till one sees them hovering with a saucy, inquiring air about barns and outbuildings,

*From John Burroughs, *Wake-Robin* (Boston: Houghton, Mifflin, 1892).

peeping into dove-cotes, and stable windows, inspecting knot-holes and pump-trees, intent only on a place to nest. They wage war against robins and wrens, pick quarrels with swallows, and seem to deliberate for days over the policy of taking forcible possession of one of the mud-houses of the latter. But as the season advances they drift more into the background. Schemes of conquest which they at first seemed bent upon are abandoned, and they settle down very quietly in their old quarters in remote stumpy fields.

Not long after the bluebird comes the robin, sometimes in March, but in most of the Northern States April is the month of the robin. In large numbers they scour the fields and groves. You hear their piping in the meadow, in the pasture, on the hill-side. Walk in the woods, and the dry leaves rustle with the whir of their wings, the air is vocal with their cheery call. In excess of joy and vivacity, they run, leap, scream, chase each other through the air, diving and sweeping among the trees with perilous rapidity.

In that free, fascinating, half-work and half-play pursuit,—sugar-making,—a pursuit which still lingers in many parts of New York, as in New England, the robin is one's constant companion. When the day is sunny and the ground bare, you meet him at all points and hear him at all hours. At sunset, on the tops of the tall maples, with look heavenward, and in a spirit of utter abandonment, he carols his simple strain. And sitting thus amid the stark, silent trees, above the wet, cold earth, with the chill of winter still in the air, there is no fitter or sweeter songster in the whole round year. It is in keeping with the scene and the occasion. How round and genuine the notes are, and how eagerly our ears drink them in! The first utterance, and the spell of winter is thoroughly broken, and the remembrance of it afar off.

Robin is one of the most native and democratic of our birds; he is one of the family, and seems much nearer to us than those rare, exotic visitants, as the orchard starling or rose-breasted grossbeak, with their distant, high-bred ways. Hardy, noisy, frolicsome, neighborly and domestic in his habits, strong of wing and bold in spirit, he is the pioneer of the thrush family, and well worthy of the finer artists whose coming he heralds and in a measure prepares us for.

I could wish Robin less native and plebeian in one respect,—the building of his nest. Its coarse material and rough masonry are creditable neither to his skill as a workman nor to his taste as an artist. I am the more forcibly reminded of his deficiency in this respect from observing yonder humming-bird's nest, which is a marvel of fitness and adaptation, a proper setting for this winged gem,—the body of it composed of a white, felt-like substance, probably the down of some plant or the wool of some worm, and toned down in keeping with the branch on which it sits by minute tree-lichens, woven together by threads as fine and frail as gossamer. From Robin's good looks and musical turn we might reasonably predict a domicile of equal fitness and elegance. At least I demand of him as clean and handsome a nest as the king-bird's, whose harsh jingle, compared with Robin's evening melody, is as the clatter of pots and kettles beside the tone of a flute. I love his note and ways better even than those of the orchard starling or the Baltimore oriole; yet his next, compared with theirs, is a half-subterranean hut contrasted with a Roman villa. There is something courtly and poetical in a pensile nest. Next to a castle in the air is a dwelling suspended to the slender branch of a tall tree, swayed and rocked forever by the wind. Why need wings be afraid of falling? Why build only where boys can climb? After all, we must set it down to the account of Robin's democratic turn; he is no aristocrat, but one of the people; and therefore we should expect stability in his workmanship, rather than elegance.

Another April bird, which makes appearance sometimes earlier and sometimes later than Robin, and whose memory I fondly cherish, is the Phoebe-bird (*Muscicapa nunciola*), the pioneer of the flycatchers. In the inland farming districts, I used to notice her, on some bright morning about Easter-day, proclaiming her arrival with much variety of motion and attitude, from the peak of the barn or hay-shed. As yet, you may have heard only the plaintive, homesick note of the bluebird, or the faint trill of the song-sparrow; and Phoebe's clear, vivacious assurance of her veritable bodily presence among us again is welcomed by all ears. At agreeable intervals in her lay she describes a circle or an ellipse in the air, ostensibly prospecting for insects, but really, I suspect, as an artistic flourish, thrown in to make up in some way for the deficiency of her musical performance. If plainness of dress indicates powers of song, as it usually does, then Phoebe ought to be unrivaled in musical ability, for surely that ashen-gray suit is the superlative of plainness; and that form, likewise, would hardly pass for a "perfect figure" of a bird. The seasonableness of her coming, however, and her civil, neighborly ways, shall make up for all deficiencies in song and plumage. After a few weeks Phoebe is seldom seen, except as she darts from her moss-covered nest beneath some bridge or shelving cliff.

Another April comer, who arrives shortly after Robin-redbreast, with whom he associates both at this season and in the autumn, is the gold-winged woodpecker, *alias* "high-hole," *alias* "flicker," *alias* "yarup." He is an old favorite of my boyhood, and his note to me means very much. He announces his arrival by a long, loud call, repeated from the dry branch of some tree, or a stake in the fence—a thoroughly melodious April sound. I think how Solomon finished that beautiful description of spring, "And the voice of the turtle is heard in the land," and see that a description of spring in this farming country, to be equally characteristic, should culminate in like manner,—"And the call of the high-hole comes up from the wood."

It is a loud, strong, sonorous call, and does not seem to imply an answer, but rather to subserve some purpose of love or music. It is "Yarup's" proclamation of peace and good-will to all. On looking at the matter closely, I perceive that most birds, not denominated songsters, have, in the spring, some note or sound or call that hints of a song, and answers imperfectly the end of beauty and art. As a "livelier iris changes on the burnished dove," and the fancy of the young man turns lightly to thoughts of his pretty cousin, so the same renewing spirit touches the "silent singers," and they are no longer dumb; faintly they lisp the first syllables of the marvelous tale. Witness the clear, sweet whistle of the gray-crested titmouse,—the soft, nasal piping of the nuthatch,—the amorous, vivacious warble of the bluebird,—the long, rich note of the meadow-lark,—the, whistle of the quail,—the drumming of the partridge,—the animation and loquacity of the swallows, and the like. Even the hen has a homely, contented carol; and I credit the owls with a desire to fill the night with music. All birds are incipient or would-be songsters in the spring. I find corroborative evidence of this even in the crowing of the cock. The flowering of the maple is not so obvious as that of the magnolia; nevertheless, there is actual inflorescence.

Few writers award any song to that familiar little sparrow, the *Socialis;* yet who that has observed him sitting by the way-side, and repeating, with devout attitude, that fine sliding chant, does not recognize the neglect? Who has heard the snow-bird sing? Yet he has a lisping warble very savory to the ear. I have heard him indulge in it even in February.

Even the cow-bunting feels the musical tendency, and aspires to its expression, with the rest. Perched upon the topmost branch beside his mate or mates,—for he is quite a polygamist, and usually has two or three demure little ladies in faded black beside him—generally in the early part of the day, he seems literally to vomit up his notes. Apparently with much labor and effort, they gurgle and blubber up out of him, falling on the ear with a peculiar subtile ring, as of turning water from a glass bottle, and not without a certain pleasing cadence.

Neither is the common woodpecker entirely insensible to the wooing of the spring, and, like the partridge, testifies his appreciation of melody after quite a primitive fashion. Passing through the woods, on some clear, still morning in March, while the metallic ring and tension of winter are still in the earth and air, the silence is suddenly broken by long, resonant hammering upon a dry limb or stub. It is Downy beating a reveille to spring. In the utter stillness and amid the rigid forms we listen with pleasure; and as it comes to my ear oftener at this season than at any other, I freely exonerate the author of it from the imputation of any gastronomic motives, and credit him with a genuine musical performance.

It is to be expected, therefore, that "Yellow-hammer" will respond to the general tendency, and contribute his part to the spring chorus. His April call is his finest touch, his most musical expression.

I recall an ancient maple standing sentry to a large sugar-bush, that, year after year, afforded protection to a brood of yellow-hammers in its decayed heart. A week or two before the nesting seemed actually to have begun, three or four of these birds might be seen, on almost any bright morning, gamboling and courting amid its decayed branches. Sometimes you would hear only a gentle, persuasive cooing, or a quiet, confidential chattering,—then that long, loud call, taken up by first one, then another, as they sat about upon the naked limbs,—anon, a sort of wild, rollicking laughter, intermingled with various cries, yelps, and squeals, as if some incident had excited their mirth and ridicule. Whether this social hilarity and boisterousness is in celebration of the pairing or mating ceremony, or whether it is only a sort of annual "house-warming" common among high-holes on resuming their summer quarters, is a question upon which I reserve my judgment.

Unlike most of his kinsmen, the golden-wing prefers the fields and the borders of the forest to the deeper seculsion of the woods, and hence, contrary to the habit of his tribe, obtains most of his subsistence from the ground, probing it for ants and crickets. He is not quite satisfied with being a woodpecker. He courts the society of the robin and the finches, abandons the trees for the meadow, and feeds eagerly upon berries and grain. What may be the final upshot of this course of living is a question worthy the attention of Darwin. Will his taking to the ground and his pedestrian feats result in lengthening his legs, his feeding upon berries and grains subdue his tints and soften his voice, and his associating with Robin put a song into his heart?

Indeed, what would be more interesting than the history of our birds for the last two or three centuries. There can be no doubt that the presence of man has exerted a very marked and friendly influence upon them, since they so multiply in his society. The birds of California, it is said, were mostly silent till after its settlement, and I doubt if the Indians heard the woodthrush as we hear him. Where did the bobolink disport himself before there were meadows in the North and rice fields in the South? Was he the same lithe, merry-hearted beau then as now? And the sparrow, the lark, and the goldfinch, birds that seem so indigenous to the open fields and so averse to the woods,—we cannot conceive of their existence in a vast wilderness and without man.

But to return. The song-sparrow, that universal favorite and firstling of the spring, comes before April, and its simple strain gladdens all hearts.

May is the month of the swallows and the orioles. There are many other distinguished arrivals, indeed nine tenths of the birds are here by the last week in May, yet the swallows and orioles are the most conspicuous. The bright plumage of the latter seems really like an arrival from the topics. I see them dash through the blossoming trees, and all the forenoon hear their incessant warbling and wooing. The swallows dive and chatter about the barn, or squeak and build beneath the eaves; the partridge drums in the fresh sprouting woods; the long, tender note of the meadow-lark comes up from the meadow; and at sunset, from every marsh and pond come the ten thousand voices of the hylas. May is the transition month, and exists to connect April and June, the root with the flower.

With June the cup is full, our hearts are satsified, there is no more to be desired. The perfection of the season, among other things, has brought the perfection of the song and plumage of the birds. The master artists are all here; and the expectations excited by the robin and the song-sparrow are fully justified. The thrushes have all come; and I sit down upon the first rock, with hands full of the pink azalea, to listen. With me, the cuckoo does not arrive till June; and often the goldfinch, the king-bird, the scarlet tanager delay their coming till then. In the meadows the bobolink is in all his glory; in the high pastures the field-sparrow sings his breezy vesper-hymn; and the woods are unfolding to the music of the thrushes.

The cuckoo is one of the most solitary birds of our forests, and is strangely tame and quiet, appearing equally untouched by joy or grief, fear or anger. Something remote seems ever weighing upon his mind. His note or call is as of one lost or wandering, and to the farmer is prophetic of rain. Amid the general joy and the sweet assurance of things, I love to listen to the strange clairvoyant call. Heard a quarter of a mile away, from out the depths of the forest, there is something peculiarly weird and monkish about it. Wordsworth's lines upon the European species apply equally well to ours:—

"O blithe new-comer! I have heard,
I hear thee and rejoice:
O cuckoo! shall I call thee bird?
Or but a wandering voice?

"While I am lying on the grass,
Thy loud note smites my ear!
From hill to hill it seems to pass,
At once far off and near!

. . .

"Thrice welcome, darling of the spring!
Even yet thou art to me
No bird, but an invisible thing,
A voice, a mystery."

The black-billed is the only species found in my locality, the yellow-billed abounds further south. Their note or call is nearly the same. The former sometimes suggests the voice of a turkey. The call of the latter may be suggested thus: *k-k-k-k-k-kow, kow, kow-ow, kow-ow.*

The yellow-billed will take up his stand in a tree, and explore its branches till he has caught every worm. He sits on a twig, and with a peculiar swaying movement of his head examines the surrounding foilage. When he discovers his prey, he leaps upon it in a fluttering manner.

In June the black-billed makes a tour through the orchard and garden, regaling himself upon the canker-worms. At this time he is one of the tamest of birds, and will allow you to approach within a few yards of him. I have even come within a few feet of one without seeming to excite his fear or suspicion. He is quite unsophisticated, or else royally indifferent.

The plumage of the cuckoo is a rich glossy brown, and is unrivaled in beauty by any other neutral tint with which I am acquainted. It is also remarkable for its firmness and fineness.

Notwithstanding the disparity in size and color, the black-billed species has certain peculiarities that remind one of the passenger-pigeon. His eye, with its red circle, the shape of his head, and his motions on alighting and taking flight, quickly suggest the resemblance; though in grace and speed, when on the wing, he is far inferior. His tail seems disproportionately long, like that of the red thrush, and his flight among the trees is very still, contrasting strongly with the honest clatter of the robin or pigeon.

Have you heard the song of the field-sparrow? If you have lived in a pastoral country with broad upland pastures, you could hardly have missed him. Wilson, I believe, calls him the grass-finch, and was evidently unacquainted with his powers of song. The two white lateral quills in his tail, and his habit of running and skulking a few yards in advance of you as you walk through the fields, are sufficient to identify him. Not in meadows or orchards, but in high, breezy pasture-grounds, will you look for him. His song is most noticeable after sundown, where other birds are silent; for which reason he has been aptly called the vesper-sparrow. The farmer following his team from the field at dusk catches his sweetest strain. His song is not so brisk and varied as that of the song-sparrow, being softer and wilder, sweeter and more plaintive. Add the best parts of the lay of the latter to the sweet vibrating chant of the wood-sparrow, and you have the evening hymn of the vesper-bird,—the poet of the plain, unadorned pastures. Go to those broad, smooth, uplying fields where the cattle and sheep are grazing, and sit down in the twilight on one of those warm, clean stones, and listen to this song. On every side, near and remote, from out the short grass which the herds are cropping, the strain rises. Two or three long, silver notes of peace and rest, ending in some subdued trills and quavers, constitute each separate song. Often you will catch only one or two of the bars, the breeze having blown the minor part away. Such unambitious, quiet, unconscious melody! It is one of the most characteristic sounds in Nature. The grass, the stones, the stubble, the furrow, the quiet herds, and the warm twilight among the hills, are all subtilely expressed in this song; this is what they are at last capable of.

The female builds a plain nest in the open field, without so much as a bush or thistle or tuft of grass to protect it or mark its site; you may step upon it or the cattle may tread it into the ground. But the danger from this source, I presume, the bird considers less than that from another. Skunks and foxes have a very impertinent curiosity, as Finchie well knows,—and a bank or hedge, or a rank growth of grass or thistles, that might promise protection and cover to mouse or bird, these cunning rogues would be apt to explore most thoroughly. The partridge is undoubtedly acquainted with the same process of reasoning; for, like the vesper-bird, she, too, nests in open, unprotected places, avoiding all show of concealment,—coming from the tangled and almost impenetrable parts of the forest, to the clean, open woods, where she can command all the approaches and fly with equal ease in any direction.

Another favorite sparrow, but little noticed, is the wood or bush sparrow, usually called by the ornithologists *Spizella pusilla.* Its size and form is that of the *socialis,* but is less distinctly marked, being of a duller redder tinge. He prefers remote bushy heathery fields, where his song is one of the sweetest to be heard. It is sometimes very noticeable, especially early in spring. I remember sitting one bright day in the still leafless April woods, when one of these birds struck up a few rods from me, repeating its lay at short intervals for nearly an hour. It was a perfect piece of wood-music, and was of course all the more noticeable for being projected upon such a broad unoccupied page of silence. Its song is like the words, *fe-o, fe-o, fe-o, few, few, few, fee fee fee,* uttered at first high and leisurely, but running very rapidly toward the close, which is low and soft.

Still keeping among the unrecognized, the white-eyed vireo, or fly-catcher, deserves particular mention. The song of this bird is not particularly sweet and soft; on the contrary, it is a little hard and shrill, like that of the indigo-bird or oriole; but for brightness, volubility, execution, and power of imitation, he is unsurpassed by any of our northern birds. His ordinary note is forcible and empathatic, but, as stated, not especially musical: *Chick-a-re'r-chick,* he seems to say, hiding himself in the low, dense undergrowth, and eluding your most vigilant search, as if playing some part in a game. But in July or August, if you are on good terms with the sylvan deities, you may listen to a far more rare and artistic performance. Your first impression will be that

that cluster of azalea, or that clump of swamp-huckleberry, conceals three or four different songsters of the field and forest, and uttered with the utmost clearness and rapidity, I am sure you cannot hear short of the haunts of the genuine mocking-bird. If not fully and accurately repeated, there are at least suggested the notes of the robin, wren, cat-bird, high-hole, goldfinch, and song-sparrow. The *pip, pip,* of the last is produced so accurately that I verily believe it would deceive the bird herself;—and the whole uttered in such rapid succession that it seems as if the movement that gives the concluding note of one strain must form the first note of the next. The effect is very rich, and, to my ear, entirely unique. The performer is very careful not to reveal himself in the meantime; yet there is a conscious air about the strain that impresses me with the idea that my presence is understood and my attention courted. A tone of pride and glee, and, occasionally, of bantering jocoseness, is discernible. I believe it is only rarely, and when he is sure of his audience, that he displays his parts in this manner. You are to look for him, not in tall trees or deep forests, but in low, dense shrubbery about wet places, where there are plenty of gnats and mosquitoes.

The winter-wren is another marvelous songster, in speaking of whom it is difficult to avoid superlatives. He is not so conscious of his powers and so ambitious of effect as the white-eyed fly-catcher, yet you will not be less astonished and delighted on hearing him. He possesses the fluency and copiousness for which the wrens are noted, and besides these qualities, and what is rarely found conjoined with them, a wild, sweet, rhythmical cadence that holds you entranced. I shall not soon forget that perfect June day, when, loitering in a low, ancient hemlock wood, in whose cathedral aisles the coolness and freshness seems perennial, the silence was suddenly broken by a strain so rapid and gushing, and touched with such a wild, sylvan plaintiveness, that I listened in amazement. And so shy and coy was the little minstrel, that I came twice to the woods before I was sure to whom I was listening. In summer he is one of those birds of the deep northern forests, that, like the speckled Canada warbler and the hermit-thrush, only the privileged ones hear.

The distribution of plants in a given locality is no more marked and defined than that of the birds. Show a botanist a landscape, and he will tell you where to look for the lady's-slipper, the columbine, or the harebell. On the same principles the ornithologist will direct you where to look for the greenlets, the wood-sparrow, or the chewink. In adjoining counties, in the same latitude, and equally inland, but possessing a different geological formation and different forest-timber, you will observe quite a different class of birds. In a land of the beech and sugar-maple I do not find the same songsters that I know where thrive the oak, chestnut, and laurel. In going from a district of the Old Red Sandstone to where I walk upon the old Plutonic Rock, not fifty miles distant, I miss in the woods the veery, the hermit-thrush, the chestnut-sided warbler, the blue-backed warbler, the green-backed warbler, the black and yellow warbler, and many others, and find in their stead the wood-thrush, the chewink, the redstart, the yellow-throat, the yellow-breasted fly-catcher, the white-eyed fly-catcher, the quail, and the turtle-dove.

In my neighborhood here in the Highlands the distribution is very marked. South of the village I invariably find one species of birds, north of it another. In only one locality, full of azalea and swamp-huckleberry, I am always sure of finding the hooded warbler. In a dense undergrowth of spice-bush, witch-hazel, and alder, I meet the worm-eating warbler. In a remote clearing, covered with heath and fern, with here and there a chestnut and an oak, I go to hear in July the wood-sparrow, and returning by a stumpy, shallow pond, I am sure to find the water-thrush.

Only one locality within my range seems to possess attractions for all comers. Here one may study almost the entire ornithology of the State. It is a rocky piece of ground, long ago cleared, but now fast relapsing into the wildness and freedom of nature, and marked by those half-cultivated, half-wild features which birds and boys love. It is bounded on two sides by the village and highway, crossed at various points by carriage-roads, and threaded in all directions by paths and by-ways, along which soldiers, laborers, and truant school-boys are passing at all hours of the day. It is so far escaping from the axe and the bush-hook as to have opened communication with the forest and mountain beyond by straggling lines of cedar, laurel, and blackberry. The ground is mainly occupied with cedar and chestnut, with an undergrowth, in many places, of heath and bramble. The chief feature, however, is a dense growth in the centre, consisting of dogwood, water-beech, swamp-ash, alder, spice-bush, hazel, etc., with a net-work, of smilax and frost-grape. A little zigzag stream, the draining of a swamp beyond, which passes through this tangle-wood, accounts for many of its features and productions, if not for its entire existence. Birds that are not attracted by the heath or the cedar and chestnut, are sure to find some excuse for visiting this miscellaneous growth in the centre. Most of the common birds literally throng this idle-wild; and I have met here many of the rarer species, such as the great-crested fly-catcher, the solitary warbler, the blue-winged swamp-warbler, the worm-eating warbler, the fox-sparrow, etc. The absence of all birds of prey, and the great number of flies and insects, both the result of proximity to the village, are considerations which no hawk-fearing, peace-loving minstrel passes over lightly; hence the popularity of the resort.

But the crowning glory of all these robins, fly-catchers, and warblers is the wood-thrush. More abundant than all other birds, except the robin and cat-bird, he greets you from every rock and shrub. Shy and reserved when he first makes his appearance in May, before the end of June he is tame and familiar, and sings on the tree over your head, or on the rock a few paces in advance. A pair even built their nest and reared their brood within ten or twelve feet of the piazza of a large summer-house in the vicinity. But when the guests commenced to arrive and the piazza to be thronged with gay crowds, I noticed something like dread and foreboding in the manner of the mother-bird; and from her still, quiet ways, and habit of sitting long and silently within a few feet of the precious charge, it seemed as if the dear creature had resolved, if possible, to avoid all observation.

If we take the quality of melody as the test, the wood-thrush, hermit-thrush, and the veery-thrush, stand at the head of our list of songsters.

The mocking-bird undoubtedly possesses the greatest range of mere talent, the most varied executive ability, and never fails to surprise and delight one anew at each hearing; but being mostly an imitator, he never approaches the serene beauty and sublimity of the hermit-thrush. The word that best expresses my feelings, on hearing the mocking-bird, is admiration, though the first emotion is one of surprise and incredulity. That so many and such various notes should proceed from one throat is a marvel, and we regard the performance with feelings akin to those we experience on witnessing the astounding feats of the athlete or gymnast,—and this, notwithstanding many of the notes imitated have all the freshness and sweetness of the originals. The emotions excited by the songs of these thrushes belong to a higher order, springing as they do from our deepest sense of the beauty and harmony of the world.

The wood-thrush is worthy of all, and more than all, the praises he has received; and considering the number of his appreciative listeners, it is not a little surprising that his relative and equal, the hermit-thrush, should have received so little notice. Both the great ornithologists, Wilson and Audubon, are lavish in their praises of the former, but have little or nothing to say of the song of the latter. Audubon says it is sometimes agreeable, but evidently has never heard it. Nuttall, I am glad to find, is more discriminating, and does the bird fuller justice.

It is quite a rare bird, of very shy and secluded habits being found in the Middle and Eastern States, during the period of song, only in the deepest and most remote forests, usually in damp and swampy localities. On this account the people in the Adirondac region call it the "Swamp Angel." Its being so much of a recluse accounts for the comparative ignorance that prevails in regard to it.

The cast of its song is very much like that of the wood-thrush, and a good observer might easily confound the two. But hear them together and the difference is quite marked: the song of the hermit is in a higher key, and is more wild and ethereal. His instrument is a silver horn which he winds in the most solitary places. The song of the wood-thrush is more golden and leisurely. Its tone comes near to that of some rare stringed instrument. One feels that perhaps the wood-thrush has more compass and power, if he would only let himself out, but on the whole he comes a little short of the pure, serene, hymn-like strain of the hermit.

Yet those who have heard only the wood-thrush may well place him first on the list. He is truly a royal minstrel, and considering his liberal distribution throughout our Atlantic seaboard, perhaps contributes more than any other bird to our sylvan melody. One may object that he spends a little too much time in tuning his instrument, yet his careless and uncertain touches reveal its rare compass and power.

He is the only songster of my acquaintance, excepting the canary, that displays different degrees of proficiency in the exercise of his musical gifts. Not long since, while walking one Sunday in the edge of an orchard adjoining a wood, I heard one that so obviously and unmistakably surpassed all his rivals, that my companion, though slow to notice such things, remarked it wonderingly; and with one accord we paused to listen to so rare a performer. It was not different in quality so much as in quantity. Such a flood of it! Such copiousness! Such long, trilling, accelerating preludes! Such sudden ecstatic overtures, would have intoxicated the dullest ear. He was really without a compeer—a master-artist. Twice afterward I was conscious of having heard the same bird.

The wood-thrush is the handsomest species of this family. In grace and elegance of manner he has no equal. Such a gentle, high-bred air, and such inimitable ease and composure in his flight and movement! He is a poet in very word and deed. His carriage is music to the eye. His performance of the commonest act, as catching a beetle, or picking a worm from the mud, pleases like a stroke of wit or eloquence. Was he a prince in the olden time, and do the regal grace and mien still adhere to him in his transformation? What a finely proportioned form! How plain, yet rich his color,—the bright russet of his back, the clear white of his breast, with the distinct heart-shaped spots! It may be objected to Robin that he is noisy and demonstrative; he hurries away or rises to a branch with an angry note, and flirts his wings in ill-bred suspicion. The marvis, or red-thrush, sneaks and skulks like a culprit, hiding in the densest alders; the cat-bird is a coquette and a flirt, as well as a sort of female Paul Pry; and the chewink shows his inhospitality by espying your movements like a Japanese. The wood-thrush has none of these under-bred traits. He regards me unsuspiciously, or avoids me with a noble reserve,— or, if I am quiet and incurious, graciously hops toward me, as if to pay his respects, or to make my acquaintance. I have passed under his nest within a few feet of his mate and brood, when he sat near by on a branch eying me sharply, but without opening his beak; but the moment I raised my hand toward his defenseless household his anger and indignation were beautiful to behold.

What a noble pride he has! Late one October, after his mates and companions had long since gone south, I noticed one for several successive days in the dense part of this next-door wood, flitting noiselessly about, very grave and silent, as if doing penance for some violation of the code of honor. By many gentle, indirect approaches, I perceived that part of his tail-feathers were undeveloped. The sylvan prince could not think of returning to court in this plight, and so, amid the falling leaves and cold rains of autumn, was patiently biding his time.

The soft, mellow flute of the veery fills a place in the chorus of the woods that the song of the vesper sparrow fills in the chorus of the fields. It has the nightingale's habit of singing in the twilight, as indeed have all our thrushes. Walk out toward the forest in the warm twilight of a June day, and when fifty rods distant you will hear their soft, reverberating notes, rising from a dozen different throats.

It is one of the simplest strains to be heard,—as simple as the curve in form, delighting from the pure element of harmony and beauty it contains, and not from any novel or fantastic modulation of it,—thus contrasting strongly with such rollicking, hilarious songsters as the bobolink, in whom we are chiefly pleased with the tintinnabulation, the verbal and labial excellence, and the evident conceit and delight of the performer.

I hardly know whether I am more pleased or annoyed with the cat-bird. Perhaps she is a little too common, and her part in the general chorus a little too conspicuous. If you are listening for the note of another bird, she is sure to be prompted to the most loud and protracted singing, drowning all other sounds; if you sit quietly down to observe a favorite or study a new-comer, her curiosity knows no bounds, and you are scanned and ridiculed from every point of observation. Yet I would not miss her; I would only subordinate her a little, make her less conspicuous.

She is the parodist of the woods, and there is ever a mischievous, bantering, half-ironical undertone in her lay, as if she were conscious of mimicking and disconcerting some envied songster. Ambitious of song, practicing and rehearsing in private, she yet seems the least sincere and genuine of the sylvan minstrels, as if she had taken up music only to be in the fashion, or not to be outdone by the robins and thrushes. In other words, she seems to sing from some outward motive, and not from inward joyousness. She is a good versifier, but not a great poet. Vigorous, rapid, copious, not without fine touches, but destitute of any high, serene melody, her performance, like that of Thoreau's squirrel, always implies a spectator.

There is a certain air and polish about her strain, however, like that in the vivacious conversation of a well-bred lady of the world, that commands respect. Her maternal instinct, also, is very strong, and that simple structure of dead twigs and dry grass is the centre of much anxious solicitude. Not long since, while strolling through the woods, my attention was attracted to a small densely grown swamp, hedged in with eglantine, brambles, and the everlasting smilax, from which proceeded loud cries of distress and alarm, indicating that some terrible calamity was threatening my sombre-colored minstrel. On effecting an entrance, which, however, was not accomplished till I had doffed coat and hat, so as to diminish the surface exposed to the thorns and brambles, and looking around me from a square yard to terra firma, I found myself the spectator of a loathsome, yet fascinating scene. Three or four yards from me was the nest, beneath which, in long festoons, rested a huge black snake; a bird two thirds grown, was slowly disappearing between his expanded jaws. As he seemed unconscious of my presence, I quietly observed the proceedings. By slow degrees he compassed the bird about with his elastic mouth; his head flattened, his neck writhed and swelled, and two or three undulatory movements of his glistening body finished the work. Then, he cautiously raised himself up, his tongue flaming from his mouth the while, curved over the nest, and, with wavy, subtle motions, explored the interior. I can conceive of nothing more overpoweringly terrible to an unsuspecting family of birds than the sudden appearance above their domicile of the head and neck of this arch-enemy. It is enough to petrify the blood in their veins. Not finding the object of his search, he came streaming down from the nest to a lower limb, and commenced extending his researches in other directions, sliding stealthily through the branches, bent on capturing one of the parent birds. That a legless, wingless creature should move with such ease and rapidity where only birds and squirrels are considered at home, lifting himself up, letting himself down, running out on the yielding boughs, and traversing with marvelous celerity the whole length and breadth of the thicket, was truly surprising. One thinks of the great myth, of the Tempter and the "cause of all our woe," and wonders if the Arch One is not now playing off some of his pranks before him. Whether we call it snake or devil matters little. I could but admire his terrible beauty, however; his black, shining folds, his easy, gliding movement, head erect, eyes glistening, tongue playing like subtle flame, and the invisible means of his almost winged locomotion.

The parent birds, in the mean while, kept up the most agonizing cry,—at times fluttering furiously about their pursuer, and actually laying hold of his tail with their beaks and claws. On being thus attacked, the snake would suddenly double upon himself and follow his own body back, thus executing a strategic movement that at first seemed almost to paralyze his victim and place her within his grasp. Not quite, however. Before his jaws could close upon the coveted prize the bird would tear herself away, and, apparently faint and sobbing, retire to a higher branch. His reputed powers of fascination availed him little, though it is possible that a frailer and less combative bird might have been held by the fatal spell. Presently, as he came gliding down the slender body of a leaning alder, his attention was attracted by a slight movement of my arm; eying me an instant, with that crouching, utter, motionless gaze which I believe only snakes and devils can assume, he turned quickly,—a feat which necessitated something like crawling over his own body,—and glided off through the branches, evidently recognizing in me a representative of the ancient parties he once so cunningly ruined. A few moments after, as he lay carelessly disposed in the top of a rank alder, trying to look as much like a crooked branch as his supple shining form woud admit, the old vengeance overtook him. I exercised my prerogative, and a well-directed missile, in the shape of a stone, brought him looping and writhing to the ground. After I had completed his downfall and quiet had been partially restored, a half-fledged member of the bereaved household came out from his hiding-place, and, jumping upon a decayed branch, chirped vigorously, no doubt in celebration of the victory.

Till the middle of July there is a general equilibrium; the tide stands poised; the holiday-spirit is unabated. But as the harvest ripens beneath the long, hot days, the melody gradually ceases. The young are out of the nest and must be cared for, and the moulting season is at hand. After the cricket has commenced to drone his monotonous refrain beneath your window, you will not, till another season, hear the wood-thrush in all his matchless eloquence. The bobolink has become careworn and fretful, and blurts out snatches of his song between his scolding and upbraiding, as you approach the vicinity of his nest, oscillating betwen anxiety for his brood and solicitude for his musical reputation. Some of the sparrows still sing, and occasionally across the hot fields, from a tall tree in the edge of the forest, comes the rich note of the scarlet tanager. This tropical-colored bird loves the hottest weather, and I hear him even in dog-days.

The remainder of the summer is the carnival of the swallows and fly-catchers. Flies and insects, to any amount, are to be had for the catching; and the opportunity is well improved. See that sombre, ashen-colored pewee on yonder branch. A true sportsman he, who never takes his game at rest, but always on the wing. You vagrant fly, you purblind moth, beware how you come within his range! Observe his attitude, the curious movement of his head, his "eye in a fine frenzy rolling, glancing from heaven to earth, from earth to heaven."

His sight is microscopic and his aim sure. Quick as thought he has seized his victim and is back to his perch. There is no strife, no pursuit,—one fell swoop and the matter is ended. That little sparrow, as you will observe, is less skilled. It is the *Socialis,* and he finds his subsistence properly in various seeds and the larvae of insects, though he occasionally has higher aspirations, and seeks to emulate the pewee, commencing and ending his career as a fly-catcher by an awkward chase after a beetle or "miller." He is hunting around in the grass now, I suspect, with the desire to indulge his favorite whim. There!—the opportunity is afforded him. Away goes a little cream-colored meadow-moth in the most tortuous course he is capable of, and away goes *Socialis* in pursuit. The contest is quite comical, though I dare say it is serious enough to the moth. The chase continues for a few yards, when there is a sudden rushing to cover in the grass,—then a taking to wing again, when the search has become too close, and the moth has recovered his wind. *Socialis* chirps angrily, and is determined not to be beaten. Keeping, with the slightest effort, upon the heels of the fugitive, he is ever on the point of halting to snap him up, but never quite does it,—and so, between disappointment and expectation, is soon disgusted, and returns to pursue his more legitimate means of subsistence.

In striking contrast to this serio-comic strife of the sparrow and the moth, is the pigeon-hawk's pursuit of the sparrow or the goldfinch. It is a race of surprising speed and agility. It is a test of wing and wind. Every muscle is taxed, and every nerve strained. Such cries of terror and consternation on the part of the bird, tacking to the right and left, and making the most desperate efforts to escape, and such silent determination on the part of the hawk, pressing the bird so closely, flashing and turning and timing his movements with those of the pursued as accurately and as inexorably as if the two constituted one body, excite feelings of the deepest concern. You mount the fence or rush out of your way to see the issue. The only salvation for the bird is to adopt the tactics of the moth, seeking instantly the cover of some tree, bush, or hedge, where its smaller size enables it to move about more rapidly. These pirates are aware of this, and therefore prefer to take their prey by one fell swoop. You may see one of them prowling through an orchard, with the yellow-birds hovering about him, crying, *Pi-ty, pi-ty,* in the most desponding tone; yet he seems not to regard them, knowing as do they, that in the close branches they are as safe as if in a wall of adamant.

August is the month of the high sailing hawks. The hen-hawk is the most noticeable. He likes the haze and calm of these long, warm days. He is a bird of leisure, and seems always at his ease. How beautiful and majestic are his movements! So self-poised and easy, such an entire absence of haste, such a magnificent amplitude of circles and spirals, such a haughty, imperial grace, and, occasionally, such daring aërial evolutions!

With slow, leisurely movement, rarely vibrating his pinions, he mounts and mounts in an ascending spiral till he appears a mere speck against the summer sky; then, if the mood seizes him, with wings half-closed; like a bent bow, he will cleave the air almost perpendicularly, as if intent on dashing himself to pieces against the earth; but on nearing the ground, he suddenly mounts again on broad, expanded wing, as if rebounding upon the air, and sails leisurely away. It is the sublimest feat of the season. One holds his breath till he sees him rise again.

If inclined to a more gradual and less precipitous descent, he fixes his eye on some distant point in the earth beneath him, and thither bends his course. He is still almost meteoric in his speed and boldness. You see his path down the heavens, straight as a line; if near, you hear the rush of his wings; his shadow hurtles across the fields, and in an instant you see him quietly perched upon some low tree or decayed stub in a swamp or meadow, with reminiscences of frogs and mice stirring in his maw.

When the south wind blows, it is a study to see three or four of these air-kings at the head of the valley far up toward the mountain, balancing and oscillating upon the strong current: now quite stationary, except a slight tremulous motion like the poise of a rope-dancer, then rising and falling in long undulations, and seeming to resign themselves passively to the wind; or, again, sailing high and level far above the mountain's peak, no bluster and haste, but, as stated, occasionally a terrible earnestness and speed. Fire at one as he sails overhead, and, unless wounded badly he will not change his course or gait.

His flight is a perfect picture of repose in motion. It strikes the eye as more surprising than the flight of the pigeon and swallow even, in that the effort put forth is so uniform and delicate as to escape observation, giving to the movement an air of buoyancy and perpetuity, the effluence of power rather than the conscious application of it.

The calmness and dignity of this hawk, when attacked by crows or the king-bird, are well worthy of him. He seldom deigns to notice his noisy and furious antagonists, but deliberately wheels about in that aërial spiral, and mounts and mounts till his pursuers grow dizzy and return to earth again. It is quite original, this mode of getting rid of an unworthy opponent, rising to heights where the braggart is dazed and bewildered and loses his reckoning! I am not sure but it is worthy of imitation.

But summer wanes, and autumn approaches. The songsters of the seed-time are silent at the reaping of the harvest. Other minstrels take up the strain. It is the heyday of insect life. The day is canopied with musical sound. All the songs of the spring and summer appear to be floating, softened and refined, in the upper air. The birds in a new, but less holiday suit, turn their faces southward. The swallows flock and go; the bobolinks flock and go; silently and unobserved, the thrushes go. Autumn arrives, bringing finches, warblers, sparrows and kinglets from the North. Silently the procession passes. Yonder hawk, sailing peacefully away till he is lost in the horizon, is a symbol of the closing season and the departing birds.

John Muir
1838-1914

Traveler, explorer, mountaineer, inventor, author, and free spirit, John Muir made his living—whether as sheepherder, factory or mill hand, fruit farmer, or guide—only as he needed to support his life of roaming, noting, sketching, and studying nature. He possessed great physical and intellectual energy; his friends knew him as a vivid, quick-witted, fascinating talker who preferred to sleep outdoors rather than in, and as a man who loved storms as much as fair weather.

Muir was Scottish by birth and came to America only in 1849 when his father emigrated with the three oldest children to establish a family homestead in the Wisconsin frontier. *The Story of My Boyhood and Youth* (1913) is a fascinating autobiography concerned mostly with his experiences on a frontier farm. He had been "fond of everything that was wild" even while a youth in Scotland, but his American experiences reaffirmed and deepened his fondness for the wilderness. He was a voracious reader who taught himself enough to enter the University of Wisconsin by age twenty-one. But he left without a degree in 1863 because he preferred to choose his studies rather than conform to the curriculum. At the university he learned his basic chemistry, geology, and botany.

Muir immediately began his career, in his words, as a "poetico-trampo-geologist-bot. and ornith-natural, etc.—etc.!—etc.!" with walking tours to Canada and the Gulf of Mexico. And during his life he made geological tours throughout the U.S., Canada, Alaska, Europe, the South Pacific, and South America. He published no books until he was nearly sixty, but kept detailed journals of all his experiences and observations and did attract national attention by his magazine articles and by his debunking of the traditional scientific explanation for the formation of the Yosemite Valley; Muir proved that the Valley was glacially formed.

In 1868, Muir found his spiritual homeland in the Yosemite, which he discovered, as the story goes, after arriving in San Francisco and immediately asking, "What's the quickest way out of town?" In his first book, *The Mountains of California* (1894), and later in such books as *My First Summer in the Sierra* (1911) and *The Yosemite* (1912), Muir showed the glory and grandeur of the California wilderness to Americans.

Muir's chief interests were the glaciers, great primitive forests, mountains, and storms of the American Northwest. By the turn of the century he had become the preeminent voice for the nascent American conservation movement. With Robert Underwood Johnson, editor of the influential *Century Magazine,* for example, Muir undertook a public campaign to establish the Yosemite as a national preserve against destructive sheep farming practices. "Hoofed locusts" was what Muir called the sheep. By 1880, Congress established the Yosemite as a national park and the following year gave the President power to establish forest reserves.

By 1897 and during the early years of the new century, Muir was fully engaged in what he called the "battle between landscape righteousness and the devil." His tone became increasingly invective and prophetic in such articles as "Forest Reservations and National Parks" and "The American Forests." Against greed, ignorance, and short-term goals, Muir argued for leaving the country as we found it for the life and enjoyment of future generations. President Roosevelt, who hiked and camped with Muir (as did Burroughs), established 148,000,000 additional acres of reserves and parks, and sixteen national monuments. As first President of the Sierra Club, as indefatigable lobbyist and author, Muir spent the rest of his life continuing the fight on behalf of the spiritual energy and "Majesty of the Inanimate," which, he believed, our own spiritual self needed for its health and vigor.

from JOHN MUIR SUMMERING IN THE SIERRA*

A Winter Storm in June

GENTRY'S STATION, NEAR YOSEMITE, JUNE 17TH

June storms are not altogether rare in the Sierra, yet they are seldom so extensive as the one just completed. A foot or more of snow and hail fell on the mountains adjacent to Yosemite on the 15th and 16th ultimo, covering flowers and ferns, and loading down the branches of the Pine trees. On the morning of the 15th, Half Dome was encircled with clouds, and the Upper Fall was torn into shreds and streamers by gusty storm winds like those of winter, and every pine and cedar waved their green plumes in lively expectation of a storm. Our party[1] were unwilling to wait fair weather, and at once began to climb out of the valley in long cavalcade with the inevitable

*From *John Muir Summering in the Sierra,* ed. Robert Engberg (Madison, WI: University of Wisconsin Press).

1. Muir was accompanied by John Swett, William Keith, and J. B. McChesney, whom Muir later refers to as "Mack."

mules, mustangs and camp *debris*. Before we had fairly passed the brow of El Capitan rain began to fall, and dark swift-moving clouds descended on many a beetling cliff and rock-front, finally forming a dense continuous ceiling from wall to wall. On reaching Gentry's Station—1,800 feet above the Valley—the storm began to abate, and we deliberated whether to push on to the Eagle Meadows, lying to the north of the Valley, or to camp where we were. Mack and Swett seemed inclined to go on, when Keith suddenly broke up the council by declaring, with a scowl darker than a storm-cloud, that it was "perfect madness for poets, painters and mountaineers to seek the darksome dripping, snow-dusted woods in such wild, woeful weather." Keith contains a poem, whose appearance is momentarily expected, which fact explains the waving rhythm of his prose. His storm advice was followed, and we speedily found ourselves beneath a sugarpine roof and around a blazing fire. After partaking of a grotesque supper, Keith showed us to rooms in the abandoned hotel here, with a fine display of obsequious smiles and good-nights. It was a wild, tempestuous night; rain alternated with wind-driven hail and snow, and vivid lightning flashes seemed completely to fill the river canyon beneath, and the thunder rolled in heavy-rounded reverberations from cliff to cliff in grand accord.

A WINTRY SCENE—MOUNTAIN PLANTS

Next morning the mountains far and near were white as winter, and the forests, rising in snowy ranks, shone resplendent with the snow lodged in their dark green foliage. No tree in the Sierra forests seems to enjoy snow so much as the sugar pine. It spreads its giant arms into the welcome storm and gathers the crystal benefaction with absolute enthusiasm. The ferns and flowers were mostly buried; here and there a green, feathery frond appearing above the lavish snow-bloom, with a tall, wandy grass tuft. Not a violet or gilia to be seen. A few of the rare California Cypridpedium grows here.[2] They weathered the storm bravely. Not so the Mariposa tulip.[3] The hailstones broke their wide-open corollas and bent their slender stalks. The blue penstimon fared hardly better, and all the finest gardens, with larkspurs and columbines seemed hopelessly ruined. Fortunately the big Washington lily was not yet in flower, and but few of the bush eriogonums. It would seem as if nature were dealing but harshly with her tender plant children, as if she sought to destroy them. Yet all that we call destruction is creating, and it is just where storms fall most violently that the greatest quantity of beauteous, joyous life appear. These Sierra gardens and forests have been stormed upon for tens of thousands of years, yet we see the upshot of all their long continued violence in the tender and exquisite loveliness that fills them today.

THE GLACIAL PERIOD

Could we have visited this Yosemite region during the glacial epoch, we would have found only fathomless wastes of ice, with not one hint of the

2. An apparent reference to the Sierra rein orchid (*Habenaria dilatata.*)

3. The reference is probably to the Leichtin's Mariposa tulip (*Calochortus leichtlini*), more common known as the Mariposa lily, found around Crane Flat and other open areas from middle elevations to timberline.

glorious landscapes that were being sculptured in the silence and darkness beneath, nor of the gardens and green meadows and glad sun-born pines. Yet the glaciers were the implements of all this lavish predestined beauty—plowing the slates, and granite to flowing hill and dale, dome and ridge; grinding the rocks to soil, and spreading it out in long curving moraines and broad fielded beds. And since the planting of the first hardy pines and frost-enduring sedges there has been a constant development toward higher and yet higher beauty. We are camped on the right lateral moraine of the Yosemite trunk glacier, which flowed through and out of the valley with a current over 2,000 feet in depth, and the excellence of the sugar pines and firs, many of them over 200 feet high, without a decayed fibre, shows how perfect is nature's system of forestry.

THE SIERRA IN JUNE

June is too early to make excursions into the high Sierra, not only because of the frequency of small rain and snow storms, but because feed for animals is scarce. July, August, September and October are better months, being made up chiefly of pure uninterrupted sunshine. Yet June snows are not greatly to be feared. They disappear in the sun as if by magic. Yesterday the flowers were buried, and the woods were in universal snowbloom; to-day not a flake or hailstone is to be seen, and not a cloud in the sky. Bees drone and zigzag from flower to flower. A ruby humming bird is within a foot of my hand as I write, sipping from the purple tubes of the Menzies penstimon.[4] More than fifty butterflies have winged past me in half an hour, all dry and vigorous, and a gray squirrel is at this moment sitting on his haunches two rods distant, pulling down the seeded pods of a rock-cress with his paws, and nibbling them on the spot, like a bear eating manzanita berries.

MOUNTAIN STREAMS—SUMMER SNOW LINE

Cascade creek goes brawling by, pouring from pool to pool with its waters, more than doubled by the melting snow. Yosemite falls are no doubt similarly increased, which will be a fine thing for tourists.

The lowest point reached by the snow was about 5,500 feet above the level of the sea. Since morning this summer snow line has receded more than a thousand feet. The breaking up of the storm last evening was a most brilliant affair. The empty clouds changed to purple and pure snowy white, shot through and through with the sun, and the dripping trees were laden with flashing, irised crystals that burned on every leaf. The clouds moved hither and thither, now down among the canyon rocks, now up among the rejoicing forests, as if reviewing their accomplished work. But my letter must be closed. To-morrow we ride through many a mile of silver fir,[5] cross Yosemite creek

4. Probably the meadow penstemon (*Penstemon heterodoxus*), which blooms in summer near subalpine meadows.

5. The nomenclature of many Sierra trees has changed over the last century. Muir is probably here referring to the white fir (*Abies concolor*), as silver firs do not grow in California.

two miles above where it leaps down into the valley and before sunset we will be camped at Lake Tenaya, one of the brightest glacier lakes in this whole Merced regions.

GENTRY'S STATION,[6]
JUNE 17, 1875

The Royal Sequoia

A few days ago while camped in the fir woods on the head of one of the southmost tributaries of the Merced, I caught sight of a lofty granite dome, called Wa-mello by the Indians,[7] looming into the free sky far above the forest, and though now studying trees, I soon found myself upon its commanding summit. Here I obtained glorious views of the wide fertile valleys of the Fresno [River], filled with forests; innumerable spires of yellow pines towering above one another on the sloping heights; miles of sugar-pine with feathery arms outstreteched in the sunshine; and toward the southwest I beheld the lofty dome-like crowns of the sequoia, rising here and there out of the green slopes and levels of the pines, singly or densed together in imposing congregations. There is something wonderfully impressive in this tree, even when beheld from a great distance; their dense foliage and smoothly rounded outlines enables one to recognize them at once in any company, to say nothing of their superior size and kingliness. They grow upon ridge tops as well as in sheltered ravines, and when one of the oldest kings attains full stature on some commanding height, he seems the very god of the woods. No tree in the Sierra forest has foliage so densely massed, or presents outlines so constant in form or so finely drawn as Sequoia. Fortunate old trees that have reached their three thousandth birthday without injury from fire or frost, present a mound like summit of warm yellow green foliage. Younger trees are darker in color, and shoot up with summits comparatively sharp, but not at all arrowy like those of the fir or pine. Their colossal brown trunks finely tapered and furrowed, may often be seen glowing in the sun, branchless, to a height of 150 feet, yet not altogether leafless, for green sprays occur at intervals, making flecks of shadow, and seeming to have been pinned on as ornamental rosettes for the sake of beauty alone. The ripe cones are green as cucumbers, and measure about two inches in length and one and a half in diameter, made up of about forty diamond-shaped scales, densely packed with from five to eight seeds at the base of each. Each cone, therefore, contains from two to three hundred seeds. The seeds resemble those of the common parsnips, and are about one-fourth of an inch long by three-sixteenths of an inch wide, the greater portion of the bulk being taken up by a thin, flat, scale-like wing, which when the seed is set free to seek its fortune, makes it fly off glancingly to its growing place like a boy's kite. The seeds are nearly ripe now, and there

6. Gentry's was a stagecoach stopover on the Big Oak Flat wagon road.

7. This is the Fresno Dome, located some fifty miles south of Yosemite Valley.

is sufficient in this grove alone to plant the globe. No other California conifer produces anything like as many seeds. Some trees certainly ripen more than a million, while one might easily number the nuts of the most fruitful pine in a single day.

COLORING MATTER—TIMBER OF THE BIG TREE

At the base of the scales and in contact with the seeds there is a considerable quantity of a dark, gritty substance, which dissolves readily in water and yields a magnificient purple color which may probably be utilized; certainly it seems well worthy of careful experiment, as it may be obtained in large quantities at a very slight cost, and the quantity of coloring matter, to say nothing of other properties, must make it exceedingly valuable should it prove available. A single cone will color a bucket of water a delicious transparent purple, that seems perfectly constant. I have myself used it as ink, and I find it first-rate; and I have also drank it, hoping thereby to improve my color and render myself more tree-wise and sequoical.[8]

The timber of the Big Tree, besides being beautiful, is easily worked, and is more enduring than any other that I know of. Build a house of sequoia logs and lay the foundation upon solid granite, and that house will last about as long as the rock. Or fell a sequoia in the dank decomposing woods and with it lay any species of oak, pine or fir, and these will be rotted and weathered out of sight before the main body of sequoia will have suffered the slightest appreciable decay or changed color. Indeed, fire seems to be the only decomposing agent that has any effect upon it. I have in my possession a specimen of the wood of the Sierra sequoia, which neither in color, strength or any other property can be distinguished from specimens cut from living trees; yet the trunk from which this specimen was obtained has lain upon the damp ground exposed to all kinds of weathering for at least three hundred and eighty years, and probably twice as long or more. The evidence in the case is simply this: a tree fifteen or twenty feet in diameter fell upon one of these Fresno hillsides, and in falling, the ponderous trunk sunk into the ground, thus making a wide ditch or furrow about five or six feet deep, and in the middle of this ditch, where a portion of the trunk had been removed by fire, I found a silver fir (*Picea Grandiss*) growing, that is four feet in diameter and three hundred and eighty years old, demonstrating that the age of my specimen must be this great at least. But in order to arrive at the whole age it would of course be necessary to know how many years elapsed before the portion of the ditch occupied by this silver fir was laid bare by fire and also how much time passed after the clearing of the ditch ere the seed was planted from which the silver fir sprung. This instance of the durability of sequoia timber is by no means a rare one. Fragments of trunks quite as ancient are to be found all through the grove, showing the same wonderful state of preservation, and manifesting their ages by various phenomena whose interpretation can hardly be missed. With regard to the strength of the timber I can say little, never having made any measured tests, yet it appears to be quite as strong as the best fir. When a large tree falls its branches break like the chalky bones of an old man. The main trunk also

8. Several of the letters Muir wrote using this sequoia ink continue to possess a distinctive purplish tone.

breaks straight across several times even where the ground is level. One noble specimen that stood two hundred and seventy-five feet high and measured twenty-two feet in diameter at the base was felled a short distance from here by digging around and cutting the main roots, and in falling, the trunk broke straight across in no less than ten places. Although I have observed several trunks of young trees five or six feet in diameter that were felled on rough ground without breaking at all. I also examined some seasoned saplings from three inches to a foot in thickness and found the wood exceedingly tough and elastic.

A DECAYING SPECIES

The big tree is sometimes regarded as a sort of companionless species whose relations have disappeared and as not properly belonging to the flora of the present geological age. These views, however, are mostly erroneous; for though it is true that as a species this mastodon of the vegetable kingdom has come to its period of decadence, many other species among our mountain flora are in the very same condition. Species develop and die like individuals, animals as well as plants; and man, at once the noblest and most conceited species on the globe, will as surely become extinct as mastodon or sequoia. But unless destroyed by man sequoia is in no immediate danger of extinction; it is perhaps scarcely farther past prime than either of our two silver firs, and judging from present conditions and its history as far as I have been able to read, it will live until A.D. 15,000 at least. The other day I counted no less than 536 sequoia saplings and sproutings growing promisingly upon a piece of ground not exceeding two acres, and specimens of every age, from one year to three or four thousand, occur in this one grove. The causes at work to effect the extinction of the species are chiefly the decay of the soil on which they are growing, changes in drainage, changes in climate, and the invasions of other trees, together with fire and the ax.[9]

THE DOOM OF THE CONIFERAE

As far as the uses of man are concerned the Sierra crop of coniferae is ripe, and in all probability will be speedily harvested. New lumber companies are coming into existence almost every year. Mills have just been built here, and a flume which is to extend down the Fresno [River] to the railroad is being vigorously pushed toward completion, when the magnificent firs and pines of the Fresno woods, together with the big trees, will be unsparingly lumbered and floated to market.

A FOREST HERMIT

A while ago I came drifting through the gorges and woods from the Mariposa trees, arriving here when the grove was full of noon sunshine, and in sauntering from tree to tree, making my way through hazel and dogwood

9. Recent investigations point to the necessity of periodic fires to clear the underbrush from the sequoia groves, thus enabling the seeds to sprout and young sequoia saplings to survive. The National Park Service has recently experimented with man-made fires within several of the sequoia forests. The Fresno Grove Muir describes in this letter was logged extensively in the 1880s. The surviving trees are known as the Nelder Grove.

and over huge brown logs, I came suddenly upon a handsome cottage with quaint, old-fashioned chimney and gables, every way uncommon, and so new and fresh that it still smelled of balsom and rosin, like a newly felled tree. Strolling forward, wondering to what my strange discovery would lead, I found an old, gray-haired man, sitting at the door upon a bark stool, weary-eyed and unspeculative and seemingly surprised that his fine forest hermitage had been discovered. After drinking at the burn that trickles past the door, I sat down beside him and bit by bit he gave me his history, which, in the main, is only a sad illustration of early California life during the gold period, full of intense experiences, now up in exciting success, now down in crushing reverses, the day of life waning meanwhile far into the afternoon, and long shadows turning to the east; health gone and gold; the game played and lost; and now, creeping into this solitude, where he may at least maintain independence, he awaits the coming of night. How sad the tones of the invisible undercurrent of many a life here, now the clang and excitements of the gold battles are over. What wrecks of hopes and health, and how truly interesting are those wrecks. Perhaps no other country in the world contains so many rare and interesting men. The name of my hermit friend is John A. Nelder, a man of broad sympathies, and a keen intuitive observer of nature. Birds, squirrels, plants all receive loving attention, and it is delightful to see how sensitively he feels the silent influences of the woods. How his eye brightens as he gazes upon the grand sequoia kings that stand guard around his cabin. How he pets and feeds the wild quails and Douglass Squirrels, and how tenderly he strokes the sapling sequoias, hoping that they will yet reach the full stature of their race and rule the woods.

To-morrow I will push on southward along the sequoia belt, making special studies of the species and visiting every grove as far as its southern-most limits.

FRESNO GROVE OF BIG TREES
SEPTEMBER 1875

Sarah Orne Jewett
1849-1909

Daughter of a learned country doctor, Sarah Orne Jewett wrote, with a firm sense of locality and character, largely from recollections of her experiences traveling with her physician father on his rounds. His fictional biography, *A Country Doctor* (1884), Jewett based on such medical travels, often to far inland farms. They lived in South Berwick, Maine, a seaport twelve miles up the tidal river from the busy port of Portsmouth, New Hampshire. South Berwick was an old colonial port with cultural traditions that changed in the nineteenth century as the maritime economy began to collapse. Jewett writes about the traditions and the changes, and about those human values and characteristics that survive dramatic change. Her education, stimulated by her father, consisted mostly of her own reading.

After her stories began to appear in *The Atlantic* about 1869 under the editorship of William Dean Howells, and with her tales coming out in collected volumes, including her masterpiece *The Country of the Pointed Firs* (1896), Jewett did travel widely abroad with her friend Anne Fields, and developed a circle of cosmopolitan and literary friends, but most of her life, like her work, focused on the Maine and New England that she knew and loved.

The titled piece of her sixth volume, "A White Heron" (1886), is remarkable not only for its unity of atmosphere and character, but for its theme of the conflicts between rural and city, emotional and scientific, and natural and economic values at a time of great change in America.

A WHITE HERON*

1 The woods were already filled with shadows one June evening, just before eight o'clock, though a bright sunset still glimmered faintly among the trunks of the trees. A little girl was driving home her cow, a plodding, dilatory, provoking creature in her behavior, but a valued companion for all that. They were going away from the western light, and striking deep into the dark woods, but their feet were familiar with the path, and it was no matter whether their eyes could see it or not.

There was hardly a night the summer through when the old cow could be found waiting at the pasture bars; on the contrary, it was her greatest pleasure to hide herself away among the high huckleberry bushes, and though she wore a loud bell she had made the discovery that if one stood perfectly still it would not ring. So Sylvia had to hunt for her until she found her, and call Co'! Co'! with never an answering Moo, until her childish patience was quite spent. If the creature had not given good milk and plenty of it, the case would have seemed very different to her owners. Besides, Sylvia had all the time there was, and very little use to make of it. Sometimes in pleasant weather it was a consolation to look upon the cow's pranks as an intelligent attempt to play hide and seek, and as the child had no playmates she lent herself to this amusement with a good deal of zest. Though this chase had been so long that the wary animal herself had given an unusual signal of her whereabouts, Sylvia had only laughed when she came upon Mistress Moolly at the swamp-side, and urged her affectionatly homeward with a twig of birch leaves. The old cow was not inclined to wander farther, she even turned in the right direction for once as they left the pasture, and stepped along the road at a good pace. She was quite ready to be milked now, and seldom stopped to browse. Sylvia wondered what her grandmother would say because they were so late. It was a great while since she had left home at half past five o'clock, but everybody knew the difficulty of making this errand a short one. Mrs. Tilley had chased the hornéd torment too many summer evenings herself to blame any one else for lingering, and was only thankful as she waited that she had Sylvia, nowadays, to give such valuable assistance. The good woman suspected that Sylvia loitered occasionally on her own account; there never was such a child for straying about out-of-doors since the world was made! Everybody said that it was a good change for a little maid who had tried to grow for eight years in a crowded manufacturing town, but, as for Sylvia herself, it seemed as if she never had been alive at all before she came to live at the farm. She thought often with wistful compassion of a wretched dry geranium that belonged to a town neighbor.

" 'Afraid of folks,' " old Mrs. Tilley said to herself, with a smile, after she had made the unlikely choice of Sylvia from her daughter's houseful of children, and was returning to the farm. " 'Afraid of folks,' they said! I guess she won't be troubled no great with 'em up to the old place!" When they reached the door of the lonely house and stopped to unlock it, and the cat came to purr loudly, and rub against them, a deserted pussy, indeed, but

*From *The Country of the Pointed Firs and Other Stories,* ed. Willa Cather (Garden City, NY: Doubleday, 1956).

fat with young robins, Sylvia whispered that this was a beautiful place to live in, and she never should wish to go home.

The companions followed the shady woodroad, the cow taking slow steps, and the child very fast ones. The cows stopped long at the brook to drink, as if the pasture were not half a swamp, and Sylvia stood still and waited, letting her bare feet cool themselves in the shoal water, while the great twilight moths struck softly against her. She waded on through the brook as the cow moved away, and listened to the thrushes with a heart that beat fast with pleasure. There was a stirring in the great boughs overhead. They were full of little birds and beasts that seemed to be wide-awake, and going about their world, or else saying good-night to each other in sleepy twitters. Sylvia herself felt sleepy as she walked along. However, it was not much farther to the house, and the air was soft and sweet. She was not often in the woods so late as this, and it made her feel as if she were a part of the gray shadows and the moving leaves. She was just thinking how long it seemed since she first came to the farm a year ago, and wondering if everything went on in the noisy town just the same as when she was there; the thought of the great red-faced boy who used to chase and frighten her made her hurry along the path to escape from the shadow of the trees.

Suddenly this little woods-girl is horror-stricken to hear a clear whistle not very far away. Not a bird's whistle, which would have a sort of friendliness, but a boy's whistle, determined, and somewhat aggressive. Sylvia left the cow to whatever sad fate might await her, and stepped discreetly aside into the bushes, but she was just too late. The enemy had discovered her, and called out in a very cheerful and persuasive tone, "Halloa, little girl, how far is it to the road?" and trembling Sylvia answered almost inaudibly, "A good ways."

She did not dare to look boldly at the tall young man, who carried a gun over his shoulder, but she came out of her bush and again followed the cow, while he walked alongside.

"I have been hunting for some birds," the stranger said kindly, "and I have lost my way, and need a friend very much. Don't be afraid," he added gallantly. "Speak up and tell me what your name is, and whether you think I can spend the night at your house, and go out gunning early in the morning."

Sylvia was more alarmed than before. Would not her grandmother consider her much to blame? But who could have foreseen such an accident as this? It did not appear to be her fault, and she hung her head as if the stem of it were broken, but managed to answer "Sylvy," with much effort when her companion again asked her name.

Mrs. Tillely was standing in the doorway when the trio came into view. The cow gave a loud moo by way of explanation.

"Yes, you'd better speak up for yourself, you old trial! Where'd she tuck herself away this time, Sylvy?" Sylvia kept an awed silence; she knew by instinct that her grandmother did not comprehend the gravity of the situation. She must be mistaking the stranger for one of the farmer-lads of the region.

The young man stood his gun beside the door, and dropped a heavy game-bag beside it; then he bade Mrs.Tilley good-evening,and repeated his wayfarer's story, and asked if he could have a night's lodging.

"Put me anywhere you like," he said. "I must be off early in the morning, before day; but I am very hungry, indeed. You can give me some milk at any rate, that's plain."

"Dear sakes, yes," responded the hostess, whose long slumbering hospitality seemed to be easily awakened. "You might fare better if you went out on the main road a mile or so, but you're welcome to what we've got. I'll milk right off, and you make yourself at home. You can sleep on husks or feathers," she proffered graciously, "I raised them all myself. There's good pasturing for geese just below there towards the ma'sh. Now step round and set a plate for the gentleman, Sylvy!" And Sylvia promptly stepped. She was glad to have something to do, and she was hungry herself.

It was a surprise to find so clean and comfortable a little dwelling in this New England wilderness. The young man had known the horrors of its most primitive housekeeping, and the dreary squalor of that level of society which does not rebel at the companionship of hens. This was the best thrift of an old-fashioned farmstead, though on such a small scale that it seemed like a hermitage. He listened eagerly to the old woman's quaint talk, he watched Sylvia's pale face and shining gray eyes with ever growing enthusiasm, and insisted that this was the best supper he had eaten for a month; then, afterward, the new-made friends sat down in the doorway together while the moon came up.

Soon it would be berry-time, and Sylvia was a great help at picking. The cow was a good milker, though a plaguy thing to keep track of, the hostess gossiped frankly, adding presently that she had buried four children, so that Sylvia's mother, and a son (who might be dead) in California were all the children she had left. "Dan, my boy, was a great hand to go gunning," she explained sadly. "I never wanted for pa'tridges or gray squer'ls while he was to home. He's been a great wand'rer, I expect, and he's no hand to write letters. There, I don't blame him, I'd ha' seen the world myself if it had been so I could.

"Sylvia takes after him," the grandmother continued affectionatly, after a minute's pause. "There ain't a foot o' ground she don't know her way over, and the wild creatur's counts her one o' themselves. Squer'ls she'll tame to come an' feed right out o' her hands, and all sorts o' birds. Last winter she got the jay-birds to bangeing here, and I believe she'd 'a' scanted herself of her own meals to have plenty to throw out amongst 'em, if I hadn't kep' watch. Anything but crows, I tell her, I'm willin' to help support,—though Dan he went an' tamed one o' them that did seem to have reason same as folks. It was round here a good spell after he went away. Dan an' his father they didn't hitch,—but he never held up his head ag'in after Dan had dared him an' gone off."

The guest did not notice this hint of family sorrows in his eager interest in something else.

"So Sylvy knows all about birds, does she?" he exclaimed, as he looked round at the little girl who sat, very demure but increasingly sleepy, in the moonlight. "I am making a collection of birds myself. I have been at it ever since I was a boy." (Mrs. Tilley smiled.) "There are two or three very rare ones I have been hunting for these five years. I mean to get them on my own ground if they can be found."

"Do you cage 'em up?" asked Mrs. Tilley doubtfully, in response to this enthusiastic announcement.

"Oh, no, they're stuffed and preserved, dozens and dozens of them," said the ornithologist," and I have shot or snared every one myself. I caught a glimpse of a white heron three miles from here on Saturday, and I have followed it in this direction. They have never been found in this district at all. The little white heron, it is," and he turned again to look at Sylvia with the hope of discovering that the rare bird was one of her acquaintances.

But Sylvia was watching a hop-toad in the narrow foot-path.

"You would know the heron if you saw it,' the stranger continued eagerly. "A queer tall white bird with soft feathers and long thin legs. And it would have a nest perhaps in the top of a high tree, made of sticks, something like a hawk's nest."

Sylvia's heart gave a wild beat; she knew that strange white bird, and had once stolen softly near where it stood in some bright green swamp grass, away over at the other side of the woods. There was an open place where the sunshine always seemed strangely yellow and hot, where tall, nodding rushes grew, and her grandmother had warned her that she might sink in the soft black mud underneath and never be heard of more. Not far beyond were the salt marshes and beyond those was the sea, the sea which Sylvia wondered and dreamed about, but never had looked upon, though its great voice could often be heard above the noise of the woods on stormy nights.

"I can't think of anything I should like so much as to find that heron's nest," the handsome stranger was saying. "I would give ten dollars to anybody who could show it to me," he added desperately, "and I mean to spend my whole vacation hunting for it if need be. Perhaps it was only migrating, or had been chased out of its own region by some bird of prey."

Mrs. Tilley gave amazed attention to all this, but Sylvia still watched the toad, not divining, as she might have done at some calmer time, that the creature wished to get to its hole under the doorstep, and was much hindered by the unusual spectators at that hour of the evening. No amount of thought, that night, could decide how many wished-for treasures the ten dollars, so lightly spoken of, would buy.

The next day the young sportsman hovered about the woods, and Sylvia kept him company, having lost her first fear of the friendly lad, who proved to be most kind and sympathetic. He told her many things about the birds and what they knew and where they lived and what they did with themselves. And he gave her a jack-knife, which she thought as great a treasure as if she were a desert-islander. All day long he did not once make her troubled or afraid except when he brought down some unsuspecting singing creature from its bough. Sylvia would have liked him vastly better without his gun; she could not understand why he killed the very birds he seemed to like so much. But as the day waned, Sylvia still watched the young man with loving admiration. She had never seen anybody so charming and delightful; the woman's heart, asleep in the child, was vaguely thrilled by a dream of love. Some premonition of that great power stirred and swayed these young foresters who traversed the solemn woodlands with soft-footed silent care. They stopped to listen to a bird's song; they pressed forward again eagerly, parting the branches,—speaking to each other rarely and in whispers; the young man going first and Sylvia following, fascinated, a few steps behind, with her gray eyes dark with excitement.

She grieved because the longed-for white heron was elusive, but she did not lead the guest, she only followed, and there was no such thing as speaking first. The sound of her own unquestioned voice would have terrified her,—it was hard enough to answer yes or no when there was need of that. At last evening began to fall, and they drove the cow home together, and Sylvia smiled with pleasure when they came to the place where she heard the whistle and was afraid only the night before.

2 Half a mile from home, at the farther edge of the woods, where the land was highest, a great pine-tree stood, the last of its generation. Whether it was left for a boundary mark, or for what reason, no one could say; the woodchoppers who had felled its mates were dead and gone long ago, and a whole forest of sturdy trees, pines and oaks and maples, had grown again. But the stately head of this old pine towered above them all and made a landmark for sea and shore miles and miles away. Sylvia knew it well. She had always believed that whoever climbed to the top of it could see the ocean; and the little girl had often laid her hand on the great rough trunk and looked up wistfully at those dark boughs that the wind always stirred, no matter how hot and still the air might be below. Now she thought of the tree with a new excitement, for why, if one climbed it at break of day, could not one see all the world, and easily discover whence the white heron flew, and mark the place, and find the hidden nest?

What a spirit of adventure, what wild ambition! What fancied triumph and delight and glory for the later morning when she could make known the secret! It was almost too real and too great for the childish heart to bear.

All night the door of the little house stood open, and the whippoorwills came and sang upon the very step. The young sportsman and his old hostess were sound asleep, but Sylvia's great design kept her broad awake and watching. She forgot to think of sleep. The short summer night seemed as long as the winter darkness, and at last when the whippoorwills ceased, and she was afraid the morning would after all come too soon, she stole out of the house and followed the pasture path through the woods, hastening toward the open ground beyond, listening with a sense of comfort and companionship to the drowsy twitter of a half-awakened bird, whose perch she had jarred in passing. Alas, if the great wave of human interest which flooded for the first time this dull little life should sweep away the satisfactions of an existence heart to heart with nature and the dumb life of the forest!

There was the huge tree asleep yet in the paling moonlight, and small and hopeful Sylvia began with utmost bravery to mount to the top of it, with tingling, eager blood coursing the channels of her whole frame, with her bare feet and fingers, that pinched and held like bird's claws to the monstrous ladder reaching up, up, almost to the sky itself. First she must mount the white oak tree that grew alongside, where she was almost lost among the dark branches and the green leaves heavy and wet with dew; a bird fluttered off its nest, and a red squirrel ran to and fro and scolded pettishly at the harmless housebreaker. Sylvia felt her way easily. She had often climbed there, and knew that higher still one of the oak's upper branches chafed against the pine trunk, just where its lower boughs were set close together. There, when she made the dangerous pass from one tree to the other, the great enterprise would really begin.

She crept out along the swaying oak limb at last, and took the daring step across into the old pine-tree. The way was harder than she thought; she must reach far and hold fast, the sharp dry twigs caught and held her and scratched her like angry talons, the pitch made her thin little fingers clumsy and stiff as she went round and round the tree's great stem, higher and higher upward. The sparrows and robins in the woods below were beginning to wake and twitter to the dawn, yet it seemed much lighter there aloft in the pine-tree, and the child knew that she must hurry if her project were to be of any use.

The tree seemed to lengthen itself out as she went up, and to reach farther and farther upward. It was like a great main-mast to the voyaging earth; it must truly have been amazed that morning through all its ponderous frame as it felt this determined spark of human spirit creeping and climbing from higher branch to branch. Who knows how steadily the least twigs held themselves to advantage this light, weak creature on her way! The old pine must have loved his new dependent. More than all the hawks, and bats, and moths, and even the sweet-voiced thrushes, was the brave, beating heart of the solitary gray-eyed child. And the tree stood still and held away the winds that June morning while the dawn grew bright in the east.

Sylvia's face was like a pale star, if one had seen it from the ground, when the last thorny bough was past, and she stood trembling and tired but wholly triumphant, high in the tree-top. Yes, there was the sea with the dawning sun making a golden dazzle over it, and toward that glorious east flew two hawks with slow-moving pinions. How low they looked in the air from that height when before one had only seen them far up, and dark against the blue sky. Their gray feathers were as soft as moths; they seemed only a little way from the tree, and Sylvia felt as if she too could go flying away among the clouds. Westward, the woodlands and farms reached miles and miles into the distance; here and there were church steeples, and white villages; truly it was a vast and awesome world.

The birds sang louder and louder. At last the sun came up bewilderingly bright. Sylvia could see the white sails of ships out at sea, and the clouds that were purple and rose-colored and yellow at first began to fade away. Where was the white heron's nest in the sea of green branches, and was this wonderful sight and pageant of the world the only reward for having climbed to such a giddy height? Now look down again, Sylvia, where the green marsh is set among the shining birches and dark hemlocks; there where you saw the white heron once you will see him again; look, look! a white spot of him like a single floating feather comes up from the dead hemlock and grows larger, and rises, and comes close at last, and goes by the landmark pine with steady sweep of wing and outstretched slender neck and crested head. And wait! wait! do not move a foot or a finger, little girl, do not send an arrow of light and consciousness from your two eager eyes, for the heron has perched on a pine bough not far beyond yours, and cries back to his mate on the nest, and plumes his feathers for the new day!

The child gives a long sigh a minute later when a company of shouting cat-birds comes also to the tree, and vexed by their fluttering and lawlessness the solemn heron goes away. She knows his secret now, the wild, light, slender bird that floats and wavers, and goes back like an arrow presently to his home in the green world beneath. Then Sylvia, well satisfied, makes her perilous way down again, not daring to look far below the branch she stands on, ready to cry sometimes because her fingers ache and her lamed feet slip. Wondering over and over again what the stranger would say to her, and what he would think when she told him how to find his way straight to the heron's nest.

"Sylvy, Sylvy!" called the busy old grandmother again and again, but nobody answered, and the small husk bed was empty and Sylvia had disappeared.

The guest waked from a dream, and remembering his day's pleasure hurried to dress himself that it might sooner begin. He was sure from the way the shy little girl looked once or twice yesterday that she had at least seen the white heron, and now she must really be persuaded to tell. Here she comes now, paler than ever, and her worn old frock is torn and tattered, and smeared with pine pitch. The grandmother and the sportsman stand in the door together and question her, and the splendid moment has come to speak of the dead hemlock-tree by the green marsh.

But Sylvia does not speak after all, though the old grandmother fretfully rebukes her, and the young man's kind appealing eyes are looking straight in her own. He can make them rich with money; he has promised it, and they are poor now. He is so well worth making happy, and he waits to hear the story she can tell.

No, she must keep silence! What is it that suddenly forbids her and makes her dumb? Has she been nine years growing, and now, when the great world for the first time puts out a hand to her, must she thrust it aside for a bird's sake? The murmur of the pine's green branches is in her ears, she remembers how the white heron came flying through the golden air and how they watched the sea and the morning together, and Sylvia cannot speak; she cannot tell the heron's secret and give its life away.

Dear loyalty, that suffered a sharp pang as the guest went away disappointed later in the day, that could have served and followed him and loved him as a dog loves! Many a night Slvia heard the echo of his whistle haunting the pasture path as she came home with the loitering cow. She forgot even her sorrow at the sharp report of his gun and the piteous sight of thrushes and sparrows dropping silent to the ground, their songs hushed and their pretty feathers stained and wet with blood. Were the birds better friends than their hunter might have been,—who can tell? Whatever treasures were lost to her, woodlands and summer-time, remember! Bring your gifts and graces and tell your secrets to this lonely country child!

Twentieth-Century British Nature Writing: The Tradition Endures

Throughout the twentieth century, British nature writing has extended the themes that allowed it to dominate the literary tradition of the nineteenth century: reflective observation of natural history; depiction of the texture of rural life; and, above all, personal exploration of nature as a means to renew human spirit. The intensification of industrialization and urbanization in the twentieth century has continued to attract audiences to works that contemplate the natural world, and that have increasingly articulated the need for practical conservation. As new learning, especially new scientific learning, has created competing intellectual interests, nature literature has responded with deeper explorations of how nature may be defined, and the ways in which humans may be defined as "a part of nature." Though no longer dominant, nature writing has remained a viable tradition in twentieth-century British literature, making distinct responses to the new intellectual milieu as well as to changes in land and social structure.

Toward the end of the nineteenth century the traditions of nature writing began to be adapted to the new century by three seminal writers: the essayists Richard Jefferies (1848-1887) and W. H. Hudson (1841-1922), and the famous poet and novelist Thomas Hardy (1840-1928). They appealed to the modern audience by describing nature in dynamic, autonomous terms, their vision informed (though not dominated) by the accumulating data of modern science. Discarding the older view that the world was governed by a personal, benevolent deity, they nonetheless continued to find profound meaning in the life of the earth; implicitly they criticized the sterility of modern industrial society. Often rooting their work in description of rural regions, these and subsequent nature writers recorded the life of the countryside for urban readers who wished to remember how they or their parents had once lived, or who simply wished to remember pleasant country holidays. In this way nature literature has served as a counterbalance to the century's predominantly urban, social literary themes.

Generally, twentieth-century British nature literature has focused upon the rural. Lacking the vast wilderness that shaped the American experience, Great Britain instead enjoys richly variegated landscapes in which ancient agricultural traditions are rooted. Twentieth-century British nature writers have joined Jefferies in appreciating the "genius of a place . . ." where "man and nature have dwelt side by side time out of mind." Hudson, likewise, came to "recognize and appreciate the enormous difference which human associations make in the effect produced on us by visible nature." The main thrust of the tradition, then, is toward the interaction between humans and the land, often viewed from historical perspectives, including the historical fact of nature literature itself. Conservation efforts, often stimulated by nature writing, have sought primarily to preserve rural landscapes, for both species habitat and for "amenity," that is, for accommodation of human demand to take pleasure in the landscape. The response of the twentieth-century British nature writers to the "shrinking" of their own land may foreshadow future responses as the world's wild places are increasingly tamed and its open spaces developed.

NEW SOCIAL FORCES

By the beginning of the twentieth century, systems of industrial manufacture and commercial distribution had largely reorganized British society, depopulating the countryside, averting human timetables from the natural signs of sunrise and season, in favor of the artificial signals of factory whistle and appointment book. By the beginning of the twentieth century the internal combustion engine joined the steam engine in the process of emptying old rural villages and also spreading urban populations out into the countryside.

As the new century unfolded, habits of life changed radically with a startling array of technological innovations. During the last quarter of the nineteenth century the sewing machine and aniline dyes rendered clothing cheaper and more colorful; the phonograph, mass-produced canned food, electric lights, and the cinema made life comfortable and entertaining; the typewriter, the telephone and the wireless telegraph, the automobile, faster ships and railways, and—three years into the twentieth century—the airplane, conspired to shrink the world, while creating occupations undreamed of a hundred years before.

Such technical progress resulted in great optimism, but beneath it, for some, lay a feeling of uneasiness, a sense of lost direction. If technology had increased comforts, it also increased the pace of life; if urban life offered variety and entertainment, it also diminished the rooted feelings of rural society. The world shrunk by telegraph and steamship was troubled by the Gatling gun, the submarine, dynamite and a growing militarism among European nations. Militarism and nationalism were, perhaps, reactions to the modern sense that life was increasingly crowded, fast-paced, and alienating.

Alienation was also provoked by developments in the history of ideas. The late nineteenth-century "crisis of faith" had been precipitated by evolutionary theory and historical criticism of the Bible, both challenging long-held assumptions about human nature. By 1900 Sigmund Freud argued in *The Interpretation of Dreams* that the "unconscious" was an irrational but pervasive influence upon human behavior. Within another ten years Albert Einstein would formulate the Special Theory of Relativity, establishing a new physics counter to "common sense," and Ivan Pavlov would demonstrate the conditioned reflex, establishing a rigidly mechanistic model for the human mind. Science was depicting a universe that seemed increasingly complex and abstract.

IMPERSONALNESS OF NATURE

One way that nature writers responded to the new intellectual milieu was to contemplate the impersonalness of nature, that is, its permanence and its domination of human culture. The novelist and poet Thomas Hardy, a central figure in the history of British literature, helped initiate this major theme. An often quoted passage from his novel *The Return of the Native* (1878), titled "A Face on Which Time Makes But Little Impression," demonstrates the somber qualities of "Haggard Egdon Heath":

> The spot was, indeed, a near relation of night, and when night showed itself an apparent tendency to gravitate together could be perceived in its shades and the scene. The sombre stretch of rounds and hollows seemed to rise and meet the evening gloom in pure sympathy, the heath exhaling darkness as rapidly as the heavens precipitate it. And so the obscurity in the air and the obscurity in the land closed together in a black fraternization towards which each advanced halfway. . . . Haggard Egdon Heath appealed to a subtler and a scarcer instinct, to a more recently learned emotion, than that which responds to the sort of beauty called charming and fair.

The uncongenial face of nature here portrayed reflects Hardy's belief that the universe is distinterested in human aspiration. Much influenced by evolutionary theory, Hardy treats nature as a complex, enduring system which engulfs human activity.

The absence of homocentric morality in nature did not limit Richard Jefferies. In *The Story of My Heart* (1883) Jefferies confesses disbelief in a personal benevolent god directing the universe. Instead he prays to the earth itself: "Leaning against the oak's massive trunk, and feeling the rough bark and the lichen at my back, looking southwards over the grassy fields, cowslip-yellow, at the woods on the slope, I thought of my desire of deeper soul-life." The creed expressed here is akin to the pantheism of the ancient world, Jefferies' "dearest Greece." Accepting the premises of evolution, he did not shrink from depicting the predatory violence by which natural balances are maintained, even in his children's books *Wood Magic* (1881) and *Bevis* (1882).

REGIONALISM

A second response of nature literature to the new century was preoccupation with regions, born partly out of nostalgia, partly out of the rootlessness of urban existence. Regional writers in rural society deliberately strove to record the details of disappearing landscape and folkways. English regionalism, in comparison with that of America, drew upon relatively ancient human relationships with the land.

The most famous and influential regionalist was Hardy. His novels and poems were set in the still-wild heath county of Dorset, which he called by its antique name, "Wessex." The Dorset setting provides a good example of the motivation for regional literature: during the period 1811-1860, two thirds of the wild heath in Dorset was lost to agriculture and development.

Regionalism in England involved not frontier but history. Hardy attempts to capture the feel of the older cultures—Saxon, Roman, and Celt—that had inhabited his native county by depicting ancient rural ritual, such as the autumn bonfire in *The Return of the Native*. The Wessex novels of Hardy are much more highly valued than the work of other regionalists, though regional writing, some of it tuned closely to the natural world, has continued as a popular genre throughout the twentieth century. Eden Philpotts (1862-1960), strongly influenced by Hardy, uses the West Country as a setting for a long list of novels. Emily Hilda Young (1880-1947) writes about Bristol and Somerset, and Constance Holme (1880-1955) sets her novels in coastal Lancashire. Sussex is the setting for Sheila Kaye-Smith (1887-1956), who focused upon character rather than landscape. The outlook of one of her characters shows one approach of the regional novel:

> As a rule he did not think much about the beauty of the things he saw. He took his countryside for granted, loving it as one loves a familiar face, without caring whether it is beautiful or not.

A somewhat different approach appears in the work of Mary Webb, whose narrator in *The House in Dormer Forest* asserts that "The love of nature is a passion for those in whom it once lodges: It cannot be removed."

Her description well describes Jefferies' appreciative familiarity with rural life in his native region of North Wiltshire. His descriptions of Coate Farm in Wiltshire, where he spent his boyhood, are preoccupied with spirit of place, and provide tangible expressions of rural experience. As his biographer W. J. Keith notes, Jefferies is one of the first to write consciously for an essentially urban audience, who appreciated his practical guides to country scenes that they, or their ancestors, had left not so many years before. *Nature Near London* (1883) and *Wild Life in a Southern County* (1879) demonstrate Jefferies' ability to share the joy he found in field and hedgerow, birds and flowers, sun and sky, observing not only natural phenomena but human engagement with them. He understood the experience of farm manager and farm laborer, gamekeeper and poacher, and portrayed the experience in works such as *The Gamekeeper at Home* (1878) and *The Amateur Poacher* (1879).

TRAVEL LITERATURE

The trend toward the old and the primitive in regional literature was but one expression of an attempt to escape the monotony of modern culture. In 1891 the French painter Gauguin (1848-1903) epitomized European longing for simplicity when he settled on the tropical island of Tahiti that had inspired his art. Interest in primitive cultures living close to nature was shared by contemporary painters, such as Pablo Picasso (1881-1973) and Paul Klee (1879-1940, and fueled the popularity of travel literature, a tradition that includes the early records of exploration in wild America.

Twentieth-century nature literature became enriched by works describing exotic, untamed lands in a variety of genres: travel memoir, novel, fantasy, spiritual quest. During the last quarter of the nineteenth century the continued growth of the British Empire created a taste for exotic settings. Indian landscapes provided settings for the popular stories and poems of Rudyard Kipling (1865-1936), who chronicled the adventures of her Majesty's soldiers while describing native culture. Kipling's *The Jungle Book* (1894) presented modern beast fables based upon behavioral characteristics of different species. Another major writer, Joseph Conrad (1857-1924), a former sea captain, depicted exotic landscapes in Africa, South America, and the Orient to symbolize the mystery of human motivation.

Probably the most widely read of the exotic nature writers was W. H. Hudson, who was raised on the Argentine pampas—vast, treeless, plains, sparsely settled by cattle ranchers. After his move to England, his ancestors' native land, Hudson drew upon his experience on the pampas in books attuned to vastness and isolation. His descriptions of exotic species continued a theme introduced by the naturalists Darwin and Wallace. *Idle Days in Patagonia* (1893) recounts the spiritual insights as well as the sense preceptions Hudson experienced while wandering on the plains. *The Naturalist in La Plata* (1892) reveals Hudson's knowledge and powers of observation, and offers interesting criticism of Darwin's evolutionary theory. It was immensely popular in its time. South America was also the subject of Henry Major Tomlinson's *The Sea and the Jungle* (1912), a true narrative of the author's escape from a bleak and boring London life into the jungles surrounding the Amazon River, a passage through spiritual realms as well as through colorful, sinister landscapes.

A world shrunk by new inventions demanded exploration of its most remote regions. Early in the century Antarctic expeditions were recorded by Sir Ernest Shackleton and the now-controversial figure Robert Falcon Scott (1868-1912), who wrote *The Voyage of the Discovery* (1905). *Scott's Last Expedition* (1914), an account of his journey to the South Pole, from which he did not return, was assembled from the journals later found on Scott's frozen body; it served as a popular tale of heroism.

Vitality inspired by Italian and Mexican landscapes dominates the travel writing of the novelist D. H. Lawrence (1885-1930). His *Sea and Sardania, Etruscan Places,* and *Mornings in Mexico* express the essential theme of travel books that qualify as literature: the search for spirit of place, a search motivated at least in part by a sense of emptiness.

AESTHETICISM AND THE GEORGIANS

A different response to the sense of spiritual emptiness emerged at the turn of the century and established a continuing literary tradition counter to that of nature writing. During the 1980's there arose a movement which attempted, with much of the force formerly felt only in religion, to locate the meaning of life in art itself. The doctrine of aestheticism embraced artificiality, that is, human artistic rendering, as the essential quality of civilization; in this it marked a return to the assumptions of the Renaissance.

Even while the aesthetic movement remained influential in the early years of the twentieth century, it became an urbane fashion to enjoy the countryside. The reign of King Edward VII (1901-1910) has become synonymous with the aristocratic hunting party and the middle-class "country weekend" in a cottage. French Impressionalism had produced the delicate, soft landscapes of Manet, Monet, and Renoir. In England impressionism provoked appreciation of riverside and flower garden. As the first World War drew closer, the escape to a domesticated countryside became the theme of a group of educated, urbane poets. The "Georgian" poets, named for the reign of King George VII, tended to deal with rural themes. They deliberately shunned the sophistication of the aesthetes in favor of sentimental, consciously simple, lovely impressions of the natural world; in doing so they were imitating the Romantic era nature poetry, though without capturing the power and creativity of the original.

Among the Georgian poets was Edward Thomas (1878-1917), a nature essayist who was influenced to begin writing poems by the great American nature writer Robert Frost. William Henry Davies (1871-1940) spent his youth in poverty as a tramp—including rambles in the United States; *Raptures* (1918) shows the happiness he had learned to enjoy in close contact with the natural scenes. Ralph Hodgson (1871-1940) wrote poems about animals, describing their natural behavior rather than interpreting them in terms of human sentimentality.

CLASSICISM AND THE NATURISTS

After the carnage of the first World War became evident, many felt repulsed by the modern society that had been involved in such horrors. One response was a revival of "classicism" in art and literature. Classicism radically rejected what it considered the assumptions of modern culture: democracy, commerce, and the primacy of science. Moreover, it questioned the romantic conception of nature as an organic system from which humanity could draw meaning.

The objective world, wrote T. E. Hulme, in what would be published after his death as *Speculations* (1917), was "a chaos, a cinder heap." The only order or meaning in nature was what human intellect placed there. Order was to be found in the spiritual truth of orthodox religion and in artistic form; tradition and morality were superior to individuality and vitality.

Yet during the same period this disparagement of nature was countered by a different set of intellectual forces. The legacy of evolutionary theory and the new science of depth psychology laid the foundation for a group of early twentieth-century writers whom John Alcorn defines as "naturists" in *The Nature Novel from Hardy To Lawrence* (1977). Also repulsed by the materialist assumptions of modern society, the naturists saw positive, even utopian potential for humanity as part of the dynamic, purposeful biological system. Older socialist utopian visions, such as that of William Morris, had been based upon consciousness, indebted to the Wordsworthian "observing, thinking, feeling first-person," as Alcorn puts it. The naturist tendency was "for closing the personal subject within the impersonal world of nature."

The intellectual foundation of the naturists rested upon evolutionary theory, which had initially disturbed traditional belief in Christianity. Darwin's ideas gradually became the nucleus of a compensatory faith in the dynamic, self-regulating system of nature. The shock that humans might have evolved from "lower" animals gradually gave way—among some thinkers—to the idea that humanity makes up a part, even if a small part, of a biological system of incredible variety and complexity, moving according to its own logic toward some final end. If the endpoint itself was inscrutable, the process of change powered by biological drives assumed a kind of holiness. The "impersonalness" of nature in Hardy's work might provide more than a backdrop for tragedy. From another perspective one may make a positive interpretation: enclosed within the system of nature is a wisdom that human consciousness can only dimly perceive because human desire and behavior is submerged within the very system.

The concepts of depth psychology reinforced the naturists' belief that humanity participated in a self-regulating biological system. The goal of the naturist writers was to liberate the human psyche from the narrow, rationalist limitations imposed by modern society. Their writing reveals attempts to reunite human characters with the old gods of woodland, stream, and harvest. A passage from Hardy's novel *The Return of the Native* demonstrates the assimilation of human behavior within a web of biological activity. A character's voice seems inseparable from voices of vegetation:

> Suddenly, on the barrow, there mingled with all this wild rhetoric of night a sound which modulated so naturally with the rest that its beginning and ending were hardly to be distinguished. The bluffs, and the bushes, and the heather-bells had broken silence; at last, so did the woman; and her articulation was but another phrase of the same discourse as theirs.

D. H. Lawrence (1885-1930) shares Hardy's conviction that the earth's natural processes provide a more enduring and meaningful basis for the individual than the restrictions of civilized society. But Lawrence, living a generation later than Hardy, had greater access to new psychological and anthropological tools for discovering underlying human desires. The physical passions that act through the human psyche Lawrence called the "life urge." Ever active beneath the surface of consciousness, the life-urge manifests itself in images, dreams, and feelings, and forceful behavior; if repressed, in destructive behavior. Thus Lawrence validated for humans the biological basis that, according to Darwin, influenced evolutionary destiny.

To be in touch with the life-urge is to have contact with the natural world, not to "know" it as the scientist does, by objective analysis, but to feel its rhythm, to be influenced by its primordial forces of wave, sunlight, predation, procreation. In "Pan in America" Lawrence describes an encounter with the power of a pine tree:

> The tree gathers up earth power from the dark bowels of the earth, and a roaming sky-glitter from above. And all unto itself, which is a tree, woody, enormous, slow but unyielding with life, bristling with acquisitive energy, obscurity radiates some of its strength . . .

Lawrence argued for opening "doors of receptivity" that had been closed by reliance upon thinking at the expense of feeling, and upon rationalism at the expense of intuition. For Lawrence the truly destructive agent was modern industrialism. Industrialism makes us see the pine tree as part of "an inanimate forest of standing lumber, marketable in St. Louis." The heart of Lawrence's attack on modern industrialized society was his repudiation of its assumption that the earth is a dead source of economic material rather than a mysterious sharer of life.

In the controversial novel, *Lady Chatterly's Lover* (1929), Lawrence dramatizes an essential conflict between industrial society and wholeness of life for the individual. Industrialism is personified in the character of a wealthy young aristocrat, who, crippled during World War I, devotes his life to development of coal mines on his inherited estate. The aristocrat's wife, her sexual and emotional needs neglected, finds fulfillment with her husband's gamekeeper, a sensitive man whose sensuality is sharpened by daily interaction with the land he patrols. Flowers, animals, and landscape are intertwined with descriptions of the love affair.

In his depiction of industrialism and nature Lawrence laid a "naturist" foundation for subsequent twentieth-century thought. Mass society, he argued, separated humans from their nourishing roots and destroyed their ability to integrate the physical with the spiritual. A prime symbol of disintegration, for Lawrence and others, was World War I.

The monumental violence of the war convinced many survivors that modern civilization had indeed failed. A classic retreat was that of Henry Williamson (1897-1977), who emerged from the war shell shocked and fatigued, unable to function in society. Gradually his boyhood habit of observing nature on walks reasserted itself and restored meaning to his life. The contrast between the positive effects of nature and the destructive forces of society led to a series of autobiographical novels, together called *The Flax of Dreams* (1928).

Not only Lawrence and Williamson, but a whole generation had been shocked by the world war. Many post-war writers looked for compensation in religion, in communism, in tradition, or in classicism. Others turned to agrarian values, both natural and social, to find a source of stability

THE RURALISTS

Several groups of post-war writers attempted not only to praise the value of rural life, but also to promote it within an increasingly urban, industrial society. During the apparent failure of industrial society in the depression years of the thirties, the ruralist movement became more widespread. The ruralists' goal was to record and revitalize the life of farm and village, which was disappearing along with its landscape. Because of attempts to stimulate the depressed economy, agricultural land decreased by eight percent in the period between 1931-1935. By 1940, after the beginning of World War II, 150,000 acres of farmland were being transferred to industrial use each year.

One group of rural writers was the agricultural novelists, who in some ways continued the regionalist movement. *Precious Bane* (1926), a story of a Shropshire farming family during the Napoleonic Wars, won for author Mary Webb a commendation from Prime Minister Baldwin: "One who reads some passages in Whitehall has almost the physical sense of being in the Shropshire cornfields."

Among the agricultural novelists there was, moreover, an intertwining of economic and personal relationships with the land. In H. W. Freeman's *Joseph and His Brethren* (1929), for example, a farm dominates a family's destiny, calling first one, then another brother back from temptations: free land in Canada, adventure in the army, marriage. Even after their father's remarriage disinherits the sons, they eventually come back to work the land as tenants because their love for that particular property is so strong. In this work the villains are foreign investment and monoculture, while farm chores—tending sheep, haying a meadow—appear intrinsically satisfying. The novel recalls the conventions of the georgic tradition in its realistic, appreciative depiction of farm labor.

The intrinsic value of husbanding one's own land, a theme suggested at the end of the eighteenth century by William Wordsworth as an argument against land enclosure, is also a theme in the novels of A. G. Street. *The Endless Furrow* (1935) chronicles the restoration of farm property to a family whose declined fortune has forced them "down" into the commercial class. The theme is common in the agricultural novel. When the protagonist attempts to gain ownership of a farm, he

> was obeying the call of a piece of England's land as countless men have done all down the ages, and will continue to do in the future . . . he loved the scent of the countryside at each and every season of the year. The growth of his crops—*his* crops—crops which he had grown in the good earth, gave him a curious satisfaction. He revelled in the room this new calling gave to him.

After his only son is killed in the war, the farmer returns to the fields and continues the cycle of husbandry for which he is responsible. Becoming a contemporary farmer was the theme of *Corduroy* (1930), part of a series of autobiographical novels by Adrian Bell, who took up farming and celebrated both the joys and responsibilities of living on the land. The autobiographical *Lark Rise to Candleford* (1935) by Flora Thompson narrates an occupational migration from farm to post office and painstakingly details the changing milieu of agricultural society of Oxfordshire.

Both Bell and Webb argue the value of rural culture in essays, belonging to a small but intensely committed intellectual movement that championed a "return to nature." They sought to reverse the decline of agriculture during the thirties, and regenerate it upon what they considered to be natural principles. Their program called for revitalizing traditional rural society, specifically husbandry of the land. Husbandry meant, quite simply, caring for the land: following the natural law and returning to the land what one removed. They opposed monoculture, chemical fertilization, mechanization (which reduced the rural labor force), and, above all, the commercial export system that they thought caused the national debt and consequent heavy taxation on the land.

Inspired by the tradition of nature literature, the movement drew upon a growing canon of research on pre-industrial rural society, including the sociological studies of John and Barbara Hammond, who sought to recover the "folk attitude" toward life, and George Sturt (1863-1927), who wrote under the pseudonym of George Bourne. Sturt owned a wheelwright's shop, itself doomed to extinction by the advent of the motor car. He attempted to record in writing the details of work in the old rural village, a way of life that was dissolving during his lifetime. His interviews with rural laborers in *The Bettesworth Book* (1901) and his analysis of *Change in the Village* (1912) are sociology more than nature writing, but his work became a source book for those interested in nature conservation according to rural values.

Those interested in rural revival included a diffuse group: the literary critic F. R. Leavis, whose *Culture and Environment* (1933) argued for education that would produce a sustainable society based locally upon land and tradition; the economist R. H. Tawney, whose *The Acquisitive Society* (1948) delivers a plea for a functional society where workers could find satisfaction in their production; the literary scholar Edmund Blunden, "Georgian" poet and author of one of the earliest books on English nature literature; the eminent historian George Trevalyn; and diverse writers such as the novelist G. K. Chesterton.

The most productive writer in the group was H. J. Massingham. Son of a London editor, Massingham embraced the countryside and its traditions with a fervor approaching that of religious conversion. He did, in fact, convert to traditional Christian belief and came to associate Christian piety with the old life of the village. His ideal was "an integrated society in which religion, nature, and necessity all play a patterned part within a given place: life cannot separate work and play, art and vitality into disconnected functions."

Massingham published a wide variety of works dealing with old patterns of rural craftsmanship, contemporary farming, and the relation between religion and the land. These themes remain intertwined in books such as *English Downland* (1936), where he describes regions in terms of topography, archaeology, flora, fauna, and history. *Wold Without End* (1932) is a journal of a year spent in the Cotswold hills.

Toward the end of World War II Massingham gathered articles from kindred thinkers into an anthology entitled *The Natural Order: Essays in the Return to Husbandry* (1945). The intent of these writers was to turn the course of postwar England from planned, intensive re-industrialization to an agrarian base. Although their plan yielded only marginal success, their writing helped generate a strong rural conservation policy after World War II.

Between the wars the "back-to-nature" ruralists were joined by a wide variety of writers calling for rural preservation. An architect, Clough Williams-Ellis wrote *England and the Octopus* (1928), a lighthearted, but forceful condemnation of ugly, obtrusive development. Clough-Ellis helped found the Society for the Preservation of Rural England, and his book rang a timely call-to-arms for the movement:

> In the late war we were invited to fight to preserve England. We believed; we fought. It may be well to preserve England, but better to have an England worth preserving. We saved our country that we might ourselves destroy it. . . . Mercifully, and perhaps just in time, there is now a small minority, fully, even passionately alive to our misdeeds both past and present, and determined that, so far as in them lies, shall halt, then face about, and begin to regain order and beauty.

Williams outlined a practical program based upon formation of local nature trusts, and lobbying of candidates for Parliament and County Councils. He made specific recommendations for reclamation of mine tailings and other industrial sites; reforestation; preservation of the land on large estates; and, especially, building design consultation with well-educated architects. This work clearly owes much to nineteenth-century nature writers, especially the critic of architecture, John Ruskin.

The need for rural preservation is expressed by C. E. M. Joad from the perspective of the enthusiast in a pamphlet entitled " The Horrors of the Countryside" (1931). Throughout the twenties and thirties hiking or "tramping" grew in popularity, especially among the growing number of unemployed. Joad protests against the new sprawl of ugly suburbs, the motor traffic, and the gamekeepers enforcing trespass laws on behalf of "pheasant-raising stockbrokers";

his complaint is that of the landless seeking "quiet loveliness" among the fields and brooks and villages of the old countryside:

> It is, indeed, a most pathetic thing to see how the exodus of those who find life in the modern town no longer tolerable destroys the very rural amenities which they go forth to seek.

Even the authors of "guidebooks" to the countryside tried to enlighten their readers. *In Search of England* (1931), by H. V. Morton noted "the memorable system of motor coach services had created the danger of the vulgarization of the countryside." But he remained optimistic that "the average Townsman, no matter what his class, feels a deep love for that country and finds there an answer to a deep instinct"; he argued that the increasing numbers discovering the countryside would make possible its preservation.

CONSERVATION AND NATURE LITERATURE

Joad and Morton named the essential paradox of conservation in England. As the problem became more acute, a growing list of societies, organized by the Council for the Preservation of Rural England, clamored for landscape preservation. A major legislative step took place in 1937, when Parliamentary action made it financially attractive for owners of large landed estates to transfer freehold to the National Trust, ensuring public access while retaining occupancy.

The English conservation movement differs in some ways from that of the United States. The latter arose in response to enormous wilderness resources, so vast as to seem limitless. The impulse to conserve grew as limits became apparent, but began in time to save vast wild areas in the National Park and National Forest systems. The British tradition of nature literature has tended to admire the garden more than the wilderness, emphasizing human interaction with nature in a much smaller and older nation. British conservation efforts, consequently, differ from the American in two ways. The first is population density. As Sir Dudley Stamp explains in *Nature Conservation in England* (1969;1974), "shortage of land is the background of the problem." In 1970, for example, there were twelve acres of land for each resident of the United States, as opposed to only .76 acres for each resident of England and Wales.

A second contrast between British and American conservation lies in the longer tenure of habitation in the British countryside. Forestland had largely been cleared for agriculture before the end of the middle ages, several hundred years before any European settlement in America. Consequently, land use and access has long been an issue, especially since the late eighteenth century when fields formerly shared by peasant farmers were enclosed by wealthy landowners, helping to create the now characteristic "field and hedgerow" pattern of the countryside, where game management often has restricted public access. Not coincidentally, it was the depopulation and relandscaping caused by enclosure that helped stimulate the first great wave of modern nature writing at the end of the eighteenth century.

Preservation of rural "amenities" for an increasingly urbanized population, then, is the first of two major twentieth-century conservation objectives. As early as 1865 the "Commons, Open Spaces, and Footpaths Preservation Society" was formed to ensure public access to undeveloped land near London. The National Trust for Places of Historic Interest or Natural Beauty was formed in 1895 as a direct consequence of nineteenth-century nature writing, particularly that of John Ruskin. It has been concerned, as its name indicates, with historical as well as natural attractions, acquiring not only land but manorial homes, castles, art collections, even entire villages. British National Parks, likewise, established after World War II, have largely been superimposed upon utilized agricultural lands and often include settled villages.

While the American conservation movement responded to writers such as Muir, who described relatively large, relatively untouched lands, the English movement has been influenced by writers who have celebrated human ties with a long-managed, intimately known countryside. The rich variety of British landscape, far out of proportion to the country's size, has evoked abundant regionalist writing, which in turn has reinforced efforts to conserve "typical" landscapes for public visitations.

The second major objective of British conservation has been the preservation of species habitat. As a small, long-settled, insular country, Great Britain supports many fewer species of animals than America. Larger mammals, such as bears and wolves, ceased to exist there centuries ago. Furthermore, aristocratic monopoly upon the land has meant management to support game at the expense of other species of wildlife. Especially in the nineteenth century, gamekeepers systematically destroyed birds and mammals that preyed upon game species. But Britain's compensatory wealth lies in the immense variety of birds that migrate to the islands because they are located along major flyways.

Preservation of rural landscape and habitat both were encouraged by W. H. Hudson and Richard Jefferies. Hudson travelled the English countryside extensively, writing appreciatively of rural landscape and rural life. The title *Afoot in England* (1909 reveals his perspective as a traveller. Books like *A Shepherd's Life* (1910) express his admiration for the old rural culture, and throughout his works, Hudson stresses the importance of wildlife as an intergral part of landscape. An accomplished ornithologist, he created a widespread and enduring appreciation of birdlife through a series of popular works, including *British Birds* (1895), *Birds in London* (1898), and *Birds and Man* (1901). Loaded with caustic attacks on plumage gatherers, these books helped marshall support for Hudson's effort to establish The Society for the Protection of Birds in 1894. Gradually the Society and its friends effected a series of laws, culminating in the Protection of Birds Act of 1954, by which all wild fowl came under direct protection of Parliament.

Jefferies' writings about the work of gamekeeper—in which he criticized the extirpation of "nuisance species"—exhibit acute observation of diverse species and sensitivity to their significance. Although well informed of the technical changes in agriculture that had caused the shifts in population, Jefferies described the value of traditional habitat in a context his urban audience understood: a personal aesthetic need: "I do not want change," he wrote in *The Open Air* (1885) "I want the same old and loved things, the same wild-flowers, the same trees. . . ."

NATURE FANTASY AND ANIMAL LITERATURE

From Hudson and Jefferies came models of another genre of nature literature that would show unique srength for re-imagining the relationships between humans and the other species that inhabit the biosphere: the genre of nature fantasy. Nature fantasy has roots in ancient pastoral and myth, in English folklore and in Spenser's *Arcadia.* Here lies the potential for connecting the urban/suburban masses with the spiritual potential of the natural world. Since children are especially attracted to the genre, it provides opportunities for new generations to imagine roots in meadow and woodland, to imagine kinship with animals and birds. The adventure of nature fantasy is at bottom the stuff of myth, and its power touches adult readers as well as children.

In Jefferies' fantasy *Wood Magic,* a young boy can communicate with animals and learn their fears and needs; its sequel *Bevis: The Story of a Boy* (1882) describes a "coming of age" through adventures in the natural world. In *Green Mansions* (1903) Hudson creates the fantasy of a man's escape to the tropical rain forest and his romance there with a native girl, Rima, who could communicate with birds. An early fictional work that attempts to portray animals in terms of the biological needs of species was the series of *The Jungle Books* (1894;1895) of Rudyard Kipling, whose stories of India, as noted above, both slaked and sharpened British thirst for exotic setting. *The Jungle Books* employ the convention of a young boy raised by a pack of wolves, who discovers "the Law" that governs behavior in nature. Arthur Ransome's children's stories based upon his childhood adventures in the Lake District combine a texture of verisimilitude with the power of imagination.

In *The Sword in the Stone,* T. H. White (1906-1964) joins nature fantasy to England's most powerful political myth, the story of King Arthur. White's Arthur is an unimpressive boy named Wart, unprepared for his destiny until his teacher Merlin transforms him into a variety of animals whose skills and insights he must absorb to prove himself a worthy ruler. A recent work of fantasy, Richard Adams' *Watership Down* (1972) describes violent predation from the perspective of peace-loving rabbits, creating analogies to relationships in human societies.

The popular children's stories of Beatrix Potter, beginning with *The Tale of Peter Rabbit* (1900), and of Kenneth Graham carry nature fantasy to an extreme of anthropomorphism: the Toad in *The Wind in the Willows* (1908) is fond of motor cars. But these books have, nonetheless, contributed to nature literature by conveying the moods of rural life and depicting the pleasant details of rural landscapes.

The most realistic depiction of animal behavior is found in the works of Henry Williamson, whose books render the lives of salmon and otters with scientific accuracy, but also with sympathy for their non-human integrity. Through careful observation and controlled imagination Williamson created a new hybrid of natural history and fantasy with *Tarka the Otter* (1928) and *Salar the Salmon* (1935), novels in which the protagonists are animals and conflicts arise out of their actual predator/prey relationships.

Employing the genre of journal, rather than fantasy, Gavin Maxwell's *Ring of Bright Water* (1960) chronicles the movements of wildlife along the rugged northwest coast of Scotland, recording personal interactions with "animals who have shared my life." It is an attempt to counter his conviction that "man has suffered in his separation from the soil and from the living creatures of the world."

The "animal poem," an attempt to see within the animal's nature, and thus rethink its significance to human understanding, has been an important form for many major twentieth-century poets, including William Butler Yeats, W. H.

Hudson, D. H. Lawrence, who published literally dozens of animal poems, and the current poet laurerate, Ted Hughes, who examines violence in natural predation, where animals become symbols of destruction.

One of the greatest achievements of imagination in twentieth-century British literatutre may be considered within the tradition of nature fantasy. The works of J. R. R. Tolkien (1892-196) have attracted passionate and enduring popularity among audiences ranging from children to literary scholars. During his service in World War II, Tolkien became preoccupied with the flaws in European civilization. His insights and his affectionate familiarity with the English countryside inform *The Hobbit* and *The Lord of the Rings* (1954-1955), fantasies that dramatize the values of rural life in heroic terms. Drawing upon far reaches of the English tradition of nature literature, Tolkien creates a fabulous world, where ancient trees literally speak, to describe limitations on human power. His vision looks back to medieval fable and forward to the environmental need for humanity to "hear" the voices of plant and animals.

ENVIRONMENTAL WRITING

The concern over environmental degradation which began to enter popular consciousness during the 1960's and 1970's has been furthered by contributions of British writers that fuse qualities of nature literature with questions of environmental science. Three topics have evoked especially important texts: growth of population and technology, sustainable agriculture, and complex relationships between humans and the biosphere. An expert on technological planning, E. F. Schumacher (1911-1977) has integrated diverse perspectives in his writing as in his career, serving both as economic advisor to the British National Coal Board and as President of the Soil Association, one of England's oldest organic farming organizations. His *Small Is Beautiful: Economics as if People Mattered* (1973), with the often anthologized essay "Buddhist Economics," synthesizes eastern philosophy and western science in arguing for alternatives to centralized, growth-driven, power-consumptive technologies.

The second issue, sustainable agriculture, is part of a complex of issues that Great Britain has long grappled with, including competition between agriculture and species preservation, and provision for individuals in a generally urbanized population to enjoy regular contact with nature.

The policy of subsidizing expansion and industrialization on British farms has removed not only the traditional landscape of "field and hedgerow" but also, through drainage, "waste" land. Not only is wildlife habitat being eradicated, argues Marion Shoard in *The Theft of the Countryside* (1985), but scenic amenities are being destroyed. Shoard questions whether the future holds further eradication of the rural way of life and further removal of the populace from immediate contract with natural environments. These issues, along with practical interests such as gardening and hiking, have revitalized the ruralist tradition in contemporary "countryside writing," which has remained a popular genre, or mix of genres, since the early 1970's. A major countryside writer, Richard Mabey, is in fact a scholar of both Jefferies and Gilbert White. In his own work he explores the interactions between human history and the habitats of British regions. *In a Green Shade: Essays on*

Landscape (1983) collects essays that search for a "contemporary redefinition of the countryside, and of our relationships with its natural life."

The special wealth of the tradition of nature literature is that it has provided imaginative, value-laden perceptions of the earth: Shakespeare's grand metaphor, Cowper's rural recompense, White's tender observation, Wordsworth's emotional interchange with natural objects, Lawrence's re-creation of the life-urge, as well as the multitude of polemicists, who together call upon us to balance profit with beauty, "improvement" with the abiding integrity of the earth. Two disparate contemporary British writers offer particularly imaginative attempts to redefine human relationships with the life of the earth. Their work, perhaps, prepares the way for nature literature of the twenty-first century.

The first is a scientist, James Lovelock. In *Gaia: A New Look at Life on Earth* (1979) he presents a theory based upon sophisticated analysis of the earth's self-regulating mechanisms throughout geologic time. His "Gaia Hypothesis" states that the earth is literally an organism: its fiery core, its species of plants and animals, its inorganic chemicals, its atmosphere—the entire biosphere is a single living entity. But this scientific theory carries the weight of myth. The name "Gaia" Lovelock borrows deliberately from the ancient Greeks, for whom it signified the female goddess of the earth. The Gaia Hypothesis has stirred the imaginations of scientists, religious thinkers, and environmentalists who desire a more integrated philosophy of nature.

The second contemporary British writer who advocates a radical change in the way we perceive our relationships with nature is John Fowles, one of the world's foremost contemporary novelists. Although his work does not apparently bear the qualities of nature writing, Fowles has stated that the need to discover a personal relationship with nature beyond scientific analysis is the theme underlying all of his published work. In his first novel, *The Collector* (1953), a deranged suburbanite kidnaps a beautiful young girl to "observe" her. The story may be read as an allegory of our modern predisposition to suffocate life by reducing it to human-imposed categories and measurable "facts."

In *The Tree* (1980) Fowles articulates his concern that modern science (and even modern criticism), though necessary and desirable in its own right, has subtly and pervasively influenced us to keep nature at a distance. Overcome by generalizing, categorizing, and naming, we have lost the art of perceiving nature as individuals in spontaneous, vital experiences. Instead, we are led to perceive it "second-hand," reducing the experience of nature to utilitarian categories. Fowles argues that as individuals we need to rediscover the ability for "seeing nature whole." His theme is akin to the intended goal of our anthology and, perhaps, to the deepest, message of the nature writing tradition:

> But this is nature's consolation, its message. . . . It can be known and entered only by each, and in its now; not by you through me, by any you through any me; only by you through yourself, or me through myself. We still have this to learn: the inalienable otherness of each, human and non-human.

Richard Jefferies
1848-1887

Probably the best loved and most influential of twentieth-century British nature writers is Richard Jefferies. A farmer's son, Jefferies knew the life of the countryside in intimate detail, and he described it enthusiastically and companionably. His contemporary attitudes demand that Jefferies be placed with writers of the twentieth century, though his life ended before the new century began.

The title of his first major work, *The Gamekeeper at Home; or, Sketches of Natural History and Rural Life* (1878), suggests the wide range of topics explored in Jefferies' subsequent writing: agriculture, including the changing relationship of farmer to land; the customs of rural society; and natural history, described as an appreciator rather than cataloguer. The title also emphasizes Jefferies' love of sport hunting, fishing, and trapping—though for him sport was not an end in itself, but a means for closer observation and better understanding of the environment. ". . . Watching so often stayed the shot," he wrote, "that at last it grew to be a habit." His essay "The Single Barrel Gun," reprinted here, articulates Jefferies' instinctive ecological sensitivity, rare in his age. But Jefferies did enjoy the challenge of rod and gun; his writing is distinguished by a realistic, unsentimental portrayal of the apparent cruelty involved in natural predation—including the human link of the chain.

Although the theme of sport does not dominate in most of his works, a characteristic tone of personal adventure, its excitement contagious to the reader, pervades all of Jefferies' descriptions of forest and field. A substantial portion of Jefferies' audience was urban. Titles like *Nature Near London* (1883) and *Wildlife in a Southern County* indicate Jefferies' role as interpreter of nature for city dwellers whose parents or grandparents had been country people.

Jefferies' knowledge of the countryside came naturally. He grew up on Coate

Farm in Wiltshire, where farming had been the family heritage for nearly three hundred years. As a youth Jefferies was allowed great freedom to wander the farm, paddle about its lake (in a homemade canoe), and walk the surrounding downs, learning nature lore independently. Later he rendered his adventures into classic stories of boyhood, *Bevis* (1882) and the fantasy *Wood Magic* (1881). He learned about nature also from his father and from a friendly gamekeeper (who served as a model for *The Gamekeeper at Home*). *The Amateur Poacher* (1879), one of Jefferies' most popular books, shows another perspective acquired on those outdoor adventures he preferred to games and school.

Instead of attending a university or taking up farming, Jefferies at seventeen began working as a journalist for a series of provincial newspapers, which, perhaps, forced him into the habit of recording accurate detail, a distinguishing mark of his nature writing. Journalism certainly led him to a broader knowledge of human interaction with the natural environment of Wiltshire. His earliest notable writing was a series of letters to *The Times* about the Wiltshire agricultural worker. After a period spent writing novels of society life, about which he knew nothing, he began contributing to newspapers and magazine articles on what he knew best: his love for the countryside, especially his native Wiltshire. This he continued for the remainder of his brief life. After years of battle with tuberculosis, during which he dictated essays from his sickbed, he died before his fortieth birthday. Near the end of his life he wrote in his diary that he had "no desire to make money or excel in anything or fame—all I cared for and desired was the fields, the hills, and the sea."

The ecstacy that Jefferies described beneath the blue sky and the stormy night many commentators have likened to accounts of orthodox mystic experience. Jefferies, however, explicity denies belief in a diety. His most profound experiences he narrates in *The Story of My Heart* (1883), a book he said he had worked on for seventeen years.

from THE STORY OF MY HEART

The story of my heart commences seventeen years ago. In the glow of youth there were times every now and then when I felt the necessity of a strong inspiration of soul-thought. My heart was dusty, parched for want of the rain of deep feeling; my mind arid and dry, for there is a dust which settles on the heart as well as that which falls on a ledge. It is injurious to the mind as well as to the body to be always in one place and always surrounded by the same circumstances. A species of thick clothing slowly grows about the mind, the pores are choked, little habits become a part of existence, and by degrees the mind is inclosed in a husk. When this began to form I felt eager to escape from it, to throw it off like heavy clothing, to drink deeply once more at the fresh fountains of life. An inspiration—a long deep breath of the pure air of thought—could alone give health to the heart.

There was a hill to which I used to resort at such periods. The labour of walking three miles to it, all the while gradually ascending, seemed to clear my blood of the heaviness accumulated at home. On a warm summer day the slow continued rise required continual effort, which carried away the sense of oppression. The familiar everyday scene was soon out of sight; I came to other trees, meadows, and fields; I began to breathe a new air and to have a fresher aspiration. I restrained my soul till I reached the sward of the hill; psyche, the soul that longed to be loose. I would write psyche always instead of soul to avoid meanings which have become attached to the word soul, but it is awkward to do so. Clumsy indeed are all words the moment the wooden stage of commonplace life is left. I restrained psyche, my soul, till I reached and put my foot on the grass at the beginning of the green hill itself.

Moving up the sweet short turf, at every step my heart seemed to obtain a wider horizon of feeling; with every inhalation of rich pure air, a deeper desire. The very light of the sun was whiter and more brilliant here. By the time I had reached the summit I had entirely forgotten the petty circumstances and the annoyances of existence. I felt myself, myself. There was an intrenchment on the summit, and going down into the fosse I walked round it slowly to recover breath. On the south-western side there was a spot where the outer bank had partially slipped, leaving a gap. There the view was over a broad plain, beautiful with wheat, and inclosed by a perfect amphitheatre of green hills. Through these hills there was one narrow groove, or pass, southwards, where the white clouds seemed to close in the horizon. Woods hid the scattered hamlets and farmhouses, so that I was quite alone.

I was utterly alone with the sun and the earth. Lying down on the grass, I spoke in my soul to the earth, the sun, the air, and the distant sea far beyond sight. I thought of the earth's firmness—I felt it bear me up; through the grassy couch there came an influence as if I could feel the great earth speaking to me. I thought of the wandering air—its pureness, which is its beauty; the air touched me and gave me something of itself. I spoke to the sea: though so far, in my mind I saw it, green at the rim of the earth and blue in deeper ocean; I desired to have its strength, its mystery, and glory. Then I addressed the sun, desiring the soul equivalent of his light and brilliance, his endurance and unwearied race. I turned to the blue heaven over, gazing into its depth, inhaling its exquisite colour and sweetness. The rich blue of the unattainable flower of the sky drew my soul towards it, and there it rested, for pure colour is rest of heart. By all these I prayed; I felt an emotion of the soul beyond all definition; prayer is a puny thing to it, and the word is a rude sign to the feeling, but I know no other.

By the blue heaven, by the rolling sun bursting through untrodden space, a new ocean of ether everyday unveiled. By the fresh and wandering air encompassing the world; by the sea sounding on the shore—the green sea white-flecked at the margin and the deep ocean; by the strong earth under me. Then, returning, I prayed by the sweet thyme, whose little flowers I touched with my hand; by the slender grass; by the crumble of dry chalky earth I took up and let fall through my fingers. Touching the crumble of earth, the blade of grass, the thyme flower, breathing the earth-encircling air, thinking of the sea and the sky, holding out my hand for the sunbeams to touch it, prone on the sward in token of deep reverence, thus I prayed that I might touch to the unutterable existence infinitely higher than deity.

With all the intensity of feeling which exalted me, all the intense communion I held with the earth, the sun and sky, the stars hidden by the light, with the ocean—in no manner can the thrilling depth of these feelings be written—with these I prayed, as if they were the keys of an instrument, of an organ, with which I swelled forth the notes of my soul, redoubling my own voice by their power. The great sun burning with light; the strong earth, dear earth; the warm sky; the pure air; the thought of ocean; the inexpressible beauty of all filled me with a rapture, an ecstasy, an inflatus. With this inflatus, too, I prayed. Next to myself I came and recalled myself, my bodily existence. I held out my hand, the sunlight gleamed on the skin and the iridescent nails; I recalled the mystery and beauty of the flesh. I thought of the mind with which I could see the ocean sixty miles distant, and gather to myself its glory. I thought of my inner existence, that consciousness which is called the soul. These, that is, myself—I threw into the balance to weigh the prayer the heavier. My strength of body, mind, and soul, I flung into it; I put forth my strength; I wrestled and laboured, and toiled in might of prayer. The prayer, this soul-emotion was in itself—not for an object—it was a passion. I hid my face in the grass, I was wholly prostrated, I lost myself in the wrestle, I was rapt and carried away.

Becoming calmer, I returned to myself and thought, reclining in rapt thought, full of aspiration, steeped to the lips of my soul in desire. I did not then define, or analyse, or understand this. I see now that what I laboured for was soul-life, more soul-nature, to be exalted, to be full of soul-learning. Finally I rose, walked half a mile or so along the summit of the hill eastwards, to soothe myself and come to the common ways of life again. Had my shepherd accidentally seen me lying on the turf, he would only have thought that I was resting a few minutes; I made no outward show. Who could have imagined the whirlwind of passion that was going on within me as I reclined there! I was greatly exhausted when I reached home. Occasionally I went upon the hill deliberately, deeming it good to do so; then, again, this craving carried me away up there of itself. Though the principal feeling was the same, there were variations in the mode in which it affected me.

Sometimes on lying down on the sward I first looked up at the sky, gazing for a long time till I could see deep into the azure and my eyes were full of the colour; then I turned my face to the grass and thyme, placing my hands at each side of my face so as to shut out everything and hide myself. Having drunk deeply of the heaven above and felt the most glorious beauty of the day, and remembering the old, old sea which (as it seemed to me) was but just younger at the edge, I now became lost, and absorbed into the being of existence of the universe. I felt down deep into the earth under, and high above into the sky, and farther still to the sun and stars. Still farther beyond the stars into the hollow of space, and losing thus my separateness of being came to seem like a part of the whole. Then I whispered to the earth beneath, through the grass and thyme, down into the depth of its ear, and again up to the starry space hid behind the blue of day. Travelling in an instant across the distant sea, I saw as if with actual vision the palms and cocoanut trees, the bamboos of India, and the cedars of the extreme south. Like a lake with islands the ocean lay before me, as clear and vivid as the plain beneath in the midst of the amphitheatre of hills.

With the glory of the great sea, I said; with the firm, solid, and sustaining earth; the depth, distance, and expanse of ether; the age, tamelessness, and ceaseless motion of the ocean; the stars, and the unknown in space; by all those things which are most powerful known to me, and by those which exist, but of which I have no idea whatever, I pray. Further, by my own soul, that secret existence which above all other things bears the nearest resemblance to the ideal of spirit, infinitely nearer than earth, sun, or star. Speaking by an inclination towards, not in words, my soul prays that I may have something from each of these, that I may gather a flower from them, that I may have in myself the secret and meaning of the earth, the golden sun, the light, the foam-flecked sea. Let my soul become enlarged; I am not enough; I am little and contemptible. I desire a greatness of soul, an irradiance of mind, a deeper insight, a broader hope. Give me power of soul, so that I may actually effect by its will that which I strive for.

In winter, though I could not then rest on the grass, or stay long enough to form any definite expression, I still went up to the hill once now and then, for it seemed that to merely visit the spot repeated all that I had previously said. But it was not only then.

In summer I went out into the fields, and let my soul inspire these thoughts under the trees, standing against the trunk, or looking up through the branches at the sky. If trees could speak, hundreds of them would say that I had had these soul-emotions under them. Leaning against the oak's massive trunk, and feeling the rough bark and the lichen at my back, looking southwards over the grassy fields, cowslip-yellow, at the woods on the slope, I thought my desire of deeper soul-life. Or under the green firs, looking upwards, the sky was more deeply blue at their tops; then the brake fern was unrolling, the doves cooing, the thickets astir, the late ash-leaves coming forth. Under the shapely rounded elms, by the hawthorn bushes and hazel, everywhere the same deep desire for the soul-nature; to have from all green things and from the sunlight the inner meaning which was not known to them, that I might be full of light as the woods of the sun's rays. Just to touch the lichened bark of a tree, or the end of a spray projecting over the path as I walked, seemed to repeat the same prayer in me.

The long-lived summer days dried and warmed the turf in the meadows. I used to lie down in solitary corners at full length on my back, so as to feel the embrace of the earth. The grass stood high above me, and the shadows of the tree-branches danced on my face. I looked up at the sky, with half-closed eyes to bear the dazzling light. Bees buzzed over me, sometimes a butterfly passed, there was a hum in the air, greenfinches sang in the hedge. Gradually entering into the intense life of the summer days—a life which burned around as if every grass blade and leaf were a torch—I came to feel the long-drawn life of the earth back into the dimmest past, while the sun of the moment was warm on me. Sesostris on the most ancient sands of the south, in ancient, ancient days, was conscious of himself and of the sun. This sunlight linked me through the ages to that past consciousness. From all the ages my soul desired to take that soul-life which had flowed through them as the sunbeams had continually poured on earth. As the hot sands take up the heat, so would I take up that soul-energy. Dreamy in appearance, I was breathing full of existence; I was aware of the grass blades, the flowers, the leaves on hawthorn and tree. I seemed to live more largely through them, as if each were a pore through which I drank. The grasshoppers called and leaped, the greenfinches sang, the black-birds happily fluted, all the air hummed with life. I was plunged deep in existence, and with all that existence I prayed.

Through every grass blade in the thousand, thousand grasses; through the million leaves, veined and edge-cut, on bush and tree; through the song-notes and the marked feathers of the birds; through the insects' hum and the colour of the butterflies; through the soft warm air, the flecks of clouds dissolving—I used them all for prayer. With all the energy the sunbeams had poured unwearied on the earth since Sesostris was conscious of them on the ancient sands; with all the life that had been lived by vigorous man and beauteous woman since first in dearest Greece the dream of the gods was woven; with all the soul-life that had flowed a long stream down to me, I prayed that I might have a soul more than equal to, far beyond my conception of, these things of the past, the present, and the fulness of all life. Not only equal to these, but beyond, higher, and more powerful than I could imagine. That I might take from all their energy, grandeur, and beauty, and gather it into me. That my soul might be more than the cosmos of life.

I prayed with the glowing clouds of sunset and the soft light of the first star coming through the violet sky. At night with the stars, according to the season: now with the Pleiades, now with the Swan or burning Sirius, and broad Orion's whole constellation, red Aldebaran, Arcturus, and the Northern Crown; with the morning star, the light-bringer, one now and then when I saw it, a white-gold ball in the violet-purple sky, or framed about with pale summer vapour floating away as red streaks shot horizontally in the east. A diffused saffron ascended into the luminous upper azure. The disk of the sun rose over the hill, fluctuating with throbs of light; his chest heaved in fervour of brilliance. All the glory of the sunrise filled me with broader and furnace-like vehemence of prayer. That I might have the deepest of soul-life, the deepest of all, deeper far than all this greatness of the visible universe and even of the invisible; that I might have a fulness of soul till now unknown, and utterly beyond my own conception.

In the deepest darkness of the night the same thought rose in my mind as in the bright light of noontide. What is there which I have not used to strengthen the same emotion?

from THE OPEN AIR*

WILD FLOWERS

A FIR-TREE is not a flower, and yet it is associated in my mind with primroses. There was a narrow lane leading into a wood, where I used to go almost every day in the early months of the year, and at one corner it was

*From *The Open Air* by Richard Jefferies. London: Chatto & Windus, 1900.

overlooked by three spruce firs. The rugged lane there began to ascend the hill, and I paused a moment to look back. Immediately the high fir-trees guided the eye upwards, and from their tops to the deep azure of the March sky over, but a step from the tree to the heavens. So it has ever been to me, by day or by night, summer or winter, beneath trees the heart feels nearer to that depth of life the far sky means. The rest of spirit found only in beauty, ideal and pure, comes there because the distance seems within touch of thought. To the heaven thought can reach lifted by the strong arms of the oak, carried up by the ascent of the flame-shaped fir. Round the spruce top the blue was deepened, concentrated by the fixed point; the memory of that spot, as it were, of the sky is still fresh—I can see it distinctly—still beautiful and full of meaning. It is painted in bright colour in my mind, colour thrice laid, and indelible; as one passes a shrine and bows the head to the Madonna, so I recall the picture and stoop in spirit to the aspiration it yet arouses. For there is no saint like the sky, sunlight shining from its face.

. . .

But the primroses by that lane did not appear till late; they covered the banks under the thousand thousand ash-poles; foxes slipped along there frequently, whose friends in scarlet coats could not endure the pale flowers, for they might chink their spurs homewards. In one meadow near primroses were thicker than the grass, with gorse interspersed, and the rabbits that came out fed among flowers. The primroses last on to the celandines and cowslips, through the time of the bluebells, past the violets—one dies but passes on the life to another, one sets light to the next, till the ruddy oaks and singing cuckoos call up the tall mowing grass to fringe summer.

Before I had any conscious thought it was a delight to me to find wild flowers, just to see them. It was a pleasure to gather them and to take them home; a pleasure to show them to others—to keep them as long as they would live, to decorate the room with them, to arrange them carelessly with grasses, green sprays, tree-bloom—large branches of chestnut snapped off, and set by a picture perhaps. Without conscious thought of seasons and the advancing hours to light on the white wild violet, the meadow orchis, the blue veronica, the blue meadow cranesbill; feeling the warmth and delight of the increasing sun-rays, but not recognizing whence or why it was joy. All the world is young to a boy, and thought has not entered into it; even the old men with gray hair do not seem old; different but not aged, the idea of age has not been mastered. A boy has to frown and study, and then does not grasp what long years mean. The various hues of the petals pleased without any knowledge of colour-contrasts, no note even of colour except that it was bright, and the mind was made happy without consideration of those ideals and hopes afterwards associated with the azure sky above the fir-tree. A fresh footpath, a fresh flower, a fresh delight. The reeds, the grasses, the rushes—unknown and new things at every step—something always to find; no barren spot anywhere, or sameness. Every day the grass painted anew, and its green seen for the first time; not the old green, but a novel hue and spectacle, like the first view of the sea.

If we had never before looked upon the earth, but suddenly came to it man or woman grown, set down in the midst of a summer mead, would it not seem to us a radiant vision? The hues, the shapes, the song and life of birds, above all the sunlight, the breath of heaven, resting on it; the mind would be filled with its glory, unable to grasp it, hardly believing that such things could be mere matter and no more. Like a dream of some spirit-land it would appear, scarce fit to be touched least it should fall to pieces, too beautiful to be long watched least it should fade away. So it seemed to me as a boy, sweet and new like this each morning; and even now, after the years that have passed, and the lines they have worn in the forehead, the summer mead shines as bright and fresh as when my foot first touched the grass. It has another meaning now; the sunshine and the flowers speak differently, for a heart that has once known sorrow reads behind the page, and sees sadness in joy. But the freshness is still there, the dew washes the colours before dawn. Unconscious happiness in finding wild flowers—unconscious and unquestioning, and therefore unbounded.

I used to stand by the mower and follow the scythe sweeping down thousands of the broad-flowered daisies, the knotted knapweeds, the blue scabious, the yellow rattles, sweeping so close and true that nothing escaped; and yet, although I had seen so many hundreds of each, although I had lifted armfuls day after day, still they were fresh. They never lost their newness, and even now each time I gather a wild flower it feels a new thing. The greenfinches came to the fallen swathe so near to us they seemed to have no fear; but I remember the yellowhammers most, whose colour, like that of the wild flowers and the sky, has never faded from my memory. The greenfinches sank into the fallen swathe, the loose grass gave under their weight and let them bathe in flowers.

One yellowhammer set on a branch of ash the live-long morning, still singing in the sun; his bright head, his clean bright yellow, gaudy as Spain, was drawn like a brush charged heavily with colour across the retina, painting it deeply, for there on the eye's memory it endures, though that was boyhood and this is manhood, still unchanged. The field—Stewart's Mash—the very tree, young ash timber, the branch projecting over the sward, I could make a map of them. Sometimes I think sun-painted colours are brighter to me than to many, and more strongly affect the nerves of the eye. Straw going by the road on a dusky winter's day seems so pleasantly golden, the sheaves lying aslant at the top, and these bundles of yellow tubes thrown up against the dark ivy on the opposite wall. Tiles, red burned, or orange coated, the sea sometimes cleanly definite, the shadows of trees in a thin wood where there is room for shadows to form and fall; some such shadows are sharper than light, and have a faint blue tint. Not only in summer but in cold winter, and not only romantic things but plain matter-of-fact things, as a waggon freshly painted red beside the wright's shop, stand out as if wet with colour and delicately pencilled at the edges. It must be out of doors; nothing indoors looks like this.

Pictures are very dull and gloomy to it, and very contrasted colours like those the French use are necessary to fix the attention. Their dashes of pink and scarlet bring the faint shadow of the sun into the room. As for our painters, their works are hung behind a curtain, and we have to peer patiently through the dusk of evening to see what they mean. Out-of-door colours do not need to be gaudy—a mere dull stake of wood thrust in the ground often stands out sharper than the pink flashes of the French studio; a faggot; the outline of a leaf; low tints without reflecting power strike the eye as a bell the ear. To me they are intensely clear, and the clearer the greater the pleasure. It is often too great, for it takes me away from solid pursuits merely to receive the impression, as water is still to reflect the trees. To me it is very painful when illness blots the definition of outdoor things, so wearisome not to see them rightly, and more oppressive than actual pain. I feel as if I was struggling to wake up with dim, half-opened lids and heavy mind. This one yellowhammer still sits on the ash branch in Stewart's Mash over the sward, singing in the sun, his feathers freshly set with colour, the same sun-song, and will sing to me so long as the heart shall beat.

The first conscious thought about wild flowers was to find out their names—the first conscious pleasure,—and then I began to see so many that I had not previously noticed. Once you wish to identify them there is nothing escapes, down to the little white chickweed of the path and the moss of the wall. I put my hand on the bridge across the brook to lean over and look down into the water. Are there any fish? The bricks of the pier are covered with green, like a wall-painting to the surface of the stream, mosses along the lines of the mortar, and among the moss little plants—what are these? In the dry sunlit lane I look up to the top of the great wall about some domain, where the green figs look over upright on their stalks; there are dry plants on the coping—what are these? Some growing thus, high in the air,on stone, and in the chinks of the tower, suspended in dry air and sunshine; some low down under the arch of the bridge over the brook, out of sight utterly, unless you stoop by the brink of the water and project yourself forward to examine under. The kingfisher sees them as he shoots through the barrel of the culvert. There the sun direct never shines upon them, but the sunlight thrown up by the ripples runs all day in bright bars along the vault of the arch, playing on them. The stream arranges the sand in the shallow in bars, minute fixed undulations; the stream arranges the sunshine in successive flashes, undulating as if the sun, drowsy in the heat, were idly closing and unclosing his eyelids for sleep. Plants everywhere, hiding behind every tree, under the leaves, in the shady places, beside the dry furrows of the field; they are only just behind something, hidden openly. The instant you look for them they multiply a hundredfold; if you sit on the beach and begin to count the pebbles by you, their number instantly increases to infinity by virtue of that conscious act.

The bird's-foot lotus was the first. The boy must have seen it, must have trodden on it in the bare woodland pastures, certainly run about on it, with wet naked feet from the bathing; but the boy was not conscious of it. This was the first, when the desire came to identify and to know, fixing upon it by means of a pale and feeble picture. In the largest pasture there were different soils and climates; it was so large it seemed a little country of itself then—the more so because the ground rose and fell, making a ridge to divide the view and enlarge by uncertainty. The high sandy soil on the ridge where the rabbits had their warren; the rocky soil of the quarry; the long grass by the elms where the rooks built, under whose nests there were vast unpalatable mushrooms—the true mushrooms with salmon gills grew nearer the warren; the slope towards the nut-tree hedge and spring. Several climates in one field: the wintry ridge over which leaves were always driving in all four seasons of the year; the level sunny plain and fallen cromlech still tall enough for a gnomon and to cast its shadow in the treeless drought; the moist, warm, grassy depression; the lotus-grown slope, warm and dry.

If you have been living in one house in the country for some time, and then go on a visit to another, though hardly half a mile distant, you will find a change in the air, the feeling, and tone of the place. It is close by, but it is not the same. To discover these minute differences, which make one locality healthy and home happy, and the next adjoining unhealthy, the Chinese have invented the science of Feng-shui, spying about with cabalistic mystery, casting the horoscope of an acre. There is something in all superstitions; they are often the foundation of science. Superstition having made the discovery, science composes a lecture on the reason why, and claims the credit. Bird's-foot lotus means a fortunate spot, dry, warm—so far as soil is concerned. If you were going to live out of doors, you might safely build your kibitka where you found it. Wandering with the pictured flower-book, just purchased, over the windy ridge where last year's skeleton leaves, blown out from the alder copse below, came on with grasshopper motion—lifted and laid down by the wind, lifted and laid down—I sat on the sward of the sheltered slope, and instantly recognized the orange-red claws of the flower beside me. That was the first; and this very morning, I dread to consider how many years afterwards, I found a plant on a wall which I do not know. I shall have to trace out its genealogy and emblazon its shield. So many years and still only at the beginning—the beginning, too, of the beginning—for as yet I have not thought of the garden or conservatory flowers (which are wild flowers somewhere), or of the tropics, or the prairies.

The great stone of the fallen cromlech, crouching down afar off in the plain behind me, cast its shadow in the sunny morn as it had done, so many summers, for centuries—for thousands of years: worn white by the endless sunbeams—the ceaseless flood of light—the sunbeams of centuries, the impalpable beams polishing and grinding like rushing water: silent, yet witnessing of the Past; shadowing the Present on the dial of the field: a mere dull stone; but what is it the mind will not employ to express to itself its own thoughts?

There was a hollow near in which hundreds of skeleton leaves had settled, a stage on their journey from the alder copse, so thick as to cover the thin grass, and at the side of the hollow a wasp's nest had been torn out by a badger. On the soft and spreading sand thrown out from his burrow the print of his foot looked as large as an elephant might make. The wild animals of our fields are so small that the badger's foot seemed foreign in its size, calling up the thought of the great game of distant forests. He was a bold badger to make his burrow there in the open warren, unprotected by park walls or preserve laws, where every one might see who chose. I never saw him by daylight: that they do get about in daytime is, however, certain, for one was shot in Surrey recently by sportsmen; they say he weighed forty pounds.

In the mind all things are written in pictures—there is no alphabetical combination of letters and words; all things are pictures and symbols. The bird's-foot lotus is the picture to me of sunshine and summer, and of that summer in the heart which is known only in youth, and then not alone. No words could write that feeling: the bird's-foot lotus writes it.

When the efforts to photograph began, the difficulty was to fix the scene thrown by the lens upon the plate. There the view appeared perfect to the least of details, worked out by the sun, and made as complete in miniature as that he shone upon in nature. But it faded like the shadows as the summer sun declines. Have you watched them in the fields among the flowers?—the deep strong mark of the noonday shadow of a tree such as the pen makes drawn heavily on the paper; gradually it loses its darkness and becomes paler and thinner at the edge as it lengthens and spreads, till shadow and grass mingle together. Image after image faded from the plates, no more to be fixed than the reflection in water of the trees by the shore. Memory, like the sun, paints to me bright pictures of the golden summer time of lotus; I can see them, but how shall I fix them for you? By no process can that be accomplished. It is like a story that cannot be told because he who knows it is tongue-tied and dumb. Motions of hands, wavings and gestures, rudely convey the framework, but the finish is not there.

To-day, and day after day, fresh pictures are coloured instantaneously in the retina as bright and perfect in detail and hue. This very power is often, I think, the cause of pain to me. To see so clearly is to value so highly and to feel too deeply. The smallest of the pencilled branches of the bare ash-tree drawn distinctly against the winter sky, waving lines one within the other, yet following and partly parallel, reproducing in the curve of the twig the curve of the great trunk; is it not a pleasure to trace each to its ending? The raindrops as they slide from leaf to leaf in June, the balmy shower that reperfumes each wild flower and green thing, drops lit with the sun, and falling to the chorus of the refreshed birds; is not this beautiful to see? On the grasses tall and heavy the purplish blue pollen, a shimmering dust, sown broadcast over the ripening meadow from July's warm hand—the bluish pollen, the lilac pollen of the grasses, a delicate mist of blue floating on the surface, has always been an especial delight to me. Finches shake it from the stalks as they rise. No day, no hour of summer, no step but brings new mazes—there is no word to express design without plan, and these designs of flower and leaf and colours of the sun cannot be reduced to set order. The eye is for ever drawn onward and finds no end. To see these always so sharply, wet and fresh, is almost too much sometimes for the wearied yet insatiate eye. I am obliged to turn away—to shut my eyes and say I *will* not see, I will not observe; I will concentrate my mind on my own little path of life, and steadily gaze downwards. In vain. Who can do so? who can care alone for his or her petty trifles of existence, that has once entered amongst the wild flowers? How shall I shut out the sun? Shall I deny the constellations of the night? They are there; the Mystery is for ever about us—the question, the hope, the aspiration cannot be put out. So that it is almost a pain not to be able to cease observing and tracing the untraceable maze of beauty.

. . .

There shone on the banks white stars among the grass. Petals delicately white in a whorl of rays—light that had started radiating from a centre and become fixed—shining among the flowerless green. The slender stem had grown so fast it had drawn its own root partly out of the ground, and when I tried to gather it, flower, stem and root came away together. The wheat was springing, the soft air full of the growth and moisture, blackbirds whistling, wood-pigeons nesting, young oak-leaves out; a sense of swelling, sunny fulness in the atmosphere. The plain road was made beautiful by the advanced boughs that overhung and cast their shadows on the dust—boughs of ash-green, shadows that lay still, listening to the nightingale. A place of enchantment in the mornings, where was felt the power of some subtle influence working behind bough and grass and bird-song. The orange-golden dandelion in the sward was deeply laden with colour brought to it anew again and again by the ships of the flower, the humble-bees—to their quays they come, unlading priceless essences of sweet odours brought from the East over the green seas of wheat, unlading priceless colours on the broad dandelion disks, bartering these things for honey and pollen. Slowly tacking aslant, the pollen ship hums in the south wind. The little brown wren finds her way through the great thicket of hawthorn. How does she know her path, hidden by a thousand thousand leaves? Tangled and crushed together by their own growth, a crown of thorns hangs over the thrush's nest; thorns of the mother, hope for the young. Is there a crown of thorns over your heart? A spike has gone deep enough into mine. The stile looks farther away because boughs have pushed forward and made it smaller. The willow scarce holds the sap that tightens the bark and would burst it if it did not enlarge to the pressure.

Two things can go through the solid oak; the lightning of the clouds that rends the iron timber, the lightning of the spring—the electricity of the sunbeams forcing him to stretch forth and lengthen his arms with joy. Bathed in buttercups to the dewlap, the roan cows standing in the golden lake watched the hours with calm frontlet; watched the light descending the meadows filling, with knowledge of long months of succulent clover. On their broad brows the year falls gently; their great, beautiful eyes, which need but a tear or a smile to make them human,—without these, such eyes, so large and full, seem above human life, eyes of the immortals enduring without passion,—in these eyes, as a mirror, nature is reflected.

I came every day to walk slowly up and down the plain road, by the starry flowers under the ash-green boughs; ash is the coolest, softest green. The bees went drifting over by my head; as they cleared the hedges they passed by my ears, the wind singing in their shrill wings. White tent-walls of cloud—a warm white, being full to overflowing of sunshine—stretched across from ash-top to ash-top, a cloud-canvas roof, a tent-palace of the delicious air. For of all things there is none so sweet as sweet air—one great flower it is, drawn round about, over, and enclosing, like Aphrodite's arms; as if the dome of the sky were a bell-flower drooping down over us, and the magical essence of it filling all the room of the earth. Sweetest of all things is wild-flower air. Full of their ideal the starry flowers strained upwards on the bank, striving to keep above the rude grasses that pushed by them; genius has ever had such a struggle. The plain road was made beautiful by the many thoughts it gave. I came every morning to stay by the star-lit bank.

A friend said, "Why do you go the same road every day? Why not have a change and walk somewhere else sometimes? Why keep on up and down the same place?" I could not answer; till then it had not occurred to me that I did always go one way; as for the reason of it I could not tell; I continued in my old mind while the summers went away. Not till years afterwards was I able to see why I went the same round and did not care for change. I do not want change: I want the same old and loved things, the same wild-flowers, the same trees and soft ash-green; the turtle-doves, the blackbirds, the coloured yellowhammer sing, sing, singing so long as there is light to cast a shadow on the dial, for such is the measure of his song, and I want them in the same place. Let me find them morning after morning, the starry-white petals radiating, striving upwards to their ideal. Let me see the idle shadows resting on the white dust; let me hear the humble-bees, and stay to look down on the rich dandelion disk. Let me see the very thistles opening their great crowns—I should miss the thistles; the reed-grasses hiding the moorhen; the bryony bine, at first crudely ambitious and lifted by force of youthful sap straight above the hedgerow to sink of its own weight presently and progress with crafty tendrils; swifts shot through the air with outstretched wings like crescent-headed shaftless arrows darted from the clouds; the chaffinch with a feather in her bill; all the living staircase of the spring, step by step, upwards to the great gallery of the summer—let me watch the same succession year by year.

Why, I knew the very dates of them all—the reddening elm, the arum, the hawthorn leaf, the celandine, the may; the yellow iris of the waters, the heath of the hillside. The time of the nightingale—the place to hear the first note; onwards to the drooping fern and the time of the redwing—the place of *his* first note, so welcome to the sportsman as the acorn ripens and the pheasant, come to the age of manhood, feeds himself; onwards to the shadowless days—the long shadowless winter, for in winter it is the shadows we miss as much as the light. They lie over the summer sward, design upon design, dark lace on green and gold; they glorify the sunlight: they repose on the distant hills like gods upon Olympus; without shadow, what even is the sun? At the foot of the great cliffs by the sea you may know this, it is dry glare; mighty ocean is dearer as the shadows of the clouds sweep over as they sweep over the green corn. Past the shadowless winter, when it is all shade, and therefore no shadow; onwards to the first coltsfoot and on to the seed-time again; I knew the dates of all of them. I did not want change; I wanted the same flowers to return on the same day, the titlark to rise soaring from the same oak to fetch down love with a song from heaven to his mate on the nest beneath. No change, no new thing; if I found a fresh wildflower in a fresh place, still it wove at once into the old garland. In vain, the very next year was different even in the same place—*that* has been a year of rain, and the flag flowers were wonderful to see; *this* was a dry year, and the flags not half the height, the gold of the flower not so deep; next year the fatal billhook came and swept away a slow-grown hedge that had given me crab-blossom in cuckoo-time and hazelnuts in harvest. Never again the same, even in the same place.

A little feather droops downwards to the ground—a swallow's feather fuller of miracle than the Pentateuch—how shall that feather be placed again in the breast where it grew? Nothing twice. Time changes the places that knew us, and if we go back in after years, still even then it is not the old spot; the gate swings differently, new thatch has been put on the old gables, the road has been widened and the sward the driven sheep lingered on is gone. Who dares to think then? For faces fade as flowers, and there is no consolation. So now I am sure I was right in always walking the same way by the starry flowers striving upwards on a slender ancestry of stem; I would follow the plain old road to-day if I could. Let change be far from me; that irresistible change must come is bitter indeed. Give me the old road,the same flowers—they were only stitchwort—the old succession of days and garland, ever weaving into it fresh wildflowers from far and near. Fetch them from distant mountains, discover them on decaying walls, in unsuspected corners; though never seen before, still they are the same: there has been a place in the heart waiting for them.

THE SINGLE-BARREL GUN

The single-barrel gun has passed out of modern sport; but I remember mine with regret, and think I shall some day buy another. I still find that the best double-barrel seems top-heavy in comparison; in poising it the barrels have a tendency to droop. Guns, of course, are built to balance and lie level in the hand, so as to almost aim themselves as they come to the shoulder; and those who have always shot with a double-barrel are probably quite satisfied with the gun on that score. To me there seems too much weight in the left hand and towards the end of the gun. Quickness of firing keeps the double-barrel to the front; but suppose a repeater were to be invented, some day, capable of discharging two cartridges in immediate succession? And if two cartridges, why not three? An easy thought, but a very difficult one to realize. Something in the *power* of the double-barrel—the overwhelming odds it affords the sportsman over bird and animal—pleases. A man feels master of the copse with a double-barrel; and such a sense of power, though only over feeble creatures, is fascinating. Besides, there is the delight of effect; for a clever right and left is sure of applause, and makes the gunner feel "good" in himself. Doubtless, if three barrels could be managed, three barrels would be more salable than doubles. One gunmaker has a four-barrel gun, quite a light weight too, which would be a tremendous success if the creatures would obligingly run and fly a little slower, so that all four cartridges could be got in. But that they will not do. For the present, the double-barrel is the gun of the time.

Still I mean some day to buy a single-barrel, and wander with it as of old along the hedges, aware that if I am not skilful enough to bring down with the first shot I shall lose my game. It is surprising how confident of that one shot you may get after a while. On the one hand, it is necessary to be extremely keen; on the other, to be sure of your own self-control, not to fire uselessly. The bramble-bushes on the shore of the ditch ahead might cover a hare. Through the dank and dark-green aftermath a rabbit might suddenly come bounding, disturbed from the furrow where he had been feeding. On the sandy paths which the rabbits have made aslant up the mound, and on their terraces, where they sit and look out from under the boughs, acorns have dropped ripe from the tree. Where there are acorns there may be pheasants; they may crouch in the fern and dry grey grass of the hedge thinking you do not see them, or else rush through and take wing on the opposite side. The only chance of a shot is as the bird passes a gap—visible while flying a yard—just time to pull the trigger. But I would rather have that chance than have to fire between the bars of a gate; for the horizontal lines cause an optical illusion, making the object appear in a different position from what it really is in, and half the pellets are sure to be buried in the rails. Wood-pigeons, when eagerly stuffing their crops with acorns, sometimes forget their usual caution; and, walking slowly, I have often got right underneath one—as unconscious of his presence as he was of mine, till a sudden dashing of wings against boughs and leaves announced his departure. This he always makes on the opposite side of the oak, so as to have the screen of the thick branches between himself and the gunner. The wood-pigeon, starting like this from a tree, usually descends in the first part of his flight, a gentle downward curve followed by an upward rise, and thus comes into view at the lower part of the curve. He still seems within shot, and to afford a good mark; and yet experience has taught me that it is generally in vain to fire. His stout quills protect him at the full range of the gun. Besides, a wasted shot alarms everything within several hundred yards; and in stalking with a single-barrel it needs as much knowledge to choose when not to fire as when you may.

The most exciting work with the single-barrel was woodcock shooting; woodcock being by virtue of rarity a sort of royal game, and a miss at a woodcock a terrible disappointment. They have a trick of skimming along the very summit of a hedge, and looking so easy to kill; but, as they fly, the tops of tall briers here, willow-rods next, or an ash-pole often intervene, and the result is apt to be a bough cut off and nothing more. Snipes, on the contrary, I felt sure of with the single-barrel, and never could hit them so well with a double. Either at starting, before the snipe got into his twist, or waiting till he had finished that uncertain movement, the single-barrel seemed to drop the shot with certainty. This was probably because of its perfect natural balance, so that it moved as if on a pivot. With the single I had nothing to manage but my own arms; with the other I was conscious that I had a gun also. With the single I could kill farther, no matter what it was. The single was quicker at short shots—snap-shots, as at rabbits darting across a narrow lane; and surer at long shots, as at a hare put out a good way ahead by the dog.

For everything but the multiplication of slaughter I liked the single best; I had more of the sense of woodcraft with it. When we consider how helpless a partridge is, for instance, before the fierce blow of shot, it does seem fairer that the gunner should have but one chance at the bird. Partridges at least might be kept for single-barrels: great bags of partridges never seemed to me quite right. Somehow it seems to me that to take so much advantage as the double-barrel confers is not altogether in the spirit of sport. The double-barrel gives no "law." At least to those who love the fields, the streams, and woods for their own sake, the single-barrel will fill the bag sufficiently, and will permit them to enjoy something of the zest men knew before the invention of weapons not only of precision but of repetition: inventions that rendered them too absolute masters of the situation. A single-barrel will soon make a sportsman the keenest of shots. The gun itself can be built to an exquisite perfection—lightness, handiness, workmanship, and performance of the very best. It is said that you can change from a single-barrel shot-gun to a sporting rifle and shoot with the rifle almost at once; while many who have been used to the slap-dash double cannot do anything for some time with a rifle. More than one African explorer has found his single-barrel smooth-bore the most useful of all the pieces in his battery; though, of course, of much larger calibre than required in our fields.

Thomas Hardy
1840-1928

Influencd by contemporary ideas on evolution and theology, Thomas Hardy established a distinct new direction for English nature writing. In his novels and poems Hardy sets human tragedy in tiny perspective against the immense, ancient, enduring world of nature. Unlike the Romantic writers who found in nature an active, benevolent principle, Hardy depicts it as essentially indifferent. Only those whose vitality has not been eroded by the restrictions of modern society—Hardy's peasants and sensitive souls—remain attuned to the elemental forces of nature. Like the characters in the following poems, they can find some solace in birdsong or waterfall, the sensual evidence that nature endures eternally, not for the sake of humanity, but to continue her own mysterious purpose.

Natural description in Hardy's work bears an authenticity accountable to his intimate familiarity with his native Dorsetshire: its wild moors and villages, and its peasant folkways. His father was a builder, and Hardy apprenticed with an architect for six years. Afterwards, he worked in London, where he encountered the controversial ideas of Darwin and Spencer that were challenging traditional Christian belief.

While working as an architect, Hardy struggled for nearly ten years to become a novelist, turning out several unsuccessful attempts. Then, at age thirty-four, he published a masterpiece, *Far from the Madding Crowd* (1974), which soon won enormous popularity. But his career as a novelist was controversial. Hardy's belief that sexual passion was the force of nature acting through individuals, and his insistence that it be explored in the novel drew such bitter criticism that after publishing *Jude the Obscure* (1895) he abandoned novel writing and concentrated on poetry. Eventually he composed over nine hundred short poems, many of them set amidst startlingly beautiful natural scenes.

UNDER THE WATERFALL*

"Whenever I plunge my arm, like this,
In a basin of water, I never miss
The sweet sharp sense of a fugitive day
Fetched back from its thickening shroud of gray.
Hence the only prime
And real love-rhyme
That I know by heart,
And that leaves no smart,
Is the purl of a little valley fall
About three spans wide and two spans tall
Over a table of solid rock,
And into a scoop of the self-same block;
The purl of a runlet that never ceases
In stir of kingdoms, in wars, in peaces;
With a hollow boiling voice it speaks
And has spoken since hills were turfless peaks."

"And why gives this the only prime
Idea to you of a real love-rhyme?
And why does plunging your arm in a bowl
Full of spring water, bring throbs to your soul?"

"Well, under the fall, in a crease of the stone,
Though where precisely none ever has known,
Jammed darkly, nothing to show how prized,
And by now with its smoothness opalized,
Is a drinking-glass:
For, down that pass
My lover and I
Walked under a sky
Of blue with a leaf-wove awning of green.
In the burn of August, to paint the scene,
And we placed our basket of fruit and wine
By the runlet's rim, where we sat to dine;
And when we had drunk from the glass together,
Arched by the oak-copse from the weather,
I held the vessel to rinse in the fall,
Where it slipped, and sank, and was past recall,
Though we stooped and plumbed the little abyss
With long bared arms. There the glass still is.
And, as said, if I thrust my arm below
Cold water in basin or bowl, a throe
From the past awakens a sense of that time,
And the glass we used, and the cascade's rhyme.
The basin seems the pool, and its edge

*From *The Complete Poems of Thomas Hardy,* edited by James Gibson (New York: Macmillan, 1978).

The hard smooth face of the brook-side ledge,
And the leafy pattern of china-ware
The hanging plants that were bathing there.

"By night, by day, when it shines or lours,
There lies intact that chalice of ours,
And its presence adds to the rhyme of love
Persistently sung by the fall above.
No lip has touched it since his and mine
In turns therefrom sipped lovers' wine."

THE DARKLING THRUSH

I leant upon a coppice gate
When Frost was spectre-gray.
And Winter's dregs made desolate
The weakening eye of day.
The tangled bine-stems scored the sky
Like strings of broken lyres,
And all mankind that haunted nigh
Had sought their household fires.

The land's sharp features seemed to be
The Century's corpse outleant,
His crypt the cloudy canopy,
The wind his death-lament.
The ancient pulse of germ and birth
Was shrunken hard and dry,
And every spirit upon earth
Seemed fervourless as I.

At once a voice arose among
The bleak twigs overhead
In a full-hearted evensong
Of joy illimited;
An aged thrush, frail, gaunt, and small,
In blast-beruffled plume,
Had chosen thus to fling his soul
Upon the growing gloom.

So little cause for carollings
Of such ecstatic sound
Was written on terrestrial things
Afar or nigh around,
That I could think there trembled through
His happy good-night air
Some blessed Hope, whereof he knew
And I was unaware.

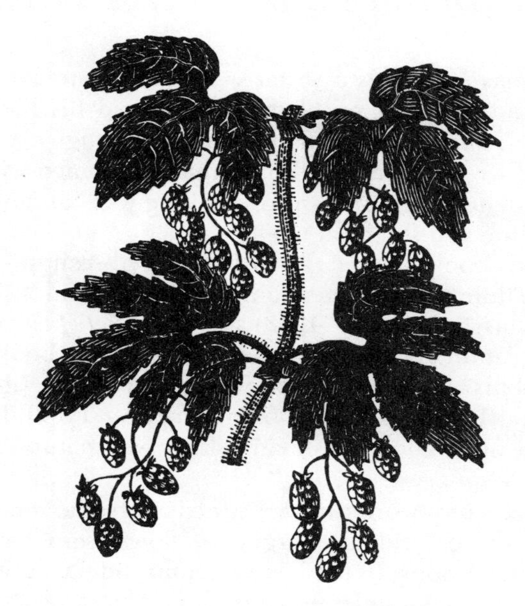

Edward Thomas
1878-1917

World War I prematurely ended the career of Edward Thomas and stunted a potential major influence on twentieth-century nature literature. Just a few years before his death, Thomas had, at the urging of his friend Robert Frost, begun to write poetry, where lies his finest work. It is both dense with meaning and yet at the same time clear. As W. J. Keith suggests, Thomas concentrated in his poetry the ideas and images of his earlier prose, eliminating less important details and refining his written "voice" so that moods and insights, though often subtle, seem delivered as easily as conversation from an old friend.

His vivid description and thoughtful reflection show the influence of the nineteenth-century nature writers. That, and his indignation over urban encroachment upon natural resources, mark Thomas as a connecting path between older nature writers and the twentieth century.

Growing up in grey London suburbs, the son of an austere civil servant, Thomas found escape in exploring the nearby Commons of London and Surrey; on holidays he roamed the Welsh countryside from which his parents had migrated and the Wiltshire fields that Richard Jefferies had described. He found escape, also, in reading Jefferies (whose biography he would write) as well as Shelley, Wordsworth, Tennyson, Darwin and a host of other nature writers. Later he became close friends with a great nature writer of the previous generation, W. H. Hudson.

Thomas attended Battersea Grammar School and then, at the insistence of his father, spent two terms at the elite St. Paul's. But he was stimulated less by school assignments than by his outdoor adventures—fishing, collecting, journal writing—and by Jefferies' books. At Oxford, where he secretly married, he decided to make writing his career, disappointing his father, who had hoped his oldest son would follow into the Civil Service.

The living Thomas earned as a writer was never quite adequate to support a growing family, and financial problems exacerbated his lifelong subjection to bouts of depression. These he treated by rambling through the countryside, where he researched and wrote the nature books that, combined with literary reviews, provided employment. Much of his prose writing was composed under the twin pressures of deadline and financial need.

Many of his travel books tapped the early twentieth-century passion to visit the countryside and, Thomas sometimes complained, to build "villas" upon it. Some of the essays, such as *Icknield Way* (1913) and *In Pursuit of Spring* (1914), are travel guides, recording landmarks, inns, and roads. His first book, *The Woodland Life* (1897), established his talent for minute description of natural details; later works emphasized, variously, introspection (*Horae Salitarae* 1902), landscape (*Beautiful Wales* 1905), or the integration of human culture with natural history (*The Heart of England* 1906; *The South Country* 1909).

Through Thomas's best work runs a distinctly personal tone, allowing an open demonstration of the emotional energy that flows from natural scenes to the author. His bitter reflections on the loss of countryside to suburban development just as clearly demonstrate a different energy.

EARLY ONE MORNING*

Early one morning in May I set out,
And nobody I knew was about.
    I'm bound away for ever,
    Away somewhere, away for ever.

There was no wind to trouble the weathercocks.
I had burnt my letters and darned my socks.

No one knew I was going away,
I thought myself I should come back some day.

I heard the brook through the town gardens run.
O sweet was the mud turned to dust by the sun.

A gate banged in a fence and banged in my head.
'A fine morning, sir', a shepherd said.

I could not return from my liberty,
To my youth and my love and my misery.

The past is the only dead thing that smells sweet,
The only sweet thing that is not also fleet.
    I'm bound away for ever,
    Away somewhere, away for ever.

*From *Collected Poems* by Edward Thomas (London: Faber & Faber Ltd.: 1936). Courtesy of Myfanwy Thomas and Faber & Faber Ltd.

THE CHERRY TREES*

The cherry trees bend over and are shedding,
On the old road where all that passed are dead,
Their petals, strewing the grass as for a wedding
This early May morn when there is none to wed.

HOW AT ONCE

How at once should I know,
When stretched in the harvest blue
I saw the swift's black bow,
That I would not have that view
Another day
Until next May
Again it is due?

The same year after year—
But with the swift alone.
With other things I but fear
That they will be over and done
Suddenly
And I only see
Them to know them gone.

A DREAM

Over known fields with an old friend in dream
I walked, but came sudden to a strange stream.
Its dark waters were bursting out most bright
From a great mountain's heart into the light.
They ran a short course under the sun, then back
Into a pit they plunged, once more as black
As at their birth; and I stood thinking there
How white, had the day shown on them, they were,
Heaving and coiling. So by the roar and hiss
And by the mighty motion of the abyss
I was bemused, that I forgot my friend
And neither saw nor sought him till the end,
When I awoke from waters unto men
Saying: 'I shall be here some day again.'

*The image of a wedding in this poem was inspired by Thomas's tiny daughter Myfanwy, who mistook the fallen blossoms for confetti.

SEDGE-WARBLERS

This beauty made me dream there was a time
Long past and irrecoverable, a clime
Where any brook so radiant racing clear
Through buttercup and kingcup bright as brass
But gentle, nourishing the meadow grass
That leans and scurries in the wind, would bear
Another beauty, divine and feminine,
Child to the sun, a nymph whose soul unstained
Could love all day, and never hate or tire,
A lover of mortal or immortal kin.

And yet, rid of this dream, ere I had drained
Its poison, quieted was my desire
So that I only looked into the water,
Clearer than any goddess or man's daughter,
And hearkened while it combed the dark green hair
And shook the millions of the blossoms white
Of water-crowfoot, and curdled to one sheet
The flowers fallen from the chestnuts in the park
Far off. And sedge-warblers, clinging so light
To willow twigs, sang longer than the lark,
Quick, shrill, or grating, a song to match the heat
Of the strong sun, nor less the water's cool,
Gushing through narrows, swirling in the pool.
Their song that lacks all words, all melody,
All sweetness almost, was dearer then to me
Than sweetest voice that sings in tune sweet words.
This was the best of May—the small brown birds
Wisely reiterating endlessly
What no man learnt yet, in or out of school.

UNDER THE WOODS

When these old woods were young
The thrushes' ancestors
As sweetly sung
In the old years.

There was no garden here,
Apples nor mistletoe;
No children dear
Ran to and fro.

New then was this thatched cot,
But the keeper was old,

And he had not
Much lead or gold.

Most silent beech and yew:
As he went round about
The woods to view
Seldom he shot.

But now that he is gone
Out of most memories,
Still lingers on,
A stoat of his,

But one, shrivelled and green,
And with no scent at all,
And barely seen
On this shed wall.

from THE WOODLAND LIFE

WILD FRUITS

It is a bright autumn afternoon, and here in a remote and unfrequented corner of a glorious common, quite close to London, pheasants in twos and threes are continually rising from the leaf-strewn ditch beneath the great oaks of the hedgerow. Their heavy flight—heavier even than it is wont to be—and their reluctance to leave the ground, tell of some great attraction there. It is not far to seek. Heaped among the long grass at the edge of the ditch, and upon the dead black leaves beneath, are bushels of ripe acorns. Many of these have burst open on falling, from very ripeness, and their numbers and size allow of no wonder that the birds lingered over them so long. The tints of the acorns are those of the season. One might say that the woods are orchards with infinite numbers of fruit-gatherers at this time of harvest. No yellow of cultivated fruit could excel the soft flow that is diffused in streaks over the acorns, as they lie on the greensward, and the many shades of gold and brown, varying almost from whiteness to a deep hazel-nut tinge. All this wealth of colour and ripeness is spread before the wild creatures of the woods in rich October. Many of the browns of the acorns might find a match on the pheasant's mottled back, and he harmonises completely with the surroundings he has chosen.

But the pheasants are not left alone to enjoy the feast. The grave rooks and pert daws come in large foraging bands and make havoc and rejoicing among the mellow heaps. The red squirrel is there also, but he is wiser than the heedless birds, and lays up great store for the harsh season that is coming. Beneath the crab-tree in the coppice, gnarled and lichened, there is rarer fruit than the oak provide. Never surely was there such a pile of wild apples. They lie broad-spread, layer on layer, some already covered with the dead leaves. Their colouring is yellow, softly golden, but their looks are not justified by their flavour; hence it is, perhaps, that they lie untouched, left to rot beneath November's frost-bitten leaves.

The present glory of the leaves is such as was not approached at harvest-home, or when the cultivated fruits were gathered. Each leaf now is tinged with apple-yellow and acorn gold and brown. As the sun comes pouring in through the leafy screen, the gay-hued leaves flash back something of their own colour into the atmosphere, and lend to the autumn air a peculiar charm. Each tree has a special hue of its own. Many of the glossy beech leaves are of an exquisite pale gold, while oaks are reddening later than the rest; the sunbeams on the willow-leaves produce a faint, soft, amber light, and the osiers flash deeply ruddy; on the dogwood-trees, which are even now in flower, there is a bronze colour that is almost unique, while the hawthorns wear their own purplish bloom. The nut-trees alone show little in their foliage that speaks of autumn, but the catkins are there, telling the season in spite of all, and even the leaves must soon succumb. One bird, more than any other, fits in with this changed aspect of the woods. The robin's crimson breast is perfectly matched by the combination of gold and red and hazel that floods the woodland scene; the brown of his plumage goes admirably with the leaves among which he wanders, and the fallen masses that are scattered about. His very song seems to harmonize with the air that inspires it; above all, it is passionate and softly mellow, and the depth of colour about him helps to convey its meaning. It is one of the few songs of the wild creatures' thanksgiving; the blackbird and thrush give him little aid, though the lark—that does not enter the woods—occasionally mounts high in song, unable to forget the summer days when he soared to the unsullied azure, with the carols of his rivals ringing about him.

Above all others, perhaps, the blackberry is the fruit most significant of the season in the woods and hedgerows. The great harvest has indeed passed, yet the berries that remain are sweeter than ever before and more welcome in their comparative rarity. The bloom on the sloe, or blackthorn plum, is unrivalled, and can scarcely be adequately described. It is purplish, toned with lilac, becoming almost pale blue; the colour is in fact almost that of the last scabious that is flowering beneath. Wreathed in amongst the lower oak-sprays a bine of honeysuckle yet bears one crown of fragrant blossom. This single flower calls up memories of June, with its wild roses, its song of Philomel, and its long happy days rung in and out by the wild music of the blackcap: there is summer in its faint perfume, and it is almost out of place among the ruddy oak leaves that are heralding cruel frosts and damp destroying mists. The festoons of bindweed are the palest of pale yellows, and the few white trumpet flowers hardly hold up their heads; they are fast going with the fall of the year.

The haws seem more scattered than usual, and give no character to the hedges as a whole. Here and there, however, a tree is one mass of deep crimson, which lends to it at a distance that peculiar purplish hue given by the combination of the sumptuous colour with the duller tints of the fading leaves. As yet the rose-bushes are untouched with the flush that the hips give them; the leaves are hardy, and many of the berries are hidden by them, and so their colouring is lost for a while. This makes them far less prominent till the finches and redwings come among them, when the leaves have dropped away.

The fruit of the bittersweet is brightest among the hedge berries. Hanging as it does over the thorn-bush or sapling which the plant has chosen to climb, the effect of the many oval bunches is that of ruby pendants mixed with polished emeralds. The bryony berries, like bright red beads strung on invisible threads, are larger and almost equally gay; and where these beautiful berries are abundant, autumn's many-coloured vesture gains a new opulence of splendour.

The many wild fruits give a character to the hedges and woods, and never are they more lovely than at sunset. The faint rays steal in through the fretted foliage, lighting up the dewy green grass beneath and the silvery trunks of the frail birches, and brightening the ruddy brier-stems and the few flowers that remain; whilst over the hill-top the firs of the ridge are reddened for a while by the glow which lingers after sundown is announced by the homeward-flying rooks and daws, and the clatter of the lesser birds assembling in the rosy light amid the trees.

from THE HEART OF ENGLAND

AN OLD WOOD

The chestnut blossom is raining steadily and noiselessly down upon a path whose naked pebbles receive mosaic of emerald light from the interlacing boughs. At intervals, once or twice an hour, the wings of a lonely swallow pass that way, when alone the shower stirs from its perpendicular fall. Cool and moist, the perfumed air flows, without lifting the most nervous leaf or letting fall a suspended bead of the night's rain from a honeysuckle bud. In an indefinite sky of grey, through which one ponderous cloud billows into sight and is lost again, no sun shines: yet there is light—I know not whence; for the brass trappings of the horses beam so as to be extinguished in their own fire. There is no song in wood or sky. Some one of summer's wandering voices—bullfinch or willow wren—might be singing, but unheard, at least unrealised. From the dead nettle spires, with dull green leaves stained by purple and becoming more and more purple towards the crest, which is of a sombre uniform purple, to the elms reposing at the horizon, all things have bowed the head, hushed, settled into a perfect sleep. Those elms are just visible, no more. The path has no sooner emerged from one shade than another succeeds, and so, on and on, the eye wins no broad dominion.

It is a land that uses a soft compulsion upon the passer-by, a compulsion to meditation, which is necessary before he is attached to a scene rather featureless, to a land that hence owes much of its power to a mood of generous reverie which it bestows. And yet it is a land that gives much. Companionable it is, reassuring to the solitary; he soon has a feeling of ease and seclusion there. The cool-leaved wood! The limitless, unoccupied fields of marsh marigold, seen through the trees, most beautiful when the evening rain falls slowly, dimming and almost putting out the lustrous bloom! Gold of the minute willows underfoot! Leagues of lonely grass where the slow herds tread the daisies and spare them yet!

Towards night, under the sweet rain, at this warm, skyless close of the day, the trees, far off in an indolent, rolling landscape, stand as if disengaged from the world, in a reticent and pensive repose.

But suddenly the rain has ceased. In an old, dense wood the last horizontal beams of the sun embrace the trunks of the trees and they glow red under their moist ceiling of green. A stile to be crossed at its edge, where a little stream, unseen, sways the stiff exuberant angelica that grows from it, gives the word to pause, and with a rush the silence and the solitude fill the brain. The wood is of uncounted age; the ground on which it stands is more ancient than the surrounding fields, for it rises and falls stormily, with huge boulders here and there; not a path intrudes upon it; the undergrowth is impenetrable to all but fox and bird and this cool red light about the trunks of the trees.

Far away a gate is loudly shut, and the rich blue evening comes on and severs me irrevocably from all but the light in the old wood and the ghostly white cow-parsley flowers suspended on unseen stalks. And there, among the trees and their shadows, not understood, speaking a forgotten tongue, old dreads and formless awes and fascinations discover themselves and address the comfortable soul, troubling it, recalling to it unremembered years not so long past but that in the end it settles down into a gloomy tranquility and satisfied discontent, as when we see the place where we were unhappy as children once. Druid and devilish deity and lean wild beast, harmless now, are revolving many memories with me under the strange, sudden red light in the old wood, and not more remote is the league-deep emerald sea-cave from the storm above than I am from the world.

from IN PURSUIT OF SPRING

LONDON TO GUILDFORD

The rain returned as I was crossing the railway bridge by Haydon's Road station. It was raining hard when the gypsy left the "Sultan," and still harder when I turned to the right along Merton Road. Rather than be soaked thus early, I took the shelter offered by a bird-shop on the left hand. This was not a cheerful or a pretty place. Overhead hung a row of cages containing chaffinches—battered ones at a shilling, a neater one at eighteen-pence—that sang every now and then,—

"My life and soul, as if he were a Greek."

Inside the shop, linnets at half a crown were rushing ceaselessly against the bars of six-inch cages, their bosoms ruffled and bloody as if from the strife, themselves like wild hearts beating in breasts too narrow. "House-moulted" goldfinches (price 5s. 6d.) were making sounds which I should have recognized as the twittering of goldfinches had I heard them among thistles on the Down tops. Little, bright foreign birds, that would have been hardly more at home there than here, looked more contented. A gold-fish, six inches long, squirmed about a globe with a diameter of six inches, in the most complete exile imaginable. The birds at least breathed air not parted entirely from the south-west wind which was now soaking the street; but the fish was in a living grave. The place was perhaps more cheerless to look at than to live in, but in a short time three more persons took shelter by it, and after glancing at the birds, stood looking out at the rain, at the dull street, the tobacconist's, news-agent's, and confectioner's shops alone being unshuttered. Presently one of the three shelterers entered a bird-shop, which I had supposed shut; the proprietor came out for a chaffinch; and in a minute or two the customer left with an uncomfortable air and something fluttering in a paper bag such as would hold a penn'orth of sweets. He mounted a bicycle, and I after him, for the rain had forgotten to fall. He turned up to the left towards Morden station, which was my way also. Not far up the road he was apparently unable to bear the fluttering in the paper bag any longer; he got down, and with an awkward air, as if he knew how many great men had done it before, released the flutterer. A dingy cock chaffinch flew off among the lilacs of a garden, saying "Chink." The deliverer was up and away again.

For some distance yet the land was level. The only hill was made by the necessity of crossing a railway at Morden station. At that point rows of houses were discontinued; shops and public-houses with a lot of plate-glass had already ceased. The open stretches were wider and wider, of dark earth, of vegetables in squares, or florists' plantations, divided by hedges low and few, or by lines of tall elm trees or Lombardy poplars. Not quite rustic men and women stooped or moved to and fro among the vegetables: carts were waiting under the elms. A new house, a gasometer, an old house and its trees, lay on the farther side of the big field: behind them the Crystal Palace. On my right, in the opposite direction, the trees massed themselves together into one wood.

It is so easy to make this flat land sordid. The roads, hedges, and fences on it have hardly a reason for being anything but straight. More and more the kind of estate disappears that might preserve trees and various wasteful and pretty things: it is replaced by small villas and market gardens. If any waste be left under the new order, it will be used for conspicuously depositing rubbish. Little or no wildness of form or arrangement can survive, and with no wildness a landscape cannot be beautiful. Barbed wire and ugly and cruel fences, used against the large and irresponsible population of townsmen, add to the charmless artificiality. It was a relief to see a boy stealing up one of the hedges, looking for birds' nests. And then close up against this eager agriculture and its barbed wires are the hotels, inns, tea-shops, and cottages with ginger-beer for the townsman who is looking for country of a more easy-going nature. This was inhospitable. On many a fence and gate had been newly written up in chalk by some prophet:

"Eternity," "Believe," "Come unto Me."

I welcomed the fences for the sake of what lay behind them. Now it was a shrubbery, now a copse, and perhaps a rookery, or a field running up mysteriously to the curved edge of a wood, and at Morden Hall it was a herd of deer among the trees. The hedges were good in themselves, and for the lush grass, the cuckoo-pint, goose-grass, and celandine upon their banks. Walking up all the slightest hills because of the south-west wind, I could see everything, from the celandines one by one and the crowding new chestnut leaves, to the genial red brick tower of St. Laurence's Church at Morden and the inns one after another—the "George," the "Lord Nelson," the "Organ," the "Brick Kiln," the "Victoria."

. . .

D. H. Lawrence
1885-1930

Reviled during his lifetime for his frank treatment of sexuality and his antimilitaristic pronouncements, D. H. Lawrence has come to be recognized as one of the greatest English writers of the twentieth century. He is praised today for forging new forms in both fiction and poetry, and for showing the importance of the unconscious, irrational, "dark" aspects of human nature, especially the force of sexuality. His ability to portray the deep yearnings and complex needs of sexual relationships has brought critical acclaim to at least three novels: the autobiographical *Sons and Lovers* (1913), as well as *The Rainbow* (1915) and *Woman in Love* (1920), which together trace the relationships of three generations of English women.

But Lawrence is essentially a nature writer. The sexual need he investigates is part of humanity's connection with the rest of organic nature, what he calls "the underground roots" or "blood-knowledge." Metaphors like these color Lawrence's portrayals of human sexuality in novels and poems. "Gloire de Dijon," for example, describes a woman bathing:

> . . . down her sides the mellow golden shadow glows
> as she stoops to the sponge, and the swung breasts
> sway like full-blown yellow Gloire de Dijon roses.

The idea that humanity's connection with nature has been severed runs parallel to the theme of troubled sexuality in Lawrence's work. Blame for both problems Lawrence places upon the mechanical assumptions of modern industrial society. His essay "Pan in America," included below, is one of his most thoughtful critiques of alienation from nature. In his final novel, *Lady Chatterly's Lover* (1928), Lawrence bluntly linked inadequate sexuality with what he considered the exploitation of nature by industrial capitalism.

Lawrence was raised in the very heart of British industrialism, the coal fields of Nottinghamshire. In *Sons and Lovers* he contrasts industrial ugliness with adjacent natural loveliness and shows the alienation of both working-class father and middle-class mother from the "underground roots" that might lend balance to their lives.

Soon after *The Rainbow* was banned by the British government, Lawrence and his German-born wife left England in a self-imposed exile, and lived in Italy, Australia, Mexico, and New Mexico. Profound nature writing appears in the novels and travel books he wrote during this period: *Kangaroo* (1923), *The Plumed Serpent* (1926), *Sea and Sardinia* (1921). Several volumes of his poetry, collected in *Complete Poems* (1964), are devoted to animals and flowers. "Snake," for example, was first published in *Birds, Beasts, and Flowers* (1923). It shows how Lawrence's insight transforms a chance encounter into a glimpse at "one of the lords of life."

LOVE ON THE FARM*

What large, dark hands are those at the window
Grasping in the golden light
Which weaves its way through the evening wind
At my heart's delight?

Ah, only the leaves! But in the west
I see a redness suddenly come
Into the evening's anxious breast—
'Tis the wound of love goes home!

The woodbine creeps abroad
Calling low to her lover:
The sun-lit flirt who all the day
Has poised above her lips in play
And stolen kisses, shallow and gay,
Of pollen, now has gone away—
She woos the moth with her sweet, low word;
And when above her his moth-wings hover
Then her bright breast she will uncover
And yield her honey-drop to her lover.

Into the yellow, evening glow
Saunters a man from the farm below;
Leans, and looks in at the low-built shed
Where the swallow has hung her marriage bed.
The bird lies warm against the wall.
She glances quick her startled eyes
Towards him, then she turns away
Her small head, making warm display

*From *The Complete Poems of D. H. Lawrence*, ed. Vivian de Sola Pinto and F. Warren Roberts.

  Of red upon the throat. Her terrors sway
  Her out of the nest's warm, busy ball,
  Whose plaintive cry is heard as she flies
  In one blue stoop from out the sties
  Into the twilight's empty hall.

Oh, water-hen, beside the rushes
Hide your quaintly scarlet blushes,
Still your quick tail, lie still as dead,
Till the distance folds over his ominous tread!

The rabbit presses back her ears,
Turns back her liquid, anguished eyes
And crouches low; then with wild spring
Spurts from the terror of *his* oncoming;
To be choked back, the wire ring
Her frantic effort throttling:
  Piteous brown ball of quivering fears!
Ah, soon in his large, hard hands she dies,
And swings all loose from the swing of his walk!
Yet calm and kindly are his eyes
And ready to open in brown surprise
Should I not answer to his talk
Or should he my tears surmise.

I hear his hand on the latch, and rise from my chair
Watching the door open; he flashes bare
His strong teeth in a smile, and flashes his eyes
In a smile like triumph upon me; then careless-wise
He flings the rabbit soft on the table board
And comes towards me: ah! the uplifted sword
Of his hand against my bosom! and oh, the broad
Blade of his glance that asks me to applaud
His coming! With his hand he turns my face to him
And caresses me with his fingers that still smell grim
Of the rabbit's fur! God, I am caught in a snare!
I know not what fine wire is round my throat;
I only know I let him finger there
My pulse of life, and let him nose like a stoat
Who sniffs with joy before he drinks the blood.

And down his mouth comes to my mouth! and down
His bright dark eyes come over me, like a hood
Upon my mind! his lips meet mine, and a flood
Of sweet fire sweeps across me, so I drown
Against him, die, and find death good.

SNAKE

A snake came to my water-trough
On a hot, hot day, and I in pyjamas for the heat,
To drink there.

In the deep, strange-scented shade of the great dark carob-tree
I came down the steps with my pitcher
And must wait, must stand and wait, for there he was
at the trough before me.

He reached down from a fissure in the earth-wall in
the gloom
And trailed his yellow-brown slackness soft-bellied down,
over the edge of the stone trough
And rested his throat upon the stone bottom,
And where the water had dripped from the tap, in a
small clearness,
He sipped with his straight mouth,
Softly drank through his straight gums, into his slack
long body,
Silently.

Someone was before me at my water-trough,
And I, like a second comer, waiting.

He lifted his head from his drinking, as cattle do,
And looked at me vaguely, as drinking cattle do,
And flickered his two-forked tongue from his lips, and
mused a moment,
And stooped and drank a little more,
Being earth-brown, earth-golden from the burning bowels
of the earth
On the day of Sicilian July, with Etna smoking.

The voice of my education said to me
He must be killed,
For in Sicily the black, black snakes are innocent, the
gold are venomous.

And voices in me said, If you were a man
You would take a stick and break him now, and finish
him off.

But must I confess how I liked him,
How glad I was he had come like a guest in quiet, to
drink at my water-trough
And depart peaceful, pacified, and thankless,
Into the burning bowels of this earth?

Was it cowardice, that I dared not kill him?
Was it perversity, that I longed to talk to him?
Was it humility, to feel so honoured?
I felt so honoured.

And yet those voices:
If you were not afraid, you would kill him!

And truly I was afraid, I was most afraid,
But even so, honoured still more
That he should seek my hospitality
From out the dark door of the secret earth.

He drank enough
And lifted his head, dreamily, as one who has drunken,
And flickered his tongue like a forked night on the air,
so black,
Seeming to lick his lips,
And looked around like a god, unseeing, into the air,
And slowly turned his head,
And slowly, very slowly, as if thrice adream,
Proceeded to draw his slow length curving round
And climb again the broken bank of my wall-face.

And as he put his head into that dreadful hole,
And as he slowly drew up, snake-easing his shoulders,
and entered farther,
A sort of horror, a sort of protest against his with-
drawing into that horrid black hole,
Deliberately going into the blackness, and slowly drawing
himself after,
Overcame me now his back was turned.

I looked round, I put down my pitcher,
I picked up a clumsy log
And threw it at the water-trough with a clatter.

I think it did not hit him,
But suddenly that part of him that was left behind
convulsed in undignified haste,
Writhed like lightning, and was gone
Into the black hole, the earth-lipped fissue in the wall-
front,
At which, in the intense still noon, I stared with fasci-
nation.

And immediately I regretted it.
I thought how paltry, how vulgar, what a mean act!

I despised myself and the voices of my accursed human
    education.
And I thought of the albatross,
And I wished he would come back, my snake.

For he seemed to me again like a king,
Like a king in exile, uncrowned in the underworld,
Now due to be crowned again.

And so, I missed my chance with one of the lords
Of life.
And I have something to expiate;
A pettiness.

PAN IN AMERICA*

At the beginning of the Christian era, voices were heard off the coasts of Greece, out to sea, on the Mediterranean, wailing: "Pan is dead! Great Pan is dead!"

The father of fauns and nymphs, satyrs and dryads and naiads was dead, with only the voices in the air to lament him. Humanity hardly noticed.

But who was he, really? Down the long lanes and overgrown ridings of history we catch odd glimpses of a lurking rustic god with a goat's white lightning in his eyes. A sort of fugitive, hidden among leaves, and laughing with the uncanny derision of one who feels himself defeated by something lesser than himself.

An outlaw, even in the early days of the gods. A sort of Ishmael among the bushes.

Yet always his lingering title: The Great God Pan. As if he was, or had been, the greatest.

Lurking among the leafy recesses, he was almost more demon than god. To be feared, not loved or approached. A man who should see Pan by daylight fell dead, as if blasted by lightning.

Yet you might dimly see him in the night, a dark body within the darkness. And then, it was a vision filling the limbs and the trunk of a man with power, as with new, strong-mounting sap. The Pan-power! You went on your way in the darkness secretly and subtly elated with blind energy, and you could cast a spell, by your mere presence, on women and on men. But particularly on women.

In the woods and the remote places ran the children of Pan, all the nymphs and fauns of the forest and the spring and the river and the rocks. These, too, it was dangerous to see by day. The man who looked up to see the white arms of a nymph flash as she darted behind the thick wild laurels away from him followed helplessly. He was a nympholept. Fascinated by the swift limbs and the wild, fresh sides of the nymph, he followed for ever,

*From *Phoenix: The Posthumous Papers* by D. H. Lawrence.

for ever, in the endless monotony of his desire. Unless came some wise being who could absolve him from the spell.

But the nymphs, running among the trees and curling to sleep under the bushes, made the myrtles blossom more gaily, and the spring bubble up with greater urge, and the birds splash with a strength of life. And the lithe flanks of the faun gave life to the oakgroves, the vast trees hummed with energy. And the wheat sprouted like green rain returning out of the ground, in the little fields, and the vine hung its black drops in abundance, urging a secret.

Gradually men moved into cities. And they loved the display of people better than the display of a tree. They liked the glory they got of overpowering one another in war. And above all, they loved the vainglory of their own words, the pomp of argument and the vanity of ideas.

So Pan became old and grey-bearded and goat-legged, and his passion was degraded with the lust of senility. His power to blast and to brighten dwindled. His nymphs became coarse and vulgar.

Till at last the old Pan died, and was turned into the devil of the Christians. The old god Pan became the Christian devil, with the cloven hoofs and the horns, the tail, and the laugh of derision. Old Nick, the Old Gentlemen who is responsible for all our wickedness, but especially our sensual excesses—this is all that is left of the Great God Pan.

It is strange. It is a most strange ending for a god with such a name. Pan! All! That which is everything has goat's feet and a tail! With a black face!

This really is curious.

Yet this was all that remained of Pan, except that he acquired brimstone and hell-fire, for many, many centuries. The nymphs turned into the nasty-smelling witches of a Walpurgis night, and the fauns that danced became sorcerers riding the air, or fairies no bigger than your thumb.

But Pan keeps on being reborn, in all kinds of strange shapes. There he was, at the Renaissance. And in the eighteenth century he had quite a vogue. He gave rise to an "ism," and there were many pantheists, Wordsworth one of the first. They worshipped Nature in her sweet-and-pure aspect, her Lucy Gray aspect.

"Oft have I heard of Lucy Gray," the school-child began to recite, on examination-day.

"So have I," interrupted the bored inspector.

Lucy Gray, alas, was the form that William Wordsworth thought fit to give to the Great God Pan.

And then he crossed over to the United States: I mean Pan did. Suddenly he gets a new name. He becomes the Oversoul, the Allness of everything. To this new Lucifer Gray of a Pan Whitman sings the famous *Song of Myself:* "I am all, and All is Me." That is: "I am Pan, and Pan is me."

The old goat-legged gentlemen from Greece thoughtfully strokes his beard, and answers: "All A is B, but all B is not A." Aristotle did not live for nothing. All Walt is Pan, but all Pan is not Walt.

This, even to Whitman, is incontrovertible. So the new American pantheism collapses.

Then the poets dress up a few fauns and nymphs, to let them run riskily—

oh, would there were any risk!—in their private "grounds." But, alas, these tame guinea-pigs soon became boring. Change the game.

We still *pretend* to believe that there is One mysterious Something-or-other back to Everything, ordaining all things for the ultimate good of humanity. It wasn't back of the Germans in 1914, of course, and whether it's back of the bolshevist is still a grave question. But still, it's back of *us,* so that's all right.

Alas, poor Pan! Is this what you've come to? Legless, hornless, faceless, even smileless, you are less than everything or anything, except a lie.

And yet here, in America, the oldest of all, old Pan is still alive. When Pan was greatest, he was not even Pan. He was nameless and unconceived, mentally. Just as a small baby new from the womb may say Mama! Dada! whereas in the womb it said nothing; so humanity, in the womb of Pan, said nought. But when humanity was born into a separate idea of itself, it said *Pan.*

In the days before man got too much separated off from the universe, he *was* Pan, along with all the rest.

As a tree still is. A strong-willed, powerful thing-in-itself, reaching up and reaching down. With a powerful will of its own it thrusts green hands and huge limbs at the light above and sends huge legs and gripping toes down, down between the earth and rocks, to the earth's middle.

Here, on this little ranch under the Rocky Mountains, a big pine tree rises like a guardian spirit in front of the cabin where we live. Long, long ago the Indians blazed it. And the lightning, or the storm, has cut off its crest. Yet its column is always there, alive and changeless, alive and changing. The tree has its own aura of life. And in winter the snow slips off it, and in June it sprinkles down its little catkin-like pollen-tips, and it hisses in the wind, and it makes a silence within a silence. It is a great tree, under which the house is built. And the tree is still within the allness of Pan. At night, when the lamplight shines out of the window, the great trunk dimly shows, in the near darkness, like an Egyptian column, supporting some powerful mystery in the over-branching darkness. By day, it is just a tree.

It is just a tree. The chipmunks skelter a little way up it, the little black-and-white birds, tree-creepers, walk quick as mice on its rough perpendicular, tapping; the bluejays throng on its branches, high up, at dawn, and in the afternoon you hear the faintest rustle of many little wild doves alighting in its upper remoteness. It is a tree, which is still Pan.

And we live beneath it, without noticing. Yet sometimes, when one suddenly looks far up and sees those wild doves there, or when one glances quickly at the inhuman-human hammering of a woodpecker, one realizes that the tree is asserting itself as much as I am. It gives out life, as I give out life. Our two lives meet and cross one another, unknowingly: the tree's life penetrates my life, and my life the tree's. We cannot live near one another, as we do, without affecting one another.

The tree gathers up earth-power from the dark bowels of the earth, and a roaming sky-glitter from above. And all unto itself, which is a tree, woody, enormous, slow but unyielding with life, bristling with acquisitive energy, obscurely radiating some of its great strength.

It vibrates its presence into my soul, and I am with Pan. I think no man could live near a pine tree and remain quite suave and supple and compliant. Something fierce and bristling is communicated. The piny sweetness is rousing and defiant, like turpentine, the noise of the needles is keen with aeons of sharpness. In the volleys of wind from the western desert, the tree hisses and resists. It does not lean eastward at all. It resists with a vast force of resistance, from within itself, and its column is a ribbed, magnificent assertion.

I have become conscious of the tree, and of its interpenetration into my life. Long ago, the Indians must have been even more acutely conscious of it, when they blazed it to leave their mark on it.

I am conscious that it helps to change me, vitally. I am even conscious that shivers of energy cross my living plasm, from the tree, and I become a degree more like unto the tree, more bristling and turpentiney, in Pan. And the tree gets a certain shade and alertness of my life, within itself.

Of course, if I like to cut myself off, and say it is all bunk, a tree is merely so much lumber not yet sawn, then in a great measure I shall *be* cut off. So much depends on one's attitude. One can shut many, many doors of receptivity in oneself; or one can open many doors that are shut.

I prefer to open my doors to the coming of the tree. Its raw earth-power and its raw sky-power, its resinous erectness and resistance, its sharpness of hissing needles and relentlessness of roots, all that goes to the primitive savageness of a pine tree, goes also to the strength of man.

Give me of your power, then, oh tree! And I will give you of mine.

And this is what men must have said, more naïvely, less sophisticatedly, in the days when all was Pan. It is what, in a way, the aboriginal Indians still say, and still *mean,* intensely: especially when they dance the sacred dance, with the tree; or with the spruce twigs tied above their elbows.

Give me your power, oh tree, to help me in my life. And I will give you my power: even symbolized in a rag torn from my clothing.

This is the oldest Pan.

Or again, I say: "Oh you, you big tree, standing so strong and swallowing juice from the earth's inner body, warmth from the sky, beware of me. Beware of me, because I am strongest. I am going to cut you down and take your life and take you into beams for my house, and into a fire. Prepare to deliver up your life to me."

Is this any less true than when the lumberman glances at a pine tree, sees if it will cut good lumber, dabs a mark or a number upon it, and goes his way absolutely without further thought or feeling. Is he truer to life? Is it truer to life to insulate oneself entirely from the influence of the tree's life, and to walk about in an inanimate forest of standing lumber, marketable in St. Louis, Mo.? Or is it truer to life to know with a pantheistic sensuality, that the tree has its own life, its own assertive existence, its own living relatedness to me: that my life is added to, or militated against, by the tree's life?

Which is really truer?

Which is truer, to live among the living, or to run on wheels?

And who can sit with the Indians around a big camp-fire of logs in the mountains at night, when a man rises and turns his breast and his curiously-smiling bronze face away from the blaze, and stands voluptuously warming his thighs and buttocks and loins, his back to the fire, faintly smiling the inscrutable Pan-smile into the dark trees surrounding, without hearing him say, in the Pan voice: "Aha! Tree! Aha! Tree! Who has triumphed now? I drank the heat of your blood into my face and breast, and now I am drinking it into my loins and buttocks and legs, oh tree! I am drinking your heat right through me, oh tree! Fire is life, and I take your life for mine. I am drinking it up, oh tree, even into my buttocks. Aha! Tree! I am warm! I am strong! I am happy, tree, in this cold night in the mountains!"

And the old man, glancing up and seeing the flames flapping in flamy rags at the dark smoke, in the upper fire-hurry towards the stars and the dark spaces between the stars, sits stonily and inscrutably: yet one knows that he is saying: "Go back, oh fire! Go back like honey! Go back, honey of life, to where you came from, before you were hidden in the tree. The trees climb into the sky and steal the honey of the sun, like bears stealing from a hollow tree-trunk. But when the tree falls and is put on to the fire, the honey flames and goes straight back to where it came from. And the smell of burning pine is as the smell of honey."

So the old man says, with his lightless Indian eyes. But he is careful never to utter one word of the mystery. Speech is the death of Pan, who can but laugh and sound the reed-flute.

Is it better, I ask you, to cross the room and turn on the heat at the radiator, glancing at the thermometer and saying: "We're just a bit below the level, in here"? Then to go back to the newspaper!

What can a man do with his life but live it? And what does life consist in, save a vivid relatedness between the man and the living universe that surrounds him? Yet man insulates himself more and more into mechanism, and repudiates everything but the machine and the contrivance of which he himself is master, god in the machine.

Morning comes, and white ash lies in the fire-hollow, and the old man looks at it broodingly.

"The fire is gone," he says in the Pan silence, that is so full of unutterable things. "Look! there is no more tree. We drank his warmth, and he is gone. He is way, way off in the sky, his smoke is in the blueness, with the sweet smell of a pine-wood fire, and his yellow flame is in the sun. It is morning, with the ashes of night. There is no more tree. Tree is gone. But perhaps there is fire among the ashes. I shall blow it, and it will be alive. There is always fire, between the tree that goes and the tree that stays. One day I shall go—"

So they cook their meat, and rise, and go in silence.

There is a big rock towering up above the trees, a cliff. And silently a man glances at it. You hear him say, without speech:

"Oh you big rock! If a man fall down from you, he dies. Don't let me fall down from you. Oh, you big pale rock, you are so still, you know lots of things. You know a lot. Help me, then, with your stillness. I go to find deer. Help me find deer."

And the man slips aside, and secretly lays a twig, or a pebble, some little object in a niche of the rock, as a pact between him and the rock. The rock will give him some of its radiant-cold stillness and enduring presence, and he makes a symbolic return, of gratitude.

Is it foolish? Would it have been better to invent a gun, to shoot his game from a great distance, so that he need not approach it with any of that living stealth and preparedness with which one live thing approaches another? Is it better to have a machine in one's hands, and so avoid the life-contact: the trouble! the pains! Is it better to see the rock as a mere nothing, not worth noticing because it has no value, and you can't eat it as you can a deer?

But the old hunter steals on, in the stillness of the eternal Pan, which is so full of soundless sounds. And in his soul he is saying: "Deer! Oh, you thin-legged deer! I am coming! Where are you, with your feet like little stones bounding down a hill? I know you. Yes, I know you, But you don't know me. You don't know where I am, and you don't know me, anyhow. But I know you. I am thinking of you. I shall get you. I've got to get you. I got to; so it will be.—I shall get you, and shoot an arrow right in you."

In this state of abstraction, and subtle, hunter's communion with the quarry—a weird psychic connexion between hunter and hunted—the man creeps into the mountains.

And even a white man who is a born hunter must fall into this state. Gun or no gun! He projects his deepest, most primitive hunter's consciousness abroad, and finds his game, not by accident, nor even chiefly by looking for signs, but primarily by a psychic attraction, a sort of telepathy: the hunter's telepathy. Then when he finds his quarry, he aims with a pure, spellbound volition. If there is no flaw in his abstracted huntsman's *will,* he cannot miss. Arrow or bullet, it flies like a movement of pure will, straight to the spot. And the deer, once she has let her quivering alertness be over-mastered or stilled by the hunter's subtle, hypnotic, *following* spell, she cannot escape.

This is Pan the Pan-mystery, the Pan-power. What can men who sit at home in their studies, and drink hot milk and have lamb's-wool slippers on their feet, and write anthropology, what *can* they possibly know about men, the men of Pan?

Among the creatures of Pan there is an eternal struggle for life, between lives. Man, defenceless, rapacious man, has needed the qualities of every living thing, at one time or other. The hard, silent abidingness of rock, the surging resistance of a tree, the still evasion of a puma, the dogged earth-knowledge of the bear, the light alertness of the deer, the sky-prowling vision of the eagle: turn by turn man has needed the power of every living thing. Tree, stone, or hill, river, or little stream, or waterfall, or salmon in the fall—man can be master and complete in himself, only by assuming the living powers of each of them, as the occasion requires.

He used to make himself master by a great effort of will, and sensitive, intuitive cunning, and immense labour of body.

Then he discovered the "idea." He found that all things were related by certain *laws.* The moment man learned to abstract, he began to make engines that would do the work of his body. So, instead of concentrating upon his quarry, or upon the living things which made his universe, he concentrated upon the engines or instruments which should intervene between him and the living universe, and give him mastery.

This was the death of the great Pan. The idea and the engine came between man and all things, like a death. The old connexion, the old Allness, was severed, and can never be ideally restored. Great Pan is dead.

Yet what do we live for, except to live? Man has lived to conquer the phenomenal universe. To a great extent he has succeeded. With all the mechanism of the human world, man is to a great extent master of all life, and of most phenomena.

And what then? Once you have conquered a thing, you have lost it. Its real relation to you collapses.

A conquered world is no good to man. He sits stupefied with boredom upon his conquest.

We need the universe to live again, so that we can live with it. A conquered universe, a dead Pan, leaves us nothing to live with.

You have to abandon the conquest, before Pan will live again. You have to live to live, not to conquer. What's the good of conquering even the North Pole, if after the conquest you've nothing left but an inert fact? Better leave it a mystery.

It was better to be a hunter in the woods of Pan, than it is to be a clerk in a city store. The hunter hungered, laboured, suffered tortures of fatigue. But at least he lived in a ceaseless living relation to his surrounding universe.

At evening, when the deer was killed, he went home to the tents and threw down the deer-meat on the swept place before the tent of his women. And the women came out to greet him softly, with a sort of reverence, as he stood before the meat, the life-stuff. He came back spent, yet full of power, bringing the life-stuff. And the children looked with black eyes at the meat, and at that wonder-being the man, the bringer of meat.

Perhaps the children of the store-clerk look at their father with a *tiny* bit of the same mystery. And perhaps the clerk feels a fragment of the old glorification, when he hands his wife the paper dollars.

But about the tents the women move silently. Then when the cooking-fire dies low, the man crouches in silence and toasts meat on a stick, while the dogs lurk round like shadows and the children watch avidly. The man eats as the sun goes down. And as the glitter departs, he says: "Lo, the sun is going, and I stay. All goes, but still I stay. Power of deer-meat is in my belly, power of sun is in my body. I am tired, but it is with power. There the small moon gives her first sharp sign. So! So! I watch her. I will give her something; she is very sharp and bright, and I do not know her power. Lo! I will give the woman something for this moon, which troubles me above the sunset, and has power.Lo! how very curved and sharp she is! Lo! how she troubles me!"

Thus, always aware, always watchful, subtly poising himself in the world of Pan, among the powers of the living universe, he sustains his life and is sustained. There is no boredom, because *everything* is alive and active, and danger is inherent in all movement. The contact between all things is keen and wary: for wariness is also a sort of reverence, or respect. And nothing, in the world of Pan, may be taken for granted.

So when the fire is extinguished, and the moon sinks, the man says to the woman: "Oh, woman, be very soft, be very soft and deep towards me, with the deep silence. Oh, woman, do not speak and stir and wound me with the sharp horns of yourself. Let me come into the deep, soft places, the dark, soft places deep as between the stars. Oh, let me lose there the weariness of the day: let me come in the power of the night. Oh, do not speak to me, nor break the deep night of my silence and my power. Be softer than dust, and darker than any flower. Oh, woman, wonderful is the craft of your darkness, the distance of your dark depths. Oh, open silently the deep that has no end, and do not turn the horns of the moon against me."

This is the might of Pan, and the power of Pan.

And still, in America, among the Indians, the oldest Pan is alive. But here, also, dying fast.

It is useless to glorify the savage. For he will kill Pan with his own hands, for the sake of a motor-car. And a bored savage, for whom Pan is dead, is the stupefied image of all boredom.

And we cannot return to the primitive life, to live in tepees and hunt with bows and arrows.

Yet live we must. And once life has been conquered, it is pretty difficult to live. What are we going to do, with a conquered universe? The Pan relationship, which the world of man once had with all the world, was better than anything man has now. The savage, today, if you give him the chance, will become more mechanical and unliving than any civilized man. But civilized man, having conquered the universe, may as well leave off bossing it. Because, when all is said and done, life itself consists in a live relatedness between man and his universe: sun, moon, stars, earth, trees, flowers, birds, animals, men, everything—and not in a "conquest" of anything by anything. Even the conquest of the air makes the world smaller, tighter, and more airless.

And whether we are a store-clerk or a bus-conductor, we can still choose between the living univese of Pan, and the mechanical conquered universe of modern humanity. The machine has no windows. But even the most mechanized human being has only got his windows nailed up, or bricked in.

W. H. Hudson
1841-1922

The most eloquent—and effective—defender of bird life in England was not a native. William Henry Hudson, son of New Englanders of English ancestry, lived most of his first thirty years on his family's ranches amidst the vast Argentine prairie, or pampas. His favorite book was Gilbert White's *Natural History of Selborne,* and throughout his boyhood he was permitted great freedom to roam the pampas on horseback. He developed an acute feeling of kinship for the plants and animals—even the topography—of that isolated environment; but he felt especially drawn to its birds, in incredible number and variety, from the giant rhea (ostrich) of the pampas to the delicate wading waterfowl of the lakes.

His early ambition was to become a naturalist/scientist like Darwin, whose *Origin of Species* he had read when he was eighteen. Hudson's subsequent writings reveal detailed, precise observation as well as a tendency to debate scientific theory, principally the details of Darwin's evolutionary hypothesis.

Personal observation of nature—and personal interpretation of it—eventually replaced scientific detachment as Hudson's primary mode of relating to the natural world. The turning point came in 1871 while on a solitary expedition to the uncharted desert of Patagonia in southern Argentina. He had planned to establish his reputation as an ornithologist by discovering new specimens, but what he discovered, riding alone week after week, his mind tuned to the rhythms of the desert, was a wisdom beyond scientific knowledge: the conviction that in his humanness there survived an ancient, intimate relation with nature as a whole. *Idle Days in Patagonia* (1893), the book of naturalist and autobiographical essays he later wrote about this expedition, reveals his transformation from ambitious scientist to philosopher of nature.

In 1874 Hudson emigrated to England, where he would live in poverty most of his life and in obscurity for at least twenty years, writing articles for magazines, publishing unsuccessful novels, and collaborating on a scientific survey of *Argentine Ornithology* (1888). In 1892 publication of *The Naturalist in La Plata* achieved both critical and popular success for its exquisite descriptions of tropical habitats and its moving pleas to preserve the rare species of animals:

> . . . like immortal flowers they have drifted down to us on the ocean of time, and their strangeness and beauty bring to our imaginations a dream and a picture of that unknown world, immeasurably far removed, where man was not, and when they perish, something of gladness goes out of nature, and the sunshine loses something of its brightness.

Over the next decade Hudson continued that theme with a series of books designed to foster public appreciation of England's profuse avian life: *British Birds* (1895), *Birds in London* (1898), and *Birds and Man* (1901). During the same period he initiated a lifelong campaign for wildlife preservation, attacking not only those who fed the fashion for feathered clothing, but also the overzealous amateur collectors and the sportsmen who killed indiscriminately. His work helped establish the Society for the Protection of Birds, which won Royal support and eventually stimulated significant legislation, the *Protection of Birds* acts.

In 1900 an annual civil list pension somewhat alleviated his perennial impoverishment. That same year he published *Nature in Downland,* in which he began to analyze the value of a whole region for the appreciative observer. *Hampshire Days* (1903), *The Land's End* (1908), *Afoot in England* (1909) (about Salisbury Plain) followed, drawing from Hudson's experience on the walking tours he and his wife took whenever they could save a few shillings. Increasingly, Hudson's interest focused on the relations between humans and their environment: *A Shepherd's Life* (1910) is considered a classic in this regard.

Hudson also wrote fiction, the best of it adventures set in South America. *Green Mansion (1904),* which won distinction for its author, serves as prototype for the nature fantasy. Deep in the Venezuelan jungle, its young protagonist falls in love with a delicate girl, Rima, who can literally talk with birds.

But the essays harbor Hudson's best writing. His deceptively simple style has been praised for its rhythm, clarity, and above all its power to engage the reader's participation at a personal level. Some of his finest prose may be found in *Far Away and Long Ago* (1918), an autobiography begun in a sickbed at age seventy-five, which narrates his boyhood on the spacious pampas and recreates his development as a naturalist "in the old, original sense of the work, one who is mainly concerned with the 'life and conversations of animals.' "

from IDLE DAYS IN PATAGONIA*

SOLITUDE IN THE WILDERNESS

I spent the greater part of one winter at a point on the Rio Negro, seventy or eighty miles from the sea, where the valley on my side of the water was about five miles wide. The valley alone was habitable, where there was water for man and beast, and a thin soil producing grass and grain; it is perfectly level, and ends abruptly at the foot of the bank or terrace-like formation of the higher barren plateau. It was my custom to go out every morning on horseback with my gun, and, followed by one dog, to ride away from the valley; and no sooner would I climb the terrace and plunge into the grey universal thicket, than I would find myself as completely alone and cut off from all sight and sound of human occupacy as if five hundred instead of only five miles separated me from the hidden green valley and river. So wild and solitary and remote seemed that grey waste, stretching away into infinitude, a waste untrodden by man, and where the wild animals are so few that they have made no discoverable path in the wilderness of thorns. There I might have dropped down and died, and my flesh been devoured by birds, and my bones bleached white in sun and wind, and no person would have found them, and it would have been forgotten that one had ridden forth in the morning and had not returned. Or if, like the few wild animals there—puma, huanaco, and hare-like *Dolichotis,* or Darwin's rhea and the crested tinamou among the birds—I had been able to exist without water, I might have made myself a hermitage of brushwood or dug-out in the side of a cliff, and dwelt there until I had grown grey as the stones and trees around me, and no human foot would have stumbled on my hiding-place.

Not once, nor twice, nor thrice, but day after day I returned to this solitude, going to it in the morning as if to attend a festival, and leaving it only when hunger and thirst and the westering sun compelled me. And yet I had no object in going—no motive which could be put into words; for although I carried a gun, there was nothing to shoot—the shooting was all left behind in the valley. Sometimes a *Dolichotis,* starting up at my approach, flashed for one moment on my sight, to vanish the next moment in the continuous thicket; or a covey of tinamous sprang rocket-like into the air, and fled away with long wailing notes and loud whur of wings; or on some distant hill-side a bright patch of yellow, of a deer that was watching me, appeared and remained motionless for two or thee minutes. But the animals were few, and sometimes I would pass an entire day without seeing one mammal, and perhaps not more than a dozen birds of any size. The weather at that time was cheerless, generally with a grey film of cloud spread over the sky, and a bleak wind, often cold enough to make my bridle hand feel quite numb. Moreover, it was not possible to enjoy a canter; the bushes grew so close together that it was as much as one could do to pass through at a walk without brushing against them; and at this slow pace,

*From *Idle Days in Patagonia* (London: J. M. Dent & Sons, 1893).

which would have seemed intolerable in other circumstances, I would ride about for hours at a stretch. In the scene itself there was nothing to delight the eye. Everywhere through the light, grey mould, grey as ashes and formed by the ashes of myriads of generations of dead trees, where the wind had blown on it, or the rain had washed it away, the underlying yellow sand appeared, and the old ocean-polished pebbles, dull red, and grey, and green, and yellow. On arriving at a hill, I would slowly ride to its summit, and stand there to survey the prospect. On every side it stretched away in great undulations; but the undulations were wild and irregular; the hills were rounded and cone-shaped, they were solitary and in groups and ranges; some sloped gently, others were ridge-like and stretched away in league-long terraces, with other terraces beyond; and all alike were clothed in the grey everlasting thorny vegetation. How grey it all was! hardly less so near at hand than on the haze-wrapped horizon, where the hills were dim and the outline blurred by distance. Sometimes I would see the large eagle-like, white-breasted buzzard, *Buteo erythronotus,* perched on the summit of a bush half a mile away; and so long as it would continue stationed motionless before me my eyes would remain involuntarily fixed on it, just as one keeps his eyes on a bright light shining in the gloom; for the whiteness of this hawk seemed to exercise a fascinating power on the vision, so surpassingly bright was it by contrast in the midst of that universal unrelieved greyness. Descending from my look-out, I would take up my aimless wanderings again, and visit other elevations to gaze on the same landscape from another point; and so on for hours, and at noon I would dismount and sit or lie on my folded poncho for an hour or longer. One day, in these rambles, I discovered a small grove composed of twenty to thirty trees, about eighteen feet high and taller than the surrounding trees. They were growing at a convenient distance apart, and had evidently been resorted to by a herd of deer or other wild animals for a very long time, for the boles were polished to a glassy smoothness with much rubbing, and the ground beneath was trodden to a floor of clean, loose yellow sand. This grove was on a hill differing in shape from other hills in its neighbourhood, so that it was easy for me to find it on other occasions; and after a time I made a point of finding and using it as a resting-place every day at noon. I did not ask myself why I made choice of that one spot, sometimes going miles out of my way to sit there, instead of sitting down under any one of the millions of trees and bushes covering the country, on any other hillside. I thought nothing at all about it, but acted unconsciously; only afterwards, when revolving the subject, it seemed to me that after having rested there once, each time I wished to rest again the wish came associated with the image of that particular clump of trees, with polished stems and clean bed of sand beneath; and in a short time I formed a habit of returning, animal-like, to repose at that same spot.

It was perhaps a mistake to say that I would sit down and rest, since I was never tired: and yet without being tired, that noonday pause, during which I sat for an hour without moving, was strangely grateful. All day the silence seemed grateful, it was very perfect, very profound. There were no insects, and the only bird sound—a feeble chirp of alarm emitted by a small skulking wren-like species—was not heard oftener than two or three times an hour. The only sounds as I rode were the muffled hoof-strokes of my horse, scratching of twigs against my boot or saddle-flap, and the low panting of the dog. And it seemed to be a relief to escape even from these sounds when I dismounted and sat down: for in a few moments the dog would stretch his head out on his paws and go to sleep, and there would be no sound, not even the rustle of a leaf. For unless the wind blows strong there is no fluttering motion and no whisper in the small stiff undeciduous leaves; and the bushes stand unmoving as if carved out of stone. One day while *listening* to the silence, it occurred to my mind to wonder what the effect would be if I were to shout aloud. This seemed at the time a horrible suggestion of fancy, a "lawless and uncertain thought" which almost made me shudder, and I was anxious to dismiss it quickly from my mind. But during those solitary days it was a rare thing for any thought to cross my mind; animal forms did not cross my vision or bird-voices assail my hearing more rarely. In that novel state of mind I was in, thought had become impossible. Elsewhere I had always been able to think most freely on horseback; and on the pampas, even in the most lonely places, my mind was always most active when I travelled at a swinging gallop. This was doubtless habit; but now, with a horse under me, I had become incapable of reflection: my mind had suddenly transformed itself from a thinking machine into a machine for some other unknown purpose. To think was like setting in motion a noisy engine in my brain; and there was something there which bade me be still, and I was forced to obey. My state was one of *suspense* and *watchfulness;* yet I had no expectation of meeting with an adventure, and felt as free from apprehension as I feel now when sitting in a room in London. The change in me was just as great and wonderful as if I had changed my identity for that of another man or animal; but at the time I was powerless to wonder at or speculate about it; the state seemed familiar rather than strange, and although accompanied by a strong feeling of elation, I did not know it—did not know that something had come between me and my intellect—until I lost it and returned to my former self—to thinking, and the old insipid existence.

from THE BOOK OF A NATURALIST

THE TOAD AS TRAVELLER

One summer day I sat myself down on the rail of a small wooden foot-bridge—a very old bridge it looked, bleached to a pale grey colour with grey, green, and yellow lichen growing on it, and very creaky with age, but the rail was still strong enough to support my weight. The bridge was at the hedgeside, and the stream under it flowed out of a thick wood over the road and into a marshy meadow on the other side, overgrown with coarse tussocky grass. It was a relief to be in that open sunny spot, with the sight of water and green grass and blue sky before me, after prowling for hours in the wood—a remnant of the old Silchester forest—worried by wood-flies in the dense undergrowth. These same wood-flies and some screaming jays were all the wild creatures I had seen, and I would now perhaps see something better at that spot.

It was very still, and for some time I saw nothing, until my wandering vision lighted on a toad travelling towards the water. He was right out in the middle of the road, a most dangerous place for him, and also difficult to travel in, seeing that it had a rough surface full of loosened stones, and was very dusty. His progress was very slow; he did not hop, but crawled laboriously for about five inches, then sat up and rested four or five minutes, then crawled and rested again. When I first caught sight of him he was about forty yards from the water, and looking at him through my binocular when he sat up and rested I could see the pulsing movements of his throat as though he panted with fatigue, and the yellow eyes on the summit of his head gazing at that delicious coolness where he wished to be. If toads can see things forty yards away the stream was visible to him, as he was on that part of the road which sloped down to the stream.

Lucky for you, old toad, thought I, that it is not market day at Basingstoke or somewhere with farmers and small general dealers flying about the country in their traps, or you would be flattened by a hoof or a wheel long before the end of your pilgrimage.

By and by another creature appeared and caused me to forget the toad. A young watervole came up stream, swimming briskly from the swampy meadow on the other side of the road. As he approached I tapped the wood with my stick to make him turn back, but this only made him swim faster towards me, and determined to have my own way I jumped down and tried to stop him, but he dived past the stick and got away where he wanted to be in the wood, and I resumed my seat.

There was the toad, when I looked his way, just about where I had last seen him, within perhaps a few inches. Then a turtle-dove flew down, alighting within a yard of the water, and after eyeing me suspiciously for a few moments advanced and took one long drink and flew away. A few minutes later I heard a faint complaining and whining sound in or close to the hedge on my left hand, and turning my eyes in that direction caught sight of a stoat, his head and neck visible, peeping at me out of the wood; he was intending to cross the road, and seeing me sitting there hesitated to do so. Still having come that far he would not turn back, and by and by he drew himself snake-like out of the concealing herbage, and was just about to make a dash across the road when I tapped sharply on the wood with my stick and he fled back into cover. In a few seconds he appeared again, and I played the same trick on him with the same result; this was repeated about four times, after which he plucked up courage enough to make his dash and was quickly lost in the coarse grass by the stream on the other side.

Then a curious thing happened: flop, flop, flop, went vole following vole, escaping madly from their hiding-places along the bank into the water, all swimming for dear life to the other side of the stream. Their deadly enemy did not swim after them, and in a few seconds all was peace and quiet again.

And when I looked at the road once more, the toad was still there, still travelling, painfully crawling a few inches, then sitting up and gazing with his yellow eyes over the forty yards of that weary *via dolorosa* which still had to be got over before he could bathe and make himself young forever in that river of life. Then all at once the feared and terrific thing came upon him: a farmer's trap, drawn by a fast trotting horse, suddenly appeared at the bend of the road and came flying down the slope. That's the end of you, old toad, said I, as the horse and trap came over him; but when I had seen them cross the ford and vanish from sight at the next bend, my eyes went back, and to my amazement there sat my toad, his throat still pulsing, his prominent eyes still gazing forward. The four dread hoofs and two shining wheels had all missed him; then at long last I took pity on him, although vexed at having to play providence to a toad, and getting off the rail I went and picked him up, which made him very angry. But when I put him in the water he expanded and floated for a few moments with legs spread out, then slowly sank his body and remained with just the top of his head and the open eyes above the surface for a little while, and finally settled down into the cooler depths below.

It is strange to think that when water would appear to be so much to these water-born and amphibious creatures they yet seek it for so short a period in each year, and for the rest of the time are practically without it! The toad comes to it in the love season, and at that time one is often astonished at the number of toads seen gathered in some solitary pool, where perhaps not a toad has been seen for months past, and with no other water for miles around. The fact is, the solitary pool has drawn to itself the entire toad population of the surrounding country, which may comprise an area of several square miles. Each toad has his own home or hermitage somewhere in that area, where he spends the greater portion of the summer season practically without water excepting in wet weather, hiding by day in moist and shady places, and issuing forth in the evening. And there too he hibernates in winter. When spring returns he sets out on his annual pilgrimage of a mile or two or even a greater distance, travelling in the slow, deliberate manner of the one described, crawling and resting until he arrives at the sacred pool—his Tipperary. They arrive singly and are in hundreds, a gathering of hermits from the desert places, drunk with excitement, and filling the place with noise and commotion. A strange sound, when at intervals the leader or precentor or bandmaster for the moment blows himself out into a wind instrument—a fairy bassoon, let us say, with a tremble to it—and no sooner does he begin than a hundred more join in; and the sound, which the scientific books describe as "croaking," floats far and wide, and produces a beautiful, mysterious effect on a still evening when the last heavy-footed labourer has trudged home to his tea, leaving the world to darkness and to me.

In England we are almost as rich in toads as in serpents, since there are two species, the common toad, universally distributed, and the rarer natterjack, abundant only in the south of Surrey. The breeding habits are the same in both species, the concert-singing included, but there is a difference in the *timbre* of their voices, the sound produced by the natterjack being more resonant and musical to most ears than that of the common toad.

The music and revels over, the toads vanish, each one taking his own road, long and hard to travel, to his own solitary home. Their homing instinct, like that of many fishes and of certain serpents that hibernate in numbers together, and of migrating birds, is practically infallible. They will not go astray, and the hungriest raptorial beasts, foxes, stoats, and cats, for example, decline to poison themselves by killing and devouring them.

In the late spring or early summer one occasionally encounters a traveller on his way back to his hermitage. I met one a mile or so from the valley of the Wylie, half-way up a high down, with his face to the summit of Salisbury Plain. He was on the bank at the side of a deep narrow path, and was resting on the velvety green turf, gay with little flowers of the chalk-hills—eye-bright, squinancy-wort, daisies, and milkwort, both white and blue.

The toad, as a rule, strikes one as rather an ugly creature, but this one sitting on the green turf, with those variously coloured fairy flowers all about him, looked almost beautiful. He was very dark, almost black, and with his shining topaz eyes had something of the appearance of a yellow-eyed black cat. I sat down by his side and picked him up, which action he appeared to regard as an unwarrantable liberty on my part; but when I placed him on my knee and began stroking his blackish corrugated back with my finger-tips his anger vanished, and one could almost imagine his golden eyes and wide lipless mouth smiling with satisfaction.

A good many flies were moving about at that spot—a pretty fly whose name I do not know, a little bigger than a house-fly, all a shining blue, with head and large eyes a bright red. These flies kept lighting on my hand, and by and by I cautiously moved a hand until a fly on it was within tongue-distance of the toad, whereupon the red tongue flicked out like lightning and the fly vanished. Again the process was repeated, and altogether I put over half-a-dozen flies in his way, and they all vanished in the same manner, so quickly that the action eluded my sight. One moment and a blue and red-headed fly was on my hand sucking the moisture from the skin, and then, lo! he was gone, while the toad still sat there motionless on my knee like a toad carved out of a piece of black stone with two yellow gems for eyes.

After helping him to a dinner, I took him off my knee with a little trouble, as he squatted close down, desiring to stay where he was, and putting him back among the small flowers to get more flies for himself if he could, I went on my way.

THE HERON: A FEATHERED NOTABLE

The bird-watcher's life is an endless succession of surprises. Almost every day he appears fated to witness some habit, some action, which he had never seen or heard of before, and will perhaps never see again. Who but Waterton ever beheld herons hovering like gulls over the water, attracted by the fish swimming near the surface? And who, I wonder, except myself ever saw herons bathing and wallowing after the manner of beasts, not birds? At all events I do not remember any notice of such a habit in any account of the heron I have read; and I have read many. At noon, one hot summer day, I visited Sowley Pond, which has a heronry near it on the Hampshire coast; and peeping through the trees on the bank I spied five herons about twenty yards from the margin bathing in a curious way among the floating poa grass, where the water was about two feet deep or more. All were quietly resting in different positions in the water—one was sitting on his knees with head and neck and shoulders out of it, another was lying on one side with one half-open wing above the surface, a third had only head and neck out, the whole body being submerged; and it puzzled me to think how he could keep himself down unless it was by grasping the roots of the grass with his claws. Occasionally one of the bathers would shift his position, coming partly up or going lower down, or turning over on the other side; but there was no flutter or bird-like excitement. They rested long in one position, and moved in a leisurely, deliberate manner, lying and luxuriating in the tepid water like pigs, buffaloes, hippopotamuses, and other water-loving mammalians. I watched them for an hour or so, and when I left, two were still lying down in the water. The other three had finished their bath, and were standing drying their plumage in the hot sun.

This was not the first surprise the heron had given me, but the first was received far from this land in my early shooting and collecting days, and the species was not our well-known historical bird, the *Ardea cinerea* of Britain and Europe generally, and Asia and Africa, but the larger *Ardea cocoi* of South America, a bird with a bigger wing-spread, but so like it in colour and action that any person from England on first seeing it would take it for a very large specimen of his familiar home bird.

It happened that I was making a collection of the birds of my part of the country and was in want of a specimen of our common heron. A few of these birds haunted the river near my home, and one day when out with the gun I caught sight of one fishing in the river. It was deep there, and the bird was standing under and close to the bank, where the water came up to his feathered thighs. Moving back from the bank I got within shooting distance and then had a look at him and saw that he was very intently watching the water, with head drawn back and apparently about to strike. And just as I pulled the trigger he struck, and stricken himself at the same moment he threw himself up into the air and rose to a height of about thirty feet, then fell back to earth close to the margin and began beating with his wings. When I came up he was at his last gasp, and what was my astonishment to find a big fish impaled by his beak. It was an uneatable fish, of a peculiar South American family, its upper part cased in bony plates; an ugly and curious-looking creature called *Vieja* ("old woman") by the natives. It was a common fish in our stream and a nuisance when caught, as it invariably sucked the hook into its belly. Now I had often found dead "old women" lying on or near the bank with a hole in their bony back and wondered at it. I had concluded that some of the native boys in our neighbourhood had taken to spearing the fish, and naturally these useless ones they killed were thrown away. Now I knew that they were killed by the heron with a blow of his powerful beak; a serious mistake on the bird's part, but an inevitable one in the circumstances, since even the shining, piercing eyes of a heron would only be able to *surmise* the presence of a fish a few inches below the surface in the muddy streams of the pampas. To distinguish the species would never be possible.

In this case the iron-hard dagger-like beak had been driven right through the fish from the bone-plated back to the belly, from which it projected about an inch and a half. With such power had the blow been delivered that it was only by exerting a good deal of force that I was able to wrench the beak out. My conclusion was that the bird would never have been able to free himself, and that by shooting him I had only saved him from the torture of a lingering death from starvation. The strange thing was that bird and fish had met their end simultaneously in that way: I doubted that such a thing had ever happened before or would ever happen again. From that time I began to pay a good deal of attention to the dead "old women" I found along the river-bank with a hole in their back, and could never find one in which the beak had been driven right through the body. In every case the beak had gone in about half-way through— just far enough to enable the bird to fly to the shore with its inconvenient captive and there get rid of it.

Death by accident is common enough in wild life, and a good proportion of such deaths are due to an error of judgement, often so slight as not to seem an error at all. For example, a hawking swallow may capture and try to bolt a wasp or other dangerous insect without first killing or crusing it, and in doing so receive a fatal sting in the throat. The flight of hawking swallows and swifts is so rapid that it hardly gives them time to judge of the precise nature of the insect appearing before them which a second's delay would lose. This is seen in swallows and swifts so frequently getting hooked by dry-fly anglers. Birds of prey, too, occasionally meet their death in a similar way, as when a kite or falcon or buzzard or eagle lifts a stoat or weasel, and the lithe little creature succeeds in wriggling up and fixing its teeth in the bird's flesh. If they fall from a considerable height both are killed. Again, birds sometimes get killed by attempting to swallow too big a morsel, and I think this is oftenest the case with birds that have rather weak beaks and have developed a rapacious habit. I remember once seeing a Guira cuckoo with head hanging and wings drooping, struggling in vain to swallow a mouse stuck fast in its gullet, the tail still hanging from its beak. Undoubtedly the first perished, as I failed in my attempts to capture it and save its life by pulling the mouse out. A common tryant-bird of South America, Pitangus, preys on mice, small snakes, lizards and frogs, as well as on large insects, but invariably hammers its prey on a branch until it is bruised to a pulp and broken up. It will work at a mouse in this way until the skin is so bruised that it can be torn open with its long, weak bill, but it never attempts to bolt it whole as the cuckoo does.

One day when sitting on the bank of Beaulieu River in Hampshire I saw a cormorant come up with a good-sized eel it had captured and was holding by the neck close to the head, but the long body of the eel had wound itself serpent-wise about the bird's long neck, and the cormorant was struggling furiously to free itself. Unable to do so it dived, thinking perhaps to succeed better under water, but when it reappeared on the surface the folds of the eel appeared to have tightened and the bird's struggles were weaker. Again it dived, and then again three or four times, still keeping its hold on the eel, but struggling more feebly each time. Finally it came up without the eel and so saved itself, since if it had kept its hold a little longer it would have been drowned.

In my *Land's End* book I have given an account of a duel between a seal and a huge conger-eel it had captured by the middle of the body, the conger-eel having fastened its teeth in the seal's head.

An odd way in which birds occasionally kill themselves is by getting a foot caught in long horse-hair or thread used in building. I have seen sparrows and house-martins dead, suspended from the nest by a hair or thread under the nest in this way.

When I killed my heron, and by doing so probably saved it from a lingering death by starvation, it struck me as an odd coincidence that it was within a stone's throw of the spot where a few weeks before I had saved another bird from a like fate—not in this instance by shooting it. The bird was the painted snipe, *Rhynchaea semicollaris,* a prettily coloured and mottled species with a green curved beak, and I found it on the low grassy margin of the stream with the point of its middle toe caught in one of Nature's traps for the unwary—the closed shell of a large fresh-water clam. The stream at this spot was almost entirely overgrown with dense beds of bulrushes, and the clams were here so abundant that the bottom of the stream was covered with them. The snipe wading into the water a foot or so from the margin had set its middle toe inside a partially open shell, which had instantly closed and caught it. Only by severing the point off could the bird have delivered itself, but its soft beak was useless for such a purpose. It had succeeded in dragging the clam out, and on my approach it first tried to hide itself by crouching in the grass, and then struggled to drag itself away. It was, when I picked it up, a mere bundle of feathers and had probably been lying thus captive for three or four days in constant danger of being spied by a passing carrion-hawk and killed and eaten. But when I released the toe it managed to flutter up and go away to a distance of thirty or forty yards before it dropped down among the aquatic grasses and sedges on a marshy islet in the stream.

A large heronry is to the naturalist one of the most fascinating spectacles in the wild bird life of this country. Heaven be thanked that all our landowners are not like those of South Devon, who are anxious to extirpate the heron in that district in the interest of the angler. On account of their action one is inclined to look on the whole fraternity of dry-fly fishers as a detestable lot of Philistines. Some years ago they raised a howl about the swallows—their worst enemies, that devoured all the mayflies, so that the trout were starved! Well, they can rejoice now to know that swallow and martin return to England in ever-decreasing numbers each summer, and they must be grateful to our neighbours across the Channel who are exterminating these noxious birds on migration.

I have known and know many heronries all over England, and I think the one I liked to visit best of all was in a small wood in a flat green country in the Norfolk Broads district. It was large, containing about seventy inhabited nests—huge nests, many of them and near together, so that it looked like a rookery made by giant rooks. And it has had a troubled history, like that of an old Norfolk town in the far past when Saxons and Danes were at variance. For this heronry had been established alongside of an old populous rookery, and the rooks hated the herons and mobbed them and demolished their nests, and persecuted them in every rookish way; but they refused to quit, and at length the rooks, unable to tolerate them, shifted their rookery a little farther away, and there was an uncomfortable sort of truce between the big black hostile birds and their grey ghostly neighbours with very long, sharp, and very unghostly beaks.

On the occasion of my last visit this heronry was in the most interesting stage, when the young birds were fully grown and were to be seen standing up on their big nests or on the topmost branches of the trees waiting to be fed. At some spots in the wood where the trees stand well apart I could count as many as forty to fifty young birds standing in this way in families of two, three, and four. It was a fine sight, and the noise they made at intervals was a fine thing to hear. The heron is a bird with a big voice. When nest-building is going on, and in fact until most of the eggs are laid, herons are noisy birds, and the sounds they emit are most curious—the loud familiar squalk or "frank," which resembles the hard, powerful alarm-note of the peacock, but is more harsh, while other grinding metallic cries remind one of the carrion-crow. Other of their loud sounds are distinctly mammalian in character; there is a dog-like sound, partly bark and partly yelp, swine-like grunting, and other sounds which recall the peculiar, unhappy, desolate cries of the large felines, especially of the puma. One need not take it for granted that these strange vocal noises are nothing but love calls. They may be in part expressions of anger, since it is hardly to be believed that the members of these rude communities invariable respect one another's rights. We see how it is with the rook, which has a more developed social instince than the lonely savage heron.

During incubation quiet reigns in the heronry; when the young are out, especially when they are well grown and ravenously hungry all day long, the wood is again filled with the uproar; and a noisier heronry than the one I am describing could not have been found. For one thing, it was situated on the very edge of the wood, overlooking the green flat expanse towards Breydon Water, where the parent birds did most of their fishing, so that the returning birds were visible from the tree-tops at a great distance, travelling slowly with eel and frog and fish-laden gullets on their wide-spread blue wings—dark blue against the high shining blue of the sky. All the young birds, stretched up to their full height, would watch its approach, and each and every one of them would regard the returning bird as its own too-long absent parent with food to appease its own furious hunger; and as it came sweeping over the colony there would be a tremendous storm of wild expectant cries—strange cat- and dog-like growling, barking, yelping, whining, screaming; and this would last until the newcomer would drop upon its own tree and nest and feed its own young, whereupon the tempest would slowly subside, only to be renewed on the appearance of the next great blue bird coming down over the wood.

One of the most delightful, the most exhilarating spectacles of wild bird life is that of the soaring heron. The great blue bird, with great round wings so measured in their beats, yet so buoyant in the vast void air! It is indeed a sight which moves all men to admiration in all countries which the great bird inhabits; and I remember one of the finest passages in old Spanish poetry describes the heron rejoicing in its placid flight. "Have you seen it, beautiful in the heavens!" the poet exclaims in untranslatable lines, in which the harmonious words, *delicado y sonoroso,* and the peculiar rhythm are made to mimic the slow pulsation of the large wings. Who has not seen it and experienced something of the feeling which stirred the old writer centuries ago:

> Has visto hermosa en el cielo
> La gárza sonreárse con plácido vuélo?
> Has visto, torciendo de la mano,
> Sacra que la deribe por el suelo?

The most perfect example I know of in literature in which the sound is an echo to the sense. How artificial and paltry that ornament often seems to us in our poets, even in much-admired passages, such as Goldsmith's white-washed walls and nicely-sanded floor, and the varnished clock that clicked behind the door. The beauty of the passage quoted—the heavenward sublime flight of the heron and the furious zigzag pursuit of the falcon, who will presently overtake and hurl it back to earth—is in its perfect naturalness, its spontaneity, as if some one in delight at the spectacle had exclaimed the words.

This is one of the sights in bird life which makes me envy the sportsmen of the old time when falconry was followed and the peregrine was flown, not at skulking magpies, as the way is with our Hawking Club, but at noble heron. They saw the great bird at its best, when it mounts with powerful wing-beats almost vertically to a vast height in the sky. The heron, in their days, when all the hawks have been extirpated by our Philistine pheasant-breeders who own the country, has no need to exercise that instinct and faculty.

The question has sometimes come into my mind, Why does the heron at all times, when, seen on the wind, it strikes us as beautiful, and when only strange or quaint-looking, or actually ugly, produce in some of us a feeling akin to melancholy? We speak of it as a grey, a ghost-like bird; and grey it certainly is, a haunter of lonely waters at the dim twilight hour; mysterious in its comings and goings. Ghostly, too, it is in another sense, and here we may see that the feeling, the sense of melancholy is due to association, to the fact that the heron is a historical bird, part of the country's past, when it was more to the country gentleman than the semi-domestic pheasant and the partridge on the arable land and the blackcock and red-grouse on the moors all together to the man of to-day. The memory of that vanished time, the thought that the ruder life of the past, when men lived nearer to Nature, had a keener flavour, is accompanied with a haunting regret. It is true that the regret is for something we have not known, that we have only heard or read of it, but it has become mixed in our mind with out very own experience past—our glad beautiful "days that are no more." And when we remember that in those distant days the heron was a table-bird, we may well believe that men were healthier and had better appetites than now—that they were all and always young.

from FAR AWAY AND LONG AGO

A SERPENT MYSTERY

It was not until after the episode related in the last chapter and the discovery that a serpent was not necessarily dangerous to human beings, therefore a creature to be destroyed at sight and pounded to a pulp lest it should survive and escape before sunset, that I began to appreciate its unique beauty and singularity. Then, somewhat later, I met with an adventure which produced another and a new feeling in me, that sense of something supernatural in the serpent which appears to have been universal among peoples in a primitive state of culture and still survives in some barbarous or semi-barbarous countries, and in others, like Hindustan, which have inherited an ancient civilization.

The snakes I was familiar with as a boy up to this time were all of comparatively small size, the largest being the snake-with-a-cross, described in an early chapter. The biggest specimen I have ever found of this ophidian was under four feet in length; but the body is thick, as in all the pit vipers. Then, there was the green-and-black snake described in the last chapter, an inhabitant of the house, which seldom exceeded three feet; and another of the same genus, the most common snake in the country. One seldom took a walk or ride on the plain without seeing it. It was in size and shape like our common grass-snake, and was formerly classed by naturalists in the same genus, Coronella. It is quite beautiful, the pale greenish-grey body, mottled with black, being decorated with two parallel bright red lines extending from the neck to the tip of the fine-pointed tail. Of the others the most interesting was a still smaller snake, brightly coloured, the belly with alternate bands of crimson and bright blue. This snake was regarded by every one as exceedingly venomous and most dangerous on account of its irascible temper and habit of coming at you and hissing loudly, its head and neck raised, and striking at your legs. But this was all swagger on the snake's part: it was not venomous at all, and could do no more harm by biting than a young dove in its nest by puffing itself up and striking at an intrusive hand with its soft beak.

Then one day I came upon a snake quite unknown to me: I had never heard of the existance of such a snake in our parts, and I imagine its appearance would have strongly affected any one in any land, even in those abounding in big snakes. The spot, too, in our plantation, where I found it, served to make its singular appearance more impressive.

There existed at that time a small piece of waste ground about half an acre in extent, where there were no trees and where nothing planted by man would grow. It was at the far end of the plantation, adjoining the thicket of fennel and the big red willow tree on the edge of the moat described in another chapter. This ground had been ploughed and dug up again and again, and planted with trees and shrubs of various kinds which were supposed to grow on any soil, but they had always languished and died, and no wonder, since the soil was a hard white clay resembling china clay. But although trees refused to grow there it was always clothed in a vegetation of its own; all the hardiest weeds were there, and covered the entire barren area to the depth of a man's knees. These weeds had thin wiry stalks and small sickly leaves and flowers, and would die each summer long before their time. This barren piece of ground had a great attraction for me as a small boy, and I visited it daily and would roam about it among the miserable half-dead weeds with the sun-baked clay showing between the brown stalks, as if it delighted me as much as the alfalfa field, blue and fragrant in its flowering-time and swarming with butterflies.

One hot day in December I had been standing perfectly still for a few minutes among the dry weeds when a slight rustling sound came from near my feet, and glancing down I saw the head and neck of a large black serpent moving slowly past me. In a moment or two the flat head was lost to sight among the close-growing weeds, but the long body continued moving slowly by—so slowly that it hardly appeared to move, and as the creature must have been not less than six feet long and probably more, it took a very long time, while I stood thrilled with terror, not daring to make the slightest movement, gazing down upon it. Although so long it was not a thick snake, and as it moved on over the white ground it had the appearance of a coal-black current flowing past me—a current not of water or other liquid but of some such element as quicksilver moving on in a rope-like stream. At last it vanished, and turning I fled from the ground, thinking that never again would I venture into or near that frightfully dangerous spot in spite of its fascination.

Nevertheless I did venture. The image of that black mysterious serpent was always in my mind from the moment of waking in the morning until I fell asleep at night. Yet I never said a word about the snake to any one: it was my secret, and I knew it was a dangerous secret, but I did not want to be told not to visit that spot again. And I simply could not keep away from it; the desire to look again at that strange being was too strong. I began to visit the place again, day after day, and would hang about the borders of the barren weedy ground watching and listening, and still no black serpent appeared. Then one day I ventured, though in fear and trembling, to go right in among the weeds, and still finding nothing began to advance step by step until I was right in the middle of the weedy ground and stood there a long time, waiting and watching. All I wanted was just to see it once more, and I had made up my mind that immediately on its appearance, if it did appear, I would take to my heels. It was when standing in this central spot that once again that slight rustling sound, like that of a few days before, reached my straining sense and sent an icy chill down my back. And there, within six inches of my toes, appeared the black head and neck, followed by the long, seemingly endless body. I dared not move, since to have attempted flight might have been fatal. The weeds were thinnest here, and the black head and slow-moving black coil could be followed by the eye for a little distance. About a yard from me there was a hole in the ground about the circumference of a breakfast-cup at the top, and into this hole the serpent put his head and slowly, slowly drew himself in, while I stood waiting until the whole body to the tip of the tail had vanished and all danger was over.

I had seen my wonderful creature, my black serpent unlike any serpent in the land, and the excitement following the first thrill of terror was still on me, but I was conscious of an element of delight in it, and I would not now resolve not to visit the spot again. Still, I was in fear, and kept away three or four days. Thinking about the snake I formed the conclusion that the hole he had taken refuge in was his den, where he lived, that he was often out roaming about in search of prey, and could hear footsteps at a considerable distance, and that when I walked about at that spot my footsteps disturbed him and caused him to go straight to his hole to hide himself from a possible danger. It struck me that if I went to the middle of the ground and stationed myself near the hole, I would be sure to see him. It would indeed be difficult to see him any other way, since one could never know in which direction he had gone out to seek for food. But no, it was too dangerous: the serpent might come upon me unawares and would probably resent always finding a boy hanging about his den. Still, I could not endure to think I had seen the last of him, and day after day I continued to haunt the spot, and going a few yards into the little weedy wilderness would stand and peer, and at the slightest rustling sound of an insect or falling leaf would experience a thrill of fearful joy, and still the black majestical creature failed to appear.

One day in my eagerness and impatience I pushed my way through the crowded weeds right to the middle of the ground and gazed with a mixed delight and fear at the hole: would he find me there, as on a former occasion? Would he come? I held my breath, I strained my sight and hearing in vain, the hope and fear of his appearance gradually died out, and

I left the place bitterly disappointed and walked to a spot about fifty yards away, where mulberry trees grew on the slope of the mound inside the moat.

Looking up into the masses of big clustering leaves over my head I spied a bat hanging suspended from a twig. The bats, I must explain, in that part of the world, that illimitable plain where there were no caverns and old buildings and other dark places to hide in by day, are not so intolerant of the bright light as in other lands. They do not come forth until evening, but by day they are content to hitch themselves to the twig of a tree under a thick cluster of leaves and rest there until it is dark.

Gazing up at this bat suspended under a big green leaf, wrapped in his black and buff-coloured wings as in a mantle, I forgot my disappointment, forgot the serpent, and was so entirely taken up with the bat that I paid no attention to a sensation like a pressure or a dull pain on the instep of my right foot. Then the feeling of pressure increased and was very curious and was as if I had a heavy object like a crowbar lying across my foot, and at length I looked down at my feet, and to my amazement and horror spied the great black snake slowly drawing his long coil across my instep! I dared not move, but gazed down fascinated with the sight of that glistening black cylindrical body drawn so slowly over my foot. He had come out of the moat, which was riddled at the sides with rat-holes, and had most probably been there hunting for rats when my wandering footsteps disturbed him and sent him home to his den; and making straight for it, as his way was, he came to my foot, and instead of going round drew himself over it. After the first spasm of terror I knew I was perfectly safe, that he would not turn upon me so long as I remained quiescent, and would presently be gone from sight. And that was my last sight of him; in vain I watched and waited for him to appear on many subsequent days: but that last encounter had left in me a sense of a mysterious being, dangerous on occasion as when attacked or insulted, and able in some cases to inflict death with a sudden blow, but harmless and even friendly or beneficient towards those who regarded it with kindly and reverent feelings in place of hatred. It is in part the feeling of the Hindoo with regard to the cobra which inhabits his house and may one day accidently cause his death, but is not to be persecuted.

Possibly something of that feeling about serpents has survived in me; but in time, as my curiosity about all wild creatures grew, as I looked more on them with the naturalist's eyes, the mystery of the large black snake pressed for an answer. It seemed impossible to believe that any species of snake of large size and black as jet or anthracite coal in colour could exist in any inhabited country without being known, yet no person I interrogated on the subject had ever seen or heard of such an ophidian. The only conclusion appeared to be that this snake was the sole one of its kind in the land. Eventually I heard of the phenomenon of melanism in animals, less rare in snakes perhaps than in animals of other classes, and I was satisfied that the problem was partly solved. My serpent was a black individual of a species of some other colour. But it was not one of our common species—not one of those I knew. It was not a thick blunt-bodied serpent like our venomous pit-viper, our largest snake, and though in shape it conformed to our two common harmless species it was twice as big as the biggest specimens I had ever seen of them. Then I recalled that two years before my discovery of the black snake, our house had been visited by a large unknown snake which measured two or three inches over six feet and was similar in form to my black serpent. The colour of this strange and unwelcome visitor was a pale greenish grey, with numerous dull black mottlings and small spots. The story of its appearance is perhaps worth giving.

It happened that I had a baby sister who could just toddle about on two legs, having previously gone on all-fours. One midsummer day she was taken up and put on a rug in the shade of a tree, twenty-five yards from the sitting-room door, and left alone there to amuse herself with her dolls and toys. After half an hour or so she appeared at the door of the sitting-room where her mother was at work, and standing there with wide-open astonished eyes and moving her hand and arm as if to point to the place she came from, she uttered the mysterious word *kú-ku.* It is a wonderful word which the southern South American mother teaches her child from the moment it begins to toddle and is useful in a desert and sparsely inhabited country where biting, stinging, and other injurious creatures are common. For babies when they learn to crawl and to walk are eager to investigate and have no natural sense of danger. Take as an illustration the case of the gigantic hairy brown spider, which is excessively abundant in summer and has the habit of wandering about as if always seeking something—"something it cannot find, it knows not what"; and in these wanderings it comes in at the open door and rambles about the room. At the sight of such a creature the baby is snatched up with the cry of *kú-ku* and the intruder slain with a broom or other weapon and thrown out. *Kú-ku* means dangerous, and the terrified gestures and the expression of the nurse or mother when using the word sink into the infant mind, and when that sound or word is heard there is an instant response, as in the case of a warning note or cry uttered by a parent bird which causes the young to fly away or crouch down and hide.

The child's gestures and the word it used caused her mother to run to the spot where it had been left in the shade, and to her horror she saw there a huge serpent coiled up in the middle of the rug. Her cries brought my father on the scene, and seizing a big stick he promptly dispatched the snake.

The child, said everybody, had had a marvellous escape, and as she had never previously seen a snake and could not intuitively know it as dangerous, or *kú-ku,* it was conjectured that she had made some gesture or attempted to push the snake away when it came on to the rug, and that it had reared its head and struck viciously at her.

Recalling this incident I concluded that this unknown serpent, which had been killed because it wanted to share my baby sister's rug, and my black serpent were one and the same species—possibly they had been mates—and that they had strayed a distance away from their native place or else were the last survivors of a colony of their kind in our plantation. It was not until twelve or fourteen years later that I discovered that it was even as I had conjectured. At a distance of about forty miles from my home, or rather from the home of my boyhood where I no longer lived, I found a snake that was new to me, the *Philodryas scotti* of naturalists, a not uncommon Argentine snake, and recognized it as the same species as the one found coiled up on my little sister's rug and presumably as my mysterious black serpent. Some of the specimens which I measured exceeded six feet in length.

A BOY'S ANIMISM

These serpent memories, particularly the enduring image of that black serpent which when recalled restores most vividly the emotion experience at the time, serve to remind me of a subject not yet mentioned in my narrative: this is animism, or that sense of something in nature which to the enlightened or civilized man is not there, and in the civilized man's child if it be admitted that he has it at all, is but a faint survival of a phase of the primitive mind. And by animism I do not mean the theory of a soul in nature, but the tendency or impulse or instinct, in which all myth originates, to *animate* all things; the projection of ourselves into nature; the sense and apprehension of an intelligence like our own but more powerful in all visible things. It persists and lives in many of us, I imagine, more than we like to think, or more than we know, especially in those born and bred amidst rural surroundings, where there are hills and woods and rocks and streams and waterfalls, these being the conditions which are most favourable to it—the scenes which have "inherited association" for us, as Herbert Spencer has said. In large towns and all populous places, where nature has been tamed until it appears like a part of man's work, almost as artificial as the buildings he inhabits, it withers and dies so early in life that its faint intimations are soon forgotten and we come to believe that we have never experienced them. That such a feeling can survive in any man, or that there was ever a time since his infancy when he could have regarded this visible world as anything but what it actually is—the stage to which he has been summoned to play his brief but important part, with painted blue and green scenery for background—becomes incredible. Nevertheless, I know that in me, old as I am, this same primitive faculty which manifested itself in my early boyhood, still persists, and in those early years was so powerful that I am almost afraid to say how deeply I was moved by it.

. . .

And I can say of myself with regard to this primitive faculty and emotion—this sense of the supernatural in natural things, as I have called it—that I am on safe ground for the same reason; the feeling has never been wholly outlived. And I will add, probably to the disgust of some rigidly orthodox reader, that these are childish things which I have no desire to put away.

The first intimations of the feeling are beyond recall; I only know that my memory takes me back to a time when I was unconscious of any such element in nature, when the delight I experienced in all natural things was purely physical. I rejoiced in colours, scents, sounds, in taste and touch: the blue of the sky, the verdure of earth, the sparkle of sunlight on water, the taste of milk, of fruit, of honey, the smell of dry or moist soil, of wind and rain, of herbs and flowers; the mere feel of a blade of grass made me happy; and there were certain sounds and perfumes, and above all certain colours in flowers, and in the plumage and eggs of birds, such as the purple polished shell of the tinamou's egg, which intoxicated me with delight. When, riding on the plain, I discovered a patch of scarlet verbenas in full bloom, the creeping plants covering an area of several yards, with a moist, green sward sprinkled abundantly with the shining flower-bosses, I would throw myself from my pony with a cry of joy to lie on the turf among them and feast my sight on their brilliant colour.

It was not, I think, till my eighth year that I began to be distinctly conscious of something more than this mere childish delight in nature. It may have been there all the time from infancy—I don't know; but when I began to know it consciously it was as if some hand had surreptitiously dropped something into the honeyed cup which gave it at certain times a new flavour. It gave me little thrills, often purely pleasurable, at other times startling, and there were occasions when it became so poignant as to frighten me. The sight of a magnificent sunset was sometimes almost more than I could endure and made me wish to hide myself away. But when the feeling was roused by the sight of a small and beautiful or singular object, such as a flower, its sole effect was to intensify the object's loveliness. There were many flowers which produced this effect in but a slight degree, and as I grew up and the animistic sense lost its intensity, these too lost their magic and were almost like other flowers which had never had it. There were others which never lost what for want of a better word I have just called their magic, and of these I will give an account of one.

I was about nine years old, perhaps a month or two more, when during one of my rambles on horseback I found at a distance of two or three miles from home, a flower that was new to me. The plant, a little over a foot in height, was growing in the sheler of some large cardoon thistle, or wild artichoke, bushes. It had three stalks clothed with long, narrow, sharply-pointed leaves, which were downy, soft to the feel like the leaves of our great mullein, and pale green in colour. All three stems were crowned with clusters of flowers, the single flower a little larger than that of the red valerian, of a pale red hue and a peculiar shape, as each small pointed petal had a fold or twist at the end. Altogether it was slightly singular in appearance and pretty, though not to be compared with scores of other flowers of the plains for beauty. Nevertheless it had an extraordinary fascination for me, and from the moment of its discovery it became one of my sacred flowers. From that time onwards, when riding on the plain, I was always on the look-out for it, and as a rule I found three or four plants in a season, but never more than one at any spot. They were usually miles apart.

On first discovering it I took a spray to show to my mother, and was strangely disappointed that she admired it merely because it was a pretty flower, seen for the first time. I had actually hoped to hear from her some word which would have revealed to me why I thought so much of it: now it appeared as if it was no more to her than any other pretty flower and even less than some she was peculiarly fond of, such as the fragrant little lily called Virgin's Tears, the scented pure white and the rose-coloured verbenas, and several others. Strange that she who alone seemed always to know what was in my mind and who loved all beautiful things, especially flowers, should have failed to see what I had found in it!

Years later, when she had left us and when I had grown almost to manhood and we were living in another place, I found that we had as neighbour a Belgian gentleman who was a botanist. I could not find a specimen of my plant to show him, but gave him a minute description of it as an annual, with very large, tough, permanent roots, also that it exuded a thick milky juice when the stem was broken, and produced its yellow seeds in a long, cylindrical, sharply-pointed pod full of bright silvery down, and I gave him sketches of flower and leaf. He succeeded in finding it in his books: the species had been known upwards of thirty years, and the discoverer, who happened to be an Englishman, had sent seed and roots to the Botanical Societies abroad he corresponded with; the species had been named after him, and it was to be found now growing in some of the Botanical Gardens of Europe.

All this information was not enough to satisfy me; there was nothing about the man in his books. So I went to my father to ask him if he had ever known or heard of an Englishman of that name in the country. Yes, he said, he had known him well; he was a merchant in Buenos Ayres, a nicegentle-mannered man, a bachelor and something of a recluse in his private house, where he lived alone and spent all his week-ends and holidays roaming about the plains with his vasculum in search of rare plants. He had been long dead—oh, quite twenty or twenty-five years.

I was sorry that he was dead, and was haunted with a desire to find out his resting-place so as to plant the flower that bore his name on his grave. He, surely, when he discovered it, must have had that feeling which I had experienced when I first beheld it and could never describe. And perhaps the presence of those deep ever-living roots near his bones, and of the flower in the sunshine above him, would bring him a beautiful memory in a dream, if ever a dream visited him, in his long unawakening sleep.

No doubt in cases of this kind, when a first impression and the emotion accompanying it endures through life, the feeling changes somewhat with time; imagination has worked on it and has had its effect; nevertheless the endurance of the image and emotion serves to show how powerful the mind was moved in the first instance.

I have related this case because there were interesting circumstances connected with it; but there were other flowers which produced a similar feeling, which, when recalled, bring back the original emotion; and I would gladly travel many miles any day to look again at any one of them. The feeling, however, was evoked more powerfully by trees than by even the most supernatural of my flowers; it varied in power according to time and place and the appearance of the tree or trees, and always affected me most on moonlight nights. Frequently, after I had first begun to experience it consciously, I would go out of my way to meet it, and I used to steal out of the house alone when the moon was at its full to stand, silent and motionless, near some group of large trees, gazing at the dusky green foliage silvered by the beams; and at such times the sense of mystery would grow until a sensation of delight would change to fear, and the fear increase until it was no longer to be borne, and I would hastily escape to recover the sense of reality and safety indoors, where there was light and company. Yet on the very next night I would steal out again and go to the spot where the effect was strongest, which was usually among the large locust or white acacia trees, which gave the name of Las Acacias to our place. The loose feathery foliage of moonlight nights had a peculiar hoary aspect that made this tree seem more intensely alive than others, more conscious of my presence and watchful of me.

I never spoke of these feelings to others, not even to my mother, notwithstanding that she was always in perfect sympathy with me with regard to my love of nature. The reason of my silence was, I think, my powerlessness to convey in words what I felt; but I imagine it would be correct to describe the sensation experienced on those moonlight nights among the trees as similar to the feeling a person would have if visited by a supernatural being, if he was perfectly convinced that it was there in his presence, albeit silent and unseen, intently regarding him, and divining every thought in his mind. He would be thrilled to the marrow, but not terrified if he knew that it would take no visible shape nor speak to him out of the silence.

This faculty or instinct of the dawning mind is or has always seemed to me essentially religious in character; undoubtedly it is the root of all nature worship, from fetishism to the highest pantheistic development. It was more to me in those early days than all the religious teaching I received from my mother. Whatever she told me about our relations with the Supreme Being I believed implicitly, just as I believed everything else she told me, and as I believed that two and two make four and that the world is round in spite of its flat appearance; also that it is travelling through space and revolving round the sun instead of standing still, with the sun going round it, as one would imagine. But apart from the fact that the powers above would save me in the end from extinction, which was a great consolation, these teachings did not touch my heart as it was touched and thrilled by something nearer, more intimate, in nature, not only in moonlit trees or in a flower or serpent, but, in certain exquisite moments and moods and in certain aspects of nature, in "every grass" and in all things, animate and inanimate.

It is not my wish to create the impression that I am a peculiar person in this matter; on the contrary, it is my belief that the animistic instinct, if a mental faculty can be so called, exists and persists in many persons, and that I differ from others only in looking steadily at it and taking it for what it is, also in exhibiting it to the reader naked and without a fig-leaf expressed, to use a Baconian phrase. When the religious Cowper confesses in the opening lines of his address to the famous Yardley oak, that the sense of awe and reverence it inspired in him would have made him bow himself down and worship it but for the happy fact that his mind was illumined with the knowledge of the truth, he is but saying what many feel without in most cases recognizing the emotion for what it is—the sense of the supernatural in nature. And if they have grown up, as was the case with Cowper, with the image of an implacable anthropomorphic diety in their minds, a being who is ever jealously watching them to note which way their wandering thoughts are tending, they rigorously repress the instinctive feeling as a temptation of the evil one, or as a lawless thought born of their own inherent sinfulness. Nevertheless it is not uncommon to meet with instances of persons who appear able to reconcile their faith in revealed religion with their animistic emotion. I will give an instance. One of the most treasured memories of an old lady friend of mine, recently deceased, was of her visits, some sixty years or more ago, to a great country-house where she met many of the distinguished people of that time, and of her host, who was then old, the head of an ancient and distinguished family, and of his reverential feeling for this trees. His greatest pleasure was to sit out of doors of an evening in sight of the grand old trees in his park, and before going in he would walk round to visit them, one by one, and resting his hand on the bark he would whisper a good-night. He was convinced, he confided to his young guest, who often accompanied him in these evening walks, that they had intelligent souls and knew and encouraged his devotion.

There is nothing surprising to me in this; it is told here only because the one who cherished this feeling and belief was an orthodox Christian, a profoundly religious person; also because my informant herself, who was also deeply religious, loved the memory of this old friend of her early life mainly because of his feeling for trees, which she too cherished, believing, as she often told me, that trees and all living and growing things have souls. What has surprised me is that a form of a tree-worship is still found existing among a few of the inhabitants in some of the small rustic villages in out-of-the-world districts in England. Not such survivals as the apple tree folk-songs and ceremonies of the west, which have long become meaningless, but something living, which has a meaning for the mind, a survival such as our anthropologists go to the end of the earth to seek among barbarous and savage tribes.

The animism which persists in the adult in these scientific times has been so much acted on and changed by dry light that it is scarcely recognizable in what is somewhat loosely or vaguely called a "feeling for nature": it has become intertwined with the aesthetic feeling and may be traced in a good deal of our poetic literature, particularly from the time of the first appearance of *Lyrical Ballads,* which put an end to the eighteenth-century poetic convention and made the poet free to express what he really felt. But the feeling, whether expressed or not, was always there. Before the classic period we find in Traherne a poetry which was distinctly animistic, with

Christianity grafted on it. Wordsworth's pantheism is a subtilized animism, but there are moments when his feeling is like that of the child or savage when he is convinced that the flower enjoys the air it breathes.

. . . .

William Butler Yeats
1865-1939

As a literary personage, William Butler Yeats needs little introduction: most critics consider him the greatest poet of the twentieth century in the English language. He won the Nobel Prize for Literature in 1923.

The relation between nature and culture is a theme implicit in much of his superb poetic canon, which he began in his teens and continued into his seventies. Interested in both mysticism and politics—especially interested in the development of the individual—Yeats wrote plays and critical essays as well as poetry. A consummate craftsman, he continually revised, publishing his own definitive edition, *Collected Poems* (1933; 1951).

Born of Anglo-Irish parents in Dublin (his father was a landscape painter), Yeats spent his youth in London, Dublin and Sligo, his mother's home in the West of Ireland, where he encountered firsthand the Irish peasantry and their folk legends. Later, participation in the Irish National Theatre spurred his study of ancient Irish myth.

The selections presented below, suggesting the influence of the Romantic tradition on Yeats's early writing, showcase the poet's power to create exquisite images of fleeting natural beauty.

THE WILD SWANS AT COOLE*

The trees are in their autumn beauty,
The woodland paths are dry,
Under the October twilight the water
Mirrors a still sky;
Upon the brimming water among the stones
Are nine-and-fifty swans.

The nineteenth autumn has come upon me
Since I first made my count;
I saw, before I had well finished,
All suddenly mount
And scatter wheeling in great broken rings
Upon their clamorous wings.

I have looked upon those brilliant creatures,
And now my heart is sore.
All's changed since I, hearing at twilight,
The first time on this shore,
The bell-beat of their wings above my head,
Trod with a lighter tread.

Unwearied still, lover by lover,
They paddle in the cold
Companionable streams or climb the air;
Their hearts have not grown old;
Passion or conquest, wander where they will,
Attend upon them still.

But now they drift on the still water,
Mysterious, beautiful;
Among what rushes will they build,
By what lake's edge or pool
Delight men's eyes when I awake some day
To find they have flown away?

THE LAKE ISLE OF INNISFREE

I will arise and go now, and go to Innisfree,
And a small cabin build there, of clay and wattles made:
Nine bean-rows will I have there, a hive for the honey-bee,
And live alone in the bee-loud glade.

And I shall have some peace there, for peace comes dropping slow,
Dropping from the veils of the morning to where the cricket sings;
There midnight's all a glimmer, and noon a purple glow,
And evening full of the linnet's wings.

I will arise and go now, for always night and day
I hear lake water lapping with low sounds by the shore;
While I stand on the roadway, or on the pavements grey,
I hear it in the deep heart's core.

THE OLD MEN ADMIRING THEMSELVES IN THE WATER

I heard the old, old men say,
'Everything alters,
And one by one we drop away.'
They had hands like claws,and their knees
Were twisted like the old thorn-trees
By the waters.
I heard the old, old men say,
'All that's beautiful drifts away
Like the waters.'

Robert W. Service
1874-1958

Robert W. Service will be remembered as the poet of the Yukon, with its gold fever, frontier adventure, and its lonely, frozen landscapes. Arriving in Whitehorse in 1904, Service knew the gold rush only by report, some ten years after the flurry of thirty thousand prospectors had arrived on the Yukon basin. But Whitehorse was still a frontier town, and Service, like Jack London, was quick to appreciate a good story. He trained his own senses well upon the desolate beauty he witnessed as he snowshoed through the wilderness.

Service earned his living in the Yukon as a bank officer, a position he quickly resigned in 1908 after his first book of verse, *The Spell of the Yukon* (1907), became an immediate best seller. His respectable job with the Vancouver Bank of Commerce had begun only six years earlier. Before that his life was a series of bouts between free-spirited behavior and disastrous poverty. Raised in Glasgow, Scotland, Service was one of ten children in a family that scrimped along on a meager inheritance, looking "middle-class" on the outside, he later recalled, but feeling "proletarian" within. A natural athlete, he loved the Scottish countryside and worshipped Robert Burns. He worked as a clerk at the Commercial Bank of Scotland in order to save passage to Canada, where he intended, somewhat naively, to set up as a cattle rancher. His arrival in British Columbia with five dollars in his pocket, however, introduced him to the backbreaking life of a farm hand. "From the first," he later recalled, "I realized that I hated hard work." He spent the following winter holed up in a backwoods cabin and "energetically cultivated laziness." He dreamed of becoming a writer, and of paradise in southern California.

After another season of farming he wandered south, spiralling deeper into poverty and desolation over a period of six years. He worked occasionally as an orange picker, tunnel miner, and handyman, and he rode the rails, eventually eating at Salvation Army kitchens. His luck changed when he landed a job with the Bank of Commerce in Vancouver, from which he was transferred to a branch at Whitehorse. His adventures are recorded with wit and drama in *Ploughman of the Moon* (1945), written when he was seventy.

In a career that spanned half a century, Service published over a dozen slim volumes of verse and half a dozen novels on adventurous themes. The titles alone (e.g., *Rhymes of a Roughneck, Songs of a Sun-Lover, Carols of an Old Codger)* make interesting reading. Neither the titles nor contents were calculated to win critical acclaim. His lyrics are spirited and uncomplicated, influenced greatly by Rudyard Kipling. "Verse, not poetry," he noted, "is what I was after—something the man in the street would take notice of." And Service became a wealthy man because of the admiration of "the man in the street." As poet-critic Louis Untermeyer put it: "the red blood and guts style is carried off jauntily."

THE CALL OF THE WILD*

Have you gazed on naked grandeur where
there's nothing else to gaze on,
Set pieces and drop-curtain scenes galore,
Big mountains heaved to heaven, which the
blinding sunsets blazon,
Black canyons where the rapids rip and roar?
Have you swept the visioned valley with the
green stream streaking through it,
Searched the Vastness for a something you
have lost?
Have you strung your soul to silence? Then
for God's sake go and do it;
Hear the challenge, learn the lesson, pay the
cost.

Have you wandered in the wilderness, the sage-
brush desolation,
The bunch-grass levels where the cattle
graze?
Have you whistled bits of rag-time at the end
of all creation,
And learned to know the desert's little
ways?
Have you camped upon the foothills, have you
galloped o'er the ranges,
Have you roamed the arid sun-lands through
and through?
Have you chummed up with the mesa? Do
you know its moods and changes?
Then listen to the Wild—it's calling you.

*From *The Spell of the Yukon* (New York: Dodd, Mead & Co.).

Have you known the Great White Silence, not
a snow-gemmed twig aquiver?
(Eternal truths that shame our soothing
lies.)
Have you broken trail on snowshoes? mushed
your huskies up the river,
Dared the unknown, led the way, and
clutched the prize?
Have you marked the map's void spaces,
mingled with the mongrel races,
Felt the savage strength of brute in every
thew?
And though grim as hell the worst is, can you
round it off with curses?
Then hearken to the Wild—it's wanting
you.

Have you suffered, starved and triumphed,
groveled down, yet grasped at glory,
Grown bigger in the bigness of the whole?
"Done things" just for the doing, letting bab-
blers tell the story,
Seeing through the nice veneer the naked
soul?
Have you seen God in His splendors, heard the
text that nature renders?
(You'll never hear it in the family pew.)
The simple things, the true things, the silent
men who do things—
Then listen to the Wild—it's calling you.

They have cradled you in custom, they have
primed you with their preaching,
They have soaked you in convention through
and through;
They have put you in a showcase; you're a
credit to their teaching—
But can't you hear the Wild?—it's calling
you.
Let us probe the silent places, let us seek what
luck betide us;
Let us journey to a lonely land I know.
There's a whisper on the night-wind, there's
a star agleam to guide us,
And the Wild is calling, calling . . . let us
go.

THE SPELL OF THE YUKON

I wanted the gold, and I sought it;
  I scrabbled and mucked like a slave.
Was it famine or scurvy—I fought it;
  I hurled my youth into a grave.
I wanted the gold, and I got it—
  Came out with a fortune last fall,—
Yet somehow life's not what I thought it,
  And somehow the gold isn't all.

No! There's the land. (Have you seen it?)
  It's the cussedest land that I know,
From the big, dizzy mountains that screen it
  To the deep, deathlike valleys below.
Some say God was tired when He made it;
  Some say it's a fine land to shun;
Maybe; but there's some as would trade it
  For no land on earth—and I'm one.

You come to get rich (damned good reason);
  You feel like an exile at first;
You hate it like hell for a season,
  And then you are worse than the worst.
It grips you like some kinds of sinning;
  It twists you from foe to a friend;
It seems it's been since the beginning;
  It seems it will be to the end.

I've stood in some mighty-mouthed hollow
  That's plumb-full of hush to the brim;
I've watched the big, husky sun wallow
  In crimson and gold, and grow dim,
Till the moon set the pearly peaks gleaming,
  And the stars tumbled out, neck and crop;
And I've thought that I surely was dreaming,
  With the peace o' the world piled on top.

The summer—no sweeter was ever;
  The sunshiny woods all athrill;
The grayling aleap in the river,
  The bighorn asleep on the hill.
The strong life that never knows harness;
  The wilds where the caribou call;
The freshness, the freedom, the farness—
  O God! how I'm stuck on it all.

The winter! the brightness that blinds you,
  The white land locked tight as a drum,

The cold fear that follows and finds you,
  The silence that bludgeons you dumb.
The snows that are older than history,
  The woods where the weird shadows slant;
The stillness, the moonlight, the mystery,
  I've bade 'em good-by—but I can't.

There's a land where the mountains are name-
    less,
  And the rivers all run God knows where;
There are lives that are erring and aimless,
  And deaths that just hang by a hair;
There are hardships that nobody reckons;
  There are valleys unpeopled and still;
There's a land—oh, it beckons and beckons,
  And I want to go back—and I will.

They're making my money diminish;
  I'm sick of the taste of champagne.
Thank God! when I'm skinned to a finish
  I'll pike to the Yukon again.
I'll fight—and you bet it's no sham-fight;
  It's hell!—but I've been there before;
And it's better than this by a damsite—
  So me for the Yukon once more.

There's gold, and it's haunting and haunting;
  It's luring me on as of old;
Yet it isn't the gold that I'm wanting
  So much as just finding the gold.
It's the great, big, broad land 'way up yonder,
It's the forests where silence has lease;
It's the beauty that thrills me with wonder,
  It's the stillness that fills me with peace.

Edwin Muir
1887-1959

Edwin Muir's early life epitomizes the rural-urban dichotomy. He spent his boyhood on the family farm on the remote Orkney Islands off the coast of Scotland; when he was fourteen, his father gave up farming because of a weak heart and moved the family to Glasgow, where urban poverty so traumatized the boy that it remained a bitter memory to the end of his life. Later he recalled the change: "The migration of my family from a pre-industrial to an industrial society had a result which I believe to be typical: four of us, my father and mother and two brothers, died within two years." Muir himself earned his living in Glasgow as a clerk in a factory that processed bones.

As a consequence, Muir became involved in socialism, but literature proved a more lasting interest. In 1919 he married the novelist Willa Anderson and moved to London, where he began to make a living as a literary journalist. During the twenties the Muirs traveled through Europe, living for a time in Italy, Czechoslovakia, Germany, and Austria; later they became the translators of Franz Kafka.

The primitive environment of Muir's youth, along with the totalitarian societies he knew in Europe, gave his poetry a uniquely mature perspective. Only after age thirty-five did he begin composing in earnest; his *First Poems* was published in 1925. Even after that, he was known as a critic and translator—until he issued his *Collected Poems* in 1952. The selections that follow reveal his powerful insights into psychology and myth, especially "The Horses," which T. S. Eliot called "that great, that terrifying poem of the 'atomic age.' "

THE ANIMALS*

They do not live in the world,
Are not in time and space.
From birth to death hurled
No word do they have, not one
To plant a foot upon,
Were never in any place.

For with names the world was called
Out of the empty air,
With names was built and walled,
Line and circle and square,
Dust and emerald;
Snatched from deceiving death
By the articulate breath.

But these have never trod
Twice the familiar track,
Never never turned back
Into the memoried day.
All is new and near
In the unchanging Here
Of the fifth great day of God,
That shall remain the same,
Never shall pass away.

On the sixth day we came.

THE HORSES

Barely a twelvemonth after
The seven days war that put the world to sleep,
Late in the evening the strange horses came.
By then we had made our covenant with silence,
But in the first few days it was so still
We listened to our breathing and were afraid.
On the second day
The radios failed; we turned the knobs; no answer.
On the third day a warship passed us, heading north,
Dead bodies piled on the deck. On the sixth day
A plane plunged over us into the sea. Thereafter
Nothing. The radios dumb;
And still they stand in corners of our kitchens,
And stand, perhaps, turned on, in a million rooms
All over the world. But now if they should speak,

If on a sudden they should speak again,
If on the stroke of noon a voice should speak,
We would not listen, we would not let it bring
That old bad world that swallowed its children quick
At one great gulp. We would not have it again.
Sometimes we think of the nations lying asleep,
Curled blindly in impenetrable sorrow,
And then the thought confounds us with its strangeness.
The tractors lie about our fields; at evening
They look like dank sea-monsters couched and waiting.
We leave them where they are and let them rust:
'They'll moulder away and be like other loam'.
We make our oxen drag our rusty ploughs,
Long laid aside. We have gone back
Far past our fathers' land.
And then, that evening
Late in the summer the strange horses came.
We heard a distant tapping on the road,
A deepening drumming; it stopped, went on again
And at the corner changed to hollow thunder.
We saw the heads
Like a wild wave charging and were afraid.
We had sold our horses in our fathers' time
To buy new tractors. Now they were strange to us
As fabulous steeds set on an ancient shield
Or illustrations in a book of knights.
We did not dare go near them. Yet they waited,
Stubborn and shy, as if they had been sent
By an old command to find our whereabouts
And that long-lost archaic companionship.
In the first moment we had never a thought
That they were creatures to be owned and used.
Among them were some half-a-dozen colts
Dropped in some wilderness of the broken world,
Yet new as if they had come from their own Eden.
Since then they have pulled our ploughs and borne our loads.
But that free servitude still can pierce our hearts.
Our life is changed; their coming our beginning.

Dylan Thomas
1914-1953

Dylan Thomas was Welsh, born and raised in the seacoast town of Swansea, where his father was Senior English Master at the Swansea Grammar School. English, that is, poetry, was the only subject in which Thomas had much interest, and after graduation, instead of choosing a university, he wrote for newspapers for a year.

During his late teen years, Thomas was already composing and reworking a substantial body of poetry. Several of his poems won prizes in *The Sunday Referee's* contests. One prize-winner, "The Force That Through the Green Fuse Drives the Flower," is reprinted here. Its theme—the theme underlying Thomas's entire canon—proceeds from the insight that birth and procreation and death are all part of a single, continuous biological cycle: just as all living things begin to age and die at the moment they are born, so does death transform them into food for other living things. The eternal repetition of the biological cycle, with its implications of immortality, captured Thomas's imagination. He achieves a magical, perhaps mystical quality by describing the cycle literally: creatures are living and dying at the very same moment. The same "force" that "drives" or pushes up the new flowers destroys the roots of trees; it also empowers the passion of youth and the "wintry fever" of death.

The degree to which Thomas identifies human life with natural processes is continually startling, and the natural imagery of sea, farm, and sexuality can make for difficult reading since Thomas builds his poems from a wealth of evocative pictures. Because syntax is subordinate to imagery, it is best to read Thomas's work aloud or, better, to hear one of his own recordings. During the war he worked as a BBC broadcaster and possessed an enchanting delivery.

The readings Thomas gave on lecture tours in England and America brought him fame; his legendary behavior—drinking, story telling, and womanizing—earned him the reputation of a wild, primitive Welsh bard. The title of his autobiographical work, *Portrait of the Artist as a Young Dog* (1940), suggests the image Thomas projected. But his increasingly excessive appetite for alcohol ended in death during an American tour when he "went out for a drink" and returned bragging that he had consumed eighteen shots of whiskey. He entered a coma and died soon after.

Thomas's great theme of birth and death offers potential for both tragedy and comedy. In his later work, from which "Fern Hill" is drawn, the comic increasingly dominates his nostalgia for the happiness of childhood into which beautiful natural imagery is woven as part of a single fabric. Thomas's full range of poetry is captured in *The Collected Poems* (1953).

THE FORCE THAT THROUGH THE GREEN FUSE DRIVES THE FLOWER*

The force that through the green fuse drives the flower
Drives my green age; that blasts the roots of trees
Is my destroyer.
And I am dumb to tell the crooked rose
My youth is bent by the same wintry fever.

The force that drives the water through the rocks
Drives my red blood; that dries the mouthing streams
Turns mine to wax.
And I am dumb to mouth unto my veins
How at the mountain spring the same mouth sucks.

The hand that whirls the water in the pool
Stirs the quicksand; that ropes the blowing wind
Hauls my shroud sail.
And I am dumb to tell the hanging man
How of my clay is made the hangman's lime.

The lips of time leech to the fountain head;
Love drips and gathers, but the fallen blood
Shall calm her sores.
And I am dumb to tell a weather's wind
How time has ticked a heaven round the stars.

And I am dumb to tell the lover's tomb
How at my sheet goes the same crooked worm.

FERN HILL

Now as I was young and easy under the apple boughs
About the lilting house and happy as the grass was green,
The night above the dingle starry,
Time let me hail and climb
Golden in the heydays of his eyes,
And honoured among wagons I was prince of the apple towns
And once below a time I lordly had the trees and leaves
Trail with daisies and barley
Down the rivers of the windfall light.

And as I was green and carefree, famous among the barns
About the happy yard and singing as the farm was home,
In the sun that is young once only,
Time let me play and be
Golden in the mercy of his means,
And green and golden I was huntsman and herdsman, the calves
Sang to my horn, the foxes on the hills barked clear and cold,
And the sabbath rang slowly
In the pebbles of the holy streams.

All the sun long it was running, it was lovely, the hay
Fields high as the house, the tunes from the chimneys, it was air
And playing, lovely and watery
And fire green as grass.
And nightly under the simple stars
As I rode to sleep the owls were bearing the farm away,
All the moon long I heard, blessed among stables, the night-jars
Flying with the ricks, and the horses
Flashing into the dark.

And then to awake, and the farm, like a wanderer white
With the dew, come back, the cock on his shoulder: it was all
Shining, it was Adam and maiden,
The sky gathered again
And the sun grew round that very day.
So it must have been after the birth of the simple light
In the first, spinning place, the spellbound horses walking warm
Out of the whinnying green stable
On to the fields of praise.

And honoured among foxes and pheasants by the gay house
Under the new made clouds and happy as the heart was long,
In the sun born over and over,
I ran my heedless ways,
My wishes raced through the house high hay
And nothing I cared, at my sky blue trades, that time allows
In all his tuneful turning so few and such morning songs
Before the children green and golden
Follow him out of grace,

Nothing I cared, in the lamb white days, that time would take me
Up to the swallow thronged loft by the shadow of my hand,
        In the moon that is always rising,
            Nor that riding to sleep
        I should hear him fly with the high fields
And wake to the farm forever fled from the childless land.
Oh as I was young and easy in the mercy of his means,
            Time held me green and dying
        Though I sang in my chains like the sea.

Henry Williamson
1897-1977

More than any twentieth-century writer, Henry Williamson succeeded in capturing the perspective and experience of animals. *Tarka the Otter* (1927), for which he won the Hawthornden Prize, *Salar the Salmon* (1935), and *The Phasian Bird* (1948) are novels told from the animals' point of view. The protagonists stuggle through complex, subtle challenges and emerge as distinctly individual characters. Williamson's detailed knowledge of natural history makes for vivid, engrossing stories, lacking entirely the mawkish sentimentality often associated with writing about animals.

Williamson's love of nature was nourished by a lifelong habit of direct observation, first as a boy in Bedfordshire, where his fishing and birding expeditions—and his worshipful reading of Richard Jefferies' works—provided consolation for a poor relationship with a cold and distant father. Later, he performed the research necessary to write *Tarka* in the wild wetlands of Devonshire, where he lived after the war.

The first World War, for which he enlisted at seventeen, was the dominating experience of Williamson's life. The horrors he saw there left him disillusioned and somewhat misanthropic; his subsequent nature writing, like that of American veteran Hemingway, may be viewed as escape from and the sublimation of the wounds to his psyche. Like D. H. Lawrence, Williamson came to believe that the vast inhumanity of the war occurred because the modern masses had been shut away from direct experience of nature, because "pale-faced men" had repressed their natural instincts. His own nature writing he intended as a corrective to that imbalance.

Immediately after the war he remained near London, depressed, cynical and friendless. But in March 1921, he suddenly moved to a cottage in Georgeham,

Devonshire, where he began a productive period that lasted most of his life. By 1928 he had completed a four-volume autobiographical novel, *The Flax of Dreams* (1921-28; 1945), in which he attempted to dramatize his ideas on human alienation from nature. Subsequently, he wrote many works on natural history and rural life, including *The Story of a Norfolk Farm* (1948), a report of his experiences as a neophyte farmer. In 1936 he edited *Anthology of Modern Nature Writing* and, the following year, a selected edition of Richard Jefferies whose influence is evident in Williamson's own clear, unflinching depiction of struggles in the natural world.

from SALAR THE SALMON*

BLACK DOG

The elvers were running. They darkened the green shallows of the river. The eddies were thick tangles of them. They had come into the estuary on the flood tide, and in a gelantinous mass had moved into the still water of the tidehead. All fish in the river sped from them, for elvers were gill-twisting torture and death.

For nearly three years as thin glassy threads the young eels had been crossing the Atlantic, drifting in warm currents of the Gulf Steam from the Sargasso Sea. Here in deep water far under floating beds of clotted marine wreckage all the mature eels of the Northern Hemisphere, patient travelers from inland ponds and ditches, brooks and rivers, came together to shed themselves of life for immortal reasons. From blue dusk of ocean's depth they passed into death; and from darkness the elvers arose again, to girdle the waters of half the earth.

Salar lay in fast water between Sloping Weir and the road bridge. He lay in front of a large stone, in the swift flume rising to pass over it. The flume streamed by his head and gills and shoulders without local eddy. No elver could reach his gill without violent wriggling, which he would feel. He was swift with the swiftness of the water. There was the least friction between fish and river, for his skin exuded a mucus or lubricant by which the water slipped. The sweep of stong water guarded his life. Other salmon were lying in like lodges in the stony surges. Salar lodged there until dusk, when he moved forward again. Gralaks moved beside him. They recognized and knew each other without greeting.

Many fish were at Sloping Weir before them, waiting beside the lessening weight of white water, in the swarming bubbles of the eddy. They lay close to one another. As soon as one fish waggled tail and dipped and rose to get a grip of the water, to test its own pulse of power, another fish took its place, ready for the take-off. Salar idled, alert, apprehensive, seventeenth in line. Sometimes two or three fish left the phalanx at the same time and after nervous ranging set themselves to swim up through the heavy water.

At the edge of the turning pool, where Shiner the poacher had waited and watched during the day stood Old Nog the heron. The bird was picking up elvers as fast as he could snick them. His throat and neck ached. A continuous loose rope of elvers wove itself on the very edge of the water, where frillets sliding down the concrete apron edge scarcely washed into

*From *Salar the Salmon* by Henry Williamson (Boston: Little, Brown and Company, 1936).

the grass. Old Nog had eaten his first thousand elvers too quickly, gulping with head downheld until his tongue refused to work.

After a return to the tree-top heronry where three hernlets had craked and fought to thrust their beaks down his throat to take what he had, Old Nog flew back to the weir and picked and swallowed slowly, his excitement gone. All afternoon he flew back and forth. At dusk he rested, sleeping for three hours. By the light of the full moon rising he returned with his mate to the weir. They crammed their crops and necks and flew back to their filthy nest, where by midnight the three hernlets were crouching, huddled and dour with over-much feeding. Old Nog then flew back to the weir, to feed himself. Most of the elvers were now gone, but he managed to satisfy his hunger.

On the way home, however, an elver wriggled down his windpipe, causing him to choke and sputter and disgorge; the mass fell beside a badger below rubbing against its scratching thorn, causing it to start and grunt with alarm. Having cautiously sniffed for some minutes, from various angles, the badger dared to taste; after which it ate all up and searched for more. For the next few nights it returned specially to rub itself against the thorn, in the hope of finding such food there again. As for Old Nog, not an elver that year reached his long pot, as countrymen do call the guts.

During the time of the moon's high tides, more than two hundred salmon passed over the weir. Salar swam up on his second attempt; at first he had been unsure of himself, and dropped back almost as soon as he had got a grip on the central cord or spine of water. Swimming again with all his power, he moved slowly into the glissade of water above the white surge, stayed a third of the way up, as though motionless, vibrating; then had gained over the water and swarm strong in jubilation, and suddenly found the sill moving away under him, release of weight from his sides, and calm deep water before him. He flung himself out for joy, and a young dog-otter, who was rolling on its back on grass at the pool's edge, where a bitch-otter had touched earlier in the night, instantly lifted its head, slipped to the edge, put its head under, and slid tail last into the water.

Salar saw the otter swimming above him, shining in a broken envelop of air on head and fur and legs. The pool took the dull blows of his acceleration, and in three seconds, when the otter had swum nine yards against the current, Salar had gone twenty yards upstream in the mill pool, swerved from a sunken tree trunk lodged in the silt, zigzagged forward to the further bank, startling other salmon resting there, and hidden himself under a ledge of rock. The otter, which was not hunting salmon, since in deep water it could never catch any, unless a fish were injured, crawled out on the bank again to enjoy through its nose what it imagined visually.

An elver wriggled against Salar, and he swam on. The pool was long and deep and dark. He swam on easily, restfully, slower than the otter had pretended to chase him. The wound in his side began to ache dully, and he rested near the surface, near water noisy over a branch of alder. At dawn he was three miles above Sloping Weir, lying under a ledge of rock hollow curving above him, and therefore protecting him from behind, with an immediate way of escape from danger into deep water. The salmon slept, only the white-grey tip of the kyp—hooked end of lower jaw—showing as the mouth slightly opened. Fifteen times a minute water passed the gills, which opened imperceptibly.

Salar slept. The water lightened with sunrise. He lay in shadow. His eyes were fixed, passively susceptible to all movement. The sun rose up. Leaves and stalks of loose weed and water moss passing were seen but unnoticed by the automatic stimulus of each eye's retina. The eyes worked together with the unconscious brain, while the nerves, centres of direct feeling, rested themselves. One eye noticed a trout hovering in the water above, but Salar did not see it.

The sun rose higher, and shone down on the river, and slowly the shadow of the ledge shrank into its base. Light revealed Salar, a grey-green uncertain dimness behind a small pale spot appearing and disappearing regularly.

Down there Salar's right eye was filled with the sun's blazing fog. His left eye saw the wall of rock and the water above. The trout right forward of him swarm up, inspected that which had attracted it, and swarm down again; but Salar's eye perceived no movement. The shadow of the trout in movement did not fall on the salmon's right eye.

A few moments later there was a slight spash left forward of Salar. Something swung over, casting the thinnest shadow; but it was seen by the eye, which awakened the conscious brain. Salar was immeditately alert.

The thing vanished. A few moments later, it appeared nearer to him.

With his left eye Salar watched the thing moving overhead. It swam in small jerks, across the current and just under the surface, opening and shutting, gleaming, glinting, something trying to get away. Salar, curious and alert, watched it until it was disappearing and then he swam up and around to take it ahead of its arc of movement. The surface water, however, was flowing faster than the river at midstream, and he misjudged the opening of his mouth, and the thing which recalled sea feeding, escaped.

On the bank upriver fifteen yards away a fisherman with fourteen-foot split-cane rod said to himself, excitedly, "Rising short"; and, pulling loops of line between reel and lowest ring of rod, he took a small pair of scissors from a pocket and snipped off the thing which had attracted Salar.

No wonder Salar had felt curious about it, for human thought had ranged the entire world to imagine that lure. It was called a fly; but no fly like it ever swam in air or flew through water. Its tag, which had glinted, was of silver from Nevada and silk of a moth from Formosa; its tail, from the feather of an Indian crow; its butt, black herl of African ostrich; its body, yellow floss silk veiled with orange breast feathers of the South American toucan, and black Macclesfield silk ribbed with silver tinsel. This fly was given the additional attraction of wings for water flight, made of strips of feathers from many birds: turkey from Canada, peahen and peacock from Japan, swan from Ireland, bustard from Arabia, golden pheasant from China, teal and wild duck and mallard from the Hebrides. Its throat was made of the feather of an English speckled hen, its side of Bengal jungle cock's neck feathers, its cheeks came from a French king-fisher, its horns from the tail of an Amazonian macaw. Wax, varnish, and enamel secured the "marriage" of the feathers. It was one of hundreds of charms, or materialized riverside incantations, made by men to persuade sleepy or depressed salmon to rise and take. Invented after a bout of seasickness by a Celt as he sailed the German Ocean between England and Norway, for nearly a hundred years this fly had borne his name, Jock Scott.

While the fisherman was tying a smaller pattern of the same fly to the end of the gut cast, dark-stained by nitrate of silver against underwater glint, Salar rose to midwater and hovered there. Behind him lay the trout, which, scared by the sudden flash of the big fish turning, had dropped back a yard. So Salar had hovered three years before in his native river, when, as parr spotted like a trout, and later as silvery smolt descending to the sea, he had fed eagerly on nymphs of the olive dun and other Ephemeridae coming down with the current.

He opened his mouth and sucked in a nymph as it was swimming to the surface. The fisherman saw a swirl on the water, and threw his fly, with swish of double-handed rod, above and to the right of the swirl. Then lowering the rod point until it was almost parallel to the water, he let the current take the fly slowly across the stream, lifting the rod tip and lowering it slightly and regularly to make it appear to be swimming.

Salar saw the fly and slowly swam up to look at it. He saw it clear in the bright water and sank away again, uninterested in the lifelessness of its bright colors. Again it reappeared, well withi his skylight window. He ignored it, and it moved out of sight. Then it fell directly over him, jigging about in the water, and with it a dark thin thing which he regarded cautiously. This was the gut case. Once more it passed over, and then again, but he saw only the dark thinness moving there. It was harmless. He ignored it. Two other salmon below Salar, one in a cleft of rock and the other beside a sodden oak log wedged under the bank, also saw the too bright thing, and found no vital interest in it.

The fisherman pulled in the line through the rod rings. It was of plaited silk, tapered and enameled for ease of casting. The line fell over his boot. Standing still, he cut off the fly, and began a search for another in a metal box, wherein scores of mixed feathers were ranged on rows of metal clasps. First he moved one with his forefinger, than another, staring at this one and frowning at that one, recalling in its connection past occasions of comparative temperatures of air and river, of height and clearness of water, of sun and shade, while the angler's familiar feeling, of obscurity mingled with hope and frustration, came over him. While from the air he tried to conjure certainty for a choice of fly, Salar, who had taken several nymphs of the olive dun during the time the angler had been cogitating, leapt and fell back with a splash that made the old fellow take a small Black Doctor and tie the gut to the loop of the steel hook with a single Cairnton-jam knot.

Salar saw this lure and fixed one eye on it as it approached and then ignored it, a thing without life. As it was being withdrawn from the water a smolt which had seen it only then leapt open-mouthed at a sudden glint and fell back, having missed it.

Many times a similar sort of thing moved over Salar, who no longer heeded their passing. He enjoyed crusing the tiny nymphs on his tongue, and tasting their flavor. Salar was not feeding, he was not hungry; but he was enjoying remembrance of his river life with awareness of an unknown great excitement before him. He was living by the spirit of running water. Indeed Salar's life was now the river: as he explored it higher, so would he discover his life.

On the bank the fisherman sat down and perplexedly reëxamined his rows and rows of flies. He had tried all recommended for the water, and several others as well; and after one short rise, no fish had come to the fly. Mar Lodge and Silver Grey, Dunkeld and Black Fairy, Beauly Snow Fly, Fiery Brown, Silver Wilkinson, Thunder and Lightning, Butcher, Green Highlander, Blue Charm, Candlestick Maker, Bumbee, Little Inky Boy, all were no good. Then in one corner of the case he saw an old fly of which most of the mixed plumage was gone: a Black Dog which had belonged to his grandfather. Grubs of moths had fretted away hackle, wing, and topping. It was thin and bedraggled. Feeling that it did not matter much what fly was used, he sharpened the point with a slip of stone, tied it on, and carelessly flipped it into the water. He was no longer fishing; he was no longer intent, he was about to go home; the cast did not fall straight, but crooked; the line also was crooked. Without splash the fly moved down a little less fast than the current, coming thus into Salar's skylight. It was like the nymphs he had been taking, only larger; and with a leisurely sweep he rose and turned across the current, and took it, holding it between tongue and vomer as he went down to his lie again, where he would crush and taste it. The sudden resistance of the line to his movement caused the point of the hook to prick the corner of his mouth. He shook his head to rid himself of it, and this action drove the point into the gristle, as far as the barb.

A moment later, the fisherman, feeling a weight on the line, lifted the rod point, and tightened the line, and had hardly thought to himself, "Salmon," when the blue-grey tail of a fish broke half out of water and its descending weight bended the rod.

Salar knew of neither fisherman nor rod nor line. He swam down to the ledge of rock and tried to rub the painful thing in the corner of his mouth against it. But his head was pulled away from the rock. He saw the line, and was fearful of it. He bored down to his lodge at the base of the rock, to get away from the line, while the small brown trout swarm behind his tail, curious to know what was happening.

Salar could not reach his lodge. He shook his head violently, and, failing to get free, turned down-stream and swam away strongly, pursued by the line and a curious buzzing vibration just outside his jaw.

Below the pool the shallow water jabbled before surging in broken white crests over a succession of rocky ledges. Salar had gone about sixty yards from his lodge, swimming hard against the backward pull of line, when the pull slackened, and he turned head to current, and lay close to a stone, to hide from his enemy.

When the salmon had almost reached the jabble, the fisherman, fearing it would break away in the rough water, had started to run down the bank, pulling line from the reel as he did so. By thus releasing direct pull on the fish, he had turned it. Then, by letting the current drag line in a loop below it, he made Salar believe that the enemy was behind him. Feeling the small pull of the line from behind, Salar swam up into deeper water, to get away from it. The fisherman was now behind the salmon, in a position to make it tire itself by swimming upstream against the current.

Salar, returning to his lodge, saw it occupied by another fish, which his rush, and the humming line cutting the water, had disturbed from the lie by the sodden log. This was Gralaks the grilse. Again Salar tried to rub the thing against the rock, again the pull, sideways and upwards, was too strong for him. He swam downwards, but could make no progress towards the rock. This terrified him and he turned upwards and swam with all his strength, to shake it from his mouth. He leapt clear of the water and fell back on his side, still shaking his head.

On the top of the leap the fisherman had lowered his rod, lest the fly be torn away as the salmon struck the water.

Unable to get free by leaping, Salar sank down again and settled himself to swim away from the enemy. Drawing the line after him, and beset again by the buzzing vibration, he traveled a hundred yards to the throat of the pool, where water quickened over gravel. He lay in the riffle spreading away from a large stone, making himself heavy, his swim-bladder shrunken, trying to press himself into the gravel which was his first hiding place in life. The backward pull on his head nearly lifted him into the fast water, but he held himslef down, for nearly five minutes, until his body ached and he weakened and he found himself being taken down sideways by the force of shallow water. He recalled the sunken tree and it became a refuge,and he swam down fast,and the pull ceased with the buzz against his jaw. Feeling relief, he swam less fast over his lodge, from which Gralaks sped away, alarmed by the line following Salar.

But before he could reach the tree the weight was pulling him back, and he turned and bored down to bottom, scattering a drove of little grey shadows which were startled trout. Again the pull was too much for him, and he felt the ache of his body spreading back to his tail. He tried to turn on his side to rub the corner of his mouth on something lying on the bed of the pool—an old cartwheel—again and again, but he could not reach it.

A jackdaw flying silent over the river, paper in beak for nest lining, saw the dull yellow flashes and flew faster in alarm of them and the man with the long curving danger.

Fatigued and aching, Salar turned downstream once more, to swim away with the river, to escape the enemy which seemed so much bigger because he could not close his mouth. As he grew heavier, slower, uncertain, he desired above all to be in the deeps of the sea, to lie on ribbed sand and rest and rest and rest. He came to rough water, and let it take him down, too tired to swim. He bumped into a rock, and was carried by the current around it, on his side, while the gut cast, tautened by the dragging weight, twanged and jerked his head upstream, and he breathed again, gulping water quickly and irregularly. Still the pull was trying to take him forward, so with a renewal by fear he turned and reëntered fast water and went down and down, until he was in another deep pool at a bend of the river. Here he remembered a hole under the roots of a tree, and tried to hide there, but had not strength enough to reach the refuge of darkness.

Again he felt release, and swam forward slowly, seeking the deepest part of the pool, to lie on the bottom with his mouth open. Then he was on his side, dazed and weary, and the broken-quicksilvery surface of the pool was becoming whiter. He tried to swim away, but the water was too thick-heavy; and after a dozen sinuations it became solid. His head was out of water. A shock passed through him as he tried to breathe. He lay there, held by line taut over fisherman's shoulder. He felt himself being drawn along just under the surface, and only then did he see his enemy—flattened, tremulant-spreading image of the fisherman. A new power of fear broke in the darkness of his lost self. When it saw the tailer coming down to it, the surface of the water was lashed by the desperately scattered self. The weight of the body falling over backwards struck the taut line; the tail fin was split. The gut broke just above the hook, where it had been frayed on the rock. Salar saw himself sinking down into the pool, and he lay there, scattered about himself and unable to move away, his tail curved round a stone, feeling only a distorted head joined to the immovable river bed.

Colin Fletcher
b. 1922

Like the Scot Robert Service, Colin Fletcher left Britain early and found adventure in the American West, carrying with him sharp memories not of Scotland but of Devonshire, where as a child he had watched otters play in the streams. After service in the Royal Marines, he emigrated to Africa, working there as hotel manager, farmer, and road builder.

In 1953 he shepherded a planeload of cattle from England across the ocean. During the next years he spent summers prospecting and constructing roads in western Canada. Later he worked as a hospital janitor and a department store Santa before his writing career developed. Rcently he described himself as a "semiprofessional bum." Like the American-born Edward Abbey, Fletcher writes with self-deprecating wit and easy style, yet captures subtle insights.

His steady occupation, other than writing, is walking, a profession he has practiced from North Devon to Mount Kenya to the American High Sierra. He once spent six months walking a thousand miles from Mexico to Oregon, and later told the story in *The Thousand-Mile Summer—The Desert and the High Sierra* (1964). Fletcher has, in fact, written the definitive book on walking—and twice revised it: *The Complete Walker* (1968; 1973; 1984). It is probably the best technical book on hiking available today. We present a selection from it here because, as Fletcher notes, it is not just a "how-to" but also a "feel-how" book.

from THE COMPLETE WALKER III*

LEARN OF THE GREEN WORLD

The wilderness has a mysterious tongue.
which teaches awful doubt.

Quoted by Charles Darwin
in *The Voyage of the Beagle*

When I began this book it was my intention to examine, here at the end, the delights of walking in different kinds of country. For I was afraid that in the course of 600 fundamentally how-to pages we might have forgotten the feel-how—afraid that the ways and means might have masked the joys and insights that can come, in the end, from the simple act of walking. I am still afraid that such an eclipse may have occurred. But I see now that the delights of different places are not what I must write about. They too are only means to an end.

Now, I am the last person to deny that each kind of country—and also each season of the year and each hour of the day—has its own very special enchantments.

Mountains offer the slow unfolding of panoramas and the exhilaration of high places. Their summits, even the humble ones, are nearly always pinnacles of experience. And afterward you come back down. You ease back, step by step, from stark rock and snow into the world of observable life: first, a single tuft of vegetation in a windswept saddle; then the tracks of a small mammal; two hours later the first tree; then the first tree that can stand upright against the wind; then the tracks of a large two-footed animal that was wearing lug-sole boots; then undeniable soil; soon trees that would be trees in any company; finally, thick undergrowth beneath the trees—and you pat your pocket to make sure the snakebite kit is still there.

In the desert you rediscover, every time you go back, the cleanness that exists in spite of the dust, the complexity that underlies the apparent openness, and the intricate web of life that stretches over the apparent barrenness; but above all you rediscover the echoing silence that you had thought you would never forget.

Then there is untrodden snow country, silent with its own kind of silence. And the surging seashore. And other dominions too, each with its own signature: estuaries, the river worlds, marshland, farmlands, moors and the open plain.

But in the course of time the memories meld. For they come, all of them, from the green world.

When I open my own mind and let the memories spill out, I find a many-hued mosaic. I remember the odd excitement and the restricted yet infinitely open world I have moved through several times when I have clambered up—very late at night, and following the little pool from my flashlight beam—to the flat, grassy summit of the hill on which I wrote at

*From *The Complete Walker III* by Colin Fletcher.

last the opening chapter of this book. I remember a three-day walk along an unspoiled beach with the wind always barreling in from the Pacific and the sand dunes always humping up on my left; and I remember the ceaseless surging and drawing back of the sea, with its final, curbing excursions into smooth sand—excursions that sometimes left stranded, high and almost dry, little fragments of transparent protoplasm (which set me thinking, "This is the stuff we came from") and sometimes cast up a bottle that I could peer at (laughing at myself for being so childlike) in the hope that it might contain a message. I remember standing on snowshoes outside my half-buried tent after a four-day storm in a newly gleaming white world, and watching the guilty, cloud-bearing southwest wind trying to reassert itself; I remember feeling a northeast breeze spring up, and almost hearing it take a deep breath and say, "They shall not pass," and then begin to blow in earnest; and I remember watching, thankfully, as the line of dark clouds was held along a front, horizon to horizon, and then was driven back, slowly but inexorably, until at last it retreated behing the peaks and the sky was left to the triumphant northeast wind and the warm and welcome sun. I remember trying to clamber up a steep woodland bank after dark, somewhere in the deep South (I think it was in Alabama), and finding myself in an enchanted world of fireflies and twisted tree roots and fireflies and clumps of grass and fireflies and wildflowers and fireflies and fireflies and fireflies—a world suddenly filled with a magic that I had not glimpsed since I was ten, and had almost come to disbelieve in. I remember striding down a desert road as dusk fell, with the wind catching my pack and billowing out the poncho like a sail and carrying me almost effortlessly along before it; and I remember how, when the rain came, it stung my bare legs refreshing without hurting. I remember, in a different, sagerush desert, coming to the edge of a village and passing a wooden building with three cars and a truck parked outside, and a battered sign that said PENTECOSTAL CHURCH OF GOD, EVERYONE WELCOME; I remember that the church door stood open to the warm evening, and that I could hear a piano and the congregation following along, with only a hint of exasperation, a half-beat behind a contralto whom nature had endowed with the volume, tempo, rigidity and determination of a brass band. In another desert village—a long-dead ghost town, this one—I remember a clump of wild blue irises growing inside the worn wooden threshold of a once busy home. I remember red, red sunsets in a small desert valley when I was not alone. I remember, further back, a dead native cow in a clearing in the dry African bush; and, in the blood-softened soil beside its torn-out entrails, a single huge paw mark. I remember the small, round, furry heads of the hyraxes that would solemnly examine us from the boulders just behind our 13,000-foot camp up near Lewis Glacier on Mount Kenya. Further back still I remember three otters cavorting across a moonlit Devonshire meadow; and a stag on a Scottish moor, silhouetted, elemental; and a shoal of small fish swimming slowly over a sloping bed of brown gravel that I can still see, stone fitting into stone, down a fifty-year tunnel. And now, vaulting back into yesterday, I find I am remembering an elk that stands regally among redwood trees and the last tendrils of morning mist, and a surprised beaver that crouches almost at my feet and eyes me for clues, and a solitary evening primrose that has prospered in a desolation of desert talus, and a rainbow that arches over a dark mountain tarn, and the huge and solemn silence that encompasses, always, the buttes and mesas and cliffs and hanging terraces of the Grand Canyon of the Colorado.

Everyone who walks has his own floodlit memories—his own fluttering windwheel of scenes and sounds and scents. (It is often the scents that linger longest, through you do not know it until they come again.) But no matter what the hue of the individual memories, they all come from the green world. And in the end, when you have learned to connect—only to connect—you understand that it is simply the green world that you seek.

I suppose you could say that going out into this older world is rather like going to church. I know that it is in my case, anyway. For me, praying is no good: my god, if I have one, is a kind of space-age Pan, and is not interested in what happens to me personally. But by walking out alone into wilderness I can elude the pressures of the pounding modern world, and in the sanctity of silence and solitude—the solitude seems to be a very important part of it—I can after a while begin to see and to hear and to think and in the end to feel with a new and exciting accuracy. And that, it seems to me, is just the kind of vision you should be hoping to find when you go to church.

Now, I do not want to suggest that out in the wilderness my mind—or, I suspect, anyone else's mind—is always soaring. Most of the time it operates on a mundanely down-to-earth level. In the course of a four-day hike taken primarily so that I could sort out ideas and directions for the first edition of this book, I tried to write down before they had faded away the thoughts that had run through my head while I was climbing one afternoon up a long and fairly steep hill. What I scribbled down was, in part: "Wonder how far now, over top and down to next creek. Maybe should have half-filled canteen from that last spring. . . . Oh hell, left heel again! Hope it's not a blister. Moleskin? No, not yet. Oh, look at that squirrel! Sun caught it beautifully, coming in from behind at an angle. Hm, horse tracks. Wonder how old. . . . Phew! Pretty damned hot for January. Better take off shirt at next halt. Almost time for rest anyway. Only five minutes. That should just get me to top of hill. . . . Hey, what's that on my leg? Oh, just water dripping off wet socks, on pack. . . . Oh my God, look! It'll be at least ten or fifteen minutes to top of bloody hill. Maybe more. . . . Say, your thoughts really do run on, don't they? Normally, don't notice it much, but. . . wait a minute, better jot down what I've been thinking, as accurately and as far back as I can. Might just be worth using in the walking book. Yes, out notebook right now. . . ."

Twice more on that four-day trip I jotted down odd islets of thought that jutted up from what was no doubt a continuous stream. Once, on a slightly less mundane but still distinctly unsoaring level, I found that as I walked I had concocted a mnemonic sentence ("King Philip, come out, for God's sake!") for a sequence that often leaves me groping: the hierarchy of categories into which biologists divide the living world (kingdom, phylum, class, order, family, genus, species). And one evening I was warming myself by a campfire and looking up at the dark pine trees silhouetted against a quarter-moon and beginning to think of beauty and life and death (or so my notes assure me) when I realized with some surprise that I was at the same time singing quietly to myself the soulful and almost immortal refrain from a song that was implanted in my mind somewhere deep in half-forgotten childhood: "And the captain sat in the captain's chair, and he played his ukulele as the ship went down."

But in trying to preclude a false impression I must not overcompensate. There are, of course, times when your mind soars or floats or hangs free and impartial—or dives into the depths.

For even in wilderness you may, very occasionally, plunge into despair—into the blackness that exists, I suppose, deep down in all our lives, waiting to blot out the underpinnings and so keep us honest. I remember a desert canyon in which, as I lay quiet beneath the stars, man was a pointless imposter on the bleak and ancient surface of the earth, and I knew I would never hope again. And I remember a night on a mountain when all that existed out in the blackness beyond my campfire was a small hemlock, and even the hemlock only flickered into and out of existence at the mercy of the fickle firelight; a night on which, for an endless, empty span, that little tree with its dark, stark needles was more lasting and more real than I was, and so claimed a crushing victory; a night on which, above all, the blackness beyond the tree was tragically and incontestably more real than the fragile tree, and therefore claimed the final, aching, desolate victory. Such interludes—in which the keepers of the void ensnare you and all, all is vanity—are rare in wilderness. But they happen. And, although I would like to deny it, they are worse than in the city. While they last, the blackness is blacker, more hopeless, more desolately victorious. This time you cannot appeal to a more profound reality.

But, far more often than despair, you find elation. A squirrel leaps across a gap in the trees, a hundred feet above your head, and your mind, caught by the beauty, leaps too—across the gap between the dragging everyday world and the universals. Two swallows, bound head to tail in tight and perfect formation, bank up and away from a cliff face in a joyous arc of freedom. A quartet of beavers browses by the margin of a backwater, silent and serene, a tableau from a calmer age. Or you sit, triumphant, on a rocky peak and look and look at the whole world spread out below; and for a while, though still human, you are no longer merely human.

At such moments you do not "commune with nature" (a trite phrase that seems to classify nature as something outside and separate from us humans). At such moments you know, deep down in your fabric, with a certainty far more secure than intellect can offer, that you are a part of the web of life, and that the web of life is a part of the rock and air and water of pre-life. You know the wholeness of the universe, the great unity. And if you keep walking long enough—for several weeks or for several months—you may with care and good fortune experience whole days or even series of days during which you exist in this happy, included state.

They do not last, of course, these rich cadenzas. But their echoes linger. When you first return to the world of man there is a period of readjustment, just as there was when you left it and went out into the wilderness. After that first glorious hot shower (which is always—and always to your new surprise—a great experience in itself) you may find that for a day, or perhaps three days, or even a week, you live an unreal, cut-off-by-a-screen-of-gauze sort of existence. But once you have readjusted to hot showers and radios and orthodox beds and automobiles and parking meters and sidewalks and elevators and other people and other people's points of view, you begin to find that you have regained thrust and direction and hope and wonder and other such vital intangibles whose presence or absence color so indelibly the tenor of our lives, but which are very difficult to discuss without sententiousness. You find yourself refreshed, that is, for the eternal struggle of trying to see things as you more or less know they are, not merely as other people tell you they are. Above all, you find that you have recomprehended—totally, so that it is there behind every thought—the knowledge that we have arisen from everything that has gone before. You know, steadily, that we are more than just a fascinating and deadly and richly promising species that has begun to take over the face of the earth. You know again, fully, that this species you belong to is the current spearhead of life—and that your personal meaning is that you are a part of the spearhead. And so you find that you can take up once more the struggle we all have to make in our own several and quirky ways if we are to succeed in living lives that are truly human—the struggle to discern some glimmering of sense in the extraordinary phenomenon that is man.

And that, I guess, is quite a lot to get out of such a simple thing as walking.

John Fowles
b. 1926

John Fowles is among the foremost living British authors. Three of his novels, *The Collector* (1963), *The Magus* (1965; 1977), and *The French Lieutenant's Woman* (1969), have achieved critical acclaim and have been made into major motion pictures. His creativity and versatility have been rewarded with prestigious literary prizes: the Silver Pen Award (1969); the W. H. Smith Award (1970); and the Christopher Award (1981).

A recurrent theme in Fowles' work is the problem of individual freedom despite modern society's tremendous pressure to conform, particularly its authoritarianism. This theme literally provides the plot of his first novel, *The Collector:* a beautiful, talented young woman is kidnapped by a deranged, boorish man who keeps her locked away in a suburban house—as one might collect a butterfly in a jar.

A complementary theme is the need for each individual to take moral responsibility for action, even when one is unable to obtain a clear or complete understanding of a situation. In *The Magus,* for example, a callow young schoolteacher deserts his lover and takes a job on a remote Greek island. There he faces incredible experiences he must deal with by making difficult moral choices.

On the surface these novels do not define Fowles as a typical nature writer, but in *The Tree* (1979), he has asserted that "the key to my fiction . . . lies in my relationship with nature." In *The Tree,* an extended personal essay, he explains his conviction that there is an *art,* as well as a science, of knowing nature. This art, like any other, is not predictable, or is it subject to rules: it is as spontaneous and varied as the individual consciousness.

One of the problems we face in contemporary life, he argues, is that the art of knowing nature has been outweighed by science; because of the dominance of science, we look on nature overwhelmingly as an object to be named and analyzed. His fiction, then, is in part a labor to bring the two modes of knowing back into balance, and thus restore to the individual the spontaneous creative power necessary for the art of living.

In its insistence that the art of knowing nature cannot be learned through the mind of another, *The Tree* pushes to the boundary of nature writing, and beyond—to the "green wood" that Fowles asserts we must each come to understand for our own selves.

from THE TREE*

. . .

Scientists restrict the word symbiotic to those relationships between species that bring some detectable mutual benefit; but the true wood, the true place of any kind, is the sum of all its phenomena. They are all in some sense symbiotic, being together in a togetherness of beings. It is only because such a vast sum of interactions and coincidences in time and place is beyond science's calculation (a scientist might say, beyond useful function, even if calculable) that we so habitually ignore it, and treat the flight of the bird and the branch it flies from, the leaf in the wind and its shadow on the ground, as separate events, or riddles—what bird? which branch? what leaf? which shadow? These question-boundaries (where do I file that?) are ours, not of reality. We are led to them, caged by them not only culturally and intellectually, but quite physically, by the restlessness of our eyes and their limited field and acuity of vision. Long before the glass lens and the movie-camera were invented, they existed in our eyes and minds, both in our mode of perception and in our mode of analysing the perceived: endless short sequence and jump-cut, endless need to edit and range this raw material.

I spent all my younger life as a more or less orthodox amateur naturalist; as a pseudo-scientist, treating nature as some sort of intellectual puzzle, or game, in which being able to name names and explain behaviourisms—to identify and to understand machinery—constituted all the pleasures and the prizes. I became slowly aware of the inadequacy of this approach: that it insidiously cast nature as a kind of opponent, an opposite team to be outwitted and beaten; that in a number of very important ways it distracted from the total experience and the total meaning of nature—and not only of what I personally needed from nature, not only as I had long, if largely unconsciously, begun to feel it (which was neither scientifically nor sentimentally, but in a way for which I had, and still have, no word). I came to believe that this approach represented a major human alienation, affecting all of us, both personally and socially; moreover, that such alienation had much more ancient roots behind the historical accident of its present scientific, or pseudo-scientific, form.

Naming things is always implicitly categorizing and therefore collecting them, attempting to own them; and because man is a highly acquisitive creature, brainwashed by most modern societies into believing that the act

*From *The Tree* by John Fowles and Frank Horvat. Text and English Translation Copyright 1979 by Association for All Speech Impaired Children. By permission of Little, Brown and Company.

of acquisition is more enjoyable than the fact of having acquired, that getting beats having got, mere names and objects they are tied to soon become stale. There is a constant need, or compulsion, to seek new objects and names—in the context of nature, new species and experiences. Everyday ones grow mute with familiarity, so known they become unknown. And not only in non-human nature: only fools think our attitude to our fellow-men is a thing distinct from our attitude to 'lesser' life on this planet.

All this is an unhappy legacy from Victorian science, which was so characteristically obsessed with both the machine and exact taxonomy. . . .

But I think the most harmful change brought about by Victorian science in our attitude to nature lies in the demand that our relation with it must be purposive, industrious, always seeking greater knowledge. This dreadfully serious and puritanical approach (nowhere better exhibited in the nineteenth century than in the countless penny magazines aimed at young people) has had two very harmful effects. One is that it turned the vast majority of contemporary Western mankind away from what had become altogether too much like a duty, or a school lesson; the second is that the far saner eighteenth-century attitude, which viewed nature as a mirror for philosophers, as an evoker of emotion, as a pleasure, a poem, was forgotten. There are intellectual reasons as well for this. Darwin made sentimental innocence, nature as mainly personal or aesthetic experience, vaguely wicked. Not only did he propose a mechanism seemingly as iron as the steam-engine, but his very method of discovery, and its success in solving a great conundrum, offered an equally iron or one-sided model for the amateur naturalist himself, and made the older and more humanist approach seem childish. A 'good' amateur naturalist today merely means one whose work is valued by the professional scientists in his field. . . .

Achieving a relationship with nature is both a science and an art, beyond mere knowledge or mere feeling alone; and I now think beyond oriental mysticism, transcendentalism, 'meditation techniques' and the rest—or at least as we in the West have converted them to our use, which seems increasingly in a narcissistic way; to make ourselves feel more positive, more meaningful, more dynamic. I do not believe nature is to be reached that way either, by turning it into a therapy, a free clinic for admirers of their own sensitivity. The subtlest of our alienations from it, the most difficult to comprehend, is our eternal need to use it in some way, to derive some personal yield. We shall never fully understand nature (or ourselves), and certainly never respect it, until we dissociate the wild from the notion of usability—however innocent and harmless the use. For it is the general uselessness of so much of nature that lies at the root of our ancient hostility and indifference to it.

There is a kind of coldness, I would rather say a stillness, an empty space, at the heart of our forced co-existence with all the other species of the planet. Richard Jefferies coined a word for it: the ultra-humanity of all that is not man . . . not with us or against us, but outside and beyond us, truly alien. It may sound paradoxical, but we shall not cease to be alienated—by our knowledge, by our greed, by our vanity—from nature until we grant it its unconscious alienation from us. . . .

So I sit in the namelessness, the green phosphorus of the tree, surrounded by impenetrable misappellations. I came here really only to be sure; not to describe it, since I cannot, or only by the misappellations; to be sure that what I have written is not all lucubration, study dream, *in vitro,* as epiphytic upon reality as the ferns on the branches above my head.

It, this namelessness, is beyond our science and our arts because its secret is being, not saying. Its greatest value to us is that it cannot be reproduced, that this being can be apprehended only by other present beings, only by the living senses and consciousness. All experience of it through surrogate and replica, through selected image, gardened word, through other eyes and minds, betrays or banishes its reality. But this is nature's consolation, its message, and well beyond the Wistman's Wood of its own strict world. It can be known and entered only by each, and in its now; not by you through me, by any you through any me; only by you through yourself, or me through myself. We still have this to learn: the inalienable otherness of each, human and non-human, which may seem the prison of each, but is at heart, in the deepest of those countless million metaphorical trees for which we cannot see the wood, both the justification and the redemption.

. . .

Nature in America: From the Era of Conservation to the Contemporary Ecological Crisis

During the twentieth century, American authors have continued to translate their experiences of rural and wild America for a broad population of readers. Even as before, the American literature of nature has for the most part in this century been shaped by both agrarian and wilderness values. We have seen that since the seventeenth century an ancient pastoral tradition informed the idea of America in everything from the earliest promotional literature to the seminal agrarianism of De Crèvecoeur, Jefferson, and Cooper. Likewise, the eighteenth- and nineteenth-century tradition of naturalists and explorers like Byrd, the Bartrams, Audubon, and Wilson played a formative role in an American literary tradition that even today combines scientific detail with reverence and awe for wilderness. If the agrarian impulse emphasizes the rural, the regional, the economic and political, the wilderness impulse emphasizes the scenic, sublime, the "otherness" of nature, and nature's psychological and spiritual impact on human beings.

Another American tradition has been very much alive also. A kind of Puritanical utilitarianism is still a force in American lives and institutions. What is not useful, what we cannot shape to ourselves or dominate is still often viewed as a sort of "evil." In the twentieth century especially, "usefulness" has come to be defined by economic values alone. John Muir called the laissez-faire spirit of economics in his time "the gobble-gobble school of economics." More recently, environmentalists find themselves opposing a modern utilitarianism that is, again, based on economic values and considerations alone. One of the significant social movements in the latter half of the twentieth century, "environmentalism" intersects with most of the major social movements of our time and with them contributes to the confrontational quality and urgency of modern social and political life.

The agrarian impulse in twentieth-century American nature writing is preceded, paralleled, and influenced by a tradition of "regionalism" in literary and social thought. After the Civil War, American writers from the East, South, and West focused their attention on the local language, customs, and lives of people living in rural and wild sections of the country. In part, the widespread interest in regions arose from the war itself. Soldiers from North and South had associated with as well as fought against one another. They returned to their homes more interested in and conscious of sectional customs and differences. Westward migration also brought people from various localities together, creating further interest in one another's home regions. Such American experiences contributed to the vogue in travel articles and local color stories. Reading them today, one is struck by a vanished life shaped in large measure by landscape and climate.

In the South, for example, William Gilmore Simms (1806-1870), Joel Chandler Harris (1848-1908), George Washington Cable (1844-1925), Kate Chopin (1851-1904), and Ellen Glasgow (1874-1945) presage such later modern authors as William Faulkner and Eudora Welty who base their fiction on Southern places and themes. In the West, Bret Harte (1836-1902), Mark Twain (1835-1910), and, later, Hamlin Garland (1860-1940) and Willa Cather (1873-1947), wrote of life in the vanishing frontier from the Middle West to California. In Garland especially, we see a nostalgic return to frontier and rural life mixed with social protest against the exploitation of common men, women, and the Indians. Garland believed that literary art must above all be rooted in the local scene—a belief held by many modern writers, including even such poets with a strong narrative bent as Robert Frost or, today, David Budbill and Wesley McNair. In his youth, Garland had indeed been a real farmer on the frontier. In *Main-travelled Roads* (1891), *Prairie Folks* (1893), and other works, Garland juxtaposed the hardship and futility of farm life on the "Middle Border" (the prairies of Iowa, Minnesota, Wisconsin, Nebraska, and the Dakotas) to the beauty and richness of the land. The causes of such hardship could of course be natural, but more often were economic monopoly and greed. "I do not advocate an exchange of masters, but freedom from masters. Life, Nature—these should be our teachers," he wrote in *Crumbling Idols* (1894). The very fact that in the late nineteenth and early twentieth centuries agriculture languished while banks and manufacturers "never made more money or were in a more flourishing condition" was indictment enough, for Garland, of changing American values. To work against these changing values, Garland joined many agrarian and Populist causes.

Later in his life Garland turned to another region for his fictional themes, settings, and characters—the high country of the Continental Divide. His work after 1900 is more stereotyped and romantic, but in novels like *The Eagles's Heart* (1900) and *The Forester's Daughter* (1914) Garland gives magnificent descriptions of the mountainous country of the West. And in *The Captain of the Gray-Horse Troop* (1902) and *The Book of the American Indian* (1924), Garland joined Cooper and Thoreau in his concern for the vanishing race.

Of course, in the long-settled East, there had always been an element of the local before the Civil War, from De Crèvecoeur to Bryant to Thoreau. In particular, writers such as Harriet Beecher Stowe (1811-1896), Sarah Orne Jewett, Mary Wilkins Freeman (1852-1930) and Edith Wharton (1862-1937)—most notably in *Ethan Frome* (1911)—wrote memorable stories and novels of New England lives and locales.

After the First World War regionalism was revitalized and included not only literature but history and social theory in the 1920's and 30's. It is during this time that regionalism claims its lineage to, and impact upon, the environmental movement several decades later. The groundwork was laid by a prominent historian, Fredrick Jackson Turner (1861-1932), and a social scientist, Howard Washington Odum (1884-1954). Both advocated sectional and regional interpretations of American history and culture. Turner is most famous for his Frontier Thesis: "the existence of an area of free land, its continuous recession, and the advance of American settlement westward explain American development." Turner's thesis that the ever-receding frontier produced American democracy and individualism—the American character and civilization—has provoked a tidal wave of criticism, debate, and new research since his death, though as Henry Nash Smith pointed out in *Virgin Land* (1950; 1970), it is still "by far the most familiar interpretation of the American past." Even more useful, however, has been Turner's Sectional Thesis; that is, the uniqueness of each section or region of the country *after* the settlement of the frontier shaped American lives and culture. Especially important in the shape of regional cultures are the limits of natural resources and the necessity of humanity's ecological adjustment to the landscape. Odum argued that geography (especially natural settings and conditions) shapes history and culture. Both men viewed the Mississippi Valley ("the whole interior basin," that is loosely called the "West") with its agrarian life and economy as the true heart of the nation. Others—Garland and philosopher Josiah Royce among them—turned this theoretical emphasis on the local into a tool to critically examine the larger American culture, to see the regional as a bastion against mass culture and mob spirit. Once again we see elements of the ancient pastoral revivified.

Regions within nations arise from a sense of identity people develop with their portion of the earth. These regions may be concentric or overlapping, as the Berkshires within New England, but what gives them life is people's awareness of an image and spirit of a place that distinguishes it from other places. A region is, therefore, the result of the relationship between nature and culture, an entity established by psychological and natural boundaries rather than political. Whether from literary, historical, or sociological perspectives, regionalism emphasizes rural, traditional values over urban values. In modern America, regionalism has tended to be a non-Marxist radicalism dissenting against the urban, the mechanistic, and the overgrown. Specific regions and smaller locales have, of course, always been the source and essence of so much detailed nature writing per se, as we have seen in Gilbert White's *The Natural History of Selborne* or Thoreau's *Walden,* and today the same is true, as even the titles of later twentieth-century nature books suggest. Sally Carrighar's *One Day on Teton Marsh,* Josephine Johnson's *The Inland Island* (about an abandoned Ohio farm), John Samson's *The Pond* (placed in rural New York), Hazel Heckman's *Island Year*—as well as urban nature discoveries like John Kieran's *A Natural History of New York City* or Louis Halle's

Spring in Washington—to name but a few, all obviously celebrate and describe the life of particular places.

Regionalism, with its emphasis on love of the land and "back to nature," flourished in the 1920's and 30's because of changes in America at that time. All the regionalist articles, books, conferences, and national commissions were responding to the fact that by 1920 the majority of Americans were city-dwellers and American agriculture had already slipped into a depression that would soon engulf the country and much of the world. Regional theorists were reacting to the abuses of industrial capitalism, an increasingly global communications technology, and the ever-expanding suburb. Two of the most important regional theorists to emerge between the World Wars were Benton MacKaye (1879-1975) and Lewis Mumford (1895-1990).

MacKaye's theory demonstrates a profound appreciation of rural and wild landscapes. His analyses of regions begin with the land, its limits and potential. Influenced by Thoreau and George Perkins Marsh, his regional planning is a kind of environmental humanism based on scientific ecological concerns and traditional ideas. MacKaye saw a transcendent, sacred order in wilderness. But he was also a forester, labor economist, and conservationist who blended the romantic with the scientific. This brand of regionalism he called "geotechnics," or the applied science of making the earth more habitable for humans. He was the father of the Appalachian Trail, one of the founders of the Wilderness Society, and author of articles and longer studies of conservation and regional planning. His favorite region was New England, and one of his models for the regional reconstruction of America was the New England village—a source of intimacy and ecological balance between society and rural or wild places. It was here, MacKaye believed, that culture and environment lived together in some degree of stability. From this example we might learn to live more wisely with our primordial, rural, and urban environments. The enemy of habitability is big government, mass civilization, and the unchecked depredations of industrial technology. MacKaye did argue that technology could become a tool for the restructuring of American society, largely by decentralizing it, and that the city itself could be as important to culture as forest and rural lands. But both technology and city must be created in proportion to the ecological and human community of specific regions.

Lewis Mumford, himself a city-bred man and student of the city, likewise developed regionalism and environmentalism as tools to dismantle the "megamachine" that, he believes, has come to rule and dehumanize our lives. His purpose has been to provide the theoretical basis, as he said in *The Myth of the Machine: The Pentagon of Power* (1970), to restore to "every habitat of man" an "ecological variety and regional integrity." An omnivorous reader and generalist, he brought biology, economics, social science, and geography to bear on urban and regional planning. If our lives are determined only by contractors, speculators, and industrialists, what do we become? As we shape nature, what we shape shapes us. Might we not instead use scientific advances, community successes (again as New England villages), and the best thought of the past (Emerson, Melville, Thoreau, and Whitman, for example) to guide us and give us the instruments of transformation?

Although MacKaye's and Mumford's extensive planning for the regional and ecological transformation of America failed in any large-scale sense, and although, like the nation itself, their visions and practical successes were bogged down in economic crisis and World War, their information and ideas have potential for Americans today. Some of their principles return to influence our thought in more recent decades, as such popular books as E. F. Shumacker's *Small Is Beautiful: Economics as if People Mattered* (1973) testify.

Yet during the 1920's and 30's literary regionalism also became more urgent, agrarian, and hostile to the apparent direction of the nation at large. The traditional agrarian emphasis on life lived within the cycles of the seasons, and on cultivation of the soil as a spiritual good, attracted some of the most talented authors of our century. The most striking expression of regionalist agrarianism during this time arose in the 1920's with a group of twelve Southern writers. Their hope was to begin a discourse that might eventually lead to saving the South and even America itself from what they saw as the debasements of early twentieth-century industrialism. The publication of their symposium, entitled *I'll Take My Stand: The South and the Agrarian Tradition* (1930), on the eve of the Great Depression is something of a high-water mark in the ebb and flow of agrarian ideals in American literature and social criticism. Donald Davidson, Andrew Lytle, John Crowe Ransom, Allen Tate, Robert Penn Warren, and Stark Young were among the group. Because their exchange of ideas took place during the boom era of the 1920's, an era whose mentality at its worst was satirized by Sinclair Lewis in *Babbitt,* there is a prophetic edge to this group of regionalists' criticism of the failures of American materialism, scientism, and "progress" as defined by industrial capitalism. They hoped to express and place agrarian and humanistic values against what one forceful spokesmen for the group, Donald Davidson, called the "privilege of irresponsibility" enjoyed by the American corporation. They also hoped to see political power return to regional-based government and away from centralized federal government. Among other things, they were in part expressing certain Jeffersonian impulses that have lingered into our century. Like many modern writers who would not be considered nature writers per se, from Sinclair Lewis to Norman Mailer, the Southern Agrarians attempted through their writing to transform a society that had become in their views dehumanized, conformist, and something-like-totalitarianism.

Although the Southern Agrarians' influence on the direction of American institutions has been minimal, elements of their regionalist and agrarian attitudes are alive in such subsequent authors as Scott and Helen Nearing, Wendell Berry, and Noel Perrin, just as their attitudes derive from elements of their forebears from Jefferson and Cooper to the Transcendentalists. Indeed, this group of Southern writers was expressing for their own region a larger myth, dream, and symbol fundamental to American civilization—the myth of the Garden created by a vast agricultural community. In his classic *Virgin Land,* Henry Nash Smith emphasized the power of this myth:

> It is true that with the passage of time this symbol, like that of the Wild West, became in turn a less and less accurate description of a society transformed by commerce and industry. When the new economic and technological forces . . . had done their work, the garden was no longer a garden. But the image of an agricultural paradise in the West, embodying group memories of an earlier, and simpler and, it was believed, a happier state of society, long survived as a force in American thought and politics.

Perhaps Donald Davidson's explanation of the Southern Agrarians' philosophy of Southern life best captures their spirit. In 1935, he wrote:

> In its very backwardness, the South had clung to some secret which embodied, it seemed, the precise elements out of which its own reconstruction—and possibly even the reconstruction of America—might be achieved. With American civilization, ugly and visibly bent on ruin, before our eyes, why should we not explore this secret?
>
> Uppermost in our minds was our feeling of intense disgust with the spiritual disorder of modern life—its destruction of human integrity and its lack of purpose. . . . We believed that life determines economics. . . and that economics is not more than an instrument, around the use of which should gather many more motives than economic ones. The evil of industrial economics was that it squeezed all human motives into one narrow channel and then looked for humanitarian means to repair injury.

The regional-agrarianism of these Southerners was paralleled by other literary regionalists. Although limits of space do not permit discussion of them all, we would briefly point to one other group of literary regionalists with special interest for students of nature literature. The American West was represented by a group centered in New Mexico especially. Including Mary Austin, Witter Bynner, and Alice Corbin-Henderson these Southwest regionalists blended their agarianism with a romantic primitivism. In other words, they looked chiefly to aboriginal America and peoples for the lessons nature offers to an impoverished American culture. Mary Austin (1868-1934) is of particular importance. Often linked with Thoreau, Muir, and Burroughs as one of the significant and most talented American nature writers, she was an active environmentalist like Muir, a sophisticated urbanite who was part of the literary avant-garde in New York and California, and a feminist who connected women's rights to all humanity's roots in the earth. Her *Waldenesque* book of essays, *Land of Little Rain* (1903), is her greatest work of nature writing and focuses on the Owens Valley between the Sierras and deserts of Nevada, where she lived between 1891 and 1905. Her autobiography, *Earth Horizon* (1932), describes her discovery of natural and regional (i.e., folk) themes. She has also been linked to later desert writers like Joseph Wood Krutch and Edward Abbey, her *The Land of Journey's Ending* (1924) being an impressive study of cultural-environmental themes common to regionalism, in this case the Taos, New Mexico area. *The Ford* (1971), based on her experiences as an environmental activist, helps set the tradition for the "environmental novel" of later writers like Abbey (*Black Sun,* 1981; *The Brave Cowboy,* 1977), Ernest Callenbach (*Ecotopia,* 1975) and Farley Mowat, a Canadian who has had a wide readership and notoriety in the U.S. (*Never Cry Wolf,* 1963; *The Snow Walker,* 1976).

We have seen that American nature writing derives in part from agrarian and regionalist-ecological values. Another strain in nature writing has emphasized chiefly wilderness and conservation values, and it too has roots in a longstanding, complex tradition. Besides naturalist-authors from Bartram to Muir, there is an equally influential tradition in the mainstream of American literature from Cooper's Natty Bumpo to William Faulkner's Ike McCaslin and Norman Mailer's D. J. and Tex. Throughout the nineteenth and twentieth centuries, heroes in

American novels and stories again and again have tried to repudiate the destructive, power-hungry, materialistic, and consuming qualities in Western civilization. More than a few of Hawthorne's villains destroy themselves, or others, in their quest for unnatural intellectual and scientific power. Melville's *Moby Dick* can be read as a quest to avenge and exploit nature, as the self-destruction of a mad hero who would egotistically assault the cosmos in search of meaning. Here mysterious seas and magnificent whales are opposed to monomaniacal man. And in his South Sea books such as *Typee* and *Omoo* Melville opposes two autonomous civilizations, an aboriginal one in search of continuing stable survival and a white one in search of means to impose its views, wishes, and needs on island peoples and resources. Mark Twain places his natural hero and his great symbol of nature, adventure, and freedom—the Mississippi—against the hypocritical, dehumanizing, and unnatural antics of the people from civilized shore life in *Huckleberry Finn.* In many stories and books Sherwood Anderson places blacks, women, horses, and nature on the opposite end of the spectrum from a corrupt, shallow, and avaricious white man's psyche and culture. Ernest Hemingway's heroes often come to believe that the works of war-torn and frenetic modern man are abominations from which we might seek solace in the primitive rites of hunting and fishing or in the woods, lakes, and streams of northern Michigan or Europe. Nick Adams' retreat to the Michigan woods following the trauma of war in "Big Two-Hearted River" is one of Hemingway's, and modern literature's, most eloquent expressions of that theme. And Faulkner's Yoknopatawpha saga is as much as anything the story of an American Adam's second Fall from grace in the new Eden. That Fall is characterized in part by the loss of wilderness to industrial commercialism, by the conflict between agrarianism and materialism, by the metamorphosis of rural into urban society, and by the impulse to own and control both property and people. No American author has placed a higher value on individuality, self-sufficiency, responsibility, courage, and endurance. And perhaps no narrative in the American fictional canon better expresses the relationship between these valuable qualities and the American wilderness than Faulkner's "The Bear."

For Americans in the twentieth century, just as for America's literary masters and nature writers, the American wilderness has come to embody the myth (the moral, cultural, and psychic truth) of Arcadia, of that timeless place from which flows a source of healing, order, and knowledge. At times informing that myth, at other times more distinct from it, there has also emerged in our century an attitude toward the American wilderness as sacred space.

The Arcadian myth continues even today to conflict with urban, material, and economic values. Like the fortunes of the wilderness itself, the fortunes of this myth have fluctuated with the comings and goings of political parties, presidents, wars, and economic crises. But between 1900 and the Great Depression, a popular, Arcadian "back to nature" movement acted as a counterpoise to the enlarging industrial city and suburban sprawl. A movement expressed through a literature popular with the urban middle classes lent further clout to earlier conservation movements begun by Muir, Burroughs, and Roosevelt, among others. Though this movement shared the pastoral sources of Jeffersonian agrarianism, it emphasized above all the value of wilderness for its spiritual and psychological impact on the individual rather than the economic and political impact of agriculture. As Peter Schmitt demonstrated in *Back to Nature: The Arcadian Myth in Urban America,* the popular forms of this wilderness movement include a vision of wilderness more tamed than the wilderness of major nineteenth- and twentieth-century naturalists. A brief description of some of the central figures and ideas of this Arcadian movement may give an overview of an important social phenomenon.

The idea of the return to nature found many conduits for expression in American life—educational, scientific, and literary. Educator and author Liberty Hyde Bailey, for example, led the way in childhood education through such books as *The Nature Study Idea* (1903), *The Outlook to Nature* (1905), and *The Holy Earth* (1915). His curricular suggestion was that through preservation and nature study the natural world would become a force for social change, for a healthier physical, psychological, and spiritual life in America. Likewise, such influential psychologists and educators as G. Stanley Hall and Maurice Bigelow contributed to the study of nature in the schools. Arguing that individual psychological development recapitulates human development from primitive to sophisticated states, Hall believed that to avoid savage, tribal, and natural experiences in personal development was to avoid the balanced and healthy foundation of personality. Through nature and nature study we re-experience the psychologically necessary "ancestral experiences" of the race. Bigelow tried to put the theory into practice by starting *The Nature Study Review* in 1905, a journal that made an impact on education for two decades. It was such curricular philosophies and programs that led to such extracurricular activities and organizations as summer camps, the Boy Scouts, and other nature and woodcraft-oriented opportunities for young people. The translation of nature experience into urban schools was less successful than the extracurricular experiences, however; even today nature studies have yet to be successfully integrated into public school curricula.

A second manifestation of the Arcadian mythos was the "wilderness" novel. Popular writers of whom we seldom hear today—Gene Stratton Porter, Howard Bell Wright, Stewart White, Mary Waller, and James Oliver Curwood—depicted wilderness as inspiring but generally purified of insect pests and uncomfortable humidities or temperatures. Their heroes, rather than primitive types, tended to be educated urbanites who valued wilderness; their heroines tended toward symbolic purity, innocence, naturalness—the goal and reward of the heroes. Although fiction writers like Jack London and Hamlin Garland enjoyed success with grimmer depictions of nature, more Arcadian nature writing in the first quarter of this century enjoyed enormous popularity and led to certain abuses of truth about wilderness. Not only was wilderness tamed in popular fiction, nature was also moralized to the limits of credibility. Such fiction was a mixed blessing. Nature writers like Neltje Blanchan divided birds and animals into "good" and "bad," with predators judged wanting by such standards. What came to be called "Christian ornithology" was an anthropomorphic tendency further exacerbated by writers who described animal behavior with a literalness and sentimentality more proper to Victorian sermons or beast fables than to a naturalist's scrutiny. When animal descriptions of such authors as Ernest Thompson Seton, Charles Roberts, and William Long tended toward their most incredible, John Burroughs and Theodore Roosevelt hooted them down in the public press. The result was the infamous "Nature Fakers" controversy. When the debate finally rose to an undignified pitch, the magazine editors themselves cut it off. But from Burrough's and Roosevelt's view, the danger of phony animal heroes, moralistic nature narratives, and cute, personified creatures was that they could ultimately reduce the credibility and work of all naturalists and conservationists.

On the other hand such "abuses," as Burroughs saw them, may have actually served the purposes of conservation as well. First, the effect of popular fiction and nonfiction about nature was to increase the Arcadian impulses of city and suburb dwellers. This desire in turn increased the tourist industry and hence public support for state and federal governments to purchase and preserve wilderness. The tendency was to preserve the unique and spectacular, and the tourist industry brought its own abuses in parking lots, highways, and resorts. But even as early as 1908 there were eleven national parks. And public awareness and support helped activists like Muir and conservation organizations after him fight municipal and private interests when they threatened wilderness areas. Sometimes the wilderness values lost, of course, as in the famous controversy over Hetch-Hetchy Valley inside Yosemite Park. Though Muir, the Secretary of the Interior, and a band of conservationists lost the fight to keep the valley from being flooded as a reservoir for metropolitan San Francisco, the battle anticipated future water and resource shortages for urban areas. More importantly, it focused national attention on the issue of the Federal Government's responsibility to all its people and to future generations, not merely to the people of a particular state, city, or corporation. Moreover, it cleared the way for later successes, such as Aldo Leopold's and Robert Marshall's work within the Forest Service to establish permanent wilderness preserves.

A second positive effect of popular nature writing was that by emphasizing animal individuality, intelligence, compassion, and nobility through anthropomorphism, the popular authors countered post-Darwinian inclinations to view animals only by species or group, to view life on the planet only through a scientific materialism and determinism, and to view human society through an ever-growing pessimism and alienation. Like many nature writers today, these earlier authors focused readers' attention on the order rather than the purposelessness of the cosmos, on human responsibility for, rather than estrangement from, our fellow creatures. If we are not mere victims of chaotic forces and impulses, then we are responsible for our actions, and ethics is returned to humanity and extends to the natural world. The attitude that the natural world and its inhabitants have rights of their own is peculiarly modern and has been recently effective in helping environmentalists preserve natural landscapes and species.

With roots in American Transcendentalism and nineteenth-century landscape painting, another corollary wilderness value to the Arcadian myth has equally informed twentieth-century nature writing and public response—the sense of wilderness as, in a primitive sense, sacred. In *The Sacred and the Profane: The Nature of Religion* (1957; 59), the novelist and eminent scholar of world religions Mircea Eliade traced the ancient and contemporary sources and qualities of nature worship in premodern cultures. The "desacralization" of the world in which we live is, Eliade argues, "an integral part of the gigantic transformation of the world undertaken by the industrial societies" and made possible by momentous advances in science. Such desacralization is responsible for our modern feelings of alienation from both nature and culture, just as it is responsible for modern anti-agrarianism. "Let us think," Eliade writes, ". . . of agricultural work in desacralized society.

Here it has become a profane act, justified by the economic profit that it brings. The ground is tilled to be exploited; the end pursued is profit and food. Emptied of religious symbolism, agricultural work becomes at once opaque and exhausting; it reveals no meaning, it makes possible no opening toward the universal, toward the world of spirit." This dubious achievement, Eliade reminds us, is a recent event in human history. Nevertheless, desacralization, however complete in social forms and attitudes and in much scientific inquiry, is still incomplete in some deeper level of our experiences and psyches. Hence the lingering ability of most of us to be inexplicably moved by natural scenery and creatures. It is just this vestige of ineffable feeling for nature that even modern nature writers from Henry Beston, to Joseph Wood Krutch, Edward Abbey, and Annie Dillard track, experience, and relate to readers hungry for something so often absent from modern life.

In *Wilderness as Sacred Space* (1976) geographer Linda Graber analyzes the sources and qualities of that lingering "geopiety" which shapes our present attitudes toward wilderness preservation. Using Eliade's argument and definition of the sacralization of nature, of the worship of that power which reveals itself in nature to us (or the experience of "hierophany," in Eliade's terms), Graber traces the expression of wilderness as a source of human transcendence and sacred power, as well as a model of moral and physical perfection, in the modern world. In her consideration of nature writers in particular, Graber makes the distinction between "knowledge about" nature (i.e., the purely scientific approach) and the exploration of one person's experience of nature (the nature writer's approach). Through the examples of Leopold, Krutch, and Abbey, she looks at the varieties of literary approaches to geopiety. Only Leopold, she notes, has emerged as a latter-day Thoreau or Muir, as *the* modern authority quoted in preservationist publications. Leopold's discovery of moral directives in nature *through* science makes him especially suited to develop a "land ethic" that inextricably ties wilderness to civilization. It is that ethic which might become—some would say is now becoming—the basis for the reform of our social and economic institutions.

Between the World Wars and after World War II, the literature of wilderness values was revitalized and made more respectably scientific than it had been during the Arcadian back-to-nature movement earlier in the century. As the life sciences were becoming more specializaed and laboratory-oriented, naturalists with literary talent such as William Beebe and Robert Murphy reestablished the less sentimental tradition begun by early naturalists from the Bartrams to Muir. Through such books as Beebe's *Jungle Peace* (1918), *Pheasants of the World* (1926), *Galapago: World's End* (1924), and *Half-Mile Down* (1934), and Murphy's *Oceanic Birds of America* (1936) and *Looking for Grace* (1947) the public was once again being informed in accurate detail, and often through eminently readable prose. The post-War scientist-authors who came after them—Loren Eisely, Rachel Carson, Lorus and Margery Milne, Lewis Thomas, to name a few—greatly influenced public biological and ecological awareness during an accelerating campaign for environmental protection.

What we now know as the environmental movement or environmentalism in post-World War II America is in large part due to the work of nature writers of both agrarian and wilderness inclinations. Together with old and new conservation groups, they provoked a revolution in public consciousness; they gave birth to the age of environmental activism, often through the use of massive doses of scientific data. Of course, the literature had been there since the early nineteenth century. Wordsworth and Thoreau transformed many readers' consciousness from the start. But in the 1960's writers, scientists, conservationists, lawyers, economists, and citizens began to work together against what had seemingly become the unconscious giants of government and corporate technology.

There were stirrings of this contemporary movement during the Great Depression of the 1930's. Franklin D. Roosevelt, like his uncle Teddy, believed in the "gospel of conservation." The relationship between humanity and nature became a political issue again during the economic crisis and the parallel devastation of depleted agricultural lands. It became obvious that more than Arcadian fantasies were called for; some new balance of economics, ecology, and social structures was in order; the easy prosperity and the dream of limitless resources, like the Babbitry of the 1920's, now seemed a fool's paradise. Franklin Roosevelt realized that at this critical moment a degree of individual liberty that had resulted in waste and destruction on many fronts had to be restrained for the larger community's survival. With support of the public and Congress, he established one of his most popular economic-ecological projects—the Civilian Conservation Corps. Hundreds of thousands of unemployed young men took to restoring the wasted land: planting trees, building reservoirs and fish habitats, raising bridges and fire towers, fighting plant diseases, cleaning beaches and campgrounds. In addition, the Soil Conservation Service fought to preserve further massive soil erosion.

The two literary works that best describe the human dimension and the proportions of the economic and ecological disaster that the nation was fighting are John Steinbeck's *Grapes of Wrath* (1939) and James Agee's *Let Us Now Praise Famous Men* (1941). It has been argued that the large and zealous C.C.C. actually intruded on wilderness areas and that FDR's conservation philosophy was too anthropocentric and inadequate by current standards, but at least there had been an awakening and a massive response. After the economic and ecological disasters of the 1930's, some forms of economic and ecological ignorance might never again seem excusable.

While government and labor did their crisis work, scientists, conservationists, and writers did theirs as well. Aside from Aldo Leopold, there is probably no better embodiment of the scientist-conservationist-author, and no one who had greater impact at the time, than forester-author Robert Marshall. In *The People's Forests* (1933) he argued that private interests have come to regulate the regulators—an argument critical to environmental debate today. And he struck an early anti-utilitarian note: natural landscapes and beings should be preserved for their own sakes. His explorations of our last frontier in Alaska were recreated in *Arctic Village* (1933) and *Arctic-Wilderness* (1956, posthumously). Friend of Leopold, of conservationist-editor Robert Sterling Yard, and of Benton MacKaye, Marshall in the mid-thirties was a founding father—along with such men—of the Appalachian Trail and the Wilderness Society. In 1939 Marshall drafted regulations that empowered the Secretary of Agriculture to set aside tracts of wilderness, thereby laying the groundwork for the most important wilderness legislation of the 1950's, 60's, and 70's.

Of course during the war, the military crisis turned the nation's attention away from nature and conservation. Indeed, under the rubric of "patriotism" special interests from logging companies to the armed forces tried to encroach on public property. But after the awakening of the 1930's, the National Park Service and conservation groups were credible and powerful enough to disprove and prevent the "patriotic necessity" of such encroachment.

After the war the reconstruction of America toward a peace-time economy combined with growing prosperity and an unsympathetic Presidential Administration to extend the hiatus in environmental activism. The Eisenhower Administration and its Secretary of the Interior Douglas McKay (an ex-car dealer from Oregon known as "Giveaway McKay") piled up the worst conservation record in decades. However, the resulting incursions on wildlife refuges, especially by oil and gas companies, ultimately had a positive if delayed effect. In the first place, the Eisenhower policies forced an enduring alliance between conservationists and Democrats that would be telling in the next two decades. In the second, nature writers, authors, and scientists turned with renewed force to the issues of environmental depredation and animals' rights.

In 1948 Fairfield Osborn's *Our Plundered Planet* argued the necessity of ecological consciousness for our very survival, and William Vogt's *Road to Survival* made the issue of population control an ecological issue. Historian, columnist, and urbanite Bernard DeVoto, much impressed with Vogt's book, typifies the post-war conversion of many. He became a one-man conservation movement in the 1950's. His knowledge of history prepared him to understand the American pattern of private interests assaulting public preserves. Especially through his *Harper's Magazine* column, he demonstrated how journalism too could become an instrument for conservation by serving as a sort of clearing house of conservation issues and crises. Similarly, the urbane academic Joseph Wood Krutch left city and academia to become one of America's greatest craftsmen of nature literature. His combination of craftsmanship and scientific accuracy made him second only to Leopold in his impact on the younger generation of readers and activists. And like Leopold, he did much to shift the then-current conservation ethic (i.e., the salvation of nature for human use and survival) to the preservationist ethic—the salvation of nature for its own sake.

In the first decades after the war other activist-authors promoting wilderness values include Chief Justice William O. Douglas, Charles Lindbergh, Howard Zahniser, and Rachel Carson. Probably the most prominent conservationist in public life during the fifties and sixties, Douglas emphasized the incapacity of federal conservation agencies. He knew all the ways in which the protector turns into culprit, and he devoted himself tirelessly to numerous preservation battles. His special affinity was for the Pacific Cascades, a subject of *My Wilderness: The Pacific West* (1960), a book reflecting his personal shift from a conservationist to a preservationist ethic following his 250-mile hike in the Himalayas in 1951. The experience was a revelation. After three days in a Buddhist monastery and subsequent studies of world religions, Douglas arrived at his beliefs that all plants and animals share "being" and therefore equal value and rights, and that wilderness areas are "sacred precincts." Another public figure at the time, Charles Lindbergh joined the cause by demonstrating his own revelation and change of faith from technology to the natural world. Foreshadowing the nation's later environmental awakening, and writing out of the tradition of Lewis Mumford,

Lindbergh declared his new vision in *Of Flight and Life* (1948), and, as a lecturer, world traveler, and author, argued that the disproportionate temptation of technological or mechanistic power distorted modern life into grotesque and pathological forms, the greatest of which is technological warfare that burns, like a great flame, all nature in its path.

One of the most effective conservationist-editor-lobbyists of the day was Howard Zahniser of the Wilderness Society. Editor of *Living Wilderness,* Zahniser was by all accounts the most influential conservation lobbyist in Washington. With his more controversial counterpart in the Sierra Club, David Brower (who built that organization from a small, regional, social-outing club into the major conservation organization in the U.S.), Zahniser helped make the entire movement more public, professional, aggressive, litigious, and effective. In the wake of Aldo Leopold, these men and other activists charged Americans with the moral obligation to preserve natural areas. More than once, this change and the changes it wrought in Americans and in an international movement have been compared to an "evolutionary leap" in ethical consciousness. The early legislative activity that embodied the change in America would range from the Wilderness Bill of 1956, to the Wilderness Act of 1964. By the 1970's environmental legislation, like the $25 billion water pollution bill of 1972, was the sign of an evolving change of vision.

The two most important events of the 1960's that quickened this evolution were the Kennedy Administration with Secretary of the Interior Stewart Udall, and the publication of Rachel Carson's *Silent Spring* (1962). The renewed governmental support for wilderness values and Carson's book sparked a renaissance in the literature of nature as much as in the legislation of nature. That renaissance encompasses works and authors so diverse and numerous—from Hal Borland to a global naturalist like Peter Matthiessen, from Ann Zwinger to the newest voices like David Rains Wallace—that only a volume devoted to the subject might describe it adequately. Here we can merely suggest some of the highlights and hope that our limited selections from several texts will express the qualities and richness of this flourishing nature literature.

If the agrarian impulses in American nature literature have waned since the Second World War and *Silent Spring,* the conservationist-preservationist impulses have surged forward with the renewed vigor of an environmental awakening unequalled since the turn of the century. It is probably because our crises have grown so acute and our populations and industrial technologies so vast that nature writing has become more polemical, even apocalyptic, in tone. The agrarianism of Wendell Berry and the quieter regionalism of Noel Perrin, for example, maintain one strain of the American tradition, it is true. But even in Berry, especially, the note of urgency, and the themes of conservation, ring through. In her shift from the scientific popularization of the natural world in *Under Sea-wind* (1941), *The Sea Around Us* (1951), and *The Edge of the Sea* (1955) to *Silent Spring,* Carson represents a change of tone in our dominant approach to nature. She further set the terms and tenor for political as well as literary environmentalism since the 1960's when she brought human beings into the delicate ecological balance as an endangered species no different from the birds and insects our pesticides were indiscriminately silencing. That she chose to focus on one problem (unpredicted effects of insecticides) and one industry (chemical) in *Silent Spring* made her massively documented yet readable account so effective that it set the standard for future scientists and authors who would focus on the ecological problems of population, agri-business, atmospheric pollution, national parks, nuclear and chemical industries, etc. That she emphasized the *unseen,* cumulative effects of pollutants, the corrupting liaisons between industry, government, and academia, and the fallacy of technological solutions also set the themes for a coming decade of activism and literature. Her influence can be seen in works by biologist-authors such as Barry Commoner and Paul Ehrlich (whose *The Population Bomb* published in 1967 and 1968 is the best-selling conservation book ever). Her influence can also be seen in scientifically trained authors who write for large audiences. Anne Simon's *The Thin Edge: Coast and Man in Crisis* (1978) returns to Carson's special area of concern, the sea and its fragile, nourishing margins. But Carson's groundwork is equally a foundation for the essays and books of writers ranging from Sigurd Olsen to Edward Abbey to poet Gary Snyder. The arrogance of humanity, the jeopardy in which we have placed ourselves and other life forms, the separate but equal claims to existence of the non-human world—these are the motifs and themes of most contemporary nature writing in America. The idealizations, if not the critiques, of the pastoral and the Arcadian must have seemed an unaffordable luxury to most writers after the War.

It is true, on the other hand, that there are moments or entire works of more disinterested, or "pure," contact with the wild world in the authors mentioned so far. But nature writing today that explores the heart and reality of nature *outside* of the controversy and the crisis tends to be more unusual than common since Carson's seminal book. The separation from explicit ecological polemic of writers such as Annie Dillard in *Pilgrim at Tinker Creek* (1974) or Alaskan poet John Haines in poetry or prose books such as his *Living off the Country: Essays on Poetry and Place* (1981) does not make their work any less important. On the contrary, by their contrast and rarity such authors may be more valuable and endurable as literature per se, and as the record of profound personal contact between the human and the natural outside of the major social movements of the day.

Those social movements interact at a number of points, however, with the environmental movement that so many authors, economists, scientists, lawyers, and citizens have joined. The countercultures of the young, the feminist movement, and, eventually, the anti-war movement all have expressed varieties of dissent that connect to the environmental ethos—a certain anti-materialism, a profound skepticism of technology for its own sake or as an ultimate solution, a distaste for the city-as-megalopolis, a certain primitivism, and a desire to decentralize the concentrations of power that, in the hands of a few, have proved dangerous for personal liberty and safety, for the economy, and for the natural environment. If Earth Day on April 22, 1970, was the largest environmental demonstration in history, the debate over nuclear technologies and atmospheric pollution has made long-standing conservation issues a lasting force in the political life of America and other developed countries. At the dawn of the nuclear age Fairfield Osborn summed up the ecologically disastrous attitude of an arrogant civilization when he wrote that through our development of physical sciences funneled into vast industrial systems we have created dangerous new environments and conditions.

> These extensions of (man's) mind-fertility and his mind-restlessness are superimposed, like crusts, on the face of the earth, choking his life sources. The

conditions under which he must live are constantly changing, he himself being the cause of the changes. In this metamorphosis he has almost lost sight of the fact that the living resoures of his life are derived from his earth-home and not from his mind-power. With one hand he harnesses great waters, with the other he dries up the water sources. He must change with changing conditions or perish. He *conquers* a continent and within a century lays much of it into barren waste. He must move to find a new and unspoiled land. He must, he must—but where? His numbers are increasing, starvation taunts him—even after his wars too many are left alive. He causes the life-giving soils for his crops to wash into the oceans. He falls back on palliatives and calls upon a host of chemists to invent substitutes for the organized processes of nature. Can they do this? Can his chemists dismiss nature and take over the operation of the earth? He hopes so. Hope turns to conviction—they must, or else he perishes. Is he not nature's "crowning glory"? Can he not turn away from his creator? Who has a better right? He has seemingly "discovered" the secrets of the universe. What need, then, to live by its principles!

Robert Frost
1874-1963

As a man of several trades—shoemaking, newspaper editing, teaching, and farming—and also master poet, Robert Frost lived most of his life in rural New England, "north of Boston," and used that locality in his poetry. The natural settings, animals, and people of New England are his source and subject. Recognized relatively late in life, his first book, *A Boy's Will* (1913), was published in England during his brief residence there from 1912–15. The lyrical poetry of that book was replaced by a more narrative strain and by the exploration of character in his second book, *North of Boston* (1914), but both lyrical and narrative impulses remained essential to his poetry throughout his long and productive career. That career included Pulitzer Prizes for *New Hampshire* (1923), *Collected Poems* (1930), *A Further Range* (1936) and *A Witness Tree* (1942); teaching stints at Amherst, Michigan University, and Harvard; and recognition as America's unofficial poet laureate.

He considered himself a Synecdochist, "that figure of speech in which we use a part for the whole." And he is the best example of how an ostensibly regional writer may become universal as well. His poetry may begin in geography, but it ramifies to include us all, our relationship to one another and to the natural world. He is probably the American poet of greatest universal appeal, of the widest, enduring audience. His accessibility is in part due to his use, like Wordsworth and Whitman, of "language really used by men," to his simplicity without simple-mindedness, and to his effort to render wisdom through poetry without being didactic.

Surprise, delight, comedy and tragedy, rich and accurate detail, and emotional intensity through restraint and form—all are qualities of Frost's poetry and the materials of his craftsmanship. Influenced by the Greek and Roman classics and by the American Transcendentalists, he combines the emotive with the restrained, the organic development of an idea with poetic form, the pursuit of transcendence with the tough realities of life and nature, and the values of self-reliance with the value of brotherhood.

A PRAYER IN SPRING*

Oh, give us pleasure in the flowers today;
And give us not to think so far away
As the uncertain harvest; keep us here
All simply in the springing of the year.

Oh, give us pleasure in the orchard white,
Like nothing else by day, like ghosts by night;
And make us happy in the happy bees,
The swarm dilating round the perfect trees.

And make us happy in the darting bird
That suddenly above the bees is heard,
The meteor that thrusts in with needle bill,
And off a blossom in mid-air stands still.

For this is love and nothing else is love,
The which it is reserved for God above
To sanctify to what far ends He will,
But which it only needs that we fulfill.

IN HARDWOOD GROVES

The same leaves over and over again!
They fall from giving shade above,
To make one texture of faded brown
And fit the earth like a leather glove.

Before the leaves can mount again
To fill the trees with another shade,
They must go down past things coming up.
They must go down into the dark decayed.

They *must* be pierced by flowers and put
Beneath the feet of dancing flowers.
However it is in some other world
I know that this is the way in ours.

HYLA BROOK

By June our brook's run out of song and speed.
Sought for much after that, it will be found
Either to have gone groping underground
(And taken with it all the Hyla breed
That shouted in the mist a month ago,
Like ghost of sleigh bells in a ghost of snow)—
Or flourished and come up in jewelweed,
Weak foliage that is blown upon and bent,
Even against the way its waters went.
Its bed is left a faded paper sheet
Of dead leaves stuck together by the heat—
A brook to none but who remember long.
This as it will be seen is other far
Than with brooks taken otherwhere in song.
We love the things we love for what they are.

DUST OF SNOW

The way a crow
Shook down on me
The dust of snow
From a hemlock tree

Has given my heart
A change of mood
And saved some part
Of a day I had rued.

THE RUNAWAY

Once when the snow of the year was beginning to fall,
We stopped by a mountain pasture to say, "Whose colt?"
A little Morgan had one forefoot on the wall,
The other curled at his breast. He dipped his head
And snorted at us. And then he had to bolt.
We heard the miniature thunder where he fled,
And we saw him, or thought we saw him, dim and gray,
Like a shadow against the curtain of falling flakes.
"I think the little fellow's afraid of the snow.
He isn't winter-broken. It isn't play
With the little fellow at all. He's running away.
I doubt if even his mother could tell him, 'Sakes,
It's only weather.' He'd think she didn't know!
Where is his mother? He can't be out alone."

And now he comes again with clatter of stone,
And mounts the wall again with whited eyes
And all his tail that isn't hair up straight.
He shudders his coat as if to throw off flies.
"Whoever it is that leaves him out so late,
When other creatures have gone to stall and bin,
Ought to be told to come and take him in."

A BROOK IN THE CITY

The farmhouse lingers, though averse to square
With the new city street it has to wear
A number in. But what about the brook
That held the house as in an elbow-crook?
I ask as one who knew the brook, its strength
And impulse, having dipped a finger length
And made it leap my knuckle, having tossed
A flower to try its currents where they crossed.
The meadow grass could be cemented down
From growing under pavements of a town;
The apple trees be sent to hearthstone flame.
Is water wood to serve a brook the same?
How else dispose of an immortal force
No longer needed? Staunch it at its source
With cinder loads dumped down? The brook was thrown
Deep in a sewer dungeon under stone
In fetid darkness still to live and run—
And all for nothing it had ever done,
Except forget to go in fear perhaps.
No one would know except for ancient maps
That such a brook ran water. But I wonder
If from its being kept forever under,
The thoughts may not have risen that so keep
This new-built city from both work and sleep.

SPRING POOLS

These pools that, though in forests, still reflect
The total sky almost without defect,
And like the flowers beside them, chill and shiver,
Will like the flowers beside them soon be gone,
And yet not out by any brook or river,
But up by roots to bring dark foliage on.

The trees that have it in their pent-up buds
To darken nature and be summer woods—
Let them think twice before they use their powers
To blot out and drink up and sweep away
These flowery waters and these watery flowers
From snow that melted only yesterday.

TREE AT MY WINDOW

Tree at my window, window tree,
My sash is lowered when night comes on;
But let there never be curtain drawn
Between you and me.

Vague dream-head lifted out of the ground,
And thing next most diffuse to cloud,
Not all your light tongues talking aloud
Could be profound.

But, tree, I have seen you taken and tossed,
And if you have seen me when I slept,
You have seen me when I was taken and swept
And all but lost.

That day she put our heads together,
Fate had her imagination about her,
Your head so much concerned with outer,
Mine with inner, weather.

DIRECTIVE

Back out of all this now too much for us,
Back in a time made simple by the loss
Of detail, burned, dissolved, and broken off
Like graveyard marble sculpture in the weather,
There is a house that is no more a house
Upon a farm that is no more a farm
And in a town that is no more a town.
The road there, if you'll let a guide direct you
Who only has at heart your getting lost,
May seem as if it should have been a quarry—
Great monolithic knees the former town
Long since gave up pretense of keeping covered.
And there's a story in a book about it:
Besides the wear of iron wagon wheels
The ledges show lines ruled southeast-northwest,
The chisel work of an enormous Glacier
That braced his feet against the Arctic Pole.
You must not mind a certain coolness from him
Still said to haunt this side of Panther Mountain.
Nor need you mind the serial ordeal
Of being watched from forty cellar holes
As if by eye pairs out of forty firkins.
As for the woods' excitement over you
That sends light rustle rushes to their leaves,
Charge that to upstart inexperience.
Where were they all not twenty years ago?
They think too much of having shaded out
A few old pecker-fretted apple trees.
Make yourself up a cheering song of how
Someone's road home from work this once was,
Who may be just ahead of you on foot
Or creaking with a buggy load of grain.
The height of the adventure is the height
Of country where two village cultures faded
Into each other. Both of them are lost.
And if you're lost enough to find yourself
By now, pull in your ladder road behind you
And put a sign up CLOSED to all but me.
Then make yourself at home. The only field
Now left's no bigger than a harness gall.
First there's the children's house of make-believe,
Some shattered dishes underneath a pine,
The playthings in the playhouse of the children.
Weep for what little things could make them glad.
Then for the house that is no more a house,
But only a belilaced cellar hole,

Now slowly closing like a dent in dough.
This was no playhouse but a house in earnest.
Your destination and your destiny's
A brook that was the water of the house,
Cold as a spring as yet so near its source,
Too lofty and original to rage.
(We know the valley streams that when aroused
Will leave their tatters hung on barb and thorn.)
I have kept hidden in the instep arch
Of an old cedar at the waterside
A broken drinking goblet like the Grail
Under a spell so the wrong ones can't find it,
So can't get saved, as Saint Mark says they mustn't.
(I stole the goblet from the children's playhouse.)
Here are your waters and your watering place.
Drink and be whole again beyond confusion.

Jack London
1876-1916

A native of California and the San Francisco Bay area, Jack London grew up in rough-and-ready circumstances that influenced his adventurous and socialist writings. An illegitimate child in an unstable family along the Oakland waterfront, he left school at age fourteen, raided oyster beds, joined a sealing cruise that took him to Japan, and tramped and labored his way about the United States and Canada. Despite a semester at the University of California in 1896, he was largely self-educated with an abiding interest in sociology and socialism. Within a year after his semester at the University he was in the Klondike Gold Rush. He failed to mine gold, but throughout his writing life he continued to mine his Klondike experiences for the men, women, and dogs who faced every harshness of man and nature. Many of his heroes bear the mark of superhuman or mythic figures, a mixture of what he witnessed in the far north and his readings of Darwin, Nietzsche, Spencer, and Marx.

His stories of the Yukon began to appear as early as 1898; *The Son of Wolf* (1900) brought him national fame. Riding on the success of this and further stories and novels of life in the arctic regions, London turned to his other interest in *The People of the Abyss* (1903), his study of slum conditions in London, England, followed by *War of the Classes* (1905), *The Iron Heel* (1908), and *The Human Drift* (1917). His most famous novel is the classic *The Call of the Wild* (1903), on one hand a naturalistic treatment of a dog-hero's return to a primordial self and world, and on the other, a mythic and epic journey into the deepest instinctual sources of the self. The wolf became for London the symbol of the ultimate wild creature, the very spirit of forest and mountain, the very presence of savagery, beauty, and mystery at the heart of nature and the human subconscious. The arctic was a machineless world that brought out humanity's deepest racial instincts, and a dramatic arena where the primordial laws of life mocked our civilized, mechanized cultures. It is in the arctic, with its white silences and ghostly wastes, London said, that "if ever, man walks alone with God." London's agrarian themes are best expressed in *The Valley of the Moon* (1913) in which the prescription for economic ills is a return to the land.

One of the most popular and enduring of modern writers in America and abroad (his writings have been translated into forty languages), London—his themes, settings, and vitality—must touch some deep chord in many readers of diverse cultures.

TO BUILD A FIRE*

Day had broken cold and gray, exceedingly cold and gray, when the man turned aside from the main Yukon trail and climbed the high earth-bank, where a dim and little-travelled trail led eastward through the fat spruce timberland. It was a steep bank, and he paused for breath at the top, excusing the act to himself by looking at his watch. It was nine o'clock. There was no sun nor hint of sun, though there was not a cloud in the sky. It was a clear day, and yet there seemed an intangible pall over the face of things, a subtle gloom that made the day dark, and that was due to the absence of sun. This fact did not worry the man. He was used to the lack of sun. It had been days since he had seen the sun, and he knew that a few more days must pass before that cheerful orb, due south, would just peep above the sky-line and dip immediately from view.

The man flung a look back along the way he had come. The Yukon lay a mile wide and hidden under three feet of ice. On top of this ice were as many feet of snow. It was all pure white, rolling in gentle undulations where the ice-jams of the freeze-up had formed. North and south, as far as his eye could see, it was unbroken white, save for a dark hair-line that curved and twisted away into the north, where it disappeared behind another spruce-covered island. This dark hair-line was the trail—the main trail—that led south five hundred miles to the Chilcoot Pass, Dyea, and salt water; and that led north seventy miles to Dawson, and still on to the north a thousand miles to Nulato, and finally to St. Michael on Bering Sea, a thousand miles and half a thousand more.

But all this—the mysterious, far-reaching hair-line trail, the absence of sun from the sky, the tremendous cold, and the strangeness and weirdness of it all—made no impression on the man. It was not because he was long used to it. He was a newcomer in the land, a *chechaquo,* and this was his first winter. The trouble with him was that he was without imagination. He was quick and alert in the things of life, but only in the things, and not in the significances. Fifty degrees below zero means eighty-odd degrees of frost. Such fact impressed him as being cold and uncomfortable, and that was all. It did not lead him to meditate upon his frailty as a creature of temperature, and upon man's frailty in general, able only to live within certain narrow limits of heat and cold; and from there on it did not lead him to the conjectural field of immortality and man's place in the universe. Fifty degrees below zero stood for a bite of frost that hurt and that must be guarded against by the use of mittens, ear-flaps, warm moccasins, and thick

*From *Jack London: Novels & Stories* (New York: The Library of America, 1982).

socks. Fifty degrees below zero was to him just precisely fifty degrees below zero. That there should be anything more to it than that was a thought that never entered his head.

As he turned to go on, he spat speculatively. There was a sharp, explosive crackle that startled him. He spat again. And again, in the air, before it could fall to the snow, the spittle crackled. He knew that at fifty below spittle crackled on the snow, but this spittle had crackled in the air. Undoubtedly it was colder than fifty below—how much colder he did not know. But the temperature did not matter. He was bound for the old claim on the left fork of Henderson Creek, where the boys were already. They had come over across the divide from the Indian Creek country, while he had come the roundabout way to take a look at the possibilities of getting out logs in the spring from the islands in the Yukon. He would be in to camp by six o'clock; a bit after dark, it was true, but the boys would be there, a fire would be going, and a hot supper would be ready. As for lunch, he pressed his hand against the protruding bundle under his jacket. It was also under his shirt, wrapped up in a handkerchief and lying against the naked skin. It was the only way to keep the biscuits from freezing. He smiled agreeably to himself as he thought of those biscuits, each cut open and sopped in bacon grease, and each enclosing a generous slice of fried bacon.

He plunged in among the big spruce trees. The trail was faint. A foot of snow had fallen since the last sled had passed over, and he was glad he was without a sled, travelling light. In fact, he carried nothing but the lunch wrapped in the handkerchief. He was surprised, however, at the cold. It certainly was cold, he concluded, as he rubbed his numb nose and cheek-bones with his mittened hand. He was a warm-whiskered man, but the hair on his face did not protect the high cheek-bones and the eager nose that thrust itself aggressively into the frosty air.

At the man's heels trotted a dog, a big native husky, the proper wolf-dog, gray-coated and without any visible or temperamental difference from its brother, the wild wolf. The animal was depressed by the tremendous cold. It knew that it was no time for travelling. Its instinct told it a truer tale than was told to the man by the man's judgment. In reality, it was not merely colder than fifty below zero; it was colder than sixty below, than seventy below. It was seventy-five below zero. Since the freezing-point is thirty-two above zero, it meant that one hundred and seven degrees of frost obtained. The dog did not know anything about thermometers. Possibly in its brain there was no sharp consciousness of a condition of very cold such as was in the man's brain. But the brute had its instinct. It experienced a vague but menacing apprehension that subdued it and made it slink along at the man's heels, and that made it question eagerly every unwonted movement of the man as if expecting him to go into camp or to seek shelter somewhere and build a fire. The dog had learned fire, and it wanted fire, or else to burrow under the snow and cuddle its warmth away from the air.

The frozen moisture of its breathing had settled on its fur in a fine powder of frost, and especially were its jowls, muzzle, and eyelashes whitened by its crystalled breath. The man's red beard and mustache were likewise frosted, but more solidly, the deposit taking the form of ice and increasing with every warm, moist breath he exhaled. Also, the man was chewing tobacco, and the muzzle of ice held his lips so rigidly that he was unable to clear his chin when he expelled the juice. The result was that a crystal beard of the color and solidity of amber was increasing its length on his chin. If he fell down it would shatter itself, like glass, into brittle fragments. But he did not mind the appendage. It was the penalty all tobacco-chewers paid in that country, and he had been out before in two cold snaps. They had not been so cold as this, he knew, but by the spirit thermometer at Sixty Mile he knew they had been registered at fifty below and at fifty-five.

He held on through the level stretch of woods for several miles, crossed a wide flat of niggerheads, and dropped down a bank to the frozen bed of a small stream. This was Henderson Creek, and he knew he was ten miles from the forks. He looked at his watch. It was ten o'clock. He was making four miles an hour, and he calculated that he would arrive at the forks at half-past twelve. He decided to celebrate that event by eating his lunch there.

The dog dropped in again at his heels, with a tail drooping discouragement, as the man swung along the creek-bed. The furrow of the old sled-trail was plainly visible, but a dozen inches of snow covered the marks of the last runners. In a month no man had come up or down that silent creek. The man held steadily on. He was not much given to thinking, and just then particularly he had nothing to think about save that he would eat lunch at the forks and that at six o'clock he would be in camp with the boys. There was nobody to talk to; and, had there been, speech would have been impossible because of the ice-muzzle on his mouth. So he continued monotonously to chew tobacco and to increase the length of his amber bread.

Once in a while the thought reiterated itself that it was very cold and that he had never experienced such cold. As he walked along he rubbed his cheek-bones and nose with the back of his mittened hand. He did this automatically, now and again changing hands. But rub as he would, the instant he stopped his cheek-bones went numb, and the following instant the end of his nose went numb. He was sure to frost his cheeks; he knew that, and experienced a pang of regret that he had not devised a nose-strap of the sort Bud wore in cold snaps. Such a strap passed across the cheeks, as well, and saved them. But it didn't matter much, after all. What were frosted cheeks? A bit painful, that was all; they were never serious.

Empty as the man's mind was of thoughts, he was keenly observant, and he noticed the changes in the creek, the curves and bends and timber-jams, and always he sharply noted where he placed his feet. Once, coming around a bend, he shied abruptly like a startled horse, curved away from the place where he had been walking, and retreated several paces back along the trail. The creek he knew was frozen clear to the bottom,—no creek could contain water in that arctic winter,—but he knew also that there were springs that bubbled out from the hillsides and ran along under the snow and on top the ice of the creek. He knew that the coldest snaps never froze these springs, and he knew likewise their danger. They were traps.

They hid pools of water under the snow that might be three inches deep, or three feet. Sometimes a skin of ice half an inch thick covered them, and in turn was covered by the snow. Sometimes there were alternate layers of water and ice-skin, so that when one broke through he kept on breaking through for a while, sometimes wetting himself to the waist.

That was why he had shied in such panic. He had felt the give under his feet and heard the crackle of a snow-hidden ice-skin. And to get his feet wet in such a temperature meant trouble and danger. At the very least it meant delay, for he would be forced to stop and build a fire and under its protection to bare his feet while he dried his socks and moccasins. He stood and studied the creek-bed and its banks, and decided that the flow of water came from the right. He reflected awhile, rubbing his nose and cheeks, then skirted to the left, stepping gingerly and testing the footing for each step. Once clear of the danger, he took a fresh chew of tobacco and swung along at his four-mile gait.

In the course of the next two hours he came upon several similar traps. Usually the snow above the hidden pools had a sunken, candied appearance that advertised the danger. Once again, however, he had a close call; and once, suspecting danger, he compelled the dog to go on in front. The dog did not want to go. It hung back until the man shoved it forward, and then it went quickly across the white, unbroken surface. Suddenly it broke through, floundered to one side, and got away to firmer footing. It had wet its forefeet and legs, and almost immediately the water that clung to it turned to ice. It made quick efforts to lick the ice off its legs, then dropped down in the snow and began to bite out the ice that had formed between the toes. This was a matter of instinct. To permit the ice to remain would mean sore feet. It did not know this. It merely obeyed the mysterious prompting that arose from the deep crypts of its being. But the man knew, having achieved a judgment on the subject, and he removed the mitten from his right hand and helped tear out the ice-particles. He did not expose his fingers more than a minute, and was astonished at the swift numbness that smote them. It certainly was cold. He pulled on the mitten hastily, and beat the hand savagely across his chest.

At twelve o'clock the day was at its brightest. Yet the sun was too far south on its winter journey to clear the horizon. The bulge of the earth intervened between it and Henderson Creek, where the man walked under a clear sky at noon and cast no shadow. At half-past twelve, to the minute, he arrived at the forks of the creek. He was pleased at the speed he had made. If he kept it up, he would certainly be with the boys by six. He unbuttoned his jacket and shirt and drew forth his lunch. The action consumed no more than a quarter of a minute, yet in that brief moment the numbness laid hold of the exposed fingers. He did not put the mitten on, but, instead, struck the fingers a dozen sharp smashes against his leg. Then he sat down on a snow-covered log to eat. The sting that followed upon the striking of his fingers against his leg ceased so quickly that he was startled. He had had no chance to take a bite of biscuit. He struck the fingers repeatedly and returned them to the mitten, baring the other hand for the purpose of eating. He tried to take a mouthful, but the ice-muzzle prevented. He had forgotten to build a fire and thaw out. He chuckled at his foolishness, and as he chuckled he noted the numbness creeping into the exposed fingers. Also, he noted that the stinging which had first come to his toes when he sat down was already passing away. He wondered whether the toes were warm or numb. He moved them inside the moccasins and decided that they were numb.

He pulled the mitten on hurriedly and stood up. He was a bit frightened. He stamped up and down until the stinging returned into the feet. It certainly was cold, was his thought. That man from Sulphur Creek had spoken the truth when telling how cold it sometimes got in the country. And he had laughed at him at the time! That showed one must not be too sure of things. There was no mistake about it, it *was* cold. He strode up and down, stamping his feet and threshing his arms, until reassured by the returning warmth. Then he got out matches and proceeded to make a fire. From the under-growth, where high water of the previous spring had lodged a supply of seasoned twigs, he got his fire-wood. Working carefully from a small beginning, he soon had a roaring fire, over which he thawed the ice from his face and in the protection of which he ate his biscuits. For the moment the cold of space was outwitted. The dog took satisfaction in the fire, stretching out close enough for warmth and far enough away to escape being singed.

When the man had finished, he filled his pipe and took his comfortable time over a smoke. Then he pulled on his mittens, settled the ear-flaps of his cap firmly about his ears, and took the creek trail up the left fork. The dog was disappointed and yearned back toward the fire. This man did not know cold. Possibly all the generations of his ancestry had been ignorant of cold, of real cold, of cold one hundred and seven degrees below freezing-point. But the dog knew; all its ancestry knew, and it had inherited the knowledge. And it knew that it was not good to walk abroad in such fearful cold. It was the time to lie snug in a hole in the snow and wait for a curtain of cloud to be drawn across the face of outer space whence this cold came. On the other hand, there was no keen intimacy between the dog and the man. The one was the toil-slave of the other, and the only caresses it had ever received were the caresses of the whip-lash and of harsh and menacing throat-sounds that threatened the whip-lash. So the dog made no effort to communicate its apprehension to the man. It was not concerned in the welfare of the man; it was for its own sake that it yearned back toward the fire. But the man whistled, and spoke to it with the sound of whip-lashes, and the dog swung in at the man's heels and followed after.

The man took a chew of tobacco and proceeded to start a new amber beard. Also, his moist breath quickly powdered with white his mustache, eyebrows, and lashes. There did not seem to be so many springs on the left fork of the Henderson, and for half an hour the man saw no signs of any. And then it happened. At a place where there were no signs, where the soft, unbroken snow seemed to advertise solidity beneath, the man broke through. It was not deep. He wet himself halfway to the knees before he floundered out to the firm crust.

He was angry, and cursed his luck aloud. He had hoped to get into camp with the boys at six o'clock, and this would delay him an hour, for he would have to build a fire and dry out his foot-gear. This was imperative at that low temperature—he knew that much; and he turned aside to the bank, which he climbed. On top, tangled in the underbrush about the trunks of several small spruce trees, was a high-water deposit of dry fire-wood—sticks and twigs, principally, but also larger portions of seasoned branches and fine, dry, last-year's grasses. He threw down several large pieces on top of the snow. This served for a foundation and prevented the young flame from drowning itself in the snow it otherwise would melt. The flame he got by touching a match to a small shred of birch-bark that he took from his pocket. This burned even more readily than paper. Placing it on the foundation, he fed the young flame with wisps of dry grass and with the tiniest dry twigs.

He worked slowly and carefully, keenly aware of his danger. Gradually, as the flame grew stronger, he increased the size of the twigs with which he fed it. He squatted in the snow, pulling the twigs out from their entanglement in the brush and feeding directly to the flame. He knew there must be no failure. When it is seventy-five below zero, a man must not fail in his first attempt to build a fire—that is, if his feet are wet. If his feet are dry, and he fails, he can run along the trail for half a mile and restore his circulation. But the circulation of wet and freezing feet cannot be restored by running when it is seventy-five below. No matter how fast he runs, the wet feet will freeze the harder.

All this the man knew. The old-timer on Sulphur Creek had told him about it the previous fall, and now he was appreciating the advice. Already all sensation had gone out of his feet. To build the fire he had been forced to remove his mittens, and the fingers had quickly gone numb. His pace of four miles an hour had kept his heart pumping blood to the surface of his body and to all the extremities. But the instant he stopped, the action of the pump eased down. The cold of space smote the unprotected tip of the planet, and he, being on that unprotected tip, received the full force of the blow. The blood of his body recoiled before it. The blood was alive, like the dog, and like the dog it wanted to hide away and cover itself up from the fearful cold. So long as he walked four miles an hour, he pumped that blood, willy-nilly, to the surface; but now it ebbed away and sank down into the recesses of his body. The extremities were the first to feel its absence. His wet feet froze the faster, and his exposed fingers numbed the faster, though they had not yet begun to freeze. Nose and cheeks were already freezing, while the skin of all his body chilled as it lost its blood.

But he was safe. Toes and nose and cheeks would be only touched by the frost, for the fire was beginning to burn with strength. He was feeding it with twigs the size of his finger. In another minute he would be able to feed it with branches the size of his wrist, and then he could remove his wet foot-gear, and, while it dried, he could keep his naked feet warm by the fire, rubbing them at first, of course, with snow. The fire was a success. He was safe. He remembered the advice of the old-timer on Sulphur Creek, and smiled. The old-timer had been very serious in laying down the law that no man must travel alone in the Klondike after fifty below. Well, here he was; he had had the accident; he was alone; and he had saved himself. Those old-timers were rather womanish, some of them, he thought. All a man had to do was to keep his head, and he was all right. Any man who was a man could travel alone. But it was surprising, the rapidity with which his cheeks and nose were freezing. And he had not thought his fingers could go lifeless in so short a time. Lifeless they were, for he could scarcely make them move together to grip a twig, and they seemed remote from his body and from him. When he touched a twig, he had to look and see whether or not he had hold of it. The wires were pretty well down between him and his finger-ends.

All of which counted for little. There was the fire, snapping and crackling and promising life with every dancing flame. He started to untie his moccasins. They were coated with ice; the thick German socks were like sheaths of iron halfway to the knees; and the moccasin strings were like rods of steel all twisted and knotted as by some conflagration. For a moment he tugged with his numb fingers, then, realizing the folly of it, he drew his sheath-knife.

But before he could cut the strings, it happened. It was his own fault or, rather, his mistake. He should not have built the fire under the spruce tree. He should have built it in the open. But it had been easier to pull the twigs from the brush and drop them directly on the fire. Now the tree under which he had done this carried a weight of snow on its boughs. No wind had blown for weeks, and each bough was fully freighted. Each time he had pulled a twig he had communicated a slight agitation to the tree—an imperceptible agitation, so far as he was concerned, but an agitation sufficient to bring about the disaster. High up in the tree one bough capsized its load of snow. This fell on the boughs beneath, capsizing them. This process continued, spreading out and involving the whole tree. It grew like an avalanche, and it descended without warning upon the man and the fire, and the fire was blotted out! Where it had burned was a mantle of fresh and disordered snow.

The man was shocked. It was as though he had just heard his own sentence of death. For a moment he sat and stared at the spot where the fire had been. Then he grew very calm. Perhaps the old-timer on Sulphur Creek was right. If he had only had a trail-mate he would have been in no danger now. The trail-mate could have built the fire. Well, it was up to him to build the fire over again, and this second time there must be no failure. Even if he succeeded, he would most likely lose some toes. His feet must be badly frozen by now, and there would be some time before the second fire was ready.

Such were his thoughts, but he did not sit and think them. He was busy all the time they were passing through his mind. He made a new foundation for a fire, this time in the open, where no treacherous tree could blot it out. Next, he gathered dry grasses and tiny twigs from the high-water flotsam. He could not bring his fingers together to pull them out, but he was able to gather them by handful. In this way he got many rotten twigs and bits of green moss that were undesirable, but it was the best he could do. He worked methodically, even collecting an armful of the larger branches to be used later when the fire gathered strength. And all the while the dog sat and watched him, a certain yearning wistfulness in its eyes, for it looked upon him as the fire-provider, and the fire was slow in coming.

When all was ready, the man reached in his pocket for a second piece of birch-bark. He knew the bark was there, and, though he could not feel it with his fingers, he could hear its crisp rustling as he fumbled for it. Try as he would, he could not clutch hold of it. And all the time, in his consciousness, was the knowledge that each instant his feet were freezing. This thought tended to put him in a panic, but he fought against it and kept calm. He pulled on his mittens with his teeth, and threshed his arms back and forth, beating his hands with all his might against his sides. He did this sitting down, and he stood up to do it; and all the while the dog sat in the snow, its wolf-brush of a tail curled around warmly over its forefeet, its sharp wolf-ears pricked forward intently as it watched the man. And the man, as he beat and treshed with his arms and hands, felt a great surge of envy as he regarded the creature that was warm and secure in its natural covering.

After a time he was aware of the first faraway signals of sensation in his beaten fingers. The faint tingling grew stronger till it evolved into a stinging ache that was excruciating, but which the man hailed with satisfaction. He stripped the mitten from his right hand and fetched forth the birch-bark. The exposed fingers were quickly going numb again. Next he brought out his bunch of sulphur matches. But the tremendous cold had already driven the life out of his fingers. In his effort to separate one match from the others, the whole bunch fell in the snow. He tried to pick it out of the snow, but failed. The dead fingers could neither touch nor clutch. He was very careful. He drove the thought of his freezing feet, and nose, and cheeks, out of his mind, devoting his whole soul to the matches. He watched, using the sense of vision in place of that of touch, and when he saw his fingers on each side the bunch, he closed them—that is, he willed to close them, for the wires were down, and the fingers did not obey. He pulled the mitten on the right hand, and beat it fiercely against his knee. Then, with both mittened hands, he scooped the bunch of matches, along with much snow, into his lap. Yet he was no better off.

After some manipulation he managed to get the bunch between the heels of his mittened hands. In this fashion he carried it to his mouth. The ice crackled and snapped when by a violent effort he opened his mouth. He drew the lower jaw in, curled the upper lip out of the way, and scraped the bunch with his upper teeth in order to separate a match. He succeeded in getting one, which he dropped on his lap. He was no better off. He could not pick it up. Then he devised a way. He picked it up in his teeth and scratched it on his leg. Twenty times he scratched before he succeeded in lighting it. As it flamed he held it with his teeth to the birch-bark. But the burning brimstone went up his nostrils and into his lungs, causing him to cough spasmodically. The match fell into the snow and went out.

The old-timer on Sulphur Creek was right, he thought in the moment of controlled despair that ensued: after fifty below, a man should travel with a partner. He beat his hands, but failed in exciting any sensation. Suddenly he bared both hands, removing the mittens with his teeth. He caught the whole bunch between the heels of his hands. His arm-muscles not being frozen enabled him to press the hand-heels tightly against the matches. Then he scratched the bunch along his leg. It flared into flame, seventy sulphur matches at once! There was no wind to blow them out. He kept his head to one side to escape the strangling fumes, and held the blazing bunch to the birch-bark. As he so held it, he became aware of sensation in his hand. His flesh was burning. He could smell it. Deep down below the surface he could feel it. The sensation developed into pain that grew acute. And still he endured it, holding the flame of the matches clumsily to the bark that would not light readily because his own burning hands were in the way, absorbing most of the flame.

At last, when he could endure no more, he jerked his hands apart. The blazing matches fell sizzling into the snow, but the birch-bark was alight. He began laying dry grasses and the tiniest twigs on the flame. He could not pick and choose, for he had to lift the fuel between the heels of his hands. Small pieces of rotten wood and green moss clung to the twigs, and he bit them off as well as he could with his teeth. He cherished the flame carefully and awkwardly. It meant life, and it must not perish. The withdrawal of blood from the surface of his body now made him begin to shiver, and he grew more awkward. A large piece of green moss fell squarely on the little fire. He tried to poke it out with his fingers, but his shivering frame made him poke too far, and he disrupted the nucleus of the little fire, the burning grasses and tiny twigs separating and scattering. He tried to poke them together again but in spite of the tenseness of the effort, his shivering got away with him, and the twigs were hopelessly scattered. Each twig gushed a puff of smoke and went out. The fire-provider had failed. As he looked apathetically about him, his eyes chanced on the dog sitting across the ruins of the fire from him, in the snow, making restless, hunching movements, slightly lifting one forefoot and then the other, shifting its weight back and forth on them with wistful eagerness.

The sight of the dog put a wild idea into his head. He remembered the tale of the man, caught in a blizzard, who killed a steer and crawled inside the carcass, and so was saved. He would kill the dog and bury his hands in the warm body until the numbness went out of them. Then he could build another fire. He spoke to the dog, calling it to him; but in his voice was a strange note of fear that frightened the animal, who had never known the man to speak in such way before. Something was the matter, and its suspicious nature sensed danger—it knew not what danger, but somewhere, somehow, in its brain arose an apprehension of the man. It flattened its ears down at the sound of the man's voice and its restless, hunching movements and the liftings and shiftings of its forefeet became more pronounced; but it would not come to the man. He got on his hands and knees and crawled toward the dog. This unusual posture again excited suspicion, and the animal sidled mincingly away.

The man sat up in the snow for a moment and struggled for calmness. Then he pulled on his mittens, by means of his teeth, and got upon his feet. He glanced down at first in order to assure himself that he was really standing up, for the absence of sensation in his feet left him unrelated to the earth. His erect position in itself started to drive the webs of suspicion from the dog's mind; and when he spoke peremptorily, with the sound of whip-lashes in his voice, the dog rendered its customary allegiance and came to him. As it came within reaching distance, the man lost his control. His arms flashed out to the dog, and he experienced genuine surprise when he discoverd that his hands could not clutch, that there was neither bend nor feeling in the fingers. He had forgotten for the moment that they were frozen and that they were freezing more and more. All this happened quickly, and before the animal could get away, he encirled its body with his arms. He sat down in the snow, and in this fashion held the dog, while it snarled and whined and struggled.

But it was all he could do, hold its body encircled in his arms and sit there He realized that he could not kill the dog. There was no way to do it. With his helpless hands he could neither draw nor hold his sheath-knife nor throttle the animal. He released it, and it plunged wildly away, with tail between its legs, and still snarling. It halted forty feet away and surveyed him curiously, with ears sharply pricked forward. The man looked down at his hands in order to locate them, and found them hanging on the ends of his arms. It struck him as curious that one should have to use his eyes in order to find out where he hands were. He began threshing his arms back and forth, beating the mittened hands against his sides. He did this for five minutes, violently, and his heart pumped enough blood up to the surface to put a stop to his shivering. But no sensation was aroused in the hands. He had an impression that they hung like weights on the ends of his arms, but when he tried to run the impression down, he could not find it.

A certain fear of death, dull and oppressive, came to him. This fear quickly became poignant as he realized that it was no longer a mere matter of freezing his fingers and toes, or of losing his hands and feet, but that it was a matter of life and death with the chances against him. This threw him into a panic, and he turned and ran up the creek-bed along the old, dim trail. The dog joined in behind and kept up with him. He ran blindly, without intention, in fear such as he had never known in his life. Slowly, as he ploughed and floundered through the snow, he began to see things again,—the banks of the creek, the old timber-jams, the leafless aspens, and the sky. The running made him feel better. He did not shiver. Maybe, if he ran on, his feet would thaw out; and, anyway, if he ran far enough, he would reach camp and the boys. Without doubt he would lose some fingers and toes and some of his face; but the boys would take care of him, and save the rest of him when he got there. And at the same time there was another thought in his mind that said he would never get to the camp and the boys; that it was too many miles away, that the freezing had too great a start on him, and that he would soon be stiff and dead. This thought he kept in the background and refused to consider. Sometimes it pushed itself forward and demanded to be heard, but he thrust it back and strove to think of other things.

It struck him as curious that he could run at all on feet so frozen that he could not feel them when they struck the earth and took the weight of his body. He seemed to himself to skim along above the surface, and to have no connection with the earth. Somehwere he had once seen a winged Mercury, and he wondered if Mercury felt as he felt when skimming over the earth.

His theory of running until he reached camp and the boys had one flaw in it: he lacked the endurance. Several times he stumbled, and finally he tottered, crumpled up, and fell. When he tried to rise, he failed. He must sit and rest, he decided, and next time he would merely walk and keep on going. As he sat and regained his breath, he noted that he was feeling quite warm and comfortable. He was not shivering, and it even seemed that a warm glow had come to his chest and trunk. And yet, when he touched his nose or cheeks, there was no sensation. Running would not thaw them out. Nor would it thaw out his hands and feet. Then the thought came to him that the frozen portions of his body must be extending. He tried to keep this thought down, to forget it, to think of something else; he was aware of the panicky feeling that it caused, and he was afraid of the panic. But the thought asserted itself, and persisted, until it produced a vision of his body totally frozen. This was too much, and he made another wild run along the trail. Once he slowed down to a walk, but the thought of the freezing extending itself made him run again.

And all the time the dog ran with him, at his heels. When he fell down a second time, it curled its tail over its forefeet and sat in front of him, facing him, curiously eager and intent. The warmth and security of the animal angered him, and he cursed it till it flattened down its ears appeasingly. This time the shivering came more quickly upon the man. He was losing in his battle with the frost. It was creeping into his body from all sides. The thought of it drove him on, but he ran no more than a hundred feet, when he staggered and pitched headlong. It was his last panic. When he had recovered his breath and control, he sat up and entertained in his mind the conception of meeting death with dignity. However, the conception did not come to him in such terms. His idea of it was that he had been making a fool of himself, running around like a chicken with its head cut off—such was the simile that occurred to him. Well, he was bound to freeze anyway and he might as well take it decently. With this new-found peace of mind came the first glimering of drowsiness. A good idea, he thought, to sleep off to death. It was like taking an anaesthetic. Freezing was not so bad as people thought. There were lots worse ways to die.

He pictured the boys finding his body next day. Suddenly he found himself with them, coming along the trail and looking for himself. And, still with them, he came around a turn in the trail and found himself lying in the snow. He did not belong with himself any more, for even then he was out of himself, standing with the boys and looking at himself in the snow. It certainly was cold, was his thought. When he got back to the States he could tell the folks what real cold was. He drifted on from this to a vision of the old-timer on Sulphur Creek. He could see him quite clearly, warm and comfortable, and smoking a pipe.

"You were right, old hoss; you were right," the man mumbled to the old-timer of Sulphur Creek.

Then the man drowsed off into what seemed to him the most

comfortable and satisfying sleep he had ever known. The dog sat facing him and waiting. The brief day drew to a close in a long slow twilight. There were no signs of a fire to be made, and, besides, never in the dog's experience had it known a man to sit like that in the snow and make no fire. As the twilight drew on, its eager yearning for the fire mastered it, and with a great lifting and shifting of forefeet, it whined softly, then flattened its ears down in anticipation of being chidden by the man. But the man remained silent. Later, the dog whined loudly. And still later it crept close to the man and caught the scent of death. This made the animal bristle and back away. A little longer it delayed, howling under the stars that leaped and danced and shone brightly in the cold sky. Then it turned and trotted up the trail in the direction of the camp it knew, where were the other food-providers and fire-providers.

Aldo Leopold
1886-1948

During his lifetime Aldo Leopold's impact on conservation in America was becoming clear, but that he would become the major nature writer of our century in terms of influence, or that *A Sand County Almanac* (1949) would become the bible of later twentieth-century conservation and environmental movements did not become clear until many years after his death.

A native of Iowa, Leopold's interest in nature began when he was just a boy, observing birds of the Mississippi River bottomlands near his home. That direction of his life continued as a young man enrolled in Yale University's Sheffield Scientific School and the Yale School of Forestry, where he received his M.S. degree in 1909, and flourished in his work upon graduation in the U. S. Forest Service in Arizona and later in New Mexico, where he was deputy supervisor and then supervisor of the Carson National Forest. During this period, he started a game protection movement in the Southwest and was appointed assistant district forester in charge of game, fish, and recreation. His efforts were acknowledged by a medal awarded from the Permanent Wildlife Protection Fund. Because of his experiences in practical game management, his theories were changing at this time from a faith in the efficacy of predator elimination to a more ecological vision, ahead of its time, of the critical role of predators in complex, regional ecosystems.

By 1919 he had become an activist within the Forest Service for the preservation of wilderness, the most famous result of his activities being the establishment in 1924 of the first of seventy-eight wilderness areas (totaling 14 million acres) designated by the Forest Service—the 574,000-acre Gila Wilderness Area in New Mexico. The aesthetic, recreational, environmental, and scientific-research values of wilderness were all encompassed by his ideas and activities at this time. He also argued that wilderness areas are a symbol, or barometer, of society's capacity for self-restraint—an idea at the heart of his "land ethic" articulated much later.

His works include: *Report on Game Survey of the North Central States* (1931), one of the first game population studies in America; *Game Management* (1933), a classic text that revolutionized the field by introducing game harvesting methods that leave intact a species' reproductive capacity, and by launching basic ecological approaches to biotic systems; and *A Sand County Almanac* (1949), which changed the way Americans would define conservation and established Leopold as a writer whose personal response to nature placed him in the same class as Thoreau and Muir.

A Sand County Almanac was an unpublished manuscript in 1948 when Leopold died of heart failure while fighting a brush fire on property neighboring his Wisconsin land. Leopold's son Luna edited the manuscript and nursed it through publication, later editing and publishing further manuscripts and journals under the title *Round River* (1953). That title refers to the stream of biotic energy flowing into everything in a circuit of life. Today, Leopold's publishers place the entire collection in a single book under the *Almanac* main title. The book includes not only Leopold's observations from his restored "shack" on an abandoned sand farm in Wisconsin, but his ideas developed during a lifetime as a forester, scientist, and activist. "We abuse land because we regard it as a commodity belonging to us," Leopold wrote in his Foreword. "When we see land as a community to which we belong, we may begin to use it with love and respect." That statement is central to Leopold's development of the land ethic for which he is most famous. "Now we face the question whether a still higher 'standard of living' is worth its cost in things natural, wild, and free . . . . The whole conflict boils down to a question of degree. We of the minority see a law of diminishing returns in progress; our opponents do not."

Based on awareness and survival values, the land ethic is the lesson of ecology, which is "teaching us to search in animal populations for analogies to our own problems." Anti-ecological behavior becomes anti-social and anti-survival behavior in our century. Each of us is a member of an ecological community that includes soil, water, plants, and animals. Humans can be good or bad citizens of that community, either respecting the whole and recognizing the right of existence off all the parts, or violating it; either threatening the balance of the community, or participating healthfully in its life.

from A SAND COUNTY ALMANAC*

THE LAND ETHIC

When GOD-LIKE god-like Odysseus returned from the wars in Troy, he hanged all on one rope a dozen slave-girls of his household whom he suspected of misbehavior during his absence.

This hanging involved no question of propriety. The girls were property. The disposal of property was then, as now, a matter of expediency not of right and wrong.

Concepts of right and wrong were not lacking from Odysseus' Greece: witness the fidelity of his wife through the long years before at last his black-prowed galleys clove the wine-dark seas for home. The ethical structure of that day covered wives, but had not yet been extended to human chattels. During the three thousand years which have since elapsed, ethical criteria have been extended to many fields of conduct, with corresponding shrinkages in those judged by expediency only.

The Ethical Sequence

This extension of ethics, so far studied only by philosophers, is actually a process in ecological evolution. Its sequences may be described in ecological as well as in philosophical terms. An ethic, ecologically, is a limitation on freedom of action in the struggle for existence. An ethic, philosophically, is a differentiation of social from anti-social conduct. These are two definitions of one thing. The thing has its origin in the tendency of interdependent individuals or groups to evolve modes of co-operation. The ecologist calls these symbioses in which the original free-for-all competition has been replaced, in part, by co-operative mechanisms with an ethical content.

The complexity of co-operative mechanisms has increased with population density, and with the efficiency of tools. It was simpler, for example, to define the anti-social uses of sticks and stones in the days of the mastodons than of bullets and billboards in the age of motors.

The first ethics dealt with the relation between individuals; the Mosaic Decalogue is an example. Later accretions dealt with the relation between the individual and society. The Golden Rule tries to integrate the individual to society; democracy to integrate social organization to the individual.

There is as yet no ethic dealing with man's relation to land and to the animals and plants which grow upon it. Land, like Odysseus' slave-girls, is still property. The land-relation is still strictly economic, entailing privileges but not obligations.

The extension of ethics to this third element in human environment is, if I read the evidence correctly, an evolutionary possibility and an ecological necessity. It is the third step in a sequence. The first two have already been taken. Individual thinkers since the days of Ezekiel and Isaiah have asserted that the despoliation of land is not only inexpedient but wrong. Society, however, has not yet affirmed their belief. I regard the present conservation movement as the embryo of such an affirmation.

An ethic may be regarded as a mode of guidance for meeting ecological situations so new or intricate, or involving such deferred reactions, that the path of social expediency is not discernible to the average individual. Animal instincts are modes of guidance for the individual in meeting such situations. Ethics are possibly a kind of community instinct in-the-making.

The Community Concept

All ethics so far evolved rest upon a single premise: that the individual is a member of a community of interdependent parts. His instincts prompt him to compete for his place in the community, but his ethics prompt him also to co-operate (perhaps in order that there may be a place to compete for).

The land ethic simply enlarges the boundaries of the community to include soils, waters, plants, and animals, or collectively: the land.

This sounds simple: do we not already sing our love for and obligation to the land of the free and the home of the brave? Yes, but just what and whom do we love? Certainly not the soil, which we are sending helter-skelter downriver. Certainly not the waters, which we assume have no function except to turn turbines, float barges, and carry off sewage. Certainly not the plants, of which we exterminate whole communities without batting an eye. Certainly not the animals, of which we have already extirpated many of the largest and most beautiful species. A land ethic of course cannot prevent the alteration, management, and use of these 'resources,' but it does affirm their right to continued existence, and, at least in spots, their continued existence in a natural state.

In short, a land ethic changes the role of *Home sapiens* from conqueror of the land-community to plain member and citizen of it. It implies respect for his fellow-members, and also respect for the community as such.

In human history, we have learned (I hope) that the conqueror role is eventually self-defeating. Why? Because it is implicit in such a role that the conqueror knows, *ex cathedra,* just what makes the community clock tick, and just what and who is valuable, and what and who is worthless, in community life. It always turns out that he knows neither, and this is why his conquests eventually defeat themselves.

In the biotic community a parallel situation exists. Abraham knew exactly what the land was for: it was to drip milk and honey into Abraham's mouth. At the present moment the assurance with which we regard this assumption is inverse to the degree of our education.

The ordinary citizen today assumes that science knows what makes the community clock tick; the scientist is equally sure that he does not. He knows that the biotic mechanism is so complex that its workings may never be fully understood.

That man is, in fact, only a member of a biotic team is shown by an ecological interpretation of history. Many historical events, hitherto explained solely in terms of human enterprise, were actually biotic interactions between people and land. The characteristics of the land determined the facts quite as potently as the characteristics of the men who lived on it.

Consider, for example, the settlement of the Mississippi valley. In the years following the Revolution, three groups were contending for its control: the native Indian, and French and English traders, and the American settlers. Historians wonder what would have happened if the English at Detroit had thrown a little more weight into the Indian side of those tipsy scales which decided the outcome of the colonial migration into the cane-lands of Kentucky. It is time now to ponder the fact that the cane-lands, when subjected to the particular mixture of forces represented by the cow, plow, fire, and axe of the pioneer, became bluegrass. What if the plant succession inherent in this dark and bloody ground had, under the impact of these forces, given us some worthless sedge, shrub, or weed? Would Boone and Kenton have held out? Would there have been any overflow into Ohio, Indiana, Illinois, and Missouri? Any Louisiana Purchase? Any transcontinental union of new states? Any Civil War?

Kentucky was one sentence in the drama of history. We are commonly told what the human actors in this drama tried to do, but we are seldom told that their success, or the lack of it, hung in large degree on the reaction of particular soils to the impact of the particular forces exerted by their occupancy. In the case of Kentucky, we do not even know where the bluegrass came from—whether it is a native species, or a stowaway from Europe.

Contrast the cane-lands with what hindsight tells us about the Southwest, where the pioneers were equally brave, resourceful, and persevering. The impact of occupancy here brought no bluegrass, or other plant fitted to withstand the bumps and buffeting of hard use. This region, when grazed by livestock, reverted through a series of more and more worthless grasses, shrubs, and weeds to a condition of unstable equilibrium. Each recession of plant types bred erosion; each increment to erosion bred a further recession of plants. The result today is a progressive and mutual deterioration, not only of plants and soils, but of the animal community subsisting thereon. The early settlers did not expect this: on the ciénegas of New Mexico some even cut ditches to hasten it. So subtle has been its progress that few residents of the region are aware of it. It is quite invisible to the tourist who finds this wrecked landscape colorful and charming (as indeed it is, but it bears scant resemblance to what it was in 1848).

This same landscape was 'developed' once before, but with quite different results. The Pueblo Indians settled the Southwest in pre-Columbian times, but they happened *not* to be equipped with range livestock. Their civilization expired, but not because their land expired.

In India, regions devoid of any sod-forming grass have been settled, apparently without wrecking the land, by the simple expedient of carrying the grass to the cow, rather than vice versa. (Was this the result of some deep wisdom, or was it just good luck? I do not know.)

In short, the plant succession steered the course of history; the pioneer simple demonstrated, for good or ill, what successions inhered in the land. Is history taught in this spirit? It will be, once the concept of land as a community really penetrates our intellectual life.

The Ecological Conscience

Conservation is a state of harmony between men and land. Despite nearly a century of propaganda, conservation still proceeds at a snail's pace; progress still consists largely of letterhead pieties and convention oratory.

On the back forty we still slip two steps backward for each forward stride.

The usual answer to this dilemma is 'more conservation education.' No one will debate this, but is it certain that only the *volume* of education needs stepping up? Is something lacking in the *content* as well?

It is difficult to give a fair summary of its content in brief form, but, as I understand it, the content is substantially this: obey the law, vote right, join some organizations, and practice what conservation is profitable on your own land; the government will do the rest.

Is not this formula too easy to accomplish anything worth-while? It defines no right or wrong, assigns no obligation, calls for no sacrifice, implies no change in the current philosophy of values. In respect of land use it urges only enlightened self-interest. Just how far will such education take us? An example will perhaps yield a partial answer.

By 1930 it had become clear to all except the ecologically blind that southwestern Wisconsin's topsoil was slipping seaward. In 1933 the farmers were told that if they would adopt certain remedial practices for five years, the public would donate CCC labor to install them, plus the necessary machinery and materials. The offer was widely accepted, but the practices were widely forgotten when the five-year contract period was up. The farmers continued only those practices that yielded an immediate and visible economic gain for themselves.

This led to the idea that maybe farmers would learn more quickly if they themselves wrote the rules. Accordingly the Wisconsin Legislature in 1937 passed the Soil Conservation District Law. This said to farmers, in effect: *We, the public, will furnish you free technical service and loan you specialized machinery, if you will write your own rules of land-use. Each county may write its own rules, and these will have the force of law.* Nearly all the counties promptly organized to accept the proffered help, but after a decade of operation, *no county has yet written a single rule.* There has been visible progress in such practices as strip-cropping, pasture renovation, and soil liming, but none in fencing woodlots against grazing, and none in excluding plow and cow from steep slopes. The farmers, in short, have selected those remedial practices which were profitable anyhow, and ignored those which were profitable to the community, but not clearly profitable to themselves.

When one asks why no rules have been written, one is told that the community is not yet ready to support them; education must precede rules. But the education actually in progress makes no mention of obligations to land over and above those dictated by self-interest. The net result is that we have more education but less soil, fewer healthy woods, and as many floods as in 1937.

The puzzling aspect of such situations is that the existence of obligations over and above self-interest is taken for granted in such rural community enterprises as the betterment of roads, schools, churches, and baseball teams. Their existence is not taken for granted, nor as yet seriously discussed, in bettering the behavior of the water that falls on the land or in the preserving of the beauty or diversity of the farm landscape. Land-use ethics are still governed wholly by economic self-interest, just as social ethics were a century ago.

To sum up: we asked the farmer to do what he conveniently could to save his soil, and he has done just that, and only that. The farmer who clears the woods off a 75 per cent slope, turns his cows into the clearing, and dumps its rainfall, rocks, and soil into the community creek, is still (if otherwise decent) a respected member of society. If he puts lime on his fields and plants his crops on contour, he is still entitled to all the privileges and emoluments of his Soil Conservation District. The District is a beautiful piece of social machinery, but it is coughing along on two cylinders because we have been too timid, and too anxious for quick success, to tell the farmer the true magnitude of his obligations. Obligations have no meaning without conscience, and the problem we face is the extension of the social conscience from poeple to land.

No important change in ethics was ever accomplished without an internal change in our intellectual emphasis, loyalties, affections, and convictions. The proof that conservation has not yet touched these foundations of conduct lies in the fact that philosophy and religion have not yet heard of it. In our attempt to make conservation easy, we have made it trivial.

Substitutes for a Land Ethic

When the logic of history hungers for bread and we hand out a stone, we are at pains to explain how much the stone resembles bread. I now describe some of the stones which serve in lieu of a land ethic.

One basic weakness in a conservation system based wholly on economic motives is that most members of the land community have no economic value. Wildflowers and songbirds are examples. Of the 22,000 higher plants and animals native to Wisconsin, it is doubtful whether more than 5 per cent can be sold, fed, eaten, or otherwise put to economic use. Yet these creatures are members of the biotic community, and if (as I believe) its stability depends on its integrity, they are entitled to continuance.

When one of these non-economic categories is threatened, and if we happen to love it, we invent subterfuges to give it economic importance. At the beginning of the century songbirds were supposed to be disappearing. Ornithologists jumped to the rescue with some distinctly shaky evidence to the effect that insects would eat us up if birds failed to control them. The evidence had to be economic in order to be valid.

It is painful to read these circumlocutions today. We have no land ethic yet, but we have at least drawn nearer the point of admitting that birds should continue as a matter of biotic right, regardless of the presence or absence of economic advantage to us.

A parallel situation exists in respect of predatory mammals, raptorial birds, and fish-eating birds. Time was when biologists somewhat overworked the evidence that these creatures preserve the health of game by killing weaklings, or that they control rodents for the farmer, or that they prey only on 'worthless' species. Here again, the evidence had to be economic in order to be valid. It is only in recent years that we hear the more honest argument that predators are members of the community, and that no special interest has the right to exterminate them for the sake of a benefit, real or fancied, to itself. Unfortunately this enlightened view is still in the talk stage. In the field the extermination of predators goes merrily on: witness the impending erasure of the timber wolf by fiat of Congress, the Conservation Bureaus, and many state legislatures.

Some species of trees have been 'read out of the party' by economics-minded foresters because they grow too slowly, or have too low a sale value to pay as timber crops: white cedar, tamarack, cypress, beech, and hemlock are examples. In Europe, where forestry is ecologically more advanced, the non-commercial tree species are recognized as members of the native forest community, to be preserved as such, within reason. Moreover some (like beech) have been found to have a valuable function in building up soil fertility. The interdependence of the forest and its constituent tree species, ground flora, and fauna is taken for granted.

Lack of economic value is sometimes a character not only of species or groups, but of entire biotic communities: marshes, bogs, dunes and 'deserts' are examples. Our formula in such cases is to relegate their conservation to government as refuges, monuments, or parks. The difficulty is that these communities are usually interspersed with more valuable private lands; the government cannot possibly own or control such scattered parcels. The net effect is that we have relegated some of them to ultimate extinction over large areas. If the private owner were ecologically minded, he would be proud to be the custodian of a reasonable proportion of such areas, which add diversity and beauty to his farm and to his community.

In some instances, the assumed lack of profit in these 'waste' areas has proved to be wrong, but only after most of them had been done away with. The present scramble to reflood muskrat marshes is a case in point.

There is a clear tendency in American conservation to relegate to government all necessary jobs that private landowners fail to perform. Government ownership, operation, subsidy, or regulation is now widely prevalent in forestry, range managment, soil and watershed management, park and wilderness conservation, fisheries management, and migratory bird management, with more to come. Most of this growth in governmental conservation is proper and logical, some of it is inevitable. That I imply no disapproval of it is implicit in the fact that I have spent most of my life working for it. Nevertheless the question arises: What is the ultimate magnitude of the enterprise? Will the tax base carry its eventual ramifications? At what point will governmental conservation, like the mastodon, become handicapped by its own dimensions? The answer, if there is any, seems to be in a land ethic, or some other force which assigns more obligation to the private landowner.

Industrial landowners and users, especially lumbermen and stockmen, are inclined to wail long and loudly about the extension of government ownership and regulation to land, but (with notable exceptions) they show little disposition to develop the only visible alternative: the voluntary practice of conservation on their own lands.

When the private landowner is asked to perform some unprofitable act for the good of the community, he today assents only with outstretched palm. If the act costs him cash this is fair and proper, but when it costs only fore-thought, open-mindedness, or time, the issue is at least debatable. The overwhelming growth of land-use subsidies in recent years must be ascribed, in large part, to the government's own agencies for conservation education: the land bureaus, the agricultural colleges, and the extension services. As far as I can detect, no ethical obligation toward land is taught in these institutions.

To sum up: a system of conservation based solely on economic self-interest is hopelessly lopsided. It tends to ignore, and thus eventually to eliminate, many elements in the land community that lack commercial value, but that are (as far as we know) essential to its healthy functioning. It assumes, falsely, I think, that the economic parts of the biotic clock will function without the uneconomic parts. It tends to relegate to government many functions eventually too large, too complex, or too widely dispersed to be performed by government.

An ethical obligation on the part of the private owner is the only visible remedy for these situations.

William Faulkner
1897-1962

A native Southerner, Faulkner is an example of one of the greatest twentieth-century authors in English who uses pastoral, regional, agrarian, and wilderness themes in this work. His first book, *The Marble Faun* (1924), was a collection of pastoral poems. But it was some four novels later before he settled, in *Sartoris* (1929), on his themes and setting—the mythical Yoknopatawpha county based loosely on Lafayette county in Mississippi, where he lived in Oxford. Here, in more than a dozen books, the old and new South, agrarian and urban values, and wilderness and commercial values, struggle for supremacy. As the region is examined in novels and stories from the time of Indian possession down to the mid-twentieth century, Faulkner traces the historical development of these conflicting forces in the South and in America. His sources include true historical records: family papers, county records, and local histories through which he sought universal truths and conflicts of the human heart. The depth of his research and the transformation of it into fiction of epical and mythical stature is all the more remarkable as a sign of his genius when we consider that he never finished high school and attended the University of Mississippi for only two years of desultory study.

To communicate his psychological and historical themes (including the ways in which history or the past shapes psychology), he developed a new prose not unlike poetry, where the reader participates in an intensely subjective, flexible, and often free-associative world that expresses his characters' inner lives and visions. His work can be demanding, but it is also rich and rewarding. For such books as *A Fable* (1954) and *The Reivers* (1962) he received Pulitzer Prizes, and in 1950 he was awarded the Nobel Prize for literature. His Nobel speech is a famous statement of Faulkner's faith in humanity despite violence, tragedy, and irrationality: "man will not merely endure: he will prevail . . . because he has a soul, a spirit capable of compassion and sacrifice and endurance . . . .the writer's duty is to write about these things." Faulkner's hunting tale in *Go Down Moses* (1942), from which the following selection is taken, is of special importance to readers interested in his treatment of nature and wilderness.

THE OLD PEOPLE

1. At first there was nothing. There was the faint, cold, steady rain, the gray and constant light of the late November dawn, with the voices of the hounds converging somewhere in it and toward them. Then Sam Fathers, standing just behind the boy as he had been standing when the boy shot his first running rabbit with his first gun and almost with the first load it ever carried, touched his shoulder and he began to shake, not with any cold. Then the buck was there. He did not come into sight; he was just there, looking not like a ghost but as if all of light were condensed in him and he were the source of it, not only moving in it but disseminating it, already running, seen first as you always see the deer, in that split second after he has already seen you, already slanting away in that first soaring bound, the antlers even in that dim light looking like a small rocking-chair balanced on his head.

"Now," Sam Fathers said, "shoot quick, and slow."

The boy did not remember that shot at all. He would live to be eighty, as his father and his father's twin brother and their father in his turn had lived to be, but he would never hear that shot nor remember even the shock of the gun-butt. He didn't even remember what he did with the gun afterward. He was running. Then he was standing over the buck where it lay on the wet earth still in the attitude of speed and not looking at all dead, standing over it shaking and jerking, with Sam Fathers beside him again, extending the knife. "Don't walk up to him in front," Sam said. "If he ain't dead, he will cut you all to pieces with his feet. Walk up to him from behind and take him by the horn first, so you can hold his head down until you can jump away. Then slip your other hand down and hook your fingers in his nostrils."

The boy did that—drew the head back and the throat taut and drew Sam Fathers' knife across the throat and Sam stooped and dipped his hands in the hot smoking blood and wiped them back and forth across the boy's face. Then Sam's horn rang in the wet gray woods and again and again; there was a boiling wave of dogs about them, with Tennie's Jim and Boon Hogganbeck whipping them back after each had had a taste of the blood, then the men, the true hunters—Walter Ewell whose rifle never missed, and Major de Spain and old General Compson and the boy's cousin, McCaslin Edmonds, grandson of his father's sister, sixteen years his senior and, since both he and McCaslin were only children and the boy's father had been nearing seventy when he was born, more his brother than his cousin and more his father than either—sitting their horses and looking down at them: at the old man of seventy who had been a Negro for two generations now but whose face and bearing were still those of the Chickasaw chief who had been his father; and the white boy of twelve with the prints of the bloody hands on his face, who had nothing to do now but stand straight and not let the trembling show.

"Did he do all right, Sam?" his cousin McCaslin said.

"He done all right," Sam Fathers said.

They were the white boy, marked forever, and the old dark man sired on both sides by savage kings, who had marked him, whose bloody hands had merely formally consecrated him to that which, under the man's tutelage, he had already accepted, humbly and joyfully, with abnegation and with pride too; the hands, the touch, the first worthy blood which he had been found at last worthy to draw, joining him and the man forever, so that the man would continue to live past the boy's seventy years and then eighty years, long after the man himself had entered the earth as chiefs and kings entered it—the child, not yet a man, whose grandfather had lived in the same country and in almost the same manner as the boy himself would grow up to live, leaving his descendants in the land in his turn as his grandfather had done, and the old man past seventy whose grandfathers had owned the land long before the white men ever saw it and who had vanished from it now with all their kind, what of blood they left behind them running now in another race and for a while even in bondage and now drawing toward the end of its alien and irrevocable course, barren, since Sam Fathers had no children.

His father was Ikkemotubbe himself, who had named himself Doom. Sam told the boy about that—how Ikkemotubbe, old Issetibbeha's sister's son, had run away to New Orleans in his youth and returned seven years later with a French companion calling himself the Chevalier Soeur-Blonde de Vitry, who must have been the Ikkemotubbe of his family too and who was already addressing Ikkemotubbe as *Du Homme*—returned, came home again, with his foreign Aramis and the quadroon slave woman who was to be Sam's mother, and a gold-laced hat and coat and a wicker wine-hamper containing a litter of month-old puppies and a gold snuff-box filled with a white powder resembling fine sugar. And how he was met at the River landing by three or four companions of his bachelor youth, and while the light of a smoking torch gleamed on the glittering braid of the hat and coat Doom squatted in the mud of the land and took one of the puppies from the hamper and put a pinch of the white powder on its tongue and the puppy died before the one who was holding it could cast it away. And how they returned to the Plantation where Issetibbeha, dead now, had been succeeded by his son, Doom's fat cousin Moketubbe, and the next day Moketubbe's eight-year-old son died suddenly and that afternoon, in the presence of Moketubbe and most of the others (the People, Sam Fathers called them) Doom produced another puppy from the wine-hamper and put a pinch of the white powder on its tongue and Moketubbe abdicated and Doom became in fact The Man which his French friend already called him. And how on the day after that, during the ceremony of accession,

Doom pronounced a marriage between the pregnant quadroon and one of the slave men which he had just inherited (that was how Sam Fathers got his name, which in Chickasaw had been Had-Two-Fathers) and two years later sold the man and the woman and the child who was his own son to his white neighbor, Carothers McCaslin.

That was seventy years ago. The Sam Fathers whom the boy knew was already sixty—a man not tall, squat rather, almost sedentary, flabby-looking though he actually was not, with hair like a horse's mane which even at seventy showed no trace of white and a face which showed no age until he smiled, whose only visible trace of Negro blood was a slight dullness of the hair and the fingernails, and something else which you did notice about the eyes, which you noticed because it was not always there, only in repose and not always then—something not in their shape nor pigment but in their expression, and the boy's cousin McCaslin told him what that was: not the heritage of Ham, not the mark of servitude but of bondage; the knowledge that for a while that part of his blood had been the blood of slaves. "Like an old lion or a bear in a cage," McCaslin said. "He was born in the cage and has been in it all his life; he knows nothing else. Then he smells something. It might be anything, any breeze blowing past anything and then into his nostrils. But there for a second was the hot sand or the cane-brake that he never even saw himself, might not even know if he did see it and probably does know he couldn't hold his own with it if he got back to it. But that's not what he smells then. It was the cage he smelled. He hadn't smelled the cage until that minute. Then the hot sand or the brake blew into his nostrils and blew away, and all he could smell was the cage. That's what makes his eyes look like that."

"Then let him go!" the boy cried. "Let him go!"

His cousin laughed shortly. Then he stopped laughing, making the sound that is. It had never been laughing. "His cage ain't McCaslin's," he said. "He was a wild man. When he was born, all his blood on both sides, except the little white part, knew things that had been tamed out of our blood so long ago that we have not only forgotten them, we have to live together in herds to protect ourselves from our own sources. He was the direct son not only of a warrior but of a chief. Then he grew up and began to learn things, and all of a sudden one day he found out that he had been betrayed, the blood of the warriors and chiefs had been betrayed. Not by his father," he added quickly. "He probably never held it against old Doom for selling him and his mother into slavery, because he probably believed the damage was already done before then and it was the same warriors' and chiefs' blood in him and Doom both that was betrayed through the black blood which his mother gave him. Not betrayed by the black blood and not wilfully betrayed by his mother, but betrayed by her all the same, who had bequeathed him not only the blood of slaves but even a little of the very blood which had enslaved it; himself his own battleground, the scene of his own vanquishment and the mausoleum of his defeat. His cage ain't us," McCaslin said. "Did you ever know anybody yet, even your father and Uncle Buddy, that ever told him to do or not do anything that he ever paid any attention to?"

That was true. The boy first remembered him as sitting in the door of the plantation blacksmith-shop, where he sharpened plow-points and mended tools and even did rough carpenter-work when he was not in the woods. And sometimes, even when the woods had not drawn him, even with the shop cluttered with work which the farm waited on, Sam would sit there, doing nothing at all for half a day or a whole one, and no man, neither the boy's father and twin uncle in their day nor his cousin McCaslin after he became practical though not yet titular master, ever to say to him, "I want this finished by sundown" or "Why wasn't this done yesterday?" And once each year, in the late fall, in November, the boy would watch the wagon, the hooped canvas top erected now, being loaded—the food, hams and sausage from the smokehouse, coffee and flour and molasses from the commissary, a whole beef killed just last night for the dogs until there would be meat in camp, the crate containing the dogs themselves, then the bedding, the guns, the horns and lanterns and axes, and his cousin McCaslin and Sam Fathers in their hunting clothes would mount to the seat and with Tennie's Jim sitting on the dog-crate they would drive away to Jefferson, to join Major de Spain and General Compson and Boon Hogganbeck and Walter Ewell and go on into the big bottom of the Tallahatchie where the deer and bear were, to be gone two weeks. But before the wagon was even loaded the boy would find that he could watch no longer. He would go away, running almost, to stand behind the corner where he could not see the wagon and nobody could see him, not crying, holding himself rigid except for the trembling, whispering to himself: "Soon now. Soon now. Just three more years" (or two more or one more) "and I will be ten. Then Cass said I can go."

White man's work, when Sam did work. Because he did nothing else: farmed no allotted acres of his own, as the other ex-slaves of old Carothers McCaslin did, performed no field work for daily wages as the younger and newer Negroes did—and the boy never knew just how that had been settled betweeen Sam and old Carothers, or perhaps with old Carothers' twin sons after him. For, although Sam lived among the Negroes, in a cabin among the other cabins in the quarters, and consorted with Negroes (what of consorting with anyone Sam did after the boy got big enough to walk alone from the house to the blacksmith-shop and then to carry a gun) and dressed like them and talked like them and even went with them to the Negro church now and then, he was still the son of that Chickasaw chief and the Negroes knew it. And, it seemed to the boy, not only Negroes. Boon Hogganbeck's grandmother had been a Chickasaw woman too, and although the blood had run white since and Boon was a white man, it was not chief's blood. To the boy at least, the difference was apparent immediately you saw Boon and Sam together, and even Boon seemed to know it was there—even Boon, to whom in his tradition it had never occurred that anyone might be better born than himself. A man might be smarter, he admitted that, or richer (luckier, he called it) but not better born. Boon was a mastiff, absolutely faithful, dividing his fidelity equally between Major de Spain and the boy's cousin McCaslin, absolutely dependent for his very bread and dividing that impartially too between

Major de Spain and McCaslin, hardy, generous, courageous enough, a slave to all the appetites and almost unratiocinative. In the boy's eyes at least it was Sam Fathers, the Negro, who bore himself not only toward his cousin McCaslin and Major de Spain but toward all white men, with gravity and dignity and without servility or recourse to that impenetrable wall of ready and easy mirth which Negroes sustain between themselves and white men, bearing himself toward his cousin McCaslin not only as one man to another but as an older man to a younger.

He taught the boy the woods, to hunt, when to shoot and when not to shoot, when to kill and when not to kill, and better, what to do with it afterward. Then he would talk to the boy, the two of them sitting beneath the close fierce stars on a summer hilltop while they waited for the hounds to bring the fox back within hearing, or beside a fire in the November or December woods while the dogs worked out a coon's trail along the creek, or fireless in the pitch dark and heavy dew of April mornings while they squatted beneath a turkey-roost. The boy would never question him; Sam did not react to questions. The boy would just wait and then listen and Sam would begin, talking about the old days and the People whom he had not had time ever to know and so could not remember (he did not remember ever having seen his father's face), and in place of whom the other race into which his blood had run supplied him with no substitute.

And as he talked about those old times and those dead and vanished men of another race from either that the boy knew, gradually to the boy those old times would cease to be old time and would become a part of the boy's present, not only as if they had happened yesterday but as if they were still happening, the men who walked through them actually walking in breath and air and casting an actual shadow on the earth they had not quitted. And more: as if some of them had not happened yet but would occur tomorrow, until at last it would seem to the boy that he himself had not come into existence yet, that none of his race nor the other subject race which his people had brought with them into the land had come here yet; that although it had been his grandfather's and then his father's and uncle's and was now his cousin's and some day would be his own land which he and Sam hunted over, their hold upon it actually was as trivial and without reality as the now faded and archiac script in the chancery book in Jefferson which allocated it to them and that it was he, the boy, who was the guest here and Sam Father's voice the mouthpiece of the host.

Until three years ago there had been two of them, the other a full-blood Chickasaw, in a sense even more incredibly lost than Sam Fathers. He called himself Jobaker, as if it were one word. Nobody knew his history at all. He was a hermit, living in a foul little shack at the forks of the creek five miles from the plantation and about that far from any other habitation. He was a market hunter and fisherman and he consorted with nobody, black or white; no Negro would even cross his path and no man dared approach his hut except Sam. And perhaps once a month the boy would find them in Sam's shop—two old men squatting on their heels on the dirt floor, talking in a mixture of negroid English and flat hill dialect and now and then a phrase of that old tongue which as time went on and the boy squatted there too listening, he began to learn. Then Jobaker died. That is, nobody had seen him in some time. Then one morning Sam was missing, nobody, not even the boy, knew when nor where, until that night when some Negroes hunting in the creek bottom saw the sudden burst of flame and approached. It was Jobaker's hut, but before they got anywhere near it, someone shot at them from the shadows beyond it. It was Sam who fired, but nobody every found Jobaker's grave.

The next morning, sitting at breakfast with his cousin, the boy saw Sam pass the dining-room window and he remembered then that never in his life before had he seen Sam nearer the house than the blacksmith-shop. He stopped eating even; he sat there and he and his cousin both heard the voices from beyond the pantry door, then the door opened and Sam entered, carrying his hat in his hand but without knocking as anyone else on the place except a house servant would have done, entered just far enough for the door to close behind him and stood looking at neither of them—the Indian face above the nigger clothes, looking at something over their heads or at something not even in the room.

"I want to go," he said. "I want to go to the Big Bottom to live."

"To live?" the boy's cousin said.

"At Major de Spain's and your camp, where you go to hunt," Sam said. "I could take care of it for you all while you ain't there. I will build me a little house in the woods, if you rather I didn't stay in the big one."

"What about Isaac here?" his cousin said, "How will you get away from him? Are you going to take him with you?" But still Sam looked at neither of them, standing just inside the room with that face which showed nothing, which showed that he was an old man only when it smiled.

"I want to go," he said. "Let me go."

"Yes," the cousin said quietly. "Of course. I'll fix it with Major de Spain. You want to go soon?"

"I'm going now," Sam said. He went out. And that was all. The boy was nine then; it seemed perfectly natural that nobody, not even his cousin McCaslin, should argue with Sam. Also, since he was nine now, he could understand that Sam could leave him and their days and nights in the woods together without any wrench. He believed that he and Sam both knew that this was not only temporary but that the exigencies of his maturing, of that for which Sam had been training him all his life some day to dedicate himself, required it. They had settled that one night last summer while they listened to the hounds bringing a fox back up the creek valley; now the boy discerned in that very talk under the high, fierce August stars a presage, a warning, of this moment today. "I done taught you all there is of this settled country," Sam said. "You can hunt it good as I can now. You are ready for the Big Bottom now, for bear and deer. Hunter's meat," he said. "Next year you will be ten. You will write your age in two numbers and you will be ready to become a man. Your pa" (Sam always referred to the boy's cousin as his father, establishing even before the boy's orphanhood did that relation between them not of the ward to his guardian and kinsman and chief and head of his blood, but of the child to the man who sired his flesh and his thinking too) "promised you can go with us then." So the boy could understand Sam's going. But he couldn't understand why now, in March, six months before the moon for hunting.

"If Jobaker's dead like they say," he said, "and Sam hasn't got anybody but us at all kin to him, why does he want to go to the Big Bottom now, when it will be six months before we get there?

"Maybe that's what he wants," McCaslin said. "Maybe he wants to get away from you a little while."

But that was all right. McCaslin and other grown people often said things like that and he paid no attention to them, just as he paid no attention to Sam saying he wanted to go to the Big Bottom to live. After all, he would have to live there for six months, because there would be no use in going at all if he was going to turn right around and come back. And, as Sam himself had told him, he already knew all about hunting in this settled country that Sam or anybody else could teach him. So it would be all right. Summer, then the bright days after the first frost, then the cold and himself on the wagon with McCaslin this time and the moment would come and he would draw the blood, the big blood which would make him a man, a hunter, and Sam would come back home with them and he too would have outgrown the child's pursuit of rabbits and 'possums. Then he too would make one before the winter fire, talking of the old hunts and the hunts to come as hunters talked.

So Sam departed. He owned so little that he could carry it. He walked. He would neither let McCaslin send him in the wagon, nor take a mule to ride. No one saw him go even. He was just gone one morning, the cabin which had never had very much in it, vacant and empty, the shop in which there never had been very much done, standing idle. Then November came at last, and now the boy made one—himself and and his cousin McCaslin and Tennie's Jim, and Major de Spain and General Compson and Walter Ewell and Boon and old Uncle Ash to do the cooking, waiting for them in Jefferson with the other wagon, and the surrey in which he and McCaslin and General Compson and Major de Spain would ride.

Sam was waiting at the camp to meet them. If he was glad to see them, he did not show it. And if, when they broke camp two weeks later to return home he was sorry to see them go, he did not show that either. Because he did not come back with them. It was only the boy who returned, returning solitary and alone to the settled familiar land, to follow for eleven months the childish business of rabbits and such while he waited to go back, having brought with him, even from his brief first sojourn, an unforgettable sense of the big woods—not a quality dangerous or particularly inimical, but profound, sentient, gigantic and brooding, amid which he had been permitted to go to and fro at will, unscathed, why he knew not, but dwarfed and, until he had drawn honorably blood worthy of being drawn, alien.

Then November, and they would come back. Each morning Sam would take the boy out to the stand allotted him. It would be one of the poorer stands of course, since he was only ten and eleven and twelve and he had never even seen a deer running yet. But they would stand there, Sam a little behind him and without a gun himself, as he had been standing when the boy shot the running rabbit when he was eight years old. They would stand there in the November dawns, and after a while they would hear the dogs. Sometimes the chase would sweep up and past quite close, belling and invisible; once they heard the two heavy reports of Boon Hogganbeck's old gun with which he had never killed anything larger than a squirrel and that sitting, and twice they heard the flat unreverberant clap of Walter Ewell's rifle, following which you did not even wait to hear his horn.

"I'll never get a shot," the boy said. "I'll never kill one."

"Yes you will," Sam said. "You wait. You'll be a hunter. You'll be a man."

But Sam wouldn't come out. They would leave him there. He would come as far as the road where the surrey waited, to take the riding horses back, and that was all. The men would ride the horses and Uncle Ash and Tennie's Jim and the boy would follow in the wagon with Sam, with the camp equipment and the trophies, the meat, the heads, the antlers, the good ones, the wagon winding on among the tremendous gums and cypresses and oaks where no axe save that of the hunter had ever sounded, between the impenetrable walls of cane and brier—the two changing yet constant walls just beyond which the wilderness whose mark he had brought away forever on his spirit even from that first two weeks seemed to lean, stooping a little, watching them and listening, not quite inimical because they were too small, even those such as Walter and Major de Spain and old General Compson who had killed many deer and bear, their sojourn too brief and too harmless to excite to that, but just brooding, secret, tremendous, almost inattentive.

Then they would emerge, they would be out of it, the line as sharp as the demarcation of a doored wall. Suddenly skeleton cotton- and corn-fields would flow away on either hand, gaunt and motionless beneath the gray rain; there would be a house, barns, fences, where the hand of man had clawed for an instant, holding, the wall of the wilderness behind them now, tremendous and still and seemingly impenetrable in the gray and fading light, the very tiny orifice through which they had emerged apparently swallowed up. The surrey would be waiting, his cousin McCaslin and Major de Spain and General Compson and Walter and Boon dismounted beside it. Then Sam would get down from the wagon and mount one of the horses and, with the others on a rope behind him, he would turn back. The boy would watch him for a while against that tall and secret wall, growing smaller and smaller against it, never looking back. Then he would enter it, returning to what the boy believed, and thought that his cousin McCaslin believed, was his loneliness and solitude.

2. So the instant came. He pulled trigger and Sam Fathers marked his face with the hot blood which he had spilled and he ceased to be a child and became a hunter and a man. It was the last day. They broke camp that afternoon and went out, his cousin and Major de Spain and General Compson and Boon on the horses, Walter Ewell and the Negroes in he wagon with him and Sam and his hide and antlers. There could have been (and were) other trophies in the wagon. But for him they did not exist, just as for all practical purposes he and Sam Fathers were still alone together as they had been that morning. The wagon wound and jolted between the slow and shifting yet constant walls from beyond and above which the wilderness watched them pass, less than inimical now and never to be inimical again since the buck still and forever leaped, the shaking gunbarrels coming constantly and forever steady at last, crashing, and still out of his instant of immortality the buck sprang, forever immortal; the wagon jolting and bouncing on, the moment of the buck, the shot, Sam Fathers and himself and the blood with which Sam had marked him forever one with the wilderness which had accepted him since Sam said that he had done all right, when suddenly Sam reined back and stopped the wagon and they all heard the unmistakable and unforgettable sound of a deer breaking cover.

Then Boon shouted from beyond the bend of the trail and while they sat motionless in the halted wagon, Walter and the boy already reaching for their guns, Boon came galloping back, flogging his mule with his hat, his face wild and amazed as he shouted down at them. Then the other riders came around the bend, also spurring.

"Get the dogs!" Boon cried, "Get the dogs! If he had a nub on his head, he had fourteen points! Laying right there by the road in that pawpaw thicket! If I'd a knowed he was there, I could have cut his throat with my pocket knife!"

"Maybe that's why he run," Walter said. "He saw you never had your gun." He was already out of the wagon with his rifle. Then the boy was out too with his gun, and the other riders came up and Boon got off his mule somehow and was scrabbling and clawing among the duffel in the wagon, still shouting, "Get the dogs! Get the dogs!" And it seemed to the boy too that it would take them forever to decide what to do—the old men in whom the blood ran cold and slow, in whom during the intervening years between them and himself the blood had become a different and colder substance from that which ran in him and even in Boon and Walter.

"What about it, Sam?" Major de Spain said. "Could the dogs bring him back?"

"We won't need the dogs," Sam said. "If he don't hear the dogs behind him, he will circle back in here about sundown to bed."

"All right," Major de Spain said. "You boys take the horses. We'll go on out to the road in the wagon and wait there." He and General Compson and McCaslin got into the wagon and Boon and Walter and Sam and the boy mounted the horses and turned back and out of the trail. Sam led them for an hour through the gray and unmarked afternoon whose light was little different from what it had been at dawn and which would become darkness without any graduation between. Then Sam stopped them.

"This is far enough," he said. "He'll be coming upwind, and he don't want to smell the mules." They tied the mounts in a thicket. Sam led them on foot now, unpathed through the markless afternoon, the boy pressing close behind him, the two others, or so it seemed to the boy, on his heels. But they were not. Twice Sam turned his head slightly and spoke back to him across his shoulder, still walking: "You got time. We'll get there 'fore he does."

So he tried to go slower. He tried deliberately to decelerate the dizzy rushing of time in which the buck which he had not even seen was moving, which it seemed to him must be carrying the buck farther and farther and more and more irretrievably away from them even though there were no dogs behind him now to make him run, even though, according to Sam, he must have completed his circle now and was heading back toward them. They went on; it could have been another hour or twice that or less than half, the boy could not have said. Then they were on a ridge. He had never been in here before and he could not see that it was a ridge. He just knew that the earth had risen slightly because the underbrush had thinned a little, the ground sloping invisibly away toward a dense wall of cane. Sam stopped. "This is it," he said. He spoke to Walter and Boon: "Follow this ridge and you will come to two crossings. You will see the tracks. If he crosses, it will be at one of these three."

Walter looked about for a moment. "I know it," he said. "I've even seen your deer. I was in here last Monday. He ain't nothing but a yearling."

"A yearling?" Boon said. He was panting from the walking. His face still looked a little wild. "If the one I saw was any yearling, I'm still in kindergarten."

"Then I must have seen a rabbit," Walter said. "I always heard you quit school altogether two years before the first grade."

Boon glared at Walter. "If you don't want to shoot him, get out of the way," he said. "Set down somewhere. By God, I—"

"Ain't nobody going to shoot him standing here," Sam said quietly.

"Sam's right," Walter said. He moved, slanting the worn, silver-colored barrel of his rifle downward to walk with it again. "A little more moving and a little more quiet too. Five miles is still Hogganbeck range, even if we wasn't downwind." They went on. The boy could still hear Boon talking, though presently that ceased too. Then once more he and Sam stood motionless together against a tremendous pin oak in a little thicket, and again there was nothing. There was only the soaring and sombre solitude in the dim light, there was the thin murmur of the faint cold rain which had not ceased all day. Then, as if it had waited for them to find their positions and become still, the wilderness breathed again. It seemed to lean inward above them, above himself and Sam and Walter and Boon in their separate lurking-places, tremendous, attentive, impartial and omniscient, the buck moving in it somewhere, not running yet since he had not been pursued, not frightened yet and never fearsome but just alert also as they were alert, perhaps already circling back, perhaps quite near, perhaps conscious also of the eye of the ancient immortal Umpire. Because he was just twelve then, and that morning something had happened to him: in less than a second he had ceased forever to be the child he was yesterday. Or perhaps that made no difference, perhaps even a city-bred man, let alone a child, could not have understood it; perhaps only a country-bred one could comprehend loving the life he spills. He began to shake again.

"I'm glad it's started now," he whispered. He did not move to speak; only his lips shaped the expiring words: "Then it will be gone when I raise the gun—"

Nor did Sam. "Hush," he said.

"Is he that near?" the boy whispered. "Do you think—"

"Hush," Sam said. So he hushed. But he could not stop the shaking. He did not try, because he knew it would go away when he needed the steadiness—had not Sam Fathers already consecrated and absolved him from weakness and regret too?—not from love and pity for all which lived and ran and then ceased to live in a second in the very midst of splendor and speed, but from weakness and regret. So they stood motionless, breathing deep and quiet and steady. If there had been any sun, it would be near to setting now; there was a condensing, a densifying, of what he had thought was the gray and unchanging light until he realised suddenly that it was his own breathing, his heart, his blood—something, all things, and that Sam Fathers had marked him indeed, not as a mere hunter, but with something Sam had had in his turn of his vanished and forgotten people. He stopped breathing then; there was only his heart, his blood, and in the following silence the wilderness ceased to breathe also, leaning, stooping overhead with its breath held, tremendous and impartial and waiting. Then the shaking stopped too, as he had known it would, and he drew back the two heavy hammers of the gun.

Then it had passed. It was over. The solitude did not breathe again yet; it had merely stopped watching him and was looking somewhere else, even turning its back on him, looking on away up the ridge at another point, and the boy knew as well as if he had seen him that the buck had come to the edge of the cane and had either seen or scented them and faded back into it. But the solitude did not breathe again. It should have suspired again then but it did not. It was still facing, watching, what it had been watching and it was not here, not where he and Sam stood; rigid, not breathing himself, he thought, cried *No! No!,* knowing already that it was too late, thinking with the old despair of two and three years ago: *I'll never get a shot.* Then he heard it—the flat single clap of Walter Ewell's rifle which never missed. Then the mellow sound of the horn came down the ridge and something went out of him and he knew then he had never expected to get the shot at all.

"I reckon that's it," he said. "Walter got him." He had raised the gun slightly without knowing it. He lowered it again and had lowered one of the hammers and was already moving out of the thicket when Sam spoke.

"Wait."

"Wait?" the boy cried. And he would remember that—how he turned upon Sam in the truculence of a boy's grief over the missed opportunity, the missed luck. "What for? Don't you hear that horn?"

And he would remember how Sam was standing. Sam had not moved. He was not tall, squat rather and broad, and the boy had been growing fast for the past year or so and there was not much difference between them in height, yet Sam was looking over the boy's head and up the ridge toward the sound of the horn and the boy knew that Sam did not even see him; that Sam knew he was still there beside him but he did not see the boy. Then the boy saw the buck. It was coming down the ridge, as if it were walking out of the very sound of the horn which related its death. It was not running, it was walking, tremendous, unhurried, slanting and tilting its head to pass the antlers through the undergrowth, and the boy standing with Sam beside him now instead of behind him as Sam always stood, and the gun still partly aimed and one of the hammers still cocked.

Then it saw them. And still it did not begin to run. It just stopped for an instant, taller than any man, looking at them; then its muscles suppled, gathered. It did not even alter its course, not fleeing, not even running, just moving with that winged and effortless ease with which deer move, passing within twenty feet of them, its head high and the eye not proud and not haughty but just full and wild and unafraid, and Sam standing beside the boy now, his right arm raised at full length, palm-outward, speaking in that tongue which the boy had learned from listening to him and Joe Baker in the blacksmith shop, while up the ridge Walter Ewell's horn was still blowing them into a dead buck.

"Oleh, Chief," Sam said. "Grandfather."

When they reached Walter, he was standing with his back toward them, quite still, bemused almost, looking down at his feet. He didn't look up at all.

"Come here, Sam," he said quietly. When they reached him he still did not look up, standing above a little spike buck which had still been a fawn last spring. "He was so little I pretty near let him go," Walter said. "But just look at the track he was making. It's pretty near big as a cow's. If there were any more tracks here besides the ones he is laying in, I would swear there was another buck here that I never even saw."

3. It was dark when they reached the road where the surrey waited. It was turning cold, the rain had stopped, and the sky was beginning to blow clear. His cousin and Major de Spain and General Compson had a fire going. "Did you get him?" Major de Spain said.

"Got a good-sized swamp-rabbit with spike horns," Walter said. He slid the little buck down from his mule. The boy's cousin McCaslin looked at it.

"Nobody saw the big one?" he said.

"I don't even believe Boon saw it," Walter said. "He probably jumped somebody's straw cow in that thicket." Boon started cursing, swearing at Walter and at Sam for not getting the dogs in the first place and at the buck and all.

"Never mind," Major de Spain said. "He'll be here for us next fall. Let's get started home."

It was after midnight when they let Walter out at his gate two miles from Jefferson and later still when they took General Compson to his house and then returned to Major de Spain's, where he and McCaslin would spend the rest of the night, since it was still seventeen miles home. It was cold, the sky was clear now; there would be a heavy frost by sunup and the ground was already frozen beneath the horses' feet and the wheels and beneath their own feet as they crossed Major de Spain's yard and entered the house, the warm dark house, feeling their way up the dark stairs until Major de Spain found a candle and lit it, and into the strange room and the big deep bed, the still cold sheets until they began to warm to their bodies and at last the shaking stopped and suddenly he was telling McCaslin about it while McCaslin listened, quietly until he had finished. "You don't believe it," the boy said. "I know you don't—"

"Why not?" McCaslin said. "Think of all that has happened here, on this earth. All the blood hot and strong for living, pleasuring, that has soaked back into it. For grieving and suffering too, of course, but still getting something out of it for all that, getting a lot out of it, because after all you don't have to continue to bear what you believe is suffering; you can always choose to stop that, put an end to that. And even suffering and grieving is better than nothing; there is only one thing worse then not being alive, and that's shame. But you can't be alive forever, and you always wear out life long before you have exhausted the possibilities of living. And all that must be somewhere; all that could not have been invented and created just to be thrown away. And the earth is shallow; there is not a great deal of it before you come to the rock. And the earth don't want to just keep things, hoard them; it wants to use them again. Look at the seed, the acorns, at what happens even to carrion when you try to bury it: it refuses too, seethes and struggles too until it reaches light and air again, hunting the sun still. And they—" the boy saw his hand in silhouette for a moment against the window beyond which, accustomed to the darkness now, he could see sky where the scoured and icy stars glittered "—they don't want it, need it. Besides, what would it want, itself, knocking around out there, when it never had enough time about the earth as it was, when there is plenty of room about the earth, plenty of places still unchanged from what they were when the blood used and pleasured in them while it was still blood?"

"But we want them," the boy said. "We want them too. There is plenty of room for us and them too."

"That's right," McCaslin said. "Suppose they don't have substance, can't cast a shadow—"

"But I saw it!" the boy cried. "I saw him!"

"Steady," McCaslin said. For an instant his hand touched the boy's flank beneath the covers. "Steady. I know you did. So did I. Sam took me in there once after I killed my first deer."

Joseph Wood Krutch
1893-1970

Krutch's lifetime spans the period of greatest conservation and environmentalist activity in America. In this sense and in the themes of his books he is a representative American nature writer. His naturalist's respect for scientifically accurate information, his grace and craftsmanship as a prose stylist, his broad background as a humanist, professor, journalist, and editor—all of these qualities mark his writings and set a standard for other nature writers to meet. His essays appeared in the most esteemed American periodicals, and he wrote more than twenty books on drama, literature, the modern human condition, and nature.

Although he was an eminent professor of English and dramatic literature at Columbia University and on the editorial staff of *The Nation,* Krutch retired from New York and Connecticut in 1952 to Tucson, Arizona. He devoted the rest of his life to conservation causes and to writing about nature, especially the deserts of the American Southwest. Writing his book *Henry David Thoreau* (1948) apparently worked a change within Krutch, for the next year his first real nature book appeared, *The Twelve Seasons* (1949), a testimony of his deepening awareness of the natural world as well as a foreshadowing of his retirement from urban and academic life. Such titles as *Great American Nature Writing* (1950), *The Desert Year* (1952), *Voice of the Desert* (1955), *Grand Canyon: Today and All It's Yesterdays* (1958), *Forgotten Peninsula: A Naturalist in Baja California* (1961) certainly suggest this change in Krutch's life and setting. In 1954 he was awarded the Burroughs Medal for Nature Writing.

In *The Twelve Seasons,* from which the excerpt here is taken, Krutch concluded:

> What we have actually done as we have built cities and tended to lead more and more exclusively urban lives is not to turn toward either the God-who-is-not-Nature or the Man-who-is-not-Nature but to busy ourselves and identify ourselves with that part of the natural world which is not alive rather than with

that part which is. What we have tended to become is not either the Humanist or the Worshiper but quite simply the mechanic and the technologist. We have forgotten the beast and the flower not in order to remember either ourselves or God, but in order to forget everything except the machine. . . .

What we have to decide is merely whether we shall choose to have our chief business with the obviously living or the obviously not-living—and we have made the wrong choice.

from THE TWELVE SEASONS*

APRIL

Hyla crucifer is what the biologists call him, but to most of us he is simply the Spring Peeper. The popularizers of natural histoy have by no means neglected him but even without their aid he has made himself known to many whose only wild flower is the daisy and whose only bird is the robin. Everyone who has ever visited the country in the spring has heard him trilling from the marsh at twilight, and though few have ever caught sight of him most know that he is a little, inch-long frog who has just awaked from his winter sleep. In southern Connecticut he usually begins to pipe on some day between the middle of March and the middle of April, and I, like most country dwellers, listen for the first of his shrill, cold notes.

Throughout the winter, neighbors who met in the village street have been greeting one another with the conventional question: "Is it cold enough for you?" Or, perhaps, if they are of the type which watches a bit more carefully than most the phenomenon of the seasons, they have been comparing thermometers in the hope that someone will admit to a minimum at least one degree higher than what was recorded "over my way." Now, however, one announces triumphantly: "Heard the peepers last night," and the other goes home to tell his wife. Few are High Church enough to risk a "Christ is risen" on Easter morning, but the peepers are mentioned without undue self-consciousness.

Even this, however, is not enough for me and I have often wondered that a world which pretends to mark so many days and to celebrate so many occasions should accept quite so casually the day when *Hyla crucifer* announces that winter is over. One swallow does not make a spring, and the robin arrives with all the philistine unconcern of a worldling back from his Winter at Aiken or Palm Beach. But the peeper seems to realize, rather better than we, the significance of his resurrection, and I wonder if there is any other phenomenon in the heavens above or in the earth beneath which so simply and so definitely announces that life is resurgent again.

We who have kept artificially warm and active through the winter act as though we were really independent of the seasons, but we forget how brief our immunity is and are less anxious than we might be if habit had not dulled our awareness. One summer which failed to arrive and we should realize well enough before we perished of hunger that we are only a little

*From *The Twelve Seasons* by Joseph Wood Krutch. Copyright 1949 by Joseph Wood Krutch. By permission of William Morrow & Co.

less at the mercy of the seasons than the weed that dies in October. One winter which lasted not six months but twelve and we should recognize our affinity with the insects who give up the ghost after laying the eggs that would never hatch if they did not lie chill and dead through the cold of a winter as necessary to them as warmth was to the males who fertilized and the females who laid them. We waited through the long period during which our accumulated supplies of food grew smaller and we waited calmly in a blind assurance that warmth would return and that nature would reawaken. Now, the voice of the peeper from the marsh announces the tremendous fact that our faith has been justified. A sigh of relief should go up and men should look at one another with a wild surprise. "It" has happened again though there was nothing during the long months that passed to support our conviction that it could and would.

We had, to be sure, the waiting pages of our calendars marked "June," "July," and even, of all things, "August." The sun, so the astronomers had assured us, had turned northward on a certain date and theoretically had been growing stronger day by day. But there was, often enough, little in the mercury of our thermometers or the feel of our fingers to confirm the fact. Many a March day had felt colder than the milder days of February. And merely astronomical seasons have, after all, very little relation to any actual human experience either as visible phenomena or as events bringing with them concomitant earthly effects.

Not one man out of a hundred thousand would be aware of the solstices or the equinoxes if he did not see their dates set down in the almanac or did not read about them in the newspaper. They cannot be determined without accurate instruments and they correspond to no phenomena he is aware of. But the year as we live it does have its procession of recurrring events, and it is a curious commentary on the extent to which we live by mere symbols that ten men know that the spring equinox occurs near the twenty-first of March to one who could give you even the approximate date when the peepers begin in his community; and that remains true even if he happens to be a countryman and even if he usually remarks, year after year, when they do begin.

It is true that the Day of the Peepers is a movable feast. But so is Easter, which—as a matter of fact—can come earlier or later by just about the same number of days that, on the calendar I have kept, separates the earliest from the latest date upon which *Hyla crucifer* begins to call. Moreover, the earliness or the lateness of the peepers means something, as the earliness or the lateness of Easter does not.

Whatever the stars may say or whatever the sun's altitude may be, spring has not begun until the ice has melted and life begun to stir again. Your peeper makes a calculation which would baffle a meteorologist. He takes into consideration the maximum to which the temperature has risen, the minimum to which it has fallen during the night, the relative length of the warmer and the colder periods, besides, no doubt, other factors hard to get down in tables or charts. But at last he knows that the moment has come. It has been just warm enough just long enough, and without too much cold in between. He inflates the little bubble in his throat and sends out the clear note audible for half a mile. On that day something older than any Christian God has risen. The earth is alive again.

The human tendency to prefer abstractions to phenomena is, I know, a very ancient one. Some anthropologists, noting that abstract design seems usually to come before the pictorial representation of anything in primitive man's environment, have said that the first picture drawn by any beginning culture is a picture of God. Certainly in the European world astronomy was the first of the sciences, and it is curious to remember that men knew a great deal about the intricate dance of the heavenly bodies before they had so much as noticed the phenomena of life about them. The constellations were named before any except the most obvious animals or plants and were studied before a science of botany or physiology had begun. The Greeks, who thought that bees were generated in the carcasses of dead animals and that swallows hibernated under the water, could predict eclipses, and the very Druids were concerned to mark the day on which the sun turned northward again. But the earliest of the sciences is also the most remote and the most abstract. The objects with which it deals are not living things and its crucial events do not correspond directly or immediately to any phenomena which are crucial in the procession of events as they affect animal or vegetable life.

Easter is an anniversary, and the conception of an anniversary is not only abstract but so difficult to define that the attempt to fix Easter used up an appalling proportion of the mental energy of learned men for many hundred of years—ultimately to result in nothing except a cumbersome complexity that is absolutely meaningless in the end. Why should we celebrate the first Sunday after the first full moon on or after the twenty-first of March? What possible meaning can the result of such a calculation have? Yet even that meaningless definition of Easter is not really accurate. For the purpose of determining the festival, the date of the full moon is assumed to be, not that of the actual full moon, but that on which the full moon would have fallen if the table worked out by Pope Gregory's learned men had been—as it is not—really accurate. Even the relatively few men who remember the commonly given formula will occasionally find that they have missed their attempt to determine when Easter will be because they consulted a lay calendar to find the full moon instead of concerning themselves with the Epact and considering the theoretical ecclesiastical full moon rather than the actual one. How much easier it is to celebrate the Day of the Peepers instead, and how much more meaningful too! On that day something miraculous and full of promise has actually happened, and that something announces itself in no uncertain terms.

Over any astronomically determined festival, the Day of the Peepers has, moreover, another advantage even greater than the simplicity with which it defines itself or the actuality of its relation to the season it announces, for *Hyla crucifer* is a sentient creature who shares with us the drama and the exultation; who, indeed, sings our hosannahs for us. The music of the spheres is a myth; to say that the heavens rejoice is a pathetic fallacy; but there is no missing the rejoicings from the marsh and no denying that they are something shared. Under the stars we feel alone but by the pond side we have company.

To most, to be sure. Hyla is a *vox et praterea nihil.* Out of a thousand who have heard him, hardly one has ever seen him at the time of his singing or recognized him if perchance he has happened by pure accident to see squatting on the branch of some shrub the tiny inch-long creature, gray or green according to his mood, and with a dark cross over his back. But it was this tiny creature who, some months before, had congregated with his fellows in the cold winter to sing and make love. No one could possibly humanize him as one humanizes a pet and so come to feel that he belongs to us rather than—what is infinitely more important—that we both, equally, belong to something more inclusive than ourselves.

Like all the reptiles and the amphibians he has an aspect which is inscrutable and antediluvian. His thoughts must be inconceivably different from ours and his joy hardly less so. But the fact is comforting rather than the reverse, for if we are nevertheless somehow united with him in that vast category of living things which is so sharply cut off from everything that does not live at all, then we realize how broad the base of the category is, how much besides ourselves is, as it were, on our side. Over against the atoms and the stars are set both men and frogs. Life is not something entrenched in man alone, in a creature who has not been here so very long and may not continue to be here so very much longer. We are not its sole guardians, not alone in enjoying or enduring it. It is not something that will fail if we should.

Strangely enough, however, man's development takes him farther and farther away from association with his fellows, seems to condemn him more and more to live with what is dead rather than with what is alive. It is not merely that he dwells in cities and associates with machines rather than with plants and with animals. That, indeed, is but a small and a relatively unimportant part of his growing isolation. Far more important is the fact that more and more he thinks in terms of abstractions, generalizations, and laws; less and less participates in the experience of living in a world of sights, and sounds, and natural urges.

Electricity, the most powerful of his servants, flows silently and invisibly. It isn't really there except in its effects. We plan our greatest works on paper and in adding machines. Push the button, turn the switch! Things happen. But they are things we know about only in terms of symbols and formulae. Do we inevitably, in the process, come ourselves to be more and more like the inanimate forces with which we deal, less and less like the animals among whom we arose? Yet it is of protoplasm that we are made. We cannot possibly become like atoms or like suns. Do we dare to forget as completely as we threaten to forget that we belong rejoicing by the marsh more anciently and more fundamentally than we belong by the machine or over the drawing board?

No doubt astronomy especially fascinated the first men who began to think because the world in which they lived was predominantly so immediate and so confused a thing, was composed so largely of phenomena which they could see and hear but could not understand or predict and to which they so easily fell victim.The night sky spread out above them defined itself clearly and exhibited a relatively simple pattern of surely recurring events. They could perceive an order and impose a scheme, thus satisfying an intellectual need to which the natural phenomena close about them refused to cater.

But the situation of modern man is exactly the reverse. He "understands" more and more as he sees and hears less and less. By the time he has reached high-school age he has been introduced to the paradox that the chair on which he sits is not the hard object it seems to be but a collection of dancing molecules. He learns to deal, not with objects but with statistics, and before long he is introduced to the idea that God is a mathematician, not the creator of things seen, and heard, and felt. As he is taught to trust less and less the evidence of the five senses with which he was born, he lives less and less in the world which they seem to reveal, more and more with the concepts of physics and biology. Even his body is no longer most importantly the organs and muscles of which he is aware but the hormones of which he is told.

The very works of art that he looks at when he seeks delight through the senses are no longer representations of what the eye has seen but constructions and designs—or, in other words, another order of abstractions. It is no wonder that for such a one spring should come, not when the peepers begin, but when the sun crosses the equator or rather—since that is only a human interpretation of the phenomenon—when the inclined axis of the earth is for an instant pointed neither toward nor away from the sun but out into space in such a way that it permits the sun's rays to fall upon all parts of the earth's surface for an equal length of time. For him astronomy does not, as it did for primitive man, represent the one successful attempt to intellectualize and render abstract a series of natural phenomena. It is, instead, merely one more of the many systems by which understanding is substituted for experience.

Surely one day a year might be set aside on which to celebrate our ancient loyalties and to remember our ancient origins. And I know of none more suitable for that purpose than the Day of the Peepers. "Spring is come!", I say when I hear them, and: "The most ancient of Christs has risen!" But I also add something which, for me at least, is even more important. "Don't forget," I whisper to the peepers; "we are all in this together."

Edwin Way Teale
1899-1980

As a contributing editor to *Audubon Magazine* and the prolific author and editor of nearly thirty books on nature themes, Edwin Way Teale's stature as one of the enduring figures in American nature writing is assured. To name a few of his public honors suggests his impact on American nature writing: Fellow of the American Association for the Advancement of Science, President of the Thoreau Society, member of the American Ornithologists' Union, and winner of the John Burroughs Medal (1943), the Eva L. Gordon Award of the American Nature Study Society (1965), and the Pulitzer Prize for general nonfiction in 1966 for *Wandering Through Winter.*

Teale has been acknowledged as one of the most knowledgeable and far-traveled American naturalists. A popular writer, he introduced two generations of Americans to wildlife and nature through his books and more than 20,000 photographs (which have been exhibited all over the world). The reason for his popularity in America and abroad—his books have been translated into ten languages—has much to do with his particular style in presenting nature. He created an original blend of journalism, science, and nature appreciation.

Teale first explored the natural history of a season, something of an original idea in itself, in a book about his 17,000-mile journey with the advance of spring through North America in *North With the Spring* (1951). *Journey Into Summer* (1960), *Autumn Across America* (1956), and *Wandering Through Winter* (1965) followed, with excerpts of each in the combined volume *The American Seasons* (1976). Some of his most important books include *The Lost Woods: Adventures of a Naturalist* (1945), *Circle of the Seasons* (1953), *Adventures in Nature* (1959), and *Springtime in Britain* (1970).

from JOURNEY INTO SUMMER*

NATURAL HISTORY OF NIAGARA FALLS

Twenty beams of colored light, 4,200,000,000 candle-power strong, cut through the June darkness. They began at the largest arc lamps of their kind in the world, each weighing more than a ton and rising far higher than our heads on the stone balcony where we stood. They ended, some a third of a mile away, some more than half a mile away, splashing their colors in a sequence of fifteen different hues across the vast curtain of Niagara's falling water. It was ten o'clock. We were on the Canadian side of the falls. The nightly color show, of which visitors the year around never seem to tire, was beginning.

We wandered among the huge, drum-shaped lamps. The hum of electricity, the whir of cooling fans were in our ears. We stopped at frequent intervals to lean against the balustrade and watch the play of colors across the foam of the distant cataract. As we remember that night, the tinted walls of plunging water formed a chromatic backdrop for small and unconsidered events that caught and held our attention. There were gulls—their bodies tinted, too—circling over the gorge where night was being electrically turned into day, moths streaming out of the night toward this battery of great suns ranged along our balcony, tannish caddis flies parading up the front of the lamps, their wings changing hue as each tinted filter slipped automatically into place, sweeping the wave of its new color downward across the lens. They all were part of the life of the cataract, of the ever-fascinating natural history of Niagara Falls.

The day before we had crossed the Rainbow Bridge and accompanied the parade of high-tension lines westward on the Niagara Peninsula of Ontario to Fonthill and Lookout Point and the home of our naturalist friends, the James A. Selbys. A phoebe had built its nest outside the long building of their private museum and a tame blue jay alighted on my shoulder and nibbled at my ear as a sign it wanted to be fed. For years, Al and Gertrude Selby had engaged in the delicate business of banding the minute nestlings of ruby-throated hummingbirds.

Together, late that afternoon, we all drove back to the falls. The object of our attention was a remarkable colony of common terns. They were living dangerously, nesting close to the brink of the Horseshoe Falls. A tapered mass of rock, shaped like a destroyer, cut the rush of the water and extended to hardly more than forty or fifty feet from the lip of the cataract. Here more than 600 terns were nesting. On slender wings, they swirled in white clouds above the rocky islet. Nearby, they plummeted down into the millrace of the waters to emerge with small, silvery fish gripped crosswise in their bills. Once, when a whole school of minnows was being carried over the brink, fifty or more terns milled about close to the edge of the falls. They darted down in arrowy descents and swiftly lifted free of the surface again, often only a few feet back of the spot where the river curved out and down in

*From *Journey Into Summer* (New York: Dodd, Mead & Co., Inc., 1960).

its thundering plunge with foam and mist and green water intermingled.

On this island stronghold the birds of the colony are safe from predators. Neither man nor beast can reach them. Only winged creatures have access to their rock. From birth, the young terns hatching there are surrounded by the continuous roaring of the falling water. They try their wings in first flights over the rapids and the cataract and the chasm that yawns below it. Their first fishing is done in the seething water where the river, torn among rocks, is making its last rush toward the falls. In this hazardous environment, in a life spent so close to the brink of Niagara and, it seems to us, so close to the brink of disaster, the light and graceful terns were well-equipped to survive.

Long after nine o'clock that night, we heard the clamor of the tern colony above the roaring of the falls. This was in part owing to the shrill, harsh voices of the birds and in part to the low-pitched sound of the falling water. Tests have shown that we never hear the main tumult of Niagara. It is pitched four octaves lower than the lowest chords of the piano. To our ears it is a vibration rather than a sound. And so, too, no doubt, to the ears of the terns, born amid the endless thunder of the cataract, much of the sound around them is inaudible.

We returned to see the colony again the next day, this time with Roy W. Sheppard, retired Canadian entomologist and the man who has studied the natural history of the Niagara region more thoroughly than anyone else I know. Other birds were also active now along the brink. Martins and rough-winged swallows coursed back and forth, often only inches above the tumbling water. At this time of year aquatic insects were emerging from the stream and hastening into the air, sometimes, it seemed, escaping from the water even as it was turning in space and curving downward in its fall. Always along the face of the falling water, mist billowed upward, an airy waterfall flowing in reverse. During nesting time, the swallows often dart out of the sunshine into the mist and emerge with their bills crammed with gauzy insects.

When the big floodlights were originally installed at Niagara, Canadian officials were concerned over the possibility that they might attract unwanted and injurious insects from the American side of the river. Sheppard was assigned to make an intensive study of the species that appeared at the lamps. While he encountered no new economic pests, he found the range of insects attracted was extensive. Most numerous were the moths and nocturnal beetles. The largest insect of all was the giant silk moth, the *polyphemus*. But there were a host of others: flying ants, lacewing flies, snowy tree crickets, roadside grasshoppers, giant water bugs, fish flies, fireflies, cicadas, ladybird beetles. Even that creature of the day rather than of the night, a butterfly—a red admiral, *Vanessa atalanta*—appeared at the lights. Incidentally, the phrase, "Broadway butterfly"—like that other descriptive phrase, "brown as a berry"—demonstrates the triumph of alliteration over fact. It is the moth and not the butterfly that comes to the bright lights. Butterflies are usually fast asleep by the time the lights go on.

Because the powerful beams that attract the insects are directed low over the river, they do not lead birds to their death as airport ceilometer lights, pointing straight up, sometimes do. A few years ago, a duck flew headlong into one of the lamps. But this is almost the only time they have been struck by birds. A flock of Canada geese, flying in fog, once veered away just in time and, on another occasion, a second flock landed in the illuminated street below when the birds were caught in sudden fog and rain. The gulls and terns we had seen circling over the gorge in the artificial illumination had seemed neither confused nor blinded by the glare.

During the best part of that long June day, Sheppard showed us places where he had observed special occurrences of natural-history interest in the vicinity of the falls. Here was a sunny recess deep in the gorge where mourning-cloak butterflies gathered in the spring after their winter hibernation. There, herring gulls nested on the rubble of a rock slide. Here was the place where Sheppard had watched eiders diving for crayfish and, up the river there, he had come upon the first otter seen at Niagara in recent times, and here, not far from the *Maid-of-the-Mist* docks, he had observed red and northern phalaropes whirling around and around in their surface feeding. From the floral clock in the park at the Lake Ontario end of the Niagara River to the islands above the falls, our courteous and observant companion pointed out various aspects of nature along the way.

On Navy Island, two or three miles above the cataract, he showed us a bald eagle's nest, now deserted. It was the last nest of the national bird built near the falls where once great numbers of eagles gathered. Alexander Wilson writes, in his *American Ornithology,* of these birds feeding on fish and squirrels and even bears and deer that had been carried over the cataract. When De Witt Clinton published his *Letters on the Natural History and Internal Resources of the State of New York,* in 1822, he reported seeing the greatest concentration of bald eagles he had ever encountered feeding in the gorge at the foot of Niagara Falls. In recent years the only eagles seen in the vicinity have been transients. Great horned owls raised a brood in the abandoned nest on Navy Island one year and for a time, later on, it was occupied by raccoons.

When eagles were year-round residents at Niagara, they were among the birds Sheppard used to see riding ice cakes down the rapids and toward the falls. Ducks, Canada geese, great black-backed gulls, as well as eagles, would alight on pieces of drifting ice in the calm water above the rapids and then come pitching and tilting down through the white water, navigating a natural shoot-the-chutes, giving the impression of enjoying a thrill ride at a carnival. Each time, before the floe attained the brink of the falls, its passenger would lift into the air and wing its way back upstream again.

Birds that are killed by being carried over the falls appear mainly to be waterfowl that sleep in the river and drift too close to the brink before they awaken. Trying to flee upstream against the swift run of the current, they are unable to reach sufficient speed to become airborne. The most spectacular disaster of this kind overtook whistling swans migrating in the spring of 1912. Between March 18 and April 6, nearly 200 of the great white birds were swept over the falls and perished. Each fall and spring, immense numbers of waterfowl use the gorge below the falls and the Niagara River as a water highway between Lake Erie and Lake Ontario. Since earliest times, the mortality of wildlife at the falls during these seasons has attracted attention. Peter Kalm, the Swedish botanist and pioneer traveler in America, wrote to John Bartram in 1750: "In the months of September and October such abundant quantities of dead waterfowl are found every morning below the Fall, on the shore, that the garrison of the fort for a long time live chiefly upon them. In October or thereabouts such plenty of feathers are to be found here below the Fall that a man in a day's time can gather enough of them for several beds."

When I talked to A. R. Muma, Chief Game Protector for the Niagara region in Canada, he expressed the opinion that most of the birds found dead below the falls have taken off in the gorge, have become blinded and confused in the driving rain and mist near the cataract and have flown into the plunging water. When we donned slickers to ride the *Maid-of-the-Mist* close to the foot of the Horseshoe Falls, we entered a zone where the rain never stops. In this outer fringe of the falls we were surrounded by such gales of wind, such slashing rain, such a thundering tumult of sound that we lost all sense of direction. The confusion of a flying bird is easy to understand. Clifford Keech, captain of the boat, pointed out a ring-billed gull that floated low in the water, riding listlessly with the swirls of the current in the gorge below the falls. We saw several such "waterlogged gulls." They had flown too close to the foot of the falls and had been carried down and tumbled about in the seething water. When they can reach shore, dry out and rest, they recover.

In another zone of rain that never stops, amid great rocks clad in pelts of the finest fur—the silky green alga, *Cladophora glomerata*—near the foot of the Americn Falls on the Cave of the Winds trip, we observed the birds of Niagara from a different viewpoint. We looked up, as we emerged from the plunging rain, and saw a duck skim low over the crest of the cataract and, high overhead, come scaling down into the gorge. Three grackles followed, lighter birds in the updrafts, seeming to have difficulty with their long tails as they descended. Out on the river, all three apparently alighted on masses of floating foam. A closer glance, however, revealed that in each case the froth had collected around a small piece of driftwood. After the grackles, the next bird we saw was a slate-blue pigeon. With half-closed wings, it slanted along the face of the falls, tossing in the turbulent air, disappearing and reappearing among the billows of mist.

Whenever, in our travels, we have come to a large waterfall we have always found pigeons, gone wild, living around it. Crannies in the rock provide attractive nesting sites. Aptly the original stock of the domestic pigeon was named the rock dove. Here at Niagara, the feral birds nest on little ledges of the sheer walls, far above the spume-streaked waters of the gorge.

To me, the dual character of the domestic pigeon has been a source of frequent surprise. Seen in a flock, swinging this way, turning that way, moving together in precision like a chorus line on a stage, they appear entirely regimented. Observed as individuals, they reveal unexpected independence. They exhibit idiosyncrasies. They are always doing the odd and unanticipated. I remember one pigeon in New York City that, each evening, flew up and up to spend the night at the top of the Empire State Building. Another, for several weeks, came into the tap room of the Yale Club each day to feed on proffered peanuts. A pigeon in the Wall Street district built a window-ledge nest made entirely of rubber bands and paper clips. And at the Little Church Around the Corner, just off Fifth Avenue, the birds that came to feed on rice thrown at weddings developed the habit of tapping at the windowpanes during ceremonies as though impatient for the rice throwing to begin.

During the Second World War, when a British tank commander in North Africa made friends with a pigeon by feeding it scraps of food, the bird is said to have followed his tank all the way from El Alamein to the Gothic Line in Italy. Twice a New Jersey pigeon named Edna sailed from New York Harbor on board the S.S. *Exford* and returned again after living the life of a vacationist on a Mediterranean cruise. Then there was another individualist bird that lived, some years ago, just outside a North Carolina city. Each day a veneer truck passed by on its regular run to a neighboring town. For some unaccountable reason, this snow-white pigeon always joined it, swooping down and flying for several miles just in front of the windshield.

In *Wind, Sand and Stars,* Antoine de St. Exupery tells of a group of Moorish chieftains from the Sahara Desert who were taken to see an ancient waterfall that has been flowing for a thousand years in the Alps. They gazed on and on. Their guide grew impatient and asked what they were waiting for. They replied: To see it stop. Niagara has been pouring over the dolomite-and-shale rim of a glacial basin for at least 35,000 years without a pause. Its slow advance upstream has left behind it a canyon seven miles long and about 200 feet deep. In the long view of the millenniums, all waterfalls are transitory. Niagara, now only a little more than half as high as it once was, may, in the distant future, degenerate into a series of rapids at the Lake Erie end of the river.

But today, its 200,000 cubic feet of water a second, foaming in a vertical plunge of more than 150 feet, forms one of the most famous natural wonders of the world. A million and a half persons a year come to see it. We were now in June, the traditional month of Niagara honeymoons. Vacationists were on the road. Schools were out. All day long, crowds streamed and swirled beside the falls. And all day long, whenever the sun was shining, somewhere, from some angle, rainbows glowed in the mist rising around the waterfalls. In curves and shining fragments, they took shape before our eyes. We saw them in the depths of the gorge. We saw them arching over the brink of the cataracts. Once, near sunset, two terns, fighting in the air, fluttered like white butterflies beneath the curve of a brilliant rainbow gleaming in the misty spray behind them.

Always, of course, we saw those bands of color with the sun behind us, with the white light of its rays broken up into component colors by the prism effect of innumerable droplets of moisture. But at the time, lost in our delight in the rainbow's simple beauty, we gave little thought to explanations. In the out-of-doors, knowing what things are is important. Knowing how things work is interesting. But there is more to nature than the facts of nature. There are beauty and poetry and awe and wonder. Too soon, the child's delight is left behind and "wonder in happy eyes fades, fades away." To forfeit this, to become deaf and blind to all except factual nature, to become absorbed entirely with identifying and explaining merely, is to lose the better half. It is to become as dry and literal and fact-minded as the listener who interrupted a thrilling story about a ship in a storm being driven onto jagged rocks to inquire:

"Were the rocks sedimentary or igneous?"

It is well to view the world at times—to see such things of beauty as the rainbow, the aurora, the cumulus cloud and the butterfly—as the child or the first man saw them. The celebrated American entomologist, Dr. John H. Comstock, one day was telling a group of his students at Cornell University of an exquisite butterfly he had once seen in the Alps. One of the group spoke up:

"What species was it, Professor?"

"At the time," Dr. Comstock replied, "I was not thinking of its species. I was thinking only how beautiful it was!"

On the third morning of our stay at Niagara, we bade goodbye to the Selbys and crossed to the American side again. On the bridge that carried us over the gorge we recalled another friend of ours and his curious adventure on it. Returning to Long Island from a summer vacation spent gathering botanical specimens and climbing mountains, George H. Peters had taken a short-cut across Canada from Detroit to Niagara. When he went through customs on the Canadian side, the official said:

"It's all right to take these plants out of Canada. But I don't think they will let you in the United States with them."

"Oh, that's all right," Peters assured him. "They all were collected in the United States."

A few minutes later he was telling the same thing at the American customs. But the official was adamant. The plants were coming from Canada and they could not come in. Thinking he would try another bridge, Peters turned around and drove back to the Canadian side. The man he had talked to there had just left for the day. His replacement told him:

"All I know is you are coming from the American side. You can't bring those plants into Canada!"

Faced with the prospect of endlessly going back and forth on the bridge, Peters took stock of his situation. Some of the plants were specimens he had long wanted to add to his collection. He had no intention of giving them up. Waiting until work traffic across the bridge began to mount, he pulled up once more at the American customs. He explained his predicament in detail. He went over it again and again. Cars piled up in a long line behind him. Horns honked. Finally the harassed official waved him through.

"Go ahead," he said, "and get those plants out of here!"

Most of that last day at Niagara we wandered about the mist-watered length of Goat Island, lying between the two great falls. Here, in May, 1861, Henry Thoreau had measured the circumference of bass and beech trees when, on the final journey of his life, to Minnesota, he had stopped off at Niagara Falls. Here he had watched ducks come floating down the rough water of the river, then take off, fly back and ride the rapids again. So, too, on this day, close to a hundred years later, the waterfowl were engaged in this same age-old sport.

Of all the ducks we saw that day, one—the nonchalant mallard—stands out in retrospect. It forms our last sharp memory of the cataracts. When we first caught sight of it, it was being swept by the swift slide of green water toward the brink of the American Falls. Calmly, it checked itself and clambered onto a small rock, awash and partly green with algae. There, less than a hundred feet from where the whole river disappeared and the thunder of the cataract seemed shaking the very rocks, it sunned itself unperturbed. A thin sheet of water streamed over the rock and over its webbed feet. Thousands of great gleaming bubbles, generated in the rapids above, flowed by it, turning and catching the sun.

After preening itself for a time, it slipped into the water again and let the current carry it away. Like a cork it drifted toward the falls, its speed increasing as it went. It showed no nervousness or alarm. It seemed unaware of any peril. We watched fascinated as the distance was reduced to less than sixty feet, less than forty feet from the brink of the abyss. The remaining distance seemed to us no more than thirty feet when, with a short, unhurried run, it lifted into the air and went slanting away down into the gorge, a creature of the air finding safety in its wings.

Sigurd Olson
1899-1982

Though he was widely travelled and he learned to love America's wilderness as a boy in northern Wisconsin, Sigurd Olson is commonly associated with that wilderness country of northern Minnesota that stretches to the Canadian border and is known as the Quetico-Superior country and National Forest. For years Olson explored much of it by canoe and, under Eisenhower, served on the President's Quetico-Superior Committee. He also served as a guide in the lakes and forests of this vast primitive area. One of the most famous woodsmen of our time, Olson was known by the out-of-doorsmen he guided as the Bourgeois—a title of honor given by the old *voyageurs* to their guides and leaders in this region. Olson is also well known as the author of eight books, including *Listening Post* (1958), *The Lonely Land* (1961), *Runes of the North* (1963), *The Hidden Forest* (1969), and *Reflections from the North Country* (1976).

The Singing Wilderness (1956), from which the selection here is taken, is one of his most admired books. Widely read, it was awarded distinction by the American Library Association in 1956 as one of forty-two significant books. Olson has also been given the Pi Delta Epsilon award for journalism (1959) and the Sierra Club's John Muir Award (1967). In 1963 he was named to the Hall of Fame and given the Founders Award of the Isaak Walton League, a leading American conservation society. Between 1954 and 1960 he was President of the National Parks Association and from 1968 to 1971 he was President of the Wilderness Society. Like *The Singing Wilderness,* his autobiographical *Open Horizons* (1969) is an important testament to one man's activism as a conservationist and an expression of the value of wilderness.

He described his own life and writing in the words of poet Archibald MacLeish: "The task of man is not to discover new worlds, but to discover his own world in terms of human comprehension and beauty."

from THE SINGING WILDERNESS*

MOON MAGIC

When the moon shines as it did last night, I am filled with unrest and the urge to range valleys and climb mountains. I want vistas of moonlit country from high places, must see the silver of roaring rapids and sparkling lakes. At such times I must escape houses and towns and all that is confining, be a part of the moon-drenched landscape and its continental sweep. It is only when the moon is full that I feel this way, only when it rises as it did last night, round and mellow as a great orange cheese over the horizon, slow-moving and majestic.

A quarter moon or a half or even a three-quarter moon does not do this to me, but when it is full my calm is gone and common things seem meaningless. All life is changed when the moon is full. Dogs howl madly when it comes into view and wolves make the hills resound with their wild music. Fish feed and throw themselves out of the water in sheer exuberance. Birds take to the air and sing in the glory of its light. Larger forms of game embark on galloping expeditions over their range. Under the full moon life is all adventure.

We must go back to the very beginnings of time to understand why this is so, back to the prehistoric, when the first protoplasmic droplets of life were responding to the powers of lunar attraction and the tidal cycles of the new world. The moon that moved oceans and changed the environments sheltering life in the making had a powerful and permanent effect on all protoplasm.

During the aeons that followed, this influence wove itself deeply into the entire complex of animal reaction. It is not surprising that man in his era of dawning intelligence made use of lunar periods in marking time, that the moon became not only the regulator but the mentor of his activities. Man began to feel that its various phases were good or bad, as past experience indicated. More and more it became part of the dreams and mystery that shrouded his early gropings toward the meaning of life and religion. The moon worked its magic, and for untold centuries men have greeted its rising with awe and reverence.

Is it any wonder that we still marvel at the coming of each full moon, that it makes us restless, uncertain, and adventurous? Is it any wonder, even though we no longer depend on it for good or evil omens, no longer govern our lives by its appearance, that it continues to arouse strange and indefinable feelings within us? As moderns we may have forgotten its ancient meaning, but inherently our responses to moonlight are no different from those of our ancestors—or, for that matter, from the responses of all other living things on the planet. It is still an event of cosmic significance.

So, when the moon shines as it did last night, I am apt to forget my work and responsibilities and take to the open, ranging the hills beneath its magic spell, tiring myself to the point where I can lie down and sleep in the

*From *The Singing Wilderness* (New York: Alfred A. Knopf, 1956).

full blaze of it. For me, this is the normal thing to do, and long ago I stopped trying to curb the impulse. I am merely being true to one of the most powerful influences within me, the reaction of protoplasm to lunar force.

If humans in all their sophistication permit moonlight to affect them, how much more does it affect animals? In my own moonlit wanderings I have had abundant occasion to see what it does and how animals in the wild respond to its charm. I have listened to loons go into ecstasies on wilderness lakes, have heard them call the whole night through and dash across the water as though possessed. I have heard sleepy birds begin to sing at midnight, wolves, foxes, frogs, and owls respond to the same inherent urge.

But the most delightful expression I know is the dance of the snowshoe hare in midwinter. If when the moon is bright you station yourself near a good rabbit swamp and stay quiet, you may see it, but you will need patience and endurance, for the night must be cold and still. Soon they begin to emerge, ghostly shadows with no spot of color except the black of their eyes. Down the converging trails they come, running and chasing one another up and down the runways, cavorting crazily in the light.

If you are weary and have seen enough, make a swoosh like the sound of wings and instantly each rabbit will freeze in its tracks, waiting for death to strike. But they are not still for long. As soon as the danger is past, they begin their game again. Very seldom do they leave the safety of their runways and the protecting woods, but once last winter I found the lone track of a snowshoe rabbit several hundred yards from cover and knew that the moon had got the best of him and that under its spell he had left the woods and struck out boldly across the open field. To make sure that nothing had happened, I followed his track, expecting at any moment to see that foolish trail end with a couple of broad wingtips marking it on either side, or in a bloody snarl of fur where a dog or a prowling fox had come upon him. But the tracks went on and on, circling grandly the drifts and stone piles of the meadow. At last they headed back to the woods, but the final jumps were wide and desperate and I knew that the moon magic had worn thin. That rabbit, I concluded, must have been very young and foolish or very old and sure.

Once when camped on a rocky point along the Canadian border with the moon at full and my tent pitched in the light of it, I was lying in my sleeping-bag, tent flaps open, studying the effect of pine needles etched against the sky. Suddenly I was aware of a slight rustle as though some small animal was trying to climb the silken roof of the tent. Then I saw that it was a mouse scrambling desperately up the edge of the side wall. For a moment it hesitated, then slipped backward, and I thought it surely must fall. Another wild scramble and it was on the ridge rope itself, tottering uncertainly back and forth. Then, to my amazement, the mouse launched itself out into space and slid down the smooth and shining surface of the tent to the ground below.

The action was repeated many times until the little animal became expert and reckless and lost no time between the climb back and the sheer abandon if its slide. Faster and faster it ran, intoxicated now by its new and thrilling experience; up along the edge straight toward the center of the ridge rope, a swift leap, belly down, legs spread wide to get the full effect of the exhilarating toboggan it had found, a slide of balloon silk straight to the needle-strewn ground below.

I watched the game for a long time. Eventually I stopped trying to count the slides and wondered at last how the mouse could possibly keep up its pace. As I lay there, I became convinced that it was enjoying itself hugely, that I was witnessing an activity which had no purpose but pleasure. I had seen many animals play in the moonlight—had watched a family of otters enjoying a slide into a deep pool, beaver playing a game of tag in a pond, squirrels chasing one another wildly through the silver-splashed tops of the pines. Under the magic spell of the moon, the mouse had acted no differently than the rest.

I thought as I lay there in my bag that, if nothing else, moonlight made animals and men forget for a little while the seriousness of living; that there were moments when life could be good and play the natural outlet for energy. I knew that if a man could abandon himself as my deer mouse had done and slide down the face of the earth in the moonlight once a month—or once a year, perhaps—it would be good for his soul.

Gary Snyder
b. 1930

One of America's most successful poets of the Pacific Northwest, Gary Snyder has conducted a sustained critique of Western culture from a position of "primitive" spiritual and ecological values. "As a poet," Snyder says, "I hold the most archaic values on earth. They go back to the Neolithic: the fertility of the soil, the magic of animals, the power-vision in solitude, the terrifying initiation and rebirth, the love and ecstasy of dance, the common work of the tribe." Arising out of his anthropological training and interests, his years of travels and Buddhist studies in Japan, and influences from Western authors on similar quests—D. H. Lawrence, W. B. Yeats, Ezra Pound, Robinson Jeffers, and Robert Duncan—Synder's vision of humanity's relationship to the cosmos is sacramental. His idea of a poem comes from that vision: "Each poem grows from an energy-mind-field-dance, and has its own inner grain. To let it grow, to let it speak for itself, is a large part of the work of the poet."

His quest and vision have made his life as much an unconventional critique of the dominant American political and business culture as his work. After graduating from college, he shipped from New York as seaman in 1948. Thus began his years as a world-traveler and laborer. He has worked as a seaman, logger, Forest Service trail crew and lookout in Oregon, Washington, and California, as a farmer, author, and advisor to the Governor of California on the Arts, among many other jobs. He was a member of the San Francisco group that launched the "Beat Movement" in literature during the 1950's and included Allen Ginsberg, Jack Kerouac, Philip Whalen, Michael McClure, and Philip Lamantia. He was, indeed, the hero of Kerouac's novel *The Dharma Bums*. Yet he has become a major American poet of the later twentieth century and has received many awards, including the National Academy of Arts and Letters Poetry Award in 1966, the Frank O'Hara Prize in 1967, and the Pulitzer Prize in 1974.

Synder has said that his poetry derives its rhythms from the physical work he is doing and the life he is leading at the time of writing. Hence his early *Riprap* (1959) is influenced as much by the geology of the Sierra Nevada and his work placing granite cobblestones on hard slab as by the Chinese poetry he was reading. *Myths and Texts* (1960) reflects days living in look-out cabins and the Indian songs and dances he witnessed. This book is seminal in that it focuses on the theme of the failure of Western culture as opposed to Buddhism and American Indian primitivism. Snyder has always seen America as a land of endless forest, bison, and clear water transformed into "the tired ground of the world's dominant culture."

Among his most significant books of poetry are *Six Sections from Mountains and Rivers Without End* (1965), *The Back Country* (1967), and *Turtle Island* (1974), a collection of poems and prose on the theme of nature, religion, and humanity, from which the following selections are taken. Further collections of essays develop themes in Snyder's poetry: *Earth House Hold* (1969) and *The Old Ways* (1977).

MOTHER EARTH: HER WHALES*

An owl winks in the shadows
A lizard lifts on tiptoe, breathing hard
Young male sparrow stretches up his neck,
        big head, watching—

The grasses are working in the sun. Turn it green.
Turn it sweet. That we may eat.
Grow our meat.

Brazil says "sovereign use of Natural Resources"
Thirty thousand kinds of unknown plants.
The living actual people of the jungle
        sold and tortured—
And a robot in a suit who peddles a delusion called "Brazil"
        can speak for *them?*

        The whales turn and glisten, plunge
            and sound and rise again,
        Hanging over subtly darkening deeps
        Flowing like breathing planets
            in the sparkling whorls of
                living light—

And Japan quibbles for words on
        what kinds of whales they can kill?
A once-great Buddhist nation
        dribbles methyl mercury

*Gary Snyder, *Turtle Island.*

like gonorrhea
in the sea.

Père David's Deer, the Elaphure,
Lived in the tule marshes of the Yellow River
Two thousand years ago—and lost its home to rice—
The forests of Lo-yang were logged and all the silt &
Sand flowed down, and gone, by 1200 AD—

Wild Geese hatched out in Siberia
head south over basins of the Yang, the Huang,
what we call "China"
On flyways they have used a million years.
Ah China, where are the tigers, the wild boars,
the monkeys,
like the snows of yesteryear
Gone in a mist, a flash, and the dry hard ground
Is parking space for fifty thousand trucks.
IS man most precious of all things?
—then let us love him, and his brothers, all those
Fading living beings—

North America, Turtle Island, taken by invaders
who wage war around the world.
May ants, may abalone, otters, wolves and elk
Rise! and pull away their giving
from the robot nations.

Solidarity. The People.
Standing Tree People!
Flying Bird People!
Swimming Sea People!
Four-legged, two-legged, people!

How can the head-heavy power-hungry politic scientist
Government two-world Capitalist-Imperialist
Third-world Communist paper-shuffling male
non-farmer jet-set bureaucrats
Speak for the green of the leaf? Speak for the soil?

(Ah Margaret Mead . . . do you sometimes dream of Samoa?)

The robots argue how to parcel out our Mother Earth
To last a little longer
like vultures flapping
Belching, gurgling,
near a dying Doe.

"In yonder field a slain knight lies—
We'll fly to him and eat his eyes
with a down
derry derry derry down down."

An Owl winks in the shadow
A lizard lifts on tiptoe
breathing hard
The whales turn and glisten
plunge and
Sound, and rise again
Flowing like breathing planets

In the sparkling whorls

Of living light.

Stockholm: Summer Solstice 40072

FOR THE CHILDREN

The rising hills, the slopes,
of statistics
lie before us.
the steep climb
of everything, going up,
up, as we all
go down.

In the next century
or the one beyond that,
they say,
are valleys, pastures,
we can meet there in peace
if we make it.

To climb these coming crests
one word to you, to
you and your children:

stay together
learn the flowers
go light

THE WILDERNESS*

I am a poet. My teachers are other poets, American Indians, and a few Buddhist priests in Japan. The reason I am here† is because I wish to bring a voice from the wilderness, my constituency. I wish to be a spokesman for a realm that is not usually represented either in intellectual chambers or in the chambers of government.

I was climbing Glacier Peak in the Cascades of Washington several years ago, on one of the clearest days I had ever seen. When we reached the summit of Glacier Peak we could see almost to the Selkirks in Canada. We could see south far beyond the Columbia River to Mount Hood and Mount Jefferson. And, of course, we could see Mount Adams and Mount Rainier. We could see across Puget Sound to the ranges of the Olympic Mountains. My companion, who is a poet, said: "You mean, there is a senator for all this?"

Unfortunately, there isn't a senator for all that. And I would like to think of a new definition of humanism and a new definition of democracy that would include the nonhuman, that would have representation from those spheres. This is what I think we mean by an ecological conscience.

I don't like Western culture because I think it has much in it that is inherently wrong and that is at the root of the environmental crisis that is not recent; it is very ancient; it has been building up for a millennium. There are many things in Western culture that are admirable. But a culture that alienates itself from the very ground of its own being—from the wilderness outside (that is to say, wild nature, the wild, self-contained, self-informing ecosystems) and from that other wilderness, the wilderness within—is doomed to a very destructive behavior, ultimately perhaps self-destructive behavior.

The West is not the only culture that carries these destructive seeds. China had effectively deforested itself by 1000 A.D. India had effectively deforested itself by 800 A.D. The soils of the Middle East were ruined even earlier. The forest that once covered the mountains of Yugoslavia were stripped to build the Roman fleet, and those mountains have looked like Utah ever since. The soils of southern Italy and Sicily were ruined by latifundia slave-labor farming in the Roman Empire. The soils of the Atlantic seaboard in the United States were effectively ruined before the American Revolution because of the one-crop (tobacco) farming. So the same forces have been at work in East and West.

You would not think a poet would get involved in these things. But the voice that speaks to me as a poet, what Westerners have called the Muse, is the voice of nature herself, whom the ancient poets called the great goddess, the Magna Mater. I regard that voice as a very real entity. At the root of the problem where our civilization goes wrong is the mistaken belief that nature is something less than authentic, that nature is not as alive as man is, or as intelligent, that in a sense it is dead, and that animals are of so

*Transcript of a statement made at a seminar at The Center for the Study of Democratic Institutions, Santa Barbara, California.

†The Center for the Study of Democratic Institutions, Santa Barbara, California.

low an order of intelligence and feeling, we need not take their feelings into account.

A line is drawn between primitive peoples and civilized peoples. I think there is a wisdom in the worldview of primitive peoples that we have to refer ourselves to, and learn from. If we are on the verge of postcivilization, then our next step must take account of the primitive worldview which has traditionally and intelligently tried to open and keep open lines of communication with the forces of nature. You cannot communicate with the forces of nature in the laboratory. One of the problems is that we simply do not know much about primitive people and primitive cultures. If we can tentatively accommodate the possibility that nature has a degree of authenticity and intelligence that requires that we look at it more sensitively, then we can move to the next step. "Intelligence" is not really the right word. The ecologist Eugene Odum uses the term "biomass."

Life-biomass, he says, is stored information; living matter is stored information in the cells and in the genes. He believes there is more information of a higher order of sophistication and complexity stored in a few square yards of forest than there is in all the libraries of mankind. Obviously, that is a different order of information. It is the information of the universe we live in. It is the information that has been flowing for millions of years. In this total information context, man may not be necessarily the highest or most interesting product.

Perhaps one of its most interesting experiments at the point of evolution, if we can talk about evolution in this way, is not man but a high degree of biological diversity and sophistication opening to more and more possibilities. Plants are at the bottom of the food chain; they do the primary energy transformation that makes all the life-forms possible. So perhaps plant-life is what the ancients meant by the great goddess. Since plants support the other life-forms, they became the "people" of the land. And the land—a country—is a region within which the interactions of water, air, and soil and the underlying geology and the overlying (maybe stratospheric) wind conditions all go to create both the microclimates and the large climactic patterns that make a whole sphere or realm of life possible. The people in that realm include animals, humans, and a variety of wild life.

What we must find a way to do, then, is incorporate the other people—what the Sioux Indians called the creeping people, and the standing people, and the flying people, and the swimming people—into the councils of government. This isn't as difficult as you might think. If we don't do it, they will revolt against us. They will submit non-negotiable demands about our stay on the earth. We are beginning to get non-negotiable demands right now from the air, the water, the soil.

I would like to expand on what I mean by representation here at the Center from these other fields, these other societies, these other communities. Ecologists talk about the ecology of oak communities, or pine communities. They *are* communities. This institute—this Center—is of the order of a kiva of elders. Its function is to maintain and transmit the lore of the tribe on the highest levels. If it were doing its job completely, it would have a cycle of ceremonies geared to the seasons, geared perhaps to the migrations of the fish and to the phases of the moon. It would be able to instruct in what rituals you follow when a child is born, when someone reaches puberty, when someone gets married, when someone dies. But, as you know, in these fragmented times, one council cannot perform all these functions at one time. Still it would be understood that a council of elders, the caretakers of the lore of the culture, would open themselves to representation from other life-forms. Historically this has been done through art. The paintings of bison and bears in the caves of southern France were of that order. The animals were speaking through the people and making their point. And when, in the dances of the Pueblo Indians and other peoples, certain individuals become seized, as it were, by the spirit of the deer, and danced as a deer would dance, or danced the dance of the corn maidens, or impersonated the squash blossom, they were no longer speaking for humanity, they were taking it on themselves to interpret, through their humanity, what these other life-forms were. That is about all we know so far concerning the possibilities of incorporating spokesmanship for the rest of life in our democratic society.

Let me describe how a friend of mine from a Rio Grande pueblo hunts. He is twenty-seven years old. The Pueblo Indians, and I think probably most of the other Indians of the Southwest, begin their hunt, first, by purifying themselves. They take emetics, a sweat bath, and perhaps avoid their wife for a few days. They also try not to think certain thoughts. They go out hunting in an attitude of humility. They make sure that they need to hunt, that they are not hunting without necessity. Then they improvise a song while they are in the mountains. They sing aloud or hum to themselves while they are walking along. It is a song to the deer, asking the deer to be willing to die for them. They usually still-hunt, taking a place alongside a trail. The feeling is that you are not hunting the deer, the deer is coming to you; you make yourself available for the deer that will present itself to you, that has given itself to you. Then you shoot it. After you shoot it, you cut the head off and place the head facing east. You sprinkle corn meal in front of the mouth of the deer, and you pray to the deer, asking it to forgive you for having killed it, to understnd that we all need to eat, and to please make a good report to the other deer spirits that he has been treated well. One finds this way of handling things and animals in all primitive cultures.

ON "AS FOR POETS"

"Energy is Eternal Delight"—William Blake, in *The Marriage of Heaven and Hell.* What are we to make of this? As the overdeveloped world (the U.S., Japan, etc.) approaches an "energy crisis" with shortages of oil and electric power (and some nations plan a desperate gamble with nuclear generating plants) we must remember that oil and coal are the stored energy of the sun locked by ancient plant-life in its cells. "Renewable" energy resources are the trees and flowers and all living beings of today, especially plant-life doing the primary work of energy-transfer.

On these fuels contemporary nations now depend. But there is another kind of energy, in every living being, close to the sun-source but in a different way. The power within. Whence? "Delight." The delight of being alive while knowing of impermanence and death, the acceptance and mastery of this. A definition:

Delight is the innocent joy arising
with the perception and realization of
the wonderful, empty, intricate,
inter-penetrating,
mutually-embracing, shining
single world beyond all discrimination
or opposites.*

*An alternative definition has been suggested by Dr. Edward Schafer of Berkeley, who describes himself as "an imaginative but unreasonable pedant" (but who is really a scholar of the prosody of artifacts, the poetry of tools).

Delight is the sophisticated joy arising
with the perception and realization of
the wonderful, replete, intricate,
rich-reflecting,
uniquely aloof, polychrome
complex worlds beyond all indifference
to nuances.

Barry Commoner
b. 1917

In the tradition of Rachel Carson, Barry Commoner is a professional scientist—Professor of Biology at Washington University, author of over 200 technical articles—who has been foremost in his generation to write also for wide audiences, to clearly explain the principles of ecology and the ways in which we are violating basic biological laws. He is also an activist through his many memberships, consultantships, and directorships in private and government organizations such as the Rachel Carson Trust for Living Environment and the Department of the Interior.

He has particularly emphasized the roles our population and consumption patterns have played in threatening the stability of natural resources and systems. He has best described his central theme himself: humans "have broken out of the circle of life, driven not only by biological need, but by the social organization which they have devised to 'conquer' nature; [by] means of gaining wealth that are governed by requirements conflicting with those which govern nature . . . To survive, we must close the circle. We must learn how to restore to nature the wealth we borrow from it."

His popular books *Science and Survival* (1966), the award-winning *The Closing Circle: Nature, Man, and Technology* (1971), *The Poverty of Power* (1976), and *The Politics of Energy* (1979), all in one way or another confirm the pattern of humanity dangerously divorced from biological law.

from SCIENCE AND SURVIVAL*

The Scientific Background of Technological Failures

These problems have a common scientific background. Each of them springs from a useful technological innovation. The burning of fuel by internal-combustion engines is an enormously valuable source of energy—but also pollutes the air. New synthetic chemicals, the fruits of remarkable advances in chemical technology since World War II, appear in a multitude of useful forms—but also as new pollutants of air and water. The development, about twenty-five years ago, of self-sustained nuclear reactions has given us not only new weapons and new sources of power, but unprecedented radioactive debris as well.

Most of these problems seem to crop up unexpectedly. The sunlight-induced chemical conservion of airborne hydrocarbons (such as gasoline vapor) into smog was discovered, not in a chemical laboratory but in the air over Los Angeles, long after the chief mode for disseminating these hydrocarbons—the superhighway—was well entrenched in the urban economy. The full significance of the absorption of fallout into the human body became known only some years after the establishment of massive programs of nuclear testing. Most of the medical hazards of the new insecticides were noticed only long after these substances were in wide use. All these problems have been imposed on us—sometimes to our considerable surprise—well after the causative activity was in full swing.

Could we cure these difficulties by calling a halt to science and new technologies? The present accelerating growth of science and technology—which, together with population growth, is the cause of most of our pollution problems—was set in motion more than sixty years ago. Its roots are in the scientific revolution which took place at the turn of the century, when physicists discovered that the apparently simple laws of Newton's time concealed a complex world of exceedingly small particles and immense forces. From this knowledge has come the great flowering of modern science—including the new energy sources and synthetic substances which have covered the earth with pollution. We are today witnessing the inevitable impact of the tidal wave created by a scientific revolution more than half a century old. It is simply too late to declare a moratorium on the progress of science.

The real question is not *whether* we should use our new knowledge, but *how* to use it. And to answer that, we must understand the structure of modern scientific knowledge: in which areas the new insights of science are powerful and effective guides to action; in which others they are too uncertain to support a sound technology. Since the scientific revolution which generated modern technology took place in physics, it is natural that modern science should provide better technological control over inanimate matter than over living things. This disparity is evident in our environmental problems. If basic theories of physics had not attained their present ability to explain nuclear structure, we would not now be confronted with massive dissemination of man-made radioisotopes and synthetic chemicals. If biological theory had become sufficiently advanced to master the problems of cancer—a chief hazard from modern pollutants—we might be better prepared to cope with these new environmental contaminants. We are in difficulty because of the wide disparity between the present state of the physical and the biological sciences.

The separation of the laws of nature among the different sciences is a human conceit; nature itself is an integrated whole. A nuclear test explosion is usually regarded as an experiment in engineering and physics; but it is also a vast, if poorly controlled, experiment in environmental biology. It is a convincing statement of the competence of modern physics and engineering, but also a demonstration of our poor understanding of the biology of fallout. If the physico-chemical sciences are to be safely used in the new technologies they will need to be governed by what we know—and do not know—about life and its environment.

The Biosphere

What we know about living things and about the biosphere—the community of life in the environment—is that they are enormously complex, and that this complexity is the source of their remarkable staying power. The web of relationships that ties animal to plant, prey to predator, parasite to host, and all to the air, water, and soil which they inhabit persists *because* it is complex. An old farmhouse practice is a simple illustration of this fundamental point. Farmers who keep cats to control the ravages of mice find it necessary to offer the cats a doorstep feeding. Only if the farmer provides this alternative source of food can the cats withstand a temporary shortage in the mouse supply and remain on hand to catch the mice when they reappear. A stable system that will keep mice in check must comprise all three components: cats, mice and domestic cat food. This principle is well established in environmental biology: anything which reduces the complexity of a natural biological system renders it less stable and more subject to fatal fluctuations.

The biosphere is closely governed by the connections among its numerous parts. The connections which comprise the biological food chain, for example, greatly amplify the effects of environmental pollution. If soil contains 1 unit of insecticide per gram, earthworms living in the soil will contain 10 to 40 units per gram, and in woodcocks feeding on the earthworms the insecticide level will rise to about 200 units per gram. In the biosphere the whole is always greater than the sum of its parts; animals which absorb one insecticide may become more sensitive to the damaging effects of a second one. Because of such amplifications, a small intrusion in one place in the environment may trigger a huge response elsewhere in the system. Often an amplification feeds on itself until the entire living system is engulfed by catastrophe. If the vegetation that protects the soil from erosion is killed, the soil will wash away, plants will then find no footholds for their seeds, and a permanent desert will result.

It is not surprising, then, that the introduction of any killing chemical into the environment is bound to cause a change somewhere in the tangled web of relationships. For this reason, and because we depend on so many detailed and subtle aspects of the environment, *any* change imposed on it for the sake of some economic benefit has a price. For the benefits of powerful insecticides we pay in losses of bird-life and fish. For the conveniences of automobiles we pay in the rise of respiratory disease from smog. For the widespread use of combustible fuels we may yet be forced to pay the catastrophic cost of protecting our cities from worldwide floods. Sooner or later, wittingly or unwittingly, we must pay for every intrusion on the natural environment.

Our Knowledge Is Dangerously Incomplete

There is considerable scientific disagreement about the medical hazards of the new pollutants: about the effects of DDT now found in human bodies, about the diseases due to smog, or about the long-range effects of fallout. But the crucial point is that the disagreements exist, for they reveal that we have risked these hazards before we knew what harm they might do. Unwittingly we have loaded the air with chemicals that damage the lungs, and the water with substances that interfere with the functioning of the blood. Because we wanted to build nuclear bombs and kill mosquitoes, we have burdened our bodies with strontium-90 and DDT, with consequences that no one can now predict. We have been massively intervening in the environment without being aware of many of the harmful consequences of our acts until they have been performed and the effects—which are difficult to understand and sometimes irreversible—are upon us. Like the sorcerer's apprentice, we are acting upon dangerously incomplete knowledge. We are, in effect, conducting a huge experiment *on ourselves.* A generation hence—too late to help—public health statistics may reveal what hazards are associated with these pollutants.

To those of us who are concerned with the growing risk of unintended damage to the environment, some would reply that it is the grand purpose of science to move into unknown territory to explore, and to discover. They would remind us that similar hazards have been risked before, and that science and technology cannot make progress without taking some risks. But the size and persistence of possible errors has also grown with the power of science and the expansion of technology. In the past, the risks taken in the name of technological progress—boiler explosions on the first steamboats, or the early injuries from radium—were restricted to a small place and a short time. The new hazards are neither local nor brief. Air pollution covers vast areas. Fallout is worldwide. Synthetic chemicals may remain in the soil for years. Radioactive pollutants now on the earth's surface will be found there for generations, and, in the case of carbon-14, for thousands of years. Excess carbon dioxide from fuel combustion eventually might cause floods that could cover much of the earth's present land surface for centuries. At the same time the permissible margin for error has become very much reduced. In the development of steam engines a certain number of boiler explosions were tolerated as the art was improved. If a single comparable disaster were to occur in a nuclear power plant or in a reactor-driven ship near a large city, thousands of people might die and a whole region be rendered uninhabitable—a price that the public might be unwilling to pay for nuclear power. The risk is one that private insurance companies have refused to underwrite. Modern science and technology are simply too powerful to permit a trial-and-error approach.

It can be argued that the hazards of modern pollutants are small compared to the dangers associated with other human enterprises. For us, today, the fallout hazard is, for example, much smaller than the risks we take on the highway or in the air. But what of the risks we inflict on future generations? No estimate of the actual harm that may be done by fallout, smog, or chemical pollutants can obscure the sober realization that in each case the risk was undertaken before it was fully understood. The importance of these issues to science, and to the citizen, lies not only in the associated hazards, but in the warning of an incipient abdication of one of the major duties of science—prediction and control of human interventions into nature. The true measure of the danger is not represented by the present hazards, but by the disasters that will surely be visited upon us if we dare to enter the new age before us without correcting this basic fault in the scientific enterprise. And if we are to correct this fault, we must first discover why it has developed.

. . .

Risk versus *Benefit*

It appears, then, that the problems of environmental pollution require a common approach: the principle of balancing risk against benefit. The risk can be determined by estimating the number of people exposed to the pollutant, the amounts which they may be expected to absorb, and the physical harm that might result. The benefit can be determined by estimating the economic, political, or social gains expected from the operation which produces the pollutant and the possibilities of substituting less hazardous operations.

Estimations of risk and benefit are proper subjects of scientific and technological analysis. There are scientific means for estimating how many cases of leukemia and of serious congenital defects may result from fallout radiation; such calculations have been reported in great detail by the United Nations Scientific Committee on the Effects of Atomic Radiation. Medical statistics can provide a similar estimate of the amount of respiratory disease that is related to exposure to smog. It should be possible, eventually, to determine what biological risks to humans, birds, or fish are to be expected from a given dosage of DDT.

Determination of the corresponding benefits is more difficult but nevertheless is also within the realm of technological competence. For example, if automobiles are, as they appear to be, a major source of smog in urban areas, it should be possible to evaluate their economic and social importance and to compare it with alternative forms of transport, such as electric trains, which are not smog producers. The economic value of insecticides to the farmer is readily calculable. While no money value can be placed on the benefits to be derived from the development of a new nuclear weapon, it should be possible, it would seem, to determine the necessity of such weapons to the nation, and the importance of nuclear tests to their development.

However difficult the procedures and uncertain the results, all these questions are subject to objective scientific and technological analysis. Presumably scientists who differ in their personal attitudes toward nuclear tests, superhighways, or songbirds could agree, more or less, in their estimates of the relevant benefits and of the associated hazards of fallout, smog, or DDT.

Once the hazards and benefits of new technological innovations become clear, it may be possible to find means to reduce the hazards—at a price. Automobile exhaust emissions can be partially reduced by mechanical devices, which will be required by law on all 1968 models. If we are threatened by accumulating carbon dioxide in the air, engineers can build devices, however expensive, to remove this substance from flue gases. If chemical pesticides are an unwarranted hazard to wildlife or man, we can, after all, stop using them and suffer the sting of the mosquito and the depredations of insects on our crops, while we try to learn enough about environmental biology to develop more natural means of control. If we find strontium-90 intolerable, the nuclear tests that produce fallout can be stopped, and they have in fact been sharply reduced by the test-ban treaty. What is needed is not only the development of technical means for dealing with environmental pollution, but also the willingness to undertake the extra expense and additional inconvenience to prevent the intrusion of pollutants into the environment.

Beyond the Realm of Science

With the determination of benefits and risk and the development of techniques which improve the balance between them, the applicability of scientific procedure to the problems of environmental contamination comes to an abrupt end. What then remains is a judgment which balances the stated risks against the corresponding benefits. A scientific analysis can perhaps tell us that every nuclear test will probably cause a given number of congenitally deformed births, but no scientific procedures can choose the balance point and tell us how many defective births we ought to tolerate for the sake of a new nuclear weapon.

What is the "importance" of fallout, determined scientifically? Some scientists have stated, with the full dignity of their professional preeminence, that the fallout hazard, while not zero, is "trivial." Nevertheless, I have seen a minister, upon learning for the first time that acts deliberately performed by his own nation were possibly endangering a few lives in distant lands and a future time, become so incensed at this violation of the biblical injunction against the poisoning of wells as to make an immediate determination to oppose nuclear testing. No science can gauge the relative validity of these conflicting responses to the same facts.

Scientific method cannot determine whether the proponents of urban superhighways or those who complain about the resultant smog are in the right, or whether the benefits of nuclear tests to the national interest outweigh the hazards of fallout. No scientific principle can tell us how to make the choice, which may sometimes be forced upon us by the insecticide problem, between the shade of the elm tree and the song of the robin.

Certainly science can validly describe what is known about the information to be gained from a nuclear experiment, the economic value of a highway, or the hazard of radioactive contamination or of smog. The statement will usually be hedged with uncertainty, and the proper answer may sometimes be "We don't know," but in any case these separate questions do belong within the realm of science. However, the choice of the balance point between benefit and hazard is a value judgment; it is based on ideas of social good, on morality or religion—not on science.

In the "informed judgment" of which the Federal Radiation Council so properly speaks, the scientist can justly claim to be "informed," but he can make no valid claim for a special competence in "judgment." Once the scientific evidence has been stated, or its absence made clear, the establishment of a level of tolerance for a modern pollutant is a *social* problem and must be resolved by social processes. Thus the logic of the scientific problems which are raised by environmental pollution forces the resolution of these issues into the arena of public policy.

If resolutions of the problems created by the recent failures in large-scale technology require social judgments, who is to make these judgments? Obviously scientists must be involved in some way, if only because they have in a sense created the problems. But if these issues require social, political, and moral judgments, then they must also somehow reflect the demands, opinions, and ethics of citizens generally. Because new experiments and technological processes are so costly that the government must often pay for them, and because government officials mediate many social decisions, the government and its administrators are also involved. What are the proper roles of scientist, citizen, and administrator?

The Scientist's Role: Two Approaches

Since World War II scientists have become deeply concerned with public affairs. We are all acutely aware that our work, our ideas, and our daily activities impinge with a frightening immediacy on national politics, on international conflicts, on the planet's fate as a human habitation.

Scientists have tried to live with these responsibilities in a number of ways. Sometimes, in moments of impending crisis, we are aware only that the main outcome of science is that the planet has become a kind of colossal, lightly triggered time bomb. Then all we can do is to issue an anguished cry of warning. In calmer times we try to grapple with the seemingly endless problems of unraveling the tangle of nuclear physics, seismology, electronics, radiation biology, ecology, sociology, normal and pathological psychology, which, added to the crosscurrents of local, national, and international politics, has become the frightful chaos that goes under the disarming euphemism "public affairs."

Many scientists have studied the technology of the new issues and have mastered their vocabulary: megatonnage, micromicrocuries, threshold dose, and all the rest of the new technical terms. Nuclear physicists have struggled to learn the structure of the chromosome and how cows give milk. Biologists have returned to long-discarded textbooks of freshman physics.

A good deal of the scientist's concern for public issues may be generated by a sense of responsibility for the events which have converted nuclear energy from a laboratory experiment into the force which has almost alone molded the course of human events since 1945. It was a group of scientists who, fearful of the consequences of the possible development of nuclear weapons by the Nazis, conducted a strenuous campaign to convince the American government that they should be achieved in the United States first. As it turned out, Germany never succeeded in achieving an atomic bomb, and the Allies won the war against Germany without using it. Many of the scientists who worked on the United States atomic bomb were relieved to know that the threat which motivated them was gone and the new force need never be used for destruction. But over their objections the weapon was turned against Japan, an enemy known to lack atomic arms. The human use of nuclear energy began with two explosions which took several hundred thousand lives; from this violent birth it has since grown into a destructive force of suicidal dimensions.

I believe that it is largely the weight of this burden which has caused the scientific community, since the end of the war, to examine with great care the interactions between science and society, to define the scientist's responsibilities to society, and to seek useful ways to discharge them.

For some time there has been a division of opinion within the scientific community on what responsibility the scientist has toward the social uses of his work. Some scientists have been guided by the idea that it is the scientist's duty to pursue knowledge of nature for its own sake without regard to social consequences. They believe that scientists, as scientists, have no special responsibility to foster any particular solution of the social issues that may result from their discoveries. They cling to the objectivity of the laboratory and try to keep their political views separate from their scientific duties. To other scientists such rigorous objectivity seems to imply a disregard for the nation's defense, or for the enormous destructiveness of nuclear war, or for the numerous ways in which science can serve human welfare. They seek to play a part in directing the power that they help to create.

The second of these positions is relatively new and originates in scientists' intense concern with such dangerous issues as nuclear war. The rationale of this position appears to be approximately the following: Scientists have a particular moral responsibility to counter the evil consequences of their works. They are also in possession of the relevant technical facts essential to an understanding of the major public issues which trouble the world. Since scientists are trained to analyze the complex forces at work in such issues, they have an ability for rational thought which renders them to some degree detached from the emotions that encumber the ordinary citizen's views of these calamitous issues. What is more, some assert, the scientist is now in a particularly favorable position to be heard—by government executives, Congressional committees, the press, and the people at large—and therefore has important opportunities to influence social decisions.

This position, it will be noted, is quite neutral politically. It can justify strong statements for or against disarmament, civil defense, nuclear testing, or the space program. Such arguments in support of the scientist's inherent claim to the right of political leadership are the implicit background of a number of practical activities by scientists. These include publication of petitions and newspaper advertisements, political lobbying, and the operation of scientific auxiliaries to the major political parties.

This general approach has become fairly common in the scientific community, in contrast to the viewpoint, more predominant in the past, that a scientist's political role should be exercised apart from his professional one. One result is a growing tendency for considerations of scientific issues to appear with a strong admixture of political views. Witness the following examples from recent discussions, by scientists, of space research:

"On solid scientific grounds, on the basis of popular appeal, and in the interests of our prestige as a peace-loving nation capable of great scientific enterprise, exobiology's goals of finding and exploring extra-territorial life should be acclaimed as the top-priority scientific goal of our space program."

At the 1963 Senate hearings referred to in Chapter 4, a witness who has been a leader in developing the nation's scientific space program said, following an exposition of the scientific values of space research:

"Our goals in space provide to our Nation that spirit and momentum that avoids our collapse into the easy-going days that tolerate social abuse."

In the same vein, I have seen a statement in which a number of distinguished scientists argued for a particular space experiment partly by supporting its scientific value, and partly by describing its special usefulness as a vehicle of international propaganda for the United States.

What is the harm in this approach? Why shouldn't scientists make effective use of their newly won position in society? Why not exploit political interests to further a scientific goal?

One danger has already been discussed—that the capability of science to understand nature, and to guide our efforts to control it, is being damaged by the pressure of political goals. And it is this capability alone that stands between us and man-made catastrophe. Clearly, no matter what else they do, scientists dare not act in such a way as to compromise the integrity of science or to damage its capability to seek the truth. But the notion that scientists have some special aptitude for the judgment of social issues—even of those which are due to the progress of science—runs a grave risk of damaging the integrity of science and public confidence in it. If two protagonists claim to know *as scientists,* through the merits of the methods of science, the one that nuclear testing is essential to the national interest, the other that it is destructive of the national interest, where lies the truth? I know from repetitious experience that the one question about fallout and nuclear war, and about the pesticide controversy, which most troubles the thoughtful citizen is: "How do I know which scientist is telling the truth?"

This is a painfully revealing question. It tells us that the public is no longer certain that scientists—all of them—"tell the truth," for otherwise why the question? The citizen has begun to doubt what he used to take for granted—that science is closely connected to the truth.

Now it seems to me that the citizen's confidence in the objectivity of science cannot be destroyed without disastrous consequences. We cannot really expect citizens, in general, to be capable of performing an independent check on the accuracy and validity of all of a scientist's statements about scientific matters. I am fully convincd that the citizen can and must study and come to understand the underlying facts about modern technological problems. But the citizen cannot check the calculations of the path of a rocket to the moon or question the validity of the law of radioactive decay. These conclusions he can accept, but only if he knows that they *are* subject to the scrutiny of scientists who will finally accept, reject, or modify them. The citizen must take a good deal of science as established by the simple fact that scientists agree about it. It is therefore inevitable that unresolvable disagreement among scientists will erode—and rightly so—the citizen's confidence in the ability of science to get at the truth.

When scientists voice their social judgments with the same authority that attaches to their professional pronouncements, the citizen is bound to confuse the inevitable and insolvable disagreements with scientific disputes. If scientists attach to their scientific conclusions those political views or social judgments which happen to provide support for these conclusions, scientific objectivity inevitably comes under a cloud.

In my opinion the notion that, because the world is dominated by science, scientists have a special competence in public affairs is also profoundly destructive of the democratic process. If we are guided by this view, science will not only create issues but also shield them from the customary processes of administrative decision-making and public judgment.

Nearly every facet of modern life is now so encumbered by a tangled array of nuclear physics, electronics, higher mathematics, and advanced biology as to interpose an apparently insuperable barrier between the citizen, the legislator, the administrator, and the major public issues of the day. No one seems to be wholly exempt from this estrangement. When, during the Congressional hearings on the nuclear-test-ban treaty, Senator Kuchel was confronted with a bewilderingly technical argument, he said in desperation to a scientist member of the AEC, "Let me put my tattered senatorial toga over your shoulders for a moment." When President Kennedy was questioned regarding governmental policy on the Starfish nuclear explosion, he was forced to fall back on the opinion of a scientist and closed the discussion with the remark, "After all, it's Dr. Van Allen's belt." Confronted by such examples, a citizen is likely to conclude that he must have a Ph.D. to support his judgments about nuclear war or the pesticide problem, or else be governed by the judgment of those who do.

The impact of modern science on public affairs has generated a nearly paralyzing paradox. Despite their origin in scientific knowledge and technological achievements (and failures) the issues created by the advance of science can only be resolved by moral judgment and political choice. But those who in a democratic society have the duty to make these decisions—legislators, government officials, and citizens generally—are often unable to perceive the issues behind the enveloping cloud of science and technology. And if those who have the special knowledge to comprehend the issues—the scientists—arrogate to themselves a major voice in the decision, they are likely to aggravate the very threats to the integrity of science which have helped to generate the problems in the first place.

A New Approach: An Informed Citizenry

There is no single magic word that solves this puzzle. But the same interlocking factors, looked at a little differently, do offer a solution: the scientist does have an urgent duty to *help* society solve the grave problems that have been created by the progress of science. But the problems are social and must be solved by social processes. In these processes the scientist has one vote and no claim to leadership beyond that given to any person who has the gift of moving his fellow men. But the citizen and the government official whose task it is to make the judgments cannot do so in the absence of the necessary facts and relevant evaluations. Where these are matters of science, the scientist as the custodian of this knowledge has a profound duty to impart as much of it as he can to his fellow citizens. But in doing so, he must guard against false pretensions and avoid claiming for science that which belongs to the conscience. By this means scientists can place the decisions on the grave issues which they have helped to create in the proper hands—the hands of an informed citizenry.

This is the view of the scientist's social responsibilities which was first developed by the AAAS Committee on Science in the Promotion of Human Welfare after a painstaking study of the conflict surrounding science and public policy. In its first report this committee said:

> In sum, we conclude that the scientific community should on its own initiative assume an obligation to call to public attention those issues of public policy which relate to science, and to provide for the general public the facts and estimates of the effects of alternative policies which the citizen must have if he is to participate intelligently in the solution of these problems. A citizenry thus informed is, we believe, the chief assurance that science will be devoted to the promotion of human welfare.

This view is plausible in its logic and laudable in its democratic intent. But does it work? An "informed citizenry" is the long-standing, and rarely attained, goal of social reformers. Most citizens, it can be argued, are unlikely to surmount the formidable difficulties involved in learning about fallout, pesticides, and air pollution. A scientist, once given a platform, might be unable to restrict himself to "the facts and estimates of the effects of alternative policies" and to refrain from also exhorting his audience to whatever policy he has adopted as his own. A scientist who has strong political sensibilities—and many do—may be unable to speak objectively on the data about nuclear war without developing a badly split personality. And by what means can scientists, who have no command over either the public news media or the machinery of government, overcome the governmental self-justification and journalistic inertia which so often impede public knowledge about complex, confused public affairs?

. . .

Once the problems are perceived by science, and scientists help citizens to understand the possible solutions, what actions can be taken to avoid the calamities that seem to follow so closely on the heels of modern technological progress? I have tried to show that science offers no "objective" answer to this question. There is a price attached to every solution; any judgment will necessarily reflect the value we place on the benefits yielded by a given technological advance and the harm we associate with its hazards. The benefits and the hazards can be described by scientific means, but each of us must choose that balance between them which best accords with our own belief of what is good—for ourselves, for society, and for humanity as a whole.

In discussing what ought to be done about these problems, I can speak only for myself. As a scientist, I can arrive at my own judgments—subject to the open criticism which is so essential to scientific discourse—about the scientific and technological issues. As a citizen, I can decide which of the alternative solutions my government ought to pursue, and, using the instruments of politics, act for the adoption of this course. As a human being, I can express in this action my own moral convictions.

As a biologist, I have reached this conclusion: we have come to a turning point in the human habitation of the earth. The environment is a complex, subtly balanced system, and it is this integrated whole which receives the impact of all the separate insults inflicted by pollutants. Never before in the history of this planet has its thin life-supporting surface been subjected to such diverse, novel, and potent agents. I believe that the cumulative effects of these pollutants, their interactions and amplification, can be fatal to the complex fabric of the biosphere. And, because man is, after all, a dependent part of this system, I believe that continued pollution of the earth, if unchecked, will eventually destroy the fitness of this planet as a place for human life.

My judgment of the possible effects of the most extreme assault on the biosphere—nuclear war—has already been expressed. Nuclear war would, I believe, inevitably destroy the economic, social, and political structure of the combatant nations; it would reduce their populations, industry and agriculture to chaotic remnants, incapable of supporting an organized effort for recovery. I believe that world-wide radioactive contamination, epidemics, ecological disasters, and possible climatic changes would so gravely affect the stability of the biosphere as to threaten human survival everywhere on the earth.

If we are to survive, we need to become aware of the damaging effects of technological innovations, determine their economic and social costs, balance these against the expected benefits, make the facts broadly available to the public, and take the action needed to achieve an acceptable balance of benefits and hazards. Obviously, all this should be done *before* we become massively committed to a new technology. One of our most urgent needs is to establish within the scientific community some means of estimating and reporting on the expected benefits and hazards of proposed environmental interventions *in advance.* Such advance consideration could have averted many of our present difficulties with detergents, insecticides, and radioactive contaminants. It could have warned us of the tragic futility of attempting to defend the nation's security by a means that can only lead to the nation's destruction.

We have not yet learned this lesson. Despite our earlier experience with nondegradable detergents, the degradable detergents which replaced them were massively marketed, by joint action of the industry in 1965, without any pilot study of their ecological effects. The phosphates which even the new detergents introduce into surface waters may force their eventual withdrawal. The United States, Great Britain, and France are already committed to costly programs for supersonic transport planes but have thus far failed to produce a comprehensive evaluation of the hazards from sonic boom, from cosmic radioactivity, and from the physiological effects of rapid transport from one time zone to another. The security of every nation in the world remains tied to nuclear armaments, and we continue to evade an open public discussion of the basic question: do we wish to commit the security of nations to a military system which is likely to destroy them?

It is urgent that we face this issue openly, now, before by accident or design we are overtaken by nuclear catastrophe. U Thant has proposed that the United Nations prepare a report on the effects of nuclear war and disseminate it throughout the world. Such a report could become the cornerstone of world peace. For the world would then know that, so long as nuclear war remains possible, we are all counters in a colossal gamble with the survival of civilization.

The costs of correcting past mistakes and preventing the threatened ones are already staggering, for the technologies which have produced them are now deeply embedded in our economic, social, and political structure. From what is know known about the smog problem, I think it unlikely that gasoline-driven automobiles can long continue to serve as the chief vehicle of urban and suburban transportation without imposing a health hazard which most of us would be unwilling to accept. Some improvement will probably result from the use of new devices to reduce emission of waste gasoline. But in view of the increasing demand for urban transportation any really effective effort to reduce the emission of waste fuel, carbon monoxide, and lead will probably require electric-powered vehicles and the replacement of urban highway systems by rapid transit lines. Added to current demands of highway-safe cars, the demand for smog-free transportation is certain to have an important impact on the powerful and deeply entrenched automobile industry.

The rapidly accelerating pollution of our surface waters with excessive phosphate and nitrate from sewage and detergents will, I believe, necessitate a drastic revision of urban waste systems. It may be possible to remove phosphates effectively by major modifications of sewage and water treatment plants, but there are no methods in sight that might counter the accumulation of nitrate. Hence, control will probably need to be based chiefly on preventing the entry of these pollutants into surface waters.

According to a report by the Committee on Pollution, National Academy of Sciences, we need to plan for a complete transformation of urban waste-removal systems, in particular to end the present practice of using water to get rid of solid wastes. The technological problems involved are so complex that the report recommends, as an initial step, the construction of a small pilot city to try out the new approach.

The high productivity of American agriculture, and therefore its economic structure, is based on the use of large amounts of mineral fertilizer in which phosphate and nitrate are major components. This fertilizer is not entirely absorbed by the crops and the remainder runs off into streams and lakes. As a result, by nourishing our crops and raising agricultural production, we help to kill off our lakes and rivers. Since there is no foreseeable means of removing fertilizer runoff from surface waters, it will become necessary, it seems to me, to impose severe restrictions on the present unlimited use of mineral fertilizers in agriculture. Proposed restraints on the use of synthetic pesticides have already aroused a great deal of opposition from the chemical industry and from agriculture. Judged by this response, an attempt to regulate the use of mineral fertilizers will confront us with an explosive economic and political problem.

And suppose that, as it may, the accumulation of carbon dioxide begins to threaten the entire globe with catastrophic floods. Control of this danger would require the modification, throughout the world, of domestic furnaces and industrial combustion plants—for example, by the addition of devices to absorb carbon dioxide from flue gases. Combustion-driven power plants could perhaps be replaced with nuclear ones, but this would pose the problem of safely disposing of massive amounts of radioactive wastes and create the hazard of reactor accidents near centers of population. Solar power, and other techniques for the production of electrical power which do not require either combustion or nuclear reactors, may be the best solution. But here too massive technological changes will be needed in all industrial nations.

The problems of industrial and agricultural pollution, while exceedingly large, complex, and costly, are nevertheless capable of correction by the proper technological means. We are still in a period of grace, and if we are willing to pay the price, as large as it is, there is yet time to restore and preserve the biological quality of the environment. But the most immediate threat to survival—nuclear war—would be a blunder from which there would be no return. I know of no technological means, no form of civil defense or counteroffensive warfare, which could reliably protect the biosphere from the catastrophic effects of a major nuclear war. There is, in my opinion, only one way to survive the threats of nuclear war—and that is to insure that it never happens. And because of the appreciable chance of an accidental nuclear war, I believe that the only way to do so is to destroy the world's stock of nuclear weapons and to develop less self-defeating means of protecting national security. Needless to say, the political difficulties involved in international nuclear disarmament are monumental.

Despite the dazzling successes of modern technology and the unprecedented power of modern military systems, they suffer from a common and catastrophic fault. While providing us with a bountiful supply of food, with great industrial plants, with high-speed transportation, and with military weapons of unprecedented power, they threaten our very survival. Technology has not only built the magnificent material base of modern society, but also confronts us with threats to survival which cannot be corrected unless we solve very grave economic, social, and political problems.

How can we explain this paradox? The answer is, I believe, that our technological society has committed a blunder familiar to us from the nineteenth century, when the dominant industries of the day, especially lumbering and mining, were successfully developed—by plundering the earth's natural resources. These industries provided cheap materials for constructing a new industrial society, but they accumulated a huge debt in destroyed and depleted resources, which had to be paid by later generations. The conservation movement was created in the United States to control these greedy assaults on our resources. The same thing is happening today, but now we are stealing from future generations not just their lumber or their coal, but the basic necessities of life: air, water, and soil. A new conservation movement is needed to preserve life itself.

The earlier ravages of our resources made very visible marks, but the new attacks are largely hidden. Thoughtless lumbering practices left vast scars on the land, but thoughtless development of modern industrial, agricultural, and military methods only gradually poison the air and water. Many of the pollutants—carbon dioxide, radioisotopes, pesticides, and excess nitrate—are invisible and go largely unnoticed until a lake dies, a river becomes foul, or children sicken. This time the world is being plundered in secret.

The earlier depredations on our resources were usually made with a fair knowledge of the harmful consequences, for it is difficult to escape the fact that erosion quickly follows the deforestation of a hillside. The difficulty lay not in scientific ignorance, but in willful greed. In the present situation, the hazards of modern pollutants are generally not appreciated until after the technologies which produce them are well established in the economy. While this ignorance absolves us from the immorality of the knowingly destructive acts that characterized the nineteenth century raids on our resources, the present fault is more serious. It signifies that the capability of science to guide us in our interventions into nature has been seriously eroded—that science has, indeed, got out of hand.

In this situation, scientists bear a very grave responsibility, for they are the guardians of the integrity of science. In the last few decades serious weaknesses in this system of principles have begun to appear. Secrecy has hampered free discourse. Major scientific enterprises have been governed by narrow national aims. In some cases, especially in the exploration of space, scientists have become so closely tied to basically political aims as to relinquish their traditional devotion to open discussion of conflicting views on what are often doubtful scientific conclusions.

What can scientists do to restore the integrity of science and to provide the kind of careful guidance to technology that is essential if we are to avoid catastrophic mistakes? No new principles are needed; instead, scientists need to find new ways to protect science itself from the encroachment of political pressures. This is not a new problem, for science and scholarship have often been under assault when their freedom to seek and to discuss the truth becomes a threat to existing economic or political power. The internal strength of science and its capability to understand nature have been weakened whenever the principles of scientific discourse were compromised, and restored when these principles were defended. The medieval suppressions of natural science, the perversion of science by Nazi racial theories, Soviet restraints on theories of genetics, and the suppression by the United States military secrecy of open discussion of the Starfish project, have all been paid for in the most costly coin—knowledge. The lesson of all these experiences is the same. If science is to perform its duty to society, which is to guide, by objective knowledge, human interactions with the rest of nature, its integrity must be defended. Scientists must find ways to remove the restraints of secrecy, to insist on open discussion of the possible consequences of large-scale experiments *before* they are undertaken, to resist the hasty and unconditional support of conclusions that conform to the demands of current political or economic policy.

Apart from these duties toward science, I believe that scientists have a responsibility in relation to the technological uses which are made of scientific developments. In my opinion, the proper duty of the scientist to the social consequence of his work cannot be fulfilled by aloofness or by an approach which arrogates to scientists alone the social and moral judgments which are the right of every citizen. I propose that scientists are now bound by a new duty which adds to and extends their older responsibility for scholarship and teaching. We have the duty to inform, and to inform in keeping with the traditional principles of science, taking into account all relevant data and interpretations. This is an involuntary obligation to society; we have no right to withhold information from our fellow citizens, or to color its meaning with our own social judgments.

Scientists alone cannot accomplish these aims, for despite its tradition of independent scholarship, science is a dependent segment of society. In this sense defense of the integrity of science is a task for every citizen. And in this sense, too, the fate of science as a system of objective inquiry, and therefore its ability safely to guide the life of man on earth, will be determined by social intent. Both awareness of the grave social issues generated by new scientific knowledge, and the policy choices which these issues require, therefore become matters of public morality. Public morality will determine whether scientific inquiry remains free. Public morality will determine at what cost we shall enjoy freedom from insect pests, the convenience of automobiles, or the high productivity of agriculture. Only public morality can determine whether we ought to intrust our national security to the catastrophic potential of nuclear war.

There is a unique relationship between the scientist's social responsibilities and the general duties of citizenship. If the scientist, directly or by inferences from his actions, lays claim to a special responsibility for the resolution of the policy issues which relate to technology, he may, in effect, prevent others from performing their own political duties. If the scientist fails in his duty to inform citizens, they are precluded from the gravest acts of citizenship and lose their right of conscience.

We have been accustomed, in the past, especially in our organized systems of morality—religion—to exemplify the principles of moral life in terms which relate to Egypt under the pharaohs or Rome under the emperors. Since the establishment of Western religions, their custodians have, of course, labored to achieve a relevance to the changing states of society. In recent times the gap between traditional moral principles and the realities of modern life has become so large as to precipitate, beginning in the Catholic church, and less spectacularly in other religious denominations, urgent demands for renewal—for the development of statements of moral purpose which are directly relevant to the modern world. But in the modern world the substance of moral issues cannot be perceived in terms of the casting of stones or the theft of a neighbor's ox. The moral issues of the modern world are embedded in the complex substance of science and technology. The exercise of morality now requires the determination of right between the farmers whose pesticides poison the water and the fishermen whose livelihood may thereby be destroyed. It calls for a judgment between the advantages of replacing a smoky urban power generator with a smoke-free nuclear one which carries with it some hazard of a catastrophic accident. The ethical principles involved are no different from those invoked in earlier times, but the moral issues cannot be discerned unless the new substance in which they are expressed is understood. And since the substance of science is still often poorly perceived by most citizens, the technical content of the issues of the modern world shields them from moral judgment.

Nowhere is this more evident than in the case of nuclear war. The horrible face of nuclear war can only be described in scientific terms. It can be pictured only in the language of roentgens and megatonnage; it can be understood only by those who have some appreciation of industrial organization, of human biology, of the intricacies of world-wide ecology. The self-destructiveness of nuclear war lies hidden behind a mask of science and technology. It is this shield, I believe, which has protected this most fateful moral issue in the history of man from the judgment of human morality. The greatest moral crime of our time is the concealment of the nature of nuclear war, for it deprives humanity of the solemn right to sit in judgment on its own fate; it condemns us all, unwittingly, to the greatest dereliction of conscience.

The obligation which our technological society forces upon all of us, scientist and citizen alike, is to discover how humanity can survive the new power which science has given it. It is already clear that even our present difficulties demand far-reaching social and political actions. Solution of our pollution problems will drastically affect the economic structure of the automobile industry, the power industry, and agriculture and will require basic changes in urban organization. To remove the threat of nuclear catastrophe we will be forced at last to resolve the pervasive international conflicts that have bloodied nearly every generation with war.

Every major advance in the technological competence of man has enforced revolutionary changes in the economic and political structure of society. The present age of technology is no exception to this rule of history. We already know the enormous benefits it can bestow; we have begun to perceive its frightful threats. The political crisis generated by this knowledge is upon us.

Science can reveal the depth of this crisis, but only social action can resolve it. Science can now serve society by exposing the crisis of modern technology to the judgment of all mankind. Only this judgment can determine whether the knowledge that science has given us shall destroy humanity or advance the welfare of man.

Wendell Berry
b. 1934

Wendell Berry stands as a model of the nature writer who has carried the American agrarian tradition far into the twentieth century. A native Kentuckian, a distinguished Professor of English at the University of Kentucky, a poet, novelist, and essayist, Berry's writing reflects his deep concern for the degradation of the landscape in his region of America. This region becomes symbolic of larger American environmental and wilderness issues. Modern conflicts are still enlivened by ancient pastoral and agrarian values in his work.

Berry's work is rooted in the land and in his region so deeply that he has been accused of being a voice of past ethics and values. But Berry is a contemporary writer who continually tests long-standing values against the realities and alternatives available in the twentieth century. He is a sophisticated, educated man and teacher who also lives as a farmer and writer in his native hills and valleys, who believes that the greatest contributions to humanity are made, first, in the environment to which we are most closely attached.

His agrarian and pastoral sympathies are most clear in such books as *Farming: A Handbook* (1970), *A Continuous Harmony: Essays Cultural and Agricultural* (1972), *The Unsettling of America: Culture and Agriculture* (1977), *The Gift of Good Land: Further Essays Cultural and Agricultural* (1981), and *A Place On Earth* (1983). He has also contributed to the vast literature of the American wilderness in *The Unforeseen Wilderness: An Essay on Kentucky's Red River Gorge* (1971), from which our selections are taken, and *The Kentucky River: Two Poems* (1976). Like Thoreau and Krutch, Berry is a superb and powerful craftsman, a master of the English language.

from THE UNFORESEEN WILDERNESS: AN ESSAY ON KENTUCKY'S RED RIVER GORGE

THE ONE-INCH JOURNEY

The mollusk-shell of civilization, in which we more and more completely enclose ourselves, is lined on the inside with a nacreous layer that is opaque, rainbow-tinted, and an inch thick. It is impossible to see through it to the world; it works, rather, as a reflecting surface upon which we cast the self-flattering outlines and the optimistic tints of our preconceptions of what the world is.

These obscuring preconceptions were once superstitious or religious. Now they are mechanical. The figure representative of the earlier era was that of the otherworldly man who thought and said much more about where he would go when he died than about where he was living. Now we have the figure of the tourist-photographer who, one gathers, will never know where he is, but only, looking at his pictures, where he *was*. Between his eye and the world is interposed the mechanism of the camera—and also, perhaps, the mechanism of economics: having bought the camera, he has to keep using it to get his money's worth. For him the camera will never work as an instrument of perception or discovery. Looking through it, he is not likely to see anything that will surprise or delight or frighten him, or change his sense of things. As he uses it, the camera is in bondage to the self-oriented assumptions that thrive within the social enclosure. It is an extension of his living room in which his pictures will finally be shown. And if you think the aspect or the atmosphere of his living room might be changed somewhat by the pictures of foreign places and wonders that he has visited, then look, won't you, at the pictures themselves. He has photographed only what he has been prepared to see by other people's photographs. He has gone religiously and taken a picture of what he saw pictured in the travel brochures before he left home. He has photographed scenes that he could have bought on postcards or prepared slides at the nearest drug store, the major difference being the frequent appearance in his photographs of himself or his wife and kids. He poses the members of his household on the brink of a canyon that the wind and water have been carving at for sixty million years as if there were an absolute equality between them, as if there were no precipice for the body and no abyss for the mind. And before he leaves he adds to the view his empty film cartons and the ruins of his picnic. He is blinded by the device by which he has sought to preserve his vision. He has, in effect, been no place and seen nothing; the awesomest wonders rest against his walls, deprived of mystery and immensity, reduced to his comprehension and his size, affirmative of his assumptions, as tame and predictable as a shelf of whatnots.

Throughout their history here, most white men have moved across the North American continent following the fictive coordinates of their own self-affirming assumptions. They have followed maps, memories, dreams,

*From *The Unforeseen Wilderness: An Essay on Kentucky's Red River Gorge* by Wendell Berry. Lexington, Ky: The University Press of Kentucky, 1971.

plans, hopes, schemes, greeds. Seldom have they looked beyond the enclosure of preconception and desire to see where they were; and the few who have looked beyond have seldom been changed by what they saw. Blind to where they were, it was inevitable that they should become the destroyers of what was there.

One of the oldest and most persistent legends of the white man's occupation of Kentucky is that of John Swift's silver. Swift was a silver miner who is supposed to have wandered in the Kentucky mountains in about 1760. He left a journal describing his adventures, paramount among which was the discovery of a marvelously rich lode of silver. The journal contained directions for finding this wealth and also a map, but because of Swift's poor knowledge of the country and its landmarks both directions and map have proved meaningless.

And that very meaninglessness has assured the survival and the dispersal of the legend, and of the indefatigable dream that the legend represents. Today, according to Thomas D. Clark, there are still people in the Kentucky mountains "who had rather seek fortune by searching for nebulous silver than by plowing corn." And that region is said to be littered with vaguely defined sites where *maybe* John Swift found and then lost his silver mine. One of those places is the Red River Gorge, and a tributary of the Red is named in commemoration of Swift's passage through that country: Swift Camp Creek.

There could be no better parable of the white man's entrance into Kentucky. For John Swift is the true forefather of our history here, and his progeny have been numerous. They have descended upon this land from the eastward passes and from their mothers' wombs with their minds set on the dream of quick riches to be had, if not from a vein of precious metal, then from coal or from logs. Or from the land itself, for those who preferred to plow rather than hunt silver have all too often followed the agricultural method known as "mining," by which the growth is taken from the land and nothing given back, until the fields are exhausted like a mined-out seam of coal.

The wealth of a place is not to be reckoned by its market value at some given moment. Its real wealth is not just its present value, but its *potential* value as it continues through time; and therefore its wealth is not finally reckonable at all, for we do not know how long the world, or our species, will last.

I have heard strip miners justify the destruction of large tracts of the earth by figures showing that the value of the mineral lying under the ground was greater than the value of the crops or the forest then standing on the surface. They would be right if the world, or if people's dependence on it, should come to an end the day after the seam was mined out.

It is certainly possible that the world or the human race may come to an end pretty soon. But another possibility—and a much more demanding possibility, too—is that the human race may continue for thousands of years. We can't possibly say how many thousands it may be. But in Asia there are agricultural lands that, by wise farming methods, have been kept continuously productive of food crops for six thousand years. If the people of China and Korea and Japan have depended on their farmlands for six thousand years, we in America might reasonably prepare to be dependent for at least that long on ours. And so before we accept the arguments of the strip miners, we should ask other experts to compute for us the value of the produce of the soil overlying the coal seams for a period of six thousand years, and we should weigh that value against the value of the mineral.

When a mineral deposit is mined out, the miners are done with that place forever. When a logging crew has cut the marketable trees from a boundary of timber, it may be that a generation or more will pass before another logging crew will return. But the farmer's relation to a place, and his dependence on it, are continuous, and because of that he is the figure who most accurately represents what our relation to the earth is. And Americans who contemplate the history and the behavior of the American farmer are not apt to find him the source of much comfort. There have been, and continue to be, noble exceptions; nevertheless, the historical *tendencies* that I am talking about seem to me clearly established.

Characteristically, the American farmer, moving into new lands to the west, did not subject himself to the disciplines and restraints implicit in the nature and the topography of the new land. Instead, he pretty much ignored where he was and went about his business on the assumption that the place he had come to was the same as the place he had come from. Thus the Englishman, starting as a farmer in Virginia, was obeying not so much a vision of what a farm in Virginia might or ought to be, as a memory of what farming in England *was*. And the son of a Virginia farmer, opening a farm in the Kentucky wilderness, imitated the Virginian's imitation of an Englishman. Because of differences in soil and climate and rainfall this imitativeness has been, in general, a failure. On relatively flat lands the performance of the American farmer has often enough been poor. On steep lands his performance has been almost invariably disastrous. Kentucky farmers have often destroyed whole hillsides in only a few crop years. In some of the levelest lands they have done more damage in a generation than the thoroughly indigenous Japanese farmers did to their land in six millennia. And the Kentucky farmer, going west, overgrazed the plains—largely, I believe, on the assumption that the grass grew there the same way he had seen it growing in Kentucky.

But the American farmer has not been so destructive just because of an illusion as to his whereabouts For years, almost from the beginning, there has been in this country a social fashion that has led people to believe that life in the city is better than life in the country, that there is something degrading in any work that dirties the hands, that work of any kind has its highest meaning and reward in leisure. Many of our farmers, because of these attitudes, have come to look upon farming not as an honorable calling or as a meaningful way of life, but as a form of bondage. Consequently, the aim and the ideal of their labor has not been a wise and preserving use of the land, but escape, both from the land and from the work it requires. And so the farmers have often farmed their land not in accordance with a vision of what it is or what it ought to be, but in accordance with a dream of where they would like to go as soon as they can get the money. It is these who have "mined" the land, for to build the fertility of a field, putting back as well as taking away, is to cut the margin of immediate profit; that would be to make a long-term investment in the future of the land, and their only thought of the future is the wish that as much of it as possible will be spent somewhere else. Their hopes and dreams lying elsewhere, they can have no clear and disciplining sense of where they are, and so the old destructive ways persist. They are institutionalized, in fact, in the efficiencies and chemical shortcuts of "agri-business."

Several months ago I watched a farmer prepare the ground and plant and grow a crop of corn on a ridge draining into the North Fork of the Red River. The ridge was narrow, falling off steeply on both sides like a barn roof. It was not suited to row-cropping at all. My guess was that, like a great deal of steep Kentucky land, it had been logged off years ago, and then cropped and pastured until the land would no longer sustain a profitable growth, and then abandoned. A growth of trees and bushes had covered it again. And then, having learned nothing from experience, and perhaps driven by the adverse markets that have nearly always afflicted farmers—and farmlands—in America, this man had returned to it, to practice on it yet again the "new ground" methods of his grandfathers, cutting and burning all the bushes and trees, plowing between the stumps, and planting corn. The crop was puny, hardly worth the man's trouble and labor, much less the damage to the ridge. The erosion, beginning as soon as he uncovered the ground, will continue—and he will thus continue to invest in his crop—long after his earnings from it have been spent and forgotten.

A practice of the same vintage and wisdom is that of overgrazing such slopes. The assumption is that the only function of grass is to serve as feed for livestock, and so the stock is permitted to graze it to the root. The result, again, is the erosion of the slopes and the steady depletion not only of the watershed but of the pasture. The result is the siltation and flooding of the streams. The result is the impoverishment and degradation and displacement of the people. For the reasons I have mentioned, and doubtless for other reasons that I don't know, the obvious lesson has never been learned: You can't uncover steep land without destroying it.

And the causes of these ruinous attitudes and practices are by no means coextensive with the ridges and hollows of the Red River country. They have their origin in our life and history as a people here in America. They have their origin in our failure to this day to be able to assign any value other than economic to the land, and to the life of and on the land, and to men's labor—and in our complacent assumption that our economy will somehow turn out to be the same as nature's, that it somehow has something to do with the truth about our life in this world. Of all illusory enclosures that of the American economy is the narrowest and the worst. To be blind to everything outside the competency of a bank clerk is, as we have been told over and over, to be spiritually dead; it is also, as we are slowly learning, to be an accomplice in the death of the world. It is a form of insanity. But even in economic terms it has failed to make sense. In the intelligence of a man governed exclusively or mainly by economic concerns there appears to be an inclination, compelling as the law of gravity, toward the *quickest* profit. Cutting a stand of timber, he is apt to diminish the possibility that more timber will ever grow. Opening a strip mine, he takes out the coal, and assures in the process that there will be no more produce from that land for generations, perhaps forever. Over-pasturing a hillside this year, he reduces the number of cattle he will be able to pasture next year. And so he is not only spiritually dead and criminally destructive, on his own terms of economics he is stupid; his "practicality" is only folly. And this man—whom our grandchildren will look upon as the incarnation of evil, if they survive the results of his folly—is the man we have most honored and entrusted with power.

When a man operates in the landscape either as a dreamer of "better" places or as a simple digit of the "economy," he is operating without moral or ecological controls. And without controls himself, he destroys the controls of nature: the layers of vegetation and topsoil that, if let alone, would cover the land and preserve it. With nothing to break the fall of the rain or to absorb and hold the water, the slopes become little more than roofs, shedding the runoff into the river. And then the river begins to be known and feared as a destroyer, and the people downstream begin to cry out for "flooding control"—as if control would not exist if some human being did not invent it, and as if it were something people could cry out for and surely get.

And for this very complex problem, with its complex sources in the abused watershed and in the minds of the people, the city fathers downstream and the Army Corps of Engineers offer a stunningly simple solution: Build a dam! The downstream citizens, sealed up in their clamshell, are aware of only one phenomenon: high water. It appears to them that Nature, man's enemy, is warring against them, threatening to fill the clamshell with a muddy flood. And so the ancient battle cry is raised: Conquer nature! Nature has already been conquered on the slopes upstream, and so now it has to be conquered downstream.

The Corps of Engineers is a famous nature-conquerer, and it is always alert for that familiar battle cry. But the Corps of Engineers has its clamshell too, and when the cry is heard it feels no need to go outside, but looks instead around its rainbow-tinted walls at its charts and maps and tables and graphs and gauges showing the direction and velocity of the political wind. From the Engineer's commanding vantage point it is clear to them that what is needed is a dam. And the processes of dam making are set in motion. All this is done by the manipulation of abstractions: between two points on a topographical map a dam is to be built, requiring a certain predicted expenditure of dollars, backing the water to the level of a certain contour, able to control a certain amount of runoff from the slopes upstream and to deliver a specified number of gallons daily to the city water companies downstream. The *place* of the resulting lake does not matter, because it is not known. For the inexhaustible details and aspects and facts and mysteries of the life of the river valley there is to be substituted the abstraction of a water level tabulated upon pieces of paper. And that abstraction of mechanics attracts the most abstract of human desires—avarice. For a lake means Tourists, Recreation, Developments, Deals, Money. Thus, by what some will call human genius and others the munificence of God, an ecological disaster will be turned into an economic bonanza. Now the walls of the shell are alight with wonderful dreams; civilization is like being surrounded by a technicolor movie, and it looks like everybody's going to have plenty of ticket money.

But enter the place itself. Leave behind the theories and the propaganda, the presumptions, the charts and statistics, and go into the watershed of the Red River. Drive along the ridges where the tributaries head up, and look at the overpastured, denuded slopes. Look at the despoiled carcass of a land that was once bountifully forested, ecologically healthy and whole and of incalculable economic potential. Consider the results of methods that grew out of ignorance and misunderstanding and economic constraint.

And then consider the river itself. Even now there are stretches of it that look as wild and unspoiled, you imagine, as they did a hundred years ago. That, to be sure, is something to be thankful for—but so far you are only looking at the surface. Step into the stream and wade down it for a few hundred steps. And notice that wherever the current slows you are walking, not over the clean rocky or weedy bottom of a healthy stream, but in mud. In places the mud is more than knee deep. It is the soil of the ridges and slopes upstream, the wasted flesh of a living creature that has been stricken by a lethal disease.

To a man standing in that mud, aware of what it means, the idea of the proposed "flood control dam" is a giddy fiction, a fairy tale that reduces science to the level of the crudest superstition. It is not as obviously stupid, but it is just as stupid nevertheless, as the idea of putting a stopper in the mouth of a volcano. For what the dam will be, if the misuse of the watershed continues, is the first step in the creation of a swamp. It will have nothing to do with the control of anything, but will be only another manifestation of the lack of moral and social and economic control that made the need for "flood control" in the first place. It will finally be seen to have a good deal more to do with the illusions of the short-term investment and the quick profit and the easy remedy than with any reality of the environment.

The proponents of the dam in the Red River Gorge are the most recent heirs of John Swift in that part of the country. They have been entranced, as Swift was, by the dream of ease—of easy wealth, of easy answers, of easy fulfillments. And the dream is accompanied, necessarily, by the assumption that such ease is not destructive.

It almost always *is* destructive. For the labor of preserving the life of the world, of which our lives are a part and on which they depend, is difficult and complex and endless. In nature all that grows is finally made to augment the possibility of growth, and so nothing is wasted. This year's leaves decay and enter the intricate life and process of the soil, which assures that there will be more leaves another year. It is this pattern and only this—not any that he may conceivably invent—that man must imitate and enter into if he is to live in the world without destroying it.

The task of preserving the life of the world has little to do with the present values of American society. It has almost nothing to do with our concepts of wealth and profit and success and luxury and ease. It has nothing at all to do with short-term investments, or short-term anything else. It is not recognizable to a short-term intelligence. It involves a man in work that he can neither live to finish nor imagine the end of. It is humble work, often involving the use of the hands. It requires a tolerance and respect for mystery. Its model figures are not to be found among the great figures of our history: our artists, inventors, soldiers, statesmen—but among humble people whose lives were devoted laboriously and ceremoniously and lovingly to the life of their land: tribal people and peasants.

John Swift has other heirs in the country of his legend who will no doubt be surprised and outraged to be so considered. And yet I believe that they and the dam builders, whose activities they are apt to deplore, have this ancestor in common. They are the lovers of "scenery." Now that the Red River Gorge has become famous because of the efforts to keep it from being made into a lake, the scenery lovers cause traffic jams there on the weekends. They come by carloads and busloads, following one another, bumper-to-bumper, along the narrow blacktop, stopping only at "scenic overlooks," or perhaps not stopping at all. For them the automobile has become a censoring device. They want to see only what can be seen sitting down and at highway speeds. They supposedly are charmed by the notion of a wilderness place, but they want it neatly packaged in "views"—as if the world were a commodity, to be served up to consumers like hamburgers at a drive-in.

Like the tourist-photographer's camera, their eyes seek out only what resembles what they have already seen, or what resembles pictures they have seen, or what they have been told is "beautiful." They will exclaim over a long view of a monumental rock or cliff, but will never see the phoebe's nest clinging to its face. Still less will they be aware of the cycles of living and dying, exuberance and pain, plenty and want, eating and being eaten, growth and decay, that course through the scene they are looking at.

The conservation movement has so far concentrated too much on scenic places. This is changing, and it can't change too soon. There will have to be a concern with agricultural methods, with city environments, with the watersheds of unspectacular streams, with the widespread preservation of farm woodlands and wetlands. To preserve only the scenic places is to invite their destruction, either in the process of the destruction of their surroundings, or by the overcrowding of people who have no other places to go.

The scenery-oriented conservationists are the ones who have introduced *esthetics* into the vocabulary of conservation and then made nonsense of it by failing to see its relation to practicality or, for that matter, to reality—so that the term is now bandied about by publicists as if it referred to a *quantity* of something to be purchased by the buyer's convenience, and by strip miners and other ruiners as if it referred to a handy camouflage for disgrace. The concern with esthetics has been mostly a dealing with appearances, as if anything that "looks good" is all right. An example of the esthetic approach to conservation is the Kentucky law requiring junkyards to be surrounded by a high fence—which only conceals the problem and, in practice, often looks worse. Another is a proposal, once advanced by West Kentucky strip miners, that areas destroyed by strip mining should be landscaped along the main highways.

The truth, as always, is more difficult. Natural beauty is no more than a by-product of natural health. Decently and frugally used, the earth will be beautiful; disdained, exploited and abused, it will be ugly, as well as unhealthy, and there will be no way to "beautify" it. When one relates to the world in terms of its "scenery," then one is apt to go around talking about "beautifying" such things as strip mines and slums. But what is being destroyed cannot be made beautiful. The notion that a process of ruin can be accompanied and offset by a process of beautification, that all is well if the country looks pretty from the roadside, is only another illusion of ease, like John Swift's silver. It is another technicolor pipedream to keep us ignorant and endangered—and dangerous—shut up in our shell.

There is something suicidal, and more sinister than that, in this quest for easy wealth and easy answers, for it proposes goals that are dead ends, that imagination and desire do not go beyond. Once the precious vein of silver has been found, once the speculation in land or mineral or timber has paid off, then a man's work will be over; he will have escaped forever the drudgery of the plow or the office. But if a man has destroyed in himself the capacity to enjoy work—and he does this inevitably by working toward the goal of escape from work—then how can he possibly enjoy leisure? He can't, of course. And our country is full of men who have worked and sacrificed and deferred pleasure, and as a result achieved all that they dreamed of—and who, having now neither work nor goal, are perfectly miserable. Such a life is shallow and destructive; despising the work it has undertaken out of hatred for work, it has unwittingly learned to despise itself; destroying peace and innocent pleasure in seeking for ease, it has unwittingly destroyed itself; despising and destroying itself, it helplessly despises and destroys the world.

That is the predominant form of our life now. But there is another form that life can take. We can learn about it from exceptional people of our own culture, and from other cultures less destructive than ours. I am speaking of the life of a man who knows that the world is not given by his fathers, but borrowed from his children; who has undertaken to cherish it and do it no damage, not because he is duty-bound, but because he loves the world and loves his children; whose work serves the earth he lives on and from and with, and is therefore pleasurable and meaningful and unending; whose rewards are not deferred until "retirement," but arrive daily and seasonally out of the details of the life of his place; whose goal is the continuance of the life of the world, which for a while animates and contains him, and which he knows he can never encompass with his understanding or desire.

Comparatively few white men have ever lived this way in America. And for the ones who have, or who have attempted to, it has been difficult, for the prevailing social current has always flowed away from the land, toward the city and the abstractions of wealth and specialization and power. The pressures against a modest and preserving life on the land have been manifested most immediately in adverse agricultural markets and in an overwhelming prejudice against all things identifiable as "country." These pressures have already destroyed the small farmers of most sections of the country, and are well advanced in the destruction of the rest.

Broken from the land, contemporary Americans do not now settle down in some city, as to some extent they used to, but remain migratory from job to job and from neighborhood to neighborhood and from city to city. But these wanderings have no real function. They do not spread knowledge and skills and songs as the wanderings of artists and poets once did, and they are not linked to natural cycles as were the wanderings of Arctic peoples and desert nomads. They are artificial wanderings, unappeasable searches for John Swift's silver in all its modern manifestations: more money, shorter hours, easier work, higher status.

Not only does all this moving around destroy the integrity and continuity of marriages and families, as has been often enough said, but it destroys any possibility of a disciplined relation to the earth. For it seems a fact that most minds require, as a condition of insight and discipline, some measure of continuity, and some measure of the devotion that can only associate itself with continuity. Unchecked by any feeling that they may return soon, or at all, weekenders strew the public woodlands and streamsides with trash. Lacking any association with the disciplines of maintaining the farmlands the year round, urban hunters have become notorious as destroyers of fences and gates—and as most indiscriminate shooters.

The conservation movement has become almost exclusively a matter of power struggles between agencies and corporations and *organizations* of conservationists. The agencies and corporations are motivated by visions of power and profit. The conservation organizations are motivated by principles which very largely remain abstract, since the number of people who can *know* a place is necessarily too small to protect it, and must therefore enlist the aid of people who do not know it but are willing to protect it on principle.

I should make it clear that I recognize the need for the conservation organizations, and that I am emphatically on their side. But the organizations, by themselves, are not enough. If they are to succeed in any way that is meaningful, or perhaps if they are to succeed at all, their work must be augmented by an effort to rebuild the life of our society in terms of a decent spiritual and economic connection to the land. That can't be done by organizations, but only by individuals and by families and by small informal groups. It will have to be done by leaving the cities and the suburbs and making a bond with some place, and by *living* there—doing the work the place requires, repairing the damage other men have done to it, preserving its woods, building back its fertility and its ecological health—undertaking, that is, the labor, the necessary difficulty and clumsiness of discovering, at this late date and in the most taxing of circumstances, a form of human life that is not destructive.

In the Red River Gorge there is such a family as I am talking about: people drawn out of the city to an ancestral tract of farmland enclosed in that wilderness—drawn back by loyalty and love, and by a sense, having learned the alternatives, of what such a place and such a life mean and what they might be made to mean. The house can be reached only by footpath in wet weather, and in the best of weather only by tractor. The house sits at the edge of the woods, at the foot of a great sheer cliff, overlooking the open fields of the bottomlands. The quiet of the wilderness rises over it, enormous, a silence millions of years old concentrated in the looming gray cliff face. It is a quietness that has been accepted; the house, one senses, has over the years been cleansed of all unnecessary sounds. It seems somehow to have assumed the deeply musing inwardness of the stone that towers over it. It is the dwelling place of a sorrowing intelligence that understands the crisis of the Gorge as a part of the crisis of the world. When the Gorge is flooded and this family loses its home and its history and the disciplining and reassuring sense of its place in the world, that will be no isolated incident, not one of those sacrifices that are sometimes required of individuals for the sake of the common good. It will be another small step in the spread of an epidemic, a chronic and cancerous devaluation of the life of the world and the lives of people. When this family is forced out of its home, which has been for them not just a place to sleep and eat but a loving task and a hopeful promise and a joy, they will join the thousands of the American dispossessed who have been driven out to make room for roads and airports and lakes and such like. When people can't be secure in their homes because of the demands of the public interest, then the public interest is serving us as a foul god.

What that household promises to the world is not the possibility of better organizations, but the possibility of better life. It has taken its life knowingly and lovingly from its place. And in return it offers to the place the promise of life—a longer and more abundant and better cherished life than can be offered it by any government or organization. For if the good principles of governments and organizations can't be made to live in the lives of people and places then they are dead—or, at best, five percent alive in the bungling dutifulness of functionaries.

And that household, meaningful and promising as it is, appears doomed, for it can survive only in its particularity, and it is caught between two abstractions: the organizations that would destroy the Gorge, and the organizations that would preserve it. The forces of destruction, of course, consider nothing except their dreams of profit, and the consequent methods. And the forces of preservation cannot consider or represent private claims because the Gorge cannot be saved, or damage to it limited, except as a *public* place. There is, so far as I know, no force that represents the frail possibility that security in one's home implies the right to stay in it. The Public Interest, in some of its manifestations, is another colored lantern slide on the wall of our snug clamshell—howbeit most remunerative to some of its servants. If the public is destroyed piecemeal "in its own interest"—well, that is regrettable, for the liars in public office will have to contend with a further diminishment of confidence in the government, but the Public Interest must be served. Meanwhile, who worries about a few more dispossessed families—they're getting *paid,* aren't they?

What will cure us? At this point it seems useless to outline yet another idea of a better community, or to invoke yet another anthropological model. These already abound, and we fail to make use of them for the same reason that we continue to destroy the earth: we remain for the most part blind to our surroundings. What the world was, or *what we have agreed that it was,* obtrudes between our sight and what the world *is.* If we do not see clearly what the nature of our place is, we destroy our place. If we don't see where we are, we are more dead than alive; if we cannot see how our own lives are drawn from the life of the world, and how they are involved and joined with that greater life, then we live in a deathly sleep, and such efforts as we may make to preserve the greater life will be inept and perhaps destructive. If like John Swift we do not know the country and its landmarks, if we are unable to see where we are in relation to it, then we lose it and lose its promised abundance. We lose our lives.

The effort to clarify our sight cannot begin in the society, but only in the eye and in the mind. It is a spiritual quest, not a political function. Each man must confront the world alone, and learn to see it for himself: "first cast out the beam out of thine own eye; and then shalt thou see clearly to cast the mote out of thy brother's eye."

And so from the figure of the silver hunter John Swift, I turn to the figure of the photographic artist—not the tourist-photographer who goes to a place, bound by his intentions and preconceptions, to record what has already been recorded and what he therefore *expects* to find, but the photographer who goes into a place in search of the real news of it.

His search is a pilgrimage, for he goes along ways he does not fully understand, in search of what he does not expect and cannot anticipate. His undertaking involves a profound humility, for he has effaced himself; he has done away with his expectations; he has ceased to make demands upon the place. He keeps only the discipline of his art that informs and sharpens his vision—he keeps, that is, the practice of observation—for before a man can be a seer he must be a looker. His camera is a dark room, and he has made a dark place in his mind, exultant and fearful, by which he accepts that he does not know what he is going to see, he does not know the next picture. He has entered into the darkness—in order to see! But for the moment the dark lens holds only a vague potency, like a lentil seed, still one with the mystery of what will come next, which is one with the mystery of the wilderness and of the creation.

And then there comes a breaking of the light—and there is another shore to step out of the dark upon, lighted by a blooming flower like a candelabra.

We are invited on! We are led on as by the promise of a feast spread for us that we do not yet know. In the shadows a little stream steps down over a ledge of rock into the light. Beyond are the trees, and the darkness again.

Knowing the heaviness of the dead-end search for wealth and ease, what a relief and a joy it is to consider the photographer's pilgrimage to the earth. He is seeking, not the ultimate form of the creation, for he cannot hope to find that, but rather the inexhaustible manifestations of form within the creation. Walking through the woods, he finds within the apparent clutter of trunks and branches a row of trees, leading the eye on. He sees the entrance of the sun upon a rock face. Among the dark trees, time and again, there appears suddenly a tree of light. In the early morning the mist is white and thick in the valley so that the ridgetops seem to float in the sky; looking, one's eyes receive a kinship with the eyes of a sage in the mountains of China a thousand years ago. The light withholds itself from the darkness inside the earth, and the darkness in the earth opens out to the light. The paths and streams clamber through notches in the cliffs. In the narrow ravines the water flashes over the rock lip, enters the great calm and ease of falling, descending into shadow; and the trees strain up out of the tumbled rocks into the light. In the midst of its ageless turmoil in the Roughs of the Upper Gorge, the river breaks out of the rocks, collects in an open pool, and stands still. A small stream is flowing out of the dark tunnel it has followed down through the woods, entering the greater opening of the river—and a man is standing there, not the uproarious creature of machines, but just a man standing quietly there, almost hidden by the leaves. The photographer is nowhere to be seen. These images are the record of his pilgrimage, and he has moved on. Once, these served him as landmarks, each one defining his whereabouts and leading him on to the next, and thence on again. It is an endless quest, for it is going nowhere in terms of space and time, but only drawing deeper into the presence and into the mystery, of what is underfoot and overhead and all around. Its grace is the grace of knowing that our consciousness and the light are always arriving in the world together.

The camera is a point of reference, a bit like a compass though not nearly so predictable. It is the discipline and the opportunity of vision. In relation to the enclosure we call civilization, these pictures are not ornaments or relics, but windows and doors, enlargements of our living space, entrances into the mysterious world outside the walls, lessons in what to look for and how to see. They limit our comfort; they drain away the subtle corruption of being smug; they make us a little afraid, for they suggest always the presence of the unknown, what lies outside the picture and beyond eyesight; they suggest the possibility of the sudden accesses of delight, vision, beauty, joy that entice us to keep alive and reward us for living; they can serve as spiritual landmarks in the pilgrimage to the earth that each one of us must undertake alone.

Always in big woods when you leave familiar ground and step off alone into a new place there will be, along with the feelings of curiosity and excitement, a little nagging of dread. It is the ancient fear of the Unknown, and it is your first bond with the wilderness you are going into. What you are doing is exploring. You are undertaking the first experience, not of the place, but of yourself in that place. It is an experience of our essential loneliness, for nobody can discover the world for anybody else. It is only after we have discovered it for ourselves that it becomes a common ground and a common bond, and we cease to be alone.

And the world cannot be discovered by a journey of miles, no matter how long, but only by a spiritual journey, a journey of one inch, very arduous and humbling and joyful, by which we arrive at the ground at our feet, and learn to be at home. It is a journey we can make only by the acceptance of mystery and of mystification—by yielding to the condition that what we have expected is not there.

Annie Dillard
b. 1945

When Annie Dillard's first published book of prose, *Pilgrim at Tinker Creek,* won the Pulitzer Prize in 1974, she suddenly became a well-known and authoritative nature writer. It was clear, however, that this young poet—*Tickets for a Prayer Wheel* (1974)—and columnist—*Living Wilderness* (1973-75)—was different from contemporary nature writers. More than one critic complained that "not one genuine ecological concern [is] voiced in the entire book," and she was compared not to twentieth-century writers but to Thoreau and Herman Melville.

Like Thoreau, Dillard promises a "meteorological journal of the mind"; she composes a detailed account of solitude in nature, of the search for the "essential facts" of life, and of the interplay of close observations of natural phenomena and meditations. And, like Thoreau, she is intensely alert as she explores her small woodland territory around Tinker Creek in Virginia. Yet like Melville, Dillard also soars on metaphysical speculations of the horrible and beautiful, the wonderful and the violent in nature. Rather than moralizing, her speculations are ambiguous, as were Melville's. Likewise, her store of exotica and arcana from her vast reading in the literature of nature, science, and exploration is reminiscent of Melville. She has written, one critic remarked, "a remarkable psalm of terror and celebration."

As a pilgrim or seeker in nature, Dillard seemed to want to start from scratch. She "forgot" the polemic of social and ethical reform raging in the anti-war and environmental movements of the sixties and seventies. She met nature fundamentally, alone, and as open to wonder and terror as a child. The result is a kind of poetic of visionary nonfiction produced by a person who describes herself as a "poet and a walker with a background in theology."

An active writer as well as a teacher of writing in several colleges, Dillard has written a number of books, including *Holy the Firm* (1978), a book of meditations: *Living by Fiction* (1982) and *Encounters with Chinese Writers* (1985), two books of literary criticism and personal response; and *Teaching a Stone to Talk: Expeditions and Encounters* (1982), essays again on her nature themes.

from PILGRIM AT TINKER CREEK*

HEAVEN AND EARTH IN JEST

I used to have a cat, an old fighting tom, who would jump through the open window by my bed in the middle of the night and land on my chest. I'd half-awaken. He'd stick his skull under my nose and purr, stinking of urine and blood. Some nights he kneaded my bare chest with his front paws, powerfully, arching his back, as if sharpening his claws, or pummeling a mother for milk. And some mornings I'd wake in daylight to find my body covered with paw prints in blood; I looked as though I'd been painted with roses.

It was hot, so hot the mirror felt warm. I washed before the mirror in a daze, my twisted summer sleep still hung about me like sea kelp. What blood was this, and what roses? It could have been the rose of union, the blood of murder, or the rose of beauty bare and the blood of some unspeakable sacrifice or birth. The sign on my body could have been an emblem or a stain, the keys to the kingdom or the mark of Cain. I never knew. I never knew as I washed, and the blood streaked, faded, and finally disappeared, whether I'd purified myself or ruined the blood sign of the passover. We wake, if we ever wake at all, to mystery, rumors of death, beauty, violence .... "Seem like we're just set down here," a woman said to me recently, "and don't nobody know why."

These are morning matters, pictures you dream as the final wave heaves you up on the sand to the bright light and drying air. You remember pressure, and a curved sleep you rested against, soft, like a scallop in its shell. But the air hardens your skin; you stand; you leave the lighted shore to explore some dim headland, and soon you're lost in the leafy interior, intent, remembering nothing.

I still think of that old tomcat, mornings, when I wake. Things are tamer now; I sleep with the window shut. The cat and our rites are gone and my life is changed, but the memory remains of something powerful playing over me. I wake expectant, hoping to see a new thing. If I'm lucky I might be jogged awake by a strange birdcall. I dress in a hurry, imagining the yard flapping with auks, or flamingos. This morning it was a wood duck, down at the creek. It flew away.

*Chapter I, "Heaven and Earth in Jest," from *Pilgrim at Tinker Creek* by Annie Dillard.

I live by a creek, Tinker Creek, in a valley in Virginia's Blue Ridge. An anchorite's hermitage is called an anchor-hold; some anchor-holds were simple sheds clamped to the side of a church like a barnacle to a rock. I think of this house clamped to the side of Tinker Creek as an anchor-hold. It holds me at anchor to the rock bottom of the creek itself and it keeps me steadied in the current, as a sea anchor does, facing the stream of light pouring down. It's a good place to live; there's a lot to think about. The creeks—Tinker and Carvin's—are an active mystery, fresh every minute. Theirs is the mystery of the continuous creation and all that providence implies: the uncertainty of vision, the horror of the fixed, the dissolution of the present, the intricacy of beauty, the pressure of fecundity, the elusiveness of the free, and the flawed nature of perfection. The mountains—Tinker and Brushy, McAfee's Knob and Dead Man—are a passive mystery, the oldest of all. Theirs is the one simple mystery of creation from nothing, of matter itself, anything at all, the given. Mountains are giant, restful, absorbent. You can heave your spirit into a mountain and the mountain will keep it, folded, and not throw it back as some creeks will. The creeks are the world with all its stimulus and beauty; I live there. But the mountains are home.

The wood duck flew away. I caught only a glimpse of something like a bright torpedo that blasted the leaves where it flew. Back at the house I ate a bowl of oatmeal; much later in the day came the long slant of light that means good walking.

If the day is fine, any walk will do; it all looks good. Water in particular looks its best, reflecting blue sky in the flat, and chopping it into graveled shallows and white chute and foam in the riffles. On a dark day, or a hazy one, everything's washed-out and lackluster but the water. It carries its own lights. I set out for the railroad tracks, for the hill the flocks fly over, for the woods where the white mare lives. But I go to the water.

Today is one of those excellent January partly cloudies in which light chooses an unexpected part of the landscape to trick out in gilt, and then shadow sweeps it away. You know you're alive. You take huge steps, trying to feel the planet's roundness arc between your feet. Kazantzakis says that when he was young he had a canary and a globe. When he freed the canary, it would perch on the globe and sing. All his life, wandering the earth, he felt as though he had a canary on top of his mind, singing.

West of the house, Tinker Creek makes a sharp loop, so that the creek is both in back of the house, south of me, and also on the other side of the road, north of me. I like to go north. There the afternoon sun hits the creek just right, deepening the reflected blue and lighting the sides of trees on the banks. Steers from the pasture across the creek come down to drink; I always flush a rabbit or two there; I sit on a fallen trunk in the shade and watch the squirrels in the sun. There are two separated wooden fences suspended from cables that cross the creek just upstream from my tree-trunk bench. They keep the steers from escaping up or down the creek when they come to drink. Squirrels, the neighborhood children, and I use the downstream fence as a swaying bridge across the creek. But the steers are there today.

I sit on the downed tree and watch the black steers slip on the creek bottom. They are all bred beef: beef heart, beef hide, beef hocks. They're a human product like rayon. They're like a field of shoes. They have cast-iron shanks and tongues like foam insoles. You can't see through to their brains as you can with other animals; they have beef fat behind their eyes, beef stew.

I cross the fence six feet above the water, walking my hands down the rusty cable and tightroping my feet along the narrow edge of the planks. When I hit the other bank and terra firma, some steers are bunched in a knot between me and the barbed-wire fence I want to cross. So I suddenly rush at them in an enthusiastic sprint, flailing my arms and hollering, "Lightning! Copperhead! Swedish meatballs!" They flee, still in a knot, stumbling across the flat pasture. I stand with the wind on my face.

When I slide under a barbed-wire fence, cross a field, and run over a sycamore trunk felled across the water, I'm on a little island shaped like a tear in the middle of Tinker Creek. On one side of the creek is a steep forested bank; the water is swift and deep on that side of the island. On the other side is the level field I walked through next to the steers' pasture; the water between the field and the island is shallow and sluggish. In summer's low water, flags and bulrushes grow along a series of shallow pools cooled by the lazy current. Water striders patrol the surface film, crayfish hump along the silt bottom eating filth, frogs shout and glare, and shiners and small bream hide among roots from the sulky green heron's eye. I come to this island every month of the year. I walk around it, stopping and staring, or I straddle the sycamore log over the creek, curling my legs out of the water in winter, trying to read. Today I sit on dry grass at the end of the island by the slower side of the creek. I'm drawn to this spot. I come to it as to an oracle; I return to it as a man years later will seek out the battlefield where he lost a leg or an arm.

A couple of summers ago I was walking along the edge of the island to see what I could see in the water, and mainly to scare frogs. Frogs have an inelegant way of taking off from invisible positions on the bank just ahead of your feet, in dire panic, emitting a froggy "Yike!" and splashing into the water. Incredibly, this amused me, and, incredibly, it amuses me still. As I walked along the grassy edge of the island, I got better and better at seeing frogs both in and out of the water. I learned to recognize, slowing down, the difference in texture of the light reflected from mudbank, water, grass, or frog. Frogs were flying all around me. At the end of the island I noticed a small green frog. He was exactly half in and half out of the water, looking like a schematic diagram of an amphibian, and he didn't jump.

He didn't jump; I crept closer. At last I knelt on the island's winterkilled grass, lost, dumbstruck, staring at the frog in the creek just four feet away. He was a very small frog with wide, dull eyes. And just as I looked at him, he slowly crumpled and began to sag. The spirit vanished from his eyes as if snuffed. His skin emptied and drooped; his very skull seemed to collapse and settle like a kicked tent. He was shrinking before my eyes like a deflating football. I watched the taut, glistening skin on his shoulders ruck, and rumple, and fall. Soon, part of his skin, formless as a pricked balloon, lay in floating folds like bright scum on top of the water: it was a monstrous and terrifying thing. I gaped bewildered, appalled. An oval shadow hung in the water behind the drained frog; then the shadow glided away. The frog skin bag started to sink.

I had read about the giant water bug, but never seen one. "Giant water bug" is really the name of the creature, which is an enormous, heavy-bodied brown beetle. It eats insects, tadpoles, fish, and frogs. Its grasping forelegs are mighty and hooked inward. It seizes a victim with these legs, hugs it tight, and paralyzes it with enzymes injected during a vicious bite. That one bite is the only bite it ever takes. Through the puncture shoot the poisons that dissolve the victim's muscles and bones and organs—all but the skin—and through it the giant water bug sucks out the victim's body, reduced to a juice. This event is quite common in warm fresh water. The frog I saw was being sucked by a giant water bug. I had been kneeling on the island grass; when the unrecognizable flap of frog skin settled on the creek bottom, swaying, I stood up and brushed the knees of my pants. I couldn't catch my breath.

Of course, many carnivorous animals devour their prey alive. The usual method seems to be to subdue the victim by downing or grasping it so it can't flee, then eating it whole or in a series of bloody bites. Frogs eat everything whole, stuffing prey into their mouths with their thumbs. People have seen frogs with their wide jaws so full of live dragonflies they couldn't close them. Ants don't even have to catch their prey: in the spring they swarm over newly hatched, featherless birds in the nest and eat them tiny bite by bite.

That it's rough out there and chancy is no surprise. Every live thing is a survivor on a kind of extended emergency bivouac. But at the same time we are also created. In the Koran, Allah asks, "The heaven and the earth and all in between, thinkest thou I made them *in jest?*" It's a good question. What do we think of the created universe, spanning an unthinkable void with an unthinkable profusion of forms? Or what do we think of nothingness, those sickening reaches of time in either direction? If the giant water bug was not made in jest, was it then made in earnest? Pascal uses a nice term to describe the notion of the creator's, once having called forth the universe, turning his back to it: *Deus Absconditus.* Is this what we think happened? Was the sense of it there, and God absconded with it, ate it, like a wolf who disappears round the edge of the house with the Thanksgiving turkey? "God is subtle," Einstein said, "but not malicious." Again, Einstein said that "nature conceals her mystery by means of her essential grandeur, not by her cunning." It could be that God has not absconded but spread, as our vision and understanding of the universe have spread, to a fabric of spirit and sense so grand and subtle, so powerful in a new way, that we can only feel blindly of its hem. In making the thick darkness a swaddling band for the sea, God "set bars and doors" and said, "Hitherto shalt thou come, but no further." But have we come even that far? Have we rowed out to the thick darkness, or are we all playing pinochle in the bottom of the boat?

Cruelty is a mystery, and the waste of pain. But if we describe a world to compass these things, a world that is a long, brute game, then we bump against another mystery: the inrush of power and light, the canary that sings on the skull. Unless all ages and races of men have been deluded by the same mass hypnotist (who?), there seems to be such a thing as beauty, a grace wholly gratuitous. About five years ago I saw a mockingbird make a straight vertical descent from the roof gutter of a four-story building. It was an act as careless and spontaneous as the curl of a stem or the kindling of a star.

The mockingbird took a single step into the air and dropped. His wings were still folded against his sides as though he were singing from a limb and not falling, accelerating thirty-two feet per second per second, through empty air. Just a breath before he would have been dashed to the ground, he unfurled his wings with exact, deliberate care, revealing the broad bars of white, spread his elegant, white-banded tail, and so floated onto the grass. I had just rounded a corner when his insouciant step caught my eye; there was no one else in sight. The fact of his free fall was like the old philosophical conundrum about the tree that falls in the forest. The answer must be, I think, that beauty and grace are performed whether or not we will or sense them. The least we can do is try to be there.

Another time I saw another wonder: sharks off the Atlantic coast of Florida. There is a way a wave rises above the ocean horizon, a triangular wedge against the sky. If you stand where the ocean breaks on a shallow beach, you see the raised water in a wave is translucent, shot with lights. One late afternoon at low tide a hundred big sharks passed the beach near the mouth of a tidal river in a feeding frenzy. As each green wave rose from the churning water, it illuminated within itself the six- or eight-foot-long bodies of twisting sharks. The sharks disappeared as each wave rolled toward me; then a new wave would swell above the horizon, containing in it, like scorpions in amber, sharks that roiled and heaved. The sight held awesome wonders: power and beauty, grace tangled in a rapture with violence.

We don't know what's going on here. If these tremendous events are random combinations of matter run amok, the yield of millions of monkeys at millions of typewriters, then what is it in us, hammered out of those same typewriters, that they ignite? We don't know. Our life is a faint tracing on the surface of mystery, like the idle, curved tunnels of leaf miners on the face of a leaf. We must somehow take a wider view, look at the whole landscape, really see it, and describe what's going on here. Then we can at least wail the right question into the swaddling band of darkness, or, if it comes to that, choir the proper praise.

At the time of Lewis and Clark, setting the prairies on fire was a well-known signal that meant, "Come down to the water." It was an extravagant gesture, but we can't do less. If the landscape reveals one certainty, it is that the extravagant gesture is the very stuff of creation. After the one extravagant gesture of creation in the first place, the universe has continued to deal exclusively in extravagances, flinging intricacies and colossi down aeons of emptiness, heaping profusions on profligacies with ever-fresh vigor. The whole show has been on fire from the word go. I come down to the water to cool my eyes. But everywhere I look I see fire; that which isn't flint is tinder, and the whole world sparks and flames.

I have come to the grassy island late in the day. The creek is up; icy water sweeps under the sycamore log bridge. The frog skin, of course, is utterly gone. I have stared at that one spot on the creek bottom for so long, focusing past the rush of water, that when I stand, the opposite bank seems to stretch before my eyes and flow grassily upstream. When the bank settles down I cross the sycamore log and enter again the big plowed field next to the steers' pasture.

The wind is terrific out of the west; the sun comes and goes. I can see the shadow on the field before me deepen uniformly and spread like a plague. Everything seems so dull I am amazed I can even distinguish objects. And suddenly the light runs across the land like a comber, and up the trees, and goes again in a wink: I think I've gone blind or died. When it comes again, the light, you hold your breath, and if it stays you forget about it until it goes again.

It's the most beautiful day of the year. At four o'clock the eastern sky is a dead stratus black flecked with low white clouds. The sun in the west illuminates the ground, the mountains, and especially the bare branches of trees, so that everywhere silver trees cut into the black sky like a photographer's negative of a landscape. The air and the ground are dry; the mountains are going on and off like neon signs. Clouds slide east as if pulled from the horizon, like tablecloth whipped off a table. The hemlocks by the barbed-wire fence are flinging themselves east as though their backs would break. Purple shadows are racing east; the wind makes me face east, and again I feel the dizzying, drawn sensation I felt when the creek bank reeled.

At four-thirty the sky in the east is clear; how could that big blackness be blown? Fifteen minutes later another darkness is coming overhead from the northwest; and it's here. Everything is drained of its light as if sucked. Only at the horizon do inky black mountains give way to distant, lighted mountains—lighted not by direct illumination but rather paled by glowing sheets of mist hung before them. Now the blackness is in the east; everything is half in shadow, half in sun, every clod, tree, mountain, and hedge. I can't see Tinker Mountain through the line of hemlock, till it comes on like a streetlight, ping, *ex nihilo.* Its sandstone cliffs pink and swell. Suddenly the light goes; the cliffs recede as if pushed. The sun hits a clump of sycamores between me and the mountains; the sycamore arms light up, and *I can't see the cliffs.* They're gone. The pale network of sycamore arms, which a second ago was transparent as a screen, is suddenly opaque, glowing with light. Now the sycamore arms snuff out, the mountains come on, and there are the cliffs again.

I walk home. By five-thirty the show has pulled out. Nothing is left but an unreal blue and a few banked clouds low in the north. Some sort of carnival magician has been here, some fast-talking worker of wonders who has the act backwards. "Something in this hand," he says, "something in this hand, something up my sleeve, somethind behing my back . . ." and abracadabra, he snaps his fingers, and it's all gone. Only the bland, blank-faced magician remains, in his unruffled coat, barehanded, acknowledging a smattering of baffled applause. When you look again the whole show has pulled up stakes and moved on down the road. It never stops. New shows roll in from over the mountains and the magician reappears unannounced from a fold in the curtain you never dreamed was an opening. Scarves of clouds, rabbits in plain view, disappear into the black hat forever. Presto chango. The audience, if there is an audience at all, is dizzy from head-turning, dazed.

Like the bear who went over the mountain, I went out to see what I could see. And, I might as well warn you, like the bear, all that I could see was the other side of the mountain: more of same. On a good day I might catch a glimpse of another wooded ridge rolling under the sun like water, another bivouac. I propose to keep here what Thoreau called "a meteorological journal of the mind," telling some tales and describing some of the sights of this rather tamed valley, and exploring, in fear and trembling, some of the unmapped dim reaches and unholy fastnesses to which those tales and sights so dizzyingly lead.

I am no scientist. I explore the neighborhood. An infant who has just learned to hold his head up has a frank and forthright way of gazing about him in bewilderment. He hasn't the faintest clue where he is, and he aims to learn. In a couple of years, what he will have learned instead is how to fake it: he'll have the cocksure air of a squatter who has come to fee he owns the place. Some unwonted, taught pride diverts us from our original intent, which is to explore the neighborhood, view the landscape, to discover at least *where* it is that we have been so startlingly set down, if we can't learn why.

So I think about the valley. It is my leisure as well as my work, a game. It is a fierce game I have joined because it is being played anyway, a game of both skill and chance, played against an unseen adversary—the conditions of time—in which the payoffs, which may suddenly arrive in a blast of light at any moment, might as well come to me as anyone else. I stake the time I'm grateful to have, the energies I'm glad to direct. I risk getting stuck on the board, so to speak, unable to move in any direction, which happens enough, God knows; and I risk the searing, exhausting nightmares that plunder rest and force me face down all night long in some muddy ditch seething with hatching insects and crustaceans.

But if I can bear the nights, the days are a pleasure. I walk out; I see something, some event that would otherwise have been utterly missed and lost; or something sees me, some enormous power brushes me with its clean wing, and I resound like a beaten bell.

I am an explorer, then, and I am also a stalker, or the instrument of the hunt itself. Certain Indians used to carve long grooves along the wooden shafts of their arrows. They called the grooves "ligtning marks," because they resembled the curved fissure lightning slices down the trunks of trees. The function of lightning marks is this: if the arrow fails to kill the game, blood from a deep wound will channel along the lightning mark, streak down the arrow shaft, and spatter to the ground, laying a trail dripped on broad-leaves, on stones, that the barefoot and trembling archer can follow into whatever deep or rare wilderness it leads. I am the arrow shaft, carved along my length by unexpected lights and gashes from the very sky, and this book is the straying trail of blood.

Something pummels us, something barely sheathed. Power broods and lights. We're played on like a pipe; our breath is not our own. James Houston describes two young Eskimo girls sitting cross-legged on the ground, mouth on mouth, blowing by turns each other's throat cords, making a low, unearthly music. When I cross again the bridge that is really the steers' fence, the wind has thinned to the delicate air of twilight; it crumples the water's skin. I watch the running sheets of light raised on the creek's surface. The sight has the appeal of the purely passive, like the racing of light under clouds on a field, the beautiful dream at the moment of being dreamed. The breeze is the merest puff, but you yourself sail headlong and breathless under the gale force of the spirit.

Edward Abbey
1927-1989

A self-described "agrarian anarchist," Edward Abbey's novels and nonfiction books take an irreverent, sometimes bitter, stand against the government agencies, corporations, and tourists who are destroying wilderness, particularly in the American West, at an alarming rate. Like the poet Gary Snyder, his religious, political, and psychological affinities are with the Indians and the Aborigines everywhere, not with the predominant American culture of business and technology. Rather than presenting a "balanced" view of environmental and wilderness issues, Abbey boldly takes the side of wilderness and agrarian values—as if he believes that his side is so disproportionately underrespresented in American life that the case for the earth has to be made without balance. As Edwin Way Teale said in his review of Abbey's *Desert Solitaire* (1968), Abbey's side "needs presenting. It is a side too rarely presented. There will always be others to voice . . . the side of pressure and power and profit."

Abbey is the author of sixteen books and is probably America's foremost "environmental novelist." His six novels include *Jonathan Troy* (1956), *The Brave Cowboy* (1958), *Fire on the Mountain* (1962), *Black Sun* (1971), *The Monkey Wrench Gang* (1975), and *Good News* (1980). But he is probably best known for his personal history-environmental books such as *Desert Solitaire, The Journey Home* (1977), and *Abbey's Road* (1970) and for his collaborative natural history books like *The Hidden Canyon* (1971). He writes, as one critic put it, "natural science with a soul, poetry rooted in rocks and trees and coyotes." Although he has written about Australia, Mexico, and Alaska as well, his particular area of interest is the American Desert Southwest. He lives in Arizona, and between 1956 and 1971 he was a Park Ranger and fire lookout for the National Park Service in the Southwest.

The selection "Down the River with Henry Thoreau" is taken from Abbey's nonfiction book *Down the River*. Though the book includes several settings and many issues, this chapter is set on the Green River in Utah.

from DOWN THE RIVER*

DOWN THE RIVER WITH HENRY THOREAU

November 4, 1980

Our river is the Green River in southeast Utah. We load our boats at a place called Mineral Bottom, where prospectors once searched for gold, later for copper, still later for uranium. With little luck. With me are five friends plus the ghost of a sixth: in my ammo can—the river runner's handbag—I carry a worn and greasy paperback copy of a book called *Walden, or Life in the Woods*. Not for thirty years have I looked inside this book; now for the first time since my school days I shall. Thoreau's mind has been haunting mine for most of my life. It seems proper now to reread him. What better place than on this golden river called the Green? In the clear tranquility of November? Through the red rock canyons known as Labyrinth, Stillwater, and Cataract in one of the sweetest, brightest, grandest, and loneliest of primitive regions still remaining in our America?

Questions. Every statement raises more and newer questions. We shall never be done with questioning, so long as men and women remain human. QUESTION AUTHORITY reads a bumper sticker I saw the other day in Moab, Utah. Thoreau would doubtless have amended that to read "Always Question Authority." I would add only the word "All" before the word "Authority." Including, of course, the authority of Henry David himself.

Here we are, slipping away in the early morning of another Election Day. A couple of us did vote this morning but we are not, really, good citizens. Voting for the lesser evil on the grounds that otherwise we'd be stuck with the greater evil. Poor grounds for choice, certainly. Losing grounds.

We will not see other humans or learn of the election results for ten days to come. And so we prefer it. We like it that way. What could be older than the news? We shall treasure the bliss of our ignorance for as long as we can. "The man who goes each day to the village to hear the latest news has not heard from himself in a long time." Who said that? Henry, naturally. The arrogant, insolent village crank.

I think of another bumper sticker, one I've seen several times in several places this year: NOBODY FOR PRESIDENT Amen. The word is getting around. Henry would have approved. Heartily. For he also said, "That government is best which governs not at all."

Year by year the institutions that dominate our lives grow even bigger, more complicated, massive, impersonal, and powerful. Whether governmental, corporate, military, or technological—and how can any one of these be disentangled from the others?—they weigh on society as the pyramids of Egypt weighed on the backs of those who were conscripted to build them.

*From *Down the River* by Edward Abbey. New York: E. P. Dutton. Reprinted by permission of the author.

The pyramids of power. Five thousand years later the people of Egypt still have not recovered. They remain a passive and powerless mass of subjects. Mere fellahin, expendable and interchangeable units in a social megamachine. As if the pride and spirit had been crushed from them forever.

In many a clear conclusion we find ourselves anticipated by the hoer of beans on the shores of Walden Pond. "As for the Pyramids," wrote Henry, "there is nothing to wonder at in them so much as the fact that so many men could be found degraded enough to spend their lives constructing a tomb for some ambitious booby, whom it would have been wiser and manlier to have drowned in the Nile. . . ."

Some critic has endeavored to answer this observation by claiming that the pyramid projects provided winter employment for swarms of peasants who might otherwise have been forced to endure long seasons of idleness and hunger. But where did the funds come from, the surplus grain, to support and feed these hundreds of thousands of two-legged pismires? Why, from the taxes levied on the produce of their *useful* work in the rice fields of the Nile Delta. The slaves were twice exploited. Every year. Just as the moon rides, concrete monuments, and industrial war machines of contemporary empire-states, whether capitalist or Communist, are funded by compulsory taxation, erected and maintained by what is in effect compulsory labor.

The river flows. The river will not wait. Let's get these boats on the current. Loaded with food, bedrolls, cooking gear—four gourmet cooks in a party of six (plus ghost)—they ride on the water, tethered to shore. Two boats, one an eighteen-foot rubber raft, the other an aluminum dory. Oar-powered. We scramble on board, the swampers untie the lines, the oarsmen heave at their oars. Rennie Russell (author of *On the Loose*) operates the raft; a long-connected, lean fellow named Dusty Teale rows the dory.

We glide down the golden waters of Labyrinth Canyon. The water here is smooth as oil, the current slow. The sandstone walls rise fifteen hundred feet above us, radiant with sunlight, manganese and iron oxides, stained with old tapestries of organic residues left on the rock faces by occasional waterfalls. On shore, wheeling away from us, the stands of willow glow in autumn copper; beyond the willow are the green-gold cottonwoods. Two ravens fly along the rim, talking about us. Henry would like it here.

November 5, 1980

We did not go far yesterday. We rowed and drifted two miles down the river and then made camp for the night on a silt bank at the water's edge. There had been nobody but ourselves at Mineral Bottom but the purpose, nonetheless, was to "get away from the crowd," as Rennie Russell explained. We understood. We cooked our supper by firelight and flashlight, ate beneath the stars. Somebody uncorked a bottle of wine. Rennie played his guitar, his friend Ted Seeley played the fiddle, and Dusty Teale played the mandolin. We all sang. Our music ascended to the sky, echoing softly from the cliffs. The river poured quietly seaward, making no sound but here and there, now and then, a gurgle of bubbles, a trilling of ripples off the hulls of our half-beached boats.

Sometime during the night a deer stalks nervously past our camp. I hear the noise and, when I get up before daybreak, I see the dainty heart-shaped tracks. I kindle the fire and build the morning's first pot of black, rich, cowboy coffee, and drink in solitude the first cupful, warming my hands around the hot cup. The last stars fade, the sky becomes brighter, passing through the green glow of dawn into the fiery splendor of sunrise.

The others straggle up, one by one, and join me around the fire. We stare at the shining sky, the shining river, the high canyon walls, mostly in silence, until one among us volunteers to begin breakfast. Yes, indeed, we are a lucky little group. Privileged, no doubt. At ease out here on the edge of nowhere, loafing into the day, enjoying the very best of the luckiest of nations, while around the world billions of other humans are sweating, fighting, striving, procreating, starving. As always, I try hard to feel guilty. Once again I fail.

"If I knew for a certainty that some man was coming to my house with the conscious intention of doing me good," writes our Henry, "I would run for my life."

We Americans cannot save the world. Even Christ failed at that. We Americans have our hands full in trying to save ourselves. And we've barely tried. The Peace Corps was a lovely idea—for idle and idealistic young Americans. Gave them a chance to see a bit of the world, learn something. But as an effort to "improve" the lives of other peoples, the inhabitants of the so-called underdeveloped nations (our nation is overdeveloped), it was an act of cultural arrogance. A piece of insolence. The one thing we could do for a country like Mexico, for example, is to stop every illegal immigrant at the border, give him a good rifle and a case of ammunition, and send him home. Let the Mexicans solve their customary problems in their customary manner.

If this seems a cruel and sneering suggestion, consider the current working alternative: leaving our borders open to unlimited immigration until—and it won't take long—the social, political, economic life of the United States is reduced to the level of life in Juarez. Guadalajara. Mexico City. San Salvador. Haiti. India. To a common peneplain of overcrowding, squalor, misery, oppression, torture, and hate.

What could Henry have said to this supposition? He lived in a relatively spacious America of only 24 million people, of whom one-sixth were slaves. A mere 140 years later we have grown to a population ten times larger, and we are nearly all slaves. We are slaves in the sense that we depend for our daily survival upon an expand-or-expire agro-industrial empire—a crackpot machine—that the specialists cannot comprehend and the managers cannot manage. Which is, furthermore, devouring world resources at an exponential rate. We are, most of us, dependent employees.

What would Henry have said? He said, "In wildness is the preservation of the world." He said, somewhere deep in his thirty-nine-volume *Journal*, "I go to my solitary woodland walks as the homesick return to their homes." He said, "It would be better if there were but one inhabitant to a square mile, as where I live." Perhaps he did sense what was coming. His last words, whispered from the deathbed, are reported to us as being "moose . . . Indians . . ."

Looking upriver toward Tidwell Bottom, a half mile away, I see a lone horse grazing on the bunch grass, the Indian rice grass, the saltbush, and sand sage of the river's old floodplain. One horse, unhobbled and untended, thirty miles from the nearest ranch or human habitation, it forages on its own. That horse, I'm thinking, may be the one that got away from me years ago, in another desert place, far from here. Leave it alone. That particular horse has found at least a temporary solution to the question of survival. Survival with honor, I mean, for what other form of survival is worth the trouble? That horse has chosen, or stumbled into, solitude and independence. Let it be. Thoreau defined happiness as "simplicity, independence, magnanimity and trust."

But solitude? Horses are gregarious beasts, like us. This lone horse on Tidwell Bottom may be paying a high price for its freedom, perhaps in some form of equine madness. A desolation of the soul corresponding to the grand desolation of the landscape that lies beyond these canyon walls.

"I never found the companion that was so companionable as solitude," writes Henry. "To be in company, even with the best, is soon wearisome and dissipating."

Perhaps his ghost will forgive us if we suspect an element of *extra-vagance* in the above statement. Thoreau had a merry time in the writing of *Walden*; it is an exuberant book, crackling with humor, good humor, gaiety, with joy in the power of words and phrases, in ideas and emotions so powerful they tend constantly toward the outermost limit of communicable thought.

"The sun is but a morning star." Ah yes, but what exactly does that mean? Maybe the sun is also an evening star. Maybe the phrase had no exact meaning even in Thoreau's mind. He was, at times, what we today might call a put-on artist. He loved to shock and exasperate; Emerson complains of Henry's "contrariness." The power of Thoreau's assertion lies not in its meaning but in its exhilarating suggestiveness. Like poetry and music, the words imply more than words can make explicit.

Henry was no hermit. Hardly even a recluse. His celebrated cabin at Walden Pond—some of his neighbors called it a "shanty"—was two miles from Concord Common. A half-hour walk from pond to post office. Henry lived in it for only two years and two months. He had frequent human visitors, sometimes too many, he complained, and admitted that his daily rambles took him almost every day into Concord. When he tired of his own cooking and his own companionship he was always welcome at the Emersons' for a free dinner. Although it seems that he earned his keep there. He worked on and off for years as Emerson's household handyman, repairing and maintaining things that the great Ralph Waldo was too busy or too incompetent to attend to himself. "Emerson," noted Thoreau in a letter, "is too much the gentleman to push a wheelbarrow." When Mrs. Emerson complained that the chickens were scratching up her flower beds, Henry attached little cloth booties to the chickens' feet. A witty fellow. Better and easier than keeping them fenced in. When Emerson was off on his European lecture tours, Thoreau would look after not only Emerson's house but also Emerson's children and wife.

We shall now discuss the sexual life of Henry David Thoreau.

November 6, 1980

Awaking as usual sometime before the dawn, frost on my beard and sleeping bag, I see four powerful lights standing in a vertical row on the eastern sky. They are Saturn, Jupiter, Mars, and, pale crescent on a darkened disc, the old moon. The three great planets seem to be rising from the cusps of the moon. I stare for a long time at this strange, startling apparition, a spectacle I have never before seen in all my years on planet Earth. What does it mean? If ever I've seen a portent in the sky this must be it. Spirit both forms and informs the universe, thought the New England transcendentalists, of whom Thoreau was one; all Nature, they believed, is but symbolic of a greater spiritual reality beyond. And within.

Watching the planets, I stumble about last night's campfire, breaking twigs, filling the coffeepot. I dip waterbuckets in the river; the water chills my hands. I stare long at the beautiful, dimming lights in the sky but can find there no meaning other than the lights' intrinsic beauty. As far as I can perceive, the planets signify nothing but themselves. "Such suchness," as my Zen friends say. And that is all. And that is enough. And that is more than we can make head or tail of.

"Reality is fabulous," said Henry; "be it life or death, we crave nothing but reality." And goes on to describe in precise, accurate, glittering detail the most subtle and minute aspects of life in and about his Walden Pond; the "pulse" of water skaters, for instance, advancing from shore across the surface of the lake. Appearance *is* reality, Thoreau implies; or so it appears to me. I begin to think he outgrew transcendentalism rather early in his career, at about the same time that he was overcoming the influence of his onetime mentor Emerson; Thoreau and the transcendentalists had little in common—in the long run—but their long noses, as a friend of mine has pointed out.

Scrambled eggs, bacon, green chiles for breakfast, with hot *salsa*, toasted tortillas, and leftover baked potatoes sliced and fried. A gallon or two of coffee, tea and—for me—the usual breakfast beer. Henry would not have approved of this gourmandising. To hell with him. I do not approve of his fastidious puritanism. For one who claims to crave nothing but reality, he frets too much about *purity*. Purity, purity, he preaches, in the most unctuous of his many sermons, a chapter of *Walden* called "Higher Laws."

"The wonder is how they, how you and I," he writes, "can live this slimy, beastly life, eating and drinking. . . ." Like Dick Gregory, Thoreau recommends a diet of raw fruits and vegetables; like a Pythagorean, he finds even beans impure, since the flatulence that beans induce disturbs his more ethereal meditations. (He would not agree with most men that "farting is such sweet sorrow.") But confesses at one point to a sudden violent lust for wild woodchuck, devoured raw. No wonder: Henry was probably anemic.

He raised beans not to eat but to sell—his only cash crop. During his lifetime his beans sold better than his books. When a publisher shipped back to Thoreau 706 unsellable copies of his *A Week on the Concord and Merrimack Rivers* (the author had himself paid for the printing of the book),

Henry noted in his *Journal*, "I now have a library of 900 volumes, over 700 of which I wrote myself."

Although professing disdain for do-gooders, Thoreau once lectured a poor Irish immigrant, a neighbor, on the advisability of changing his ways. "I tried to help him with my experience . . ." but the Irishman, John Field, was only bewildered by Thoreau's earnest preaching. "Poor John Field!" Thoreau concludes: "I trust he does not read this, unless he will improve by it. . . ."

Nathaniel Hawthorne, who lived in Concord for a time and knew Thoreau, called him "an intolerable bore."

On the subject of sex, as we would expect, Henry betrays a considerable nervous agitation. "The generative energy, which, when we are loose, dissipates and makes us unclean, when we are continent invigorates and inspires us. Chastity is the flowering of man. . . ."(But not of flowers?) "We are conscious of an animal in us, which awakens in proportion as our higher nature slumbers. It is reptile and sensual. . . ." "He is blessed who is assured that the animal is dying out in him day by day. . . ." In a letter to his friend Harrison Blake, Henry writes: "What the essential difference between man and woman is, that they should be thus attracted to one another, no one has satisfactorily answered."

Poor Henry. We are reminded of that line in Whitman (another great American oddball), in which our good gray poet said of women, "They attract with a fierce, undeniable attraction," while the context of the poem makes it clear that Whitman himself found young men and boys much more undeniable.

Poor Thoreau. But he could also write, in the late essay "Walking," "The wildness of the savage is but a faint symbol of the awful ferity with which good men and lovers meet." Ferity—now there's a word. What could it have meant to Thoreau? Our greatest nature lover did not have a loving nature. A woman acquaintance of Henry's said she'd sooner take the arm of an elm tree than that of Thoreau.

Poor Henry David Thoreau. His short (forty-five years), quiet, passionate life apparently held little passion for the opposite sex. His relationship with Emerson's wife Lidian was no more than a long brother-sisterly friendship. Thoreau never married. There is no evidence that he ever enjoyed a mutual love affair with any human, female or otherwise. He once fell in love with and proposed marriage to a young woman by the name of Ellen Sewall; she rejected him, bluntly and coldly. He tried once more with a girl named Mary Russell; she turned him down. For a young man of Thoreau's hypersensitive character, these must have been cruel, perhaps disabling blows to what little male ego and confidence he possessed to begin with. It left him shattered, we may assume, on that side of life; he never again approached a woman with romantic intentions on his mind. He became a professional bachelor, scornful of wives and marriage. He lived and probably died a virgin, pure as shriven snow. Except for those sensual reptiles coiling and uncoiling down in the root cellar of his being. Ah, purity!

But we make too much of this kind of thing nowadays. Modern men and women are obsessed with the sexual; it is the only realm of primordial adventure still left to most of us. Like apes in a zoo, we spend our energies on the one field of play remaining; human lives otherwise are pretty well caged in by the walls, bars, chains, and locked gates of our industrial culture. In the relatively wild, free America of Henry's time there was plenty of opportunity for every kind of adventure, although Henry himself did not, it seems to me, take advantage of those opportunities. (He could have toured the Western plains with George Catlin!) He led an unnecessarily constrained existence, and not only in the "generative" region.

Thoreau the spinster-poet. In the year 1850, when Henry reached the age of thirty-three, Emily Dickinson in nearby Amherst became twenty. Somebody should have brought the two together. They might have hit it off. I imagine this scene, however, immediately following the honeymoon:

EMILY (raising her pen)
Henry, you haven't taken out the garbage.
HENRY (raising his flute)
Take it out yourself.

What tunes did Thoreau play on that flute of his? He never tells us; we would like to know. And what difference would a marriage—with a woman—have made in Henry's life? In his work? In that message to the world by which he challenges us, as do all the greatest writers, to change our lives? He taunts, he sermonizes, he condemns, he propounds conundrums, he orates and exhorts us:

> "Wherever a man goes, men will pursue and paw him with their dirty institutions. . . ."
>
> "I found that by working six weeks a year I could meet all the expenses of living."
>
> "Tell those who worry about their health that they may be already dead."
>
> "When thousands are thrown out of employment, it suggests they were not well-employed."
>
> "If you stand right fronting and face to face with a fact, you will see the sun glimmer on both its surfaces, as if it were a scimitar, and feel its sweet edge dividing you through the heart and marrow, and so you will happily conclude your mortal career."
>
> ". . .The hero is commonly the simplest and obscurest of men."
>
> ". . .Little is to be expected of a nation when the vegetable mould is exhausted, and it is compelled to make manure of the bones of its fathers."

"Genius is a light which makes the darkness visible, like the lightning's flash, which perchance shatters the temple of knowledge itself. . . ."

"When, in the course of ages, American liberty has become a fiction of the past—as it is to some extent a fiction of the present—the poets of the world will be inspired by American mythology."

"We should go forth on the shortest walk. . .in the spirit of undying adventure, never to return."

". . .If I repent of anything, it is very likely to be my good behavior. What demon possessed me that I behaved so well?"

"No man is so poor that he need sit on a pumpkin; that is shiftlessness."

"I would rather sit on a pumpkin and have it all myself than be crowded on a velvet cushion."

"A man is rich in proportion to the number of things which he can afford to let alone."

"We live meanly, like ants, though the fable tells us that we were long ago changed into men. . . ."

"A living dog is better than a deal lion. Shall a man go and hang himself because he belongs to a race of pygmies, and not be the biggest pygmy that he can?"

"I will endeavor to speak a good word for the truth."

"Rather than love, than money, than fame, give me truth."

"Any truth is better than make-believe."

And so forth.

November 7, 1980

On down this here Greenish river. We cast off, row south past Woodruff, Point, and Saddlehorse bottoms, past Upheaval Bottom and Hardscrabble Bottom. Wherever the river makes a bend—and this river comes near, in places, to bowknots—there is another flat area, a bottom, covered with silt, sand, gravel, grown up with grass and brush and cactus and, near shore, trees: willow, cottonwood, box elder, and jungles of tamarisk.

The tamarisk does not belong here, has become a pest, a water-loving exotic engaged in the process of driving out the cottonwoods and willows. A native of arid North Africa, the tamarisk was imported to the American Southwest fifty years ago by conservation *experts*—dirt management specialists—in hopes that it would help prevent streambank erosion. The cause of the erosion was flooding, and the primary cause of the flooding, then as now, was livestock grazing.

Oars at rest, we drift for a while. The Riverine String Band take up their instruments and play. The antique, rowdy, vibrant music from England and Ireland by way of Appalachia and the Rocky Mountains floats on the air, rises like smoke toward the high rimrock of the canyon walls, fades by infinitesimal gradations into the stillness of eternity. Where else could it go?

Ted Seeley prolongs the pause, then fills the silence with a solo on the fiddle, a Canadian invention called "Screechin' Old Woman and Growlin' Old Man." This dialogue continues for some time, concluding with a triumphant outburst from the Old Woman.

We miss the landing off the inside channel at Wild Horse Bench and have to fight our way through thickets of tamarisk and cane to the open ground of Fort Bottom. We make lunch on crackers, canned tuna, and chopped black olives in the shade of a cottonwood by the side of a long-abandoned log cabin. A trapper, prospector, or cow thief might have lived here—or all three of them—a century ago. Names and initials adorn the lintel of the doorway. The roof is open to the sky.

We climb a hill of clay and shale and limestone ledges to inspect at close hand an ancient ruin of stone on the summit. An Anasazi structure, probably seven or eight hundred years old, it commands a broad view of river and canyon for many miles both up and downstream, and offers a glimpse of the higher lands beyond. We can see the great Buttes of the Cross, Candlestick Tower, Junction Butte (where the Green River meets the Colorado River), Ekker Butte, Grandview Point, North Point, and parts of the White Rim. Nobody human lives at those places, or in the leagues of monolithic stone between them. We find pleasure in that knowledge. From this vantage point everything looks about the same as it did when Major John Wesley Powell and his mates first saw it in 1869. Photographs made by members of his party demonstrate that nothing much has changed except the vegetation types along the river, as in the case of tamarisk replacing willow.

We return to our river. A magisterial magpie sails before us across the barren fields. Two ravens and a hawk watch our lazy procession downstream past the long straightway of Potato Bottom. We make camp before sundown on an island of white sand in the middle of the river. A driftwood fire under an iron pot cooks our vegetable stew. Russel mixes a batch of heavy-duty cornbread in the Dutch oven, sets the oven on the hot coals, and piles more coals on the rimmed lid. The cornbread bakes. We drink our beer, sip our rum, and listen to a pack of coyotes yammering like idiots away off in the twilight.

"I wonder who won the election," says one member of our party—our boatwoman Lorna Corson.

"The coyotes can explain everything," says Rennie Russell.

It's going to be a cold and frosty night. We add wood to the fire and put on sweaters and coats. The nights are long in November; darkness by six.

The challenge is to keep the fire going and conversation and music alive until a decent bedtime arrives. Ten hours is too long to spend curled in a sleeping bag. The body knows this if the brain does not. That must be why I wake up every morning long before the sun appears. And why I remain sitting here, alone on my log, after the others have crept away, one by one, to their scattered beds.

Henry gazes at me through the flames of the campfire. From beyond the veil. Edward, he says, what are you doing here? Henry, I reply, what are you doing out there?

How easy for Thoreau to preach simplicity, asceticism and voluntary poverty when, as some think, he had none but himself to care for during his forty-five years. How easy to work part-time for a living when you have neither wife nor children to support. (When you have no payments to meet on house, car, pickup truck, cabin cruiser, life insurance, medical insurance, summer place, college educations, dinette set, color TVs, athletic club, real estate investments, holidays in Europe and the Caribbean. . . .)

Why Henry never took a wife has probably more to do with his own eccentric personality than with his doctrine of independence-through-simplicity. But if he had *wanted* a partner, and had been able to find one willing to share his doctrine, then it seems reasonable to suppose that the two of them—with their little Thoreaus—could have managed to live a family life on Thoreauvian principles. Henry might have been compelled to make pencils, survey woodlots, and give public lectures for twenty-four weeks, rather than only six, each year, but his integrity as a free man would still have been preserved. There is no reason—other than the comic incongruity of imagining Henry Thoreau as husband and father—to suppose that his bachelorhood invalidates his arguments. If there was tragedy in the life of Thoreau, that tragedy lies not in any theoretical contradiction between what Henry advocated and how he lived but in his basic loneliness. He was a psychic loner all his life.

But a family man nevertheless. Except for his two years and two months at Walden Pond, his student years at Harvard, and occasional excursions to Canada, Cape Cod, and Maine, Thoreau lived most of his life in and upon the bosom of family—Emerson's family, part of the time, and the Thoreau family—mother, sister, uncles, and aunts—during the remainder.

When his father died Henry took over the management of the family's pencil-making business, a cottage industry carried on in the family home. Always a clever fellow with his hands, Henry developed a better way of manufacturing pencils, and a better product. Some think that the onset of his tuberculosis, which eventually killed him, was hastened by the atmosphere of fine powdered graphite in which he earned a part of his keep.

A part of it: Thoreau had no wish to become a businessman—"Trade curses everything it handles"—and never gave to pencils more than a small part of his time.

He was considered an excellent surveyor by his townsmen and his services were much in demand. His work still serves as the basis of many property lines in and around the city of Concord. There is a document in the Morgan Library in New York, a map of Walden Pond, signed "H.D. Thoreau, Civil Engineer."

But as with pencil-making, so with surveying—Thoreau would not allow it to become a full-time career. Whatever he did, he did well; he was an expert craftsman in everything to which he put his hand. But to no wage-earning occupation would he give his life. He had, he said other business." And this other business awaited him out in the woods, where, as he wrote, "I was better known."

What was this other business? It is the subject of *Walden*, of his further books and essays, and of the thirty-nine volumes of his *Journal*, from which, to a considerable extent, the books were quarried. Thoreau's subject is the greatest available to any writer, thinker and human being, one which I cannot summarize in any but the most banal of phrases: "meaning," or "the meaning of life" (meaning *all* life, of course, not human life only), or in the technical usage preferred by professional philosophers, "the significance of existence."

It is this attempt to encircle with words the essence of being itself—with or without a capital *B*—which gives to Henry's prose-poetry the disturbing, haunting, heart-opening quality that some call mysticism. Like the most ambitious poets and artists, he was trying to get it all into his work, whatever "it" may signify, whatever "all" may include. Living a life full of wonder—wonderful—Henry tries to impart that wonder to his readers.

"There is nothing inorganic. . . . The earth is not a mere fragment of dead history, stratum upon stratum, like the leaves of a book, to be studied by geologists and antiquaries chiefly, but living poetry like the leaves of a tree, which precede flowers and fruit; not a fossil earth but a living earth. . . ."

That the earth, considered whole, is a kind of living being, might well seem like nonsense to the hardheaded among us. Worse than nonsense—mystical nonsense. But let us remember that a hard head, like any dense-hulled and thick-shelled nut, can enclose, out of necessity, only a tiny kernel of meat. Thinking meat, in this case. The hard head reveals, therefore, while attempting to conceal and shelter, its tiny, soft, delicate, and suspicious mind.

The statement about earth is clear enough. And probably true. To some, self-evident, though not empirically verifiable within the present limitations of scientific method. Such verification requires a more sophisticated science than we possess at present. It requires a science with room for more than data and information, a science that includes sympathy for the object under study, and more than sympathy, love. A love based on prolonged contact and interaction. Intercourse, if possible. Observation informed by sympathy, love, intuition. Numbers, charts, diagrams, and formulas are not in themselves sufficient. The face of science as currently constructed is a face that only a mathematician could love. The root meaning of "science" is "knowledge"; to see and to see truly, a qualitative, not merely quantitative, understanding.

For an example of science in the whole and wholesome sense read Thoreau's description of an owl's behavior in "Winter Visitors." Thoreau observes the living animal in its native habitat, and watches it for weeks. For an example of science in its debased sense take this: According to the L.A. *Times*, a psychologist in Los Angeles defends laboratory experimentation on captive dogs with the assertion that "little is known about the psychology of dogs." Anyone who has ever kept a dog knows more about dogs than that psychologist—who doubtless considers himself a legitimate scientist—will learn in a year of Sundays.

Or this: Researchers in San Francisco have confined chimpanzees in airtight glass cubicles (gas chambers) in order to study the effect of various dosages of chemically polluted air on these "manlike organisms." As if there were not already available five million human inhabitants of the Los Angeles basin, and a hundred other places, ready, willing, and eager to supply personally informed testimony on the subject under scrutiny. Leaving aside any consideration of ethics, morality, and justice, there are more intelligent ways to study living creatures. Or nonling creations: rocks have rights too.

That which today calls itself science gives us more and more information, an indigestible glut of information, and less and less understanding. Thoreau was well aware of this tendency and foresaw its fatal consequences. He could see the tendency in himself, even as he partially succumbed to it. Many of the later *Journals* are filled with little but the enumeration of statistical data concerning such local Concord phenomena as the rise and fall of lake levels, or the thickness of the ice on Flint's Pond on a January morning. Tedious reading—pages and pages on "factoids," as Norman Mailer would call them—attached to no coherent theory, illuminated by neither insight nor outlook nor speculation.

Henry may have had a long-range purpose in mind but he did not live long enough to fulfill it. Kneeling in the snow on a winter's day to count the tree rings in a stump, he caught the cold that led to his death on May 6, 1862. He succumbed not partially but finally to facticity.

Why'd you do it, Henry? I ask him through the flames.

The bearded face with the large, soft, dark eyes, mournful and thoughtful as the face of Lincoln, smiles back at me but offers no answer. He evades the question by suggesting other questions in his better-known, "mystical" vein:

"There was a dead horse in the hollow by the path to my house, which compelled me sometimes to go out of my way, especially in the night when the air was heavy, but the assurance it gave me of the strong appetite and inviolable health of Nature was my compensation for this. I love to see that Nature is so rife with life that myriads can be afforded to be sacrificed and suffered to prey on one another. . . . The impression made on a wise man is that of universal innocence. Compassion is a very untenable ground. It must be expeditious. Its pleadings will not bear to be stereotyped."

Henry, I say, what the devil do you mean?

He smiles again and says, "I observed a very small and graceful hawk, like a nighthawk, alternately soaring like a ripple and tumbling a rod or two over and over, showing the underside of its wings, which gleamed like a satin ribbon in the sun. . . . The merlin it seemed to me it might be called;

but I care not for its name. It was the most ethereal flight I have ever witnessed. It did not simply flutter like a butterfly, nor soar like the larger hawks, but it sported with proud reliance in the fields of the air. . . . It appeared to have no companion in the universe . . . and to need none but the morning and the ether with which it played. It was not lonely, but made all the earth lonely beneath it."

Very pretty, Henry. Are you speaking for yourself? I watch his lined, gentle face, the face of his middle age (though he had no later) as recorded in photographs, and cannot help but read there the expression, engraved, of a patient, melancholy resignation. All babies look identical; boys and adolescents resemble one another, in their bewildered hopefulness, more than they differ. But eventually the inner nature of the man appears on his outer surface. Character begins to shine through. Year by year a man reveals himself, while those with nothing to show, show it. Differentiation becomes individuation. By the age of forty, if not before, a man is responsible for his face. The same is true of women too, certainly, although women, obeying the biological imperative, strive harder than men to preserve an appearance of youthfulness—the reproductive look—and lose it sooner. Appearance *is* reality.

Henry replies not to my question but, as befits a ghostly seer, to my thought: "Nothing can rightly compel a simple and brave man to a vulgar sadness."

We'll go along with that, Henry; you've been accused of many things but no one, to my knowledge, has yet accused you of vulgarity. Though Emerson, reacting to your night in jail for refusing to pay the poll tax, called the gesture "mean and skulking and in bad taste." In bad taste! How typically Emersonian. Robert Louis Stevenson too called you a "skulker" on the grounds that you preached more strongly than you practiced, later recanting when he learned of your activity in the antislavery movement. The contemporary author Alan Harrington, in his book *The Immortalist*, accuses you of writing, at times, like "an accountant of the spirit." That charge he bases on your vague remarks concerning immorality, and on such lines as "Goodness is the only investment that never fails."

Still other current critics, taking their cue from those whom Nabokov specified as "the Viennese quacks," would deflect the force of your attacks on custom, organized religion, and the state by suggesting that you suffered from a complex of complexes, naturally including the castration complex and the Oedipus complex. Your defiance of authority, they maintain, was in reality no more than the rebelliousness of an adolescent rejecting his father—in this case the meek and mousy John Thoreau.

Whatever grain of truth may be in this diagnosis, such criticism betrays the paternalistic condescension of these critics toward human beings in general. The good citizen, they seem to be saying, is like the obedient child; the rebellious man is a bad boy. "The people are like children," said our own beloved, gone but not forgotten, Richard Nixon. The psychiatric approach to dissidence has been most logically applied in the Soviet Union, where opposition to the state is regarded and treated as a form of mental illness.

In any case, Henry cannot be compelled to confess to a vulgar sadness. The vulgarity resides in the tactics of literary Freudianism. Of the opposition. Psychoanalysis is the neurosis of the psychoanalyst—and of the psychoanalytic critic. Why should we bother any more with this garbage? I thought we stopped talking about Freud back in 1952. Sometime near the end of the Studebaker era.

Fading beyond the last flames of the fire, Henry lulls me to sleep with one of his more soporific homilies:

"The light which puts out our eyes is darkness to us. Only that day dawns to which we are awake. There is more day to dawn. The sun . . . "

Yes, yes, Henry, we know. How true. Whatever it means. How late it is. Whatever the hour.

I rise from my log, heap the coals of the fire together, and by their glimmering light and the cold light of the stars fumble my way back and into the luxury of my goosedown nest. Staring up at mighty Orion, trying to count six of the seven Pleiades, a solemn thought comes to me: We Are Not Alone.

I nuzzle my companion's cold nose, the only part of her not burrowed deep in her sleeping bag. She stirs but does not wake. We're not alone, I whisper in her ear. I know, she says; shut up and go to sleep. Smiling, I face the black sky and the sapphire stars. Mark Twain was right. Better the savage wasteland with Eve than Paradise without her. Where she is, there is Paradise.

Poor Henry.

And then I hear that voice again, far off but clear: "All Nature is my bride."

November 8, 1980

Who won the election? What election? Mere vapors on the gelid air, like the breath from my lungs. I rebuild the fire on the embers of last night's fire. I construct the coffee, adding fresh grounds to yesterday's. One by one, five human forms reassemble themselves about me, repeating themselves, with minor variations, for another golden day. The two vegetarians in our group—Rennie and Lorna—prepare their breakfast oatmeal, a viscous gray slime. I dump two pounds of Buck-sliced bacon into the expedition's wok, to the horror of the vegetarians, and stir it roughly about with a fork. Stir-cooking. The four carnivores look on with hungry eyes. The vegetarians smile in pity. "Pig meat," says Lorna, "for the four fat pork faces." "Eat your pussy food," says Dusty Teale, "and be quiet."

The melody of morning, Black-throated desert sparrows chatter in the willows: *chirr. . . chirr. . . chit chit chit.* The sun comes up, a glaring, cymbal, over yonder canyon rim. Quickly the temperature rises five, ten, twenty degrees, at the rate of a degree a minute, from freezing to fifty-two. Or so it feels. We peel off parkas, sweaters, shirts, thermal underwear. Ravens croak, a rock falls, the river flows.

The fluvial life. The alluvial shore. "A river is superior to a lake," writes

Henry in his *Journal*, "in its liberating influence. It has motion and indefinite length. . . . With its rapid current it is a slightly fluttering wing. River towns are winged towns."

Down the river. Lorna rows the dory, I row the raft. We are edified by water music from our string trio, a rich enchanting tune out of Peru called "Urubamba." The song goes on and on and never long enough. The Indians must have composed it for a journey down the Amazon.

Fresh slides appear on the mud banks; a beaver plops into the water ahead of us, disappears. The beavers are making a comeback on the Green. Time for D. Julien, Jim Bridger, Joe Meek, Jed Smith, and Jim Beckwourth to reappear. Eternal recurrence, announced Nietzsche. Time for the mountain men to return. The American West has not given us, so far, sufficient men to match our mountains. Or not since the death of Crazy Horse, Sitting Bull, Dull Knife, Red Cloud, Chief Joseph, Little Wolf, Red Shirt, Gall, Geronimo, Cochise, Tenaya (to name but a few), and their comrades. With their defeat died a bold, brave, heroic way of life, one as fine as anything recorded history has to show us. Speaking for myself, I'd sooner have been a liver-eating, savage horseman, riding with Red Cloud than a slave-owning sophist sipping tempered wine in Periclean Athens. For example. Even Attila the Hun, known locally as the Scourge of God, brought more fresh air and freedom into Europe than the crowd who gave us the syllogism and geometry, Aristotle and his *Categories,* Plato and his *Laws*.

Instead of mountain men we are cursed with a plague of diggers, drillers, borers, grubbers; of asphalt-spreaders, dam-builders, overgrazers, clear-cutters, and strip-miners whose object seems to be to make our mountains match our men—making molehills out of mountains for a race of rodents—for the rat race.

Oh well . . . revenge is on the way. We see it in those high thin clouds far on the northern sky. We feel it in those rumbles of discontent deep in the cupboards of the earth: tectonic crockery trembling on the continental shelves. We hear it down the slipface of the dunes, a blue wind moaning out of nowhere. We smell it on the air: the smell of danger. Death before dishonor? That's right. What else? Liberty or death? Naturally.

When no one else would do it, it was Thoreau, Henry Thoreau the intolerable bore, the mean skulker, the "quaint stump figure of a man," as William Dean Howells saw him, who rang the Concord firebell to summon the villagers to a speech by Emerson attacking slavery. And when John Brown stood on trial for his life, when all America, even the most ardent abolitionists, was denouncing him, it was himself—Henry—who delivered a public address first in Concord, then in Boston, not only defending but praising, even eulogizing, the "madman" of Harpers Ferry.

We go on. Sheer rock—the White Rim—rises from the river's left shore. We pause at noon to fill our water jugs from a series of potholes half filled with last week's rainwater. We drink, and sitting in the sunlight on the pale sandstone, make our lunch—slabs of dark bread, quite authentic, from a bohemian bakery in Moab; a serious hard-core hippie peanut butter, heavy as wet concrete, from some beatnik food coop in Durango, Colorado (where Teale and Corson live); raspberry jam; and wild honey, thick as axle grease, for esophageal lubrication.

"What is your favorite dish?" another guest asked Thoreau as they sat down to a sumptuous Emersonian dinner.

"The nearest," Henry replied.

"At Harvard they teach all branches of learning," said Ralph Waldo.

"But none of the roots," said Henry.

Refusing to pay a dollar for his Harvard diploma, he said, "Let every sheep keep its own skin." When objections were raised to his habit of exaggeration, Henry said, "You must speak loud to those who are hard of hearing." Asked to write for the *Ladies' Companion*, he declined on the grounds that he "could not write anything companionable." He defines a pearl as "the hardened tear of a diseased clam, murdered in its old age." On the art of writing he said to a correspondent, "You must work very long to write short sentences." And added that "the one great rule of composition . . . is to speak the truth." Describing the flavor of a certain wild apple, he wrote that it was "sour enough to set a squirrel's teeth on edge, or make a jay scream."

And so on. The man seemingly composed wisecracks and epigrams in his sleep. Even on his deathbed. "Henry, have you made your peach with God?" asked a relative. "I am not aware that we had quarreled, Aunt," said Henry. To another visitor, attempting to arouse in him a decent Christian concern with the the next world, Henry said, "One world at a time."

One could make a book of Henry's sayings. And call it *Essais. Areopagitica. Walden.*

Many of his friends, neighbors, relatives, and relative friends must have sighed in relief when Henry finally croaked his last, mumbling "moose . . . Indians . . ." and was safely buried under Concord sod. Peace, they thought, at long last. But, to paraphrase the corpse, they had *somewhat hastily* concluded that he was dead.

His passing did not go unnoticed outside of Concord. Thoreau had achieved regional notoriety by 1862. But at the time when the giants of New England literature were thought to be Emerson, Hawthorne, Alcott, Channing, Irving, Longfellow, Dr. Lowell, and Dr. Holmes, Thoreau was but a minor writer. Not even a major minor writer.

Today we see it differently. In the ultimate democracy of time, Henry has outlived his contemporaries. Hawthorne and Emerson are still read, at least in university English departments, and it may be that in a few elementary schools up in Maine and Minnesota children are being compelled to read Longfellow's *Hiawatha* (I doubt it; doubt that they can, even under compulsion), but as for the others they are forgotten by everyone but specialists in American literature. Thoreau, however, becomes more significant with each passing decade. The deeper our United States sinks into industrialism, urbanism, militarism—with the rest of the world doing its best to emulate America—the more poignant, strong, and appealing becomes Thoreau's demand for the right of every man, every woman, every child, every dog, every tree, every snail darter, every lousewort, every living thing, to live its own life in its own way at its own pace in its own square mile of home. Or in its own stretch of river.

Looking at my water-soaked, beer-stained, grease-spotted cheap paperback copy of *Walden*, I see that mine was from the thirty-third printing. And this is only one of at least a dozen current American editions of the book. *Walden* has been published abroad in every country where English can be read, as in India—God knows they need it there—or can be translated, as in Russia, where they need it even more. The Kremlin's commissars of literature have classified Thoreau as a nineteenth-century social reformer, proving once again that censors can read but seldom understand.

The village crank becomes a world figure. As his own Johnny Appleseed, he sows the seeds of liberty around the planet, even on what looks like the most unpromising soil. Out of Concord, apples of discord. Truth threatens power, now and always.

We walk up a small side canyon toward an area called Soda Springs Basin; the canyon branches and branches again, forming more canyons. The floor of each is flood-leveled sand, the walls perpendicular sandstone. Each canyon resembles a winding corridor in a labyrinth. We listen for the breathing of the Minotaur but find only cottonwoods glowing green and gold against the red rock, rabbitbrush with its mustard-yellow bloom, mule-ear sunflowers facing the sunlight, their coarse petals the color of butter, and the skull and curled horns of a desert bighorn ram, half buried in the auburn sand.

The canyons go on and on, twisting for miles into the plateau beyond. We turn back without reaching Soda Springs. On our return Dusty Teale takes up the bighorn trophy, carries it back to the dory and mounts it on the bow, giving his boat dignity, class, an unearned but warlike glamour.

We camp today at Anderson Bottom, across the river from Unknown Bottom. We find pictographs and petroglyphs here, pictures of deer, bighorns, warriors, and spectral figures representing—who knows—gods, spirits, demons. They do not trouble us. We cook our dinner and sing our songs and go to sleep.

November 9. 1980.

Early in the morning I hear coyotes singing again, calling up the sun. There's something about the coyotes that reminds me of Henry. What is it? After a moment the answer comes.

Down near Tucson, Arizona, where I sometimes live—a grim and grimy little-big town, swarming with nervous policemen, dope dealers, resolute rapists, and geriatric bank robbers, but let this pass for the moment—the suburban parts of the city are infested with pet dogs. Every home owner in these precincts believes that he needs whatever burglar protection he can get; and he is correct. Most evenings at twilight the wild coyotes come stealing in from the desert to penetrate the suburbs, raid garbage cans, catch and eat a few cats, dogs, and other domesticated beasts. When this occurs the dogs raise a grim clamor, roaring like maniacs, and launch themselves in hot but tentative pursuit of the coyotes. The coyotes retreat into the brush and cactus, where they stop, facing the town, to wait and sit and laugh at the dogs. They yip, yap, yelp, howl, and holler, teasing the dogs, taunting them, enticing them with the old-time call of the wild. And the dogs stand and tremble, shaking with indecision, furious, hating themselves, tempted to join the coyotes, run off with them into the hills, but—afraid. Afraid to give up the comfort, security, and safety of their housebound existence. Afraid of the unknown and dangerous.

Thoreau was our suburban coyote. Town dwellers have always found him exasperating.

"I have traveled a good deal in Concord; and everywhere, in shops and offices and fields, the inhabitants have appeared to me to be doing penance in a thousand remarkable ways. . . . By a seeming fate, commonly called necessity, they are employed, as it says in an old book, laying up treasures which moth and rust will corrupt and thieves break through and steal. It is a fool's life, as they will find when they get to the end of it, if not before. . . . I sometimes wonder that we can be so frivolous. . . . As if you could kill time without injuring eternity."

Oh, come now, Henry, stop yapping at us. Go make love to a pine tree (all Nature being your bride). Lay off. Leave us alone. But he will not stop.

"The mass of men lead lives of quiet desperation. What is called resignation is confirmed desperation. . . . A stereotyped but unconscious despair is concealed even under what are called the games and amusements of mankind. There is no play in them."

But is it *true* that the mass of men lead lives of quiet desperation? And if so, did Henry escape such desperation himself? And who, if anyone, can answer these questions?

As many have noted, the mass of men—and women—lead lives today of *un*quiet desperation. A frantic busyness ("business") pervades our society wherever we look—in city and country, among young and old and middle-aged, married and unmarried, all races, classes, sexes, in work and play, in religion, the arts, the sciences, and perhaps most conspicuously in the self-conscious cult of meditation, retreat, withdrawal. The symptoms of universal unease and dis-ease are apparent on every side. We hear the demand by conventional economists for increased "productivity," for example. Productivity of what? for whose benefit? to what end? by what means and at what cost? Those questions are not considered. We are belabored by the insistence on the part of our politicians, businessmen and military leaders, and the claque of scriveners who serve them, that "growth" and "power" are intrinsic goods, of which we can never have enough, or even too much. As if gigantism were an end in itself. As if a commendable rat were a rat twelve hands high at the shoulders—and still growing. As if we could never have peace on this planet until one state dominates all others.

The secondary symptoms show up in the lives of individuals, the banalities of everyday soap opera: crime, divorce, runaway children, loneliness, alcoholism, mental breakdown. We live in a society where suicide (in its many forms) appears to more and more as a sensible solution; as a viable alternative; as a workable option.

Yes, there are many who seem to be happy in their lives and work. But strange lives, queer work. Space technicians, for example, busily refining a new type of inertial guidance system for an intercontinental ballistic missile bearing hydrogen bombs. Laboratory biologists testing the ability of mice, dogs, and chimpanzees to cultivate cancer on a diet of cigarettes and Holsum bread, to propel a treadmill under electric stimuli, to survive zero gravity in a centrifuge. And the indefatigable R. Buckminster Fuller hurtling around the globe by supersonic jet with six wristwatches strapped to each forearm, each watch set to a different time zone. "The world is big," says Fuller, "but it is comprehensible."

And also, to be fair, young dancers in a classroom; an old sculptor hacking in fury at a block of apple wood; a pinto bean farmer in Cortez, Colorado, surveying his fields with satisfaction on a rainy day in July (those rare farmers, whom Thoreau dismissed with such contempt, we now regard with envy); a solitary fly fisherman unzipping his fly on the banks of the Madison River; wet children playing on a shining, sun-dazzled beach.

Compared with ours, Thoreau's was an open, quiet, agrarian society, relatively clean and uncluttered. The factory system was only getting under way in his time, though he took note of it when he remarked that "the shop girls have no privacy, even in their thoughts." In his day England, not America, was "the workhouse of the world." (America now in the process of being succeeded by Japan.) What would Henry think of New England, of the United States, of the Western world, in the year 1980? 1984? 2001? Would he not assert, confidently as before, that the mass of humans continue to lead lives of quiet desperation?

Quiet desperation. The bite of the phrase comes from the unexpected, incongruous juxtaposition of ordinarily antithetical words. The power of it comes from our sense of its illuminating force—"a light which makes the darkness visible." Henry's shocking pronouncement continues to resonate in our minds, with deeper vibrations, 130 years after he made it. He allows for exceptions, indicating the "mass of men," not all men, but as for the truth of his observation no Gallup Poll can tell us; each must look into his own heart and mind and then deny it if he can.

And what about Henry himself? When one of his friends, William Ellery Channing, declared morosely that no man could be happy "under present conditions," Thoreau replied without hesitation, "But I am." He spent nearly a year at his dying and near the end, too weak to write any more, he dictated the following, in answer to a letter from his friend Blake:

"You ask particularly after my health. I *suppose* that I have not many months to live; but of course I know nothing about it. I may add that I am enjoying existence as much as ever, and regret nothing."

When the town jailer, Sam Staples, the same who had locked Thoreau up for a night many years before, and had also become a friend, paid a visit to the dying man, he reported to Emerson: "Never spent an hour with more satisfaction. Never saw a man dying with so much pleasure and peace." A trifle lugubrious, but revealing. Henry's sister Sophia wrote, near his end, "It is not possible to be sad in his presence. No shadow attaches to anything connected with my precious brother. His whole life impresses me as a grand miracle. . . ."

A cheerful stoic all the way, Thoreau refused any drugs to ease the pain or let him sleep; he rejected opiates, according to Channing, "on the ground that he preferred to endure the worst sufferings with a clear mind rather than sink into a narcotic dream." As he would never admit to a vulgar sadness, so he would not allow himself to surrender to mere physical pain.

It must have seemed to Henry during his last year that his life as an author had been a failure. Only two of his books were published during his lifetime and neither received much recognition. His contemporaries, without exception—Emerson included—had consigned him to oblivion, and Henry could not have been unaware of the general opinion. But even in this he refused to acknowledge defeat. Noting the dismal sales of his books, he wrote in his *Journal*: "I believe that the result is more inspiring and better for me than if thousands had bought my wares. It affects my privacy less and leaves me freer."

Emerson declared that Thoreau was a coldly unemotional man, stoical but never cheerful; Emerson had so convinced himself of this that when, in editing some of Thoreau's letters for publication, he came across passages that indicated otherwise, he deleted them. But Ralph Waldo's son Edward, in his book *Henry Thoreau as Remembered by a Young Friend*, wrote that Henry loved to sing and dance, and was always popular with the children of Concord.

In her *Memories of Hawthorne*, Hawthorne's daughter Rose gives us this picture of Thoreau ice skating, with Emerson and Hawthorne, on the frozen Concord River: "Hawthorne," she writes, "moved like a self-impelled Greek statue, stately and grave" (the marble faun); Emerson "closed the line, evidently too weary to hold himself erect, pitching headforemost . . ."; while Thoreau, circling around them, "performed dithyrambic dances and Bacchic leaps."

But what of the photographs of Henry referred to earlier, the daguerreotype in his thirty-ninth year by B.W. Maxham, made in 1856, and the ambrotype by E.S. Dunshee, made in 1861? Trying to get some sense of the man himself, in himself, which I do not get from his words alone, or from the accounts of Thoreau by others, I find myself looking again and again at these old pictures. Yes, the eyes are unusually large, very sensitive and thoughtful, as is the expression of the whole face. The nose is too long, the chin too small, neither an ornament; the face deeply lined, the brow high, the hair and beard luxuriant. A passable face, if not a handsome one. And it still seems to me that I read in his eyes, in his look, an elemental melancholy. A resigned sadness. But the man was ailing with tuberculosis when the former picture was made, within a year of his death when the second was made. These facts should explain the thoughtful look, justify a certain weariness. In neither picture can we see what might be considered a trace of self-pity—the *vulgar* sadness. And in neither can we perceive the faintest hint of any kind of desperation. Henry may have been lonely; he was never a desperate man.

What does it matter? For us it is Henry's words and ideas that count, or more exactly, the symbiotic and synergistic mutually reinforcing logic of word and idea, and his successful efforts to embody both in symbolic acts. If it were true that he never had a happy moment (I doubt this) in his entire life, he surely had an intense empathy with the sensation of happiness:

". . .I have penetrated to those meadows on the morning of many a first spring day, jumping from hummock to hummock, from willow root to willow root, when the wild river valley and the woods were bathed in so pure and bright a light as would have waked the dead, if they had been slumbering in their graves, as some suppose. There needs no stronger proof of immortality."

The paragraph is from the springtime of Henry's life. *Walden* is a young man's book, most of it written before his thirtieth year. But the infatuation with the sun and sunlight carries on into the premature autumn of his years as well; he never gave them up, never surrendered. Near the end of his life he wrote:

"We walked [jumping has become walking, but the spirit remains the same] in so pure and bright a light, gliding the withered grass and leaves, so softly and serenely bright, I thought I had never bathed in such a golden flood, without a ripple or a murmur to it. The west side of every wood and rising ground gleamed like the boundary of Elysium, and the sun on our backs seemed like a gentle herdsman driving us home at evening."

And concluding: "So we saunter toward the Holy Land, till one day the sun shall shine more brightly than ever he has done, shall perchance shine into our minds and hearts, and light up our whole lives with a great awakening light, as warm and serene and golden as on a bankside in autumn."

November 10, 1980.

Onward, into Stillwater Canyon. We have left Labyrinth behind, though how Major Powell distinguished the two is hard to determine. The current is slow, but no slower than before, the canyons as serpentine as ever. In the few straight stretches of water we gain a view of Candlestick Tower, now behind us, and off to the southwest, ahead, the great sandstone monadnock three hundred feet high known as Cleopatra's Chair, "bathed," as Henry would say, "in a golden flood of sunlight."

We row around an anvil-shaped butte called Turk's Head. Hard to see any reason for the name. Is there any reason, out here, for any name? These huge walls and giant towers and vast mazy avenues of stone resist attempts at verbal reduction. The historical view, the geological view, the esthetical view, the rock climber's view, give us only aspects of a massive *presence* that remains fundamentally unknowable. The world is big and it is incomprehensible.

A hot, still morning in Stillwater Canyon. We row and rest and glide, at two miles per hour, between riparian jungles of rusty willow, coppery tamarisk, brown cane, and gold-leaf cottonwoods. On the shaded side the crickets sing their dirgelike monotone. They know, if we don't, that winter is coming.

But today is very warm for mid-November. An Indian-summer day. Looking at the rich brown river, jungle on both banks, I think how splendid it would be, and apposite, to see the rugose snout of an alligator come sliding through the water toward us. We need alligators here. Crocodiles, also. A few brontosauri, pteranodons, and rocs with twenty-five-foot wingspan would not be amiss. How tragic that we humans arrived too late, to the best of our conscious recollection, to have witnessed the fun and frolic of the giant thunder lizards in their time of glory. Why was that great chapter ripped too soon from the Book of Life? I would give ten years off the beginning of my life to see, only once, *Tyrannosaurus rex* come rearing up from the elms of Central Park, a Morgan police horse screaming in its jaws. We can never have enough of nature.

We explore a couple of unnamed side canyons on the right, searching for a natural stone arch I found ten years ago, on a previous river journey. Hallucination Arch, we named it then, a lovely span of two-tone rosy sandstone—not shown on any map—somewhere high in the northern fringes of the Maze. We do not find it this time. We pass without investigating a third unknown canyon; that must have been the right one.

We camp for two nights at the mouth of Jasper Canyon, spend the day between the nights exploring Jasper's higher ramifications, toward the heart of the Maze. If the Maze has a heart. We go on the following day, down the river, and come sailing out one fine afternoon into the confluence of the two great desert streams. The Green meets the Colorado. They do not immediately merge, however, but flow along side by side like traffic lanes on a freeway, the greenish Colorado, the brownish Green, with a thin line of flotsam serving as median.

Henry never was a joiner either.

"Know all men by these presents that I, Henry Thoreau, do not wish to be considered a member of any incorporated body which I have not joined."

A crusty character, Thoreau. An unpeeled man. A man with the bark on him.

We camp today at Spanish Bottom, near the first rapids of Cataract Canyon. Sitting around our fire at sundown, four of us gnawing on spareribs, the other two picking at their pussy food—tofu and spinach leaves and stewed kelp (it looks like the testicles of a sick octopus)—we hear the roar of tons of silty water plunging among the limestone molars of Brown Betty Rapid: teeth set on edge. The thunderous vibrations rise and fall, come and go, with the shifting evening winds.

We spend the next day wandering about the top of the Maze, under the shadows of Lizard Rock, Standing Rock, the Chimney, looking down into five-hundred-foot-deep canyons, into the stems, branches, and limbs of an arboreal system of part-time drainages. It took a liberal allowance of time, indeed, for the rare storms of the canyon country to carve out of solid rock these intricate canyons, each with its unscalable walls, boxlike heads, stomach-turning dropoffs. A man could spend the better part of a life exploring this one area, getting to know, so far as possible, its broad outline and its intimate details. You could make your summer camp on Pete's Mesa, your winter camp down in Ernie's Country, and use Candlestick Spire all year round for a personalized private sundial. And die, when you're ready, with the secret center of the Maze clutched to your bosom. Or, more likely, never found.

Henry spent his life—or earned his life—exploring little more than the area surrounding his hometown of Concord. His jaunts beyond his own territory do not amount to much. He traveled once to Minnesota, seeking health, but that was a failure. He never came west, although, as he says, he preferred walking in a westerly direction. He never saw our Rocky Mountains, or the Grand Canyon, or the Maze. He never reached the Amazon, Alaska, Antarctica, the Upper Nile, or the Mountains of the Moon. He journeyed once to Staten Island but was not impressed.

Instead, he made a world out of Walden Pond, Concord, and their environs. He walked, he explored, every day and many nights, he learned to know his world as few ever know any world. Once, as he walked in the woods with a friend (Thoreau had many friends, we come to realize, if not one in his lifetime with whom he could truly, deeply share his life; it is we, his readers, over a century later, who must be and are his true companions), the friend expressed his long-felt wish to find an Indian arrowhead. At once Henry stopped, bent down, and picked one up.

November 14, 1980.

Today will be our last day on the river. We plan to run the rapids of Cataract Canyon this morning, camp on Lake Powell this afternoon, go on to Hite Marina and back to civilization, such as it is, tomorrow.

I rise early, as usual, and before breakfast go for a walk into the fields of Spanish Bottom. I see two sharp-shinned hawks roosting in a cottonwood. A tree of trembling leaves, pale gold and acid green. The hawks rise at my approach, circle, return to the tree as I go on. Out in the field, one hundred yards away, I see an erect neck, a rodentian head, a pair of muley ears displayed in sharp silhouette against the redrock cliffs. I stop, we stare at each other—the transient human, the ephemeral desert mule deer. Then I notice other deer scattered beyond the first: one, two, three, four, five—nine all told. Two with antlers.

My first thought is *meat*. Unworthy thought—but there they are, waiting, half of them standing broadside to me, their dear beating hearts on level with the top of the sand sage, saltbush, rice grass. Two of them within a hundred yards—easy range for a thirty-thirty. Meat means survival. Survival, by Christ, with honor. With *honor!* When the cities lie at the monster's feet, we shall come here, my friends, my very few friends and I, my sons and my daughter, and we will survive. We shall live.

My second thought is more fitting, for the moment. Leave them in peace. Let them be. Efface yourself, for a change, and let the wild things be.

What would Henry say? Henry said, "There is a period in the history of the individual, as of the race, when the hunters are the 'best men,' as the Algonquins called them. We cannot but pity the boy who has never fired a gun; he is no more humane, while his education has been sadly neglected." But then he goes on to say: "No humane being, past the thoughtless age of boyhood, will wantonly murder any creature which holds its life by the same tenure that he does. The hare in its extremity cries like a child. I warn you, mothers, that my sympathies do not make the usual *philanthropic* distinctions." Is that his last word on the subject? Hardly. Henry had many words for every subject, and no last word for any. He also writes, "But I see that if I were to live in a wilderness, I should become . . . a fisher and hunter in earnest."

So let them be for now. I turn back to camp, making one step. The deer take alarm, finally, and move off at a walk. I watch. Their fear becomes contagious. One begins to run, they all run, bounding away toward the talus slopes of the canyon wall. I watch them leap upward into the rocks, expending energy with optimum ease, going farther and rising higher until they disappear, one by one, somewhere among the boulders and junipers at the foot of the vertical wall.

Back to camp and breakfast. We load the boats, secure the hatches, lash down all baggage, strap on life jackets, face the river and the sun, the growing roar of the rapids. First Brown Betty, then Ben Hur and Capsize Rapids, then the Big Drop and Satan's Gut. Delightful names, and fitting. We feel the familiar rush of adrenaline as it courses through our blood. We've been here before, however, and know that we'll get through. Most likely. The odds are good. Our brave boatman and boatwoman, Dusty and Lorna, ply the oars and steer our fragile craft into the glassy tongue of the first rapid. The brawling waters roar below, rainbows of broken sunlight dance in the spray. We descend.

Henry thou should be with us now.

I look for his name in the water, his face in the airy foam. He must be here. Wherever there are deer and hawks, wherever there is liberty and danger, wherever there is wilderness, wherever there is a living river, Henry Thoreau will find his eternal home.

WATCHING THE BIRDS: THE WINDHOVER

We used to live, my wife and I, in a glassy cabin on a mountain peak, surrounded by a national forest. Our job was to watch. Watch what? Well, watch just about everything. To us it seemed like the center of the world. When clouds gathered, we watched for lightning, where it struck. After the lightning we'd watch for smoke in the trees and when and if it appeared, a few hours later or a couple of days later, we'd locate the smoke with our precision fire-finder and radio the news to forest headquarters. The report generally went like this: "Phoenix, this is Aztec Peak, ten-seventy-three." (10-73 is forest radio code for fire.)

"Go ahead, Aztec."

"We've got a little smoke for you at zero-four-two degrees and thirty minutes, southwest side of Two Bar Ridge. It's a single snag, blue-gray smoke, small volume, intermittent puffs. Light wind from the west. Heavy fuel but not spreading."

"Ten-four, Aztec. Let us know if it grows."

While fire crews were dispatched to find and put out the fire, my wife and I returned to our job of watching. We watched the clouds again and the weather, and approaching and departing storms. We watched the sun go down behind Four Peaks and the Superstition Mountains, that sundown legend retold and recurring every evening, day after day after day. We saw the planet Venus bright as radium floating close to the shoulder of the new moon. We watched the stars, and meteor showers, and the snaky ripple of cloud-to-cloud lightning coursing across the sky at night.

We watched the birds. One day a little nuthatch flew into our cabin through an open window, banged its silly head against the closed window opposite, and dropped to the floor. I picked up the tiny bird, holding it in my palm. I could feel the beating of its furious heart. I set it down on the catwalk outside, in the sunlight. After a while the nuthatch came to, shook its head, lofted its wings, and fluttered off. What can you think of a bird that crashes into glass and creeps headfirst down the trunk of a pine?

The forest spread below us in summer in seventeen different shades of green. There were yellow pine and piñon pine, blue spruce and Engelmann spruce, white fir and Douglas fir, quaking aspen, New Mexican locust, alligator juniper, and four kinds of oak. Along the rimrock of the escarpment, where warm air rose from the canyons beneath, grew manzanita, agave, sotol, and several species of cactus—prickly pear, pincushion, fishhook. Far down in the canyons, where water flowed, though not always on the surface, we could see sycamore, alder, cottonwood, walnut, hackberry, wild cherry, and wild grape. And a hundred other kinds of tree, shrub, and vine that I would probably never learn to identify by name.

The naming of things is a useful mnemonic device, enabling us to distinguish and utilize and remember what otherwise might remain an undifferentiated sensory blur, but I don't think names tell us much of character, essence, meaning. Einstein thought that the most mysterious aspect of the universe (if it is, indeed, a *uni*-verse, not a pluri-verse) is what he called its "comprehensibility." Being primarily a mathematician and only secondarily a violinist, Einstein saw the world as comprehensible because so many of its properties and so much of its behavior can be described through mathematical formulas. The atomic bomb and Hiroshima made a convincing argument for his point of view. As does the ignition of juniper twigs, by the agency of friction, into heat, smoke, and flame. Mass is transformed into energy, emitting light. Employing fire lookouts.

Even so, I find something narrow and too specialized in Einstein's summary of the situation. The specialist's viewpoint may go deep but it cannot go all the way through. How could it if the world, though finite, is unbounded? Nor does its practical utility—atomic bombs—make up for its lack of breadth. All special theories suffer from this defect. The lizard sunning itself on a stone would no doubt tell us that time, space, sun, and earth exist to serve the lizard's interests; the lizard, too, must see the world as perfectly comprehensible, reducible to a rational formula. Relative to the context, the lizard's metaphysical system seems as complete as Einstein's.

But to me the most mysterious thing about the universe is not its comprehensibility but the fact that it exists. And the same mystery attaches to everything within it. The world is permeated through and through by mystery. By the incomprehensible. By creatures like you and me and Einstein and the lizards.

Modern science and technology have given us the engineering techniques to measure, analyze, and take apart the immediate neighborhood, including the neighbors. But this knowledge adds not much to our understanding of things. "Knowledge is power," said Francis Bacon, great-great-grandfather of the nuclear age. Power, exactly—that's been the point of the game all along. But power does not lead to wisdom, even less to understanding. Sympathy, love, physical contact—touching—are better means to so fine an end.

Vague talk, I agree. This blather about mystery is probably no more than a confession of intellectual laziness. Let's have no more metaphysical apologetics. Throw metaphysic to the dogs, I say, and watch the birds. I'd rather contemplate the noble turkey vulture soaring on the air, contemplating me, than speculate further on Einstein's theories, astrophysics, or the significance of the latest computer printouts from Kitt Peak Observatory and NASA. The computer tapers (tapirs?) have a word for it: GIGO. Garbage In, Garbage Out. Output equals Input. Numbers in, numbers out—nothing more. NINO, a double negation. Anything reduced to numbers and algebra is not very interesting. Useful, of course, for the processing of data, physical relations, human beings—but not interesting.

The vultures are interesting. In the morning they would rise, one by one, from their communal roost a quarter-mile below our lookout, and disperse themselves to the four quarters of the firmament. Each patrols its chosen—or allocated—territory, rising so high and sailing so far it soon becomes invisible to human eyes, even when our human eyes are aided by Bausch & Lomb 7X50 binoculars. But although we cannot always see them, the buzzards keep an eye on one another as well as on the panorama of life and death below, and when one bird descends for an actual or potential lunch its mates notice and come from miles away to join the feast. This is the principle of evolutionary success: mutual aid.

At evening, near sundown, the vultures would return. Friendly, tolerant, gregarious birds, they liked to roost each night on the same dead pine below. One by one they spiraled downward, weaving transparent figures in the air while others maintained a holding pattern, sinking slowly, gradually—as if reluctant to leave the heights—twoard the lime-spattered branches of the snag. They might even have had nests down in there somewhere, although I could never see one, with little buzzard chicks waiting for supper. Try to imagine a baby vulture.

Gathered on their favorite dead tree, heads nodding together, the vultures resembled from our vantage point a convocation of bald, politic funeral directors discussing business prospects—always good. Dependable. The mature birds have red, wrinkled, featherless heads; the heads of the young are a bluish color and also naked. The heads are bald because it's neater, safer, more sanitary, given the line of work. If you made your living by thrusting your beak and eyes and ears and neck deep into the rotting entrails, say, of a dead cow, you too would prefer to be bald as a buzzard. Feathers on the head would impede a hasty withdrawal, when necessary, and might provide lodging for maggots, beetles, worms, and bacteria. Best for the trade to keep sleek and tidy.

I respect vultures myself, even like them, I guess, in a way, and fully expect someday to join them, internally at least. One should plan one's reincarnation with care. I like especially the idea of floating among the clouds all day, seldom stirring a feather, meditating on whatever it is that vultures meditate about. It looks like a good life, from down here.

We had some golden eagles in the area too, but seldom got a look at them. Uncommon and elitist birds, aloof as warlords, they generally hang out as far as possible from human habitat. Who could blame them? Sheepmen and many others shoot them on sight, on general principles. Our hero Ernest Hemingway could not resist the temptation to bag an eagle now and then, though he hated himself afterward. Not an easy job to be, or to have been, Ernest Hemingway. Elinor Wylie advised emulation:

> Avoid the reeking herd,
> Shun the polluted flock,
> Live like that stoic bird
> The eagle of the rock.

But she spent most of her time in New York City. Can't blame her either. Every bird in its proper place.

The redtail hawk is a handsome character. I enjoyed watching the local hunter come planing through the pass between our mountaintop and the adjoining peak, there to catch the wind and hover in place for a while, head twitching back and forth as it scans the forest below. When he—or she—spots something live and edible, down she goes at an angle of forty-five degrees, feet first, talons extended, wings uplifted, feathers all aflutter, looking like a Victorian lady in skirts and ruffled pantaloons jumping off a bridge.

The hawk disappears into the woods. I watch, binoculars ready. She rises seconds later from the trees with something wriggling, alive, in her right foot. A field mouse. The hawk sails high in the air. The mouse is fighting, bites the hawk on the shank (I can see these details without difficulty), and the startled redtail drops her prey. The mouse falls down and away, also at an angle of forty-five degrees, carried eastward by the wind. The hawk stoops, swoops, and recaptures the mouse a hundred feet above the treetops, carries it to the broken-off top of a pine, perches there, still holding the struggling mouse in her claws, and makes one quick stab of beak to the mouse's head. I see a spurt of red. The mouse is still. The hawk gulps down her lunch raw and whole, in one piece, as an owl does. *Hors rodentine.* Later, after craw and gizzard have done their work, the hawk will regurgitate a tiny ball of fur and toenails.

We watched the storms of late afternoon. Sun descending in a welter of brawling purple clouds. Spokes of gold wheel across the sky, jags and jets of lightning flicker from cloud to cloud and from cloud to earth. Mighty kettledrums thunder in the distance. My wind gauge reads thirty-five knots. The trees sway, the wind booms through the forest.

Watching the vultures gather below, I noticed a disturbance. A small gray-backed falcon was diving among the vultures, harrying the laggards. It was a peregrine falcon—rare but not extinct. Watching through the glasses, I saw one vulture actually flapping its wings to escape the falcon—an unusual exertion for a vulture. The falcon strikes, their bodies collide in what appears to me as a glancing blow. A few vulture feathers float off on the wind. The vulture flaps into the shelter of the trees, swearing quietly, apparently unharmed. Tiring of this sport, the falcon skims upward in a sweeping arc, shooting through the circling vultures, winging higher and higher into the sky, and stops at the apex of its parabola to hover there, still as a star, facing the wind, the lightning, the advancing storm.

The falcon hangs in space for second after second, motionless, as if suspended on a thread, its wings, body, and spirit in perfect equilibrium with the streaming torrents of the air. Give your heart to the hawks, urged Robinson Jeffers. Okay, I thought, I'll do that. For this one splendid moment. Until the falcon sheers off on the wind and vanishes in storm and light.

Appealing as I find the idea of reincarnation, I must confess that it has a flaw: to wit, there is not a shred of evidence suggesting it might be true. The idea has nothing going for it but desire, the restless aspiration of the human mind. But when was aspiration ever intimidated by fact? Given a choice, I plan to be a long-winged fantailed bird next time around.

Which one? Vulture, eagle, hawk, falcon, crane, heron, wood ibis? Well, I believe I was a wood ibis once, back in the good old days of the Pleistocene epoch. And from what I already know of passion, violence, the intensity of the blood, I think I'll pass on eagle, hawk, or falcon this time. For a lifetime or two, or maybe three, I think I'll settle for the sedate career, serene and soaring, of the humble turkey buzzard. And if any falcon comes around making trouble I'll spit in his eye. Or hers. And contemplate this world we love from a silent and considerable height.

John Haines
b. 1924

An Alaskan by choice, John Haines has lived on our last frontier since the late 1940's, homesteading, hunting, exploring, fishing, writing, and hiring out as a carpenter and house painter. Like Thoreau, he has managed to reduce human existence to its essence and to record news from the soul of wilderness. *Winter News* (1966), his first book, is the result of twenty years of writing poetry and ten years of living in wild Alaska. Haines writes a sparse, tight, almost stingy poetry that reduces a thing described and language itself to the most essential level. Informed and shaped by his early training as a painter and sculptor, his poetry is like visual art, using color, absence of color, dream imagery, and spatial relationships to express the moods and qualities of experiences or observations. And there is a brooding, white vastness, like London's White Silence, in much that he writes.

Having ventured out to fill many university posts in Alaska, Washington, Montana, and elsewhere, and having especially divided his time between Alaska and Montana, he is a resident of Fairbanks who has received the Alaskan Governor's Award for "life contributions" to the arts. Titles of his prose books suggest his interests and themes: *Of Traps and Snares* (1982) on trapping and wilderness life; contributions to *Minus Thirty-One and the Wind Blowing: Nine Reflections about Living on Land* (1980); and *Living off the Country: Essays on Poetry and Place* (1981).

But Haines is most highly regarded as the author of a dozen books of poetry—especially *The Stone Harp* (1971), *Cicada* (1977), *News from the Glacier* (1980), and *Winter News*. He has been called "one of our best nature poets, or for that matter one of the best nature writers of any kind." In describing his own purpose and poetry, Haines uses an idea familiar to students of ecology: "If the life is open enough and serious enough, everything met with and experienced will relate in one way or another to the poet's most personal concern. Everything is connected—or ought to be."

from LIVING OFF THE COUNTRY*

THE WRITER AS ALASKAN: BEGINNINGS AND REFLECTIONS

I

As a poet I was born in a particular place, a hillside overlooking the Tanana River in central Alaska, where I built a house and lived for the better part of twenty-two years. It was there, in the winter of 1947-48, that I began writing poems seriously, and there many years later that I wrote my first mature poems. Many things went into the making of those poems and the others I've written since: the air of the place, its rocks, soil, and water; snow and ice; human history, birds, animals, and insects. Other things, surely, not directly related to the place: the words of other poets learned once, forgotten, and remembered again. Old stories from childhood, voices out of dreams. Images, a way of seeing learned partly from several years' study as a painter and sculptor. And human relationship, life shared with another person whose existence mingled with my own, so that we saw the world as one person. But it was finally the place itself that provided the means of unifying all of these into a single experience.

I must have carried in myself from an early age some vague design of such a place and such a life. I grew up more or less homeless, moved from place to place, and came, I think, to regard all residence and all relationships as only temporary. It would naturally follow that I nourished in myself a great wish for something more permanent. What I got from that early life was a good sense of geography, but also great insecurity and uncertainty about who I was. I think I knew then that I would have to find a specific place and be born over again as my own person.

Why I chose that particular place rather than another probably can't be answered completely. I might have gone elsewhere and become a very different poet and person. But there was, most likely, no other region where I might have had that original experience of the North American wilderness. Unlike other "wilderness" areas, Alaska in those days seemed open-ended. I could walk north from my homestead at Richardson all the way to the Arctic Ocean and never cross a road nor encounter a village. This kind of freedom may no longer be available, but at that time it gave to the country a limitlessness and mystery hard to find now on this planet.

From the first day I set foot in interior Alaska, and more specifically on Richardson Hill, I knew I was home. Something in me identified with that landscape. I had come, let's say, to the dream place. Not exactly, of course, for there never was an exact place, but here was something so close to it that I could accept it at once. I think such a recognition must be rare, and I was extremely fortunate to have it happen in the way that it did. Such a purity of feeling, of joy and of being in the right place, I have not often felt since.

What that experience meant to me, in terms of self-discovery and the sort

*From *Living Off the Country: Essays on Poetry and Place* (Ann Arbor, Michigan: The University of Michigan Press, 1981).

of work I was to do, could be told at great length, but I will try only to suggest in this essay some of the most important features of its personal significance.

There was, first of all, the experience of the wilderness itself, of finding life on more basic terms than those given me without thought as a child. This may seem like a strange thing to say, but perhaps it will make better sense if I link it to a more general theme. At times it becomes necessary for people to turn away from their cultural origins and return for a while to an older and simpler existence. One of the consequences of having a language and a culture is that these begin to exist for themselves in place of the original things we once lived by. Words become abstract, institutions and customs become unrelated to anything necessary or authentic. And they begin subtly to sap vitality from us; we begin to live falsely and after a while we find it necessary to turn away from them and find ourselves once more in the hard irreducible world of natural things—of rock and water, fire and wood, flesh and blood.

So here, on a steep hillside, seventy miles from Fairbanks, was a place to begin. It was for me the beginning of what I have come to understand as the myth-journey of humankind. This life of food gathering, of making for ourselves out of what we can find around us, this is what we have come from and will return to. The Scottish poet, Edwin Muir, speaks in terms of the biblical Fall from Paradise, and he may be right. Think of what we have done to the earth and to ourselves—this fallen kingdom, the landscapes we make everywhere, devoid of beauty and grandeur. I can still remember the intensity of my feeling, of actual pain and outrage, seeing the landscape of southern California once more after twelve years in the wilderness. I saw it slowly as I drove south from Alaska, through Canada—the accumulating ruin of the North American landscape.

I had when younger a habit of mind, of dreaminess, a vague drifting through the world. I was naturally observant, but unfocused. Living as I did there at Richardson, limited by circumstances to a small area, I found it necessary to learn more and more about it in order to get a living from it. I was forced to pay attention, to learn in detail many things of a kind I could not have learned if I had stayed only briefly in the country or had lived there in easier circumstances. I learned quickly because it was an adventure for me, a young person from the city unused to knowing any place intimately, to distinguish actual things, particular and exact, from the vague and general character of the world. Words began to fasten themselves to what I saw. I learned the names of the things to be found there, characteristic of the subarctic the world over: the forest trees and shrubs, their kinds and uses, what made good building material or fuel, and what did not; what could be eaten, preserved, and put up for later use. I began for the first time to make things for myself, to build shelters, to weave nets, to make sleds and harness, and to train animals for work. I learned to hunt, to watch and to listen, to think like a moose, if need be, or a marten, or a lynx. I watched the river, and saw in its gray and swirling water, heavy with silt, the probable trace of salmon, and knew where to set my nets. I read the snow and what was written there. I became familiar with the forms of frost, the seeding of the grasses, the early swelling of the birch leaves. I watched a tree, no bigger than my wrist when I first built there, grow tenfold over the years, until I had to cut away its branches from the rain gutters of the house.

Digging in the soil, picking away the rock, uprooting stumps, I became in time a grower of things sufficient to feed myself and another. Slowly finding my way into the skills of hunter and trapper, I understood what blood and bone, hide and muscle, marrow and sinew really are; not as things read about, but as things touched and handled until they became as familiar to me as my own skin. Land itself came alive for me as it never had before, more alive sometimes than the people who moved about on it. I learned that it is land, *place,* that makes people, provides for them the possibilities they will have of becoming something more than mere lumps of sucking matter. We today who live so much from the inheritance of land and culture do not understand this as well as we need to. Few of us these days are really residents anywhere, in the deep sense of that term. We live off the surface of things and places, the culture as well as the land; ours is a derivative life: we take what we find without thought, without regard for origin or consequences, unaware for the most part that the resources, both natural and cultural, are fast diminishing.

These were big lessons, basic things, and I was a long time assimilating them and understanding their significance. Never really privileged in youth, I was never in actual want, either. Like most people in our society, I did not know what it was to be hungry, to look for food and find myself short when I needed it most. That old life, unchanged for centuries, in time with the seasons, the rising and setting of the sun, the coming and going of birds and animals, the sources of food and light, became for me not a passage in a book of histories, but a matter of daily occurrence, a way still vital and full of meaning. I grew to feel that if civilization failed, I could still make my way, and in general, thrive. I still feel that way, though I am old enough to know that it would not be as easy for me now as it was twenty or thirty years ago.

The place in which I settled, Richardson, which included Banner Creek and the nearby Tenderfoot area, had been a thriving gold rush camp from around 1905 until the later years of the First World War. As with many such settlements, conditions rapidly changed; the early gold was mined, and people left for another camp, another strike. By the time I came there in 1947, only six or eight of the older residents still lived along the creeks, or in the hills above the Tanana. Most of the old buildings were gone, and it was only by listening to what the residents told me that I learned something of the history of Richardson. And what I learned seemed to confirm what Thomas Hardy said once in respect to local life, long residence in a certain place, and the changes he had witnessed in his own lifetime.

> The change at the root of this has been the recent supplanting of the class of stationary cottagers, who carried on the local traditions and humours, by a population of more or less migratory labourers, which has led to a break of continuity in local history, more fatal than any other thing to the preservation of legend, folk-lore, close inter-social

> relations and eccentric individualities. For these the indispensible conditions of existence are attachment to the soil of one particular spot by generation after generation.[Preface to *Far from the Madding Crowd* (Greenwich, Conn.: Fawcett, 1960)]

What I found at Richardson was a late beginning of just that local condition of which Hardy is speaking. The few gold rush survivors, men and women, could not have been living in the area for more than fifty years, but in their memories and the stories they told, full of humor and spite, already the place had begun to acquire the dimensions of myth. Each of the persons I came to know before the last of them died in the late 1960s had a clarity of outline, a distinctiveness of temperament that only simplicity and a certain isolation allow human character. For the first time in my life I became aware of individuals, in all their quirkiness and singularity. I was fortunate indeed, for what I found has by now nearly vanished from American life, and in its place all life takes on the same bland mediocrity one finds so plentiful in the suburbs. It may be true, as I sometimes find reason to believe, that this change has been more than just a sign of deterioration in social life. In order for a new form of life to occupy a place, another must die. When our imaginations have grown enough, perhaps we will understand that for us the local must one day include the continent and finally the planet itself. It seems likely that nothing else will allow us to thrive as a species. But it is also true that meanwhile we are painfully aware that an honored and durable way of life has disappeared, leaving an empty place in our lives.

It would be easy to say that something of the cold and clarity of the land, and much of the rest I have been talking about, just somehow got into the poems I wrote while I lived there. In a way this is true, but there is more to it. It was an awakening, profound, and disturbing. Everything was so new to me that it was like finding myself for the first time with my feet on the earth. To the extent that it was possible for me, I entered the original mystery of things, the great past out of which we came. I saw the midwinter sun sink in a cleft of the mountains to the south, and I felt I had learned a great secret. The winter solstice was an actual event, and it came on with a menace and a grandeur much older than a date on the Christian calendar.

But most important, as I have already suggested, was the meeting of place and dream. Without my being entirely conscious of it, this place and this life were what I had wanted more than any other thing. All doors seemed to open there; things hidden away, brooded upon for years, came to life: the owls I sketched as a child, the grass flowing on the hillside, the lynx track in the snow. When I was a small boy, five or six years old, my father read to me on winter evenings from Kipling's *Jungle Books*. Something took shape then and there in my mind: the wolf in the mouth of the cave, ready for the night's hunting, the forest coming awake, and far away the village of men. Thirty years went by, and that shape surfaced in a poem, "Book of the Jungle," from *Winter News*.

The animal, rising at dusk
from its bed in the trampled
grass—
    this is how it all began.

Far off the shaggy tribesmen
listened and fed their fires
with thorns.

Secret paths of the forest,
when did your children walk
unarmed, clothed only
with the shadows of leaves?

We are still kneeling
and listening,
as from the edge of a field
there rises sometimes at evening
the snort of a rutting bull.

Poetry seems to have been a natural response to my living there. My first winter in the cabin at Richardson, unable for some reason to paint, I began attempting poems in which I could express some of my feeling for this place I was coming to know, amazed at all I was seeing and learning. The poems were not, of course, very good. They were hardly poems at all. I had a lot to learn, about writing and about myself. To really know the place, I had to live there, build there, become intimate with it and know it for a long time before I could say anything about it that would be personal and distinctive. It was nearly ten years before I wrote anything that satisfied me.

On that hillside remote from many distractions, it was possible for me to see things, all things, more clearly and to think in a quiet that is hard to come by these days. The events of my life seemed to reach into both past and future. Sometimes on a fall evening, looking out on that great valley, the route of migrations, I saw, or in some way felt, a future invasion of the continent—some force out of Asia, as in the not-so-remote past. In a poem called "Foreboding" I tried to convey something of the essence of this feeling, call it a vision if you like: a suggestion of an event still to come.

Something immense and lonely
divides the earth at evening.

For nine long years I have watched
from an inner doorway:
as in a confused vision,
manlike figures approach, cover
their faces, and pass on,
heavy with iron and distance.

There is no sound but the wind
crossing the road, filling
the ruts with a dust as fine as chalk.

Like the closing of an inner door,
the day begins its dark
journey, across nine bridges
wrecked one by one.

I hope it will be clearer from this brief description how much and in what ways those years at Richardson formed me as a person and as a poet. There is one part of it I have hardly mentioned, and that concerns the two women who lived there with me much of the time, and one in particular. It seems only honest in an account of this sort not to have it appear that I was alone all the time, or that whatever was done I did all by myself. Without that companionship and support, physical and emotional, it seems unlikely that I would have gotten through those years, deprived as in some ways they were; and it seems to me not the least of things that I did finally learn to live with another human being.

It is still a place I go back to, in mind and in spirit, though it seems I cannot return to it fully in fact. The material it gave me is still part of my life, and I go back to it in poems and in prose, trying to understand as well as I can the significance of what happened to me there. The experience was so powerful that it has influenced everything else I have done. Probably I measure everything else against it. Of all things I have and am, it is something I do not lose. While writing parts of this essay I could see on a table before me a broken sandstone seed mortar that I dug up from a field in California a few years ago. When I found it I was out early in the morning, looking at some Indian rock paintings not far from where I was camped with my wife and a group of schoolchildren. Such things, and the landscapes of which they are part, would not have for me the significance they do if I had not explored for myself during those years in Alaska something of the original life of the continent.

But I no longer live at Richardson. In more ways than one, perhaps, that life is gone. Place for me has shifted from the north country wilderness to a house in suburban California; from there to some rocks in the arid California foothills, to the rainy outlines of a city in the Northwest, and to a windy street in Missoula, Montana. These places have added to the sum of what I have been; and then, returning to some enduring stillness in my life, I find myself once more in a familiar setting of broad river and sunlit hill. Behind all I write there is a landscape, partly idealized, perhaps, upon which the human figure, my own or another's, acts out a part of its life. That original place still sustains me. It gave me a way of perceiving the world that I might not have acquired otherwise, and not least, a solitude in which I could learn to listen to my own voice. But as I have tried to show, I do not think that place, outer place, alone can account for this. There must be another place, and that is within the person himself. When that interior place, formed out of dream and fantasy, and by intense imagination, finds its counterpart in a physical landscape, then some genuine human reality can be created.

The homestead at Richardson provided a place of departure from which I might go out into the world forearmed. On the evidence of my own experience, I believe that one of the most important metaphors of our time is the journey out of wilderness into culture, into the forms of our complicated and divided age, with its intense confusions and deceptions. The eventual disintegration of these cultural forms returns us once more to the wilderness. This journey can be seen both as fall and as reconciliation. And place, once again, means actual place, but also a state of mind, of consciousness. Once that place is established, we carry it with us, as we do a sense of ourselves.

II

As D. H. Lawrence has told us, there is a "spirit of place." In any landscape or region on the map, there is a potential life to be lived. The place itself offers certain possibilities, and these, combined with the capacities of those who come there, produce after a while certain kinds of life. In human terms, these may be, among other things, religions, art forms, architecture, stories, and myths, and sometimes the absence of them. This is much clearer when we look at tribal societies that have survived with little change for centuries. But it may still be true for us, mobile, and in some ways innovative contemporary people that we are. Place makes people; in the end it makes everything. Strong efforts may be made to deny the place, to silence the authentic, but the spirit of things will break through that silence to speak, if necessary, in strained and deformed accents. William Carlos Williams, in his book, *In the American Grain,* attempted to define what he felt had gone wrong with America from the start—the inability or refusal to recognize what was actually under our feet, or in the air, and to live by that. Instead we fell back on the old names for things, familiar responses to whatever lay beyond our power to see. The meaning of what he found is still with us, as potent as ever.

What do we find here in Alaska? Something absolutely new in American experience. Though it resembles all previous encounters of a people with a new country, for Americans (the great majority of people in the United States and in Canada) it is profoundly new. If we wish to read about the North, not as sensation or bald news report, we must go to Scandinavian literature, to the Russians, or to some extent, to the Canadians. I have found it clearest and strongest in the writings of Norwegian and Swedish authors, in the books of Hamsun, Vesaas, Lagerlof, and others. Strange and exotic to the experience of a southerner: the brief, intense summers, the long, sunless winters. In Edwin Muir's account of his early years in the Orkney Islands, I recognized the North: the long shadows over the treeless islands, the barely setting sun of midsummer. My second summer in Alaska I sat on the porch of my cabin at Richardson in the evenings and read through *Kristin Lavransdätter,* Sigrid Undset's trilogy on life in medieval Norway. And there on the page was the North I was coming to know. The book and the sound of the river below the house mingled, and my being there had that much more meaning for me. This is what real literature does, it seems to me; it enhances the place, the conditions under which we live, and we are more alive thereby. But there is little in English that carries the authentic mark of having been made in the North.

It is not only the land itself that faces us in the North today, as real as that is, but the entire drama of European life on this continent reenacted at a pace that leaves us stunned and gasping. The experience is hard to come to grips with; there are few names for it, and too many old responses. We see Alaska through clichés to save us from thinking: "The Last Frontier," "The Great Land." What do these really mean, aside from a great opportunity to grab? "North to the Future," that preposterous slogan once flaunted on the state auto license plates: the whole thing is a travel agent's invention. There *is* no place called Alaska, just as there is hardly anything today that can be identified as California. But of course there was, and is, such a place, though it can scarcely be found any longer for what we have done to it, and are beginning to do here. What I read about Alaska in magazines is for the most part the superficial message of the tourist—he who comes to gape, but not to understand.

How long might it take a people living here to be at home in their landscape and to produce from that experience things that could be recognized anywhere as literature of the first rank? Several hundred years? A few generations? We know from history how long a people have lived in a land and then found ways to express that living in song and the other forms of art. Closeness is needed, long residence, intimacy of a sort that demands a certain daring and risk: a surrender, an abandonment, or just a sense of somehow being stuck with it. Whatever it is that is needed, it can't be merely willed. And much of what we say about it will be conditional; in the end it will depend on the right circumstances and on the genius of a few individuals who know what they want to do, and whose material and direction cannot be predicted. All we can do is to project a few apparent needs and conditions.

The Alaskan writer faces a double task: to see, to feel, and to interpret the place itself, and then to relate that experience to what he knows of the world at large. Not simply to describe the place and what is in it (though valuable, this has been done many times already); but to give this material a life in imagination, a vitality beyond mere appearances. This alone allows the place to be seen and felt by an audience whose members are everywhere. It is not, in the end, Alaska, a place where a few people can live in perpetual self-congratulation, but humankind we are talking about. What we do and say here touches everywhere the common lot of people.

The Alaskan writer faces in addition a difficulty which is everywhere around us, and whose effect can be seen in much of the writing of today. The way we live nowadays seems intended to prevent closeness to anything outside this incubator world we have built around us. Within it, individuals face an increasingly impoverished inner world. It seems all too characteristic of us as a people that we tend to limit and confine ourselves, to specialize and restrict. We prefer anything to openness. The sort of intimacy, of being available to the land in Alaska, to the things it can reveal to one willing to stay, to observe and listen, this is prevented, or at least it is blunted, by the life most people come here to live, a life no different than one they would live anywhere. It requires of them no change, but especially no inner change. The weather is colder, the days a little longer, or shorter, but life comes boxed in the same meager pattern. To one seeing it after some absence, it seems a strange and lonely place; it is as if here, finally, the dream of frontier America must face itself. There is nowhere else to go, and it may be that deep down we are afraid that it is already a failure so enormous that we have no words for it. This furious industry over the face of the land is a distraction, and in the end it will hide nothing. If Alaska is the last frontier it may be because it represents the last full-scale attempt in North America to build a society worthy of human life, worthy of the claims made for America at the beginning. The weight of the past is heavy, and old habits hold on. The natives in Alaska have already formed themselves into "corporations"; the name is significant in that it is really *business* that runs our lives, and we are all conscripts to a system that divides and demeans us.

To see what is here, right in front of us: nothing would seem easier or more obvious, yet few things are more difficult. There are unmistakable signs that something may be dying among us: that capacity to see the world, to recognize the "other" and admit it into our lives. Invisible walls shut us out, or shut us in, and we make them stronger and thicker by the day. This may sound entirely negative, but it is frankly what I read in much that is written today. The poet Robert Bly made the observation not long ago that what most poets write about these days is not what is out there in the world, but what is passing through their own heads, filled with shapes and designs already known. Moving from the city to the country, writing about fields and ponds and hayricks doesn't change anything, though it may be a gesture of sorts. Likewise, moving from a city "outside" to another city in Alaska isn't likely to change anything either. Something else is needed, a change of an entirely different kind, and this can take place only within the individual—but by implication it would also take place between the individual and his environment.

The world of the poet has shrunk many times since the days when Wallace Stevens and William Carlos Williams took for their concern the whole of life, or at least the whole life of a place. The world with which the contemporary poet characteristically concerns himself or herself resembles the self-limited world of the adolescent. It is a deliberate limitation that comes, I believe, from despair, as if the meaning of our situation, the weight of the disasters that threaten us, is so huge that we cannot find words for it, nor perhaps even emotions. Therefore we shrink, become deliberately small and trivial, and chatter about nothing at all, huddled like apes before a storm.

An original literature is possible in Alaska, but much is against it, everything perhaps except the place itself. There is the inevitable provinciality of a newly settled place, the self-protectiveness of unsure people who tend to feel threatened by anything "outside" and possibly superior to themselves. The Alaskan writer must learn to live with the knowledge that what he or she writes may be recognized by only a few people, and the better we write the fewer those few will be. In Alaska, as in our society generally, the average person just isn't listening, and probably doesn't care. This may be unpleasant, but it is true. Everyman has no longer a culture, but sports and entertainment. Money and power are the chief motives in American life, not decency and justice, nor humanistic values generally.

I realize that there is another side to this, and that is the obvious and willing care on the part of groups and individuals to learn what the land can teach, and to live by that learning. Strong efforts are being made to rescue large areas of Alaska from the destruction inevitably following on the rapid settling of a land. Some of us, at least, are trying to change our way of living, to be more in accord with the realities that face us. These efforts matter, though they reflect the concern of relatively few people.

In January, 1976, I went on a 900 mile trip through interior and south central Alaska. In spite of the many gloomy reports being written at the time, I saw that the oil pipeline after all had not changed the land very much. The old impression of its vastness, and, in winter, at least, of the uninhabitability of much of it, is still there, and will be, I suspect, for a long time to come. That big land out there abides, as always. Projects like Alyeska are not yet the ruin of Alaska. Away from the cities, what impressed me most was how little the land has changed since I first saw it over thirty years ago. Works and days seem lost in that immensity, so much so that one feels a mixture of awe, gratitude, and a little fear: fear of what *could* happen if all restraint on settlement and development were removed.

We can hardly look to the arts for the specific answers to the difficulties that beset us, for they generally provide none. They can, however, reveal to us a range of possible human responses to life, show us what it is like to be alive now, feeling and thinking. And genuine literature shows, as only great writings and art do show, the significant shapes that lie behind appearances. We can learn from past and living examples, poets and writers whose work owes some authentic quality to the North. What does it mean to be in this place at this time? How does it relate to what is happening in the world elsewhere? It is no longer possible to live in Alaska, or anywhere else, and keep out the world. We are in it, for better or worse. One might make a categorical statement: no significant literature can be written now that does not include in its subject the human predicament everywhere.

Literature must embody some truth, in what is said and the way it is said, if it is to have any meaning for us now and in the future. And this is why, for Alaska, clichés about the "last frontier" will not do. The truth of our times, bitter and disheartening as it may turn out to be, must be faced. Honesty and imagination are needed. What counts finally in a work are not novel and interesting things, though these can be important, but the absolutely authentic. I think that there *is* a spirit of place, a presence asking to be expressed; and sometimes when we are lucky as writers, and quiet in a way few of us want to be anymore, a voice enters our own, becomes mingled with it, and we speak with a force and clarity not otherwise heard.

We live in a world, that great "other" made up of nature, the wilderness, the universe. At the same time we are compelled, because we are human and vulnerable, to make for ourselves, in imagination and in fact, another world in which we can feel at home, yet not too far removed from that other. One of the functions of the writer, the poet, is to reconcile us to our lot; in the words of William Carlos Williams, "by metaphor to reconcile the people and the stones": to tell us a story in such a way that we become the characters in a tale we can believe in. Isn't this what writing, storytelling, and the arts generally are all about? The money making, the market, "success," and all the rest of it are beside the point, though they may seem important enough from time to time. Alaska needs a literature as a matter of practical necessity, of self-identification. "A culture without dreams is finished. It has nothing to motivate it."*

A literature is made of many things, not just a few outstanding names and works, and there is room for all kinds of writing. But what has most concerned me in this essay is that literature so distinctive that it belongs unmistakably to a certain place and yet speaks for all places. It ought to be the task of the Alaskan writer to understand this, and to seek to embody it in his or her work. Otherwise, what Alaska produces as literature may go on being notable for its hymns to Mount McKinley, dead odes to dead salmon, superficial accounts of "life on the last frontier," or finally, at best, very thin copies of the many poems and stories written anywhere in this country today. My concern is with the writer who wishes above all to come to terms in some way with the truth of our times. Everything tries to prevent this, to offer instead easy rewards for saying the obvious and already known. I suppose that what this means is that the writing, the best of it, should have some commitment beyond the private self. This seems not to be a time in which anyone has a right to expect a seriousness of the kind I am asking for, but anything less will not be enough.

We need to be as clear as possible about the world we live in, and to have some ideas about our place in it; to understand and to accept, if necessary, the limitations that living on a finite and exhaustible planet imposes on us. Perhaps here in Alaska is an opportunity to deepen that understanding. It is another *place,* where we can stand and see the world and ourselves. The literature that is to come will bear the mark of an urgency, a seriousness that recognizes the dangers and choices held out to us by our involvement with the earth. And it may now and then be possible to recover, in a new land, something of that first morning of existence, when we looked at the world and saw, without motives, how beautiful it is.

*(Joseph Campbell, "Man and Myth," in *Voices and Visions,* ed. Sam Keen [New York: Harper and Row, 1974], p. 79).